TOKYO MEWMEW OMNIBUS

VOLUME ①

Written by Reiko Yoshida
Illustrated by Mia Ikumi

Translated by Elina Ishikawa
Lettered by AndWorld Design

KC
KODANSHA
COMICS

A Kodansha Comics Trade Paperback Original

Tokyo Mew Mew Omnibus volume 1 copyright © 2001
Reiko Yoshida/ Mia Ikumi
English translation copyright © 2011 Reiko Yoshida/ Mia Ikumi

Published in the United States by Kodansha Comics, an imprint of
Kodansha USA Publishing, LLC, New York.

Publication rights for this English edition arranged through
Kodansha Ltd., Tokyo.

First published in Japan in 2001 by Kodansha Ltd., Tokyo,
as *Tokyo Mew Mew,* volumes 1 and 2.

ISBN 978-1935429876

Printed and bound in Germany by GGP Media GmbH, Poessneck.

www.kodansha.us

10th printing

Translator: Satsuki Yamashita
Lettering: AndWorld Design

CONTENTS

Original Cover Design by
Mizuno Productions

About the Creator: Born on March 27th, Aries,
Blood type O, From Ôsaka Prefecture.
She won the 24th Nakayoshi New Faces Manga
Award with the manga Usagi no Furasu Hoshi in
the year 1997, which made its debut in the
January 1998 issue of Run-Run. Her featured
works are Super Doll Licca-chan and Ichigo no
Mori no Nemuri Hime. She enjoys playing with
her cat and wearing cute (weird?) clothes.

TOKYO MEW MEW OMNIBUS

Translation by Elina Ishikawa

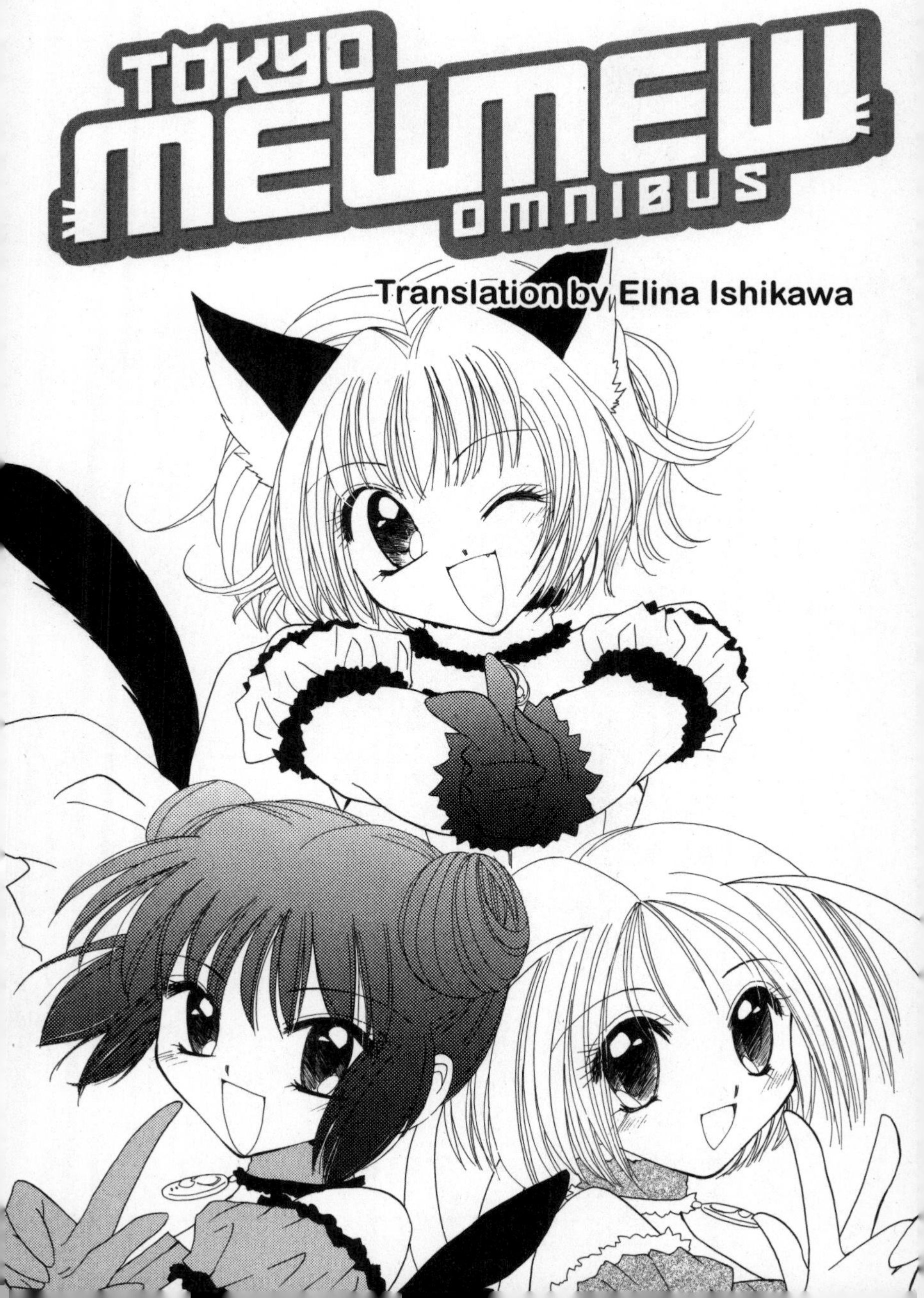

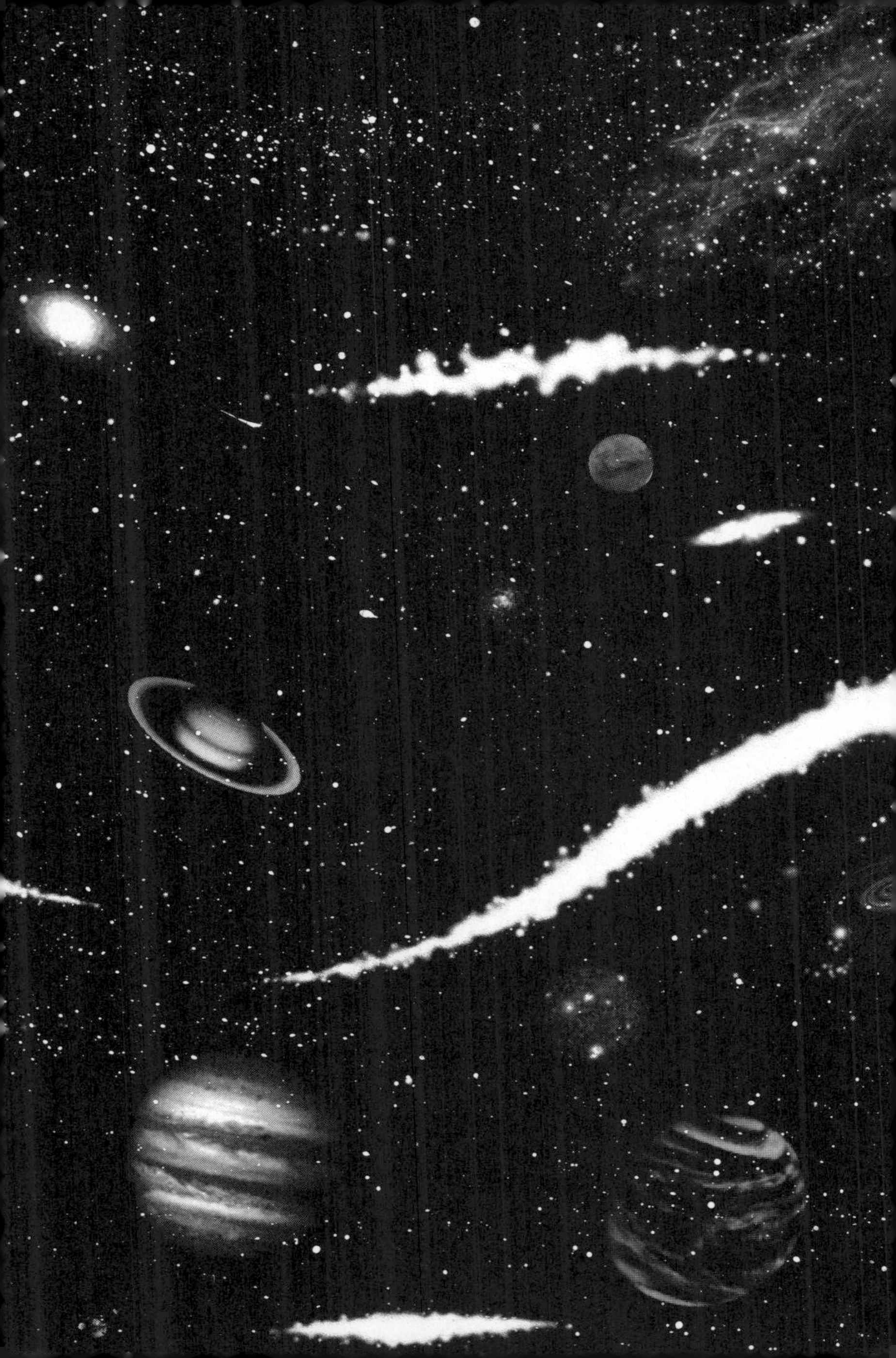

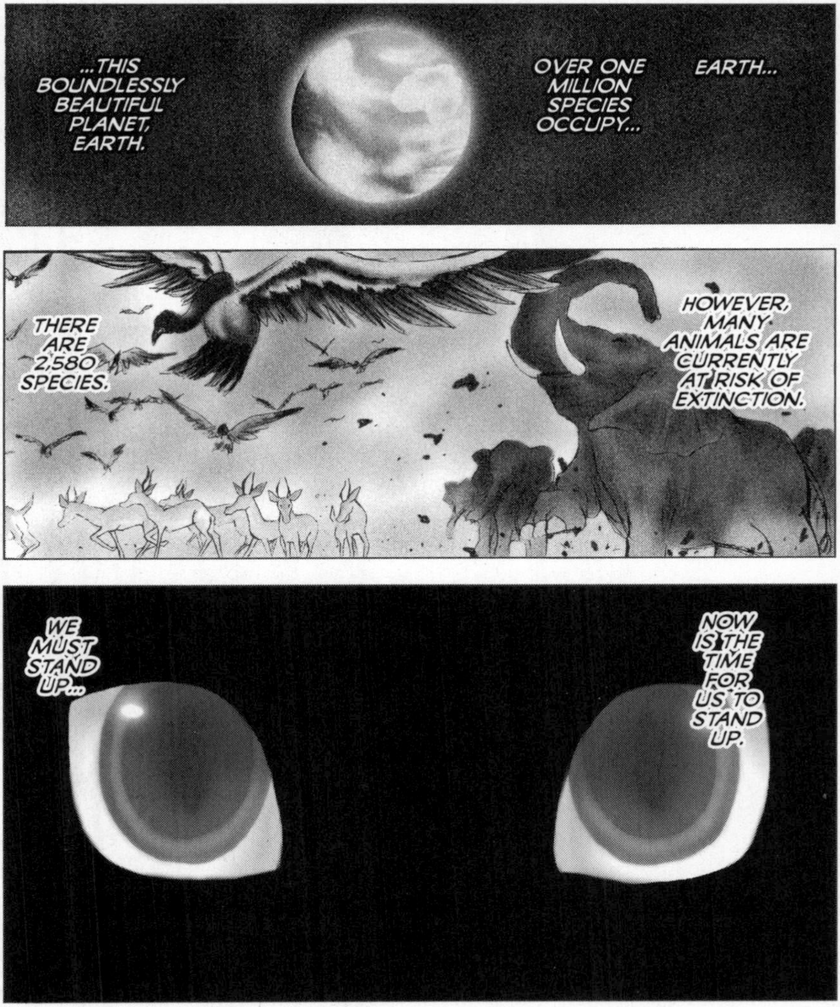
EARTH...
OVER ONE MILLION SPECIES OCCUPY...
...THIS BOUNDLESSLY BEAUTIFUL PLANET, EARTH.
HOWEVER, MANY ANIMALS ARE CURRENTLY AT RISK OF EXTINCTION.
THERE ARE 2,580 SPECIES.
NOW IS THE TIME FOR US TO STAND UP.
WE MUST STAND UP...

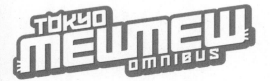

TOKYO MEWMEW OMNIBUS

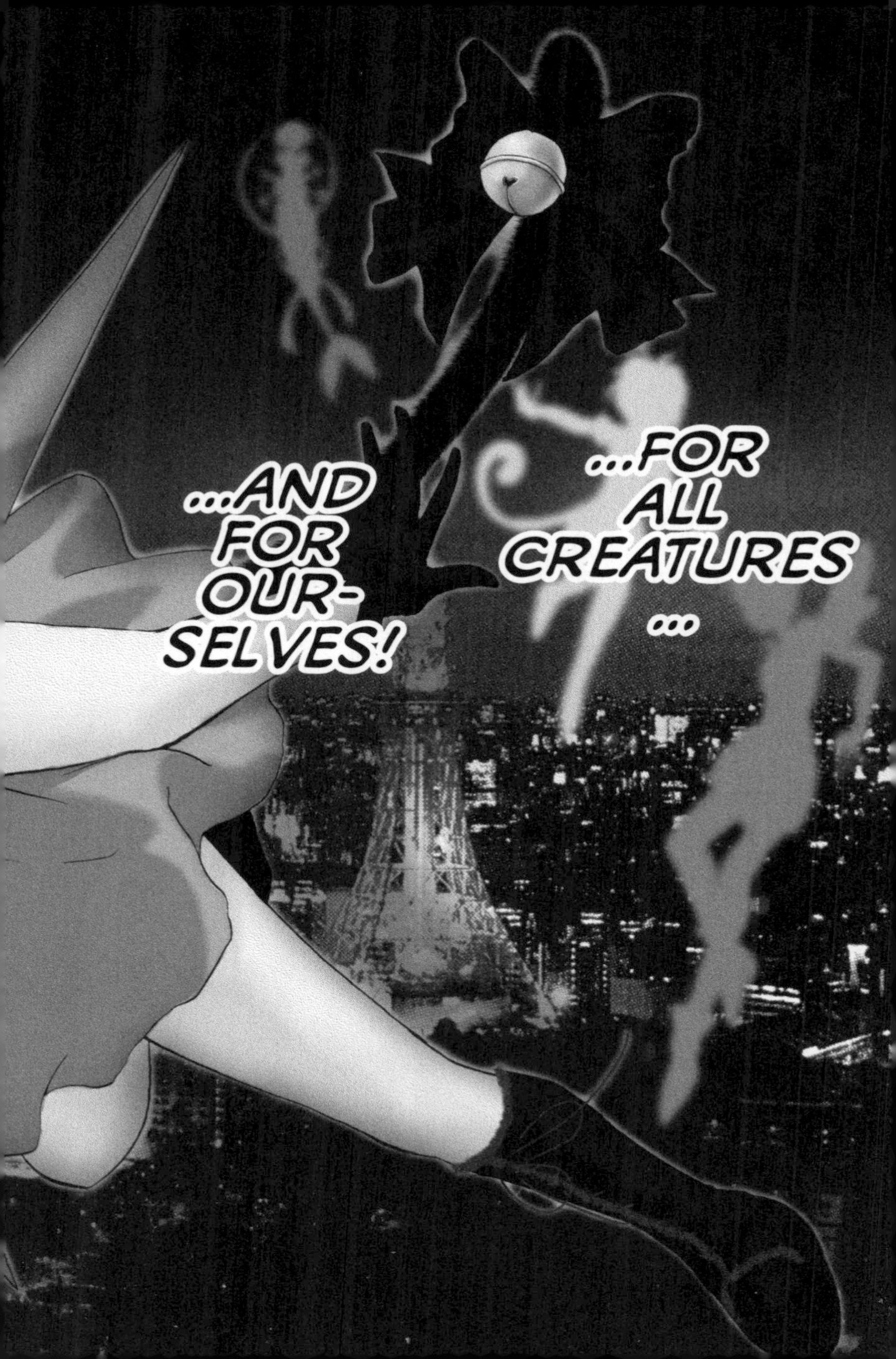
...FOR ALL CREATURES ...
...AND FOR OUR-SELVES!

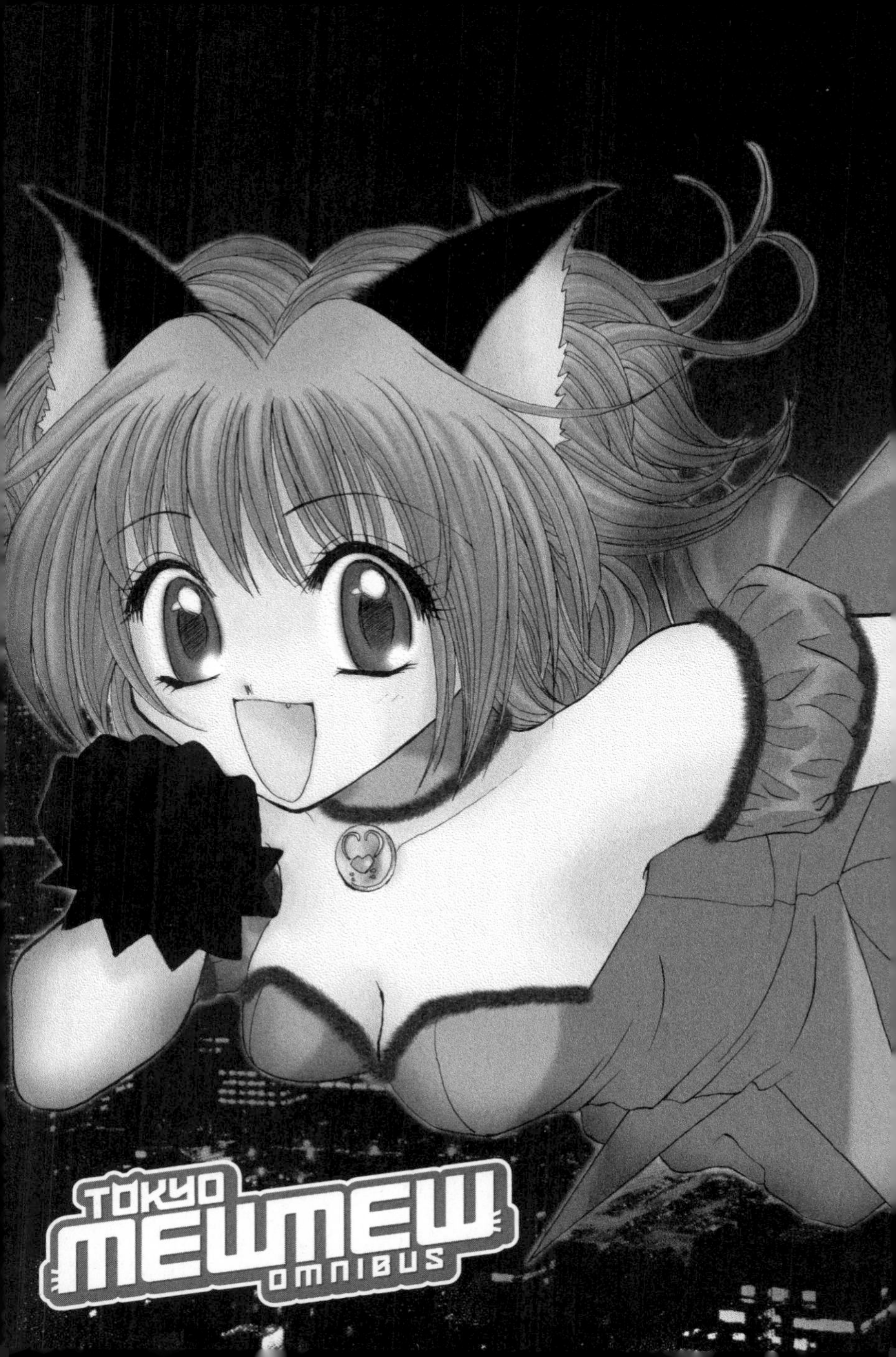
TOKYO MEWMEW OMNIBUS

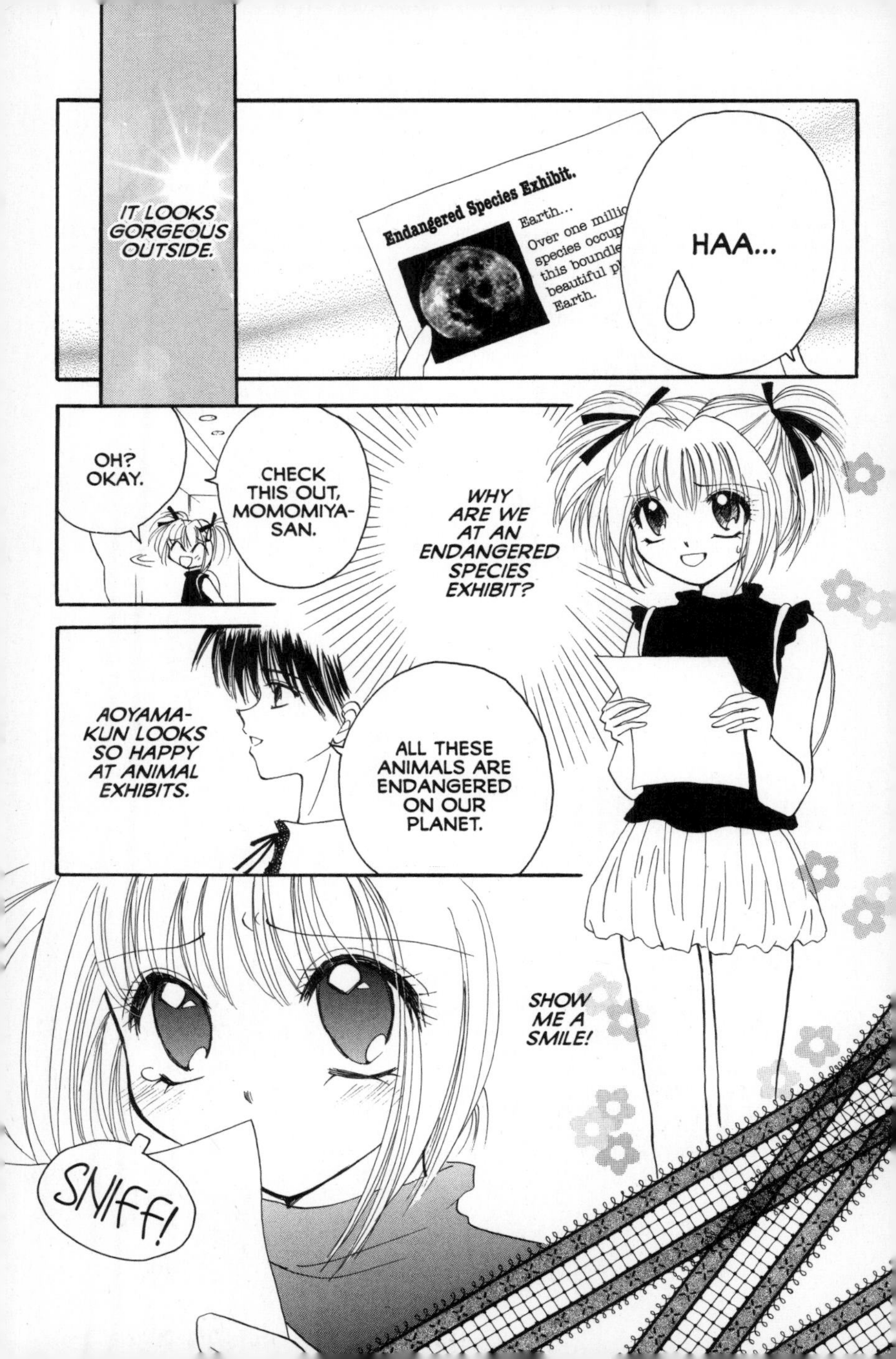
HAA...
Endangered Species Exhibit.
Earth...
Over one milli
species occup
this boundle
beautiful pl
Earth.
IT LOOKS GORGEOUS OUTSIDE.
WHY ARE WE AT AN ENDANGERED SPECIES EXHIBIT?
SHOW ME A SMILE!
CHECK THIS OUT, MOMOMIYA-SAN.
OH? OKAY.
ALL THESE ANIMALS ARE ENDANGERED ON OUR PLANET.
AOYAMA-KUN LOOKS SO HAPPY AT ANIMAL EXHIBITS.
SNIFF!

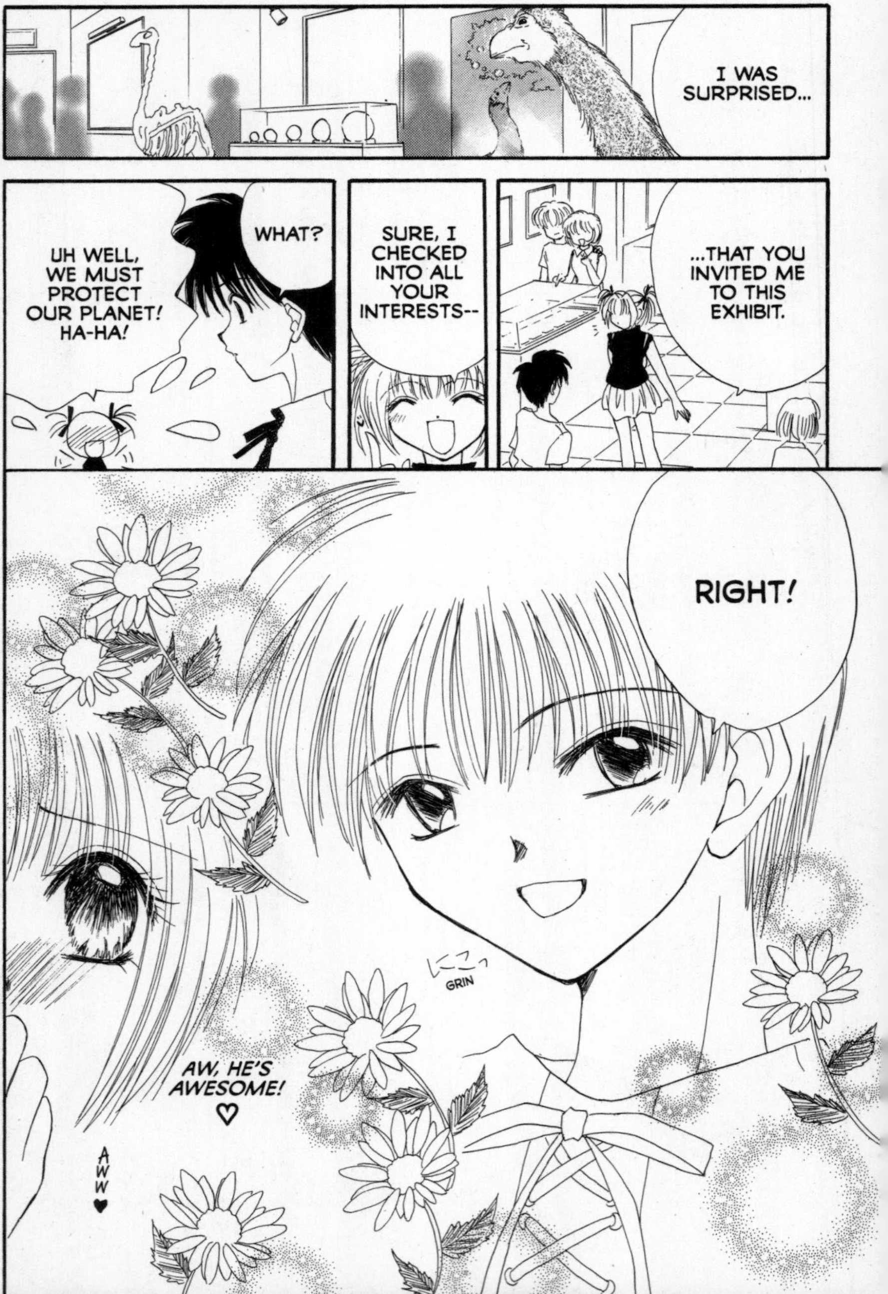
I WAS SURPRISED...
...THAT YOU INVITED ME TO THIS EXHIBIT.
SURE, I CHECKED INTO ALL YOUR INTERESTS--
WHAT?
UH WELL, WE MUST PROTECT OUR PLANET! HA-HA!
RIGHT!
にこっ
GRIN
AW, HE'S AWESOME! ♡
AWW ♥

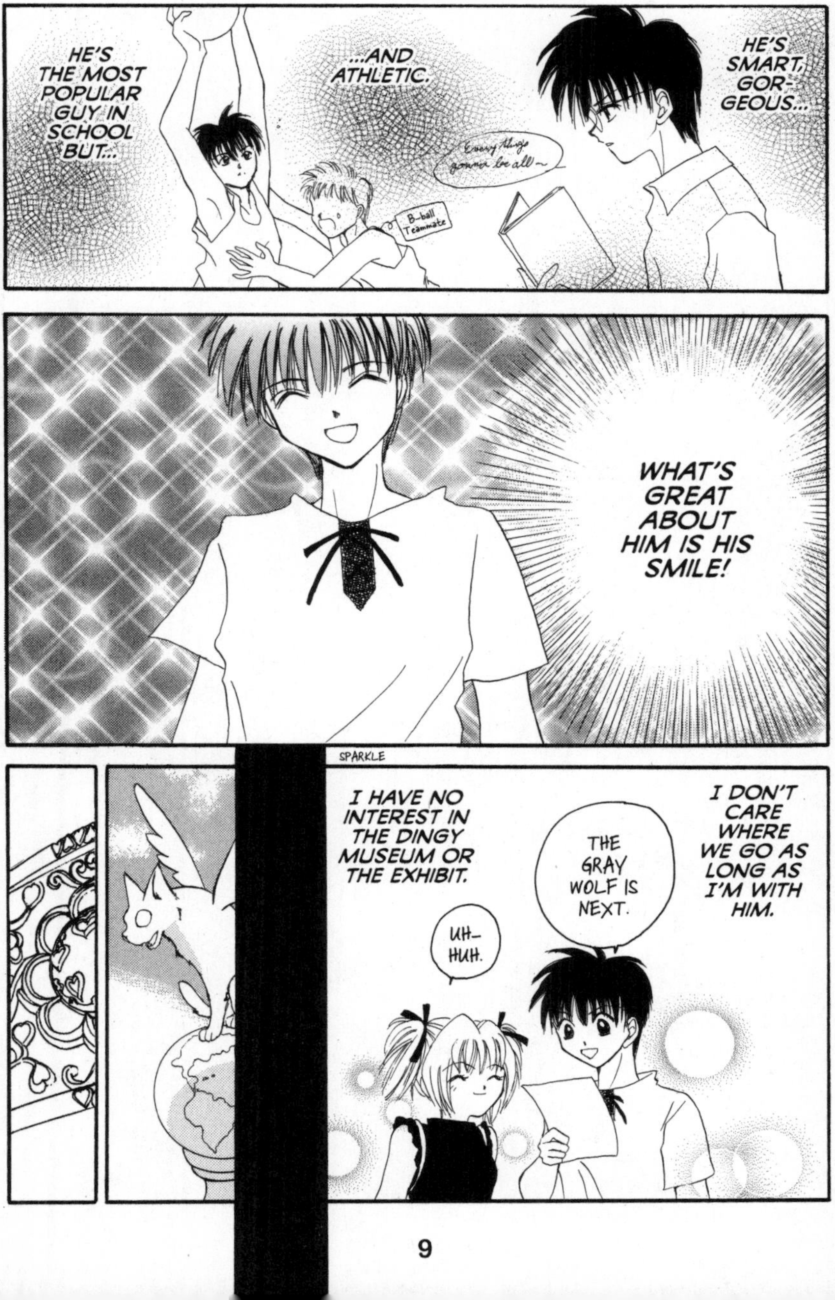
HE'S SMART, GORGEOUS...
...AND ATHLETIC.
Everything's gonna be all~
B-ball Teammate
HE'S THE MOST POPULAR GUY IN SCHOOL BUT...
WHAT'S GREAT ABOUT HIM IS HIS SMILE!
SPARKLE
I DON'T CARE WHERE WE GO AS LONG AS I'M WITH HIM.
THE GRAY WOLF IS NEXT.
I HAVE NO INTEREST IN THE DINGY MUSEUM OR THE EXHIBIT.
UH-HUH.

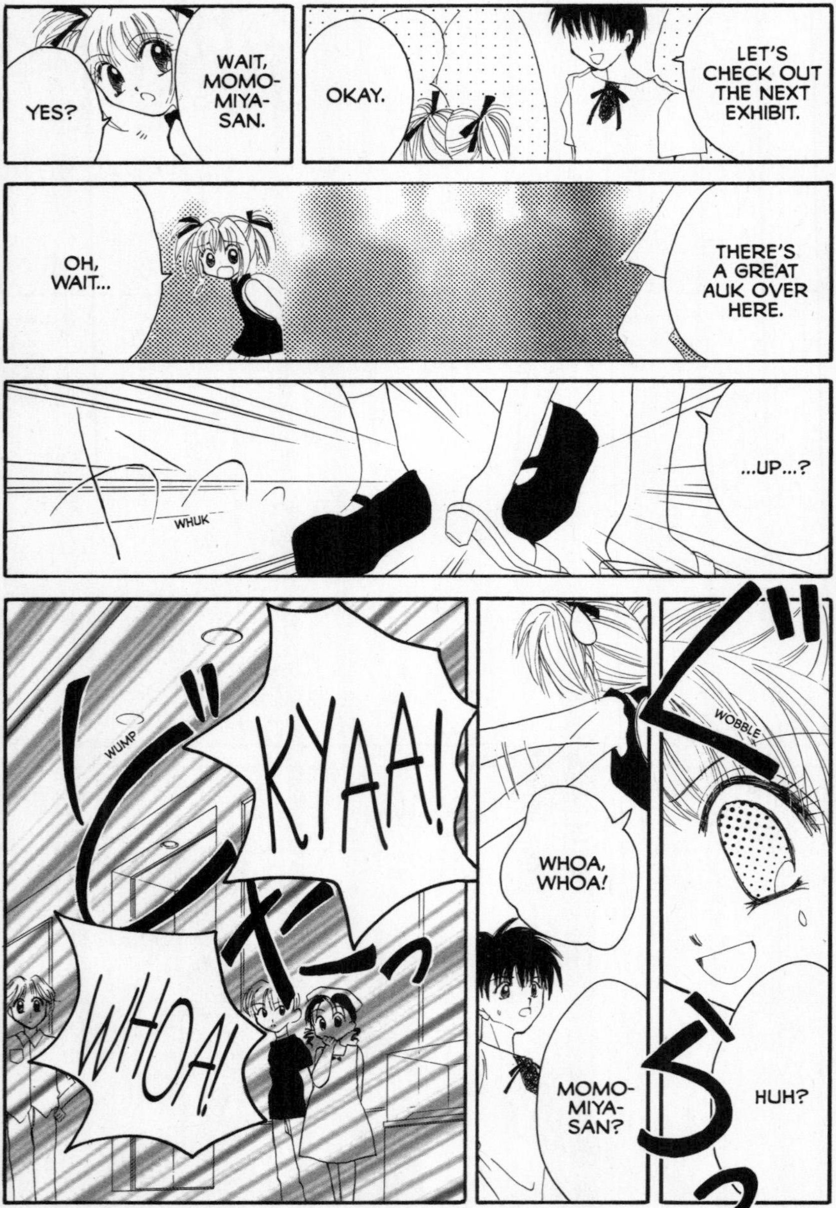

LET'S CHECK OUT THE NEXT EXHIBIT.
OKAY.
WAIT, MOMO-MIYA-SAN.
YES?
THERE'S A GREAT AUK OVER HERE.
OH, WAIT...
...UP...?
WHUK
WOBBLE
HUH?
WHOA, WHOA!
MOMO-MIYA-SAN?
KYAA!
WUMP
WHOA!

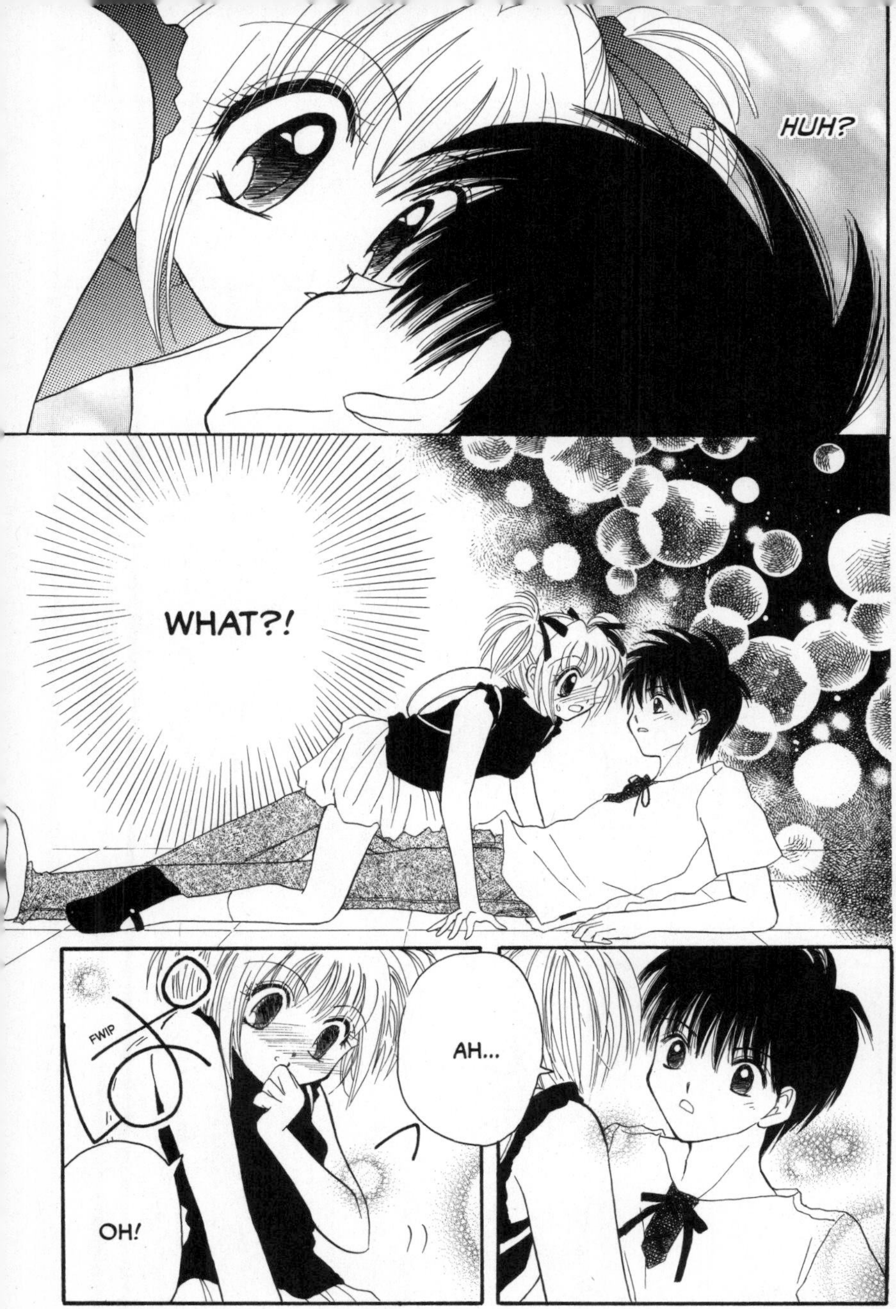
HUH?
WHAT?!
AH...
FWIP
OH!

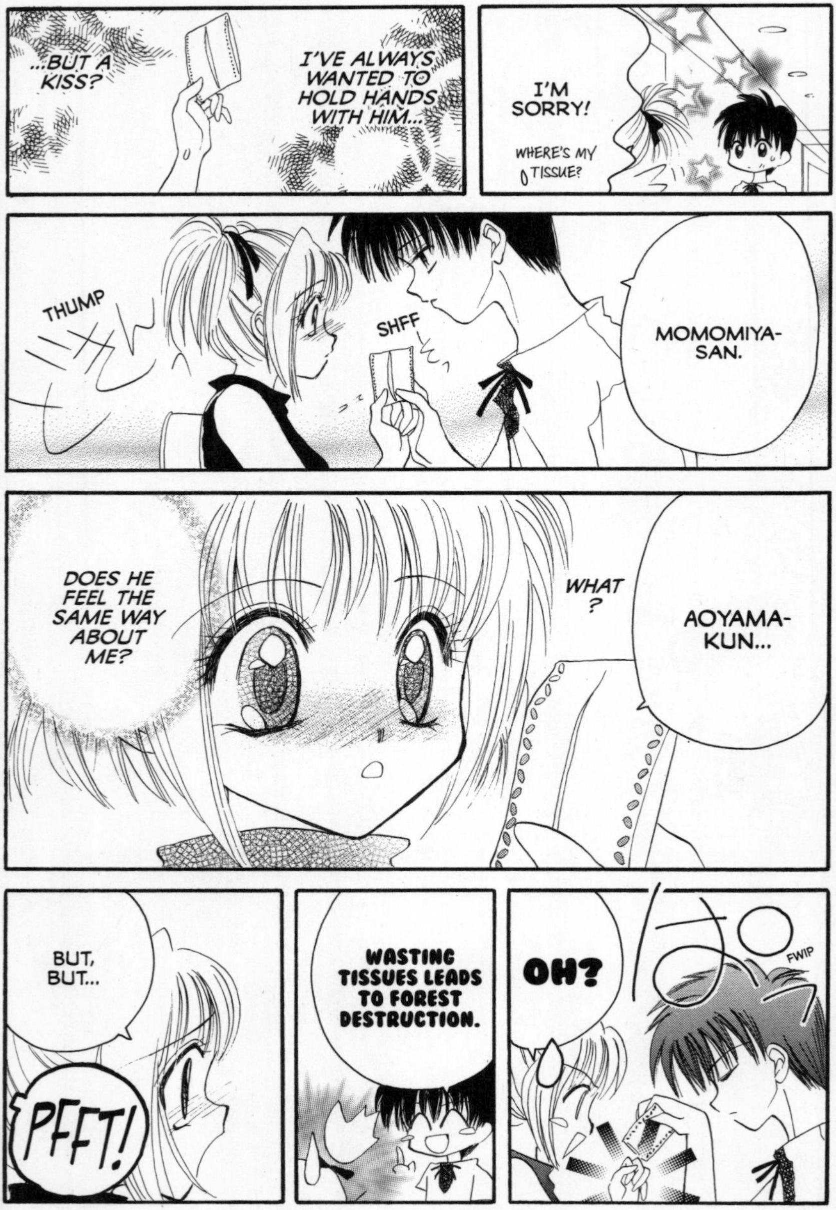
I'M SORRY!
WHERE'S MY TISSUE?
I'VE ALWAYS WANTED TO HOLD HANDS WITH HIM...
...BUT A KISS?
MOMOMIYA-SAN.
SHFF
THUMP
AOYAMA-KUN...
WHAT?
DOES HE FEEL THE SAME WAY ABOUT ME?
FWIP
OH?
WASTING TISSUES LEADS TO FOREST DESTRUCTION.
BUT, BUT...
PFFT!

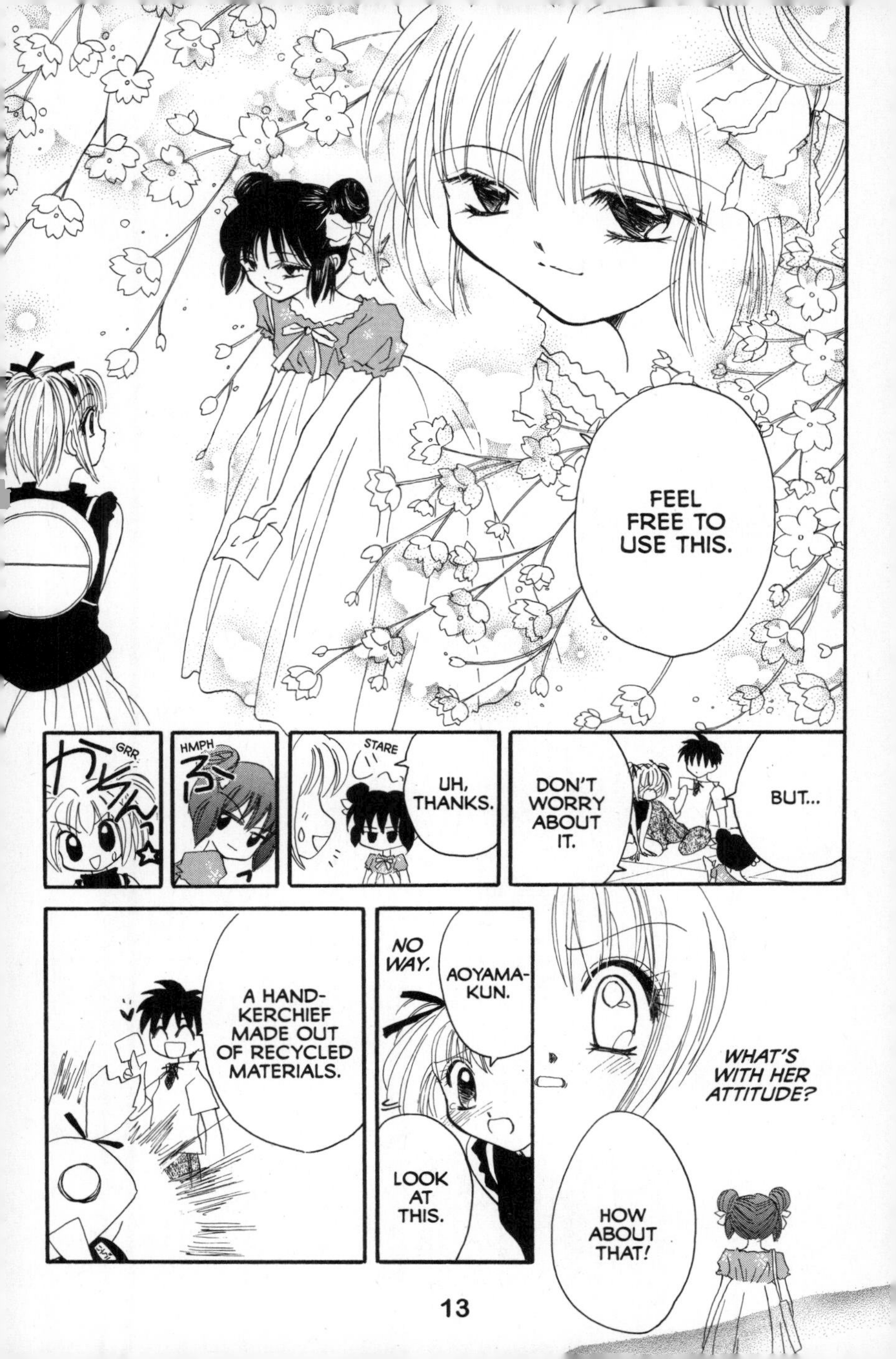
FEEL FREE TO USE THIS.
BUT...
DON'T WORRY ABOUT IT.
UH, THANKS.
STARE
HMPH
GRR
WHAT'S WITH HER ATTITUDE?
HOW ABOUT THAT!
AOYAMA-KUN.
NO WAY.
LOOK AT THIS.
A HAND-KERCHIEF MADE OUT OF RECYCLED MATERIALS.

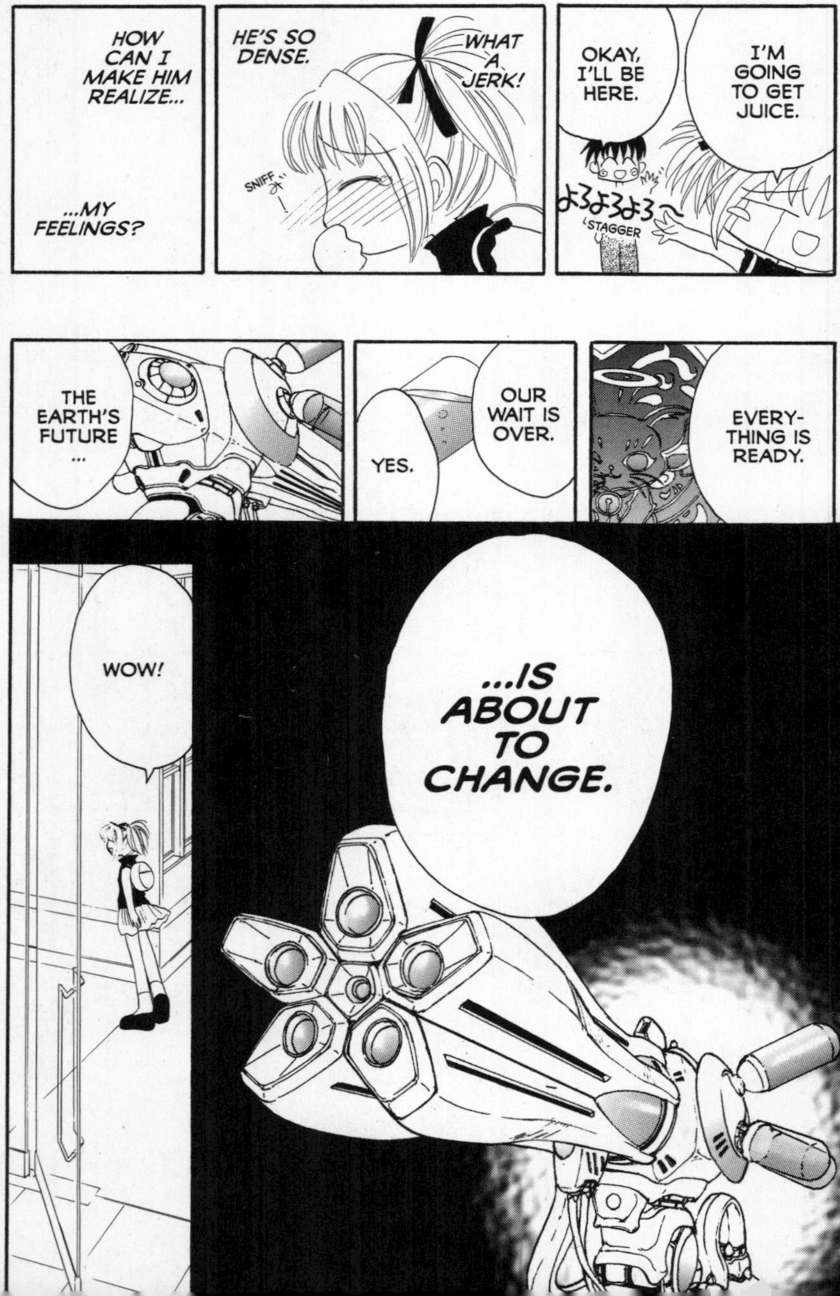
I'M GOING TO GET JUICE.
OKAY, I'LL BE HERE.
よろよろよろ〜
STAGGER
WHAT A JERK!
HE'S SO DENSE.
SNIFF
HOW CAN I MAKE HIM REALIZE...
...MY FEELINGS?
EVERY-THING IS READY.
OUR WAIT IS OVER.
YES.
THE EARTH'S FUTURE ...
...IS ABOUT TO CHANGE.
WOW!

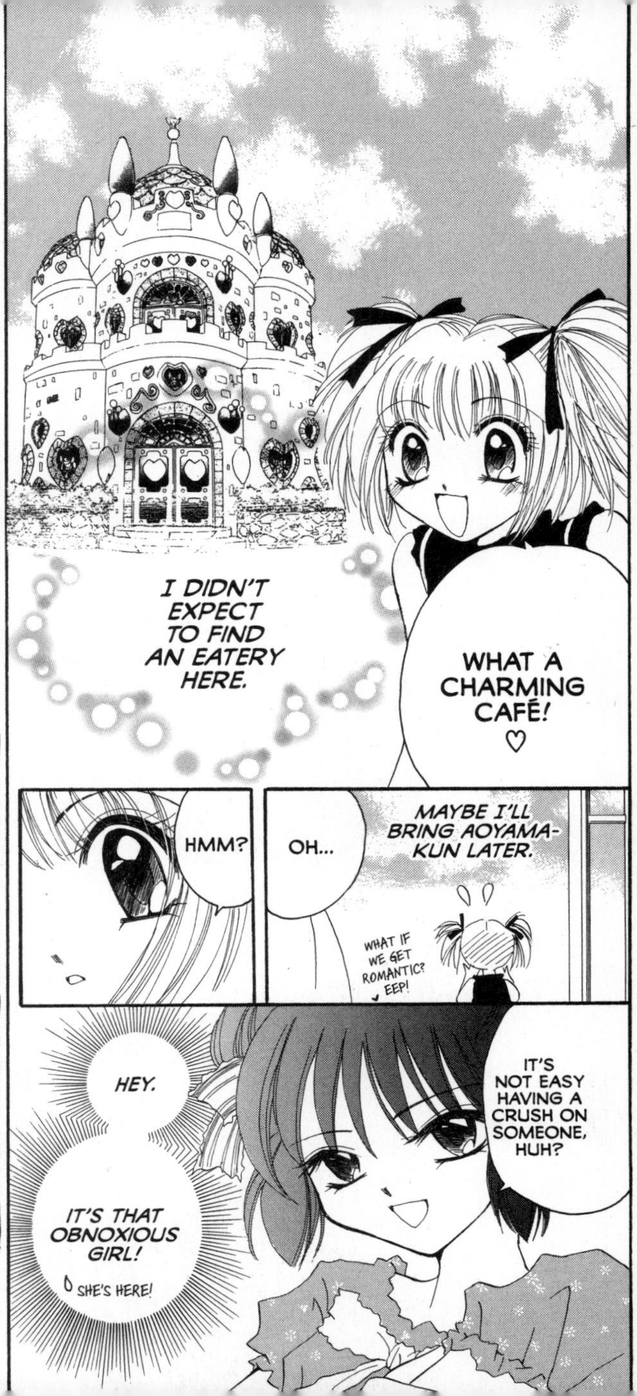
WHAT A CHARMING CAFÉ! ♡
I DIDN'T EXPECT TO FIND AN EATERY HERE.
MAYBE I'LL BRING AOYAMA-KUN LATER.
OH...
WHAT IF WE GET ROMANTIC? EEP! ♥
HMM?
IT'S NOT EASY HAVING A CRUSH ON SOMEONE, HUH?
HEY.
IT'S THAT OBNOXIOUS GIRL!
SHE'S HERE!

Meeting with My Editors: Part One

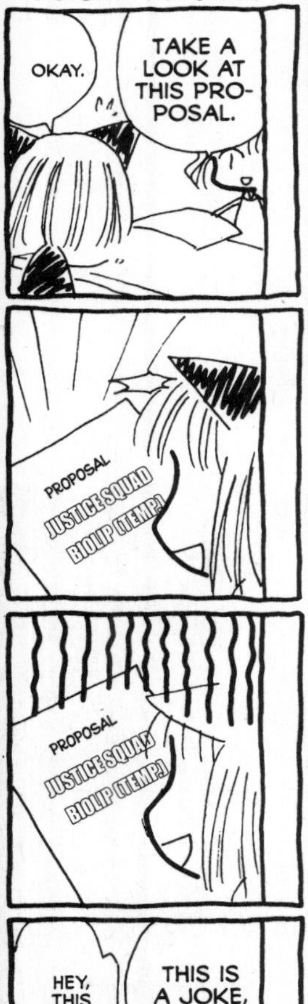
TAKE A LOOK AT THIS PROPOSAL.
OKAY.
PROPOSAL
JUSTICE SQUAD BIOLIP (TEMP.)
PROPOSAL
JUSTICE SQUAD BIOLIP (TEMP.)
THIS IS A JOKE, RIGHT?
HEY, THIS TOOK US TWO HOURS!

My editors chose the current title after this. ♡

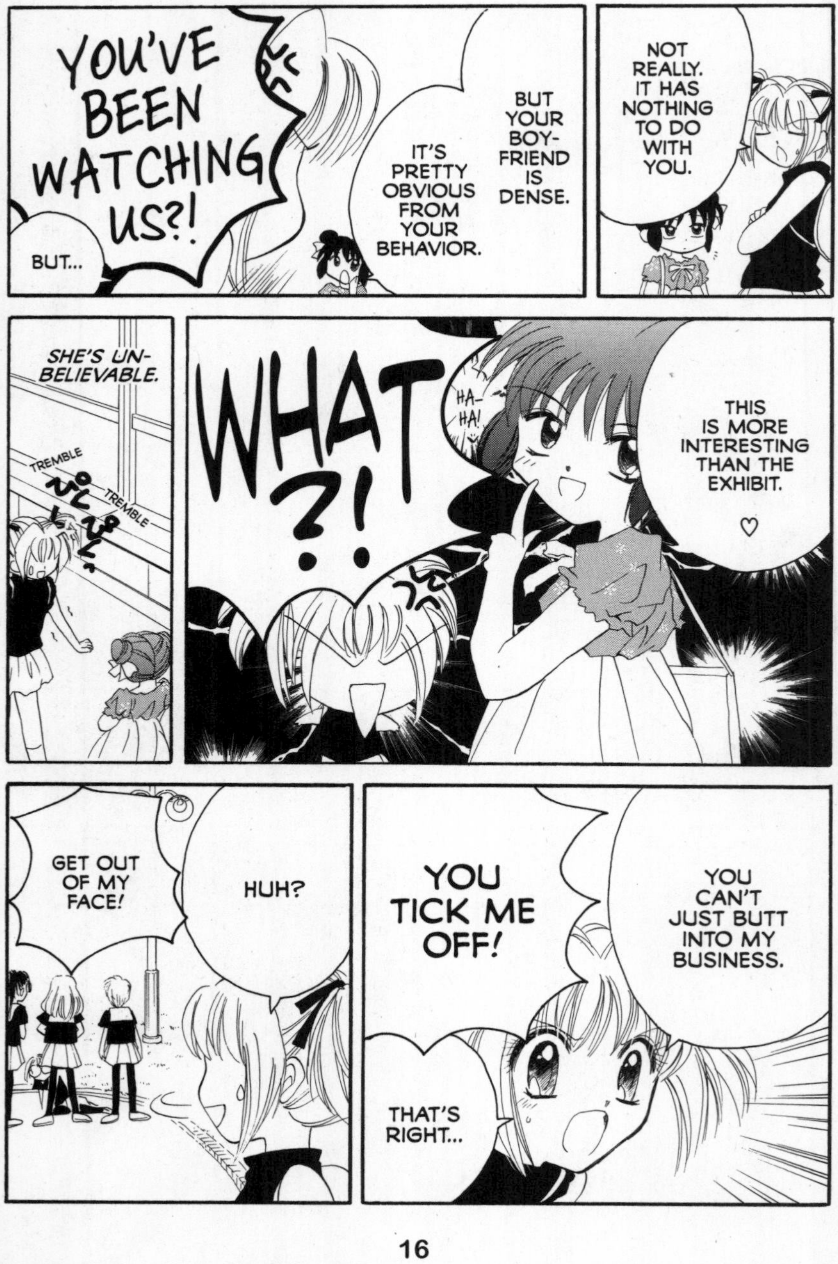
NOT REALLY. IT HAS NOTHING TO DO WITH YOU.
BUT YOUR BOY-FRIEND IS DENSE.
IT'S PRETTY OBVIOUS FROM YOUR BEHAVIOR.
YOU'VE BEEN WATCHING US?!
BUT...
THIS IS MORE INTERESTING THAN THE EXHIBIT. ♡
HA-HA!
WHAT?!
SHE'S UN-BELIEVABLE.
TREMBLE
TREMBLE
YOU CAN'T JUST BUTT INTO MY BUSINESS.
YOU TICK ME OFF!
THAT'S RIGHT...
HUH?
GET OUT OF MY FACE!

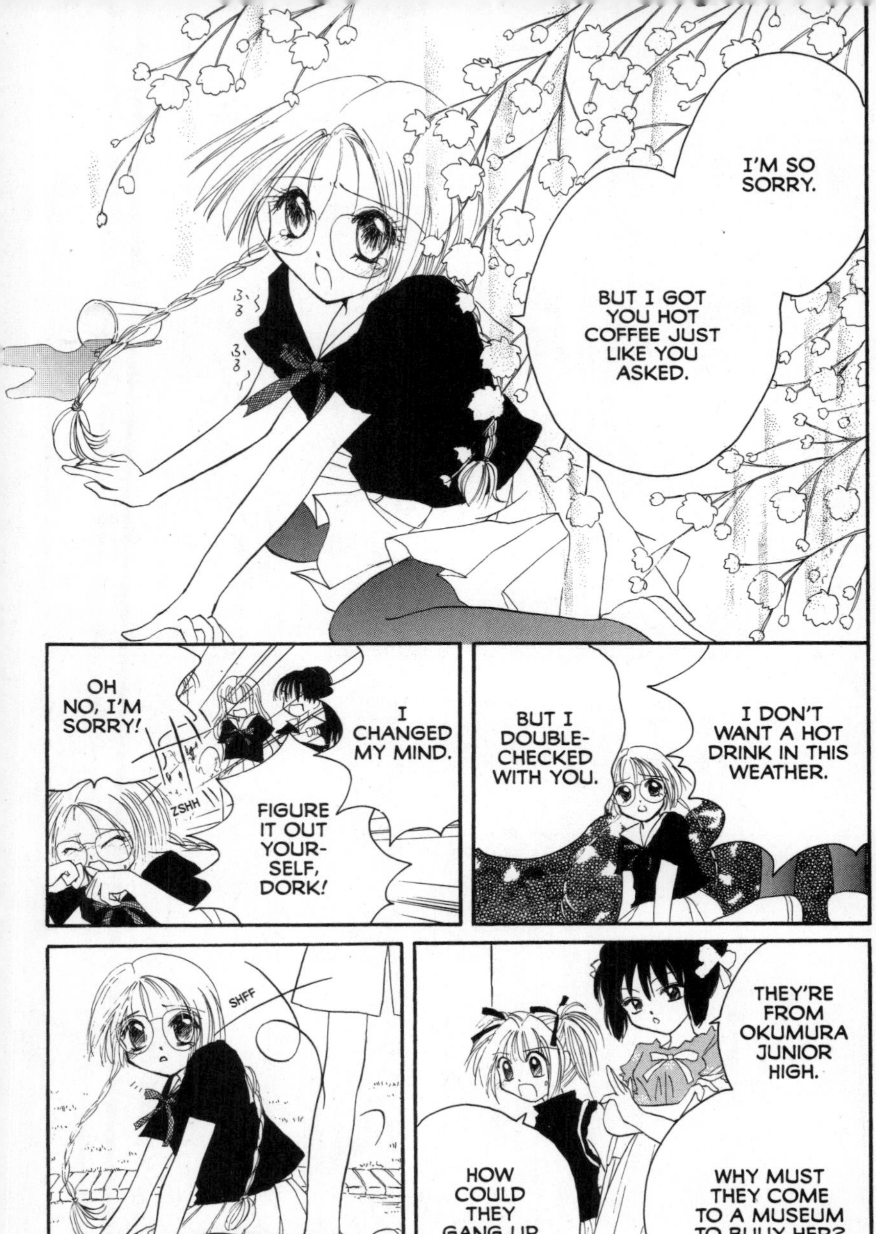
I'M SO SORRY.
BUT I GOT YOU HOT COFFEE JUST LIKE YOU ASKED.
I DON'T WANT A HOT DRINK IN THIS WEATHER.
BUT I DOUBLE-CHECKED WITH YOU.
I CHANGED MY MIND.
FIGURE IT OUT YOURSELF, DORK!
ZSHH
OH NO, I'M SORRY!
THEY'RE FROM OKUMURA JUNIOR HIGH.
WHY MUST THEY COME TO A MUSEUM TO BULLY HER?
HOW COULD THEY GANG UP ON HER?
SHFF

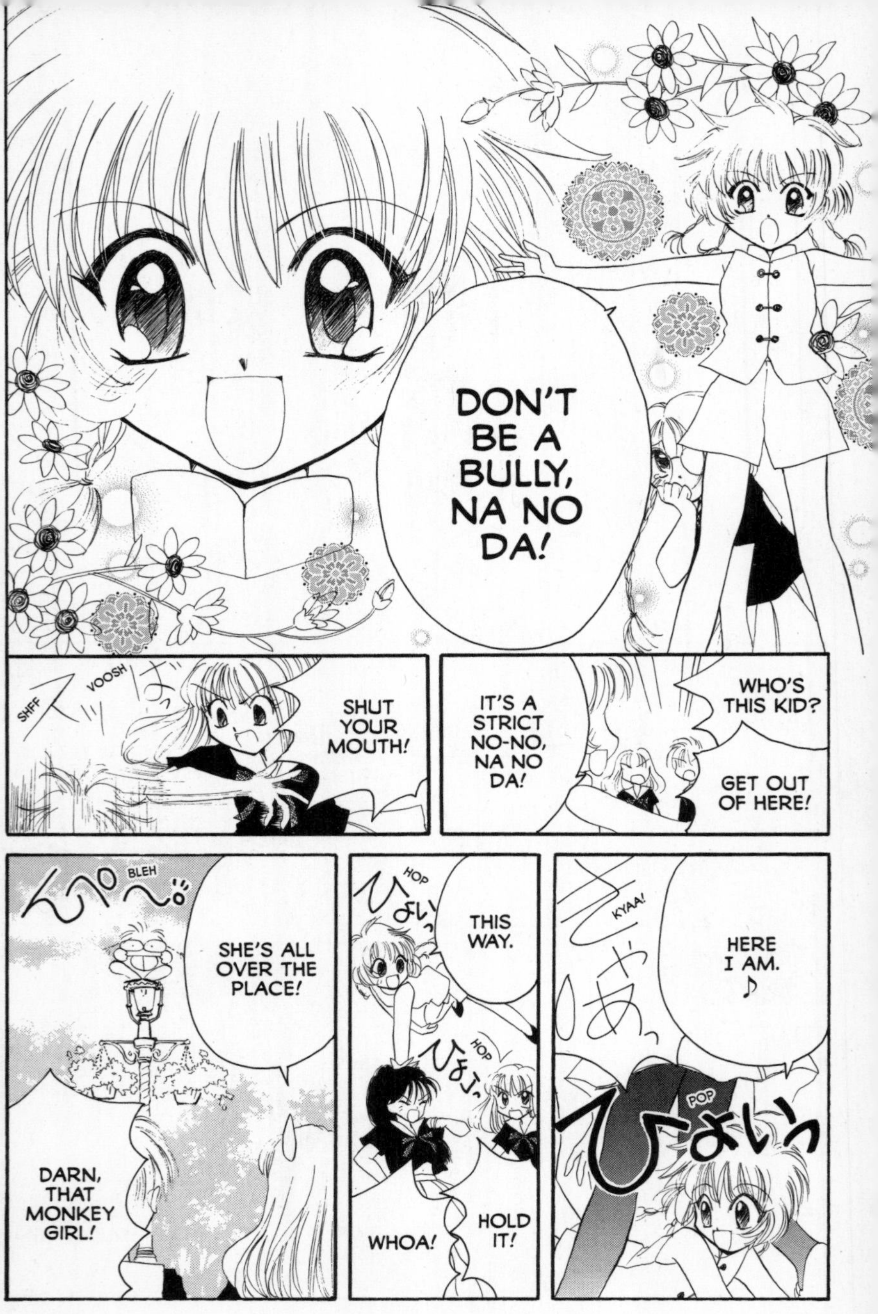
DON'T BE A BULLY, NA NO DA!
WHO'S THIS KID?
GET OUT OF HERE!
IT'S A STRICT NO-NO, NA NO DA!
VOOSH
SHFF
SHUT YOUR MOUTH!
KYAA!
HERE I AM. ♪
POP
HOP
THIS WAY.
HOP
HOLD IT!
WHOA!
BLEH
SHE'S ALL OVER THE PLACE!
DARN, THAT MONKEY GIRL!

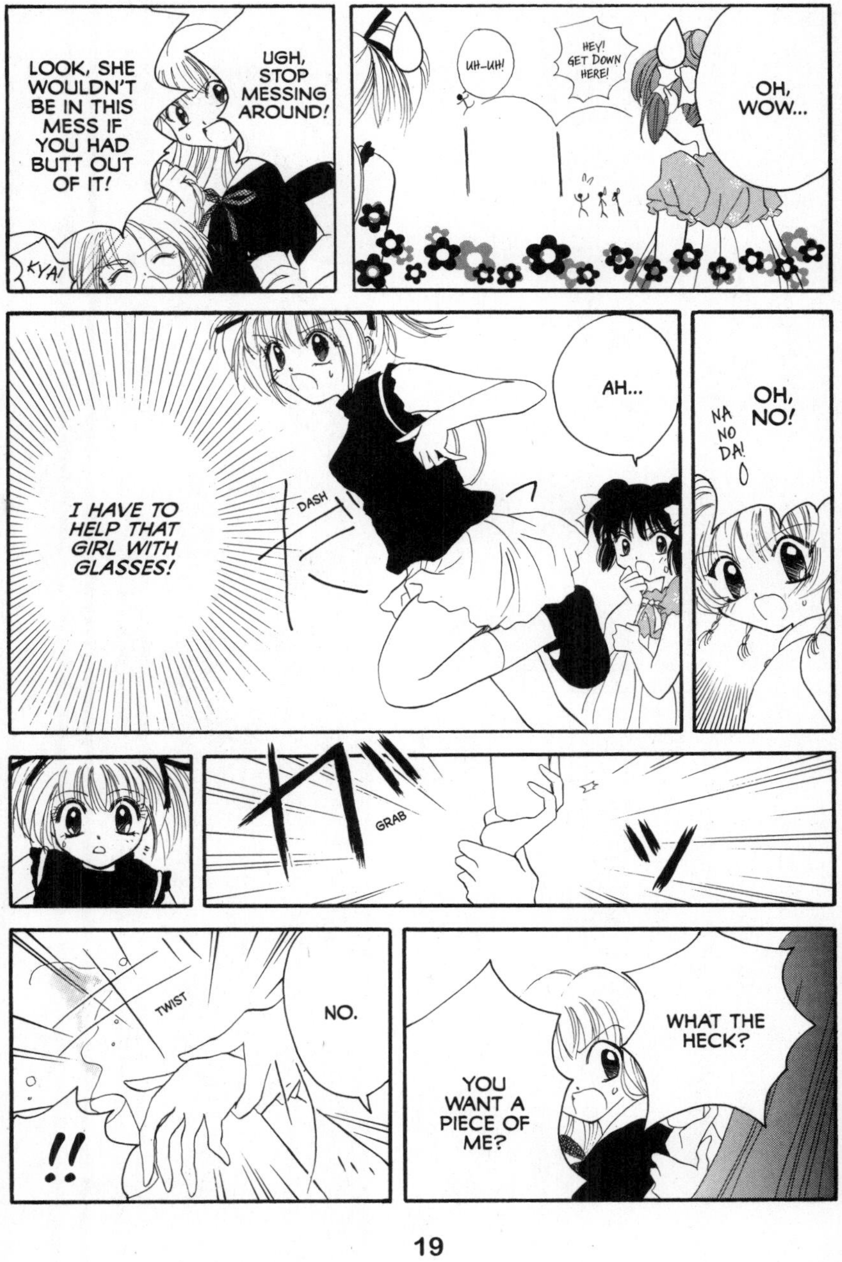
OH, WOW...
HEY! GET DOWN HERE!
UH-UH!
UGH, STOP MESSING AROUND!
LOOK, SHE WOULDN'T BE IN THIS MESS IF YOU HAD BUTT OUT OF IT!
KYA!
OH, NO!
NA NO DA!
AH...
DASH
I HAVE TO HELP THAT GIRL WITH GLASSES!
GRAB
WHAT THE HECK?
YOU WANT A PIECE OF ME?
NO.
TWIST
!!

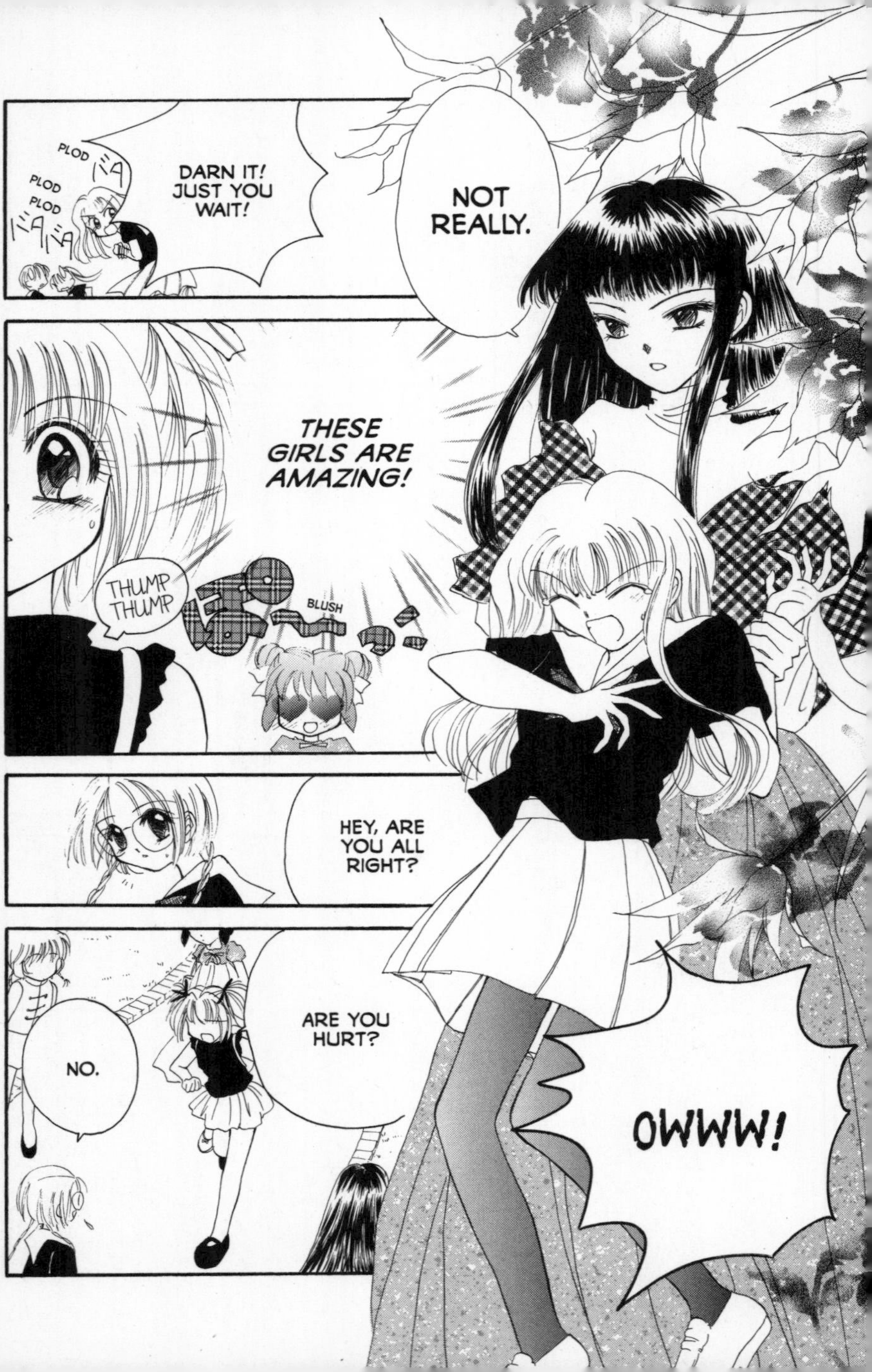
NOT REALLY.
OWWW!
DARN IT! JUST YOU WAIT!
PLOD
PLOD
PLOD
THESE GIRLS ARE AMAZING!
BLUSH
THUMP THUMP
HEY, ARE YOU ALL RIGHT?
ARE YOU HURT?
NO.

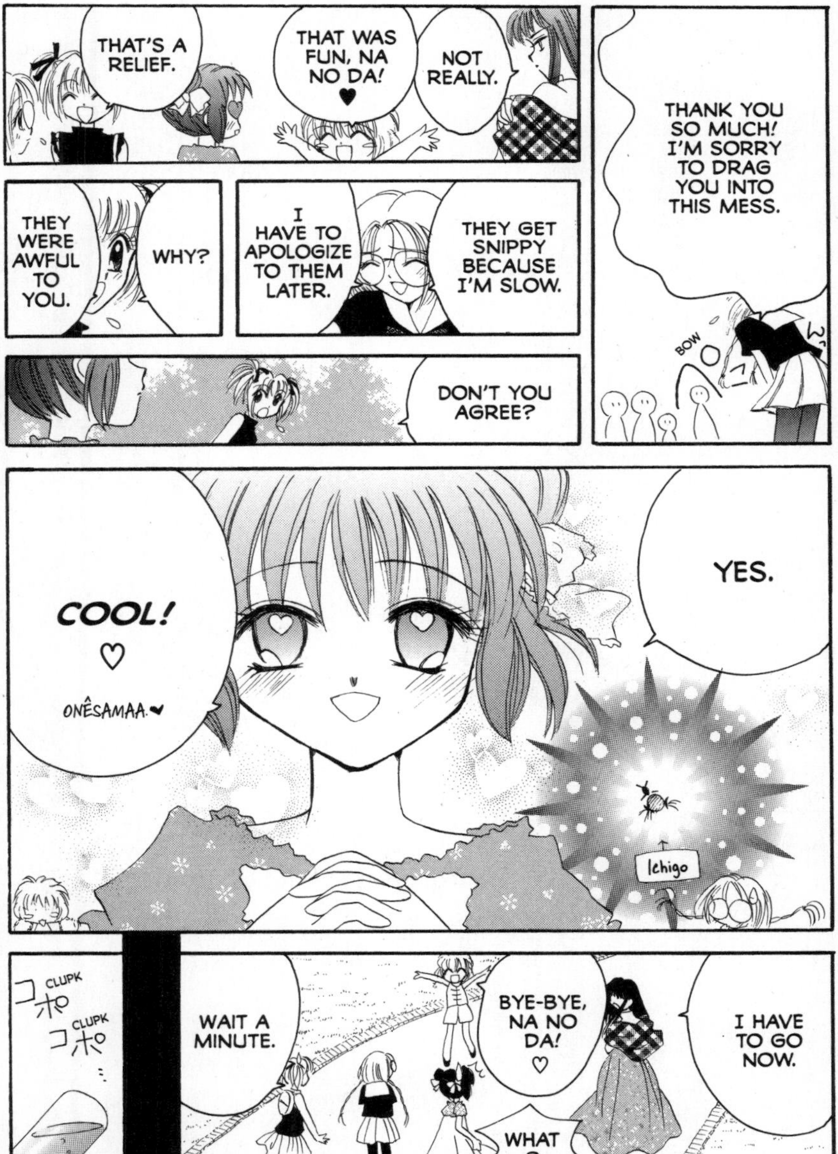

THANK YOU SO MUCH! I'M SORRY TO DRAG YOU INTO THIS MESS.
BOW
NOT REALLY.
THAT WAS FUN, NA NO DA! ♥
THAT'S A RELIEF.
THEY GET SNIPPY BECAUSE I'M SLOW.
I HAVE TO APOLOGIZE TO THEM LATER.
WHY?
THEY WERE AWFUL TO YOU.
DON'T YOU AGREE?
YES.
COOL! ♡
ONÊSAMAA.♥
Ichigo
I HAVE TO GO NOW.
BYE-BYE, NA NO DA! ♡
WHAT?
WAIT A MINUTE.
コポ CLUPK
コポ CLUPK

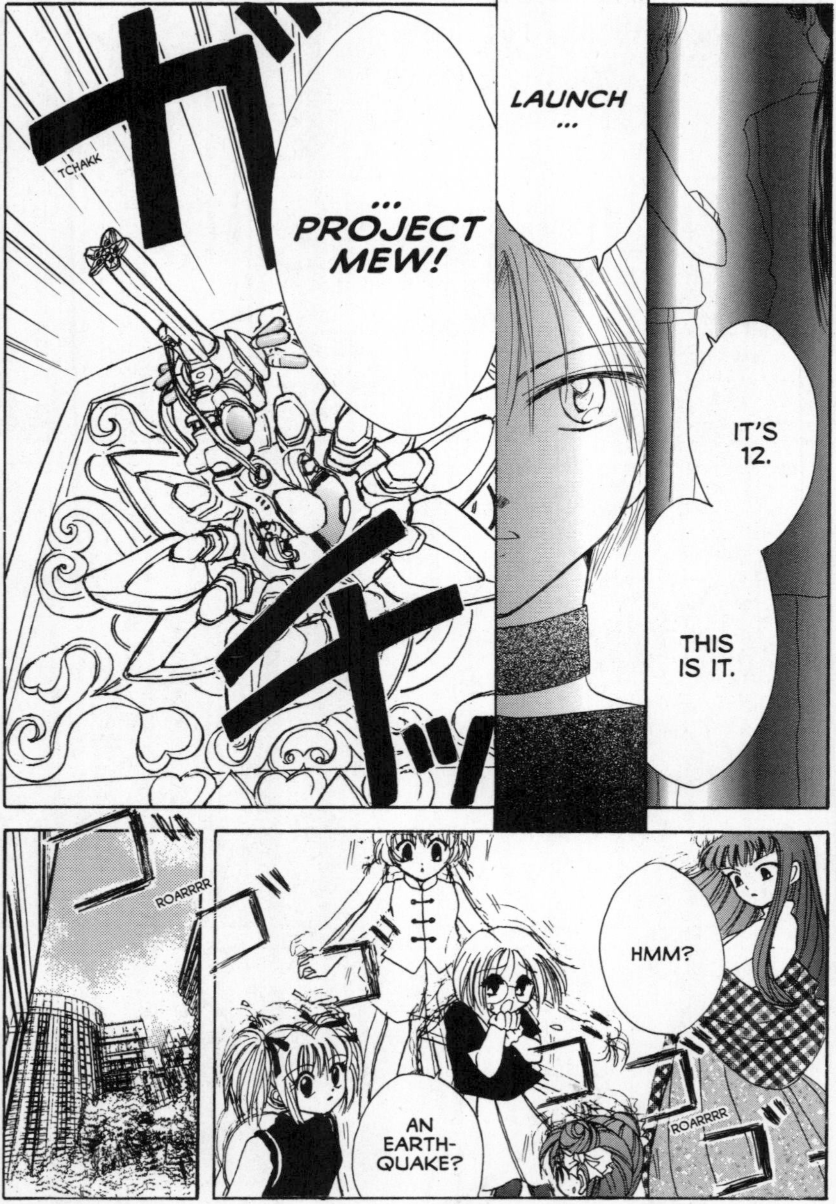
IT'S 12.
THIS IS IT.
LAUNCH ...
... PROJECT MEW!
TCHAKK
HMM?
ROARRRR
AN EARTH-QUAKE?
ROARRRR

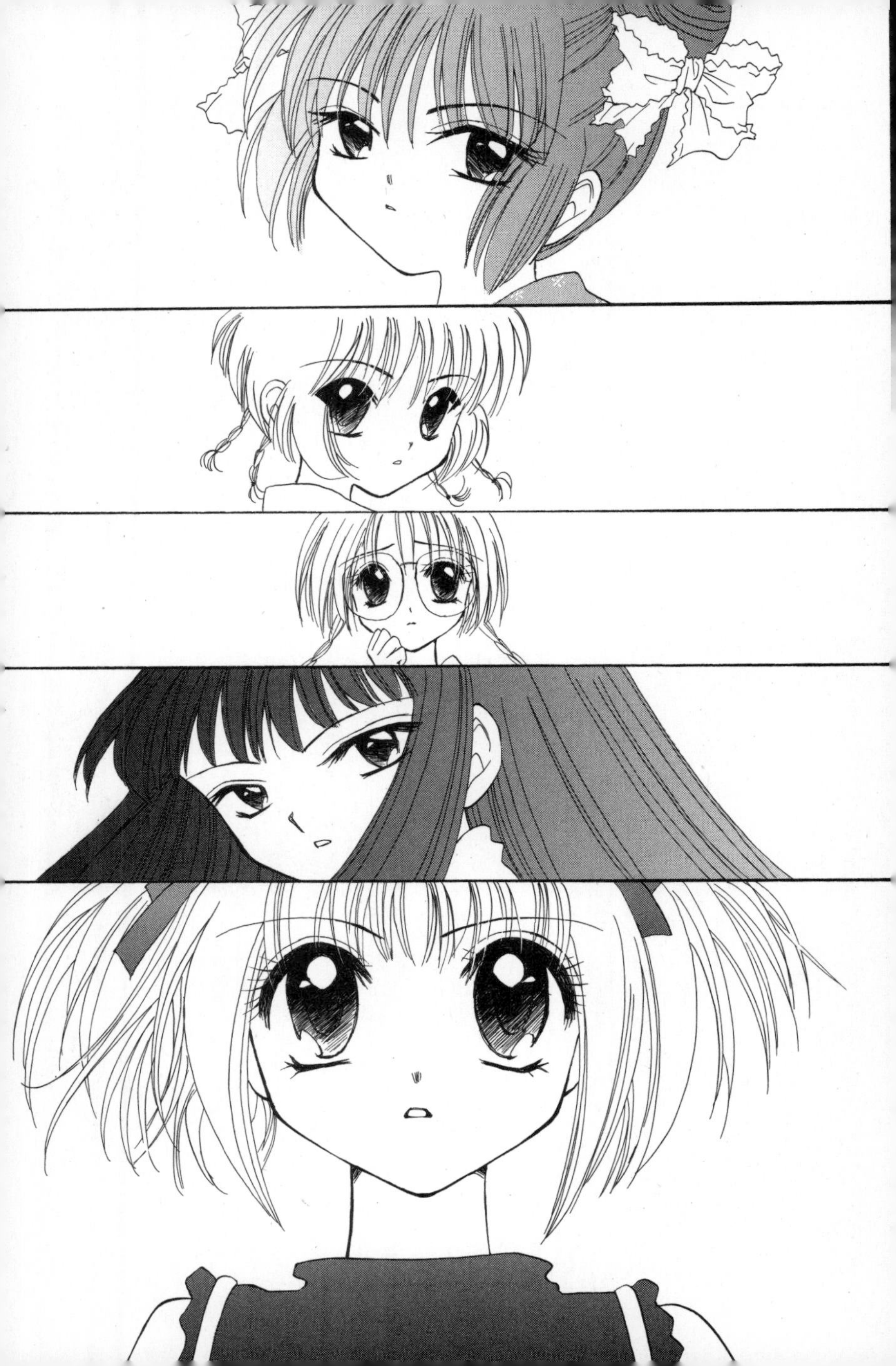

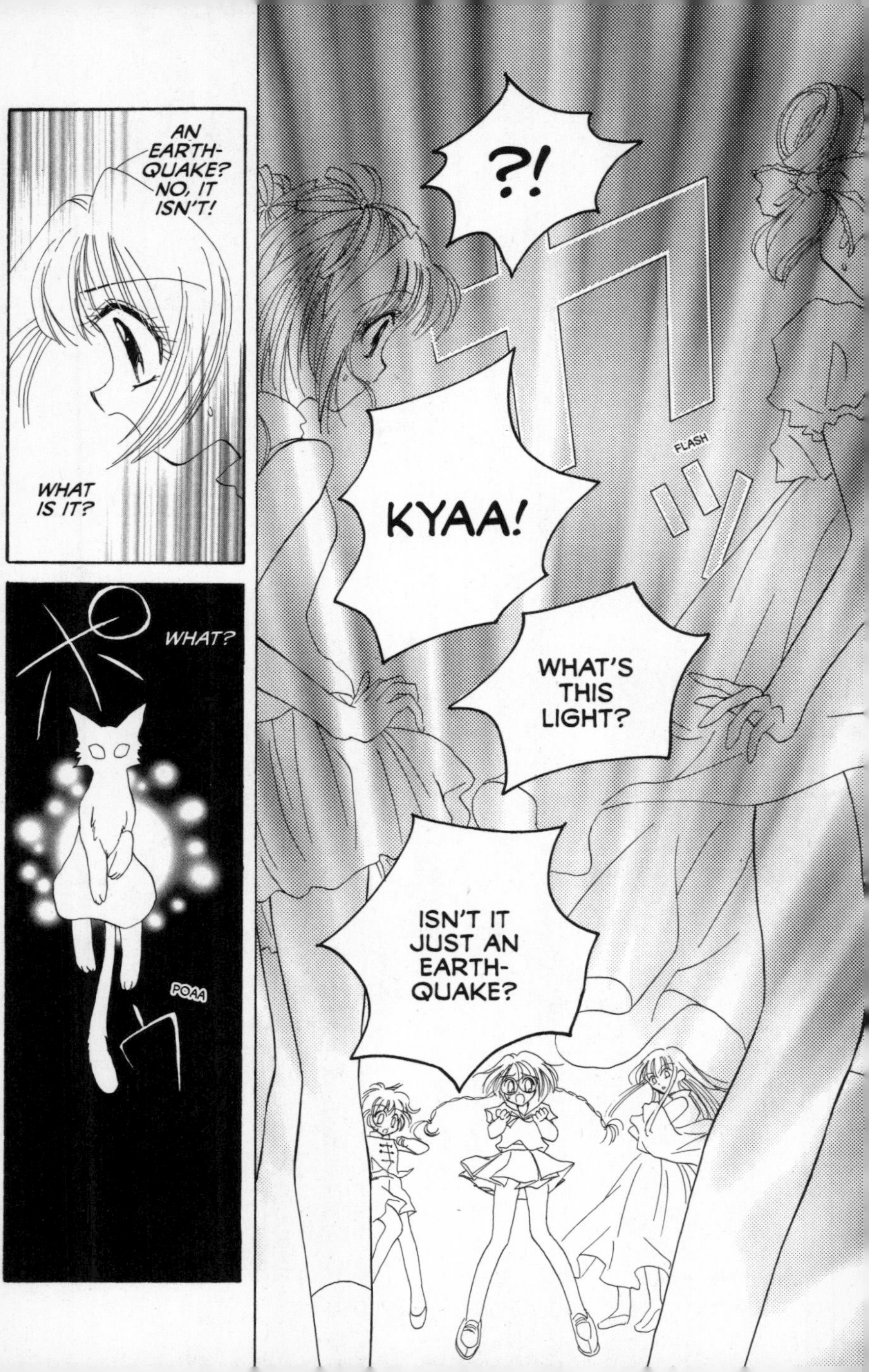
?!
FLASH
KYAA!
WHAT'S THIS LIGHT?
ISN'T IT JUST AN EARTH-QUAKE?
AN EARTH-QUAKE? NO, IT ISN'T!
WHAT IS IT?
WHAT?
POAA

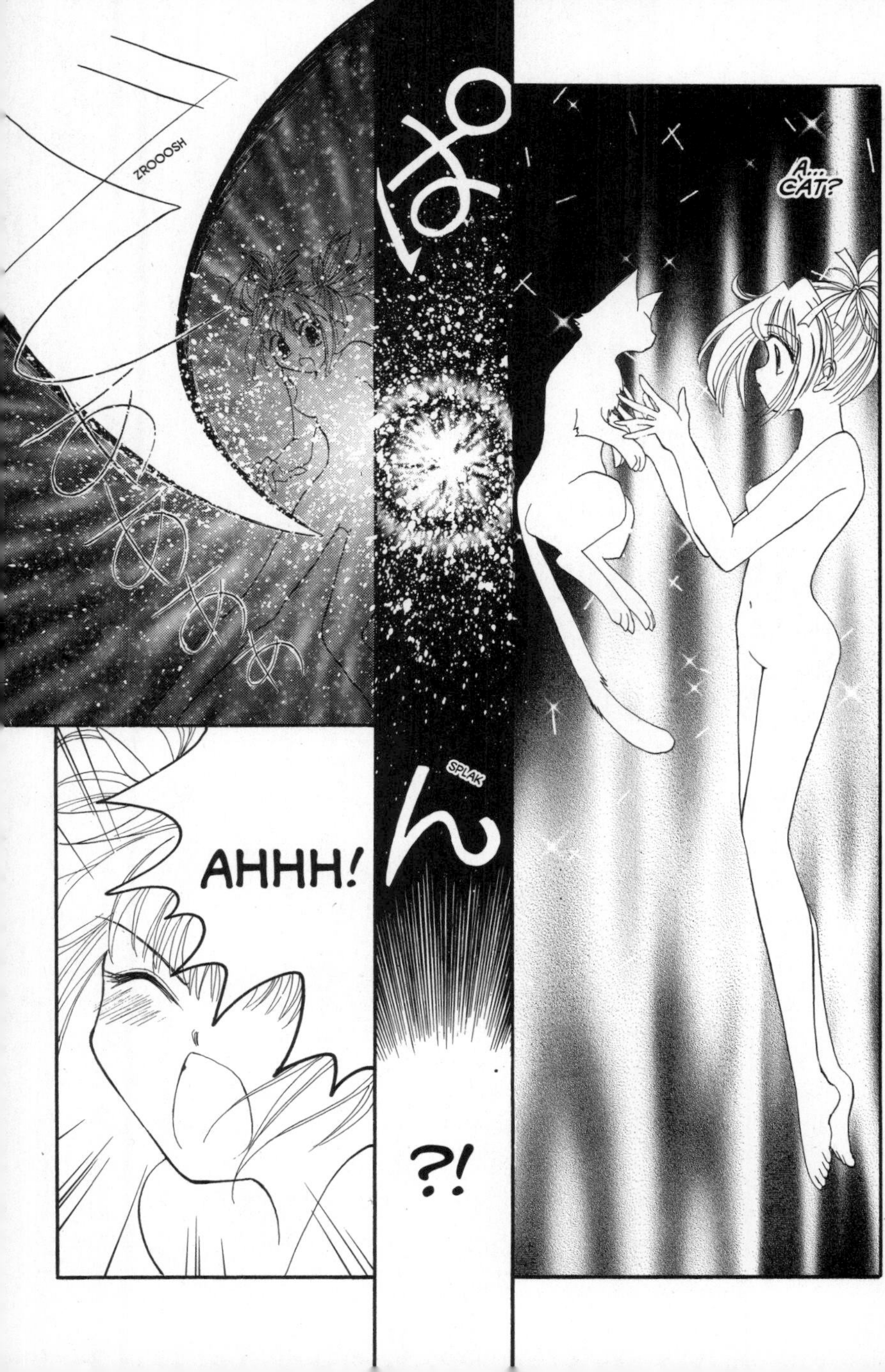
A... CAT?
ぱ
ん
SPLAK
?!
ZROOOSH
AHHH!

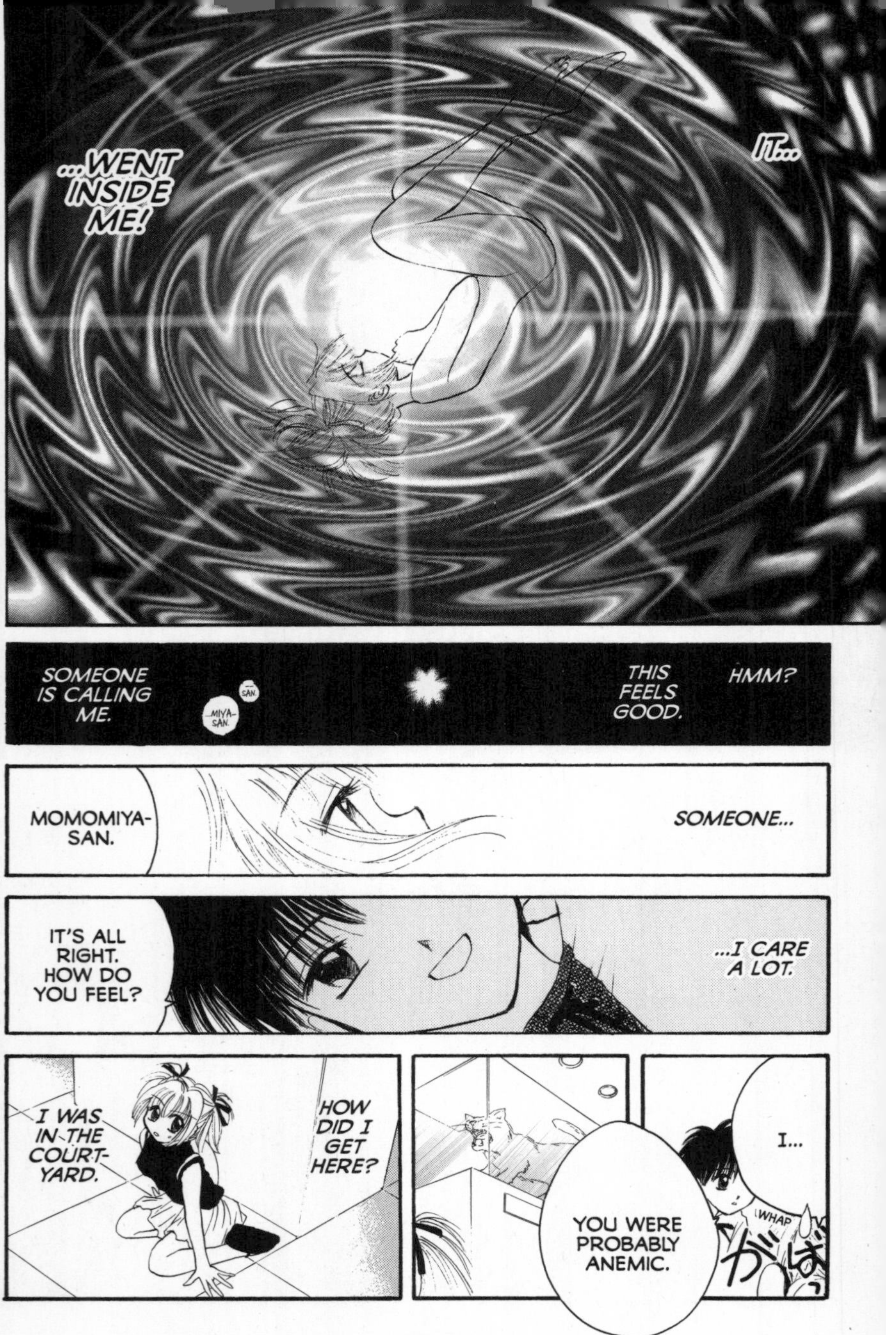

IT...
...WENT INSIDE ME!
HMM?
THIS FEELS GOOD.
—SAN.
...MIYA-SAN.
SOMEONE IS CALLING ME.
SOMEONE...
MOMOMIYA-SAN.
...I CARE A LOT.
IT'S ALL RIGHT. HOW DO YOU FEEL?
I...
WHAP
YOU WERE PROBABLY ANEMIC.
HOW DID I GET HERE?
I WAS IN THE COURTYARD.

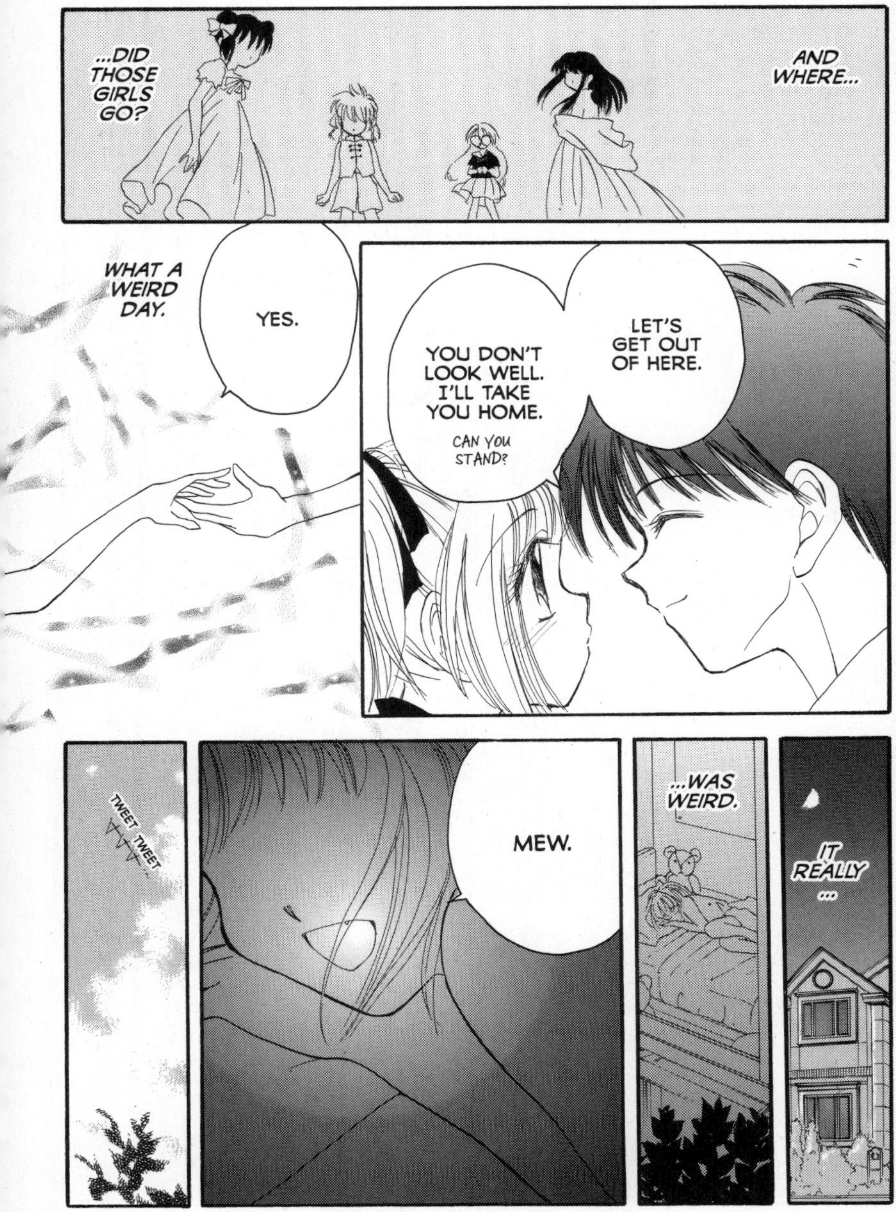
AND WHERE...
...DID THOSE GIRLS GO?
LET'S GET OUT OF HERE.
YOU DON'T LOOK WELL. I'LL TAKE YOU HOME.
CAN YOU STAND?
YES.
WHAT A WEIRD DAY.
IT REALLY ...
...WAS WEIRD.
MEW.
TWEET TWEET

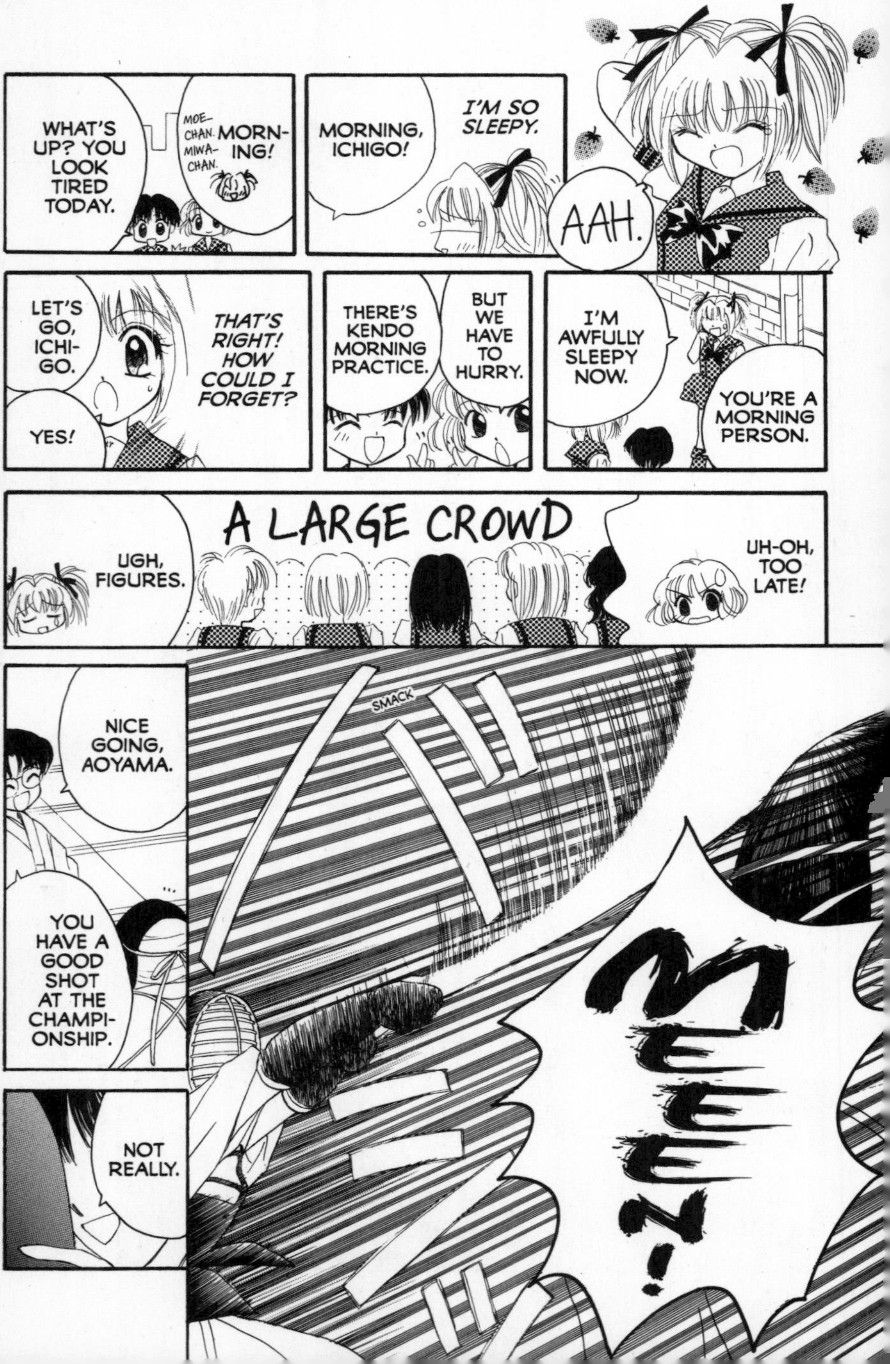
AAH.
I'M SO SLEEPY.
MORNING, ICHIGO!
MORNING!
MOE-CHAN. MIWA-CHAN.
WHAT'S UP? YOU LOOK TIRED TODAY.
I'M AWFULLY SLEEPY NOW.
YOU'RE A MORNING PERSON.
BUT WE HAVE TO HURRY.
THERE'S KENDO MORNING PRACTICE.
THAT'S RIGHT! HOW COULD I FORGET?
LET'S GO, ICHIGO.
YES!
UH-OH, TOO LATE!
A LARGE CROWD
UGH, FIGURES.
MEEEN!
SMACK
NICE GOING, AOYAMA.
...
YOU HAVE A GOOD SHOT AT THE CHAMPIONSHIP.
NOT REALLY.

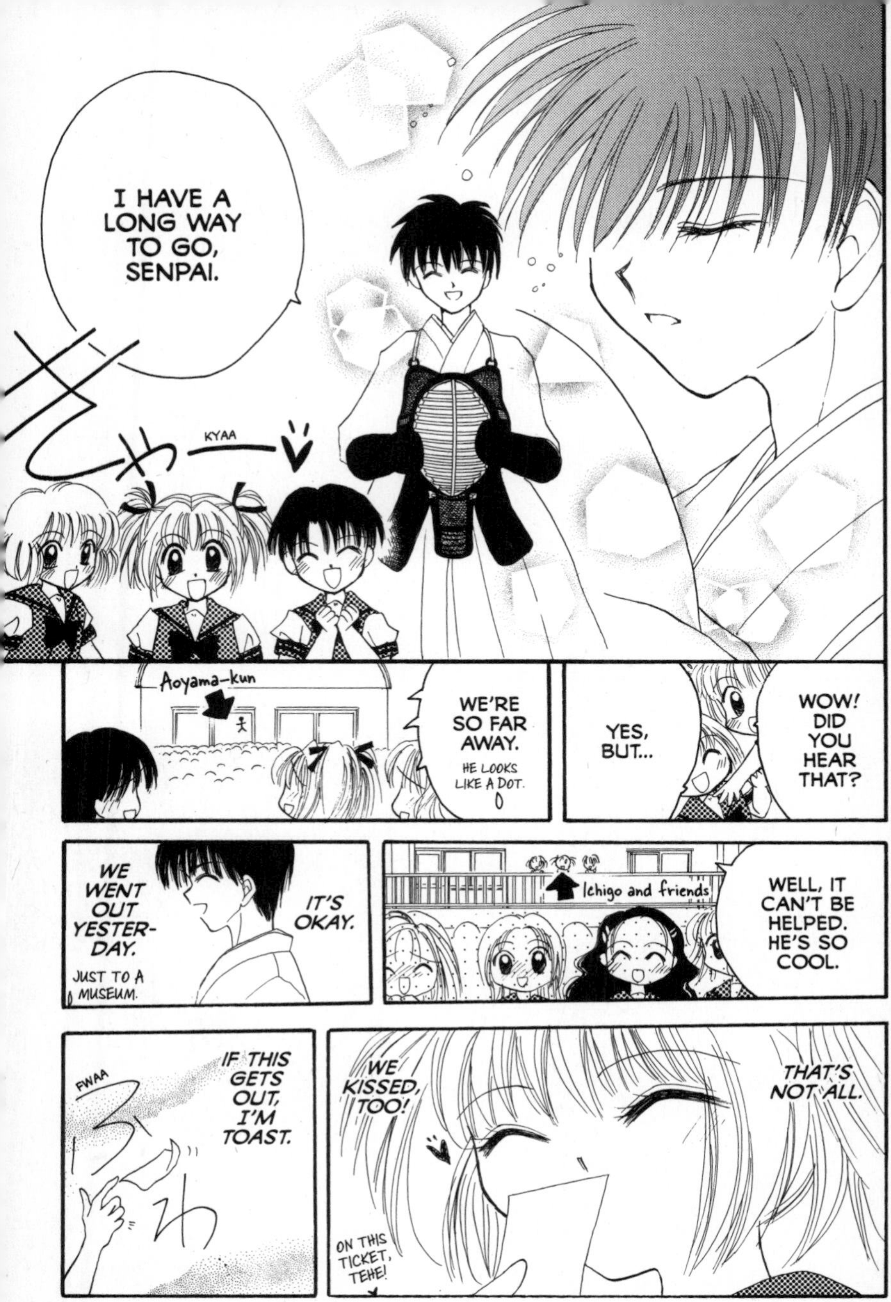
I HAVE A LONG WAY TO GO, SENPAI.
KYAA
WOW! DID YOU HEAR THAT?
YES, BUT...
WE'RE SO FAR AWAY.
HE LOOKS LIKE A DOT.
Aoyama-kun
WELL, IT CAN'T BE HELPED. HE'S SO COOL.
Ichigo and friends
IT'S OKAY.
WE WENT OUT YESTER-DAY.
JUST TO A MUSEUM.
THAT'S NOT ALL.
WE KISSED, TOO!
ON THIS TICKET, TEHE!
IF THIS GETS OUT, I'M TOAST.
FWAA

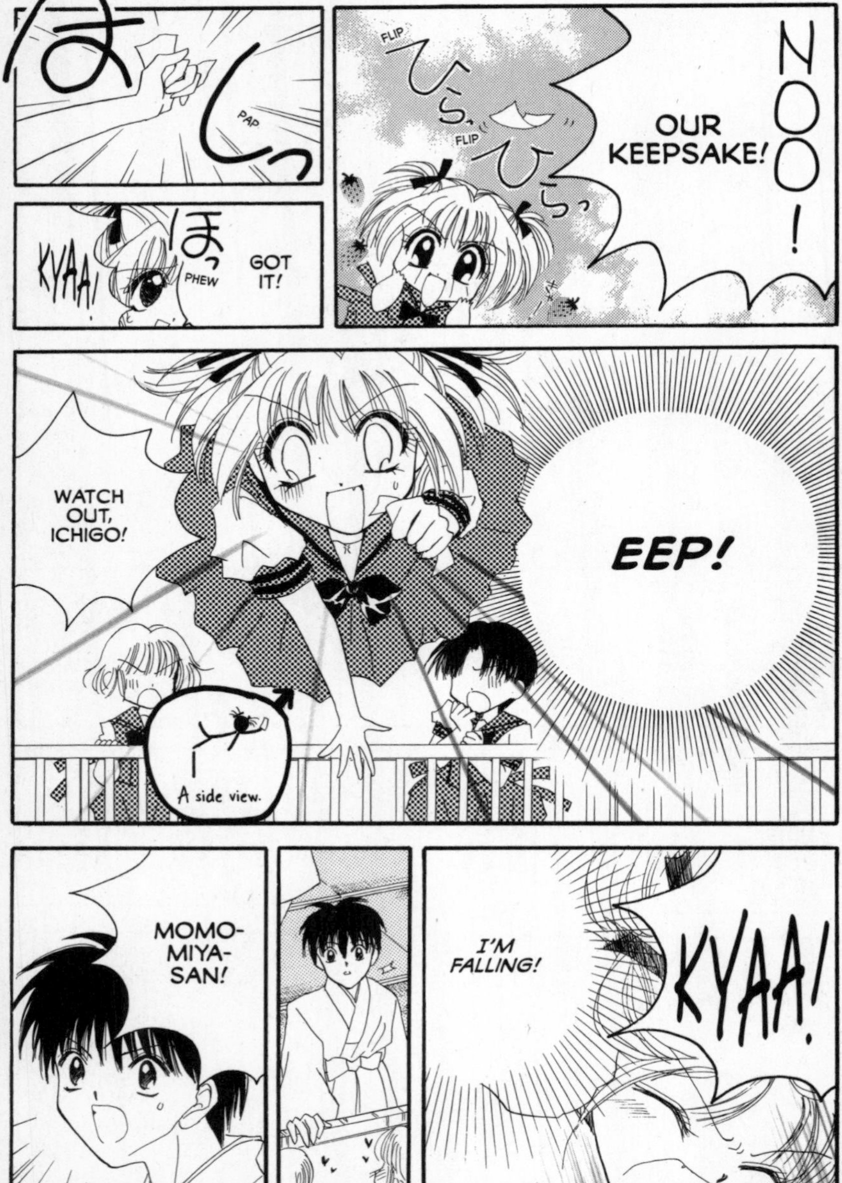
NOOO!
OUR KEEPSAKE!
ひら、ひらっ
FLIP
FLIP
ぱしっ
PAP
KYAA!
ほっ
PHEW
GOT IT!
EEP!
WATCH OUT, ICHIGO!
A side view.
KYAA!
I'M FALLING!
MOMO-MIYA-SAN!

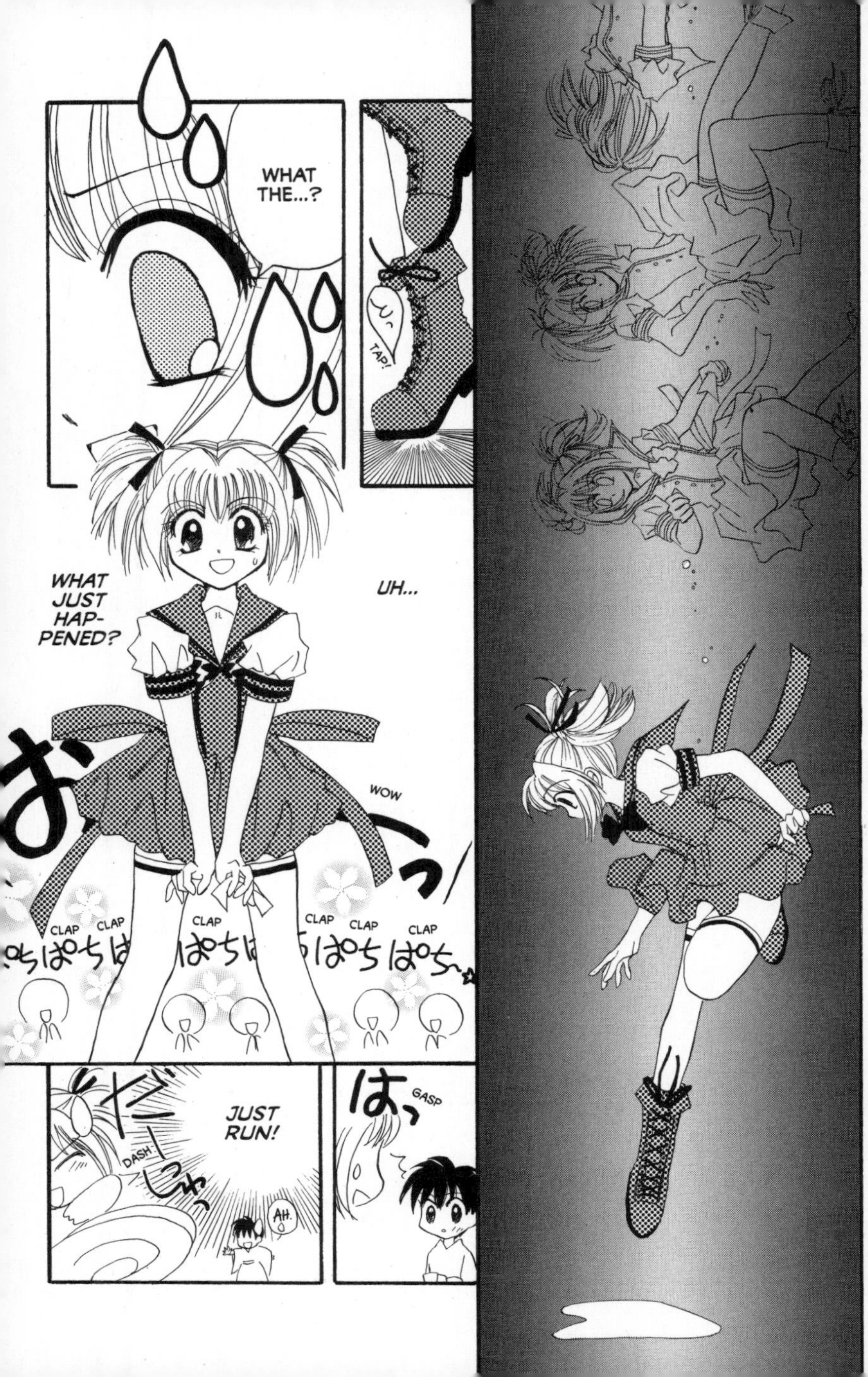
TAP!
WHAT THE...?
UH...
WHAT JUST HAP-PENED?
WOW
CLAP CLAP
CLAP
CLAP CLAP
CLAP
GASP
JUST RUN!
DASH
AH.

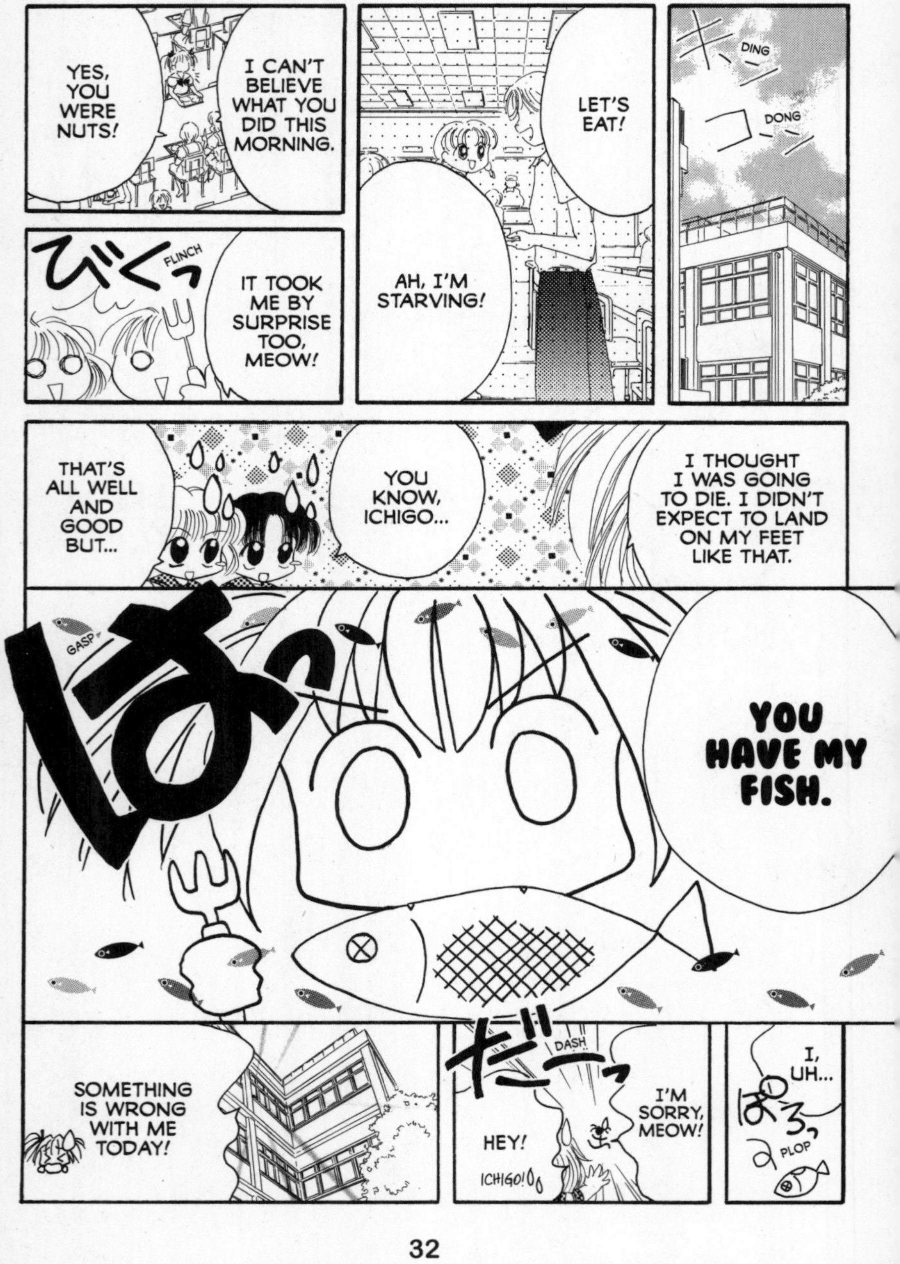
DING
DONG
LET'S EAT!
AH, I'M STARVING!
I CAN'T BELIEVE WHAT YOU DID THIS MORNING.
YES, YOU WERE NUTS!
IT TOOK ME BY SURPRISE TOO, MEOW!
びくっ
FLINCH
I THOUGHT I WAS GOING TO DIE. I DIDN'T EXPECT TO LAND ON MY FEET LIKE THAT.
YOU KNOW, ICHIGO...
THAT'S ALL WELL AND GOOD BUT...
YOU HAVE MY FISH.
はっ
GASP
I, UH...
ぽろっ
PLOP
だーっ
DASH
I'M SORRY, MEOW!
HEY!
ICHIGO!
SOMETHING IS WRONG WITH ME TODAY!

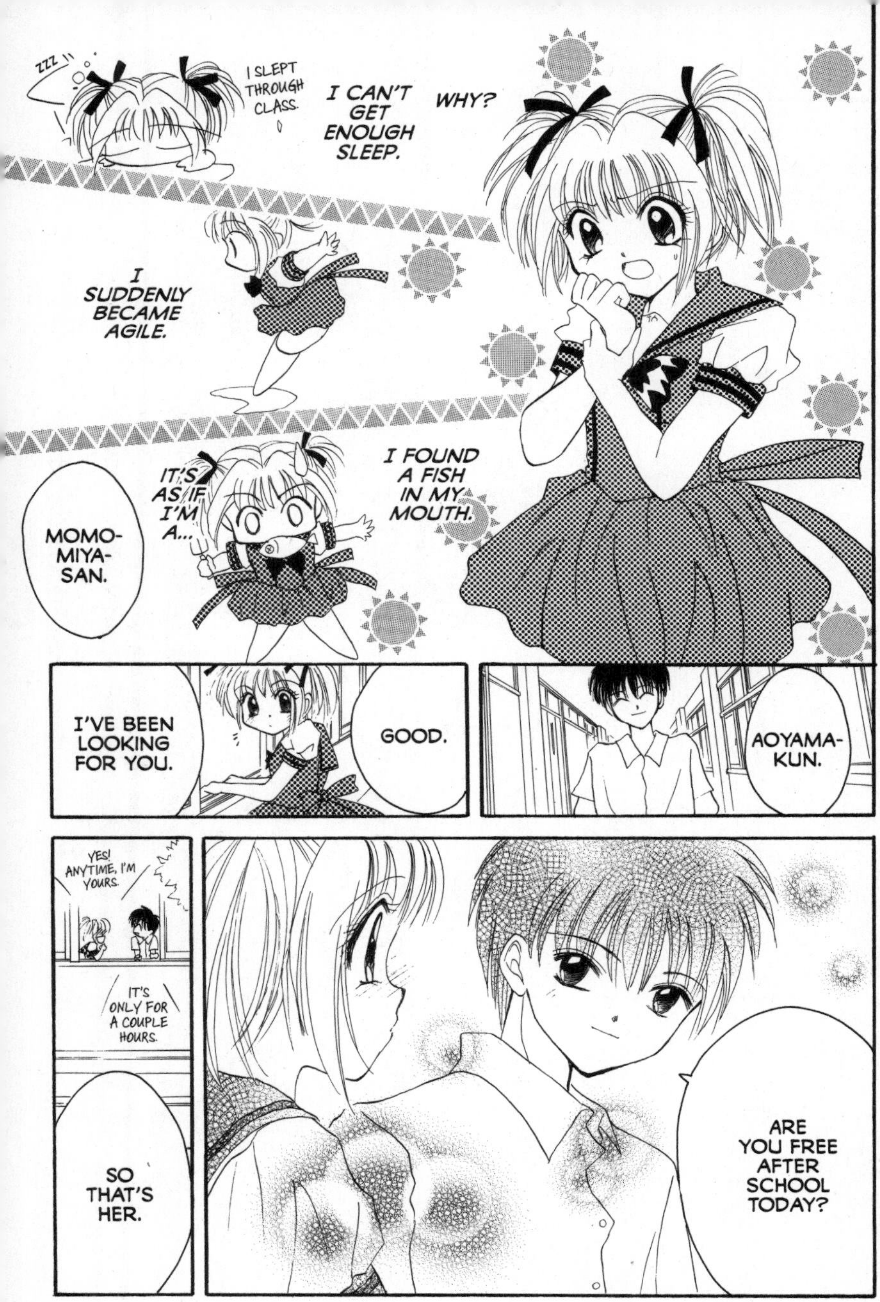
WHY?
I CAN'T GET ENOUGH SLEEP.
I SLEPT THROUGH CLASS.
ZZZ
I SUDDENLY BECAME AGILE.
I FOUND A FISH IN MY MOUTH.
IT'S AS IF I'M A...
MOMO-MIYA-SAN.
AOYAMA-KUN.
GOOD.
I'VE BEEN LOOKING FOR YOU.
ARE YOU FREE AFTER SCHOOL TODAY?
YES! ANYTIME, I'M YOURS.
IT'S ONLY FOR A COUPLE HOURS.
SO THAT'S HER.

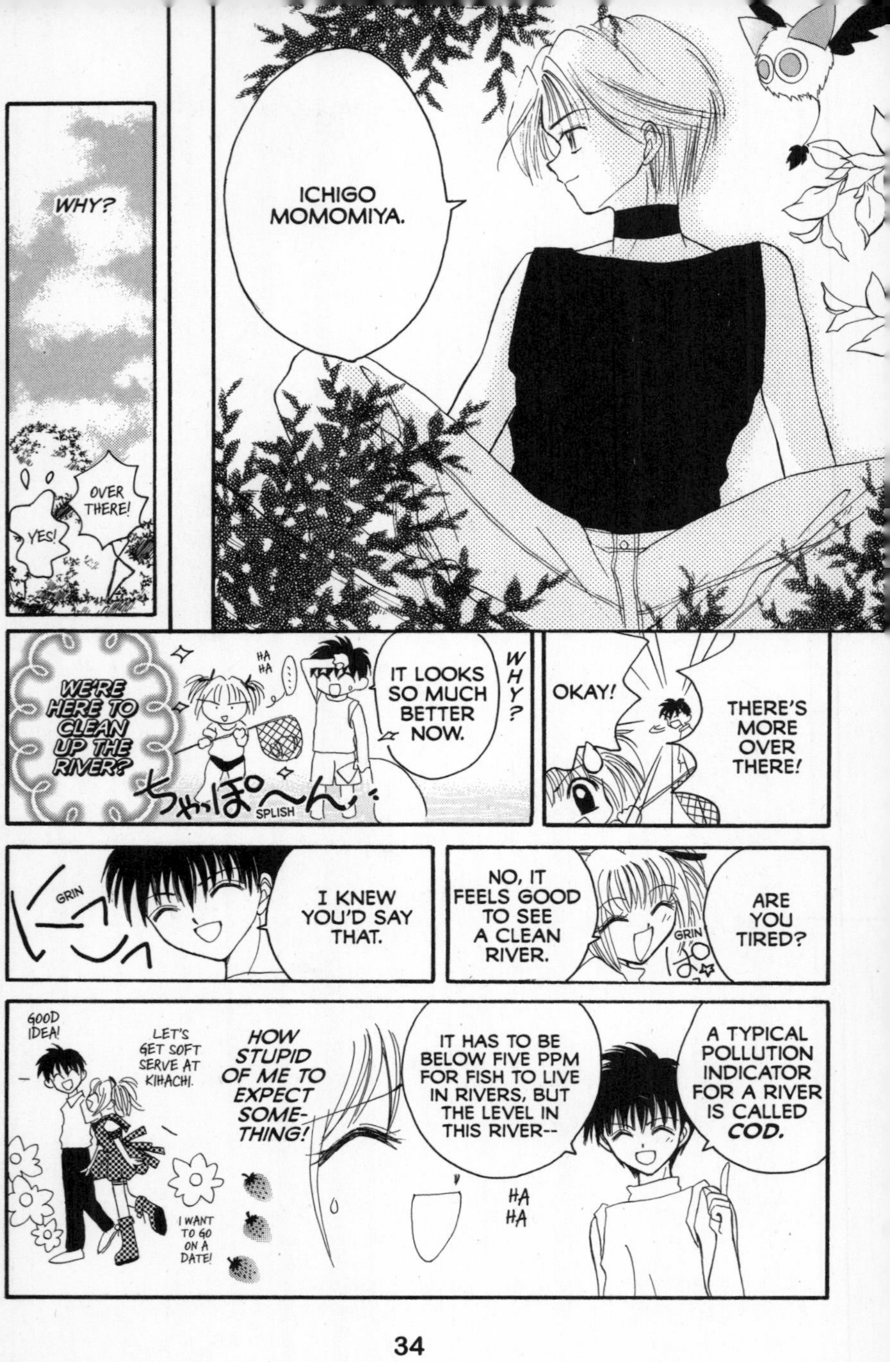
ICHIGO MOMOMIYA.
WHY?
OVER THERE!
YES!
THERE'S MORE OVER THERE!
OKAY!
WHY?
IT LOOKS SO MUCH BETTER NOW.
HA HA
WE'RE HERE TO CLEAN UP THE RIVER?
ちゃぽ～ん
SPLISH
ARE YOU TIRED?
GRIN
NO, IT FEELS GOOD TO SEE A CLEAN RIVER.
I KNEW YOU'D SAY THAT.
GRIN
A TYPICAL POLLUTION INDICATOR FOR A RIVER IS CALLED COD.
HA HA
IT HAS TO BE BELOW FIVE PPM FOR FISH TO LIVE IN RIVERS, BUT THE LEVEL IN THIS RIVER--
HOW STUPID OF ME TO EXPECT SOMETHING!
LET'S GET SOFT SERVE AT KIHACHI.
GOOD IDEA!
I WANT TO GO ON A DATE!

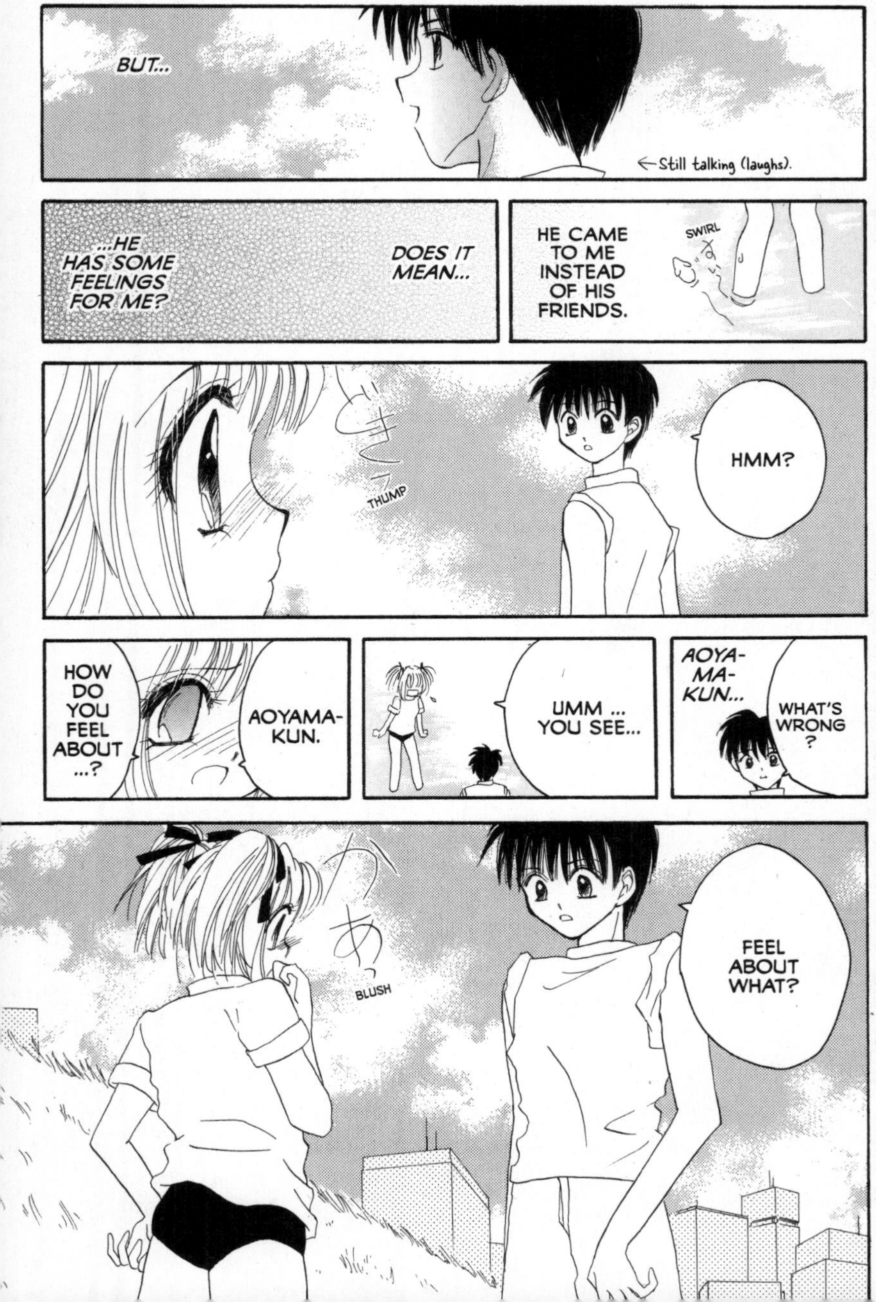
BUT...
←Still talking (laughs).
HE CAME TO ME INSTEAD OF HIS FRIENDS.
SWIRL
DOES IT MEAN...
...HE HAS SOME FEELINGS FOR ME?
HMM?
THUMP
AOYAMA-KUN...
WHAT'S WRONG?
UMM ... YOU SEE...
AOYAMA-KUN.
HOW DO YOU FEEL ABOUT ...?
FEEL ABOUT WHAT?
BLUSH

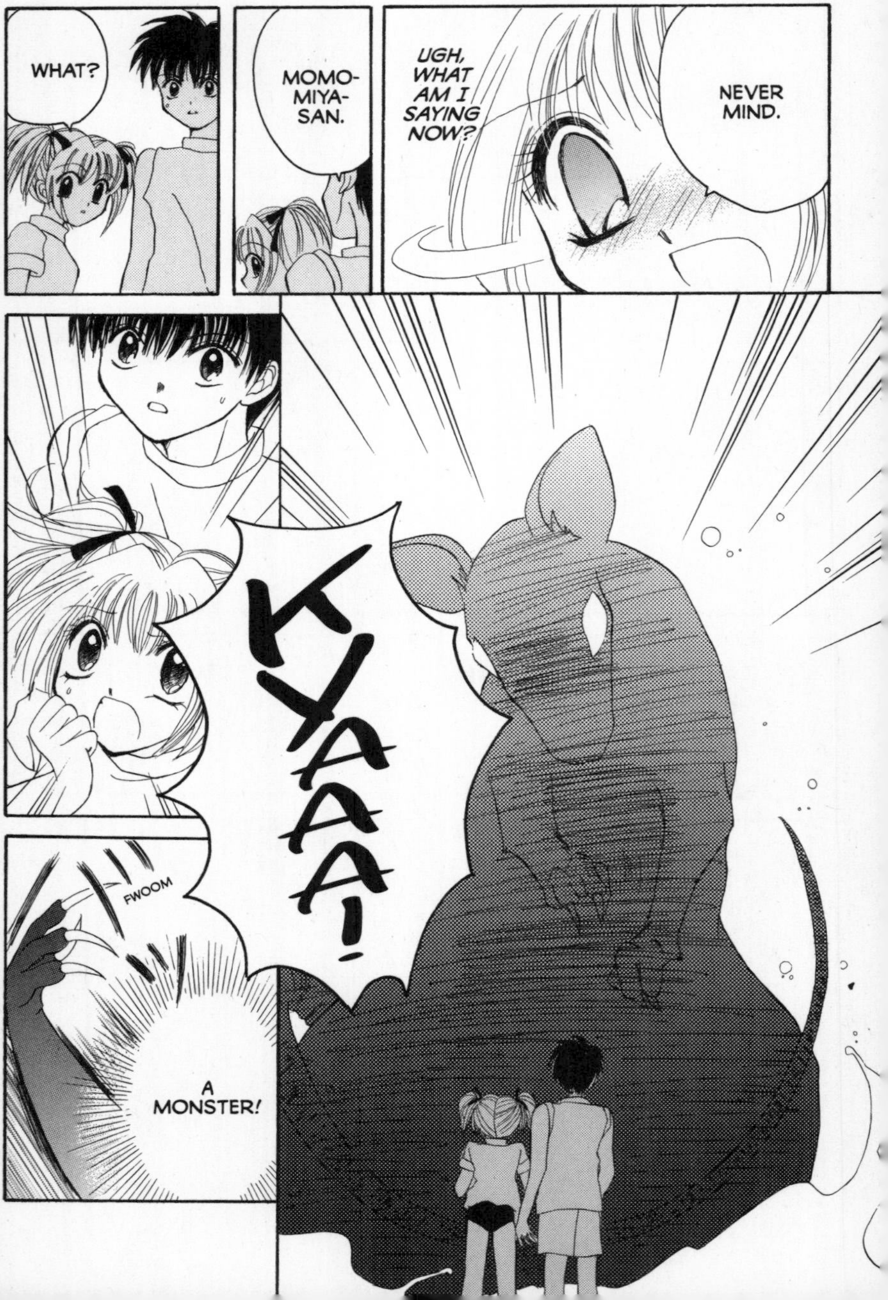
UGH, WHAT AM I SAYING NOW?
NEVER MIND.
MOMO-MIYA-SAN.
WHAT?
KYAAAA!
FWOOM
A MONSTER!

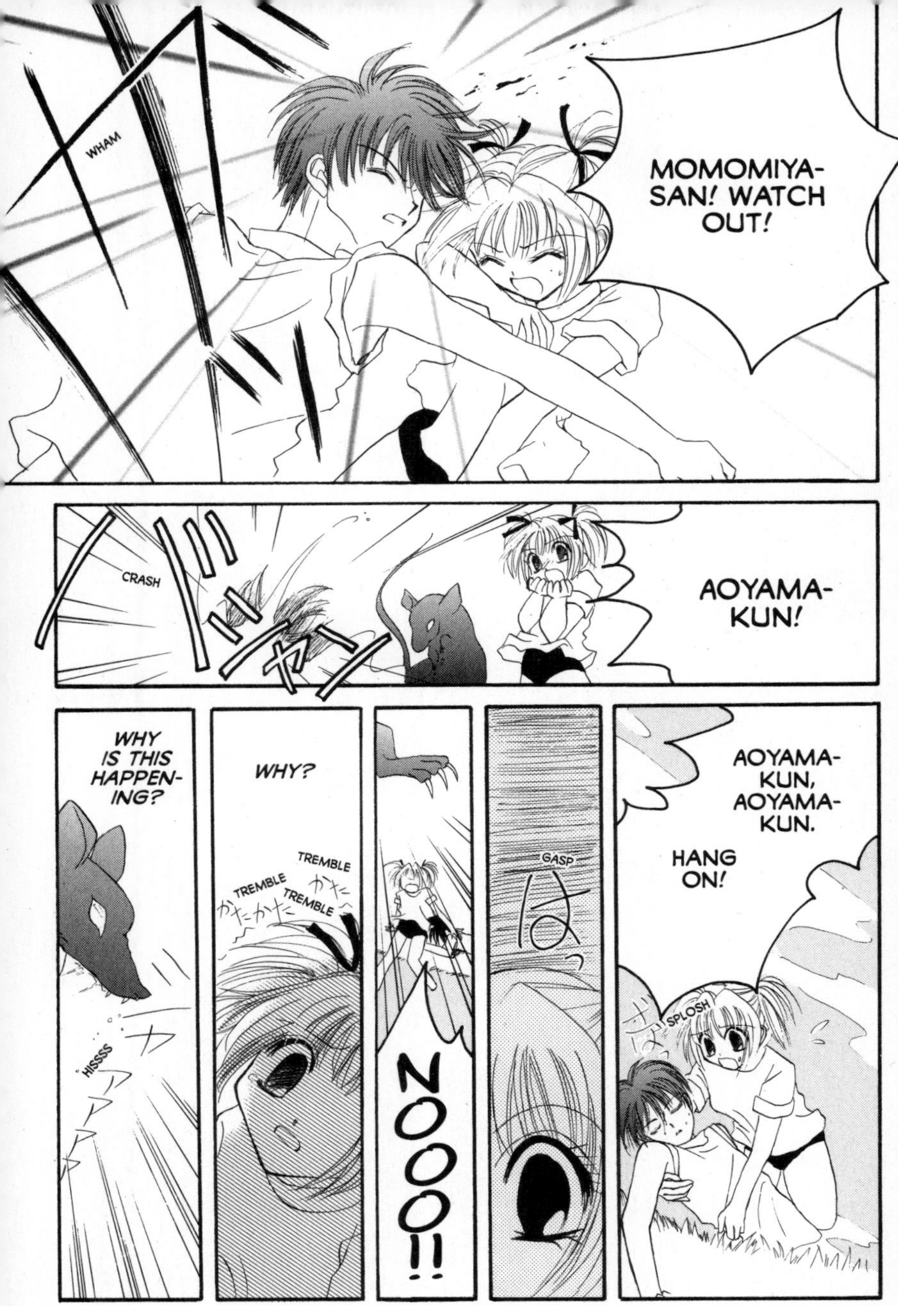
MOMOMIYA-SAN! WATCH OUT!
WHAM
AOYAMA-KUN!
CRASH
AOYAMA-KUN, AOYAMA-KUN.
HANG ON!
SPLOSH
GASP
NOOOO!!
WHY?
TREMBLE
TREMBLE
TREMBLE
WHY IS THIS HAPPENING?
HISSSS

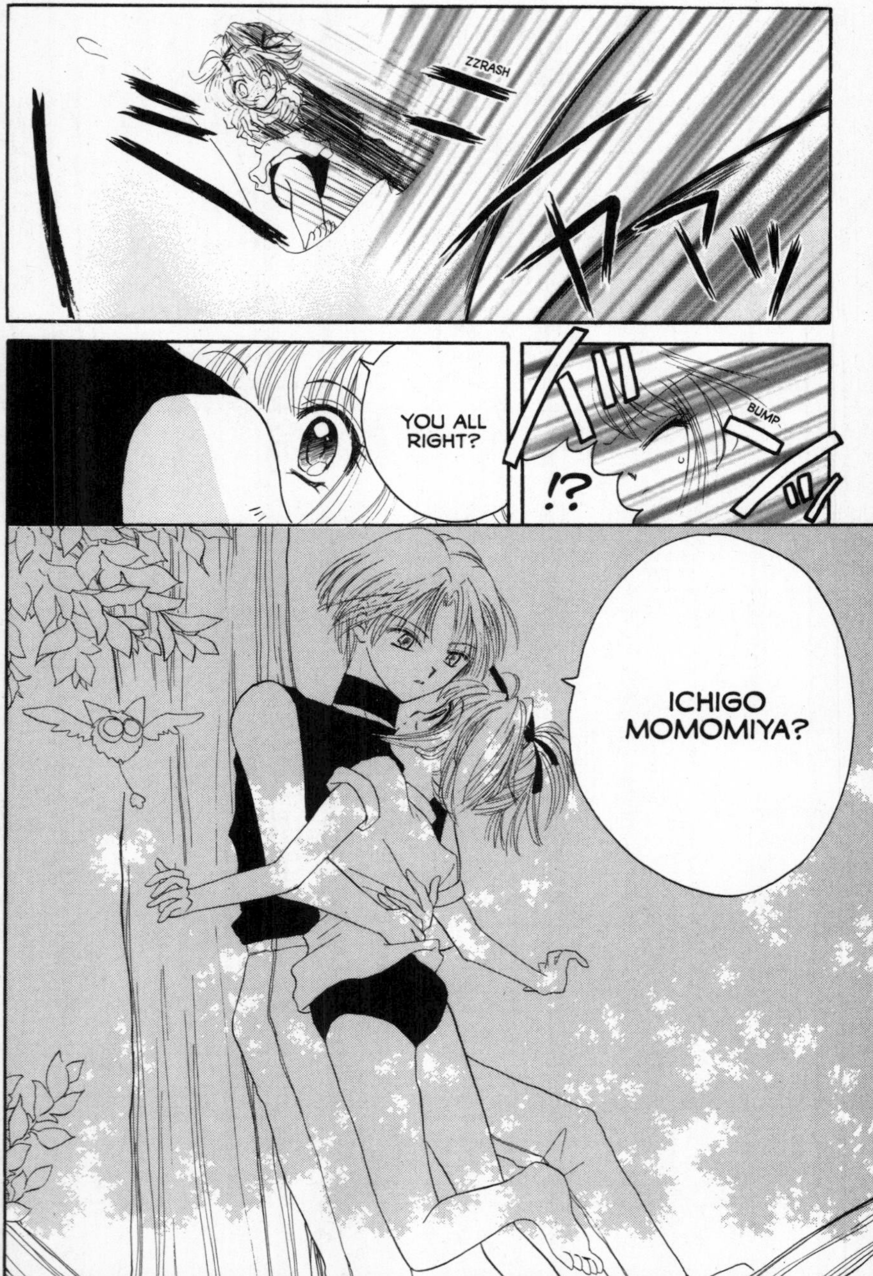
ZZRASH
BUMP
!?
YOU ALL RIGHT?
ICHIGO MOMOMIYA?

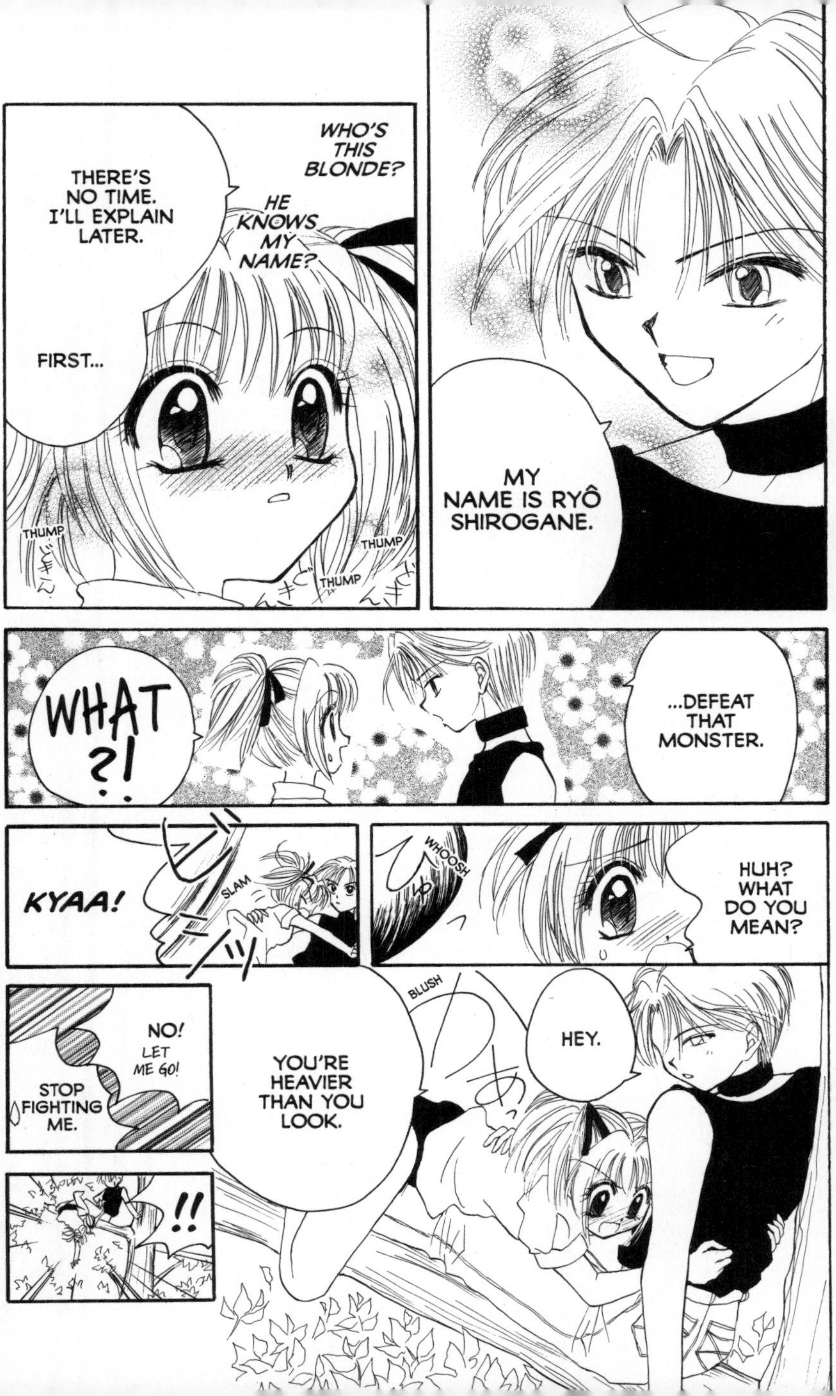
MY NAME IS RYÔ SHIROGANE.
WHO'S THIS BLONDE?
HE KNOWS MY NAME?
THERE'S NO TIME. I'LL EXPLAIN LATER.
FIRST...
THUMP
THUMP
THUMP
...DEFEAT THAT MONSTER.
WHAT ?!
WHOOSH
HUH? WHAT DO YOU MEAN?
KYAA!
SLAM
HEY.
BLUSH
YOU'RE HEAVIER THAN YOU LOOK.
NO! LET ME GO!
STOP FIGHTING ME.
!!

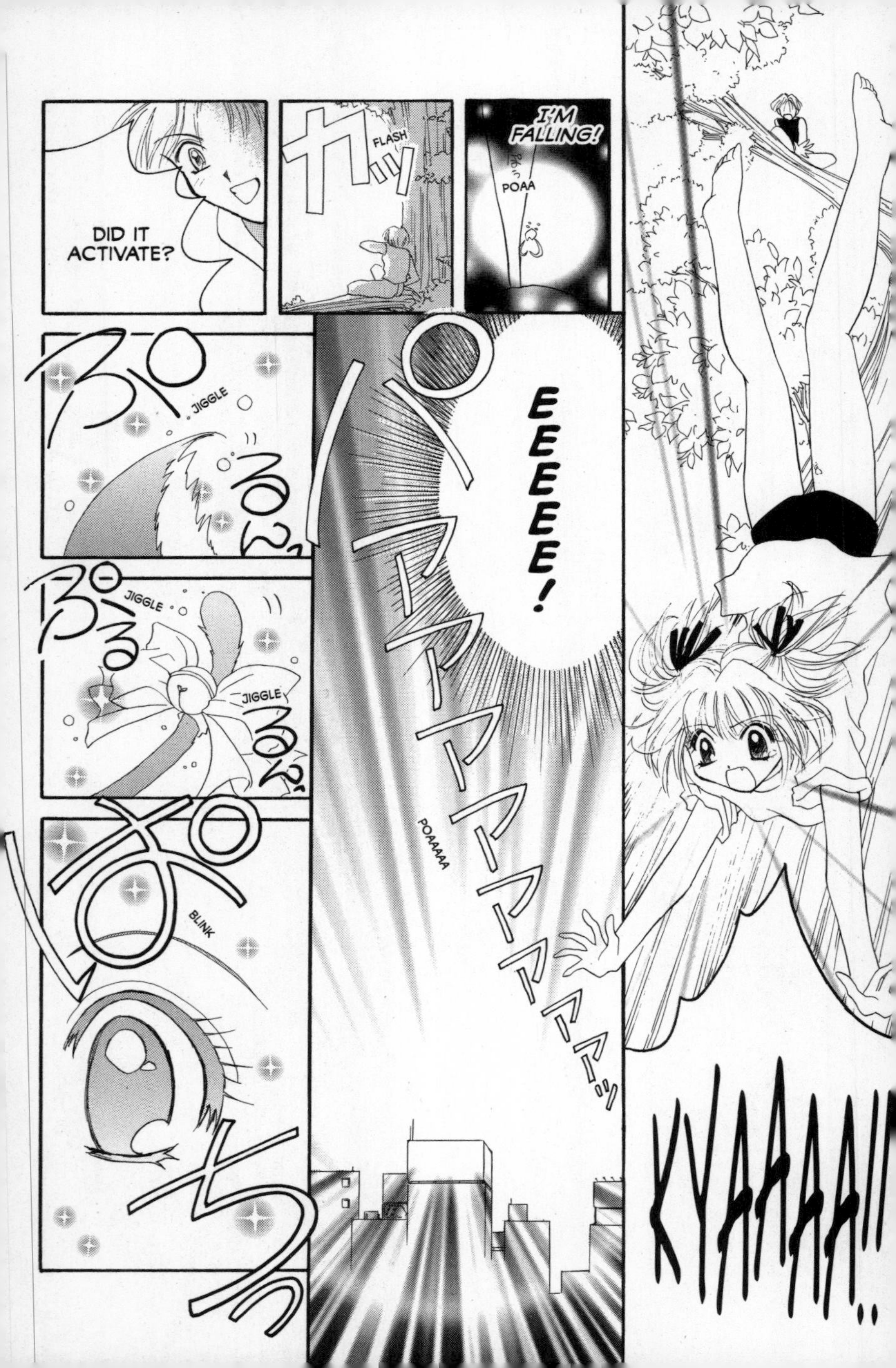
KYAAA!!..
I'M FALLING!
POAA
FLASH
DID IT ACTIVATE?
EEEEE!
POAAAAA
JIGGLE
JIGGLE
JIGGLE
BLINK

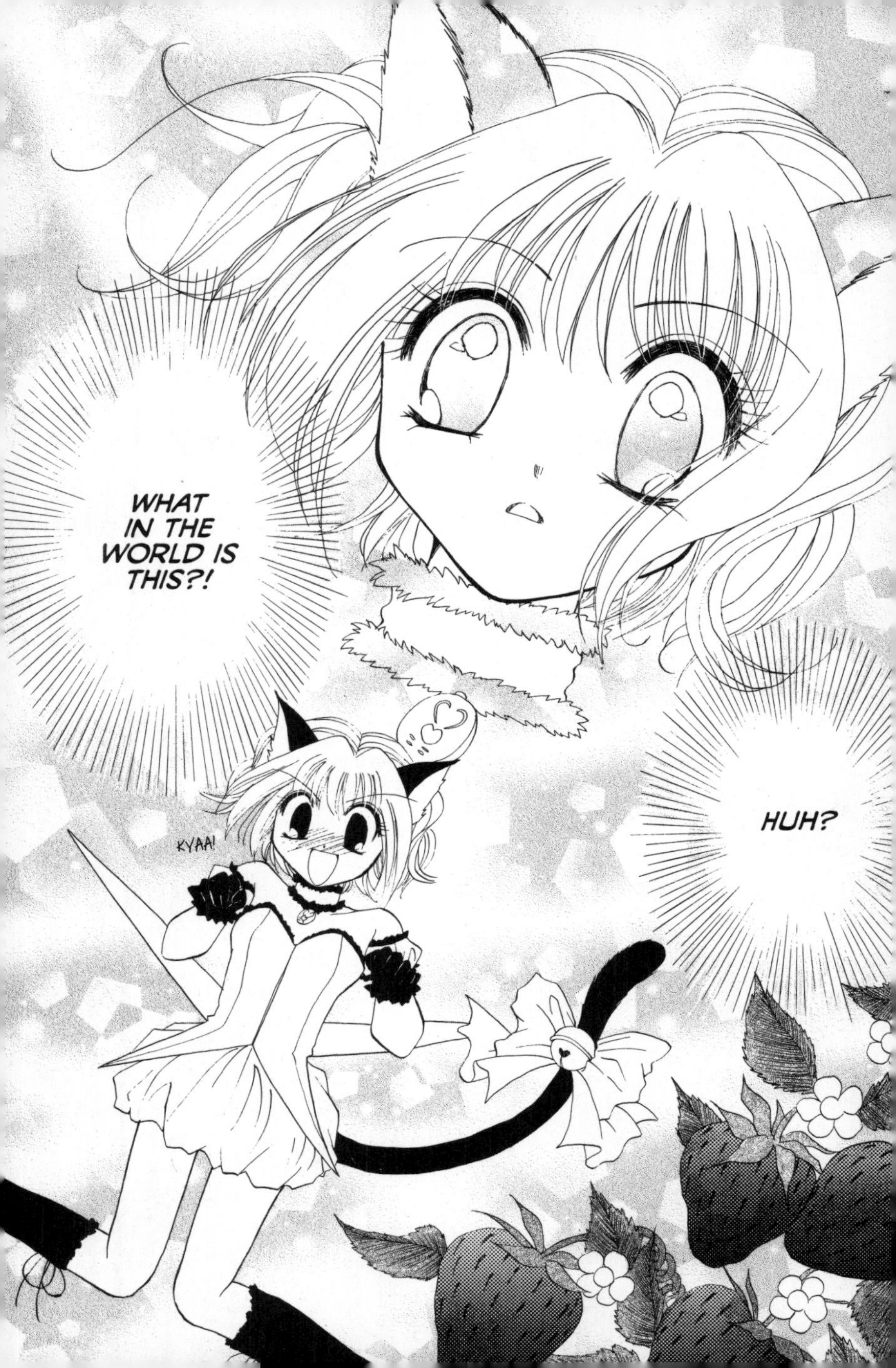
HUH?
WHAT IN THE WORLD IS THIS?!
KYAA!

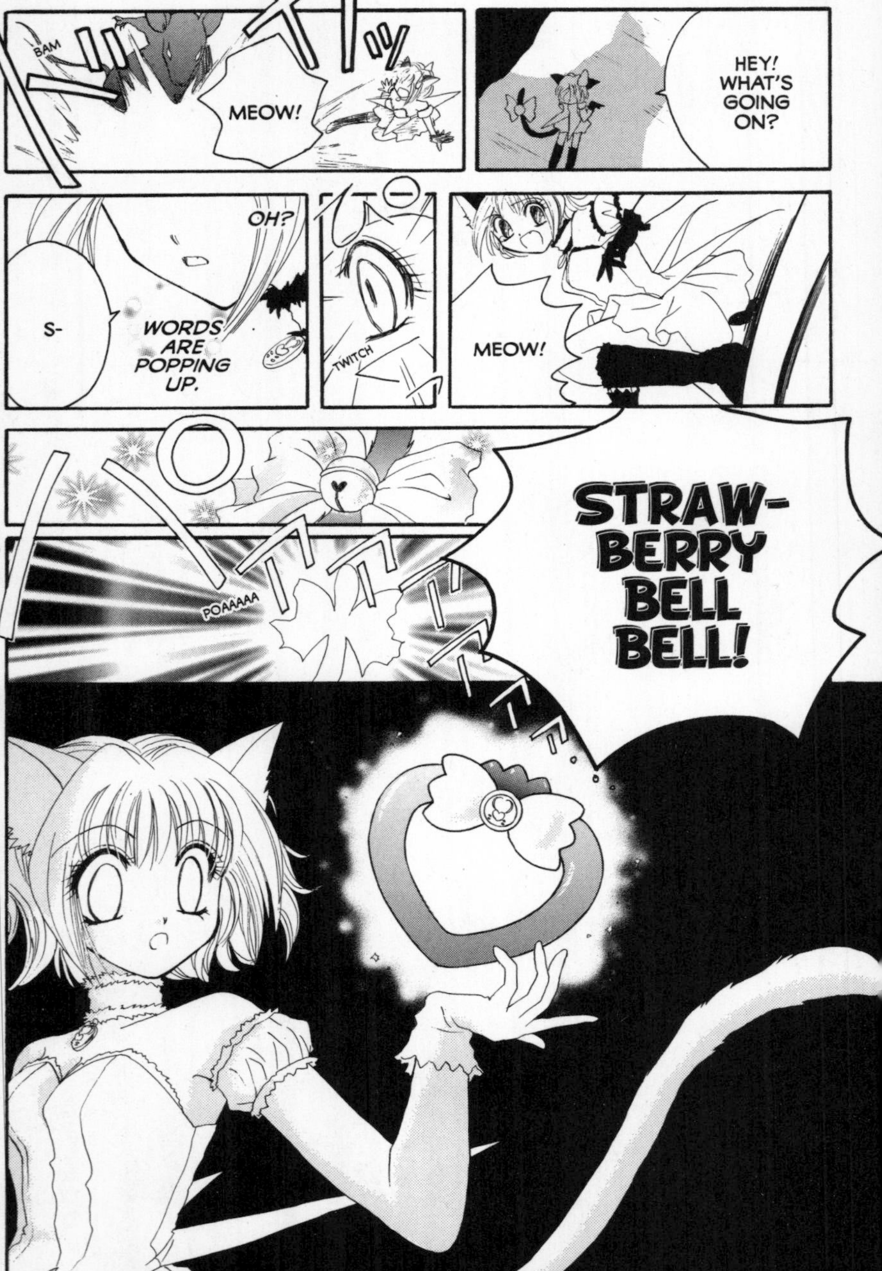
HEY! WHAT'S GOING ON?
BAM
MEOW!
MEOW!
TWITCH
OH?
S-
WORDS ARE POPPING UP.
STRAW-BERRY BELL BELL!
POAAAAA

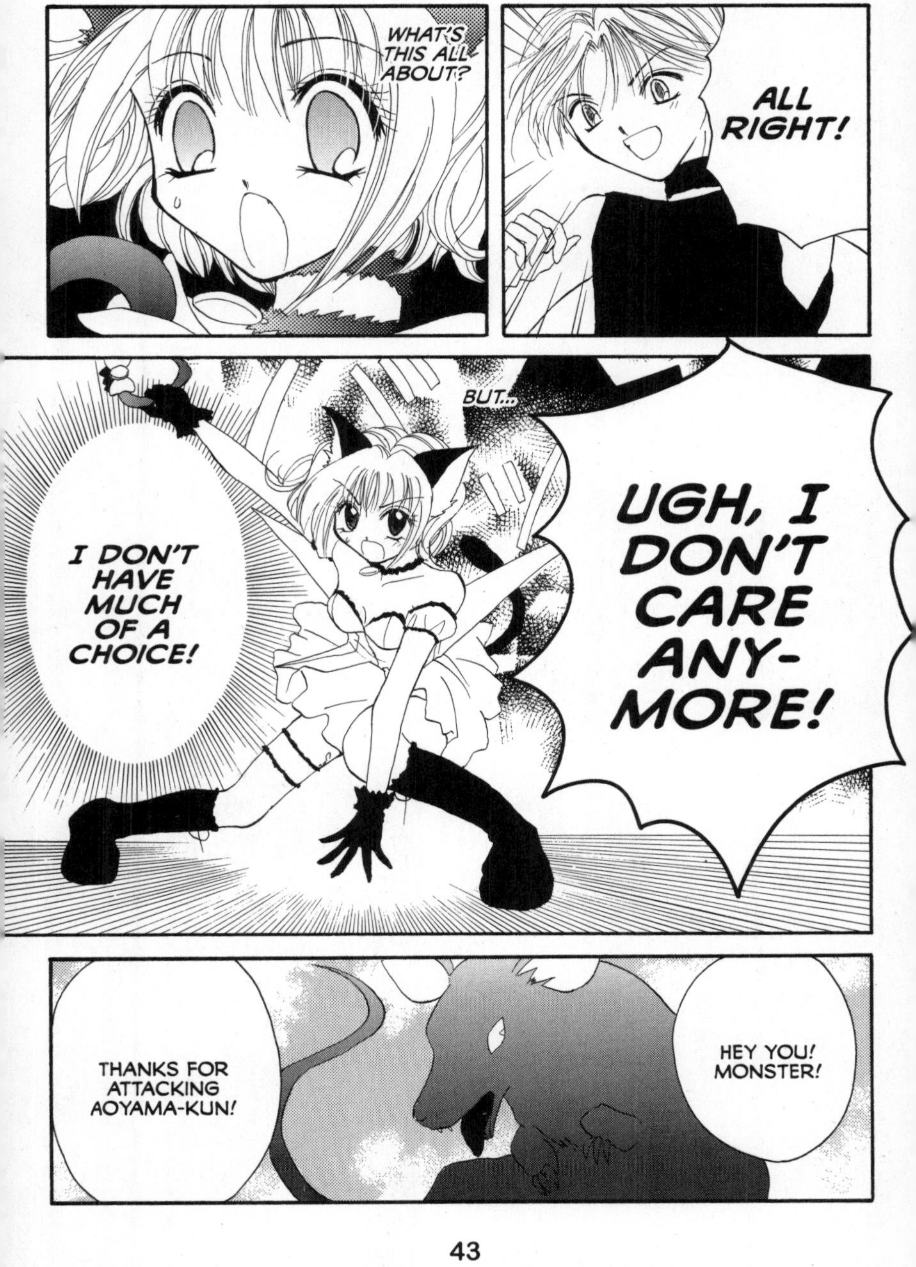
ALL RIGHT!
WHAT'S THIS ALL ABOUT?
BUT...
UGH, I DON'T CARE ANY-MORE!
I DON'T HAVE MUCH OF A CHOICE!
HEY YOU! MONSTER!
THANKS FOR ATTACKING AOYAMA-KUN!

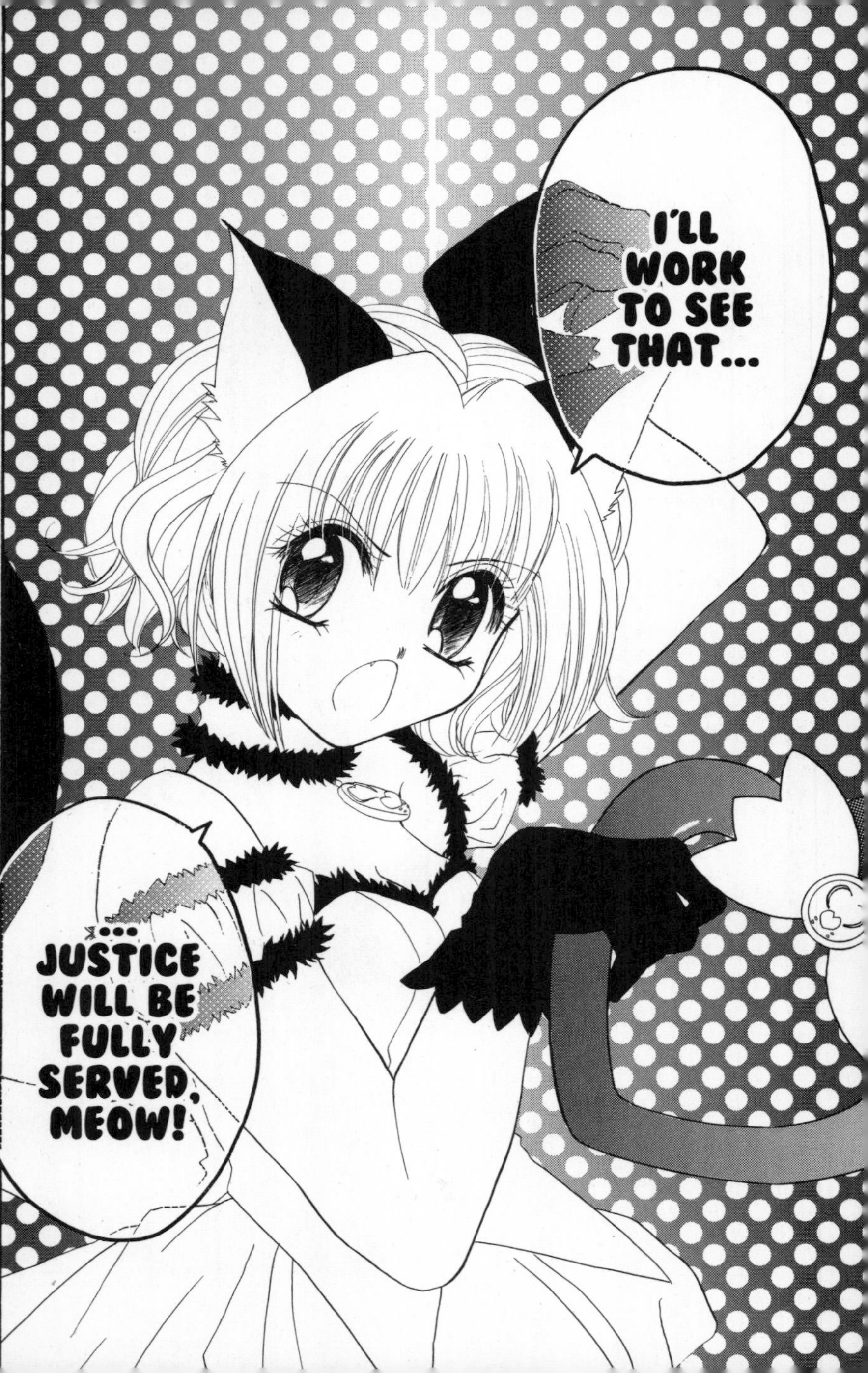
I'LL WORK TO SEE THAT...
...JUSTICE WILL BE FULLY SERVED, MEOW!

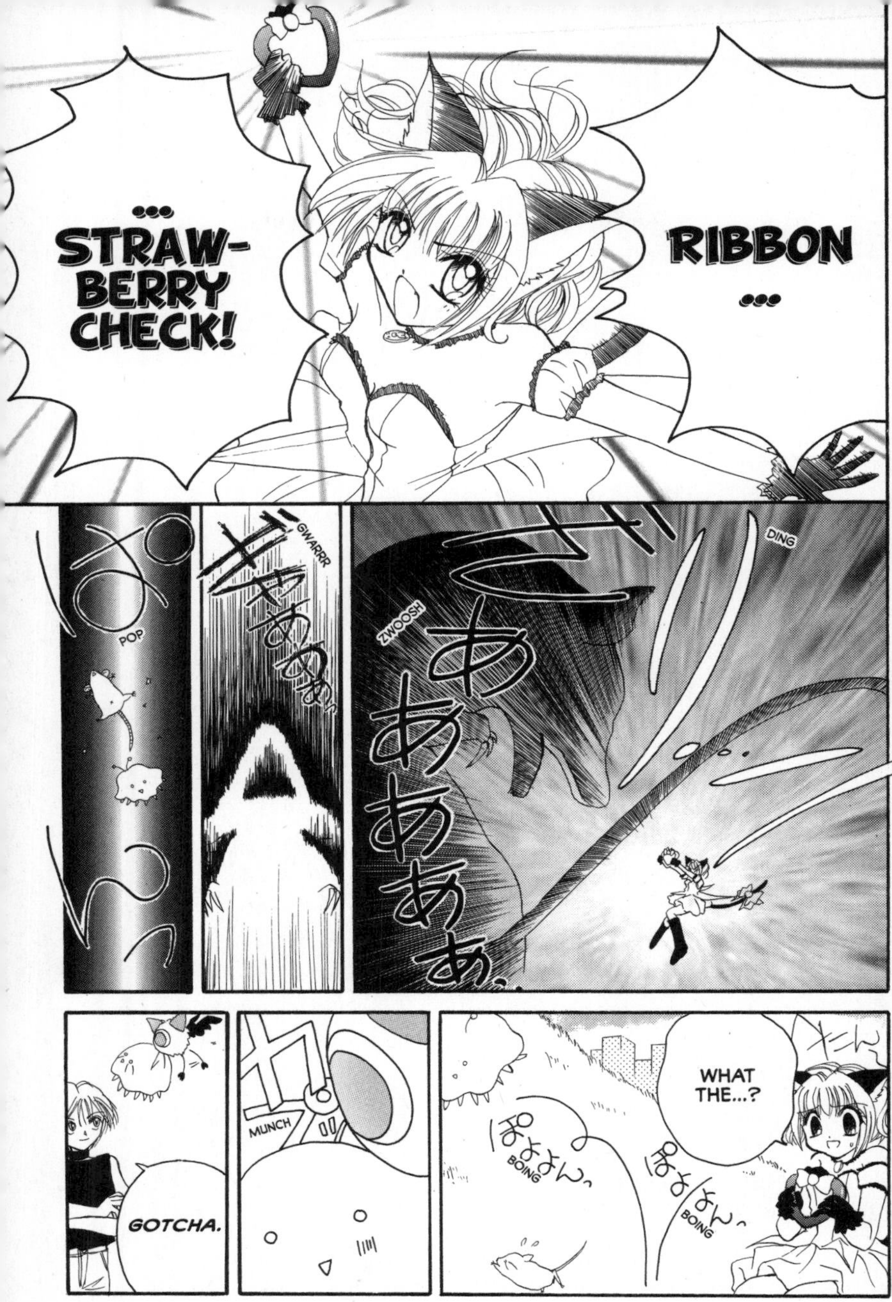
RIBBON
...
...
STRAW-
BERRY
CHECK!
DING
ZWOOSH
GWARRR
POP
WHAT THE...?
ぽよよん
BOING
ぽよよん
BOING
MUNCH
GOTCHA.

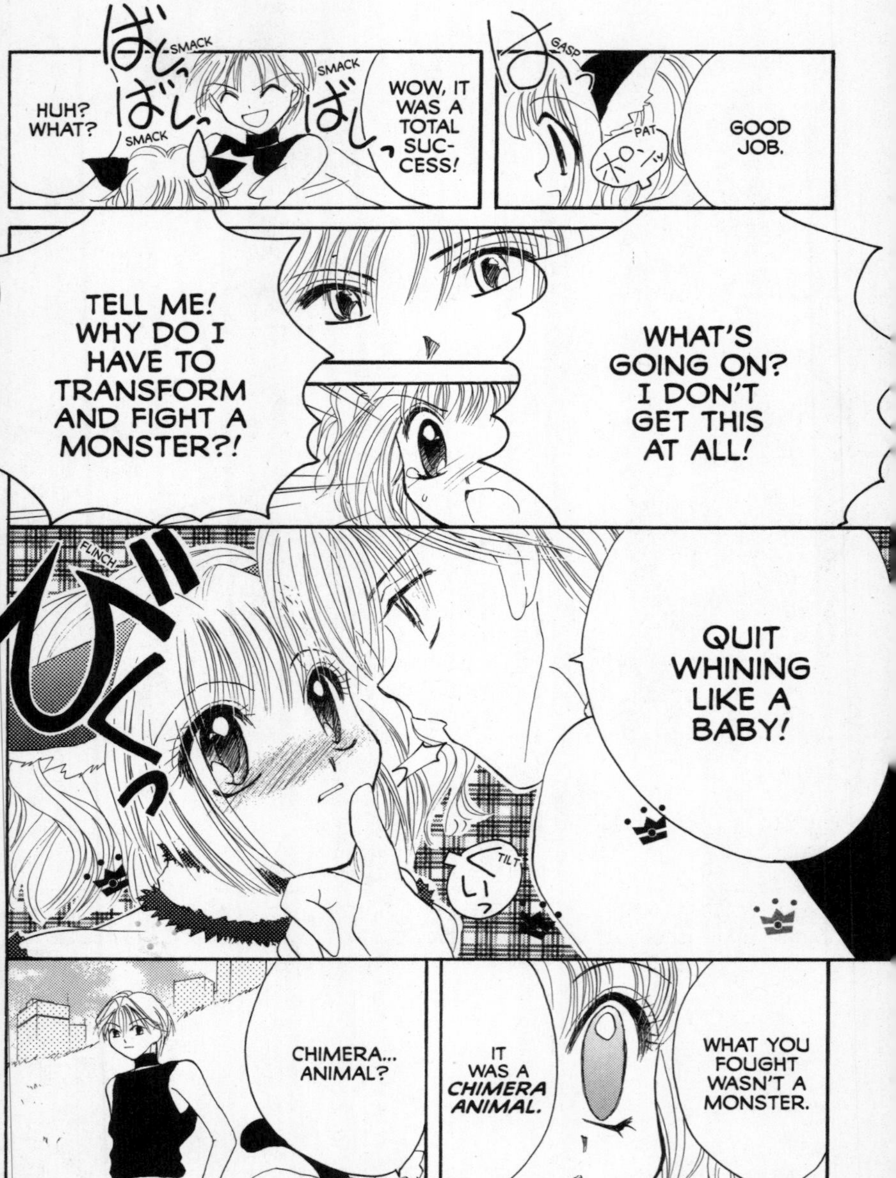
GASP
PAT
GOOD JOB.
SMACK
WOW, IT WAS A TOTAL SUC-CESS!
SMACK
SMACK
HUH? WHAT?
WHAT'S GOING ON? I DON'T GET THIS AT ALL!
TELL ME! WHY DO I HAVE TO TRANSFORM AND FIGHT A MONSTER?!
QUIT WHINING LIKE A BABY!
TILT
FLINCH
WHAT YOU FOUGHT WASN'T A MONSTER.
IT WAS A *CHIMERA ANIMAL.*
CHIMERA... ANIMAL?

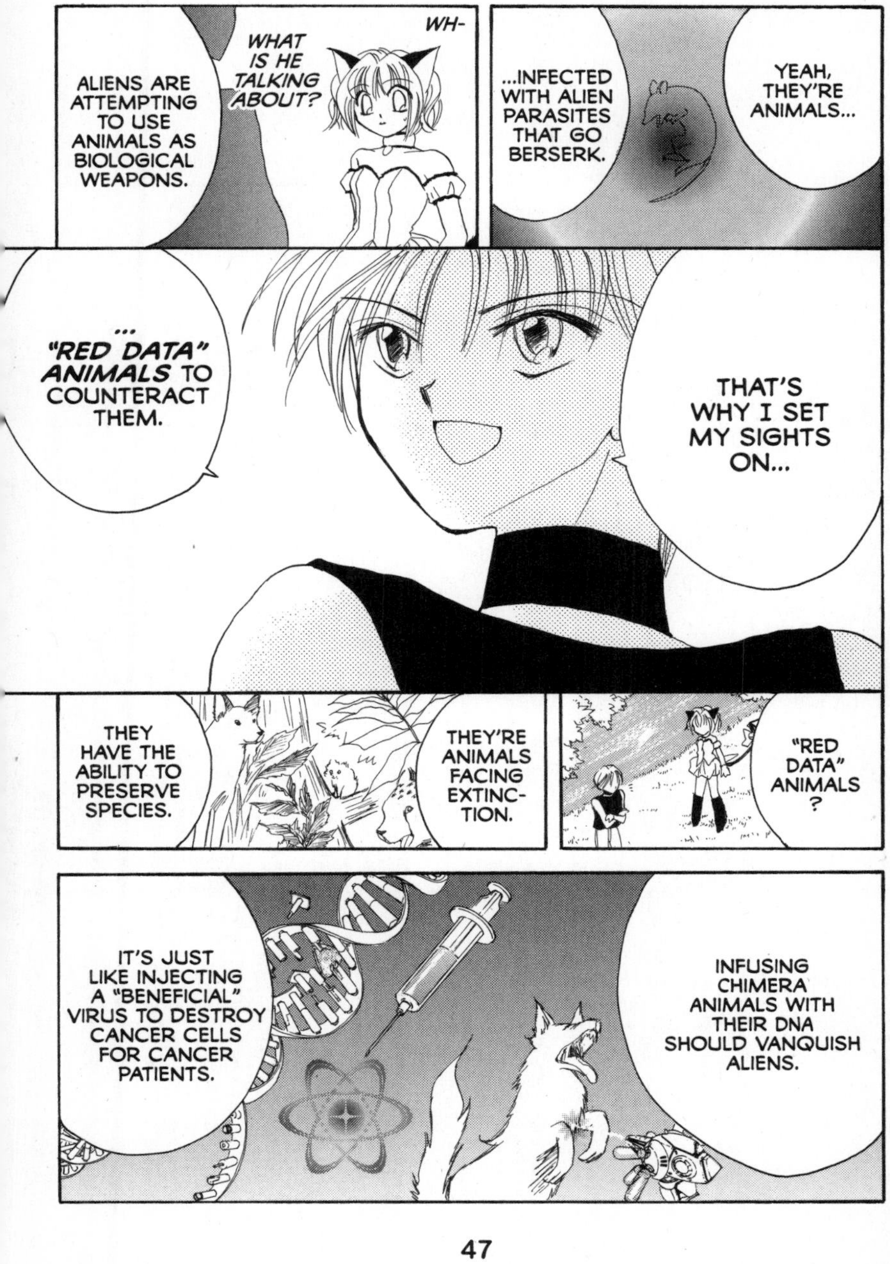

YEAH, THEY'RE ANIMALS...
...INFECTED WITH ALIEN PARASITES THAT GO BERSERK.
WH-
WHAT IS HE TALKING ABOUT?
ALIENS ARE ATTEMPTING TO USE ANIMALS AS BIOLOGICAL WEAPONS.
THAT'S WHY I SET MY SIGHTS ON...
... "RED DATA" ANIMALS TO COUNTERACT THEM.
"RED DATA" ANIMALS ?
THEY'RE ANIMALS FACING EXTINC- TION.
THEY HAVE THE ABILITY TO PRESERVE SPECIES.
INFUSING CHIMERA ANIMALS WITH THEIR DNA SHOULD VANQUISH ALIENS.
IT'S JUST LIKE INJECTING A "BENEFICIAL" VIRUS TO DESTROY CANCER CELLS FOR CANCER PATIENTS.

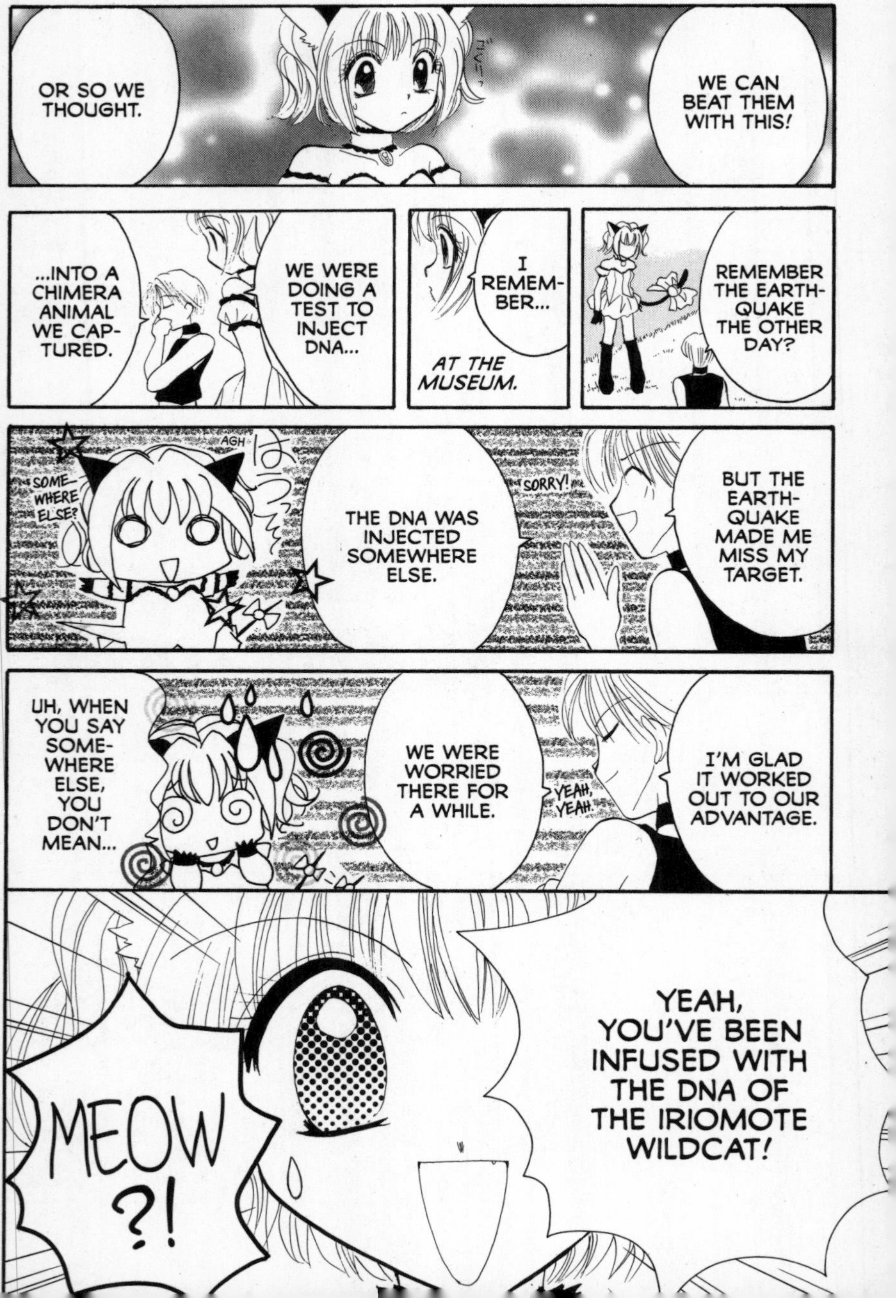
WE CAN BEAT THEM WITH THIS!
OR SO WE THOUGHT.
REMEMBER THE EARTH-QUAKE THE OTHER DAY?
I REMEM-BER...
AT THE MUSEUM.
WE WERE DOING A TEST TO INJECT DNA...
...INTO A CHIMERA ANIMAL WE CAP-TURED.
BUT THE EARTH-QUAKE MADE ME MISS MY TARGET.
SORRY!
THE DNA WAS INJECTED SOMEWHERE ELSE.
AGH
SOME-WHERE ELSE?
I'M GLAD IT WORKED OUT TO OUR ADVANTAGE.
YEAH, YEAH.
WE WERE WORRIED THERE FOR A WHILE.
UH, WHEN YOU SAY SOME-WHERE ELSE, YOU DON'T MEAN...
YEAH, YOU'VE BEEN INFUSED WITH THE DNA OF THE IRIOMOTE WILDCAT!
MEOW ?!

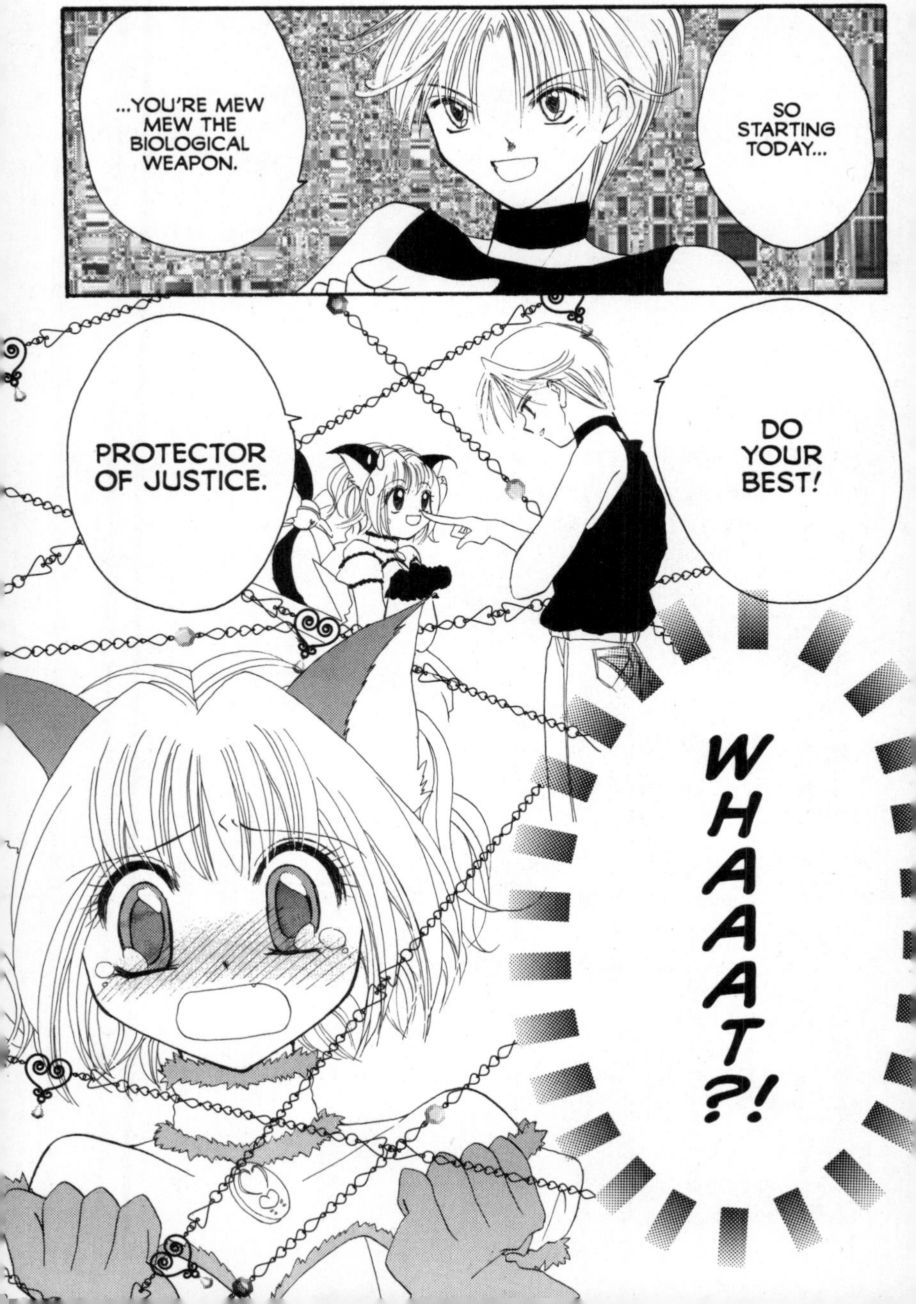
SO STARTING TODAY...
...YOU'RE MEW MEW THE BIOLOGICAL WEAPON.
DO YOUR BEST!
PROTECTOR OF JUSTICE.
WHAAAT?!

MASHA'S TOKYO MEW MEW OMNIBUS
RED DATA FILE

WHAT ARE "RED DATA" ANIMALS?

THEY ARE ANIMALS AT RISK OF EXTINCTION. CURRENTLY, THERE ARE 2,580 SPECIES WORLDWIDE. IT'S DUE TO OVERHUNTING AND ECOLOGICAL DESTRUCTION. LET'S COME TOGETHER AND SAVE THESE ENDANGERED ANIMALS!

FILE 1: IRIOMOTE WILDCAT

SIZE: ABOUT 50 CM* IN HEAD AND BODY LENGTH AND 25 CM* IN TAIL LENGTH FOR FEMALES. MALES ARE SLIGHTLY LARGER THAN FEMALES.
HABITAT: IRIOMOTE ISLAND, OKINAWA.

THE IRIOMOTE WILDCAT WAS DISCOVERED AS A NEW SPECIES OF CAT AFTER 72 YEARS AND IT ATTRACTED CONSIDERABLE ATTENTION WORLDWIDE AT THE TIME. DESIGNATED AS A PROTECTED SPECIES SINCE 1967, IT LIVES PRIMARILY ON THE GROUND BUT IS A GOOD TREE CLIMBER. CURRENTLY, FEWER THAN 100 EXIST, CALLING FOR ITS PROTECTION.

*50 CM IS ABOUT 19.7 IN. 25 CM IS ABOUT 9.8 IN.

FILE 2: BLUE LORIKEET

SIZE: ABOUT 18 CM* IN HEAD AND BODY LENGTH AND ABOUT 11 CM* IN WINGSPAN.
HABITAT: TAHITI ISLANDS.

WHILE THE BLUE LORIKEET IS RELATED TO HOUSEHOLD PARAKEETS, ONLY 1,500 TO 2,500 OF THIS RARE SPECIES EXIST. IT'S CHARACTERIZED BY A WHITE THROAT. THE BLUE LORIKEET'S ENDANGERMENT IS SAID TO BE CAUSED BY FALCONS BROUGHT TO ITS HABITAT AND AN EPIDEMIC OF AVIAN MALARIA.

CONTINUE TO PAGE 162.   *18 CM IS ABOUT 7.1 IN. 11 CM IS ABOUT 4.3 IN.

Howdy! I'm Ikumi!

Hello. It's been a while or nice to meet you. I'm Mia Ikumi. It's my first book in a while. Thank you for waiting. Because of a long preparation phase, it seemed to have taken much less time to put the book out, but it's been over a year since my last book. Did you think I had quit being a manga artist? Don't worry (?), I'm still drawing manga.
Enjoy Tokyo Mew Mew!

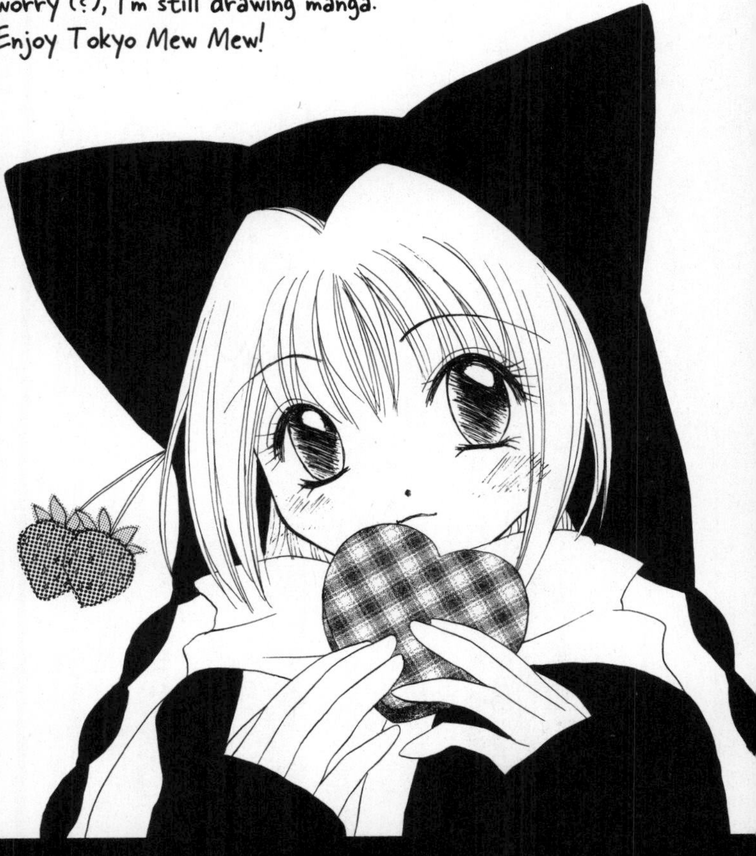

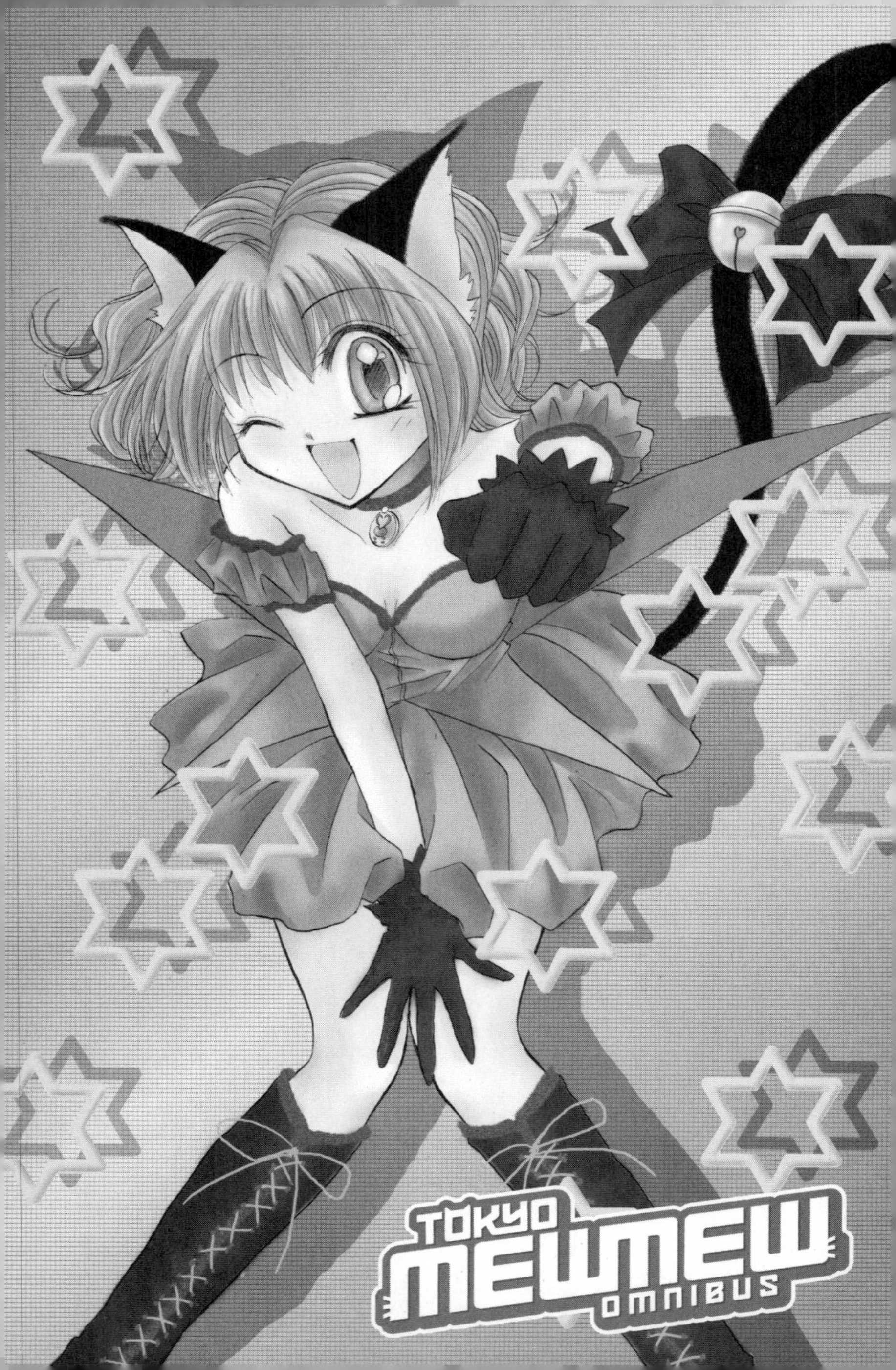
TOKYO
MEWMEW
OMNIBUS

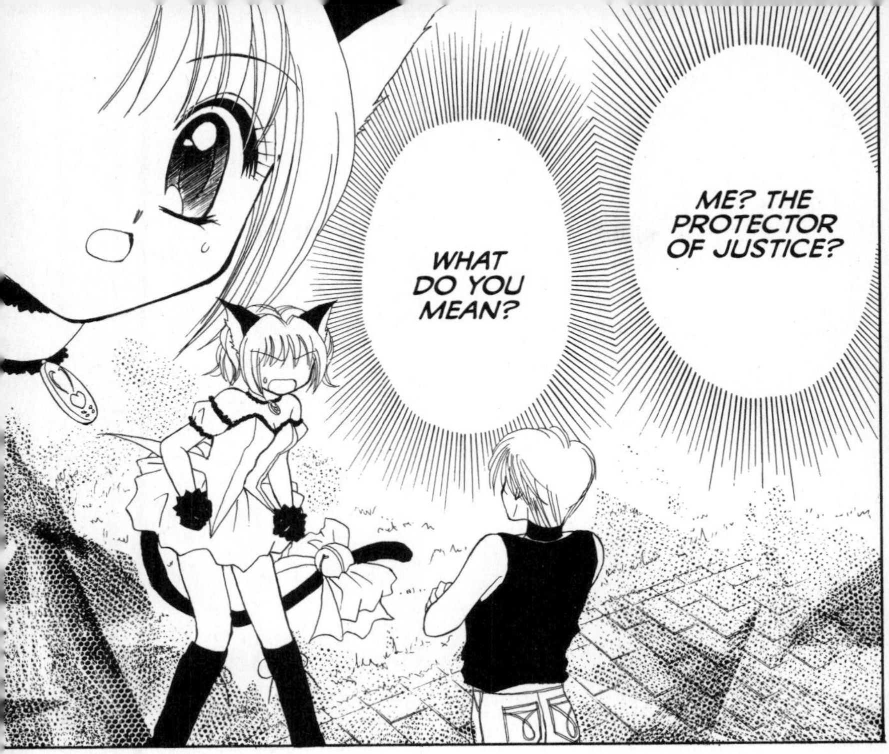
ME? THE PROTECTOR OF JUSTICE?
WHAT DO YOU MEAN?

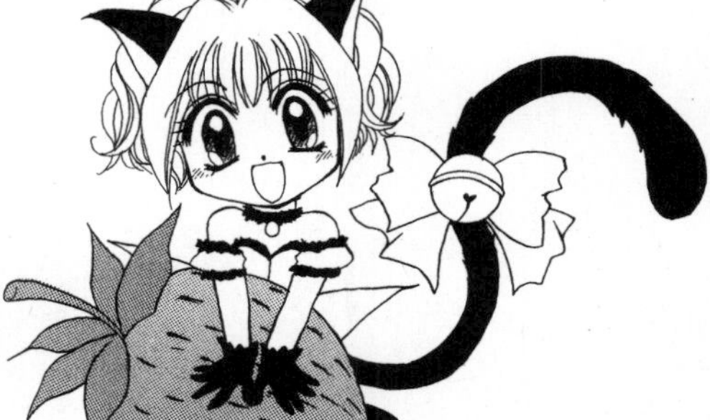

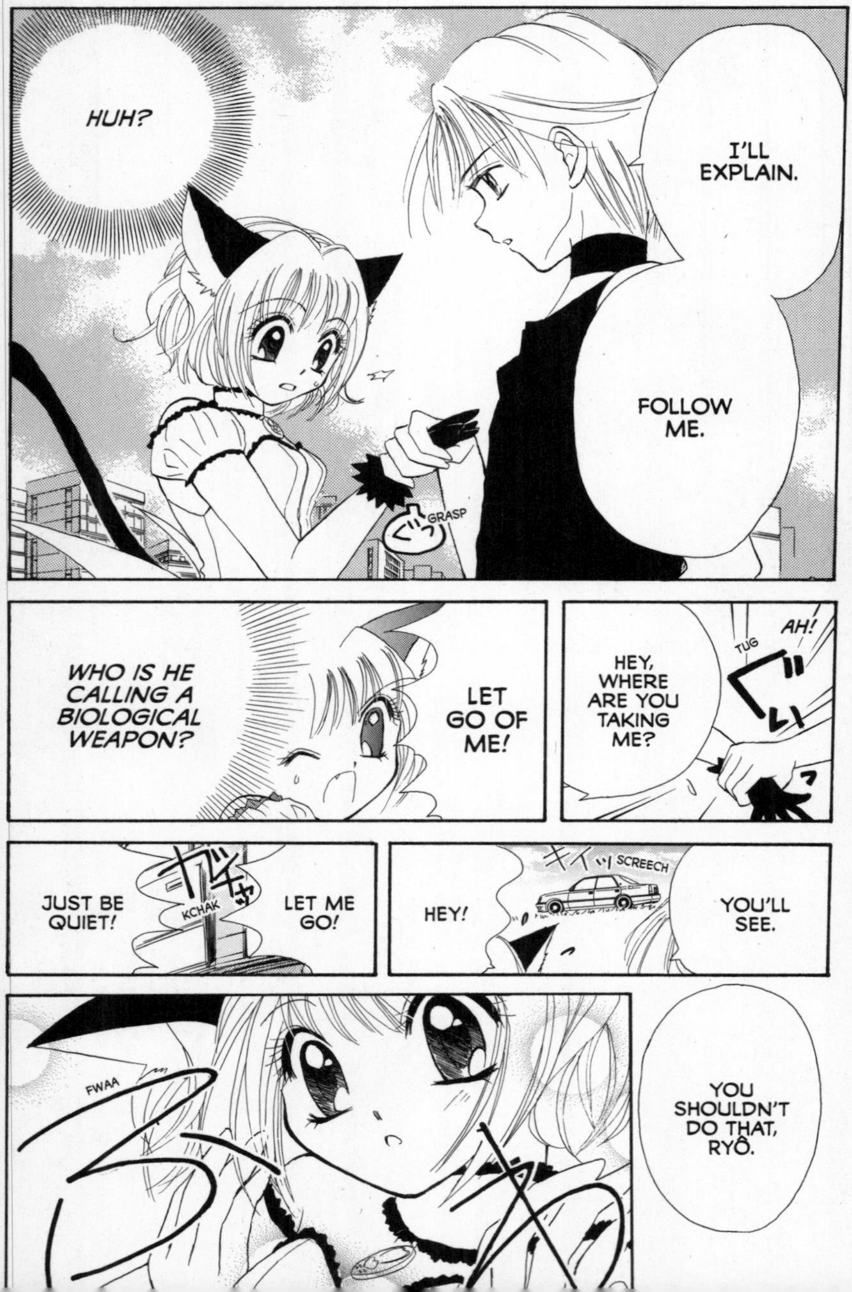
I'LL EXPLAIN.
HUH?
FOLLOW ME.
GRASP
AH!
TUG
HEY, WHERE ARE YOU TAKING ME?
LET GO OF ME!
WHO IS HE CALLING A BIOLOGICAL WEAPON?
YOU'LL SEE.
SCREECH
HEY!
LET ME GO!
KCHAK
JUST BE QUIET!
YOU SHOULDN'T DO THAT, RYÔ.
FWAA

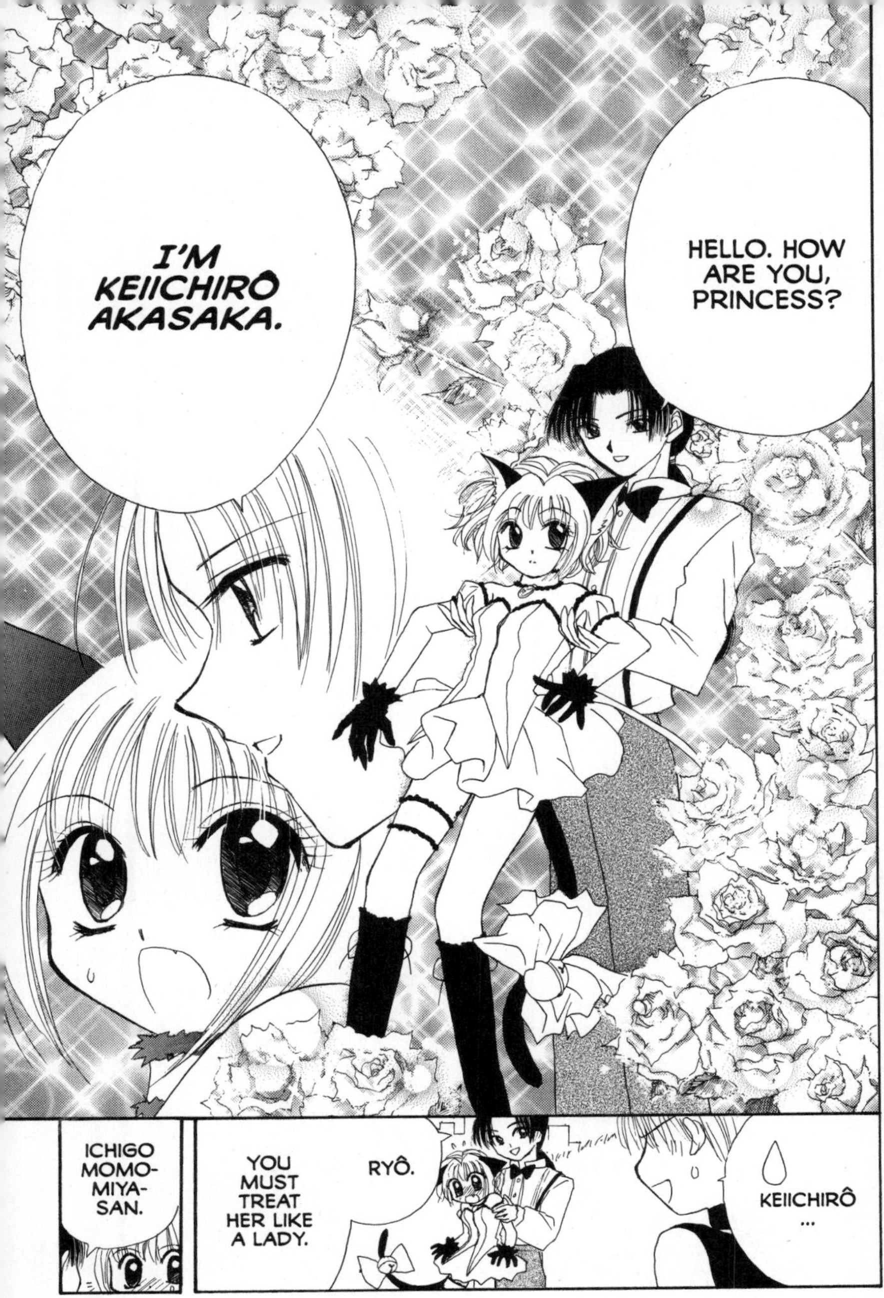
HELLO. HOW ARE YOU, PRINCESS?
I'M KEIICHIRÔ AKASAKA.
KEIICHIRÔ ...
RYÔ.
YOU MUST TREAT HER LIKE A LADY.
ICHIGO MOMO-MIYA-SAN.

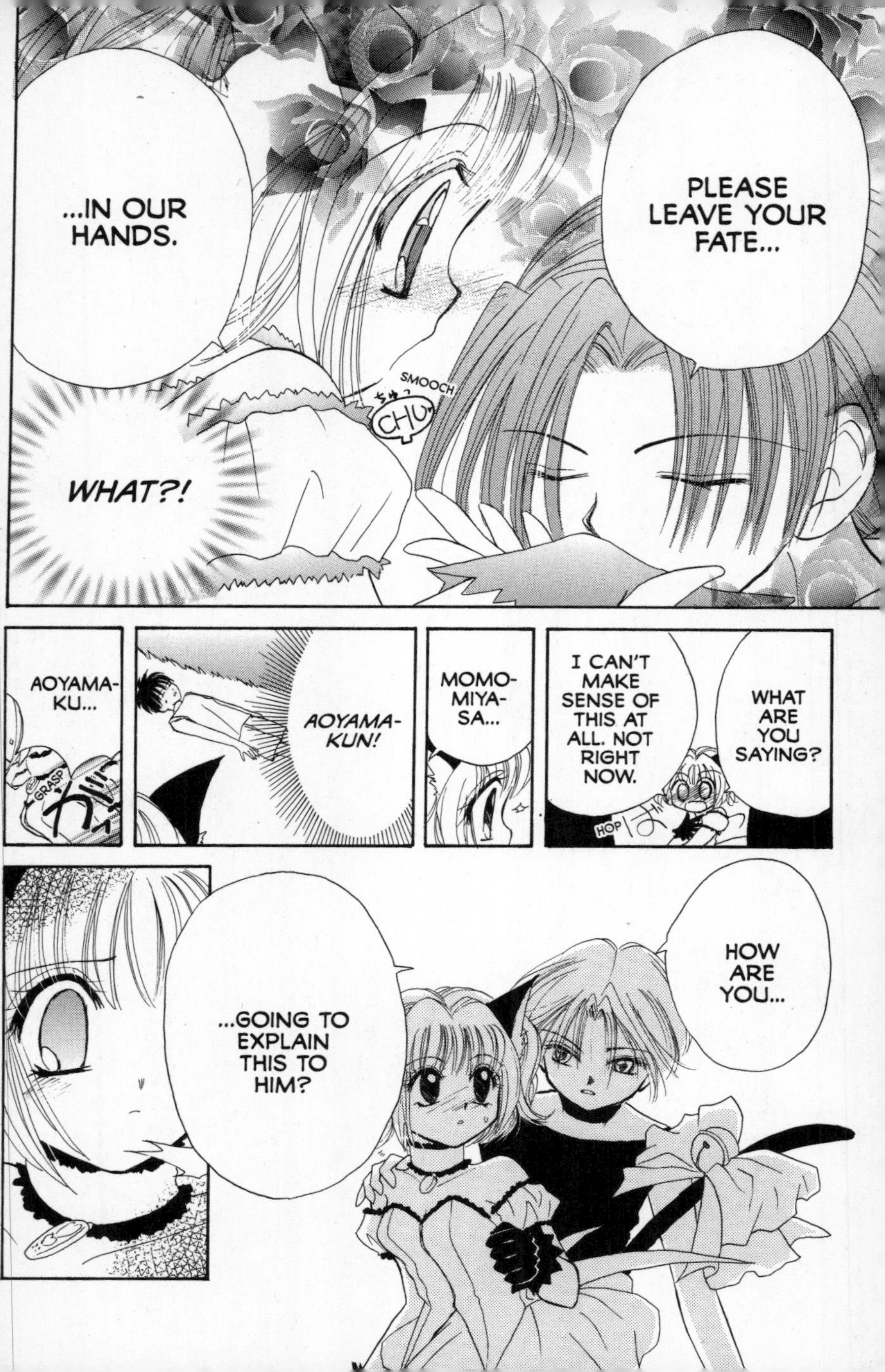
PLEASE LEAVE YOUR FATE...
...IN OUR HANDS.
SMOOCH
CHU
WHAT?!
WHAT ARE YOU SAYING?
I CAN'T MAKE SENSE OF THIS AT ALL. NOT RIGHT NOW.
HOP
MOMO-MIYA-SA...
AOYAMA-KUN!
AOYAMA-KU...
GRASP
HOW ARE YOU...
...GOING TO EXPLAIN THIS TO HIM?

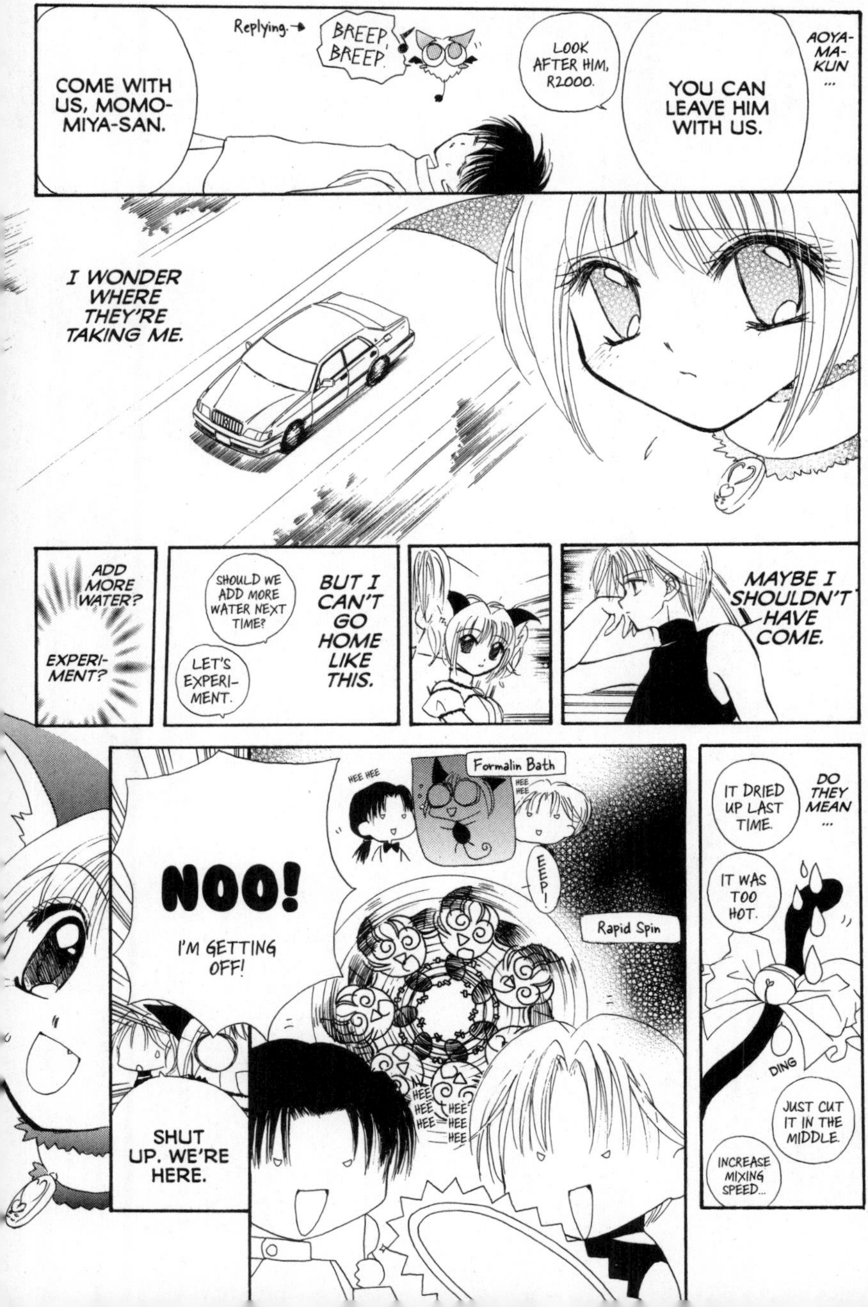
AOYAMA-KUN ...
YOU CAN LEAVE HIM WITH US.
LOOK AFTER HIM, R2000.
BREEP, BREEP.
Replying.
COME WITH US, MOMOMIYA-SAN.
I WONDER WHERE THEY'RE TAKING ME.
MAYBE I SHOULDN'T HAVE COME.
BUT I CAN'T GO HOME LIKE THIS.
SHOULD WE ADD MORE WATER NEXT TIME?
LET'S EXPERIMENT.
ADD MORE WATER?
EXPERIMENT?
DO THEY MEAN ...
IT DRIED UP LAST TIME.
IT WAS TOO HOT.
DING
JUST CUT IT IN THE MIDDLE.
INCREASE MIXING SPEED...
Formalin Bath
HEE HEE
HEE HEE
EEEP!
NOO!
I'M GETTING OFF!
Rapid Spin
HEE HEE HEE HEE
HEE HEE
SHUT UP. WE'RE HERE.

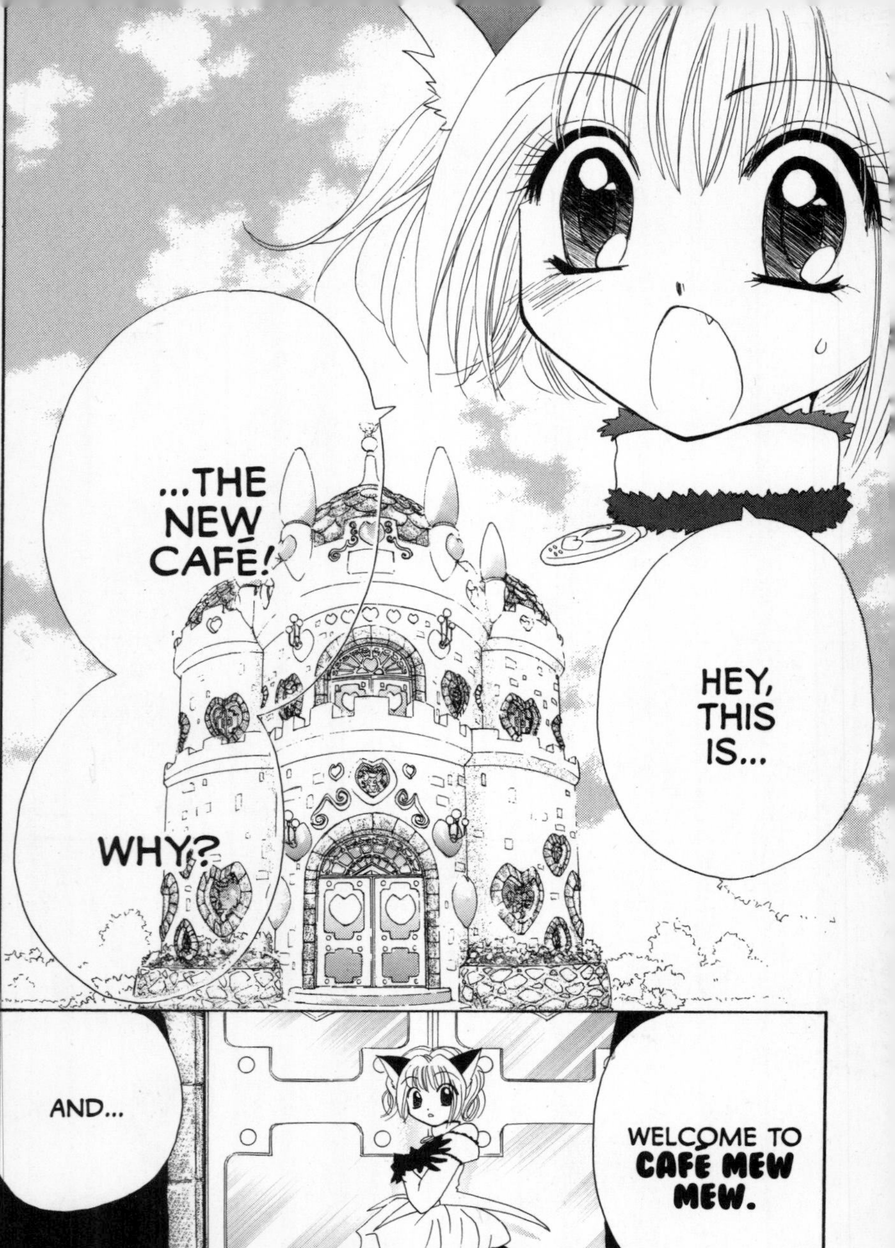
HEY, THIS IS...
...THE NEW CAFÉ!
WHY?
WELCOME TO CAFÉ MEW MEW.
AND...

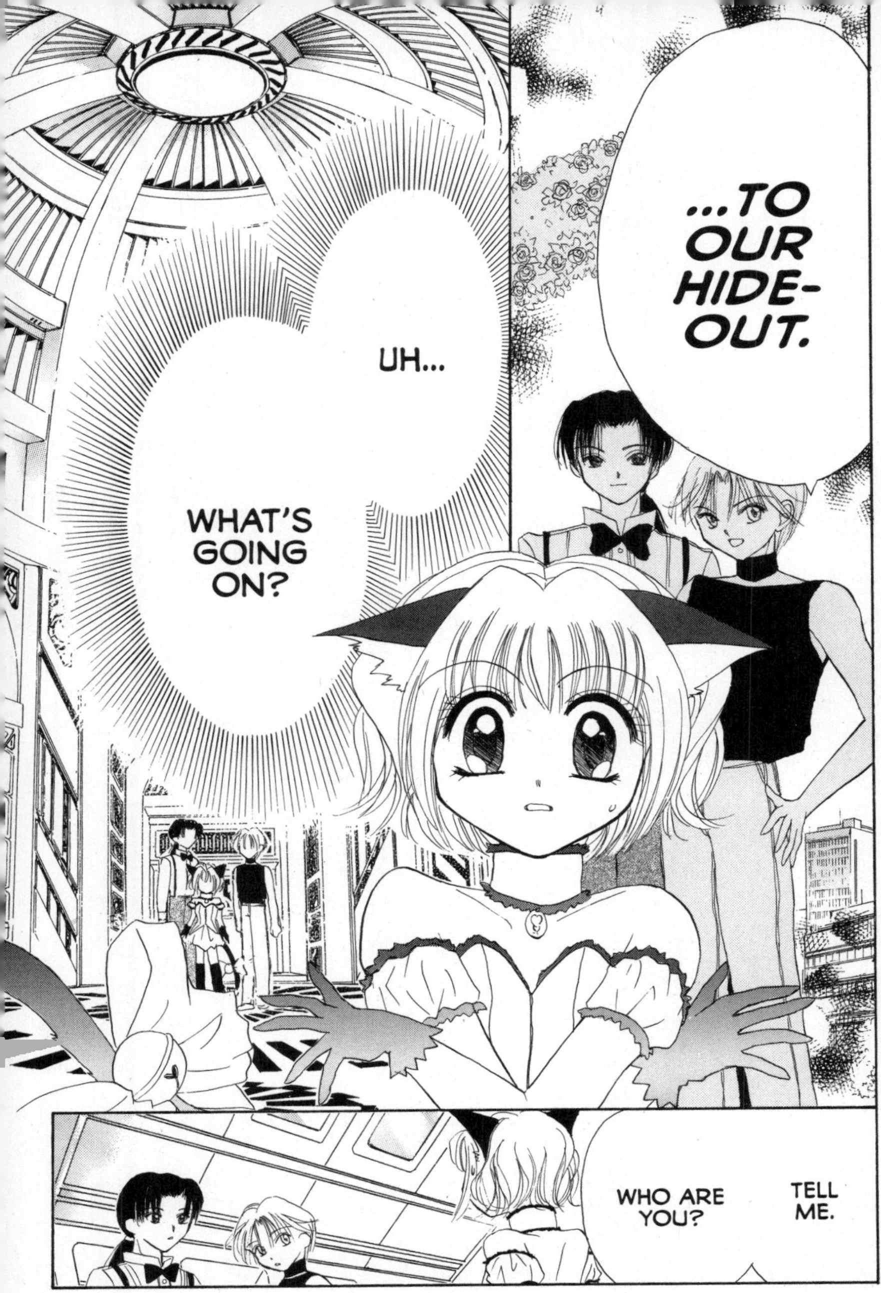
...TO OUR HIDE-OUT.
UH...
WHAT'S GOING ON?
TELL ME.
WHO ARE YOU?

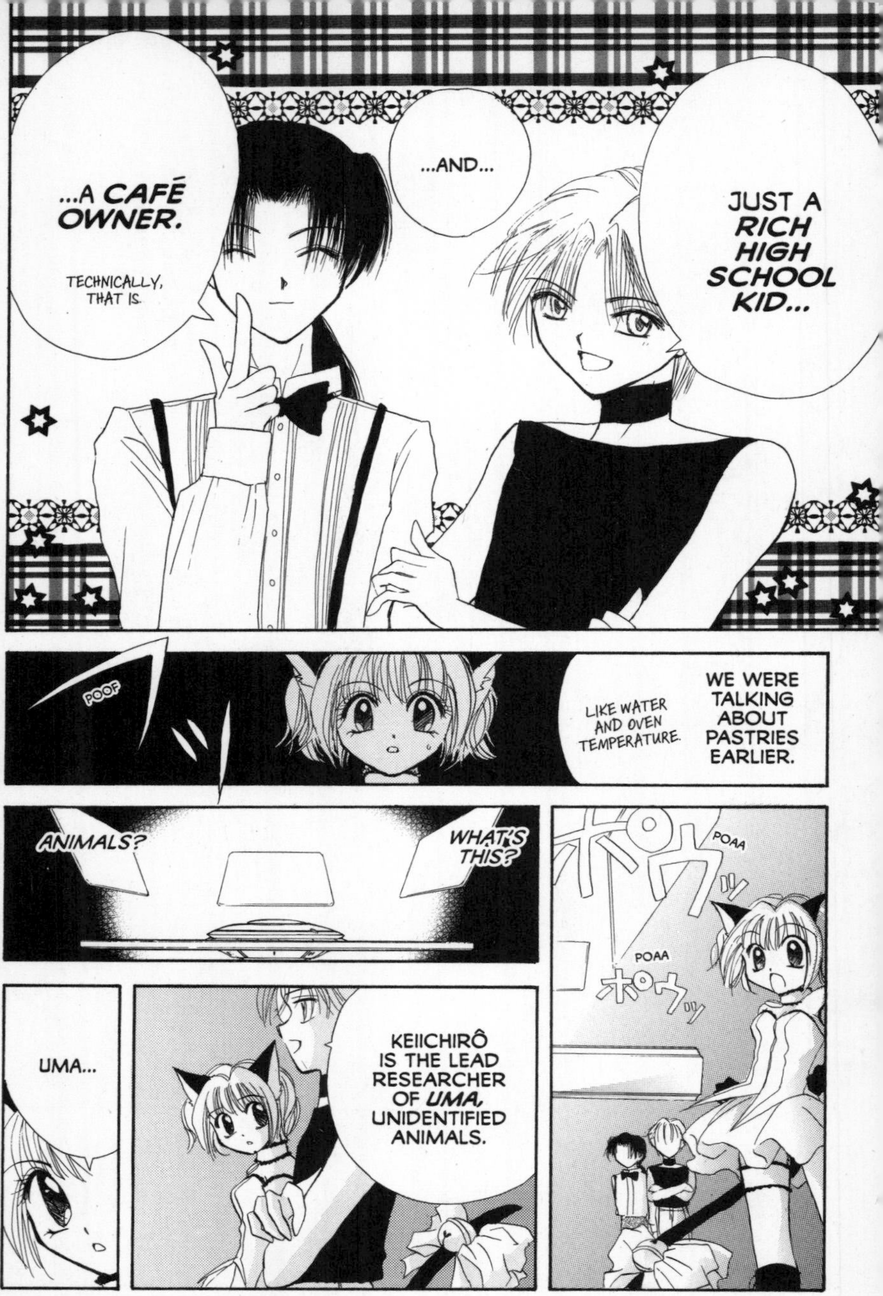
JUST A RICH HIGH SCHOOL KID...
...AND...
...A CAFÉ OWNER.
TECHNICALLY, THAT IS.
WE WERE TALKING ABOUT PASTRIES EARLIER.
LIKE WATER AND OVEN TEMPERATURE.
POOF
POAA
POAA
WHAT'S THIS?
ANIMALS?
KEIICHIRÔ IS THE LEAD RESEARCHER OF UMA, UNIDENTIFIED ANIMALS.
UMA...

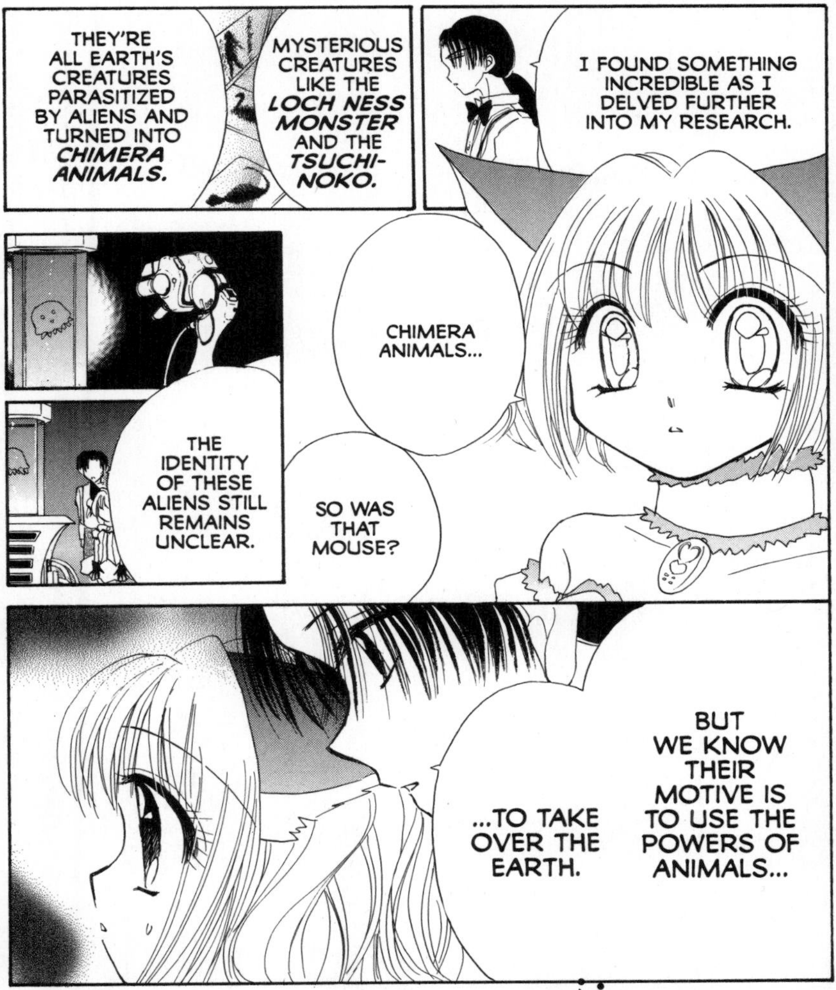

I FOUND SOMETHING INCREDIBLE AS I DELVED FURTHER INTO MY RESEARCH.
MYSTERIOUS CREATURES LIKE THE *LOCH NESS MONSTER* AND THE *TSUCHI-NOKO.*
THEY'RE ALL EARTH'S CREATURES PARASITIZED BY ALIENS AND TURNED INTO *CHIMERA ANIMALS.*
CHIMERA ANIMALS...
SO WAS THAT MOUSE?
THE IDENTITY OF THESE ALIENS STILL REMAINS UNCLEAR.
BUT WE KNOW THEIR MOTIVE IS TO USE THE POWERS OF ANIMALS...
...TO TAKE OVER THE EARTH.
SO YOU'RE GOING TO COMBAT THEM.
WHY ME?!
RAH
NICE JOB ON A SHORT AND CLEAR EXPLANATION.

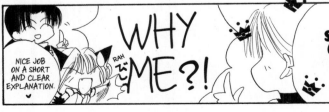

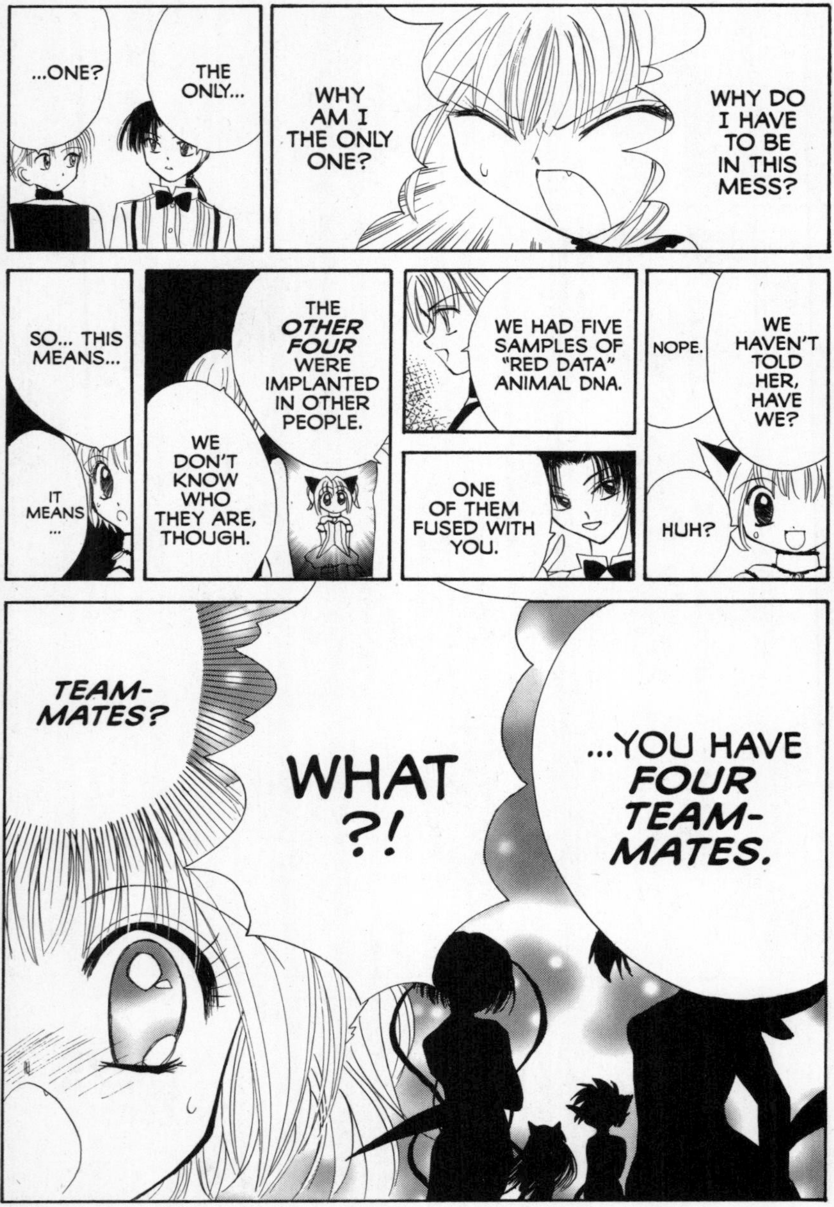
WHY DO I HAVE TO BE IN THIS MESS?
WHY AM I THE ONLY ONE?
THE ONLY...
...ONE?
WE HAVEN'T TOLD HER, HAVE WE?
NOPE.
HUH?
WE HAD FIVE SAMPLES OF "RED DATA" ANIMAL DNA.
ONE OF THEM FUSED WITH YOU.
THE *OTHER FOUR* WERE IMPLANTED IN OTHER PEOPLE.
WE DON'T KNOW WHO THEY ARE, THOUGH.
SO... THIS MEANS...
IT MEANS ...
...YOU HAVE *FOUR TEAM-MATES.*
WHAT ?!
TEAM-MATES?

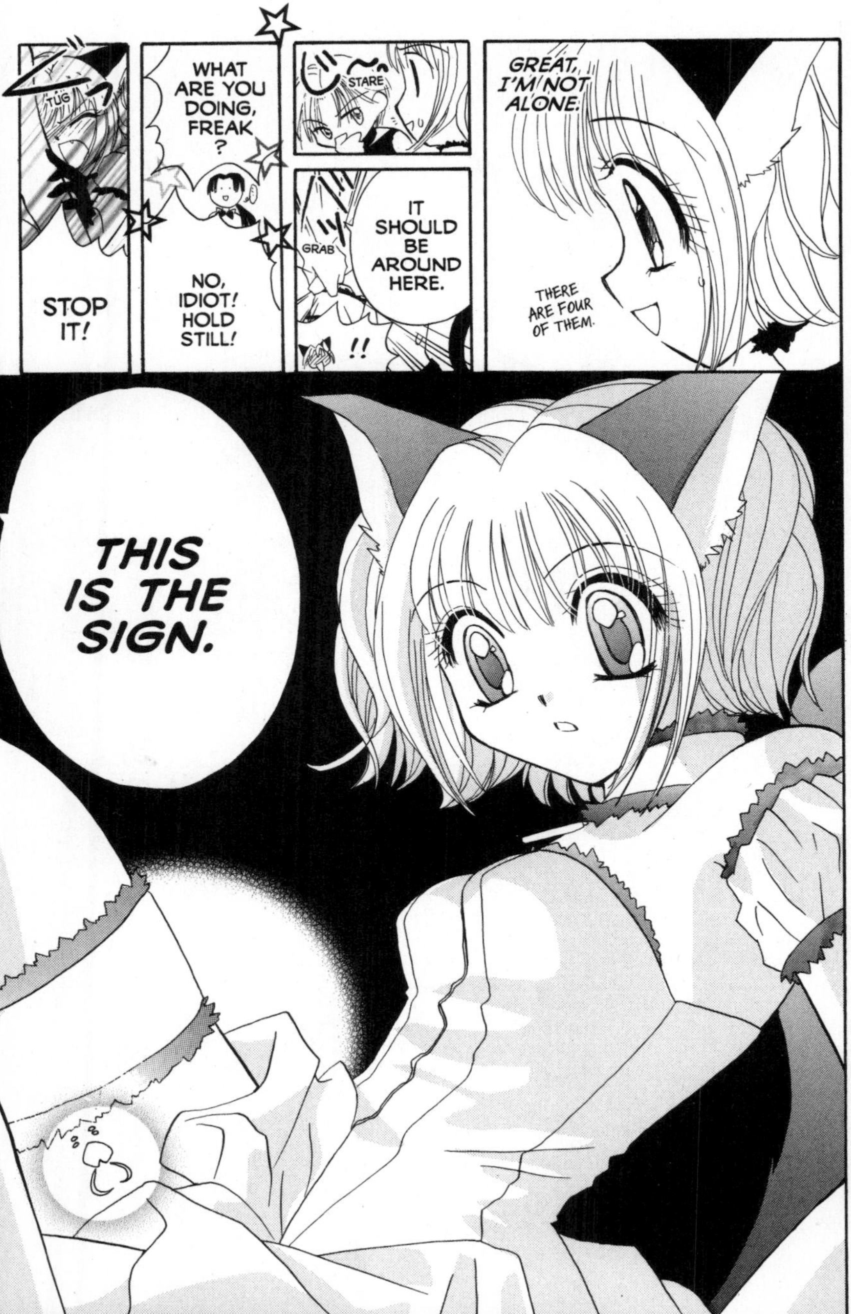
GREAT, I'M NOT ALONE.
THERE ARE FOUR OF THEM.
STARE
IT SHOULD BE AROUND HERE.
GRAB
!!
WHAT ARE YOU DOING, FREAK?
NO, IDIOT! HOLD STILL!
TUG
STOP IT!
THIS IS THE SIGN.

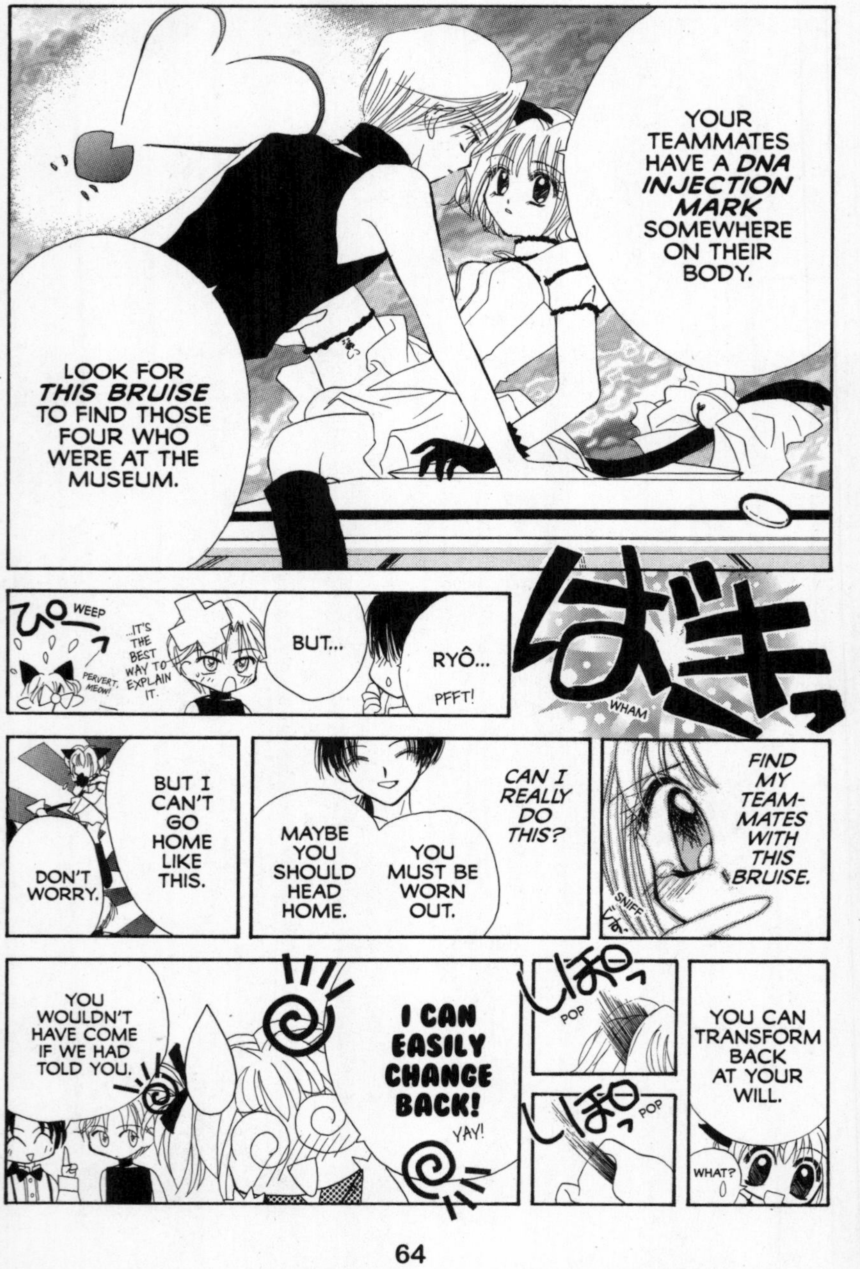
YOUR TEAMMATES HAVE A DNA INJECTION MARK SOMEWHERE ON THEIR BODY.
LOOK FOR THIS BRUISE TO FIND THOSE FOUR WHO WERE AT THE MUSEUM.
WHAM
RYÔ...
PFFT!
BUT...
...IT'S THE BEST WAY TO EXPLAIN IT.
WEEP
PERVERT, MEOW!
FIND MY TEAMMATES WITH THIS BRUISE.
SNIFF
CAN I REALLY DO THIS?
YOU MUST BE WORN OUT.
MAYBE YOU SHOULD HEAD HOME.
BUT I CAN'T GO HOME LIKE THIS.
DON'T WORRY.
YOU CAN TRANSFORM BACK AT YOUR WILL.
WHAT?
POP
POP
I CAN EASILY CHANGE BACK!
YAY!
YOU WOULDN'T HAVE COME IF WE HAD TOLD YOU.

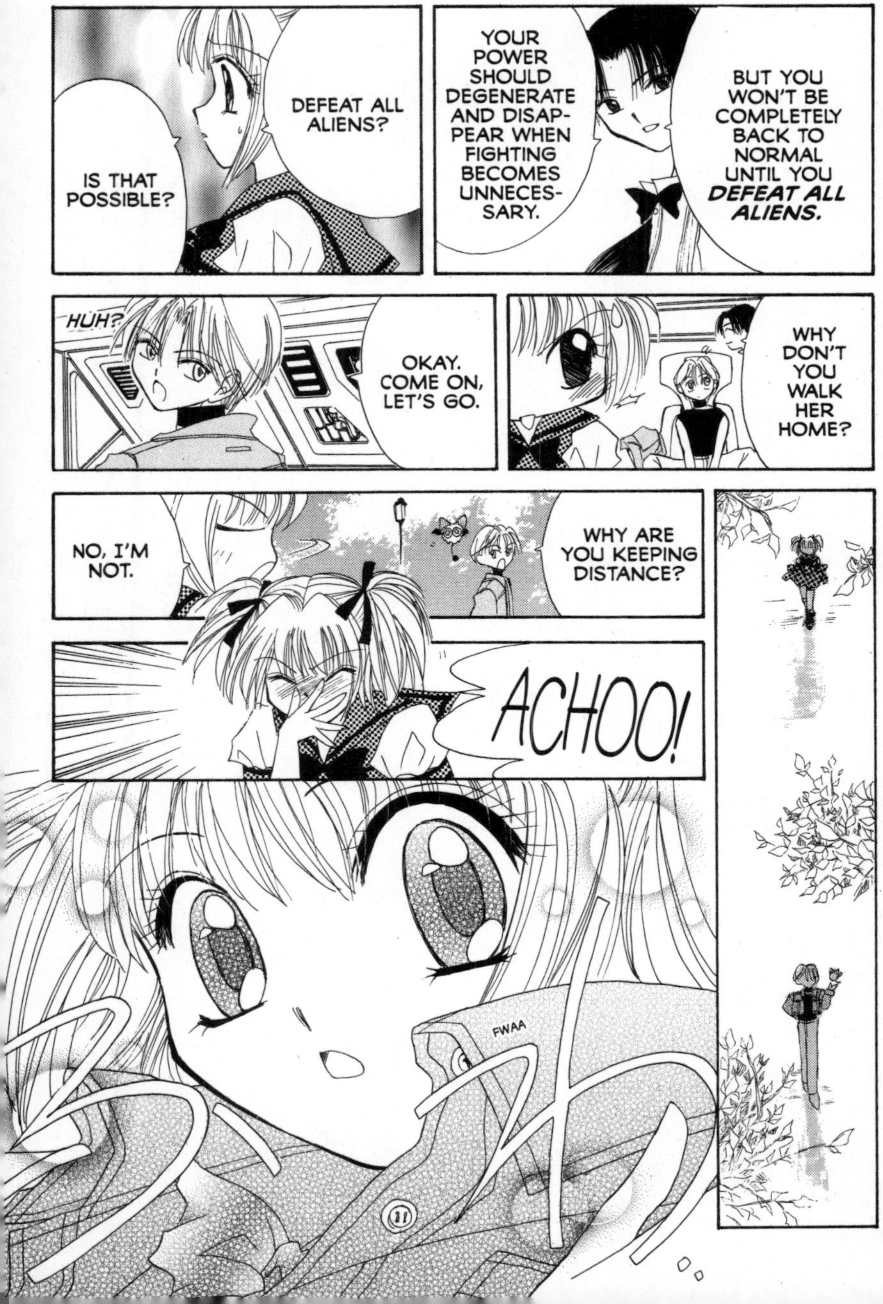

YOUR POWER SHOULD DEGENERATE AND DISAPPEAR WHEN FIGHTING BECOMES UNNECESSARY.
BUT YOU WON'T BE COMPLETELY BACK TO NORMAL UNTIL YOU ***DEFEAT ALL ALIENS.***
DEFEAT ALL ALIENS?
IS THAT POSSIBLE?
WHY DON'T YOU WALK HER HOME?
OKAY. COME ON, LET'S GO.
HUH?
WHY ARE YOU KEEPING DISTANCE?
NO, I'M NOT.
ACHOO!
FWAA

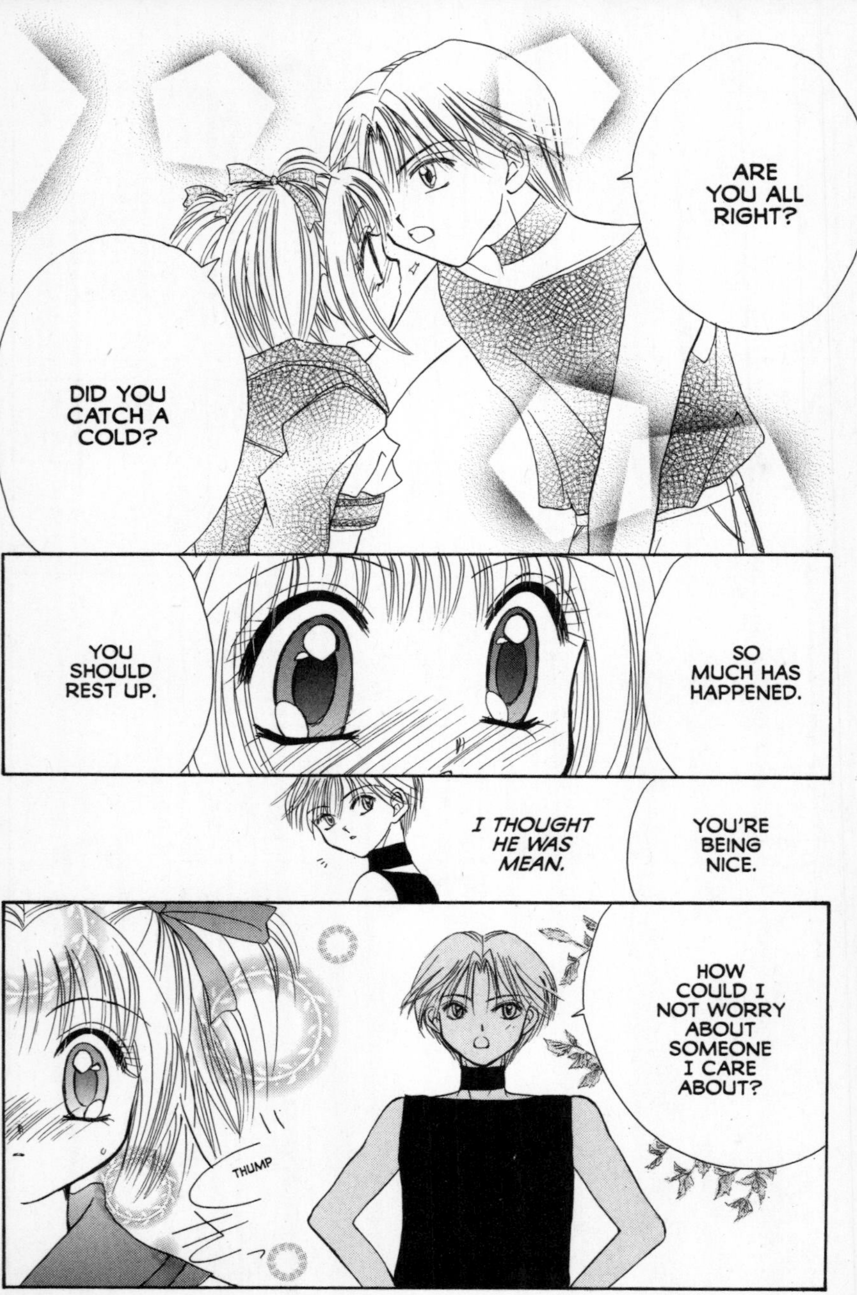
ARE YOU ALL RIGHT?
DID YOU CATCH A COLD?
SO MUCH HAS HAPPENED.
YOU SHOULD REST UP.
YOU'RE BEING NICE.
I THOUGHT HE WAS MEAN.
HOW COULD I NOT WORRY ABOUT SOMEONE I CARE ABOUT?
THUMP

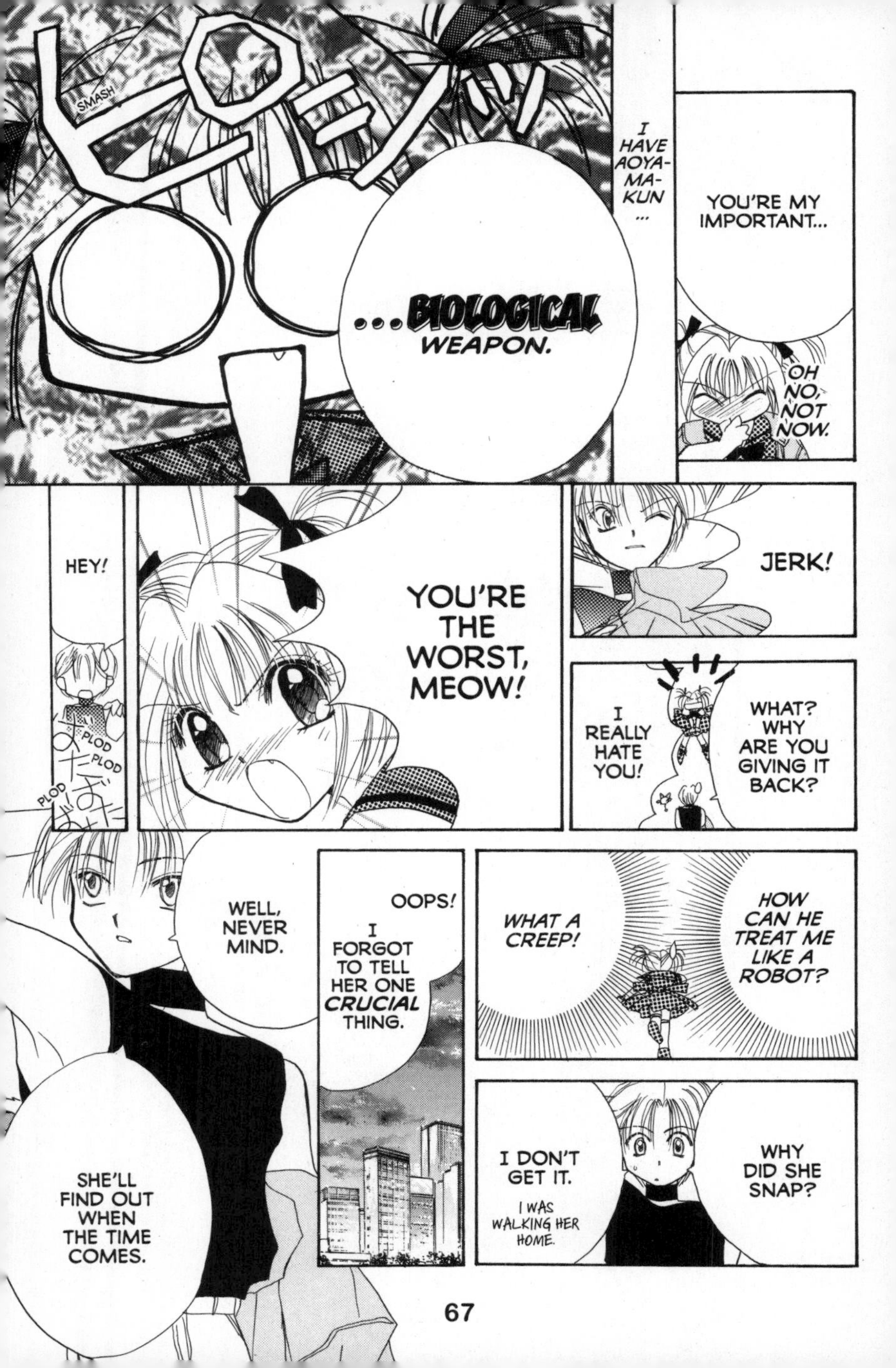
YOU'RE MY IMPORTANT...
OH NO, NOT NOW.
I HAVE AOYAMA-KUN ...
SMASH
...BIOLOGICAL WEAPON.
JERK!
WHAT? WHY ARE YOU GIVING IT BACK?
I REALLY HATE YOU!
YOU'RE THE WORST, MEOW!
HEY!
PLOD
PLOD
PLOD
HOW CAN HE TREAT ME LIKE A ROBOT?
WHAT A CREEP!
WHY DID SHE SNAP?
I DON'T GET IT.
I WAS WALKING HER HOME.
OOPS!
I FORGOT TO TELL HER ONE CRUCIAL THING.
WELL, NEVER MIND.
SHE'LL FIND OUT WHEN THE TIME COMES.

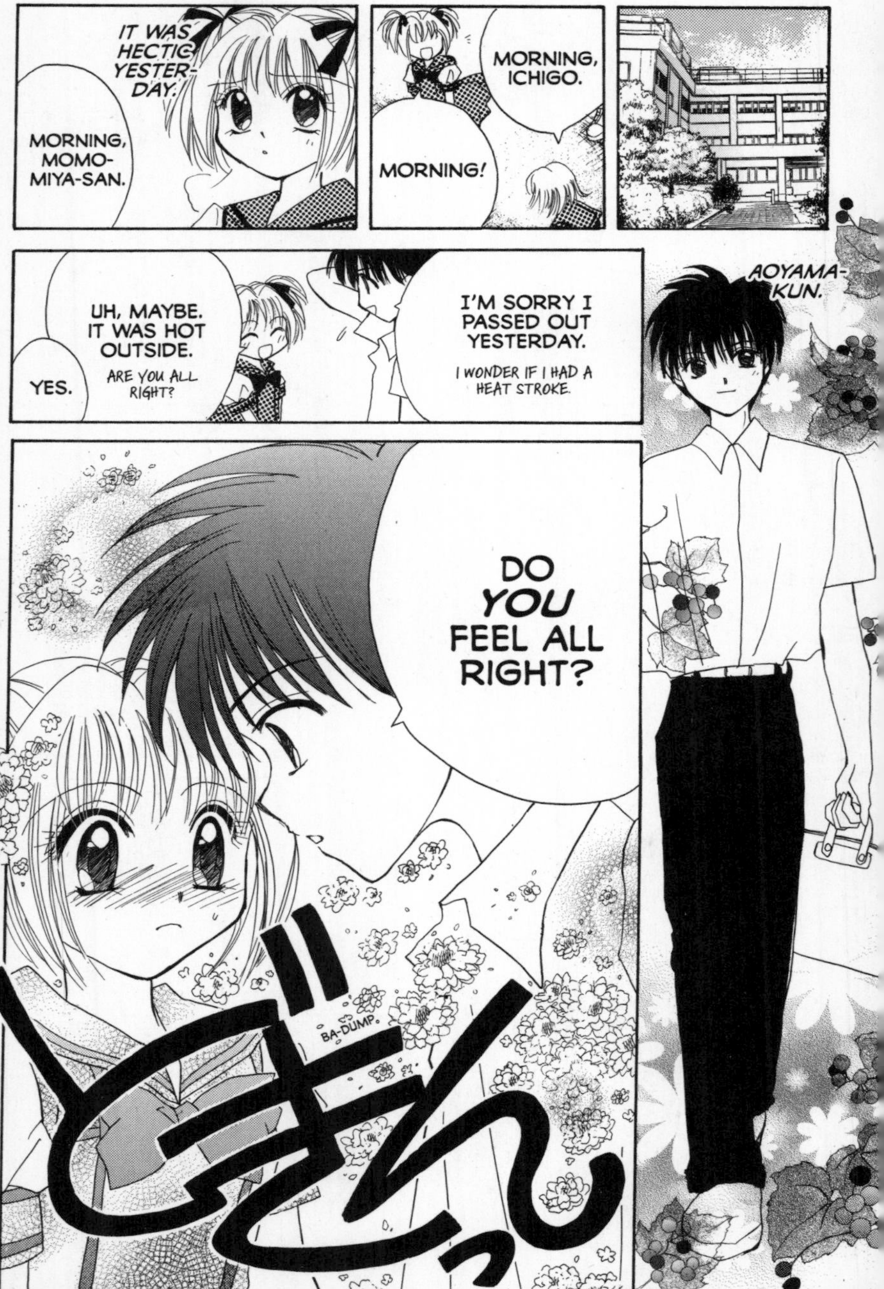
MORNING, ICHIGO.
MORNING!
IT WAS HECTIC YESTER-DAY.
MORNING, MOMO-MIYA-SAN.
AOYAMA-KUN.
I'M SORRY I PASSED OUT YESTERDAY.
I WONDER IF I HAD A HEAT STROKE.
UH, MAYBE. IT WAS HOT OUTSIDE.
ARE YOU ALL RIGHT?
YES.
DO *YOU* FEEL ALL RIGHT?
BA-DUMP.
どきんっ

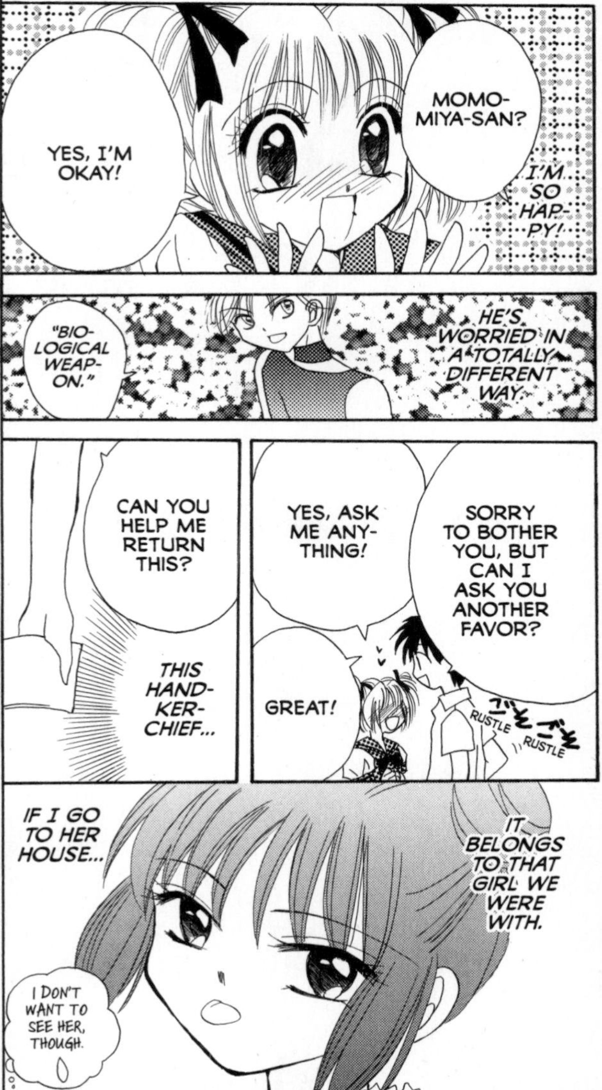
MOMO-MIYA-SAN?
I'M SO HAP-PY!
YES, I'M OKAY!
HE'S WORRIED IN A TOTALLY DIFFERENT WAY.
"BIO-LOGICAL WEAP-ON."
SORRY TO BOTHER YOU, BUT CAN I ASK YOU ANOTHER FAVOR?
YES, ASK ME ANY-THING!
RUSTLE
RUSTLE
GREAT!
CAN YOU HELP ME RETURN THIS?
THIS HAND-KER-CHIEF...
IT BELONGS TO THAT GIRL WE WERE WITH.
IF I GO TO HER HOUSE...
I DON'T WANT TO SEE HER, THOUGH.
...I COULD FIND OUT IF SHE'S MY TEAMMATE!
I'LL GO!

Meeting with My Editors: Part Two

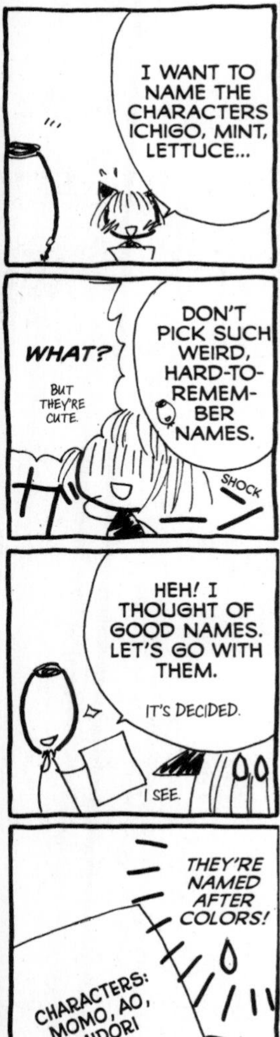
I WANT TO NAME THE CHARACTERS ICHIGO, MINT, LETTUCE...
DON'T PICK SUCH WEIRD, HARD-TO-REMEMBER NAMES.
WHAT?
BUT THEY'RE CUTE.
SHOCK
HEH! I THOUGHT OF GOOD NAMES. LET'S GO WITH THEM.
IT'S DECIDED.
I SEE.
THEY'RE NAMED AFTER COLORS!
CHARACTERS: MOMO, AO, MIDORI

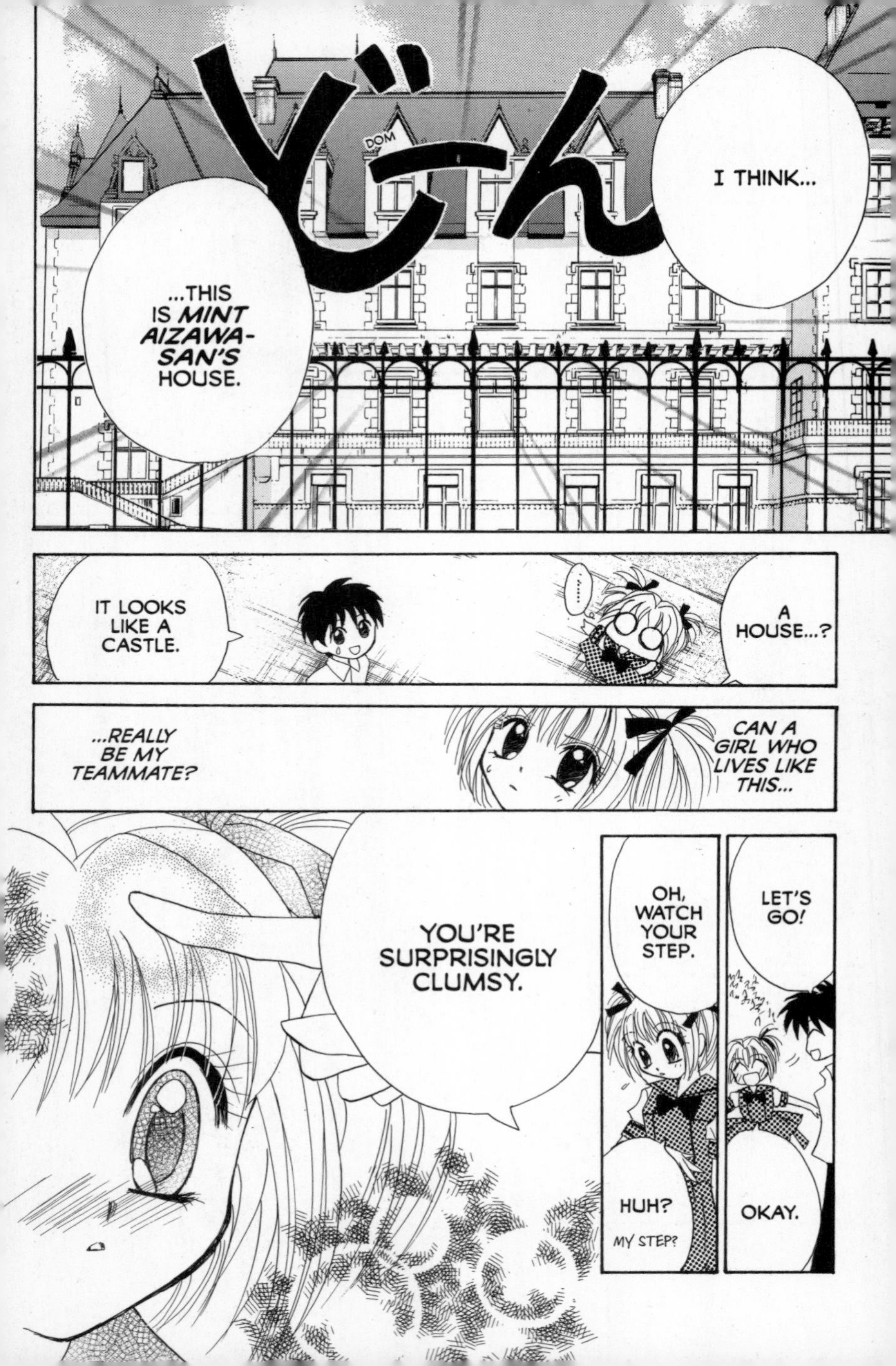

どーん
DOM
I THINK...
...THIS IS *MINT AIZAWA-SAN'S* HOUSE.
A HOUSE...?
......
IT LOOKS LIKE A CASTLE.
CAN A GIRL WHO LIVES LIKE THIS...
...REALLY BE MY TEAMMATE?
LET'S GO!
OKAY.
OH, WATCH YOUR STEP.
HUH?
MY STEP?
YOU'RE SURPRISINGLY CLUMSY.

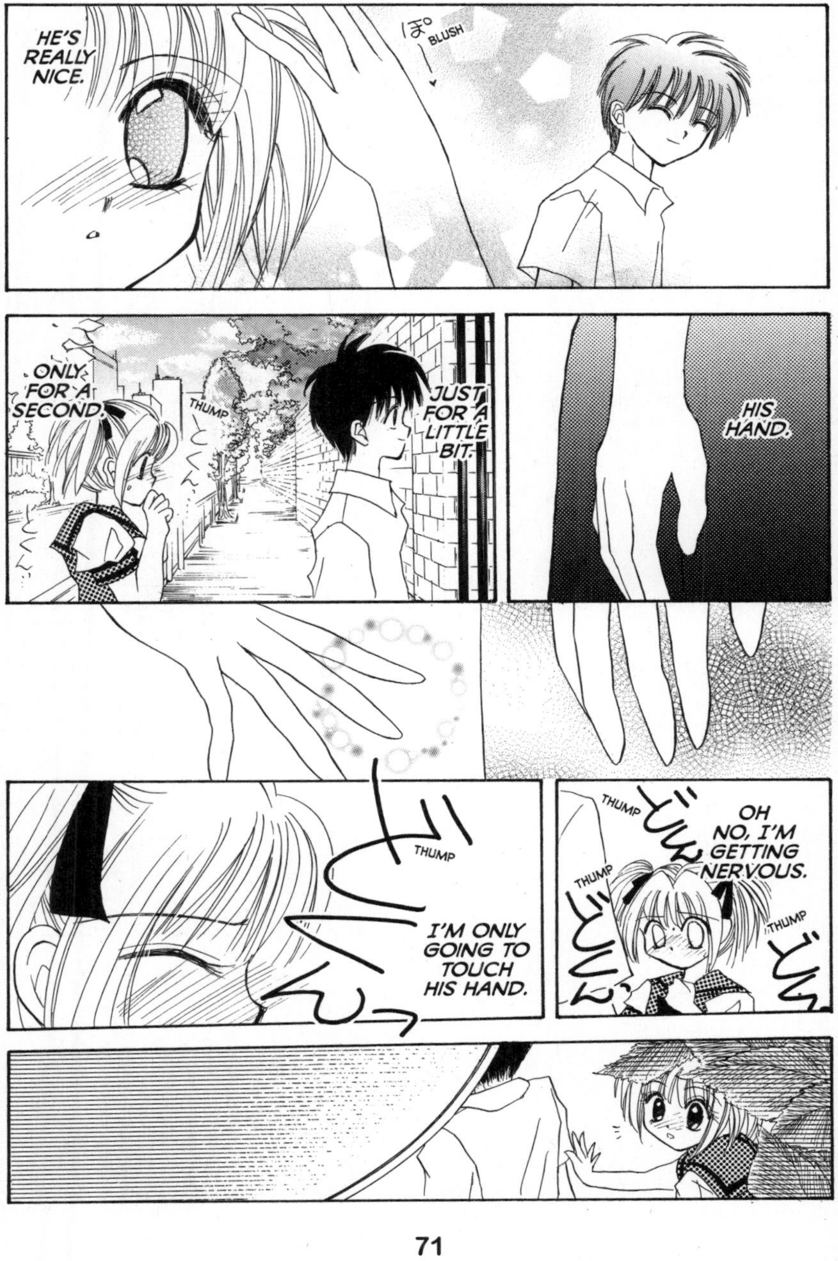
ぽー
BLUSH
HE'S REALLY NICE.
HIS HAND.
JUST FOR A LITTLE BIT.
THUMP
とくん
ONLY FOR A SECOND.
とくん
OH NO, I'M GETTING NERVOUS.
THUMP
どくん
THUMP
どくん
THUMP
どくん
どくん
THUMP
I'M ONLY GOING TO TOUCH HIS HAND.

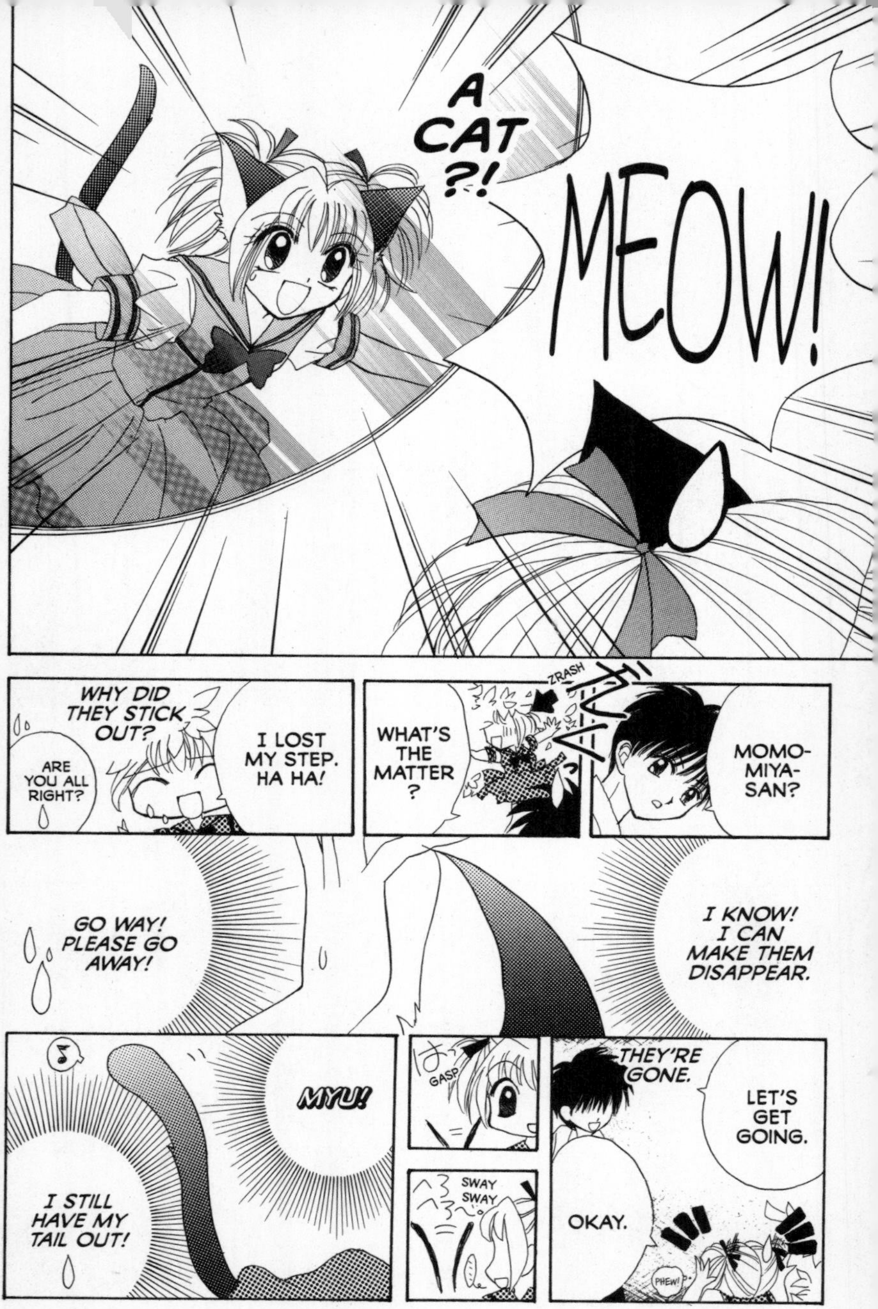
MEOW!
A CAT ?!
MOMO-MIYA-SAN?
ZRASH
WHAT'S THE MATTER ?
I LOST MY STEP. HA HA!
WHY DID THEY STICK OUT?
ARE YOU ALL RIGHT?
I KNOW! I CAN MAKE THEM DISAPPEAR.
GO WAY! PLEASE GO AWAY!
LET'S GET GOING.
THEY'RE GONE.
OKAY.
PHEW!
GASP
SWAY SWAY
MYU!
I STILL HAVE MY TAIL OUT!

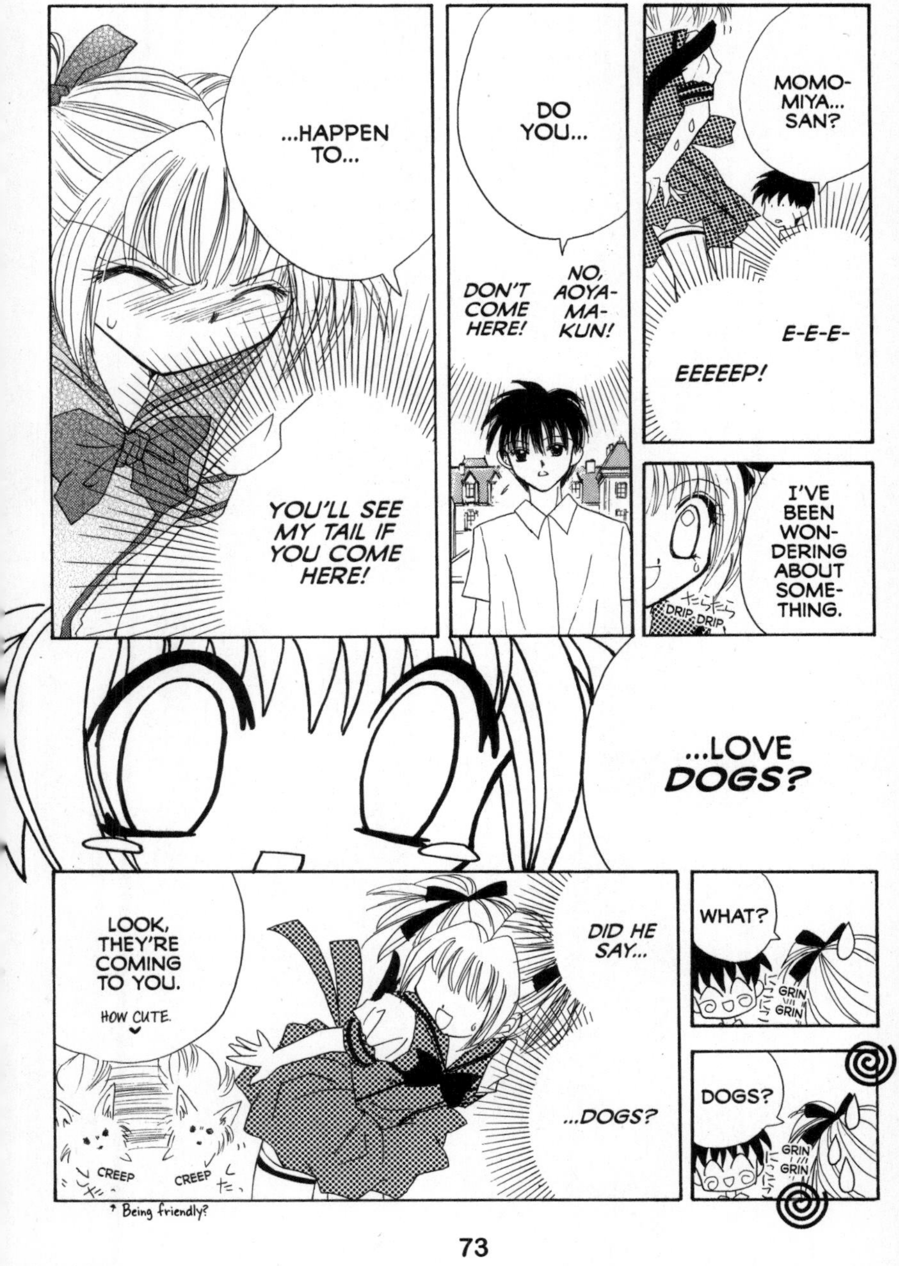
MOMO-MIYA... SAN?
E-E-E-
EEEEEP!
I'VE BEEN WONDERING ABOUT SOMETHING.
DRIP DRIP
DO YOU...
NO, AOYAMA-KUN!
DON'T COME HERE!
...HAPPEN TO...
YOU'LL SEE MY TAIL IF YOU COME HERE!
...LOVE DOGS?
WHAT?
GRIN GRIN
DOGS?
GRIN GRIN
DID HE SAY...
...DOGS?
LOOK, THEY'RE COMING TO YOU.
HOW CUTE.
CREEP
CREEP
* Being friendly?

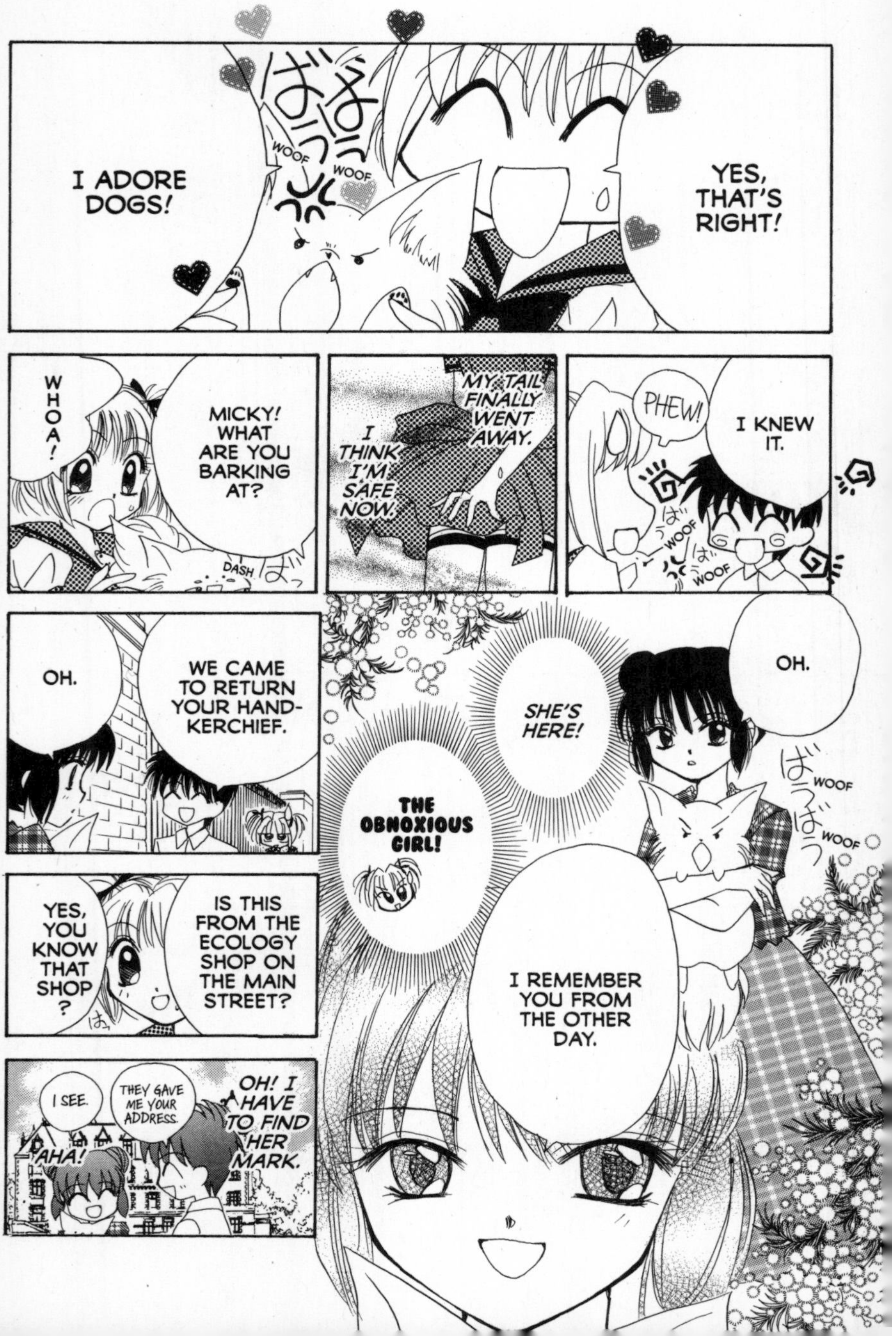
YES, THAT'S RIGHT!
WOOF
WOOF
I ADORE DOGS!
I KNEW IT.
PHEW!
WOOF
WOOF
MY TAIL FINALLY WENT AWAY.
I THINK I'M SAFE NOW.
MICKY! WHAT ARE YOU BARKING AT?
WHOA!
DASH
OH.
SHE'S HERE!
WOOF
WOOF
THE OBNOXIOUS GIRL!
I REMEMBER YOU FROM THE OTHER DAY.
WE CAME TO RETURN YOUR HAND-KERCHIEF.
OH.
IS THIS FROM THE ECOLOGY SHOP ON THE MAIN STREET?
YES, YOU KNOW THAT SHOP?
OH! I HAVE TO FIND HER MARK.
THEY GAVE ME YOUR ADDRESS.
I SEE.
AHA!

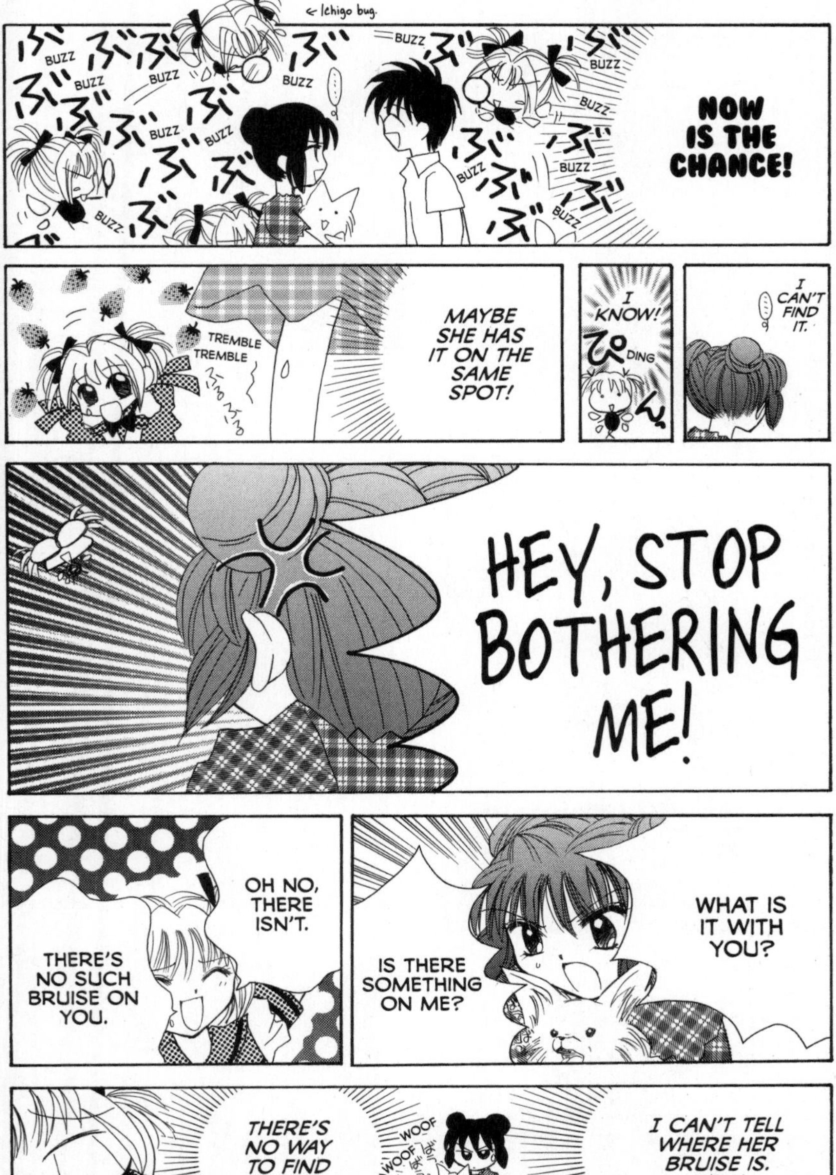

← Ichigo bug.
NOW IS THE CHANCE!
BUZZ
BUZZ
BUZZ
BUZZ
BUZZ
BUZZ
BUZZ
BUZZ
BUZZ
BUZZ
BUZZ
BUZZ
I CAN'T FIND IT.
I KNOW!
DING
MAYBE SHE HAS IT ON THE SAME SPOT!
TREMBLE TREMBLE
HEY, STOP BOTHERING ME!
WHAT IS IT WITH YOU?
IS THERE SOMETHING ON ME?
OH NO, THERE ISN'T.
THERE'S NO SUCH BRUISE ON YOU.
I CAN'T TELL WHERE HER BRUISE IS. UGH!
WOOF
WOOF
THERE'S NO WAY TO FIND OUT!

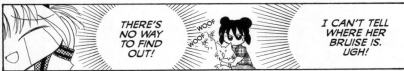

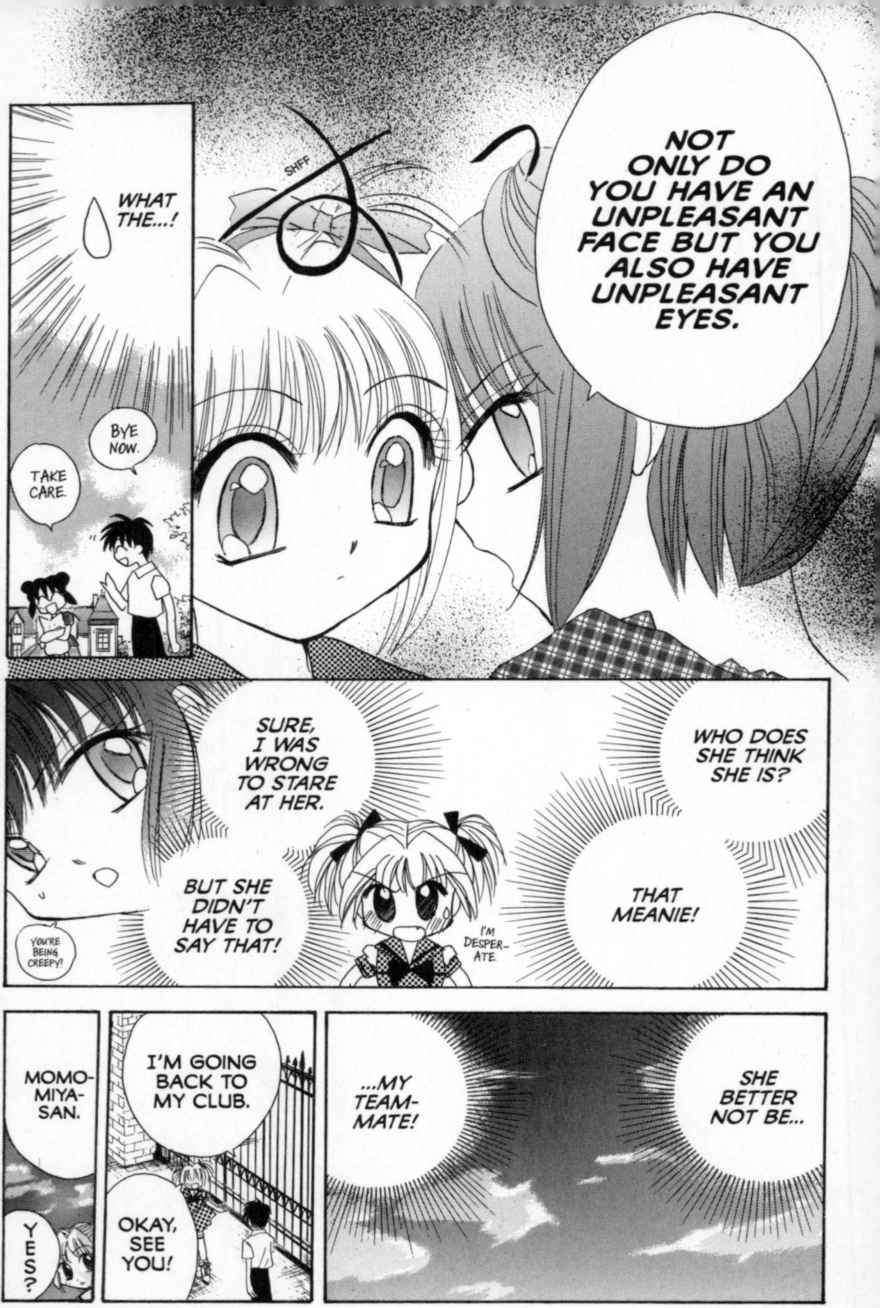

NOT ONLY DO YOU HAVE AN UNPLEASANT FACE BUT YOU ALSO HAVE UNPLEASANT EYES.
SHFF
WHAT THE...!
BYE NOW.
TAKE CARE.
WHO DOES SHE THINK SHE IS?
SURE, I WAS WRONG TO STARE AT HER.
THAT MEANIE!
I'M DESPER-ATE.
BUT SHE DIDN'T HAVE TO SAY THAT!
YOU'RE BEING CREEPY!
SHE BETTER NOT BE...
...MY TEAM-MATE!
I'M GOING BACK TO MY CLUB.
OKAY, SEE YOU!
MOMO-MIYA-SAN.
YES?

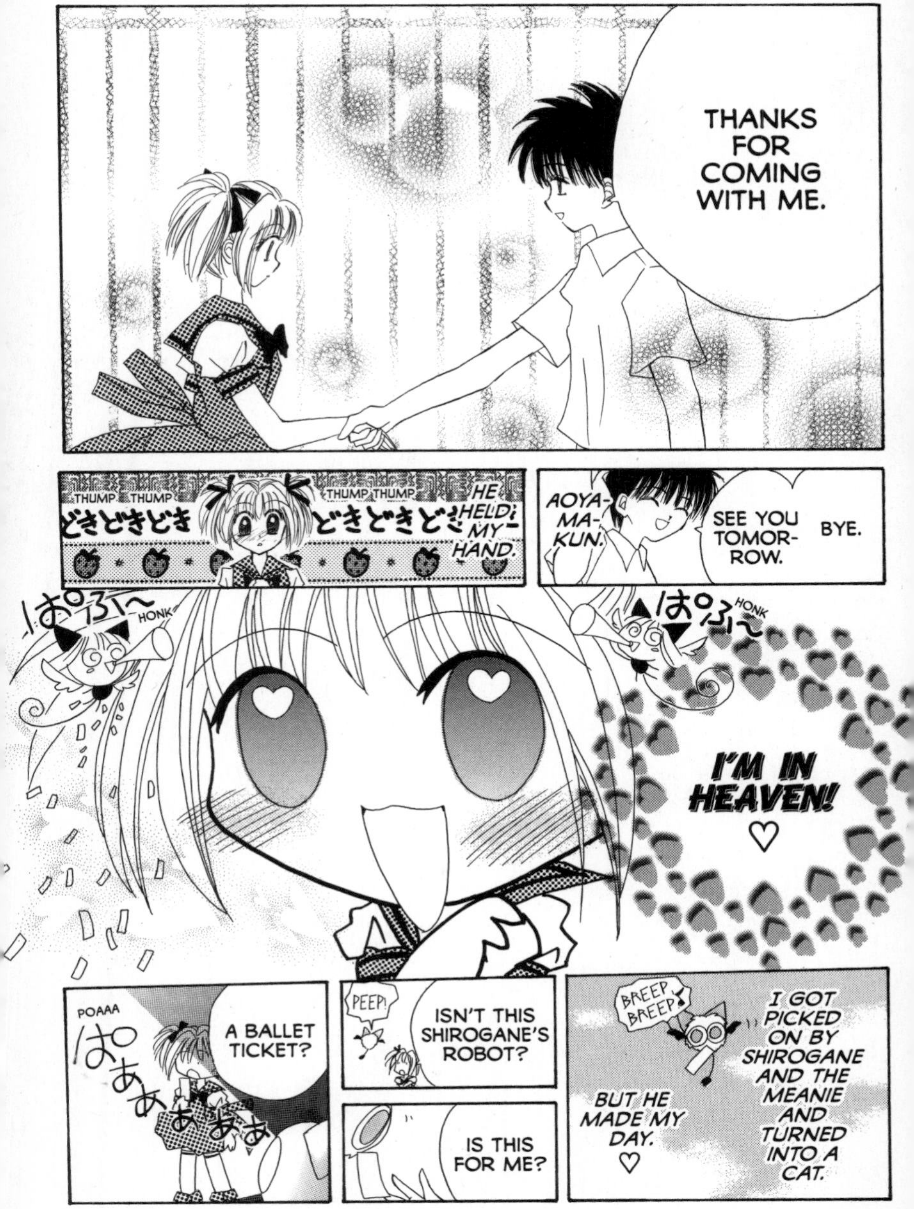
THANKS FOR COMING WITH ME.
SEE YOU TOMORROW.
BYE.
AOYAMA-KUN.
HE HELD MY HAND.
THUMP THUMP
どきどきどき
THUMP THUMP
どきどきどき
はぷふ〜
HONK
I'M IN HEAVEN! ♡
はぷふ〜
HONK
BREEP, BREEP
I GOT PICKED ON BY SHIROGANE AND THE MEANIE AND TURNED INTO A CAT.
BUT HE MADE MY DAY. ♡
PEEP!
ISN'T THIS SHIROGANE'S ROBOT?
IS THIS FOR ME?
A BALLET TICKET?
POAAA
ぱあぁぁぁぁ

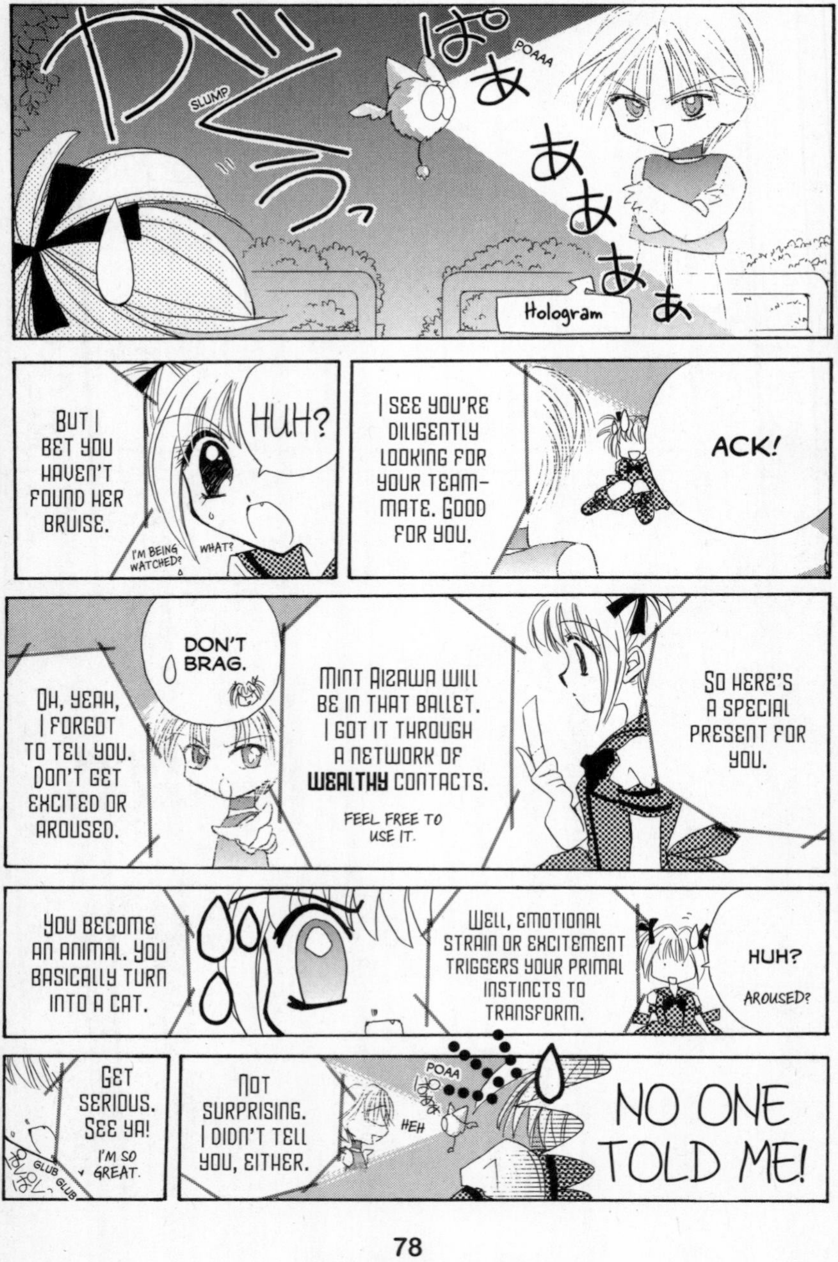
ぱああああぁ
POAAA
SLUMP
Hologram
ACK!
I SEE YOU'RE DILIGENTLY LOOKING FOR YOUR TEAM-MATE. GOOD FOR YOU.
HUH?
BUT I BET YOU HAVEN'T FOUND HER BRUISE.
WHAT?
I'M BEING WATCHED?
SO HERE'S A SPECIAL PRESENT FOR YOU.
MINT AIZAWA WILL BE IN THAT BALLET. I GOT IT THROUGH A NETWORK OF WEALTHY CONTACTS.
FEEL FREE TO USE IT.
DON'T BRAG.
OH, YEAH, I FORGOT TO TELL YOU. DON'T GET EXCITED OR AROUSED.
HUH?
AROUSED?
WELL, EMOTIONAL STRAIN OR EXCITEMENT TRIGGERS YOUR PRIMAL INSTINCTS TO TRANSFORM.
YOU BECOME AN ANIMAL. YOU BASICALLY TURN INTO A CAT.
NO ONE TOLD ME!
POAA
HEH
NOT SURPRISING. I DIDN'T TELL YOU, EITHER.
GET SERIOUS. SEE YA!
I'M SO GREAT.
GLUB GLUB

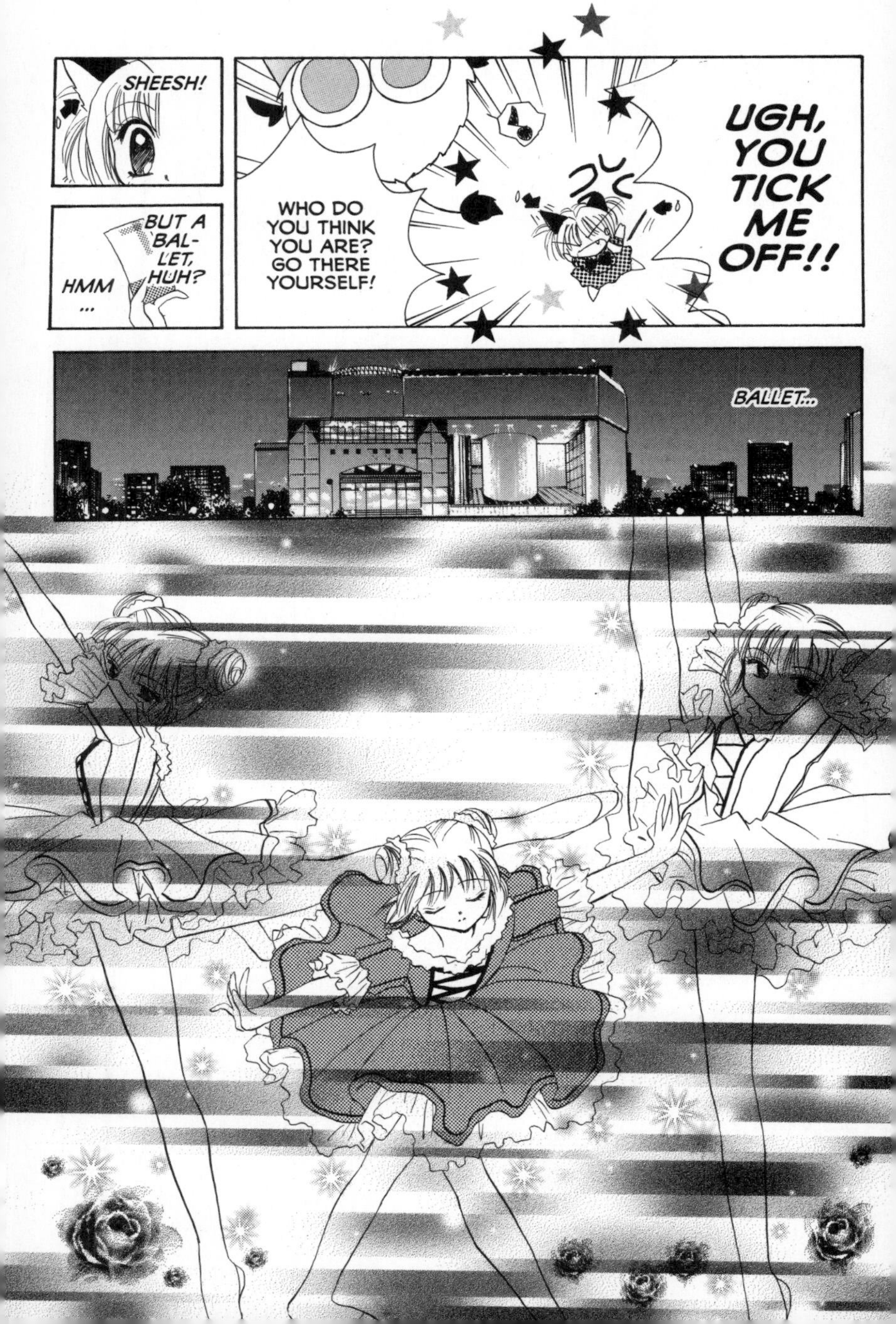
UGH, YOU TICK ME OFF!!
WHO DO YOU THINK YOU ARE? GO THERE YOURSELF!
SHEESH!
BUT A BAL-LET, HUH?
HMM ...
BALLET...

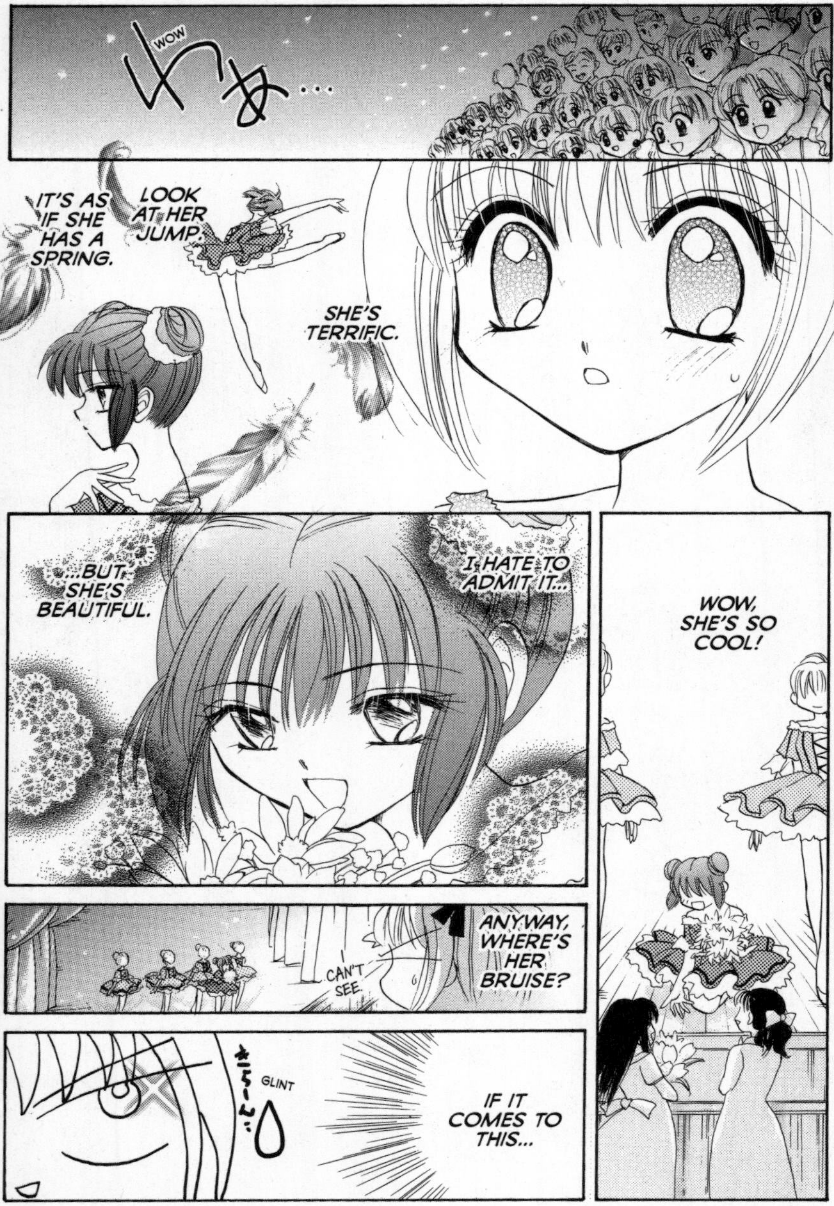
わぁ...
WOW
SHE'S TERRIFIC.
LOOK AT HER JUMP.
IT'S AS IF SHE HAS A SPRING.
WOW, SHE'S SO COOL!
I HATE TO ADMIT IT...
...BUT SHE'S BEAUTIFUL.
ANYWAY, WHERE'S HER BRUISE?
I CAN'T SEE.
IF IT COMES TO THIS...
きらーん
GLINT

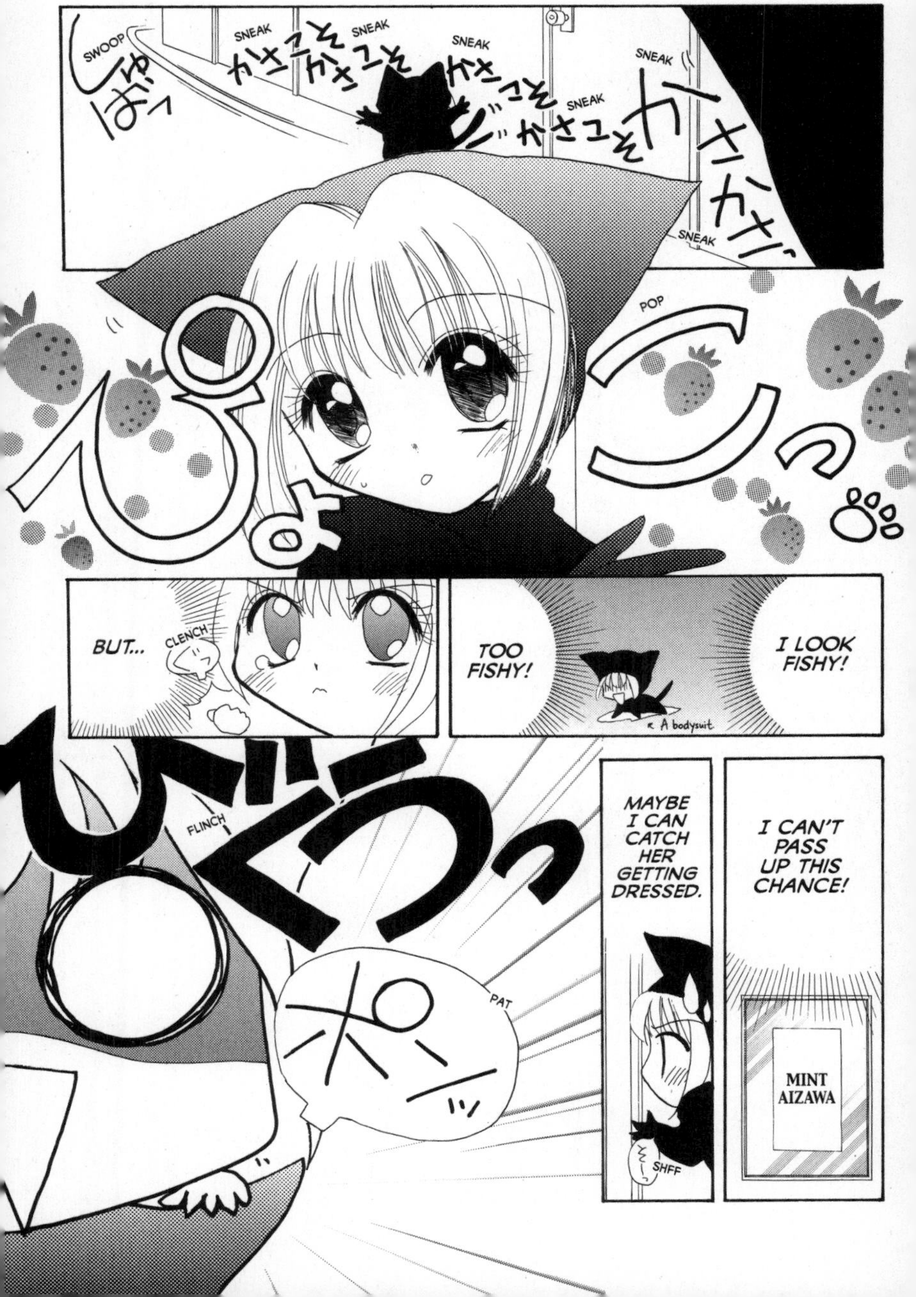
SNEAK
SNEAK
SNEAK
SNEAK
SNEAK
SWOOP
SNEAK
POP
I LOOK FISHY!
TOO FISHY!
A bodysuit
CLENCH
BUT...
I CAN'T PASS UP THIS CHANCE!
MINT AIZAWA
MAYBE I CAN CATCH HER GETTING DRESSED.
SHFF
FLINCH
PAT

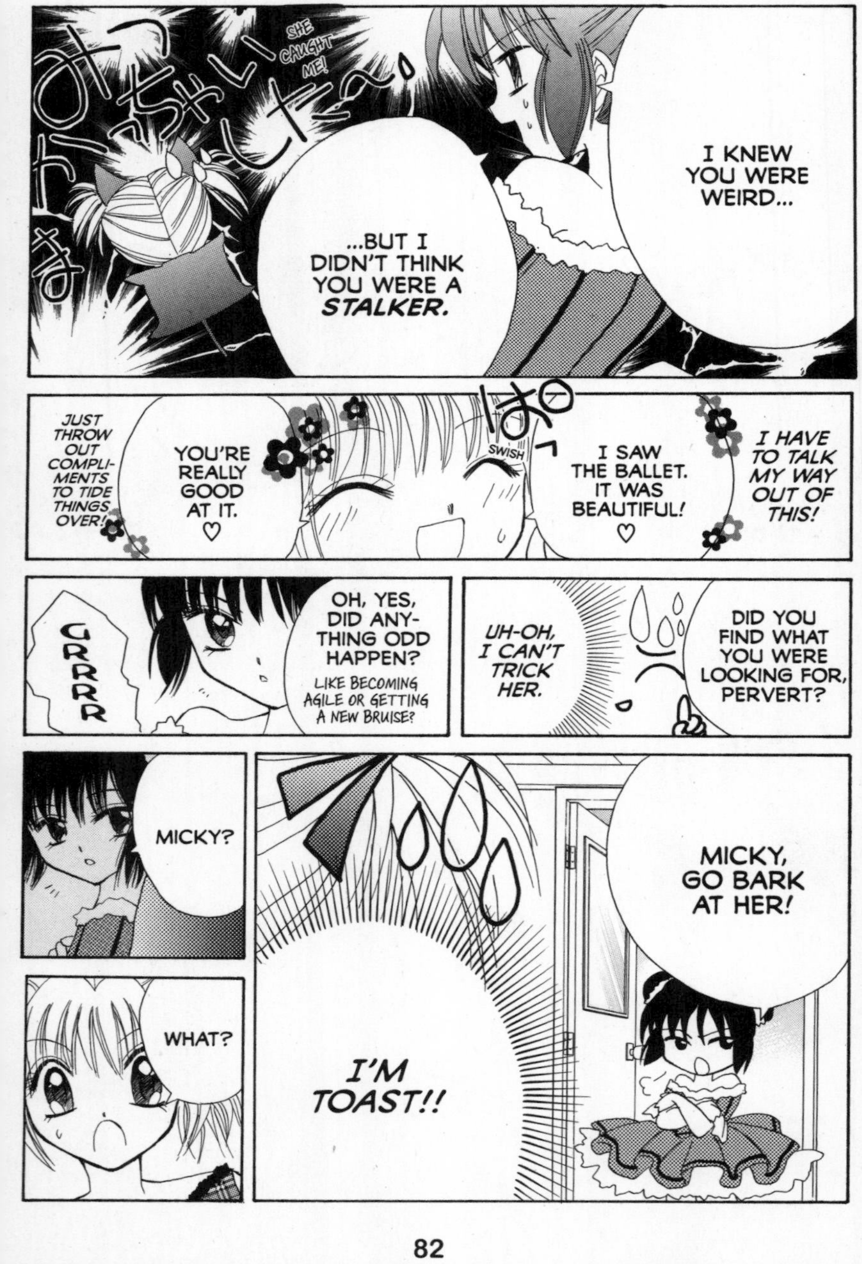
I KNEW YOU WERE WEIRD...
...BUT I DIDN'T THINK YOU WERE A *STALKER.*
SHE CAUGHT ME!
I HAVE TO TALK MY WAY OUT OF THIS!
I SAW THE BALLET. IT WAS BEAUTIFUL! ♡
SWISH
YOU'RE REALLY GOOD AT IT. ♡
JUST THROW OUT COMPLIMENTS TO TIDE THINGS OVER!
DID YOU FIND WHAT YOU WERE LOOKING FOR, PERVERT?
UH-OH, I CAN'T TRICK HER.
OH, YES, DID ANYTHING ODD HAPPEN?
LIKE BECOMING AGILE OR GETTING A NEW BRUISE?
GRRRR
MICKY, GO BARK AT HER!
I'M TOAST!!
MICKY?
WHAT?

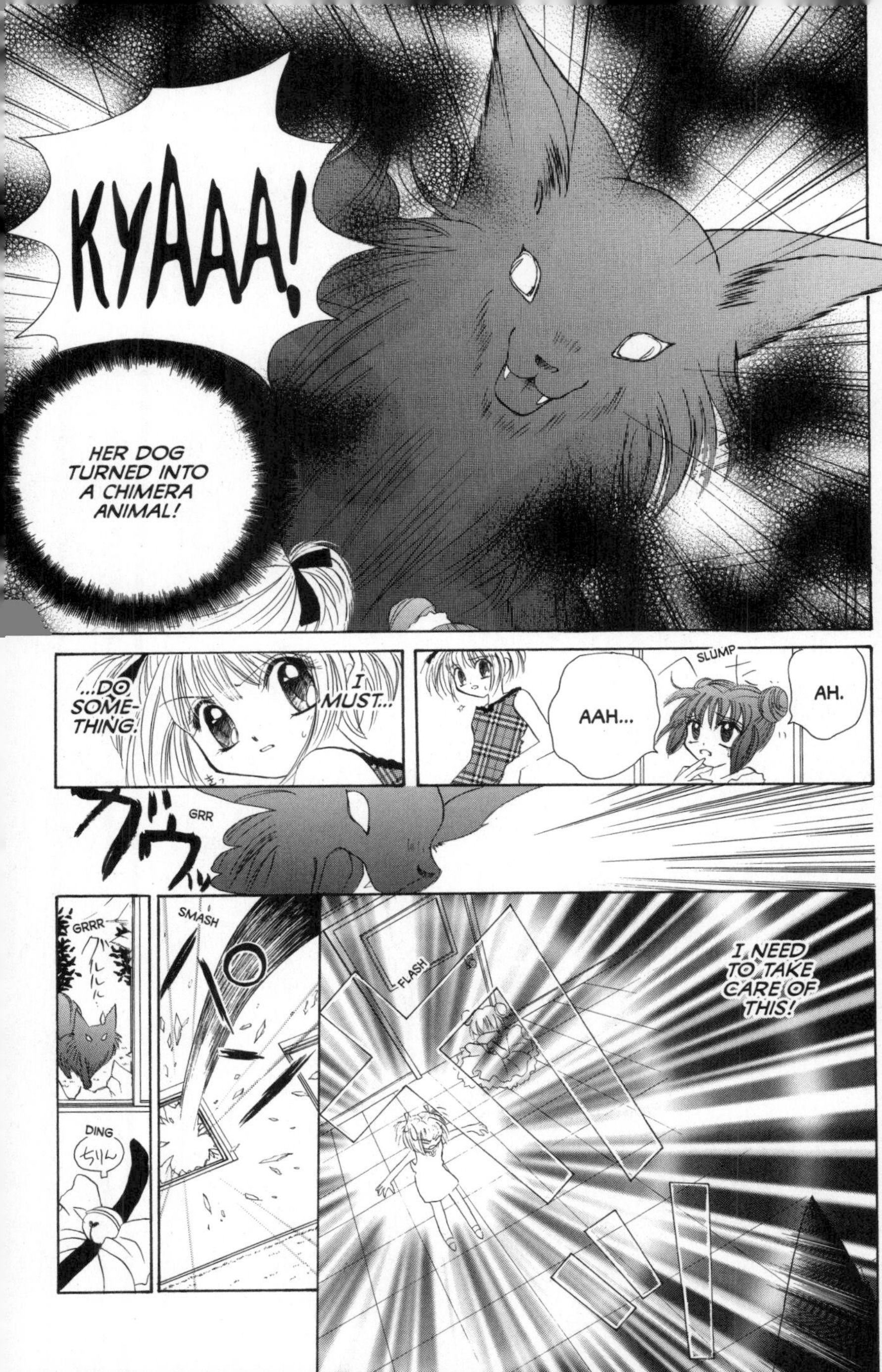
KYAAA!
HER DOG TURNED INTO A CHIMERA ANIMAL!
SLUMP
AH.
AAH...
I MUST...
...DO SOMETHING.
GRR
I NEED TO TAKE CARE OF THIS!
FLASH
SMASH
GRRR
DING
ちりん

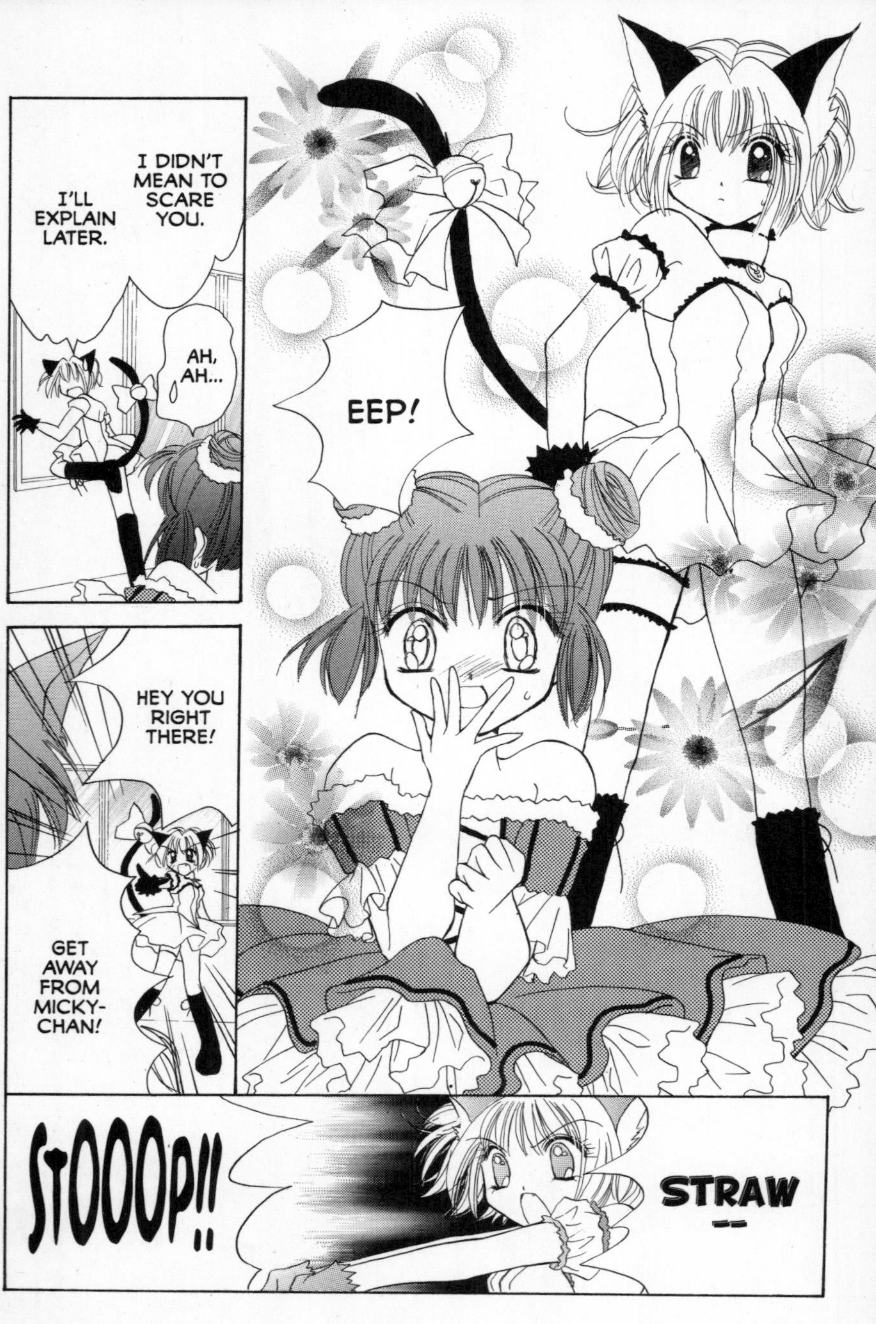
EEP!
I DIDN'T MEAN TO SCARE YOU.
I'LL EXPLAIN LATER.
AH, AH...
HEY YOU RIGHT THERE!
GET AWAY FROM MICKY-CHAN!
STRAW --
STOOOP!!

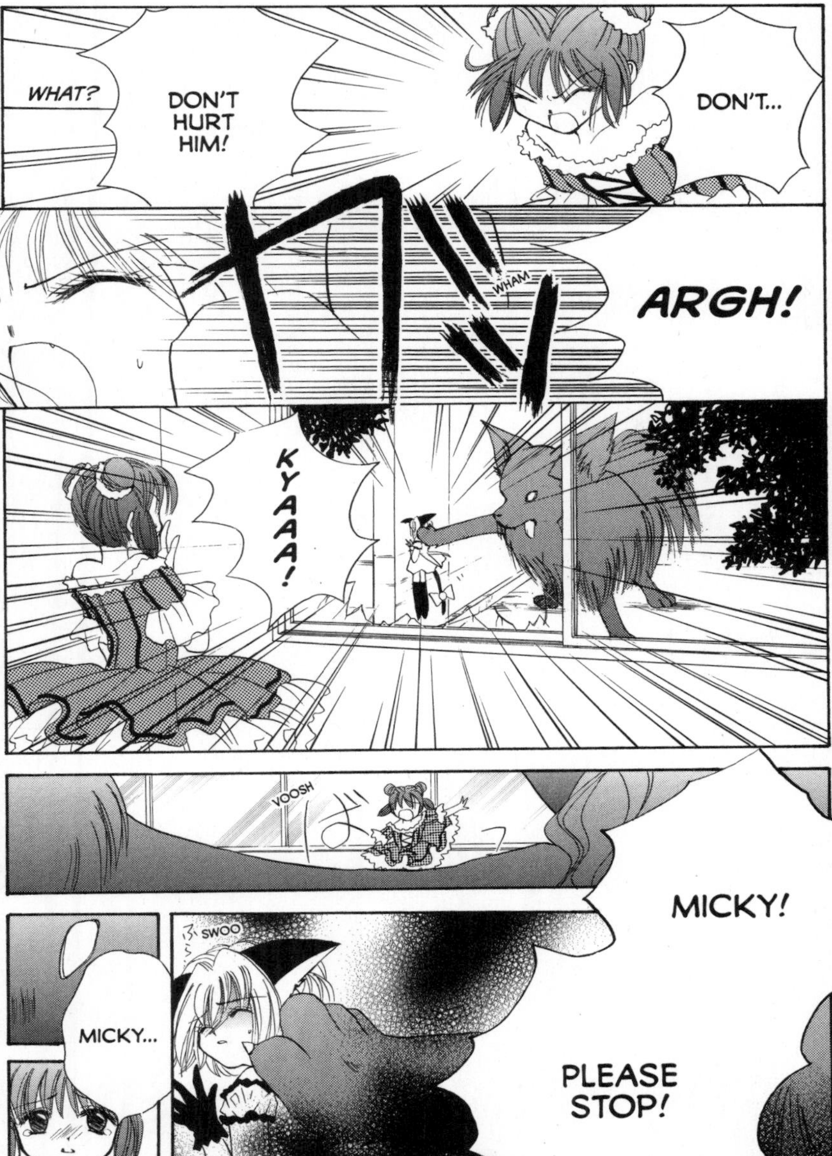
DON'T...
DON'T HURT HIM!
WHAT?
ARGH!
WHAM
KYAAAA!
VOOSH
MICKY!
SWOO
PLEASE STOP!
MICKY...

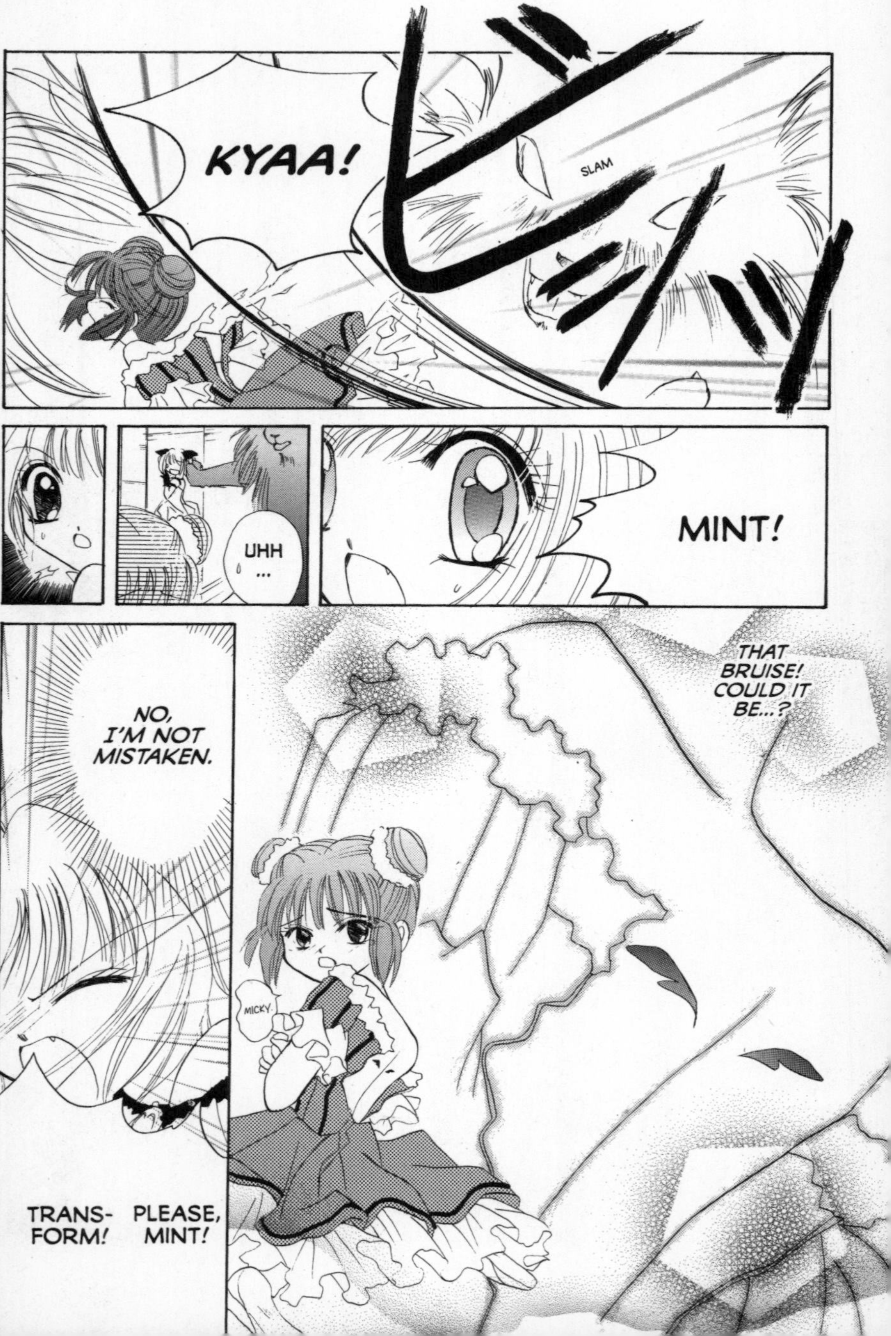
KYAA!
SLAM
MINT!
UHH ...
THAT BRUISE! COULD IT BE...?
MICKY.
NO, I'M NOT MISTAKEN.
PLEASE, MINT!
TRANS-FORM!

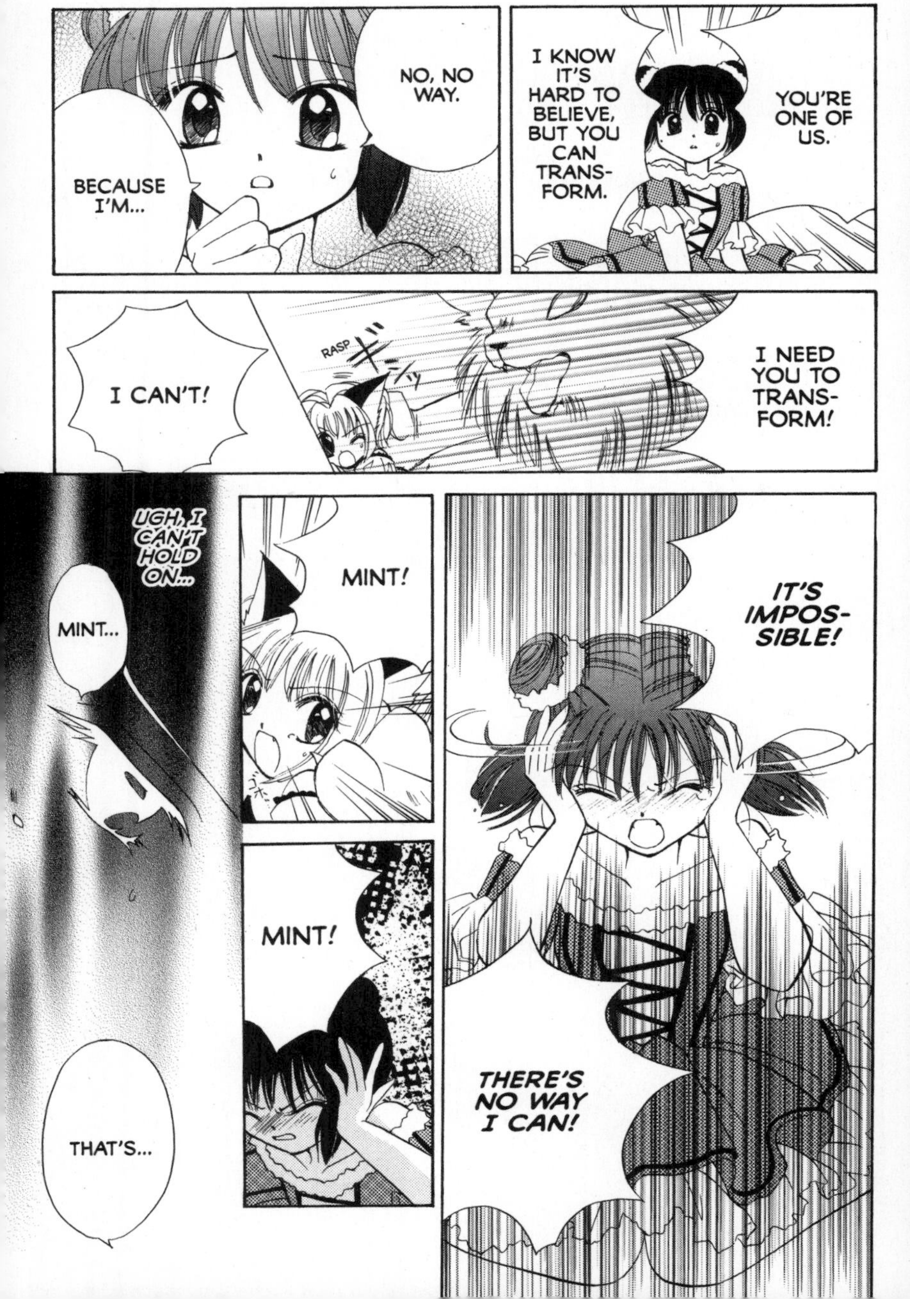
YOU'RE ONE OF US.
I KNOW IT'S HARD TO BELIEVE, BUT YOU CAN TRANS-FORM.
NO, NO WAY.
BECAUSE I'M...
I NEED YOU TO TRANS-FORM!
RASP
I CAN'T!
IT'S IMPOS-SIBLE!
THERE'S NO WAY I CAN!
MINT!
MINT!
UGH, I CAN'T HOLD ON...
MINT...
THAT'S...

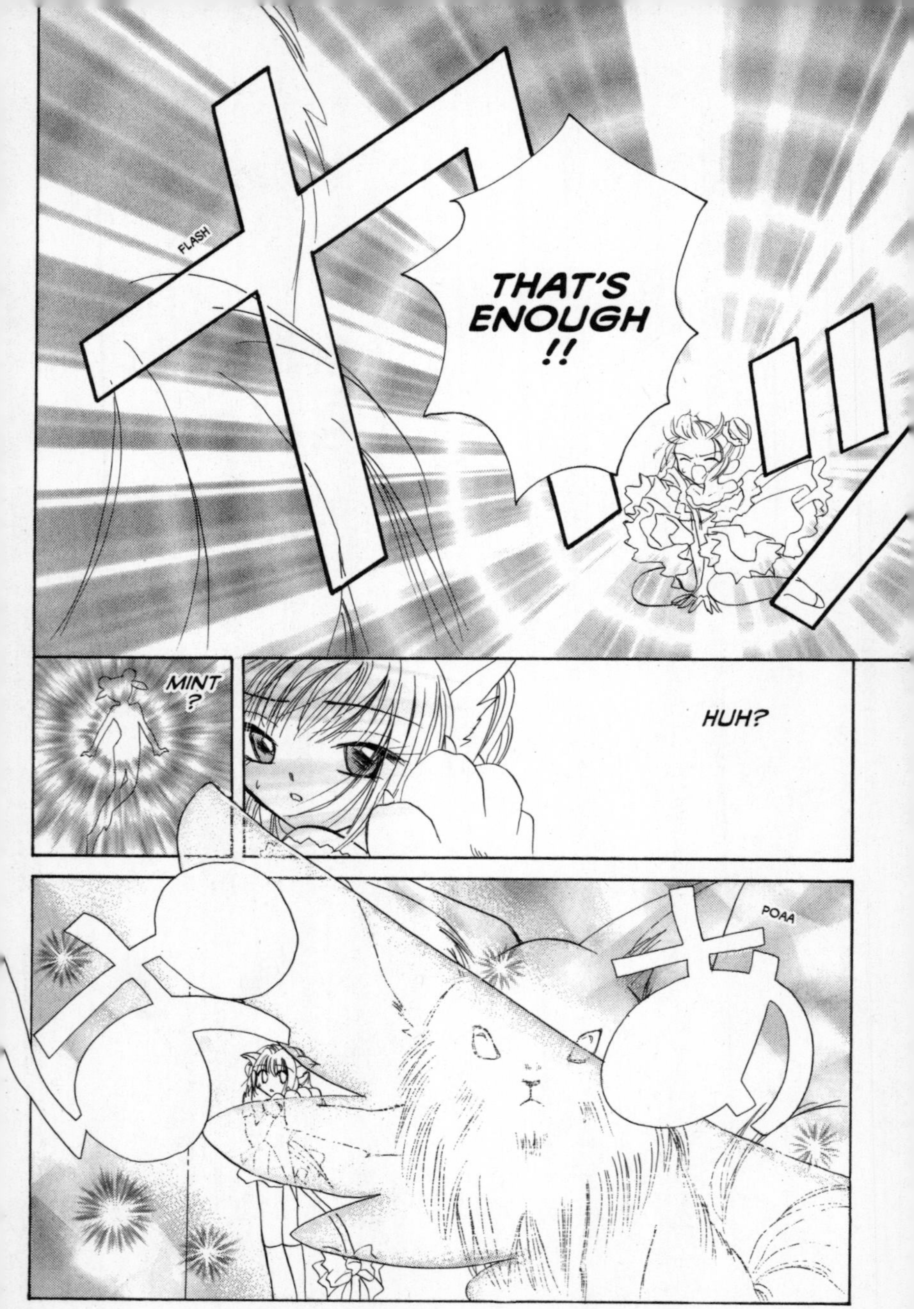
FLASH
THAT'S ENOUGH !!
HUH?
MINT ?
POAA

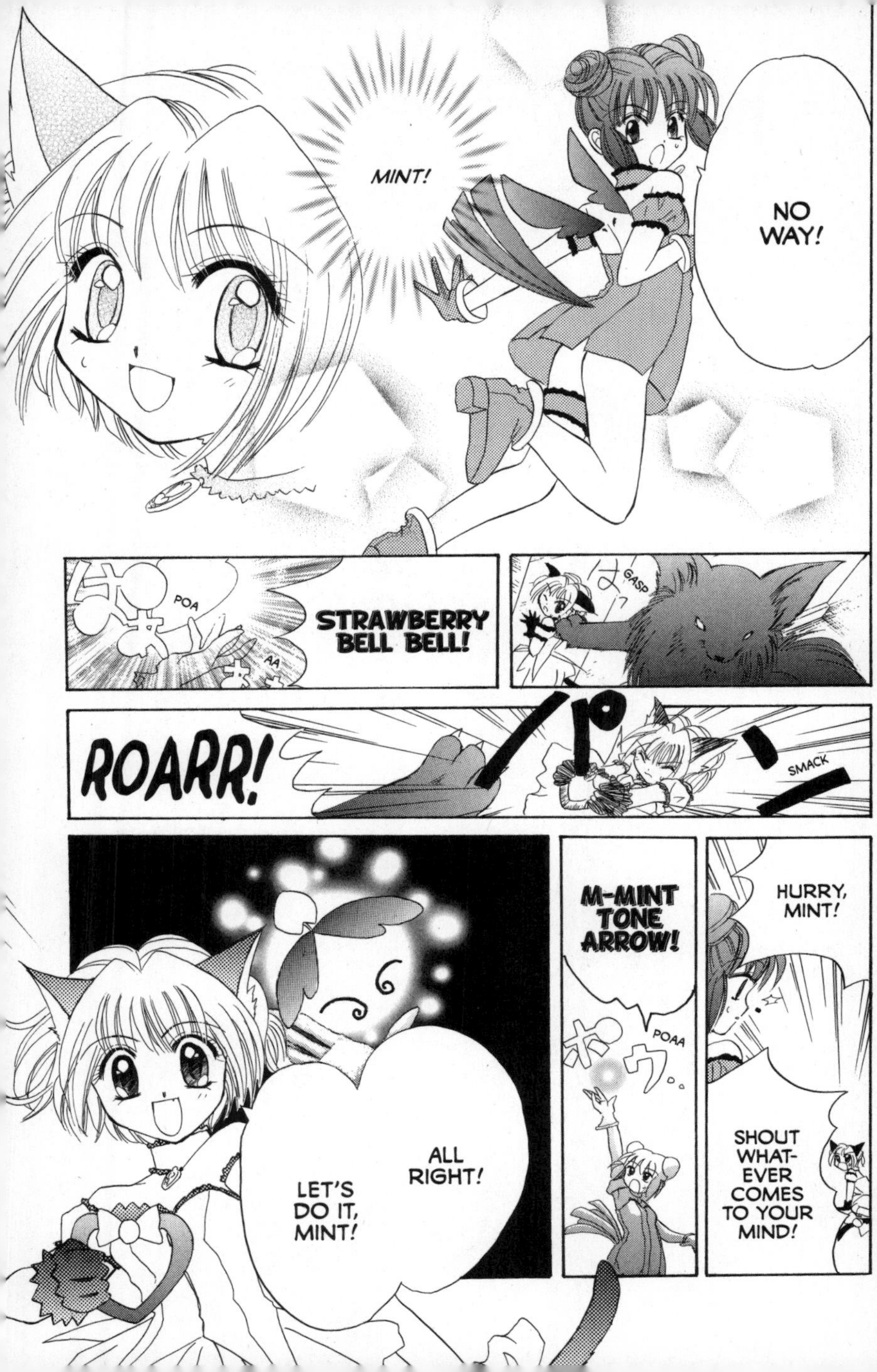

NO WAY!
MINT!
GASP
STRAWBERRY BELL BELL!
POA
AA
SMACK
ROARR!
HURRY, MINT!
SHOUT WHAT-EVER COMES TO YOUR MIND!
M-MINT TONE ARROW!
POAA
ALL RIGHT!
LET'S DO IT, MINT!

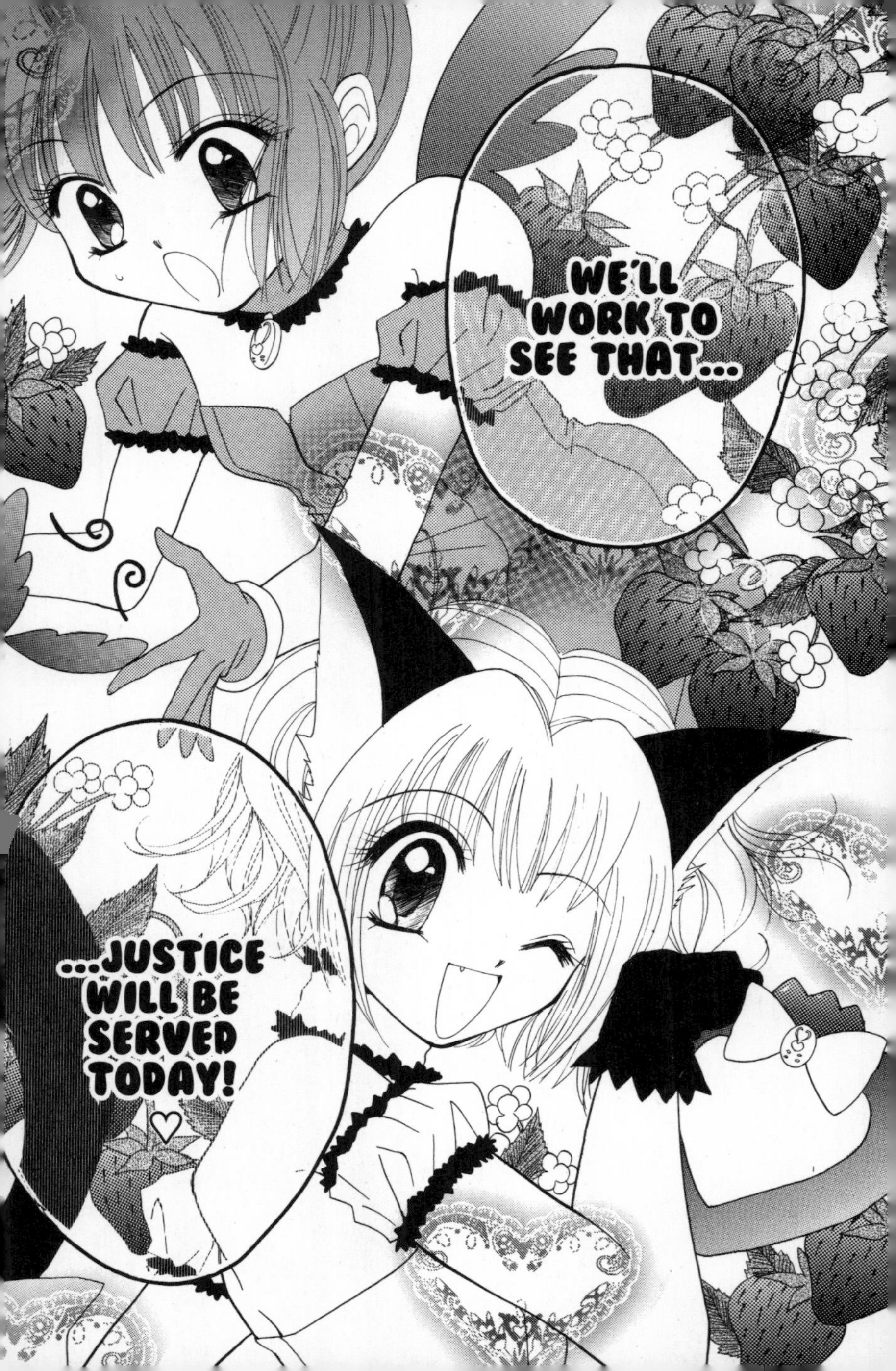
WE'LL WORK TO SEE THAT...
...JUSTICE WILL BE SERVED TODAY! ♡

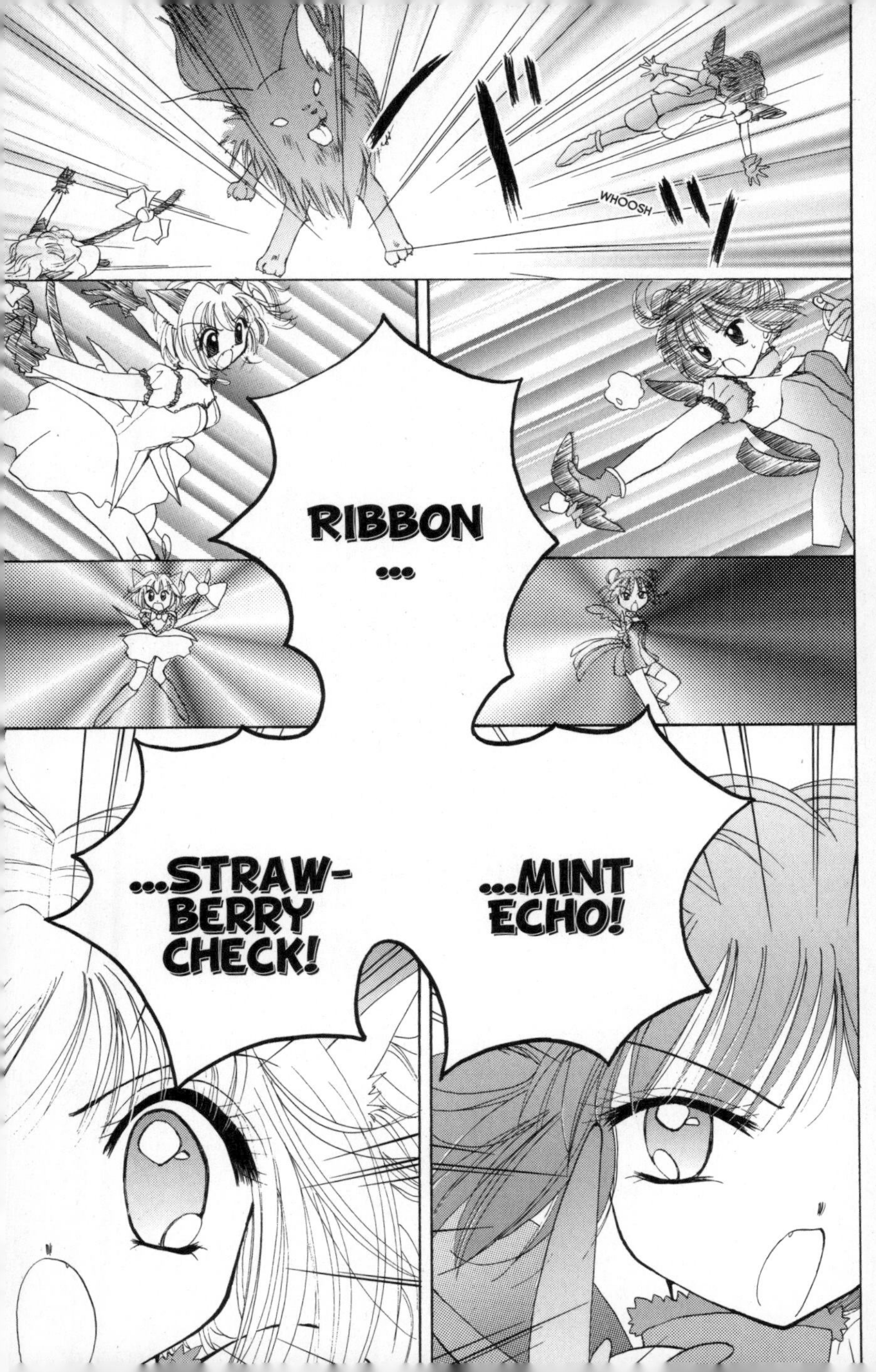
WHOOSH
RIBBON...
...MINT ECHO!
...STRAW-BERRY CHECK!

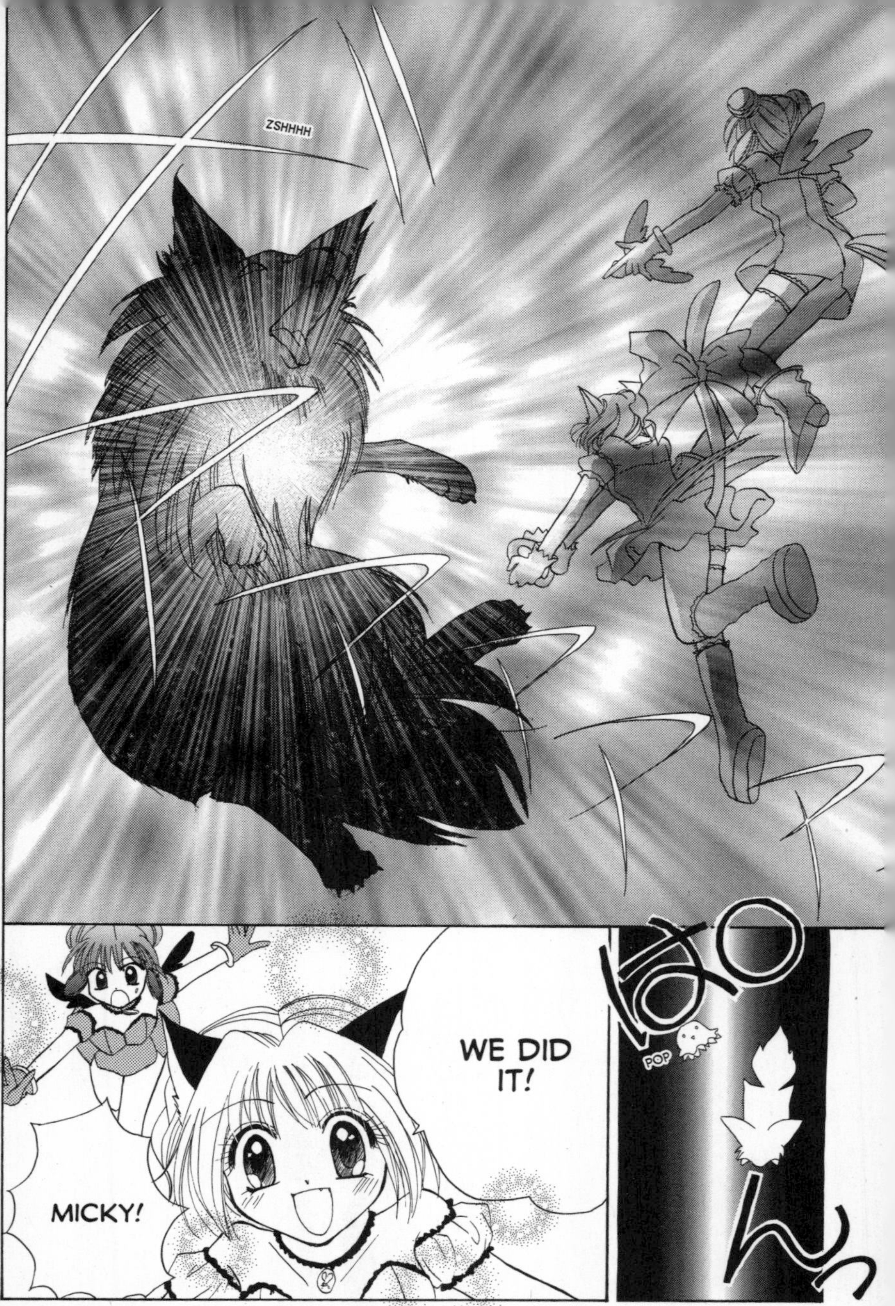
ZSHHHH
POP
WE DID IT!
MICKY!

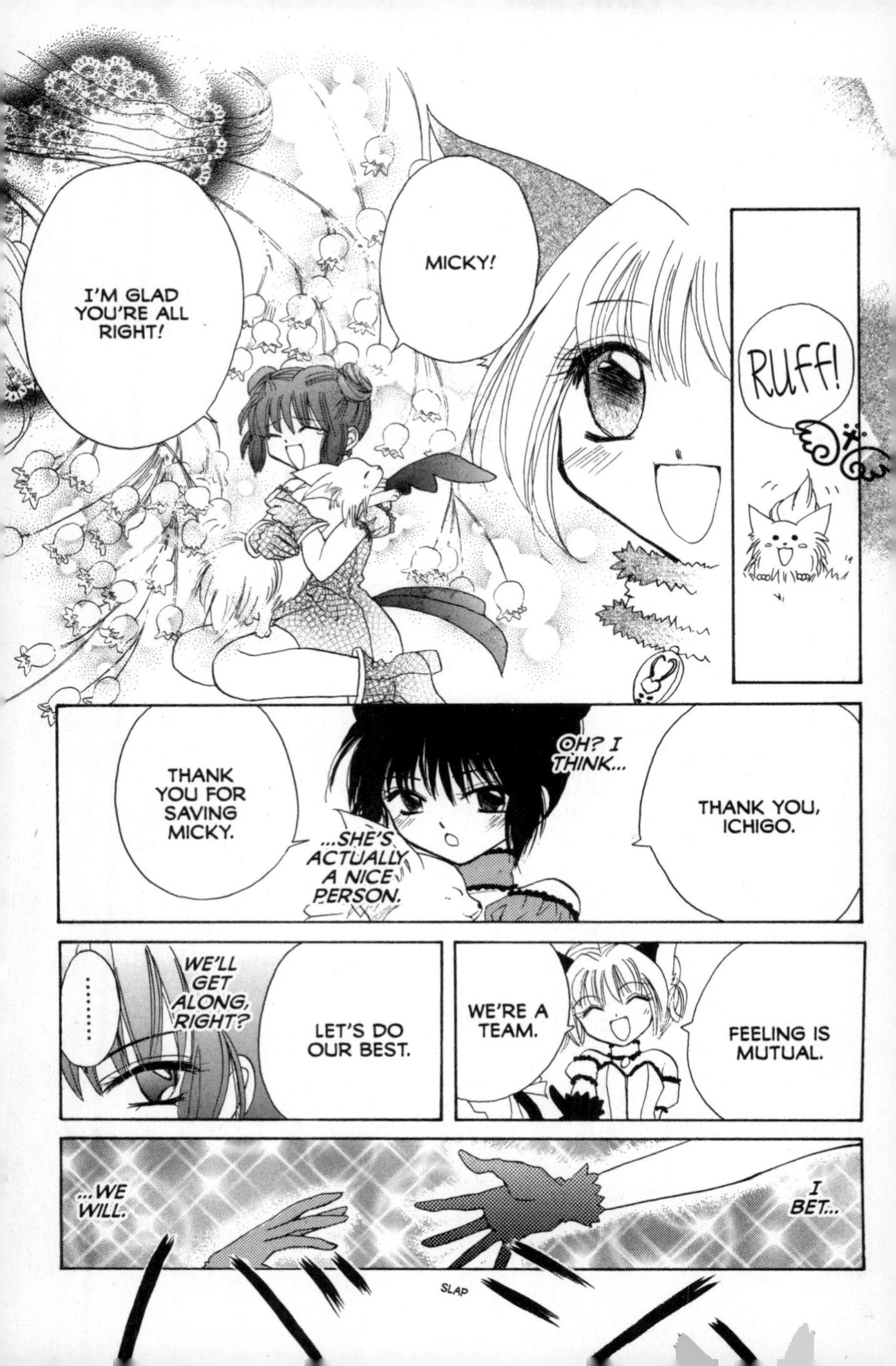
RUFF!
MICKY!
I'M GLAD YOU'RE ALL RIGHT!
THANK YOU, ICHIGO.
OH? I THINK...
...SHE'S ACTUALLY A NICE PERSON.
THANK YOU FOR SAVING MICKY.
FEELING IS MUTUAL.
WE'RE A TEAM.
LET'S DO OUR BEST.
WE'LL GET ALONG, RIGHT?
....
I BET...
...WE WILL.
SLAP

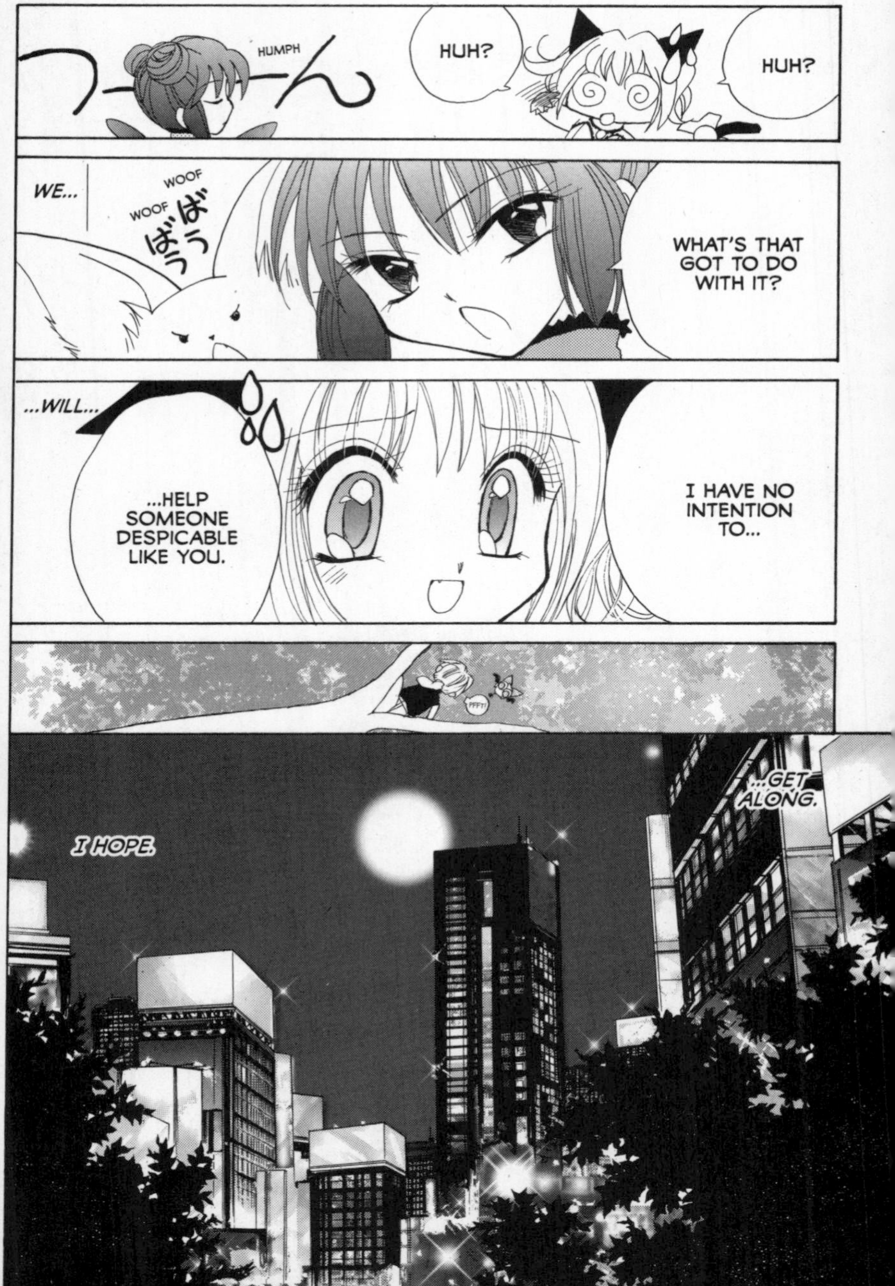
HUH?
HUH?
HUMPH
つーん
WHAT'S THAT GOT TO DO WITH IT?
WOOF WOOF
ばうばう
WE...
I HAVE NO INTENTION TO...
...HELP SOMEONE DESPICABLE LIKE YOU.
...WILL...
PFFT!
...GET ALONG.
I HOPE.

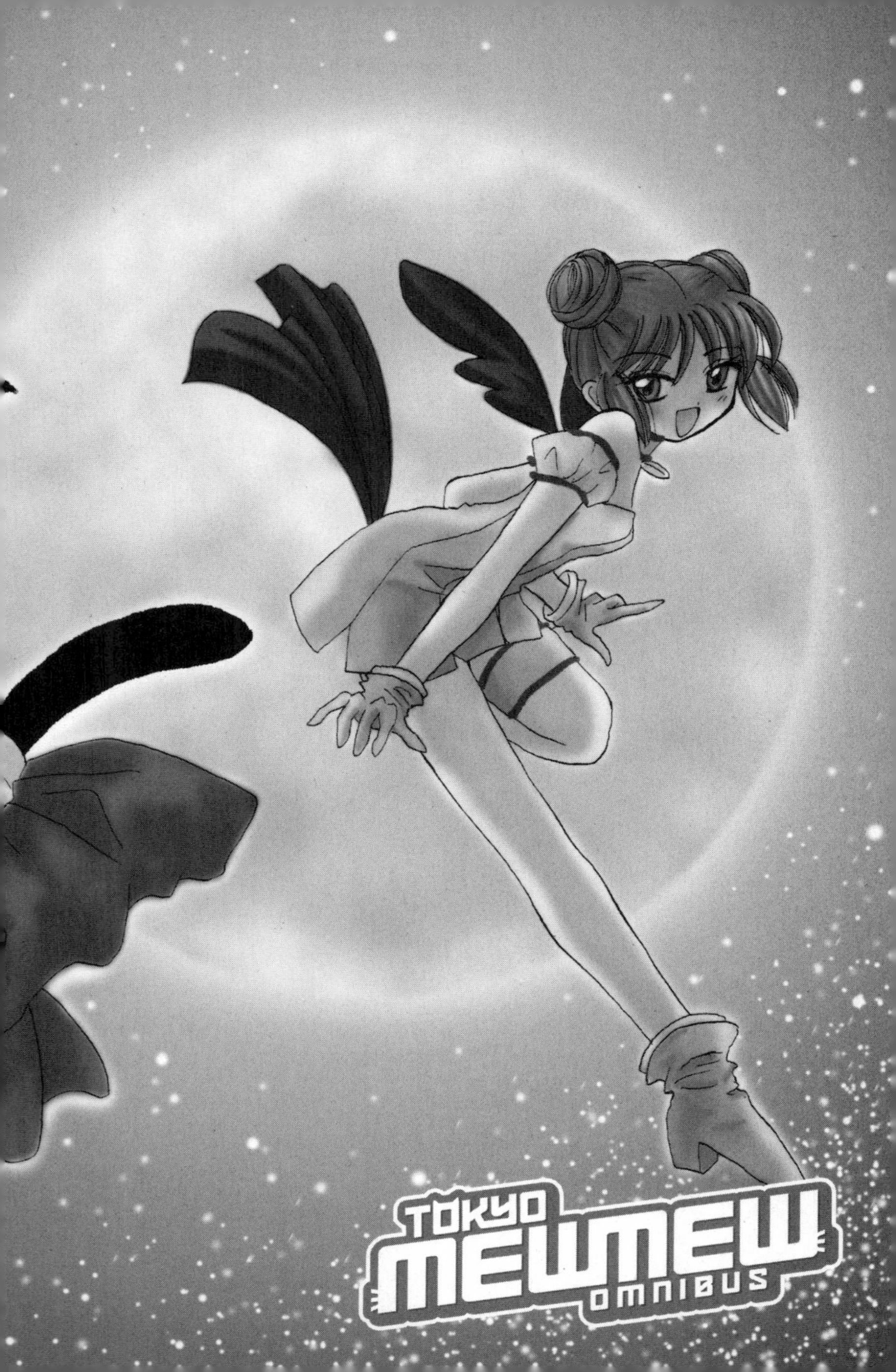
TOKYO
MEWMEW
OMNIBUS

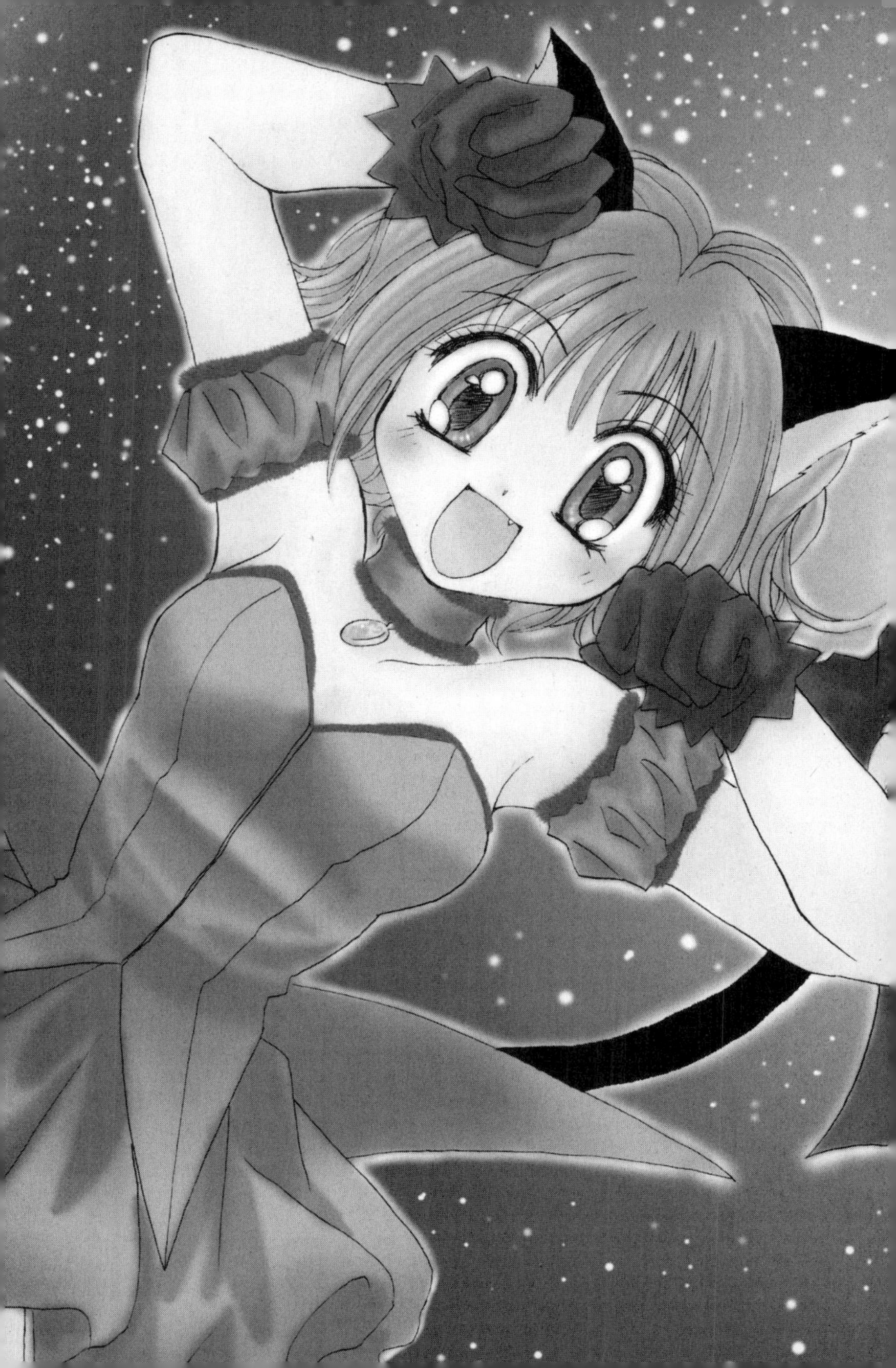

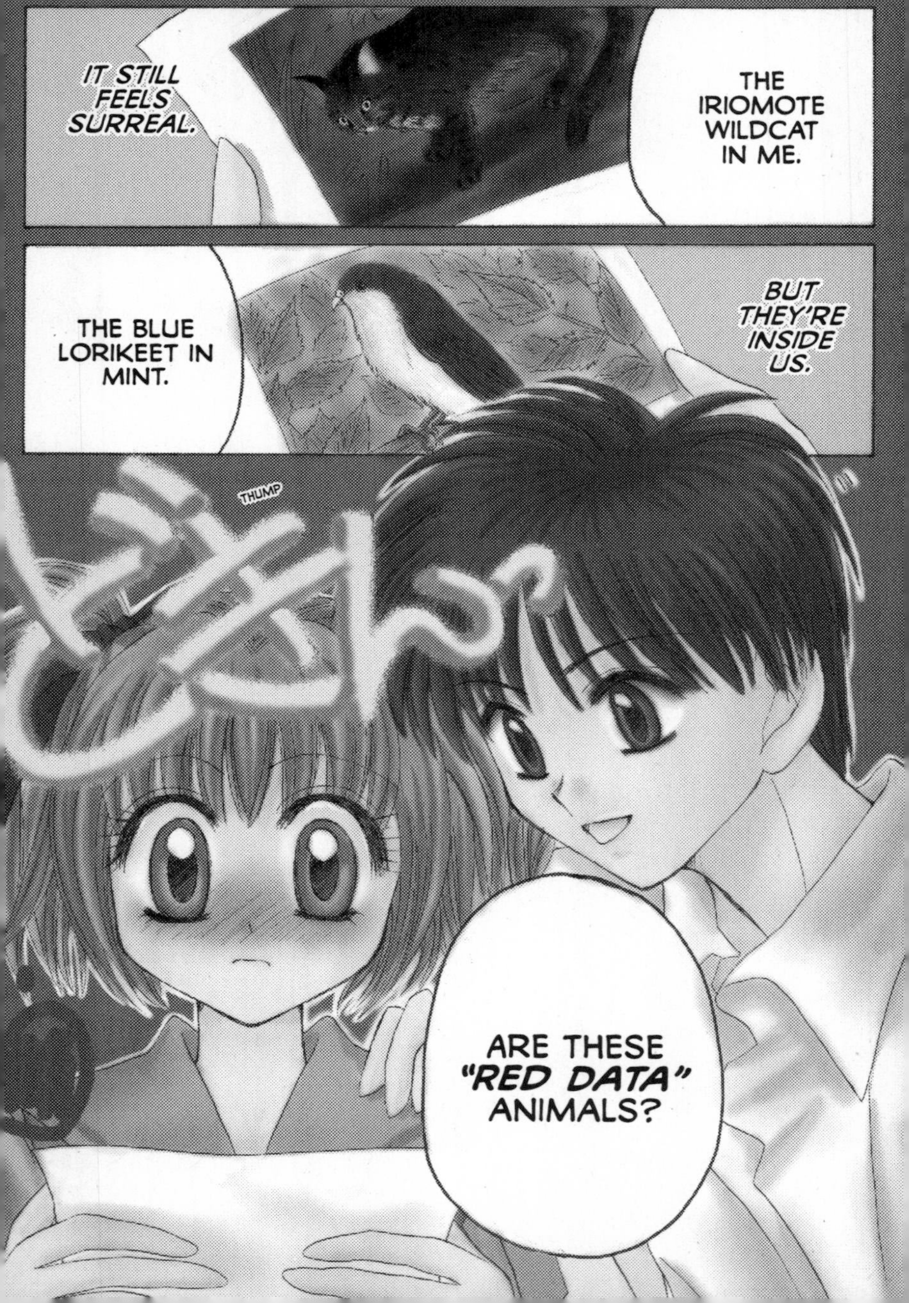
THE IRIOMOTE WILDCAT IN ME.
IT STILL FEELS SURREAL.
BUT THEY'RE INSIDE US.
THE BLUE LORIKEET IN MINT.
THUMP
ARE THESE "RED DATA" ANIMALS?

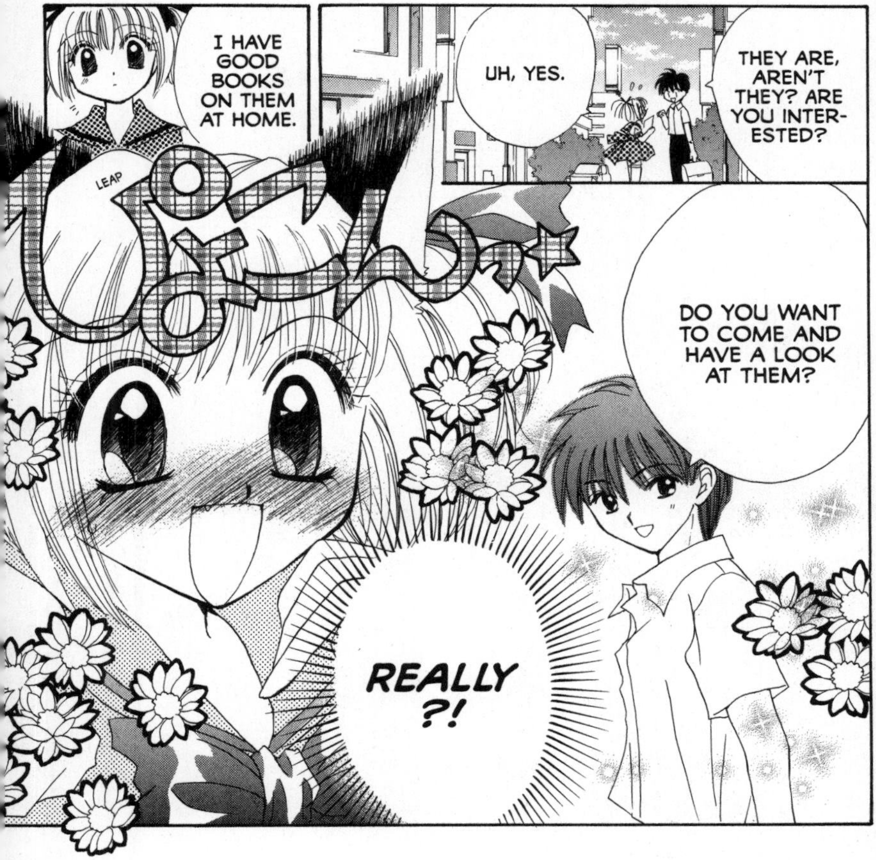
THEY ARE, AREN'T THEY? ARE YOU INTER-ESTED?
UH, YES.
I HAVE GOOD BOOKS ON THEM AT HOME.
DO YOU WANT TO COME AND HAVE A LOOK AT THEM?
LEAP
REALLY ?!

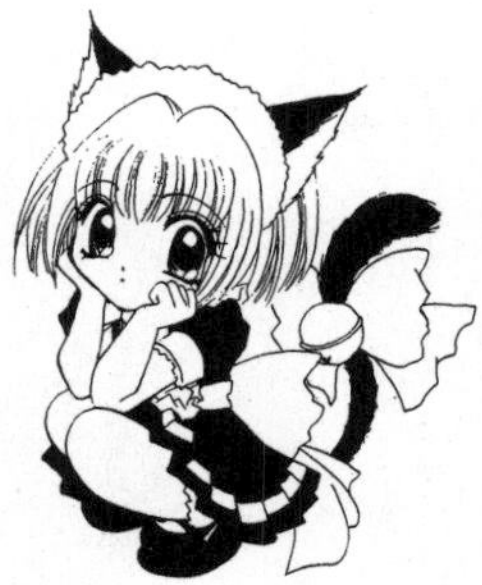

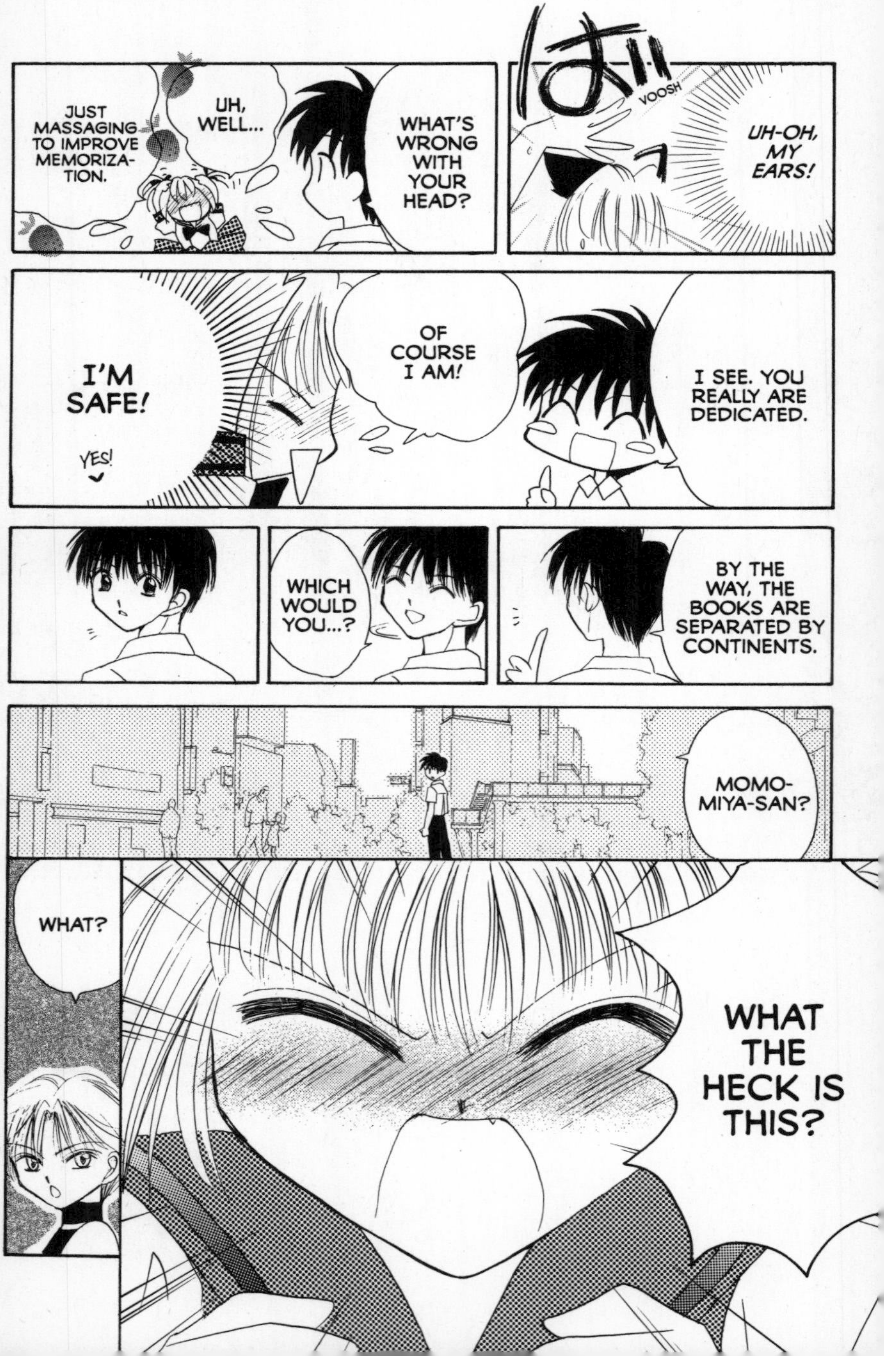
VOOSH
UH-OH, MY EARS!
WHAT'S WRONG WITH YOUR HEAD?
UH, WELL...
JUST MASSAGING TO IMPROVE MEMORIZA-TION.
I SEE. YOU REALLY ARE DEDICATED.
OF COURSE I AM!
I'M SAFE!
YES!
BY THE WAY, THE BOOKS ARE SEPARATED BY CONTINENTS.
WHICH WOULD YOU...?
MOMO-MIYA-SAN?
WHAT THE HECK IS THIS?
WHAT?

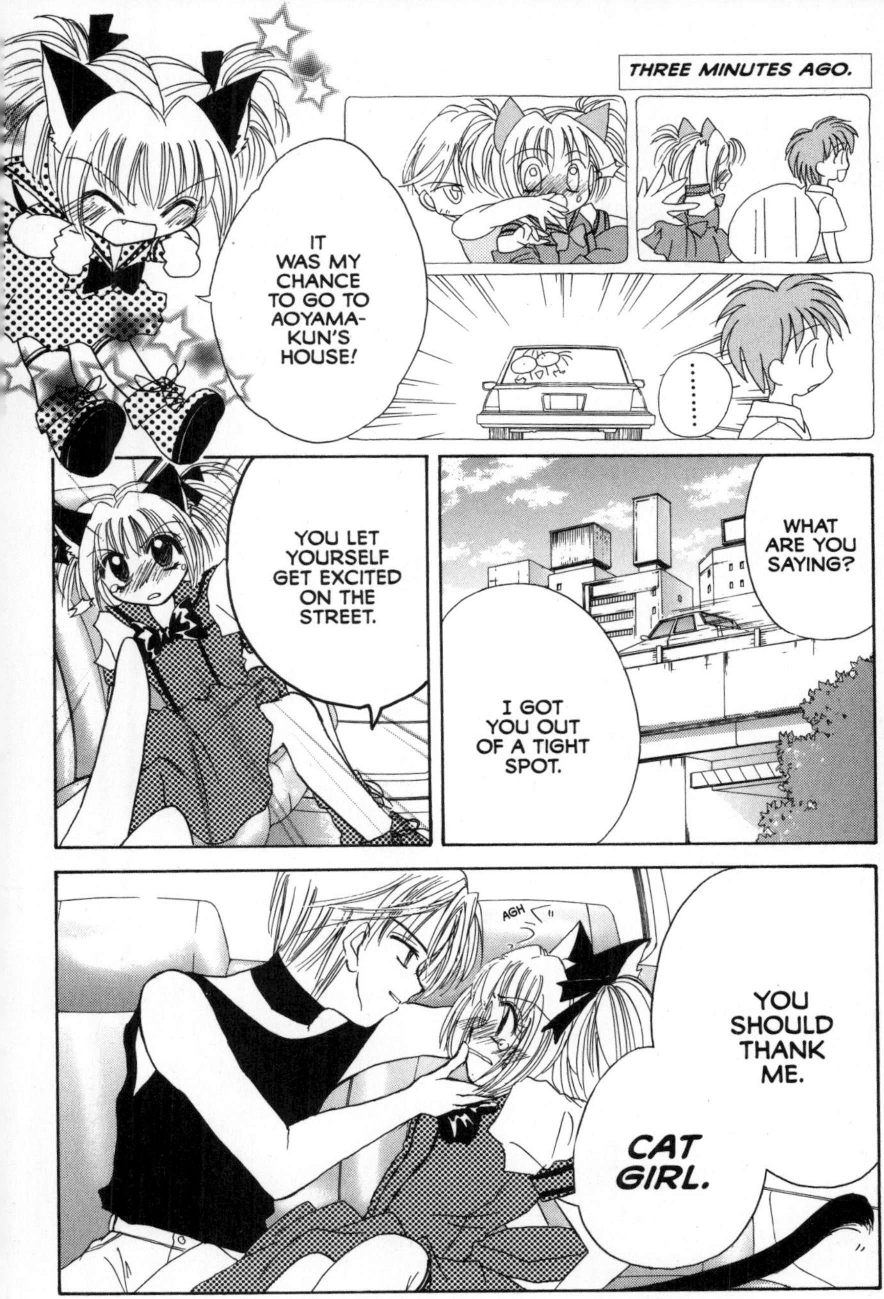
THREE MINUTES AGO.
......
IT WAS MY CHANCE TO GO TO AOYAMA-KUN'S HOUSE!
WHAT ARE YOU SAYING?
I GOT YOU OUT OF A TIGHT SPOT.
YOU LET YOURSELF GET EXCITED ON THE STREET.
AGH
YOU SHOULD THANK ME.
CAT GIRL.

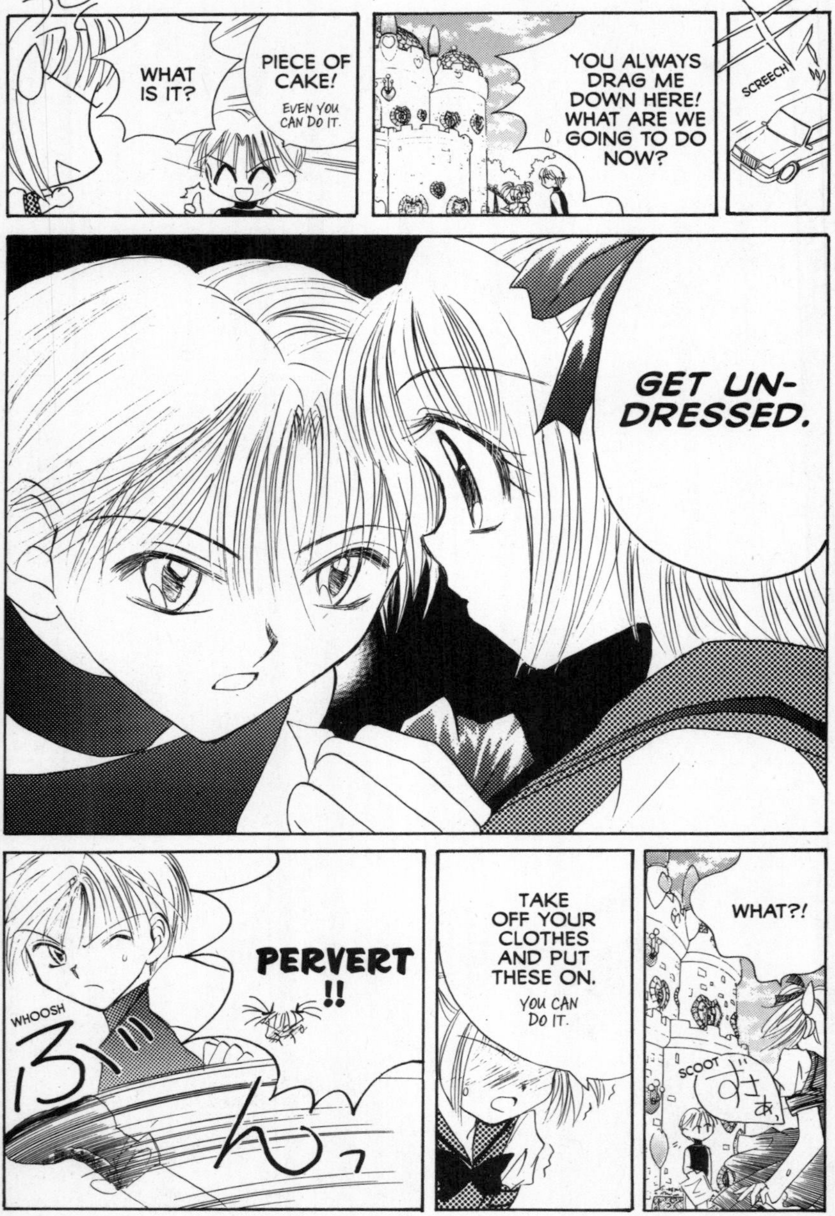
SCREECH
YOU ALWAYS DRAG ME DOWN HERE! WHAT ARE WE GOING TO DO NOW?
PIECE OF CAKE!
EVEN YOU CAN DO IT.
WHAT IS IT?
GET UN-DRESSED.
WHAT?!
SCOOT
TAKE OFF YOUR CLOTHES AND PUT THESE ON.
YOU CAN DO IT.
PERVERT !!
WHOOSH

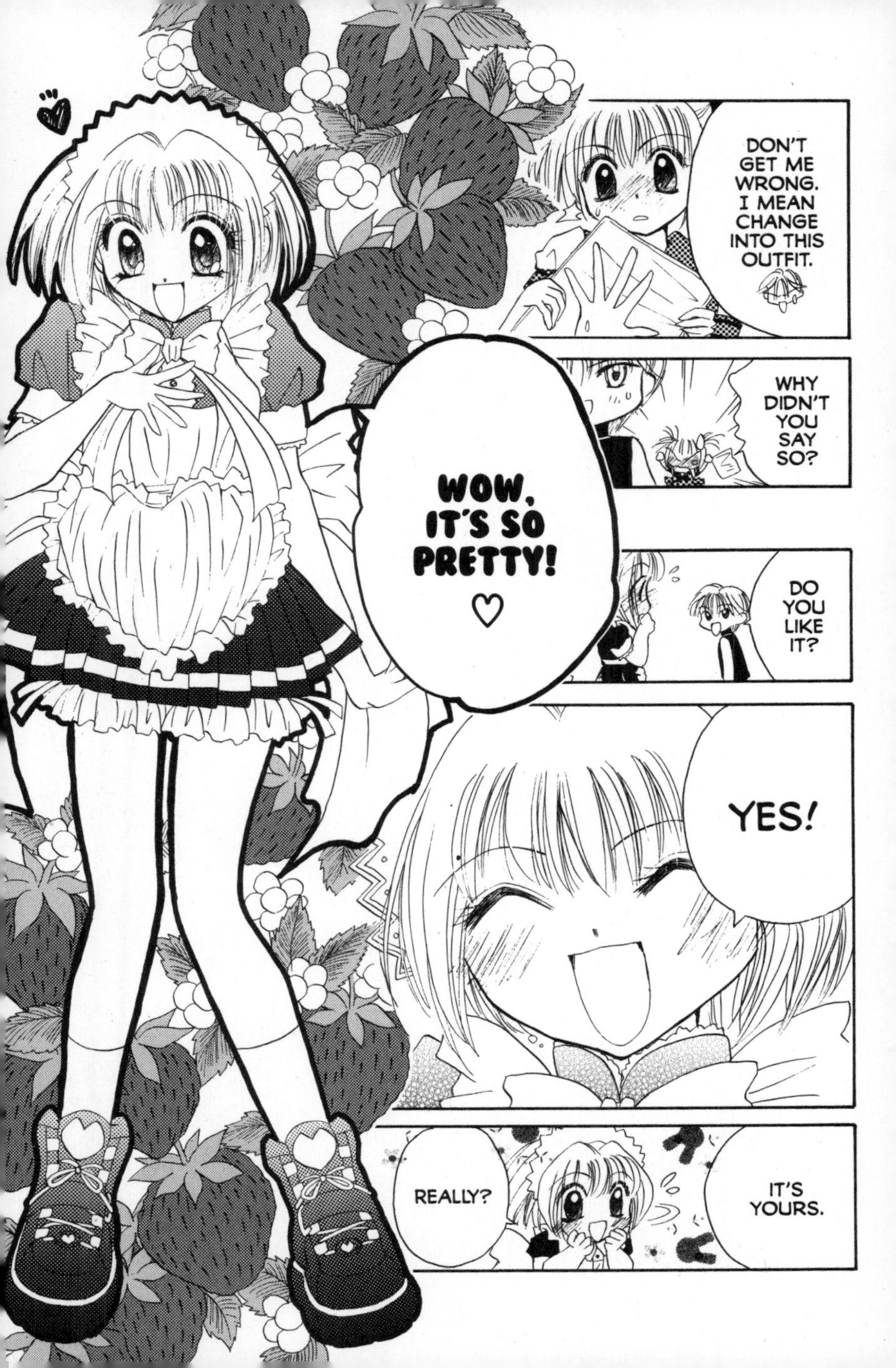
DON'T GET ME WRONG. I MEAN CHANGE INTO THIS OUTFIT.
WHY DIDN'T YOU SAY SO?
DO YOU LIKE IT?
YES!
IT'S YOURS.
REALLY?
WOW, IT'S SO PRETTY! ♡

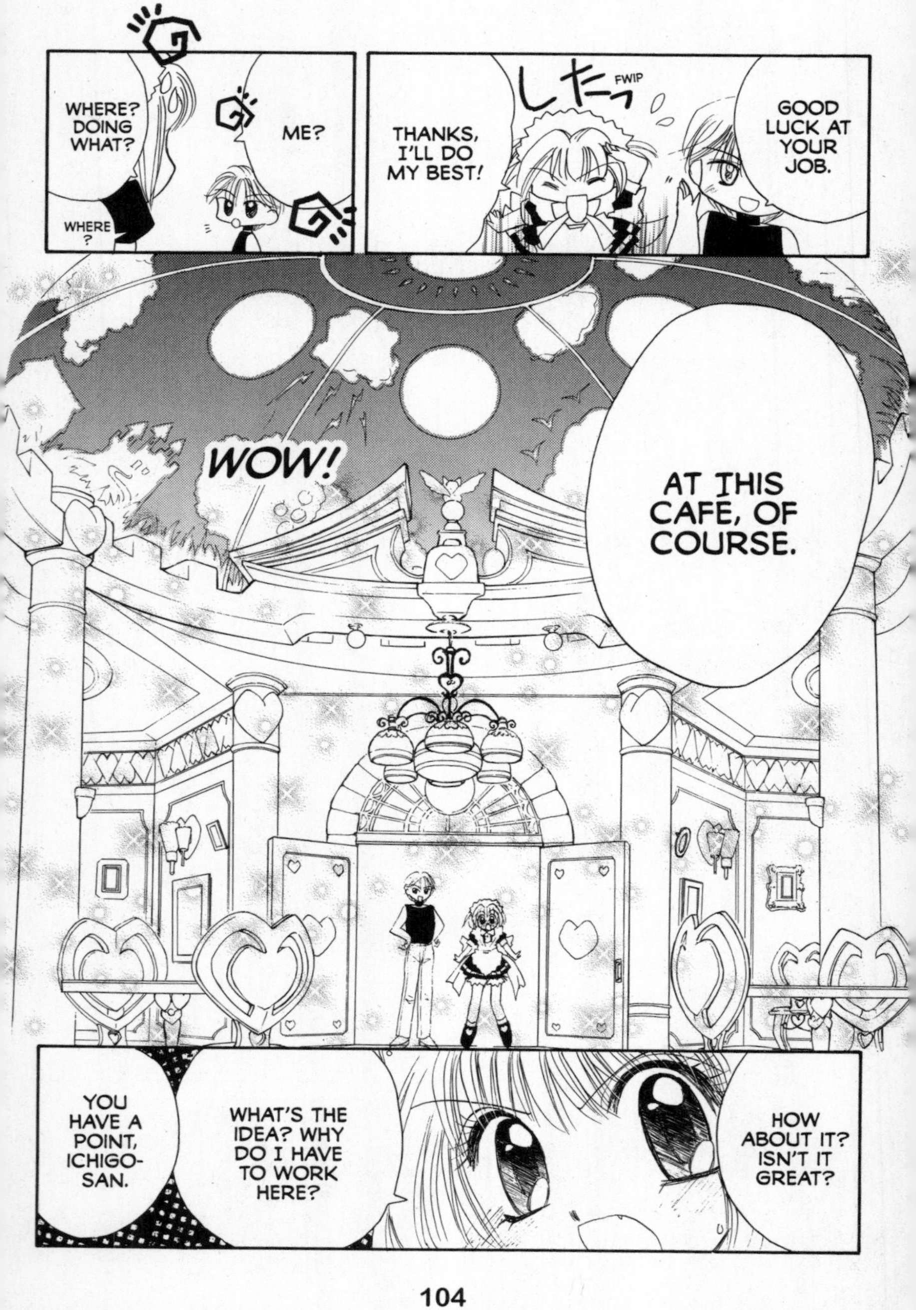
GOOD LUCK AT YOUR JOB.
FWIP
THANKS, I'LL DO MY BEST!
ME?
WHERE? DOING WHAT?
WHERE ?
AT THIS CAFE, OF COURSE.
WOW!
HOW ABOUT IT? ISN'T IT GREAT?
WHAT'S THE IDEA? WHY DO I HAVE TO WORK HERE?
YOU HAVE A POINT, ICHIGO-SAN.

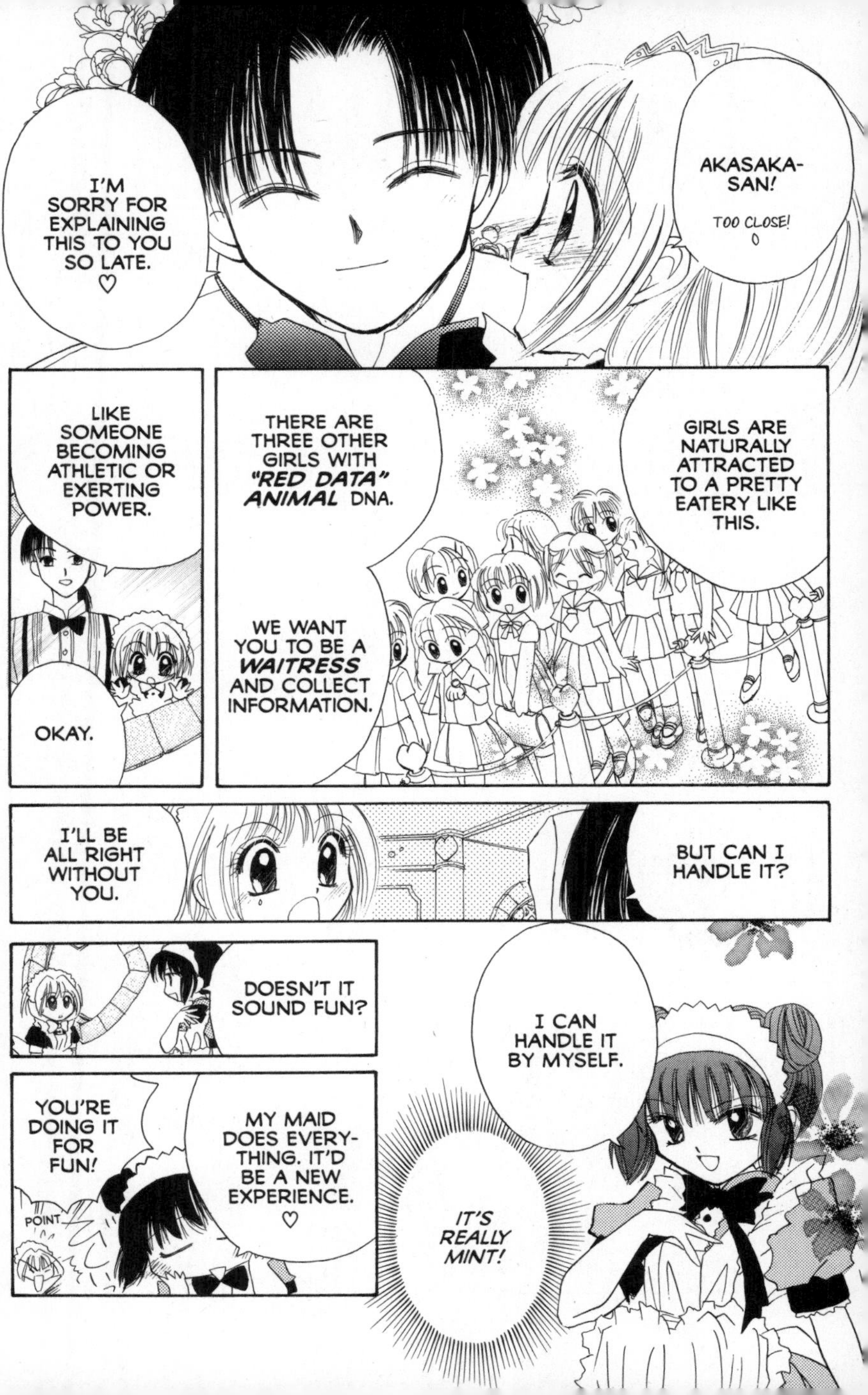
AKASAKA-SAN!
TOO CLOSE!
I'M SORRY FOR EXPLAINING THIS TO YOU SO LATE. ♡
GIRLS ARE NATURALLY ATTRACTED TO A PRETTY EATERY LIKE THIS.
THERE ARE THREE OTHER GIRLS WITH *"RED DATA" ANIMAL* DNA.
WE WANT YOU TO BE A *WAITRESS* AND COLLECT INFORMATION.
LIKE SOMEONE BECOMING ATHLETIC OR EXERTING POWER.
OKAY.
BUT CAN I HANDLE IT?
I'LL BE ALL RIGHT WITHOUT YOU.
I CAN HANDLE IT BY MYSELF.
IT'S REALLY MINT!
DOESN'T IT SOUND FUN?
MY MAID DOES EVERY-THING. IT'D BE A NEW EXPERIENCE. ♡
YOU'RE DOING IT FOR FUN!
POINT

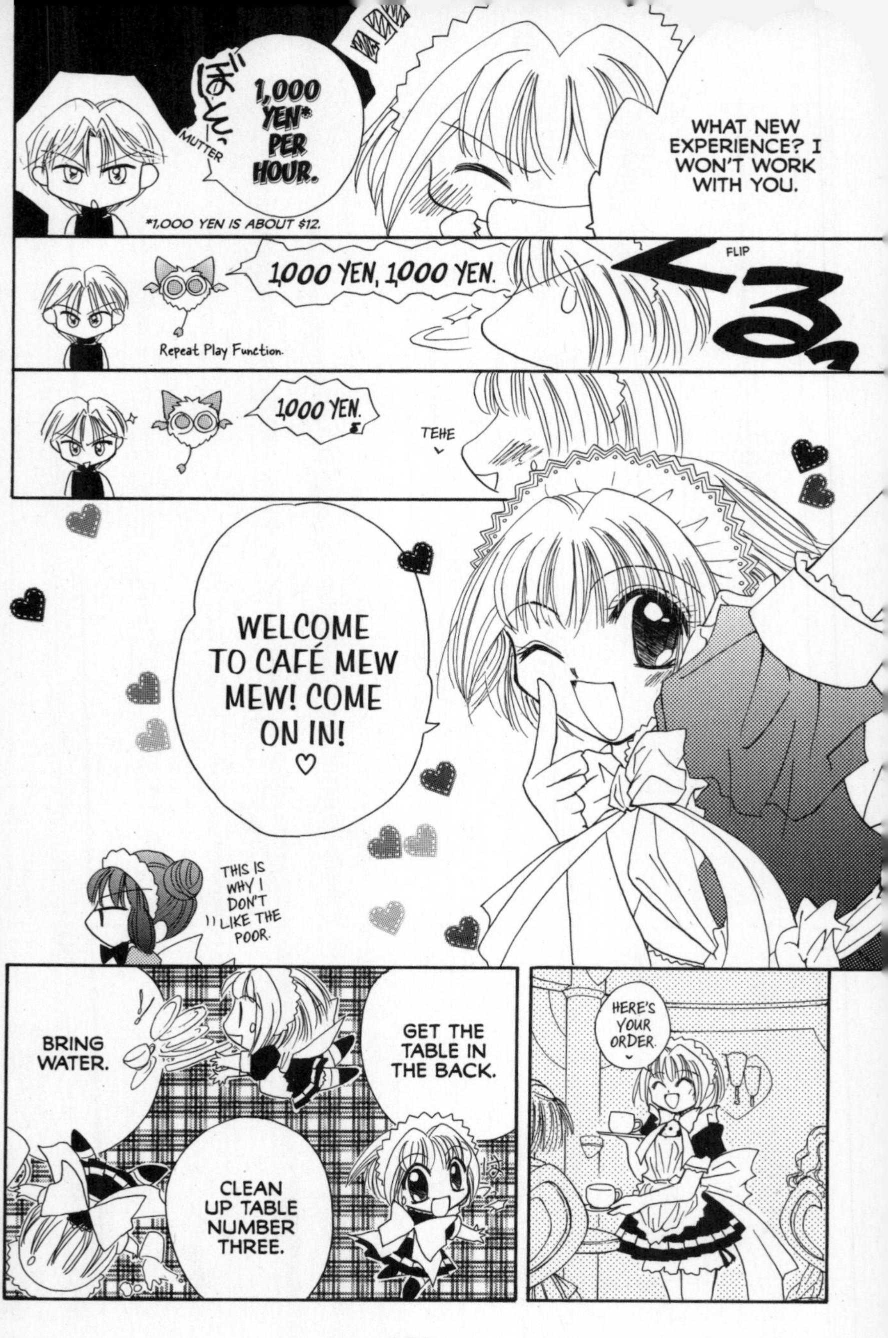

WHAT NEW EXPERIENCE? I WON'T WORK WITH YOU.
MUTTER
1,000 YEN* PER HOUR.
*1,000 YEN IS ABOUT $12.
FLIP
1,000 YEN, 1,000 YEN.
Repeat Play Function.
TEHE
1,000 YEN.
WELCOME TO CAFÉ MEW MEW! COME ON IN! ♡
THIS IS WHY I DON'T LIKE THE POOR.
HERE'S YOUR ORDER.
GET THE TABLE IN THE BACK.
BRING WATER.
CLEAN UP TABLE NUMBER THREE.

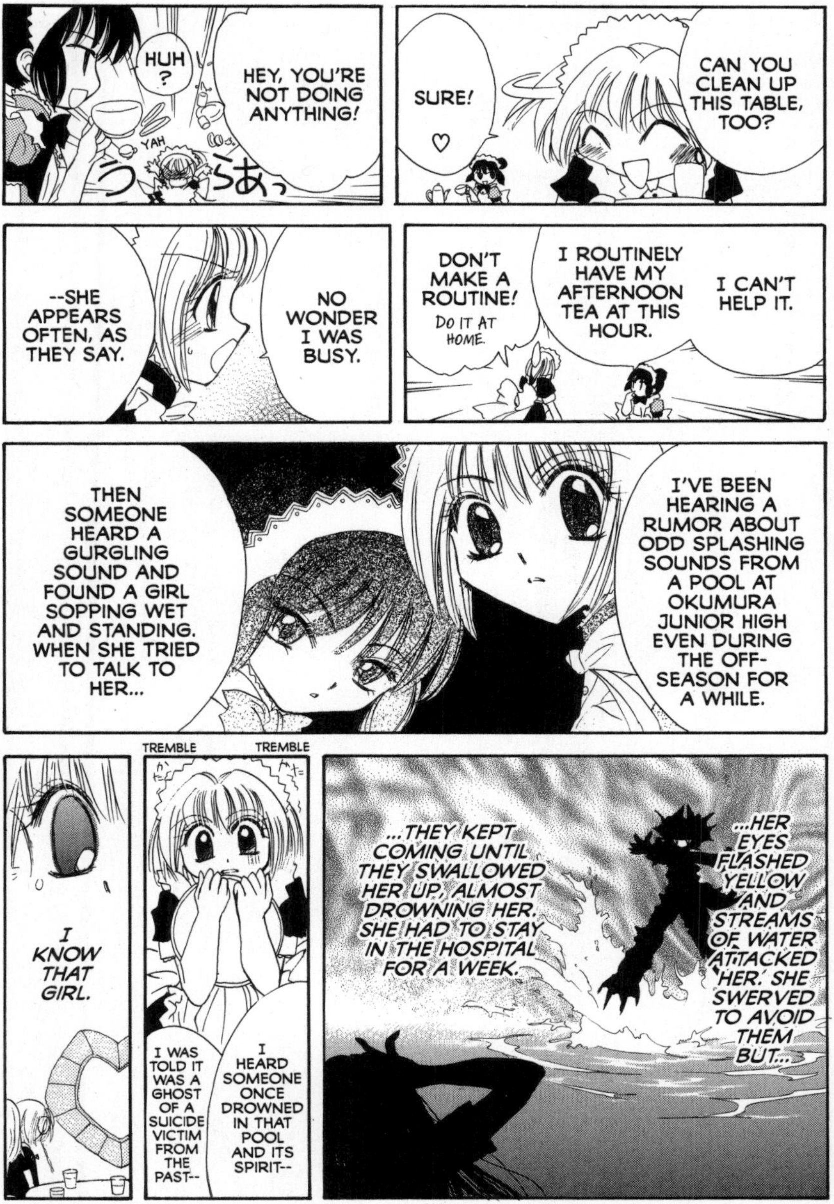
CAN YOU CLEAN UP THIS TABLE, TOO?
SURE! ♡
HEY, YOU'RE NOT DOING ANYTHING!
HUH ?
YAH
うらあっ
I CAN'T HELP IT.
I ROUTINELY HAVE MY AFTERNOON TEA AT THIS HOUR.
DON'T MAKE A ROUTINE!
DO IT AT HOME.
NO WONDER I WAS BUSY.
--SHE APPEARS OFTEN, AS THEY SAY.
I'VE BEEN HEARING A RUMOR ABOUT ODD SPLASHING SOUNDS FROM A POOL AT OKUMURA JUNIOR HIGH EVEN DURING THE OFF-SEASON FOR A WHILE.
THEN SOMEONE HEARD A GURGLING SOUND AND FOUND A GIRL SOPPING WET AND STANDING. WHEN SHE TRIED TO TALK TO HER...
...HER EYES FLASHED YELLOW AND STREAMS OF WATER ATTACKED HER. SHE SWERVED TO AVOID THEM BUT...
...THEY KEPT COMING UNTIL THEY SWALLOWED HER UP, ALMOST DROWNING HER. SHE HAD TO STAY IN THE HOSPITAL FOR A WEEK.
TREMBLE
TREMBLE
I HEARD SOMEONE ONCE DROWNED IN THAT POOL AND ITS SPIRIT--
I WAS TOLD IT WAS A GHOST OF A SUICIDE VICTIM FROM THE PAST--
I KNOW THAT GIRL.

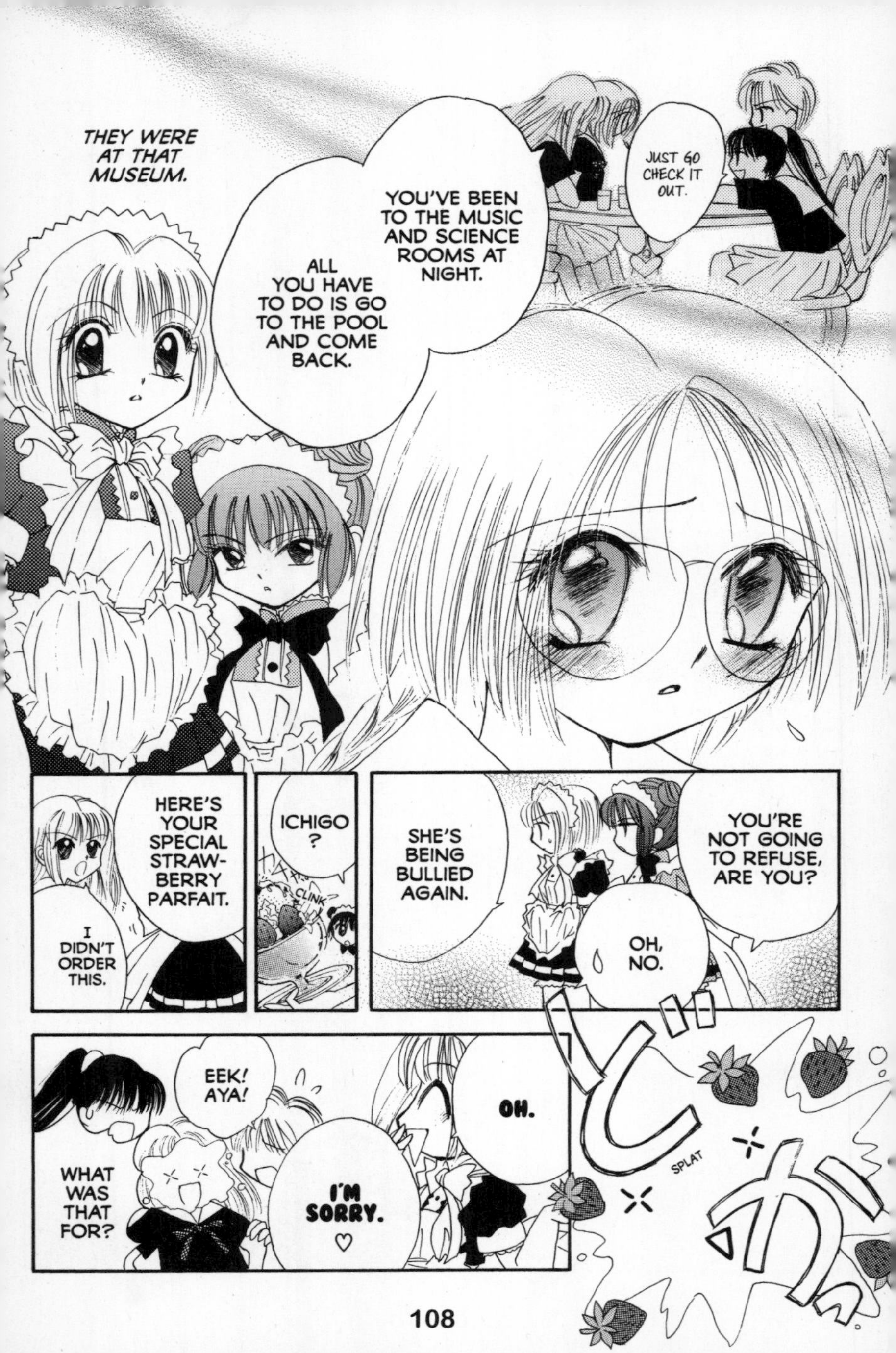
JUST GO CHECK IT OUT.
YOU'VE BEEN TO THE MUSIC AND SCIENCE ROOMS AT NIGHT.
ALL YOU HAVE TO DO IS GO TO THE POOL AND COME BACK.
THEY WERE AT THAT MUSEUM.
YOU'RE NOT GOING TO REFUSE, ARE YOU?
OH, NO.
SHE'S BEING BULLIED AGAIN.
ICHIGO?
CLINK
HERE'S YOUR SPECIAL STRAW-BERRY PARFAIT.
I DIDN'T ORDER THIS.
SPLAT
OH.
I'M SORRY. ♡
EEK! AYA!
WHAT WAS THAT FOR?

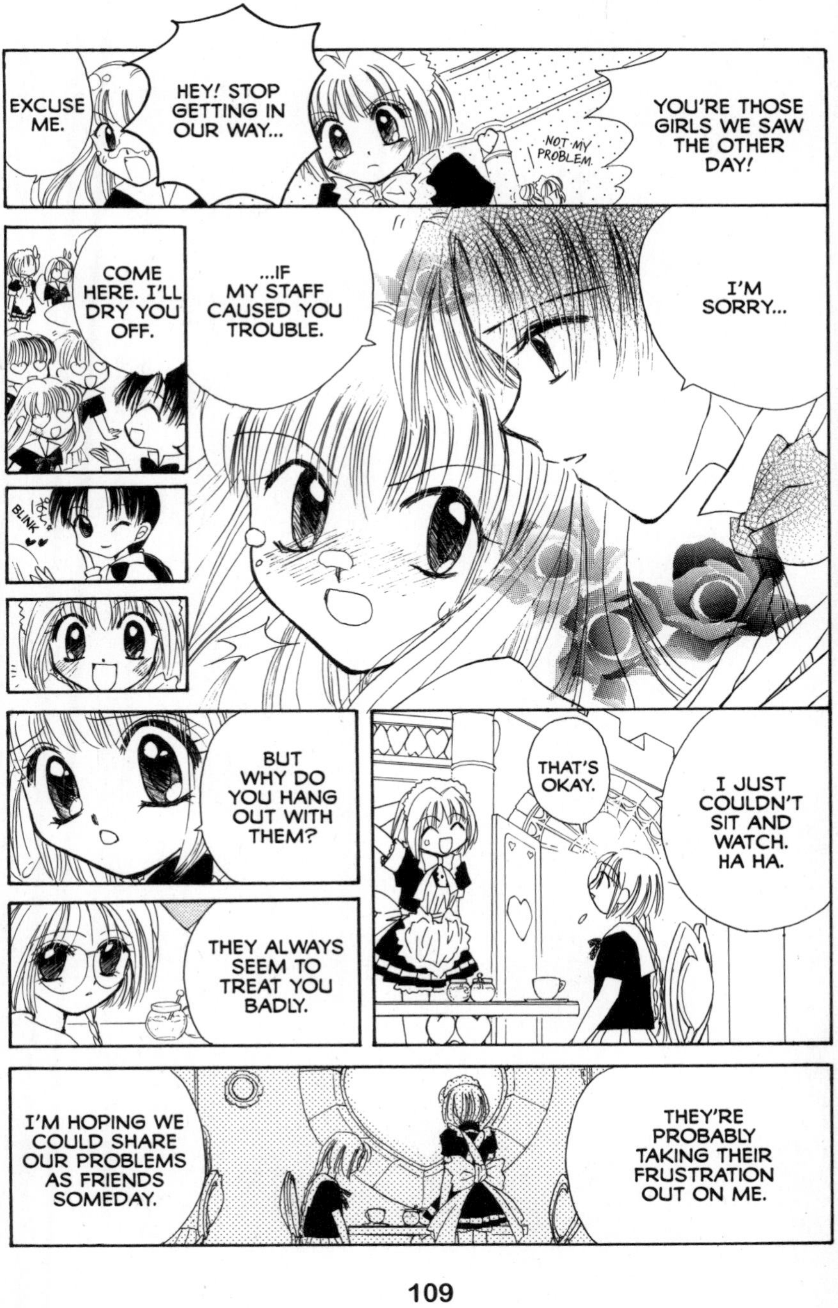
YOU'RE THOSE GIRLS WE SAW THE OTHER DAY!
NOT MY PROBLEM.
HEY! STOP GETTING IN OUR WAY...
EXCUSE ME.
I'M SORRY...
...IF MY STAFF CAUSED YOU TROUBLE.
COME HERE. I'LL DRY YOU OFF.
BLINK
I JUST COULDN'T SIT AND WATCH. HA HA.
THAT'S OKAY.
BUT WHY DO YOU HANG OUT WITH THEM?
THEY ALWAYS SEEM TO TREAT YOU BADLY.
THEY'RE PROBABLY TAKING THEIR FRUSTRATION OUT ON ME.
I'M HOPING WE COULD SHARE OUR PROBLEMS AS FRIENDS SOMEDAY.

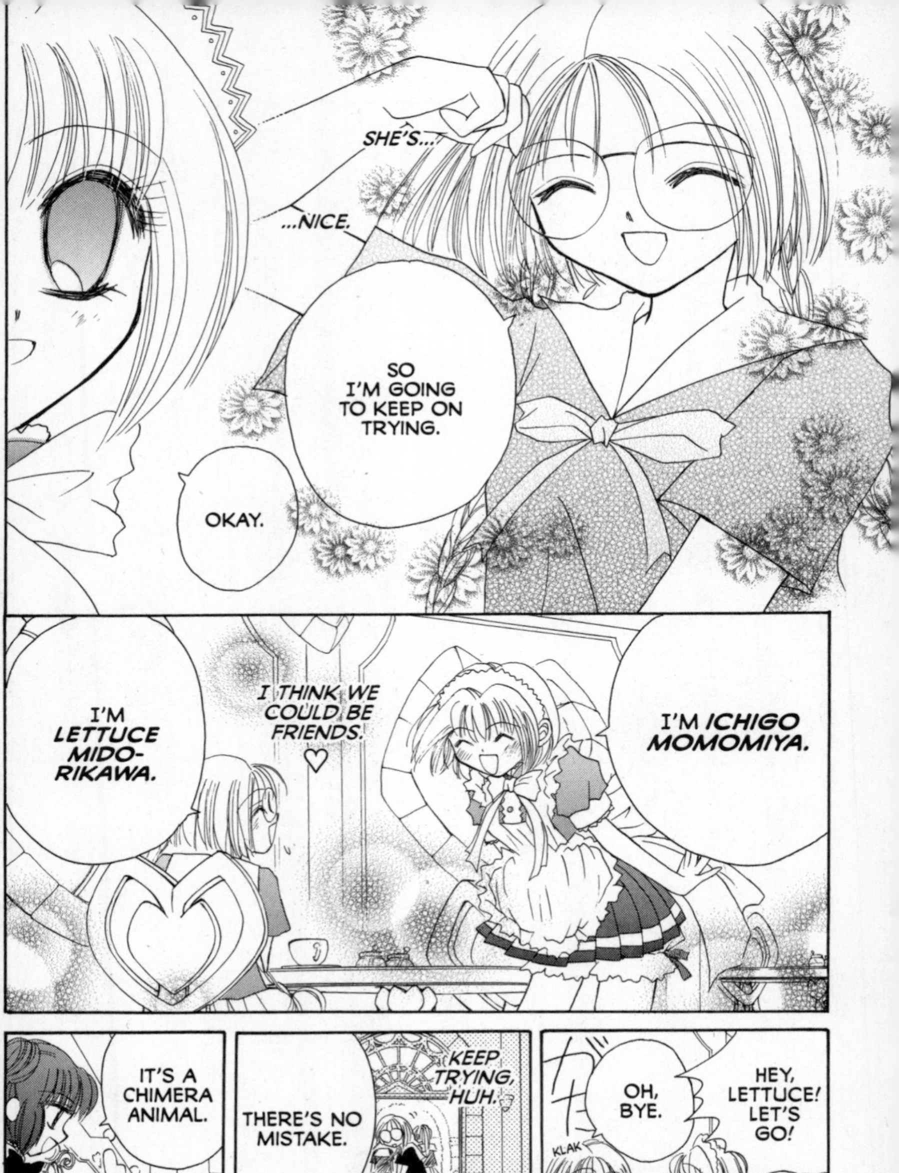
SHE'S...
...NICE.
SO I'M GOING TO KEEP ON TRYING.
OKAY.
I'M ICHIGO MOMOMIYA.
I THINK WE COULD BE FRIENDS. ♡
I'M LETTUCE MIDO-RIKAWA.
HEY, LETTUCE! LET'S GO!
OH, BYE.
KLAK
KEEP TRYING, HUH.
THERE'S NO MISTAKE.
IT'S A CHIMERA ANIMAL.
HUH?

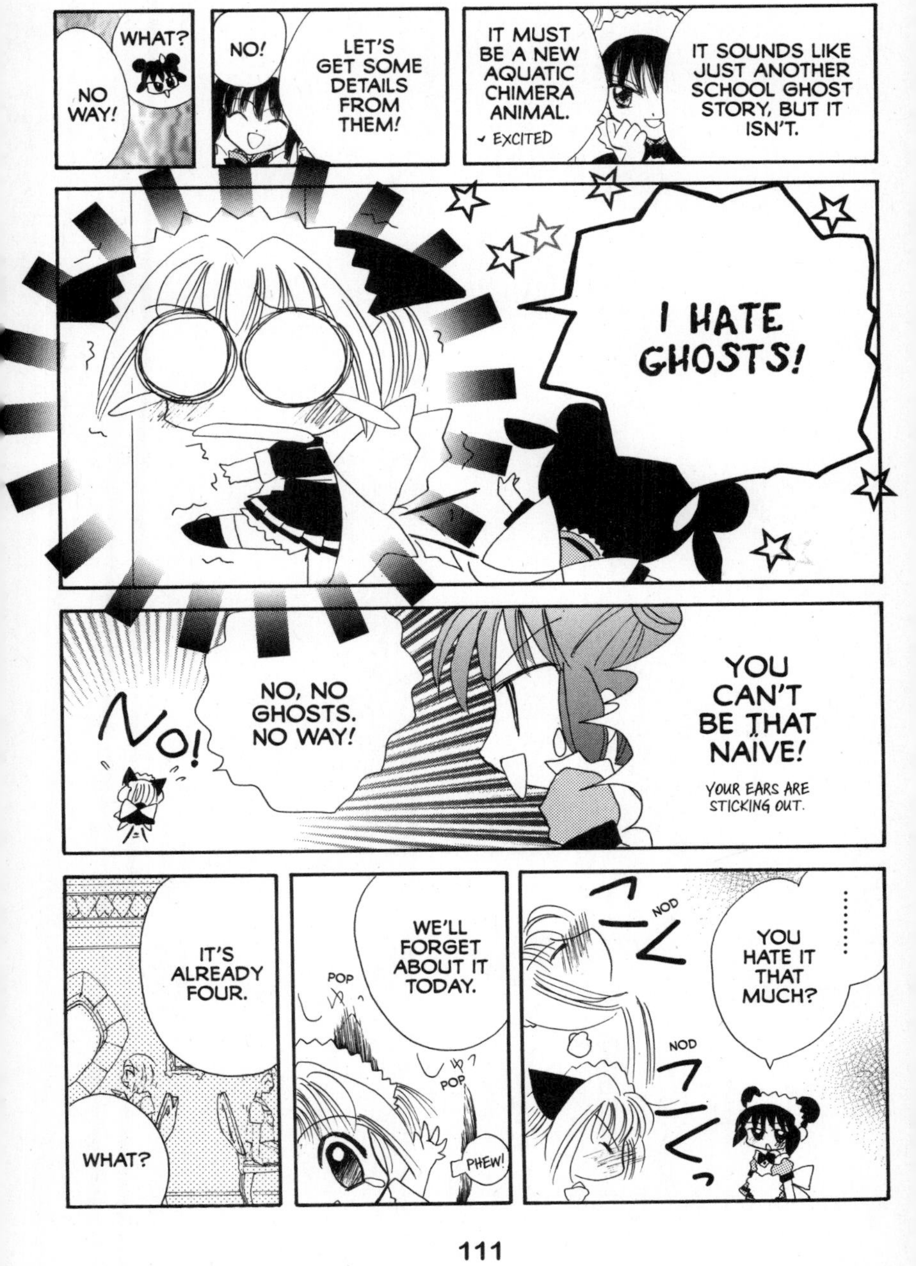
IT SOUNDS LIKE JUST ANOTHER SCHOOL GHOST STORY, BUT IT ISN'T.
IT MUST BE A NEW AQUATIC CHIMERA ANIMAL.
EXCITED
LET'S GET SOME DETAILS FROM THEM!
NO!
WHAT?
NO WAY!
I HATE GHOSTS!
YOU CAN'T BE THAT NAÏVE!
YOUR EARS ARE STICKING OUT.
NO, NO GHOSTS. NO WAY!
NO!
....
YOU HATE IT THAT MUCH?
NOD
NOD
WE'LL FORGET ABOUT IT TODAY.
POP
POP
PHEW!
IT'S ALREADY FOUR.
WHAT?

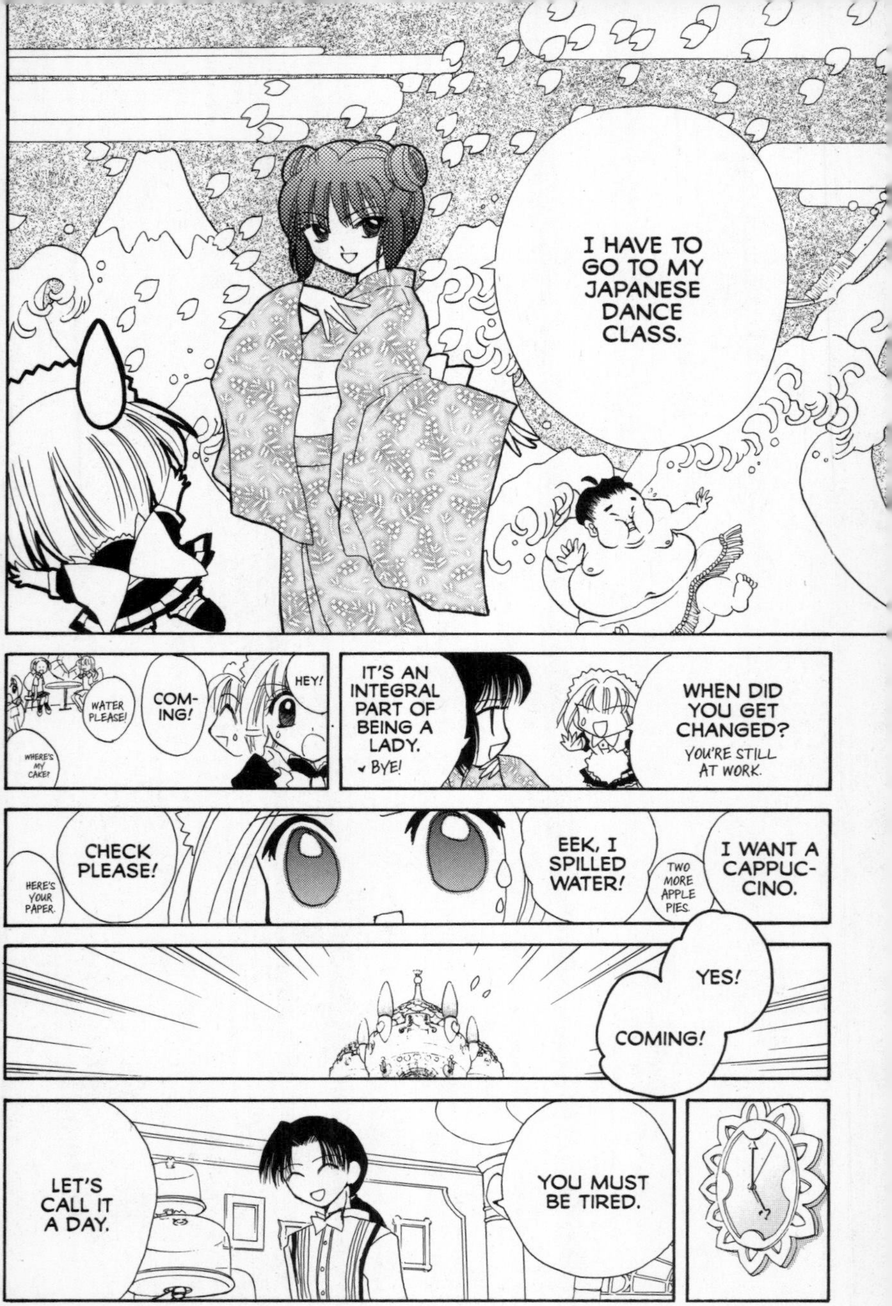
I HAVE TO GO TO MY JAPANESE DANCE CLASS.
WHEN DID YOU GET CHANGED?
YOU'RE STILL AT WORK.
IT'S AN INTEGRAL PART OF BEING A LADY.
♥ BYE!
HEY!
COM-ING!
WATER PLEASE!
WHERE'S MY CAKE?
I WANT A CAPPUC-CINO.
TWO MORE APPLE PIES.
EEK, I SPILLED WATER!
CHECK PLEASE!
HERE'S YOUR PAPER.
YES!
COMING!
YOU MUST BE TIRED.
LET'S CALL IT A DAY.

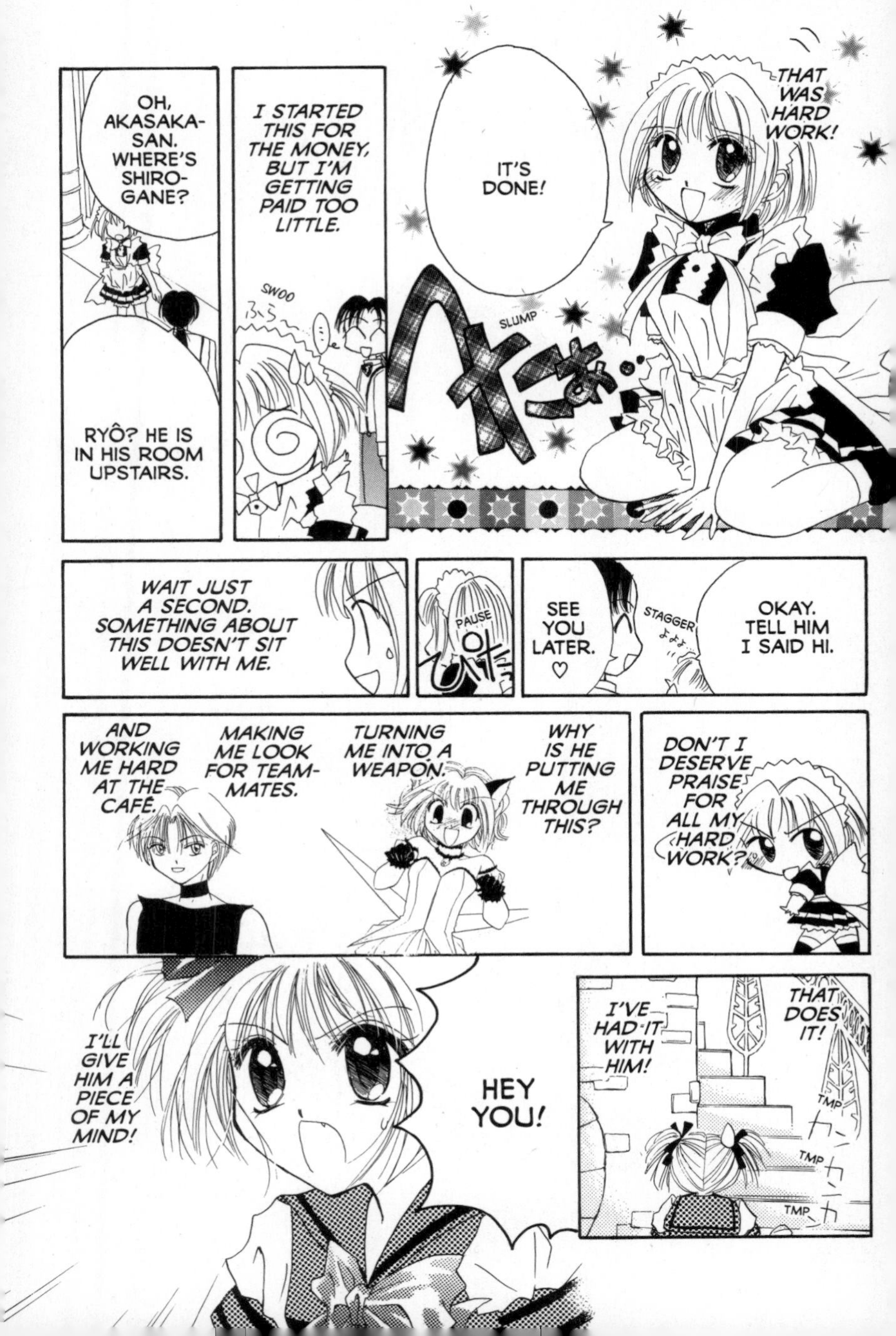
THAT WAS HARD WORK!
IT'S DONE!
SLUMP
I STARTED THIS FOR THE MONEY, BUT I'M GETTING PAID TOO LITTLE.
SWOO
OH, AKASAKA-SAN. WHERE'S SHIRO-GANE?
RYÔ? HE IS IN HIS ROOM UPSTAIRS.
OKAY. TELL HIM I SAID HI.
STAGGER
SEE YOU LATER. ♡
PAUSE
WAIT JUST A SECOND. SOMETHING ABOUT THIS DOESN'T SIT WELL WITH ME.
DON'T I DESERVE PRAISE FOR ALL MY HARD WORK?
WHY IS HE PUTTING ME THROUGH THIS?
TURNING ME INTO A WEAPON.
MAKING ME LOOK FOR TEAM-MATES.
AND WORKING ME HARD AT THE CAFÉ.
THAT DOES IT!
I'VE HAD IT WITH HIM!
TMP
TMP
TMP
HEY YOU!
I'LL GIVE HIM A PIECE OF MY MIND!

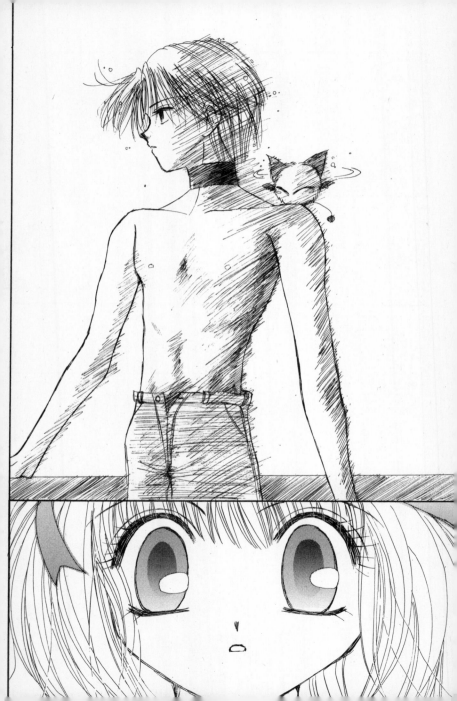

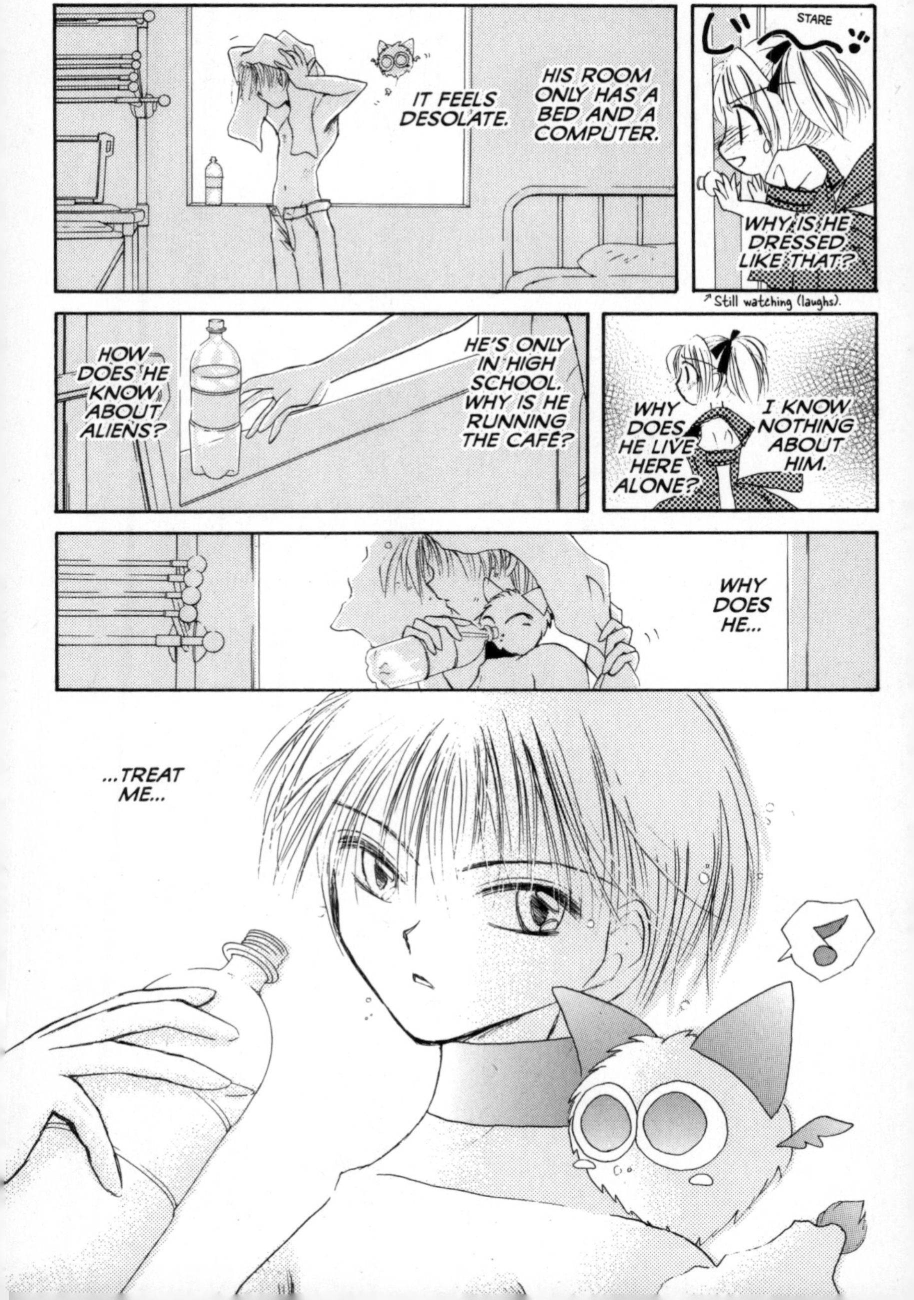
STARE
WHY IS HE DRESSED LIKE THAT?
↗Still watching (laughs).
HIS ROOM ONLY HAS A BED AND A COMPUTER.
IT FEELS DESOLATE.
I KNOW NOTHING ABOUT HIM.
WHY DOES HE LIVE HERE ALONE?
HE'S ONLY IN HIGH SCHOOL. WHY IS HE RUNNING THE CAFÉ?
HOW DOES HE KNOW ABOUT ALIENS?
WHY DOES HE...
...TREAT ME...

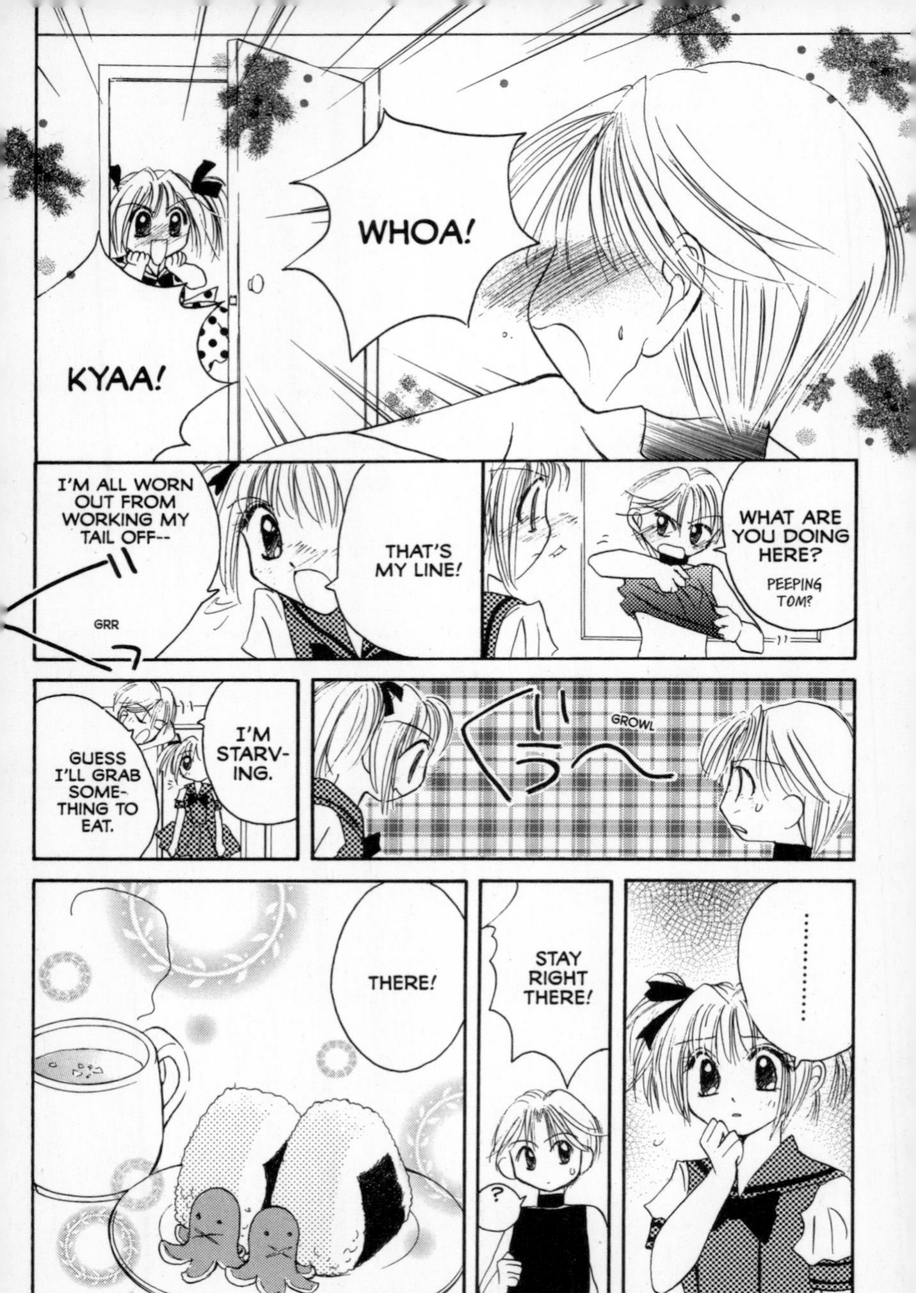
WHOA!
KYAA!
WHAT ARE YOU DOING HERE?
PEEPING TOM?
THAT'S MY LINE!
I'M ALL WORN OUT FROM WORKING MY TAIL OFF--
GRR
GROWL
I'M STARV-ING.
GUESS I'LL GRAB SOME-THING TO EAT.
....
STAY RIGHT THERE!
?
THERE!

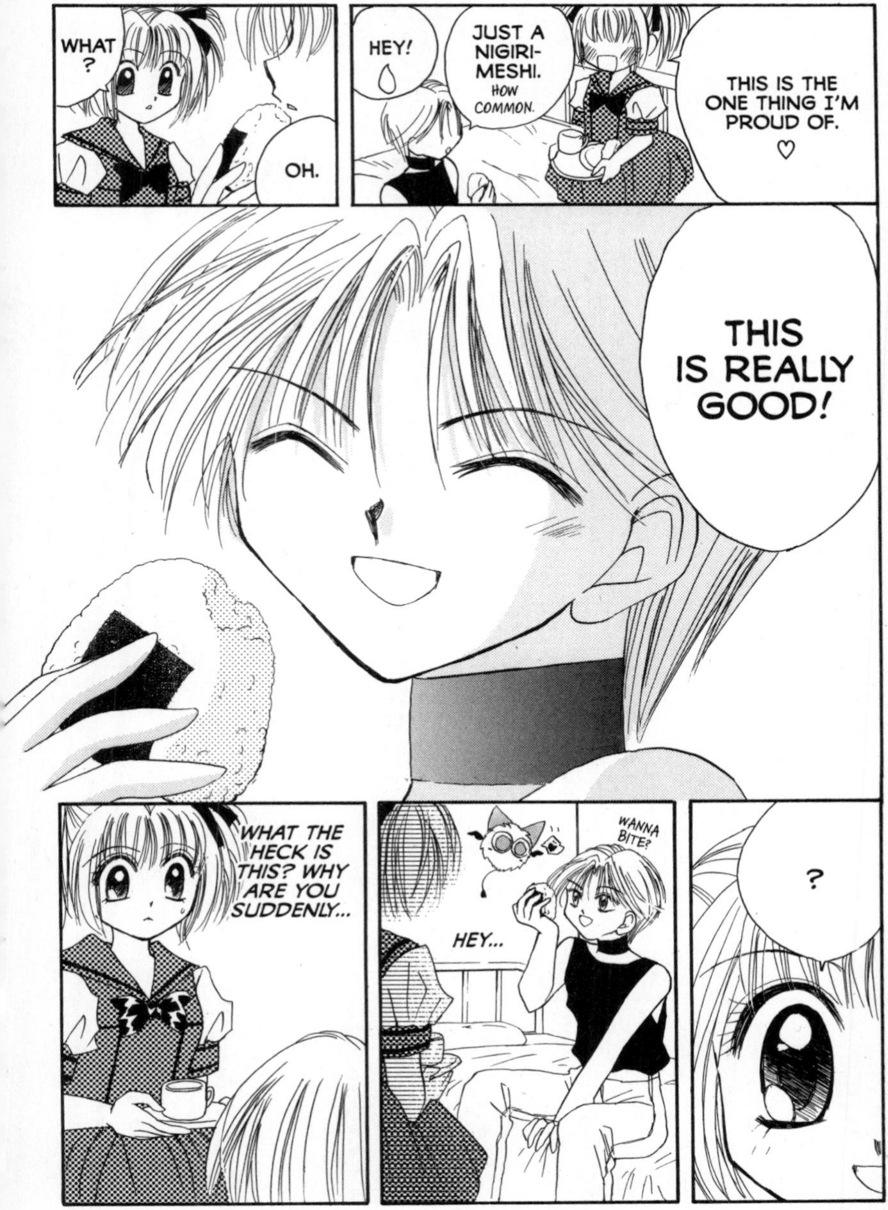
THIS IS THE ONE THING I'M PROUD OF. ♡
JUST A NIGIRI-MESHI. HOW COMMON.
HEY!
WHAT ?
OH.
THIS IS REALLY GOOD!
?
WANNA BITE?
HEY...
WHAT THE HECK IS THIS? WHY ARE YOU SUDDENLY...

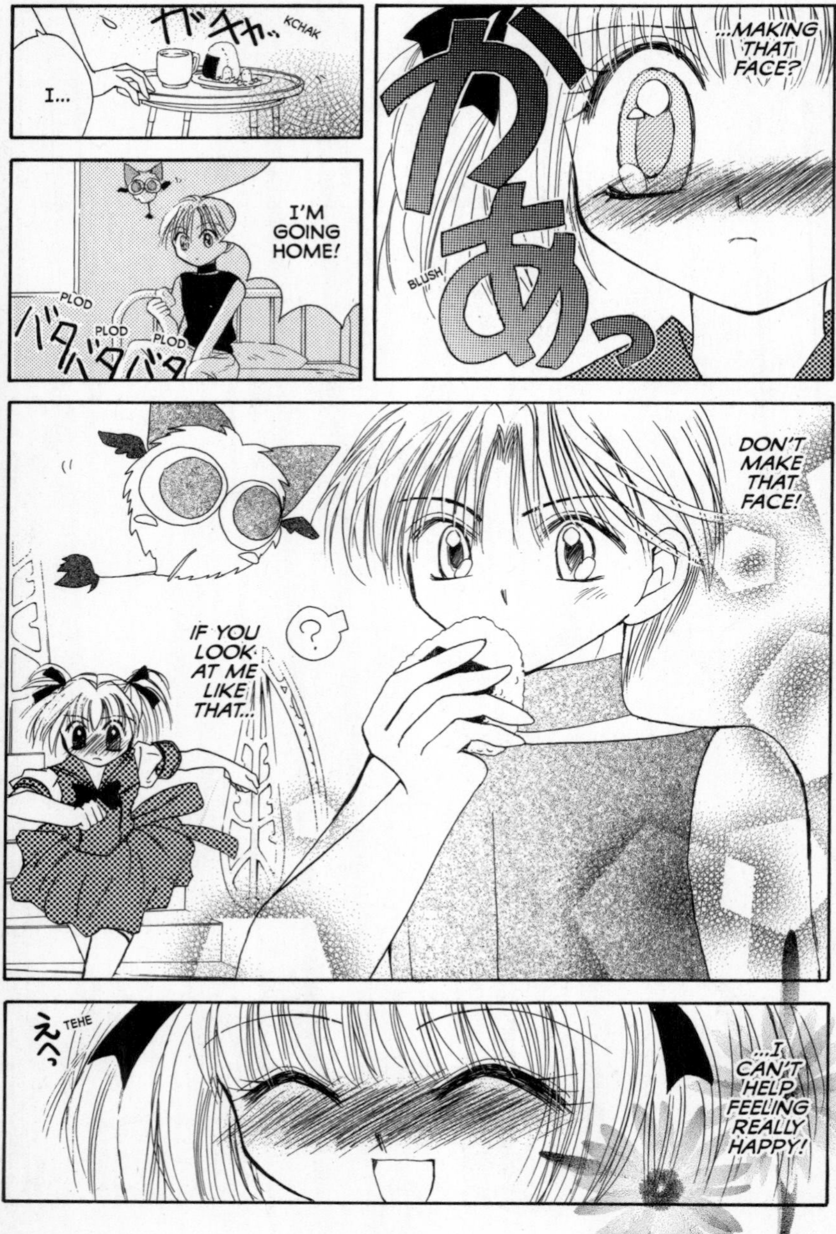
...MAKING THAT FACE?
かあっ
BLUSH
ガキャッ
KCHAK
I...
I'M GOING HOME!
バタバタバタ
PLOD
PLOD
PLOD
DON'T MAKE THAT FACE!
IF YOU LOOK AT ME LIKE THAT...
...I CAN'T HELP FEELING REALLY HAPPY!
えへっ
TEHE

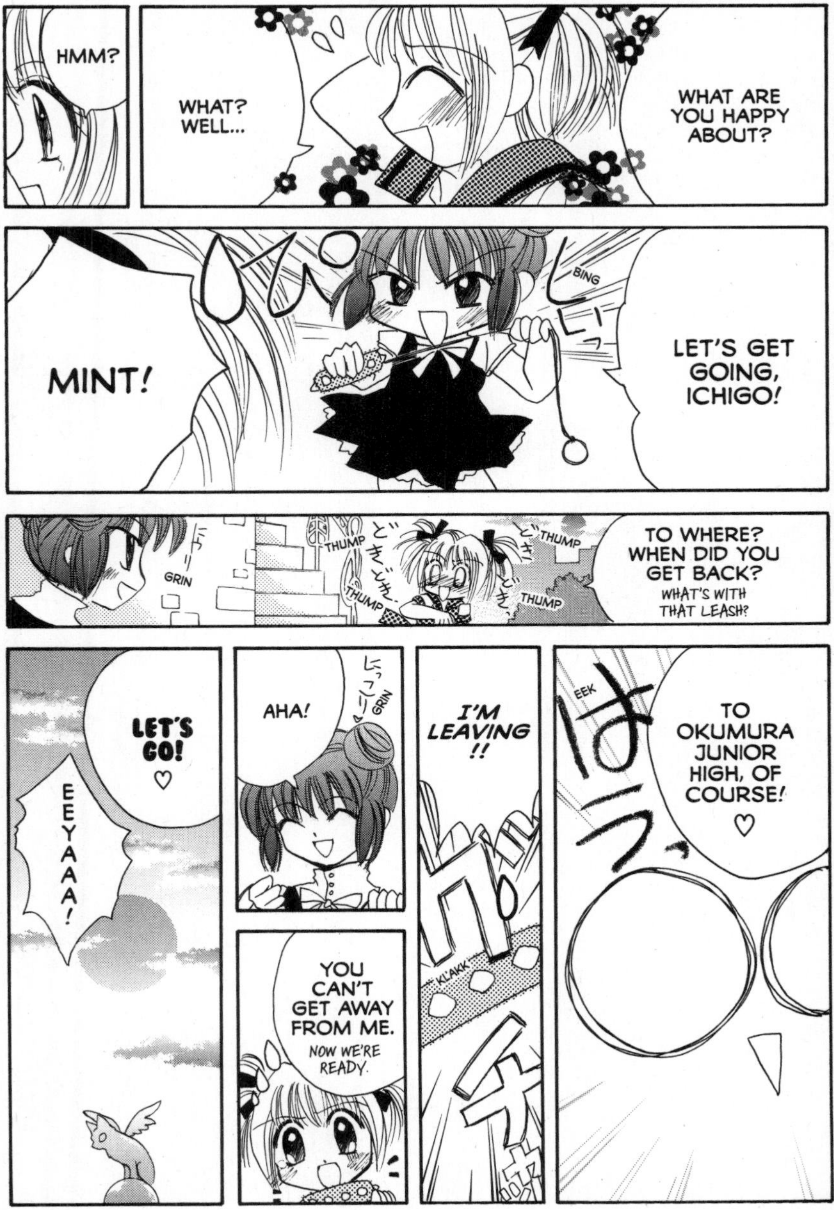
WHAT ARE YOU HAPPY ABOUT?
WHAT? WELL...
HMM?
LET'S GET GOING, ICHIGO!
BING
MINT!
TO WHERE? WHEN DID YOU GET BACK?
WHAT'S WITH THAT LEASH?
THUMP
THUMP
THUMP
THUMP
GRIN
TO OKUMURA JUNIOR HIGH, OF COURSE! ♡
EEK
I'M LEAVING!!
KLAKK
AHA!
GRIN
YOU CAN'T GET AWAY FROM ME.
NOW WE'RE READY.
LET'S GO! ♡
EEYAAAA!

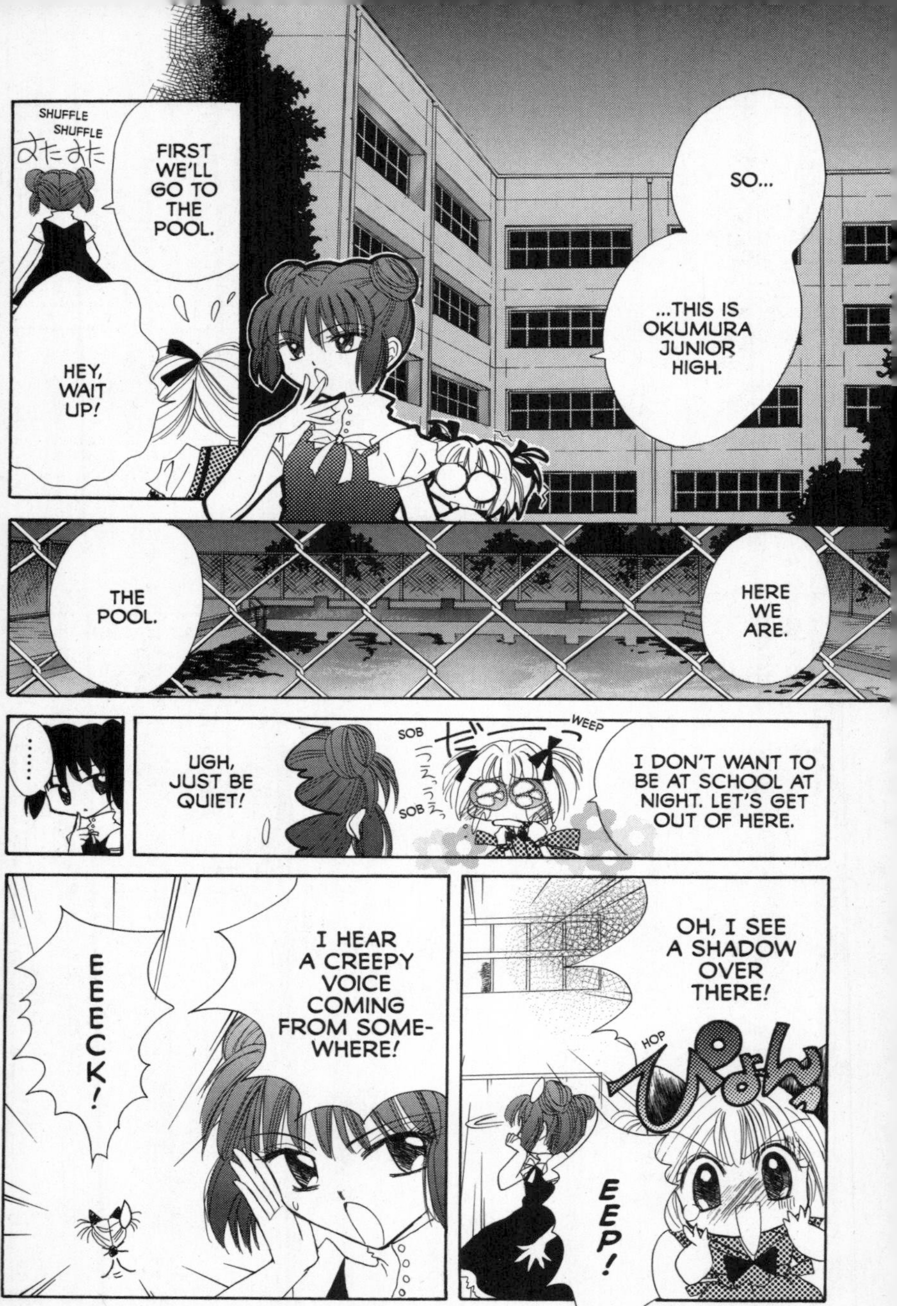
SO...
...THIS IS OKUMURA JUNIOR HIGH.
SHUFFLE SHUFFLE
FIRST WE'LL GO TO THE POOL.
HEY, WAIT UP!
HERE WE ARE.
THE POOL.
I DON'T WANT TO BE AT SCHOOL AT NIGHT. LET'S GET OUT OF HERE.
WEEP
SOB
SOB
UGH, JUST BE QUIET!
......
OH, I SEE A SHADOW OVER THERE!
HOP
EEP!
I HEAR A CREEPY VOICE COMING FROM SOME-WHERE!
EEEECK!

HUFF! ♡
SCREEEE!!
DID YOU DO THAT ON PURPOSE?
SORRY, IT WAS JUST MY IMAGINATION. ♡
WELL, NOTHING IS HAPPENING.
LET'S CHECK THE POOL AGAIN BEFORE WE GO.
WHAT? WE'RE LEAVING? ♡
KYAA!
THUD
WHAT ARE YOU DOING, ICHIGO?
MY FOOT GOT CAUGHT ON SOMETHING.
OWW.

Meeting with My Editors: Part Three

ONE YEAR BEFORE THE MANGA BEGAN.
THIS IS THE NEW CHARACTER.
SHOWING TO ANOTHER EDITOR
WHAT'S THIS ANIMAL ?
LET ME SEE.
STARE
OH, THIS.
THIS ONE.
WHY IT'S A FROG.
NO!!
IT'S A MOUSE!
CONFIDENT
じしんまんまん

SEE PAGE 171 FOR DETAILS ON THIS CHARACTER.

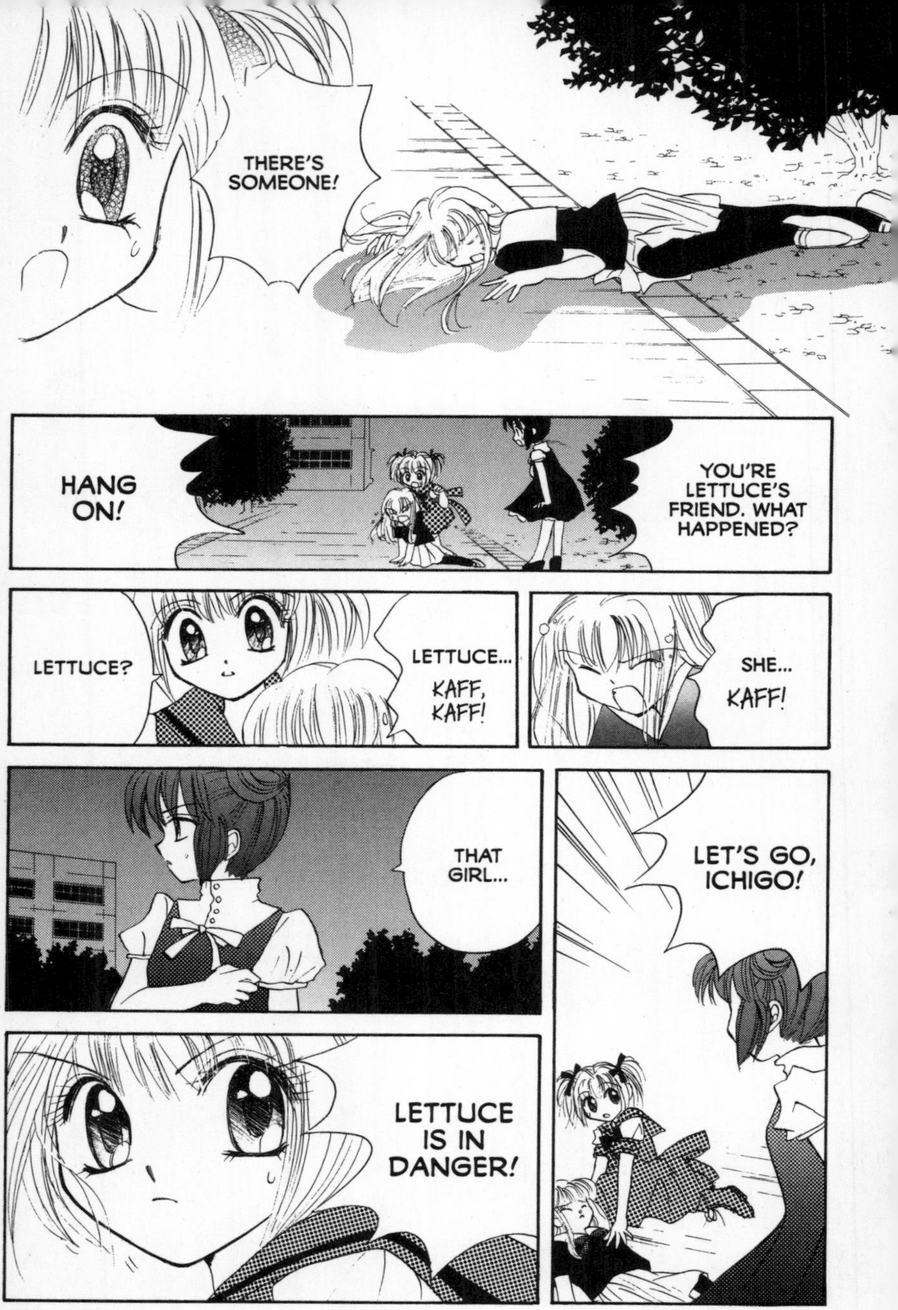
THERE'S SOMEONE!
YOU'RE LETTUCE'S FRIEND. WHAT HAPPENED?
HANG ON!
SHE... KAFF!
LETTUCE... KAFF, KAFF!
LETTUCE?
LET'S GO, ICHIGO!
THAT GIRL...
LETTUCE IS IN DANGER!

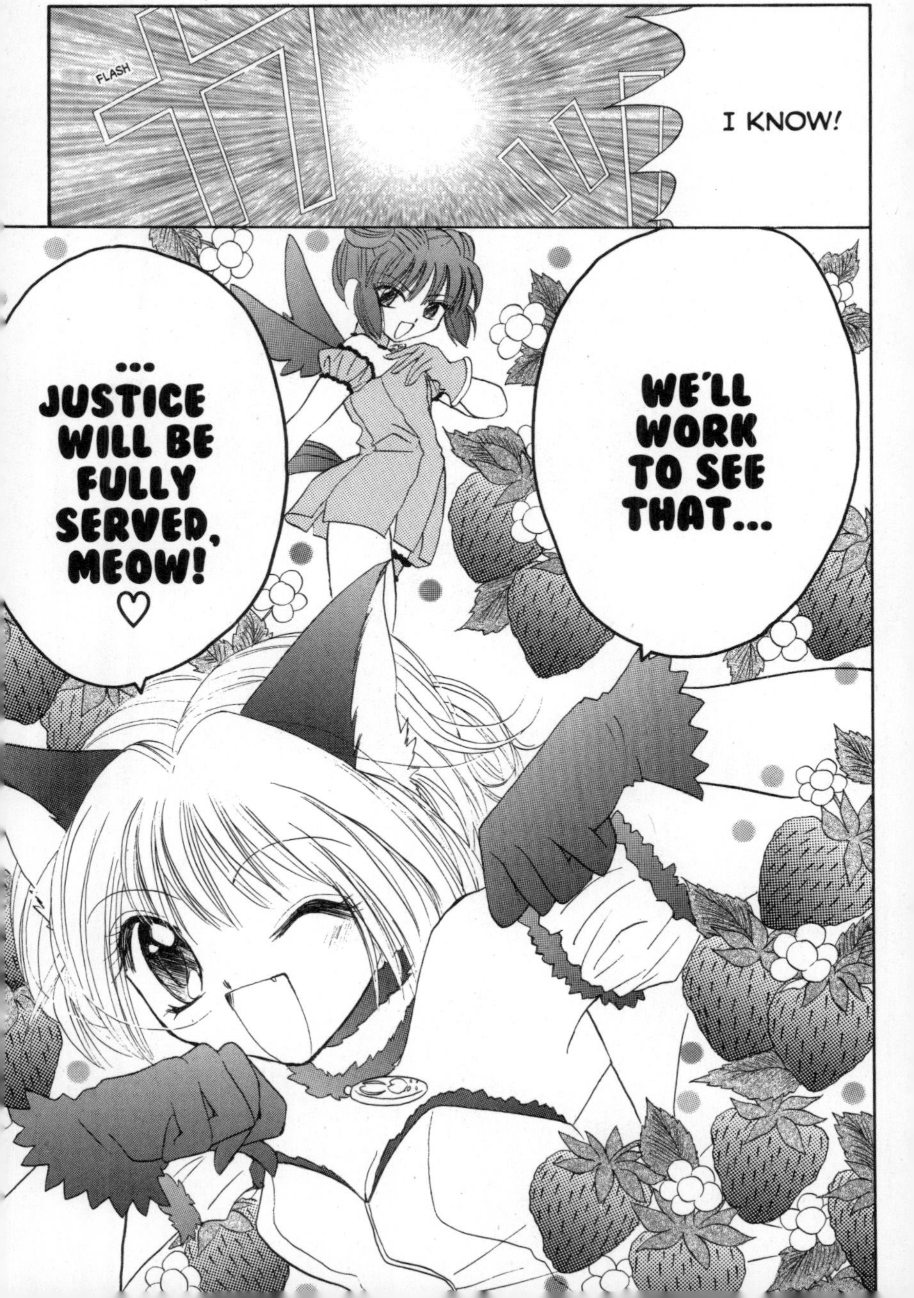
I KNOW!
FLASH
WE'LL WORK TO SEE THAT...
... JUSTICE WILL BE FULLY SERVED, MEOW! ♡

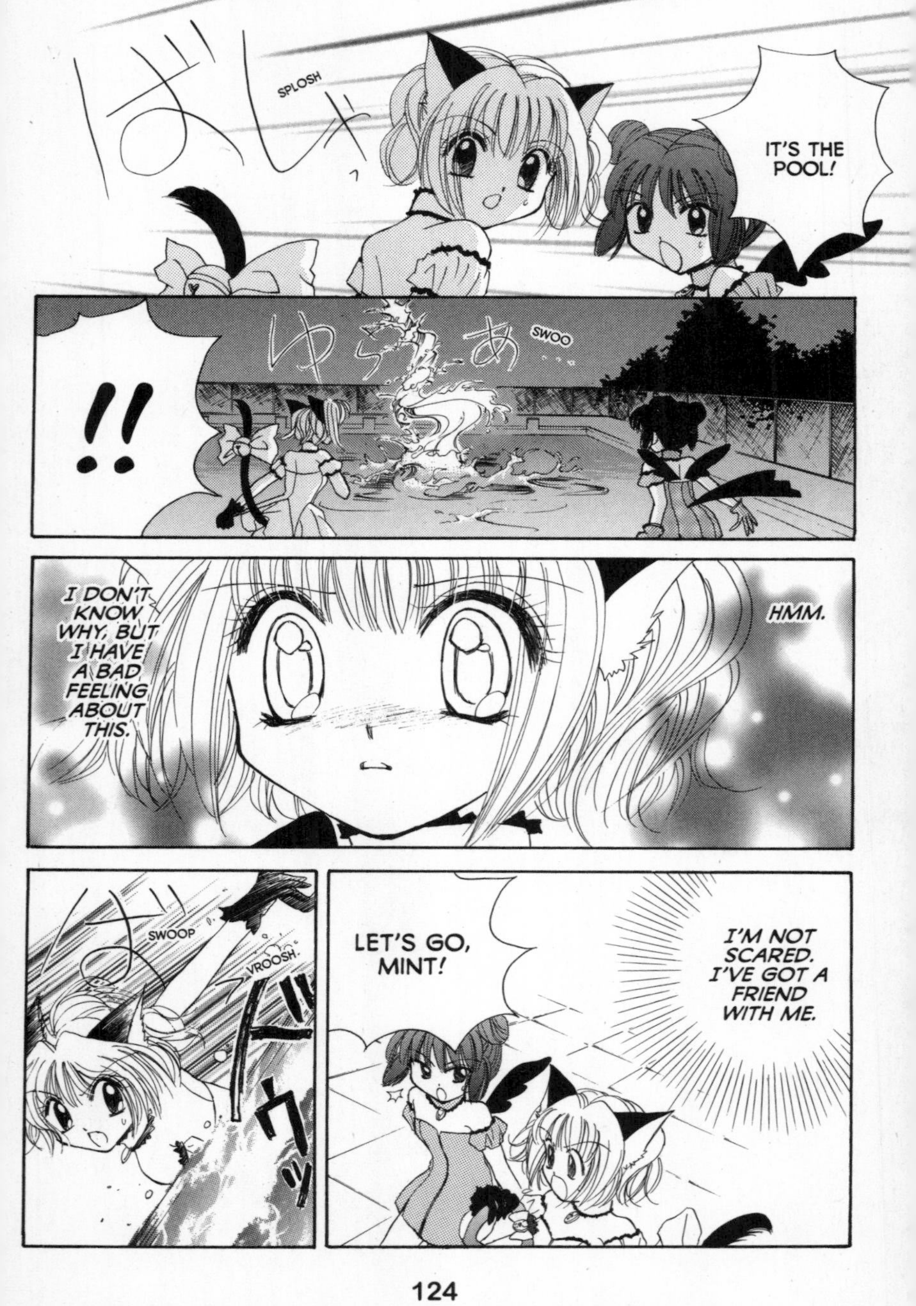
IT'S THE POOL!
SPLOSH
SWOO
!!
HMM.
I DON'T KNOW WHY, BUT I HAVE A BAD FEELING ABOUT THIS.
I'M NOT SCARED. I'VE GOT A FRIEND WITH ME.
LET'S GO, MINT!
SWOOP
VROOSH

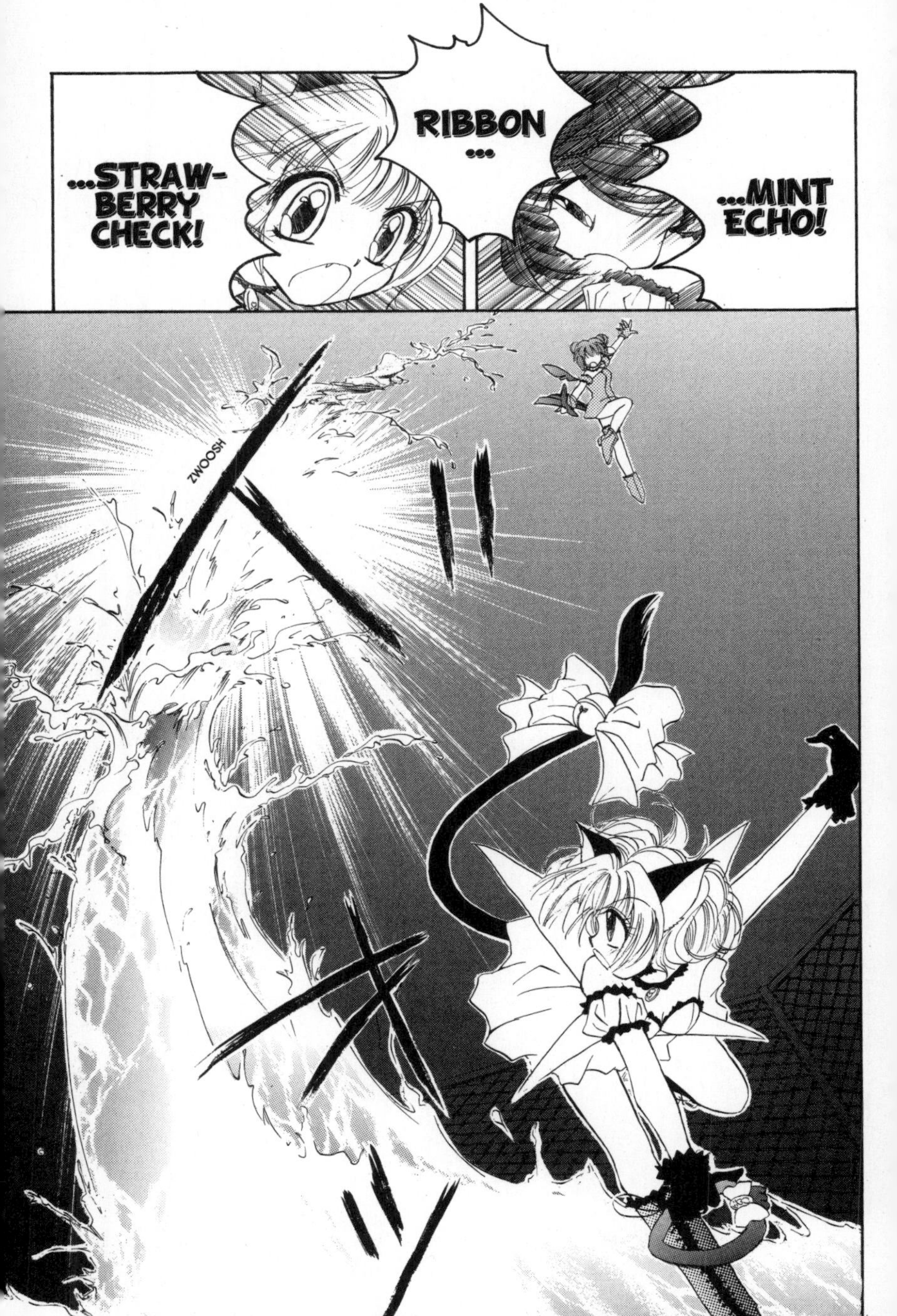
...MINT ECHO!
RIBBON ...
...STRAWBERRY CHECK!
ZWOOSH

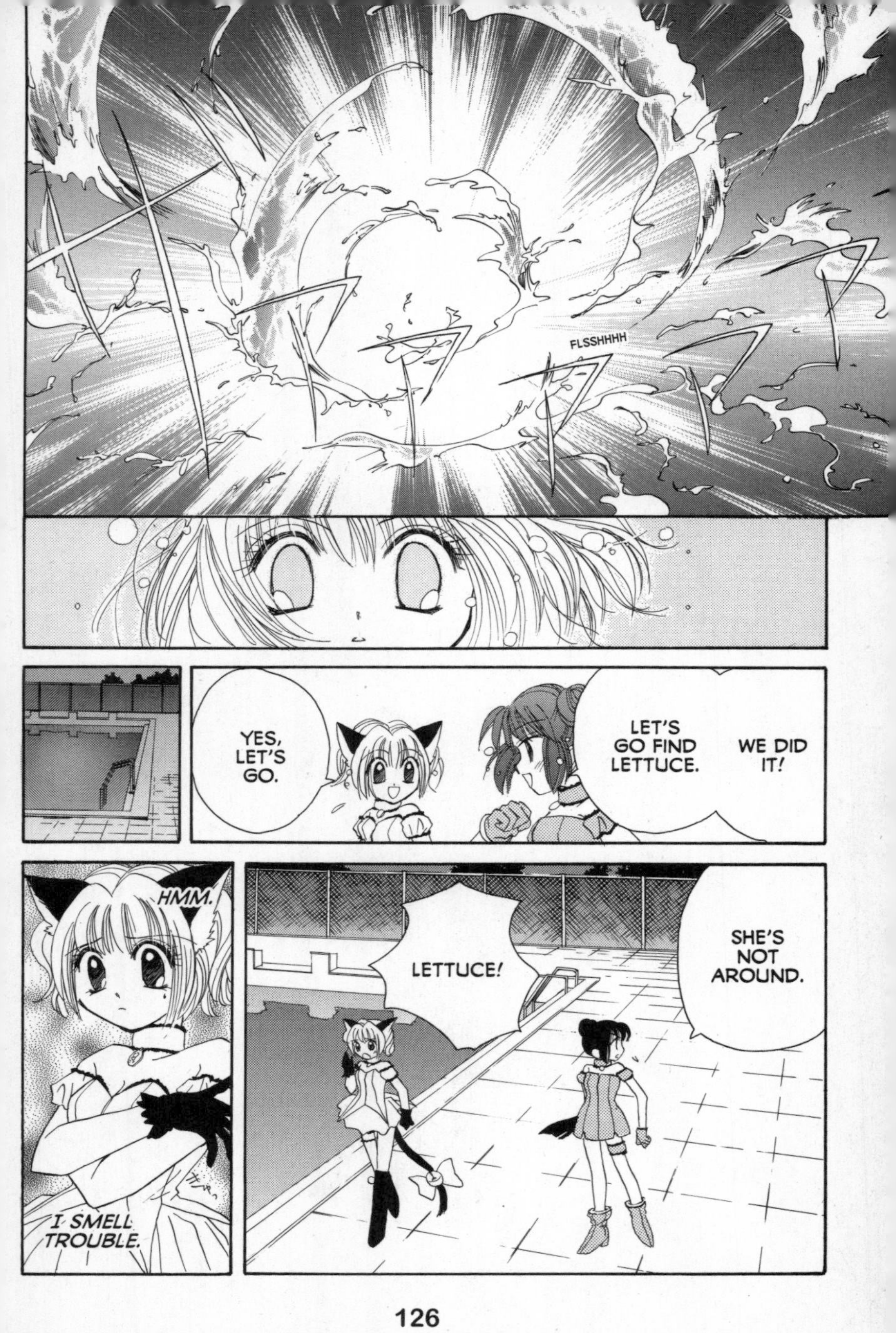
FLSSHHHH
WE DID IT!
LET'S GO FIND LETTUCE.
YES, LET'S GO.
SHE'S NOT AROUND.
LETTUCE!
HMM.
I SMELL TROUBLE.

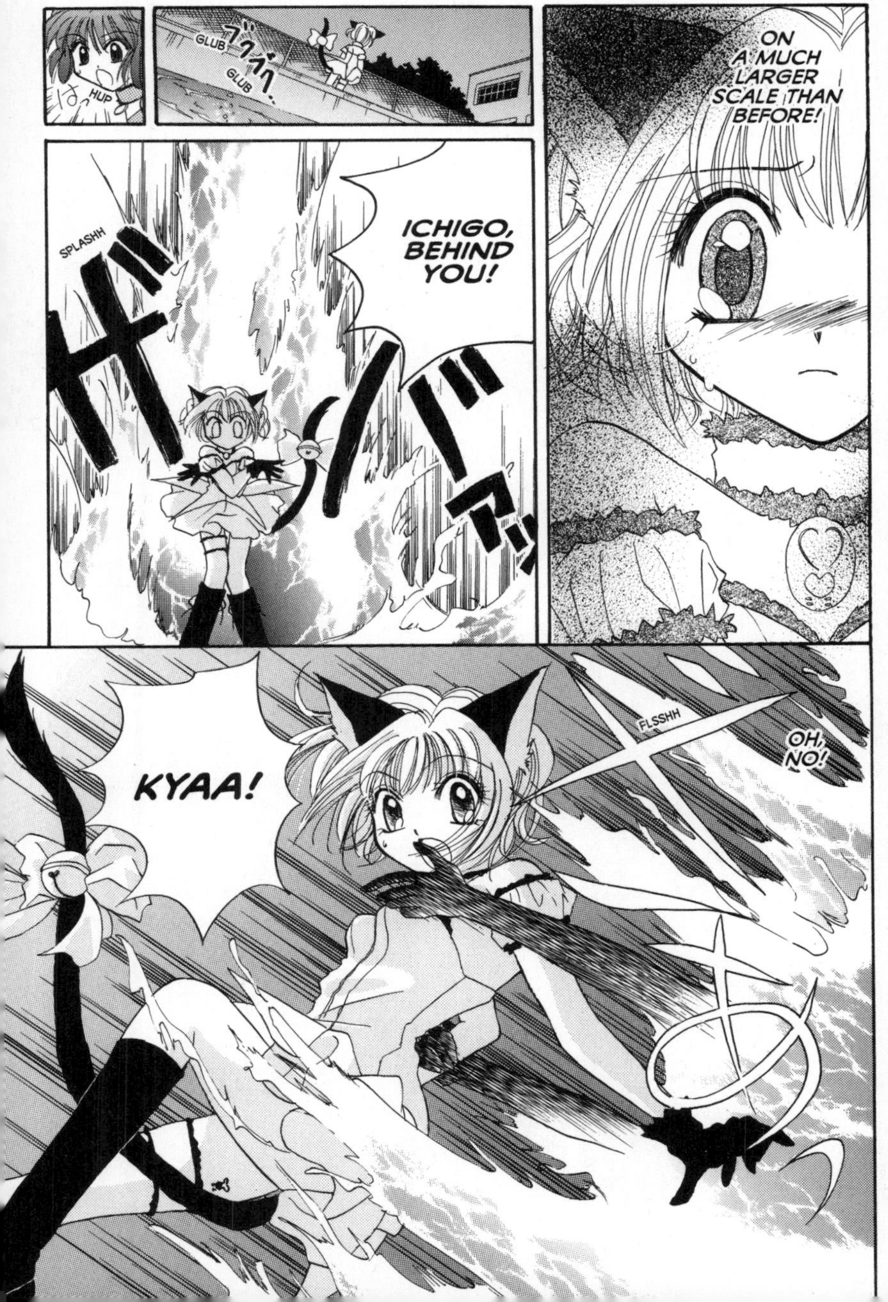
ON A MUCH LARGER SCALE THAN BEFORE!
GLUB
GLUB
HUP
ICHIGO, BEHIND YOU!
SPLASHH
OH, NO!
FLSSHH
KYAA!

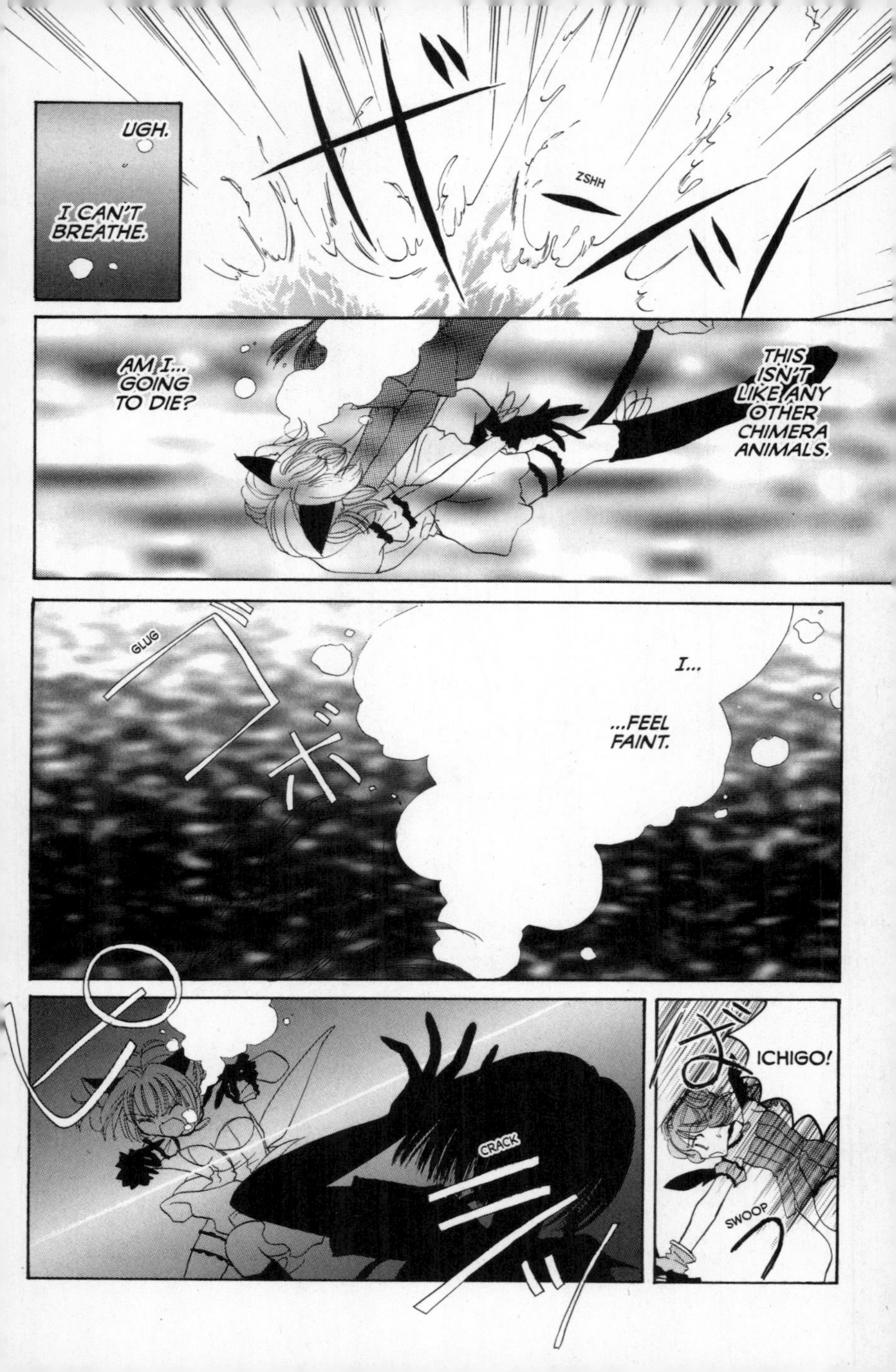
ZSHH
UGH.
I CAN'T BREATHE.
THIS ISN'T LIKE ANY OTHER CHIMERA ANIMALS.
AM I... GOING TO DIE?
I...
...FEEL FAINT.
GLUG
ICHIGO!
SWOOP
CRACK

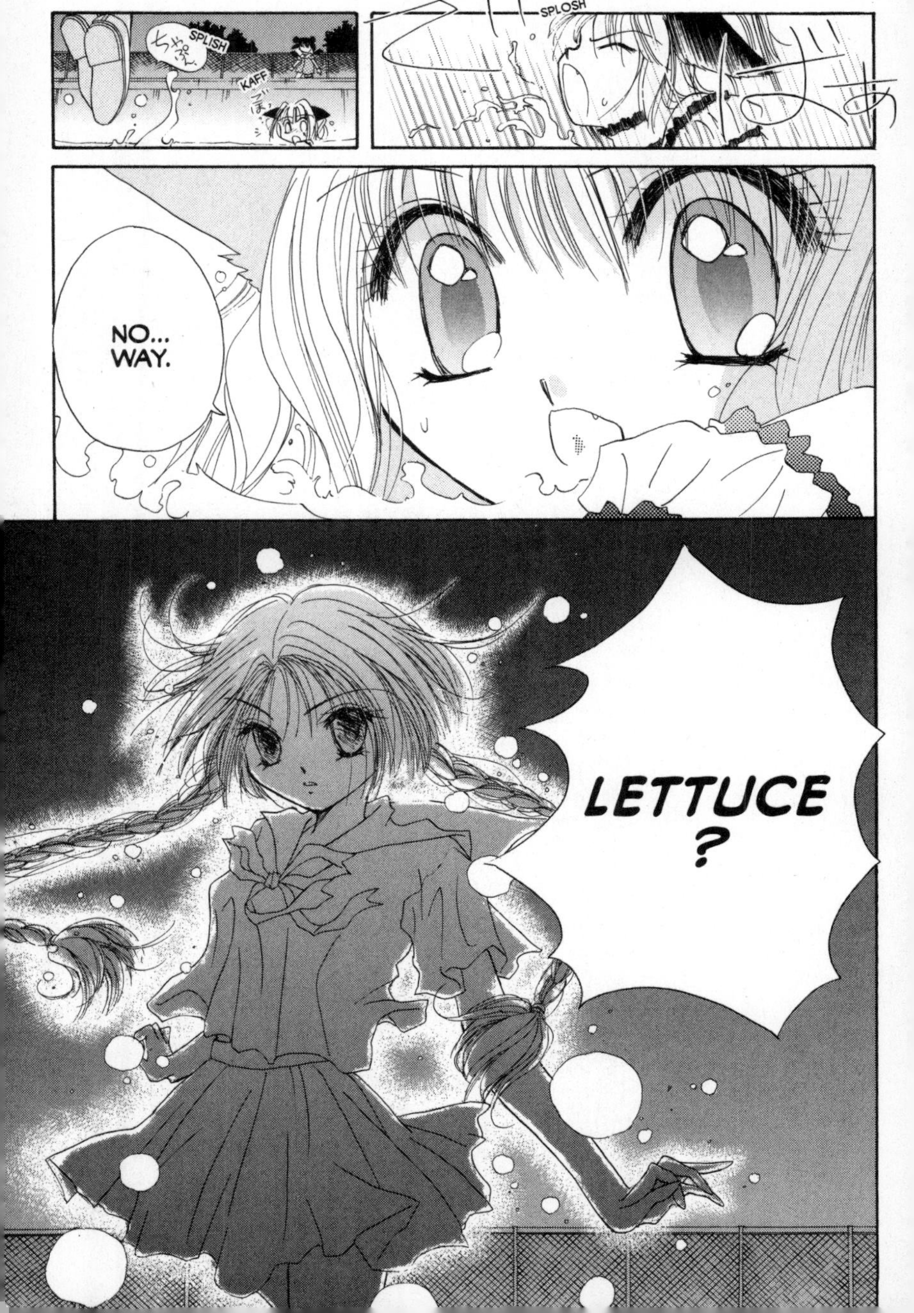
SPLOSH
SPLISH
KAFF
NO... WAY.
LETTUCE ?

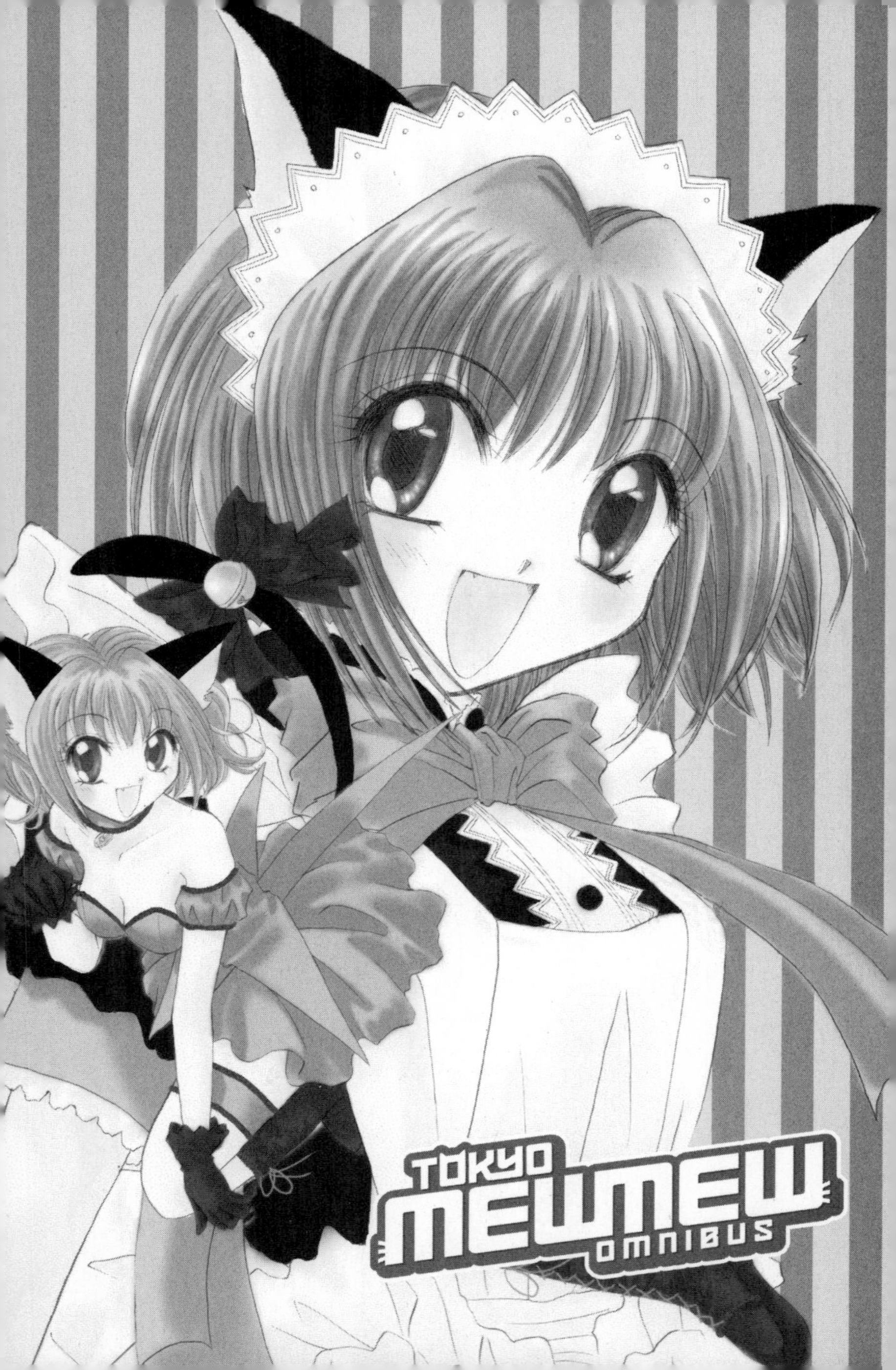
TOKYO
MEWMEW
OMNIBUS

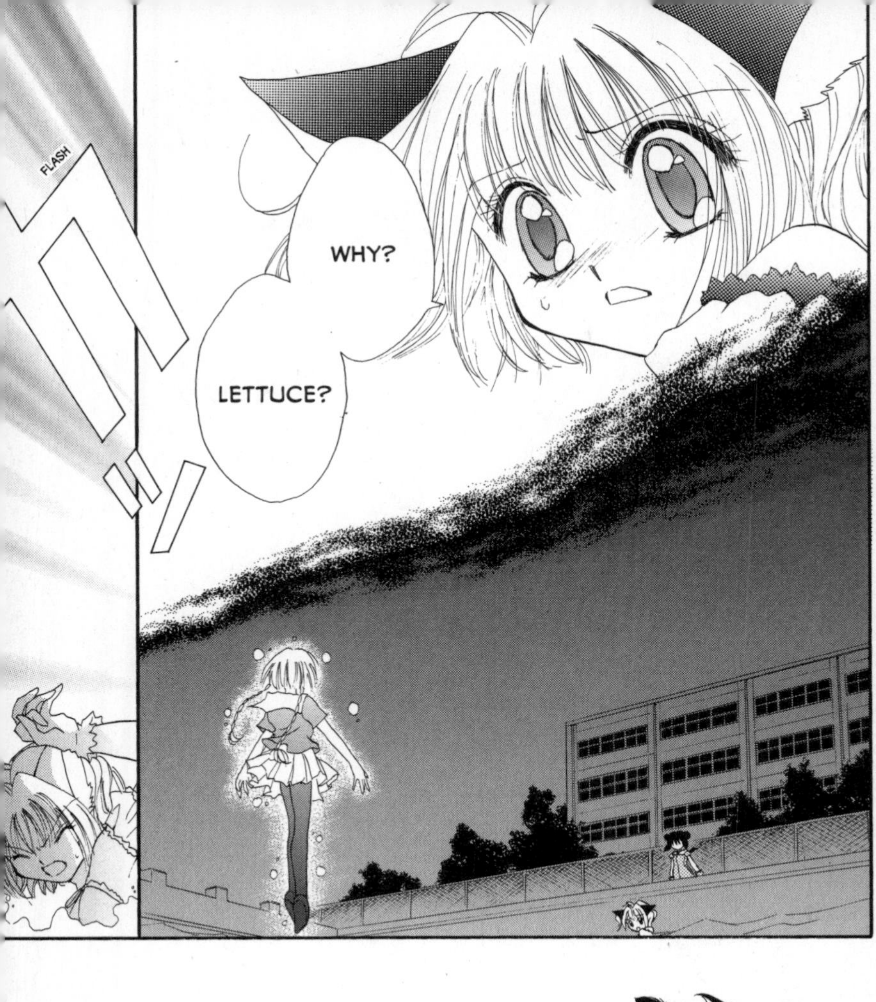
WHY?
LETTUCE?
FLASH

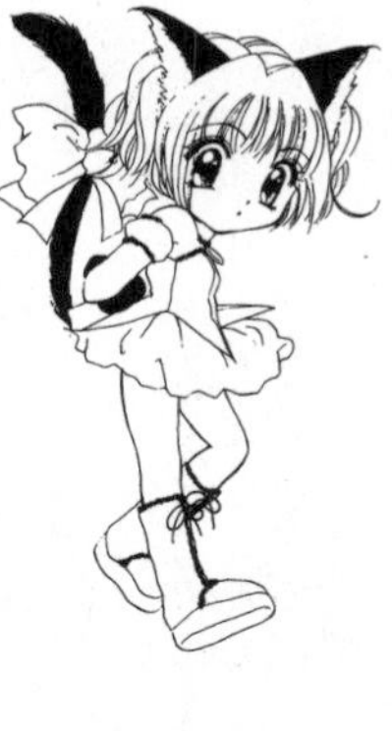

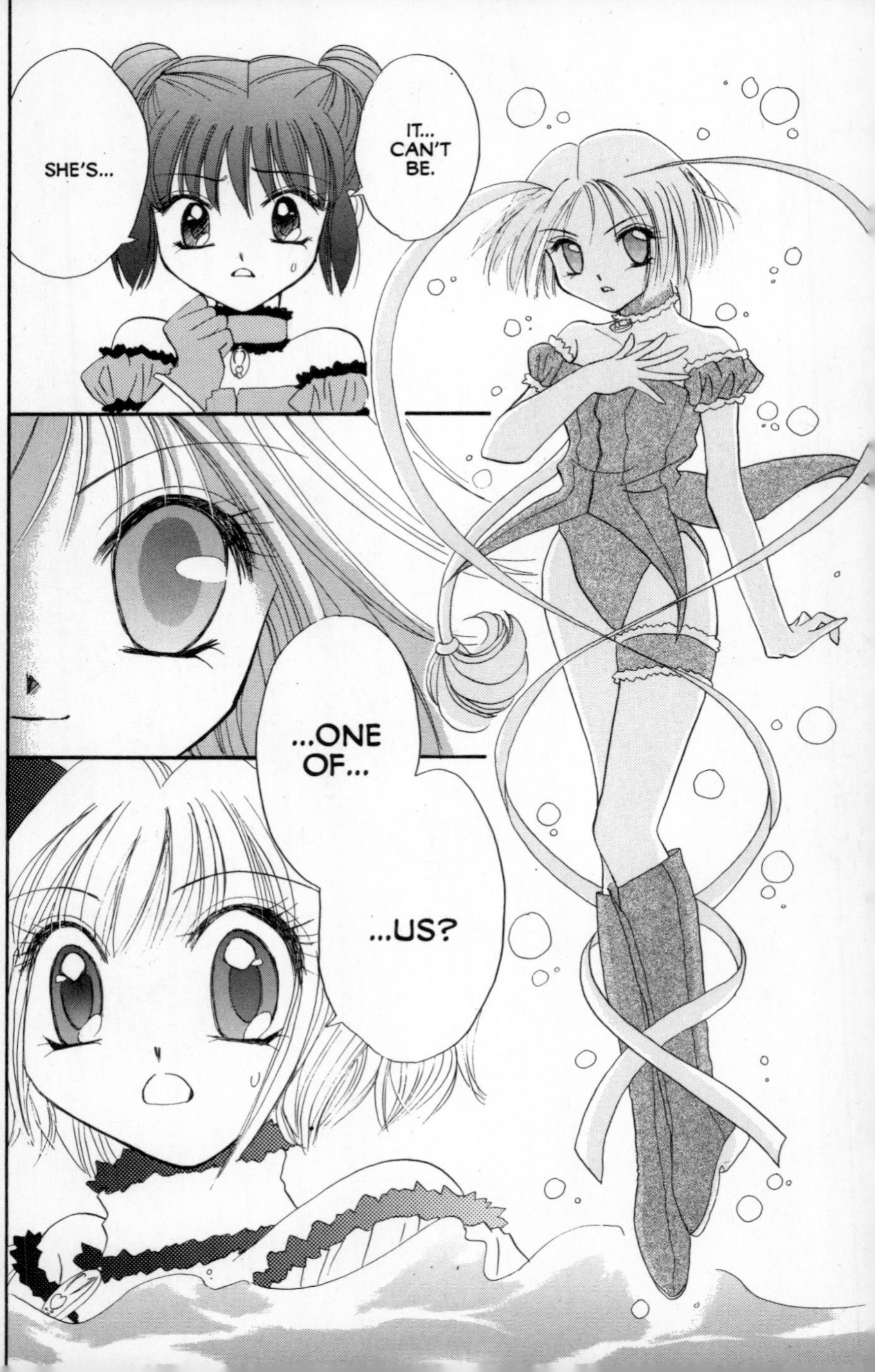
IT... CAN'T BE.
SHE'S...
...ONE OF...
...US?

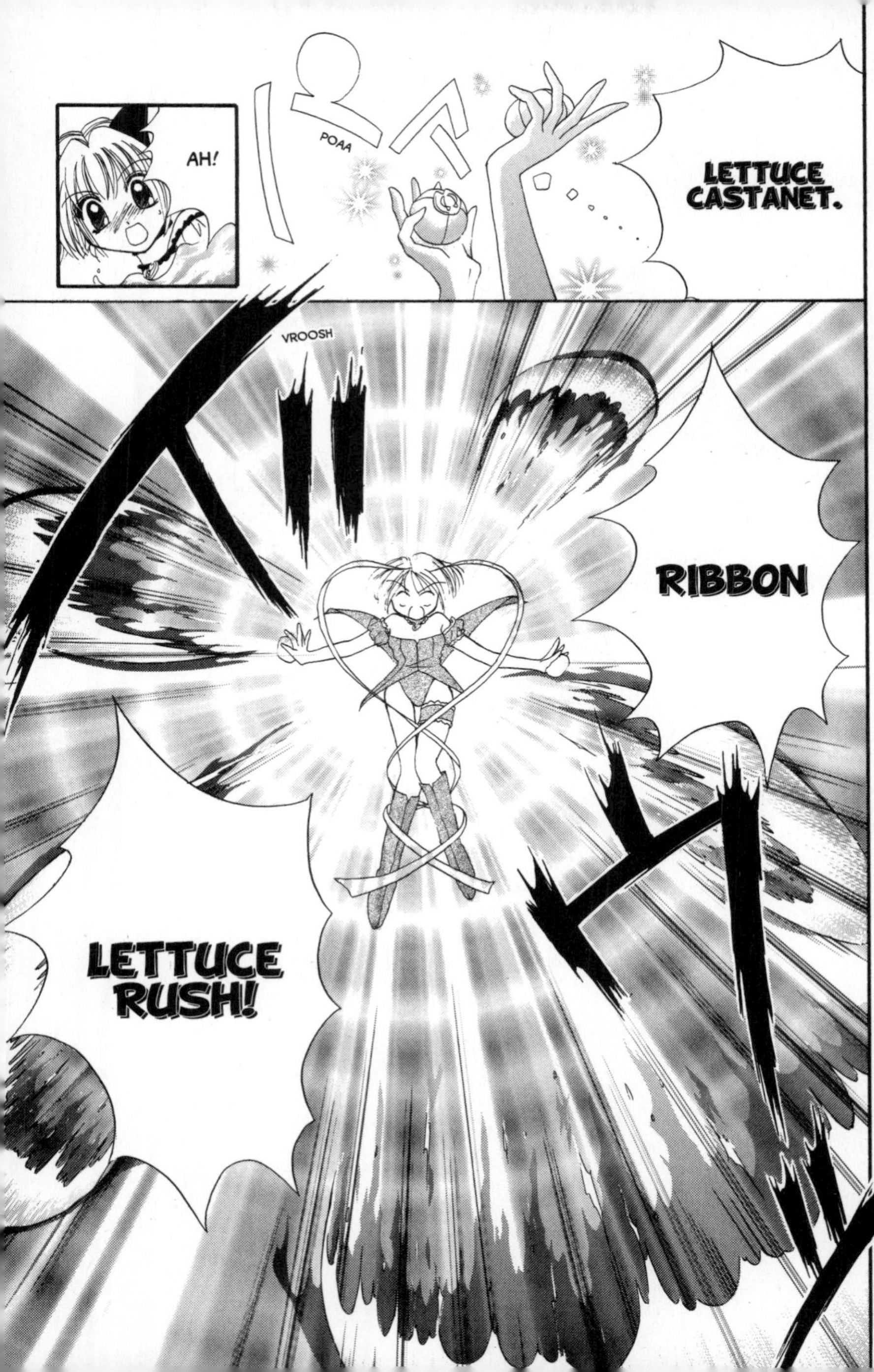
LETTUCE CASTANET.
POAA
AH!
VROOSH
RIBBON
LETTUCE RUSH!

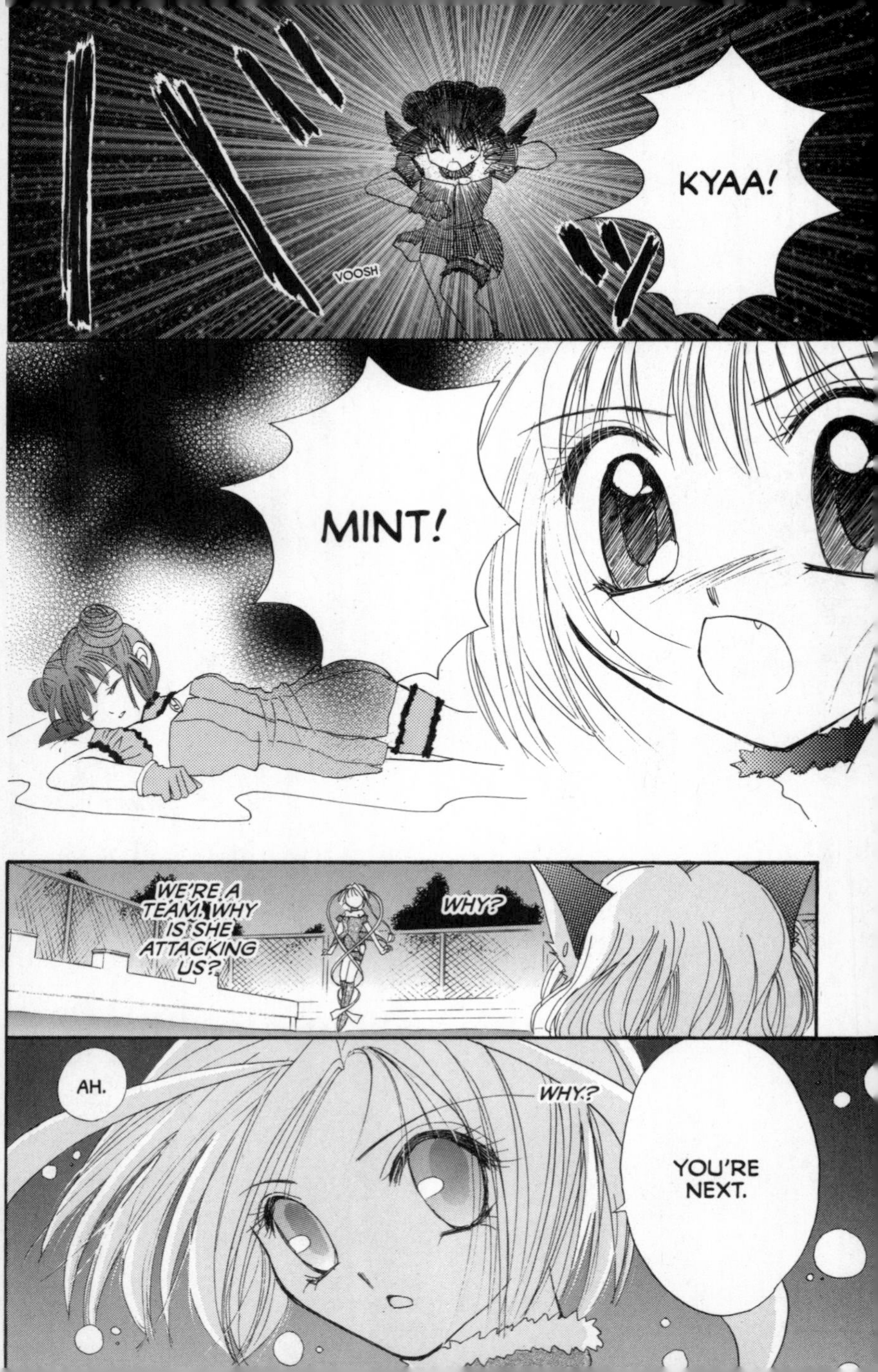
KYAA!
VOOSH
MINT!
WHY?
WE'RE A TEAM. WHY IS SHE ATTACKING US?
YOU'RE NEXT.
WHY?
AH.

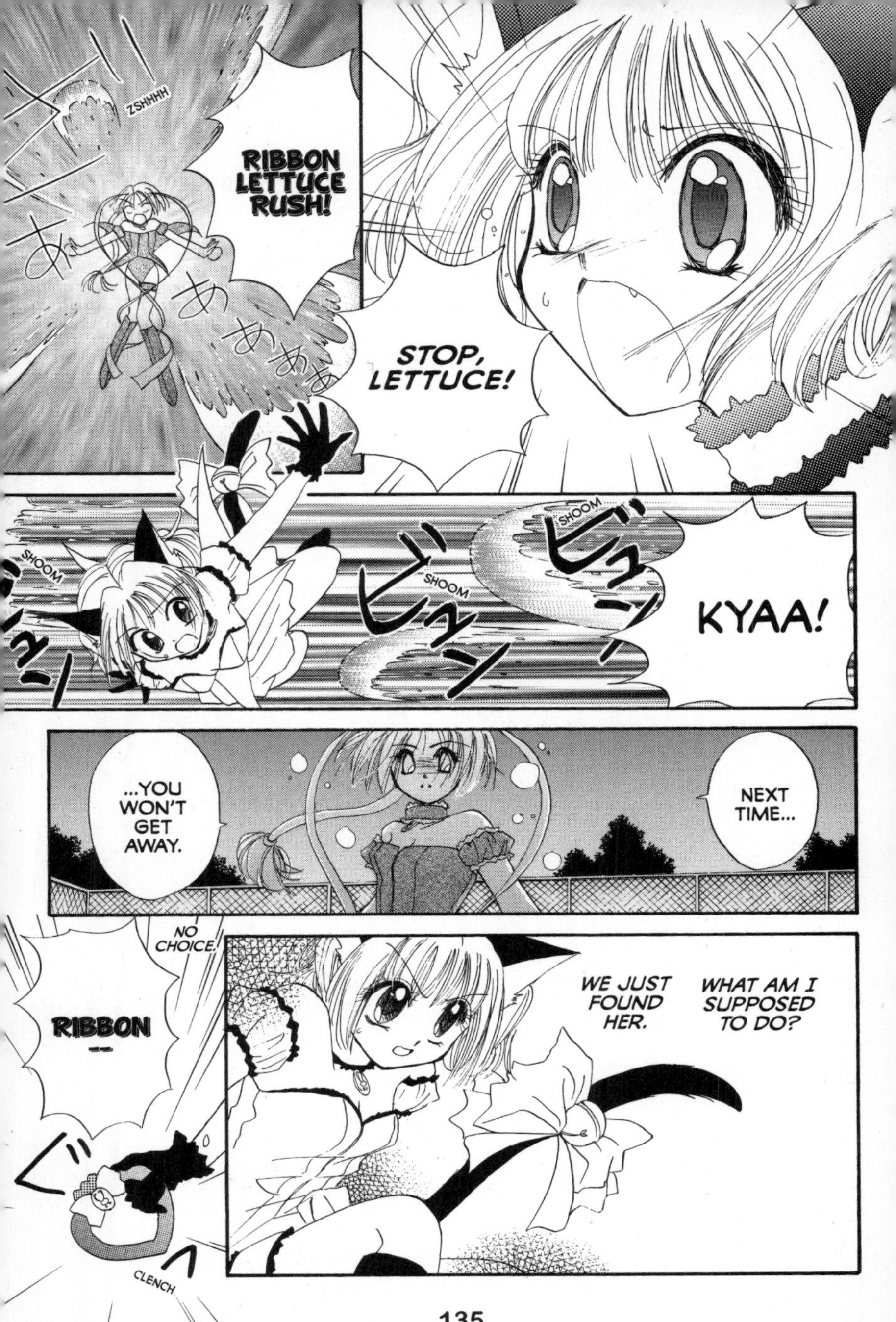
STOP, LETTUCE!
ZSHHHH
RIBBON LETTUCE RUSH!
SHOOM
KYAA!
SHOOM
SHOOM
NEXT TIME...
...YOU WON'T GET AWAY.
WHAT AM I SUPPOSED TO DO?
WE JUST FOUND HER.
NO CHOICE.
RIBBON --
CLENCH

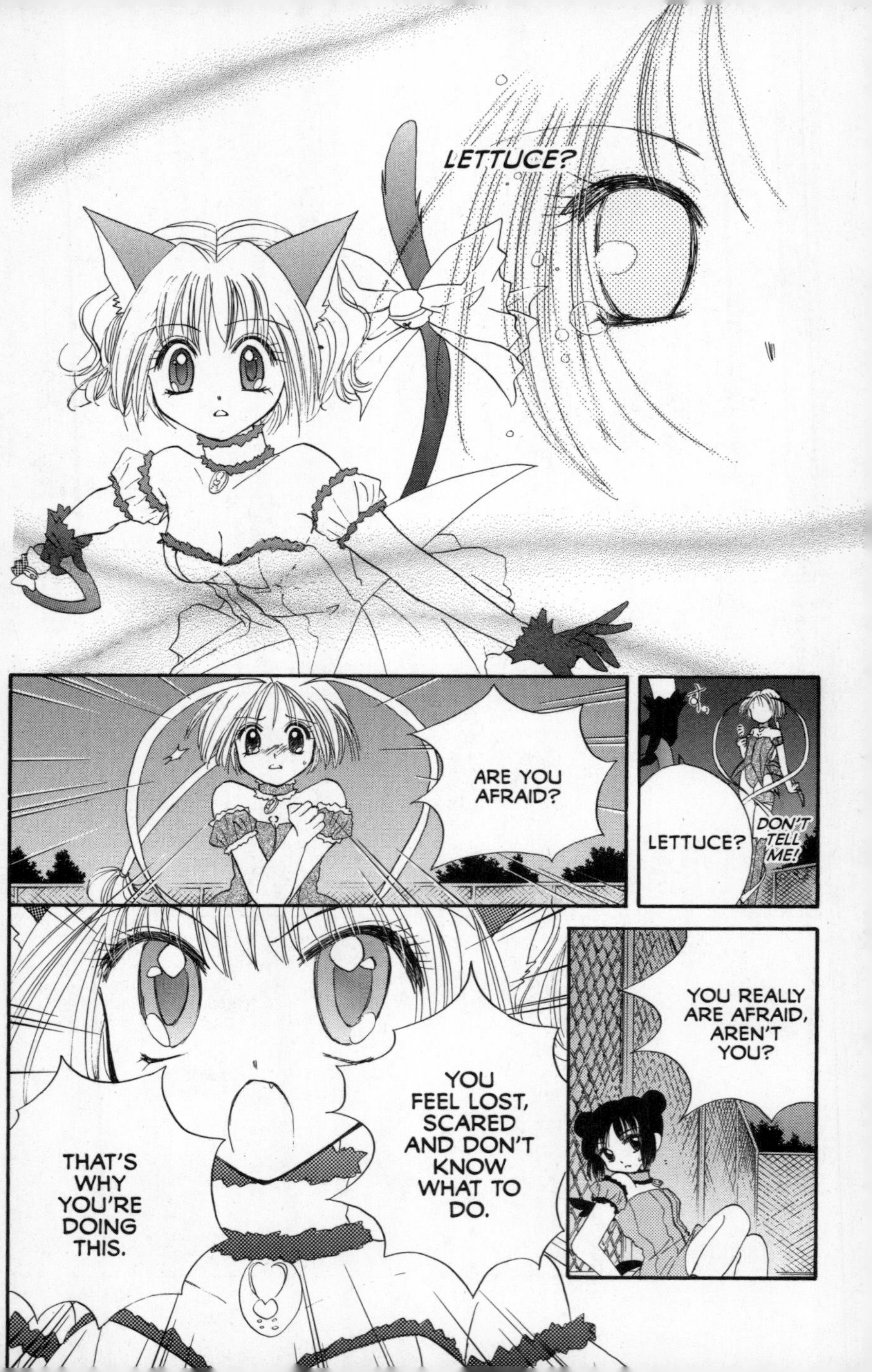
LETTUCE?
DON'T TELL ME!
LETTUCE?
ARE YOU AFRAID?
YOU REALLY ARE AFRAID, AREN'T YOU?
YOU FEEL LOST, SCARED AND DON'T KNOW WHAT TO DO.
THAT'S WHY YOU'RE DOING THIS.

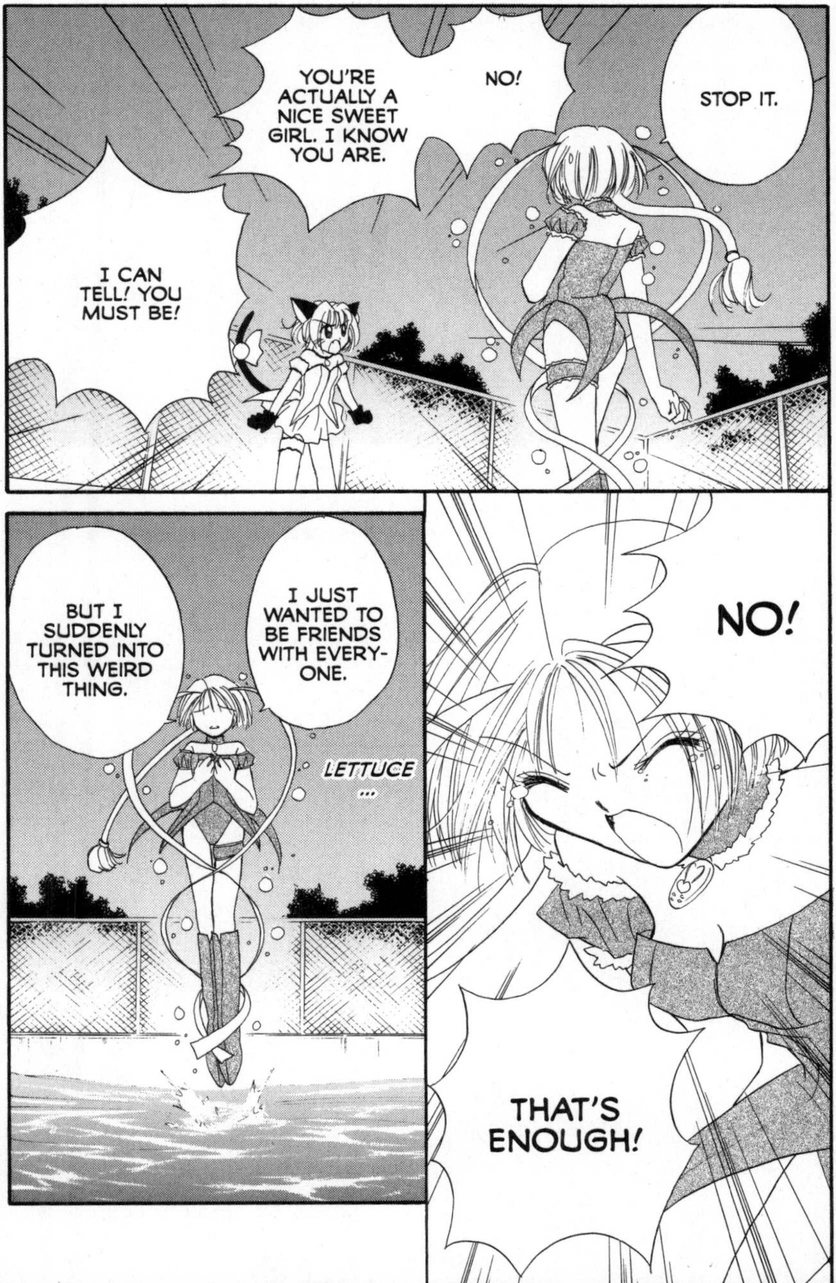
STOP IT.
NO!
YOU'RE ACTUALLY A NICE SWEET GIRL. I KNOW YOU ARE.
I CAN TELL! YOU MUST BE!
NO!
THAT'S ENOUGH!
I JUST WANTED TO BE FRIENDS WITH EVERY-ONE.
BUT I SUDDENLY TURNED INTO THIS WEIRD THING.
LETTUCE ...

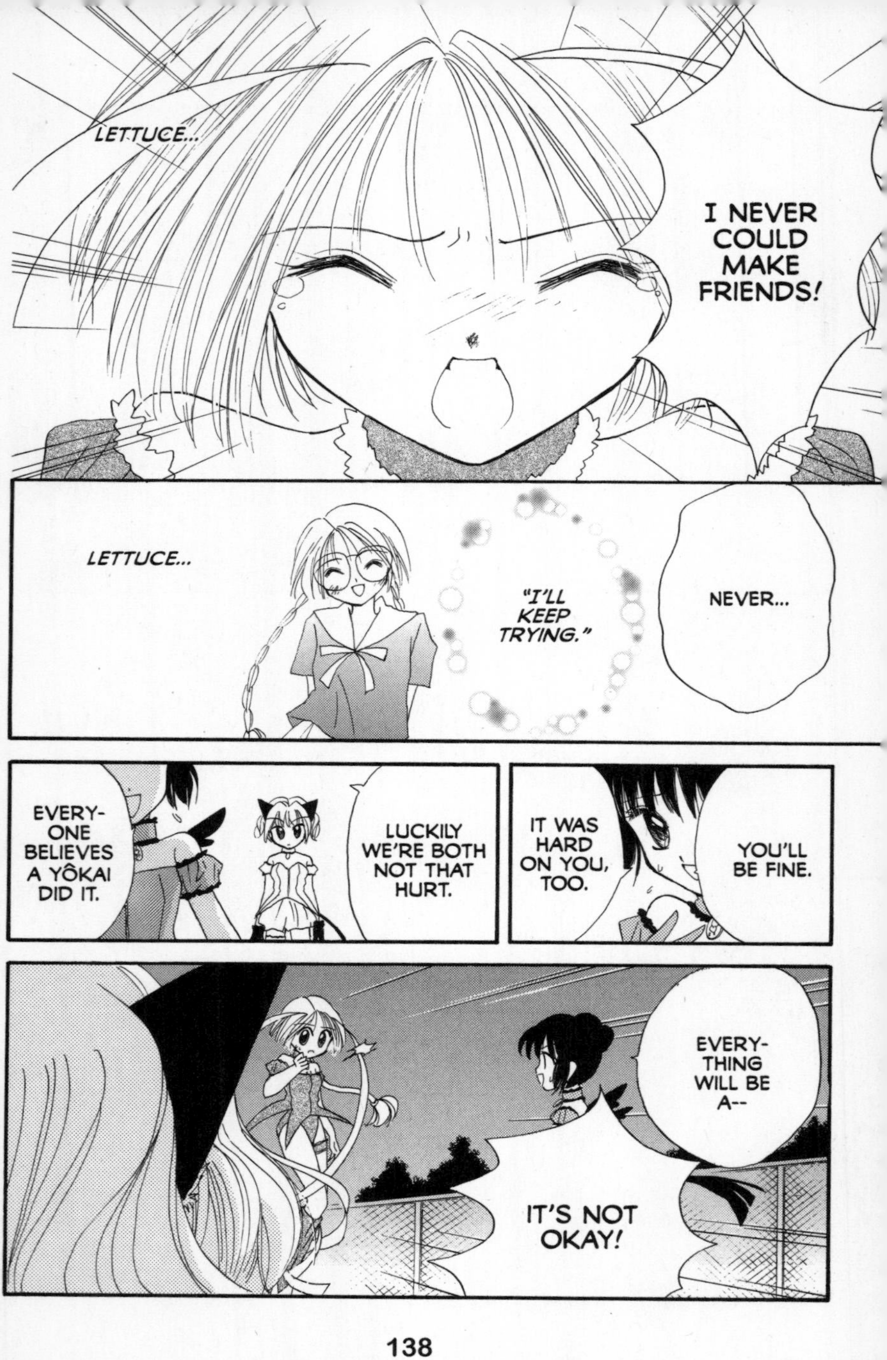
I NEVER COULD MAKE FRIENDS!
LETTUCE...
NEVER...
"I'LL KEEP TRYING."
LETTUCE...
YOU'LL BE FINE.
IT WAS HARD ON YOU, TOO.
LUCKILY WE'RE BOTH NOT THAT HURT.
EVERY-ONE BELIEVES A YÔKAI DID IT.
EVERY-THING WILL BE A--
IT'S NOT OKAY!

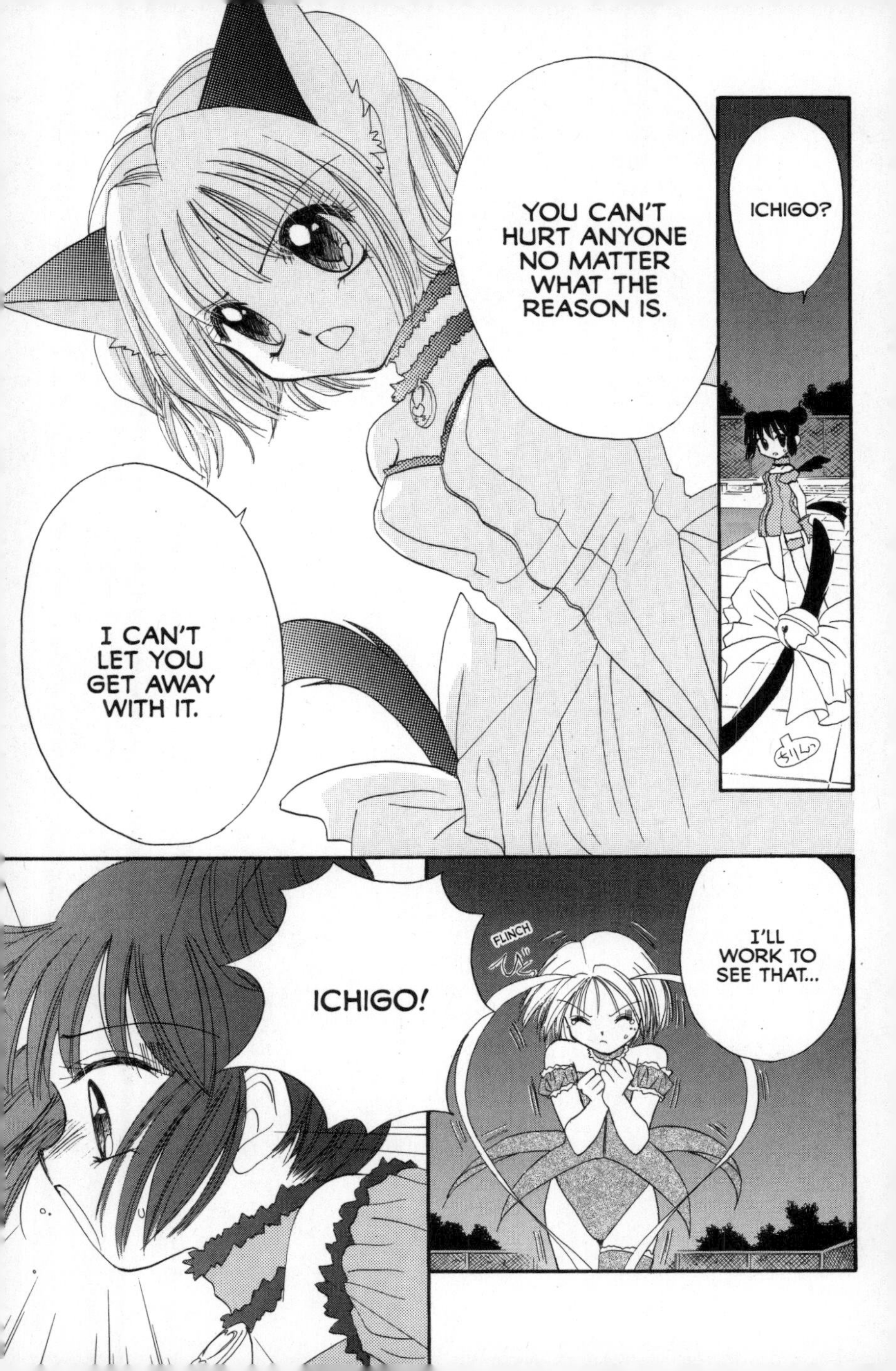
ICHIGO?
YOU CAN'T HURT ANYONE NO MATTER WHAT THE REASON IS.
I CAN'T LET YOU GET AWAY WITH IT.
I'LL WORK TO SEE THAT...
FLINCH
ICHIGO!

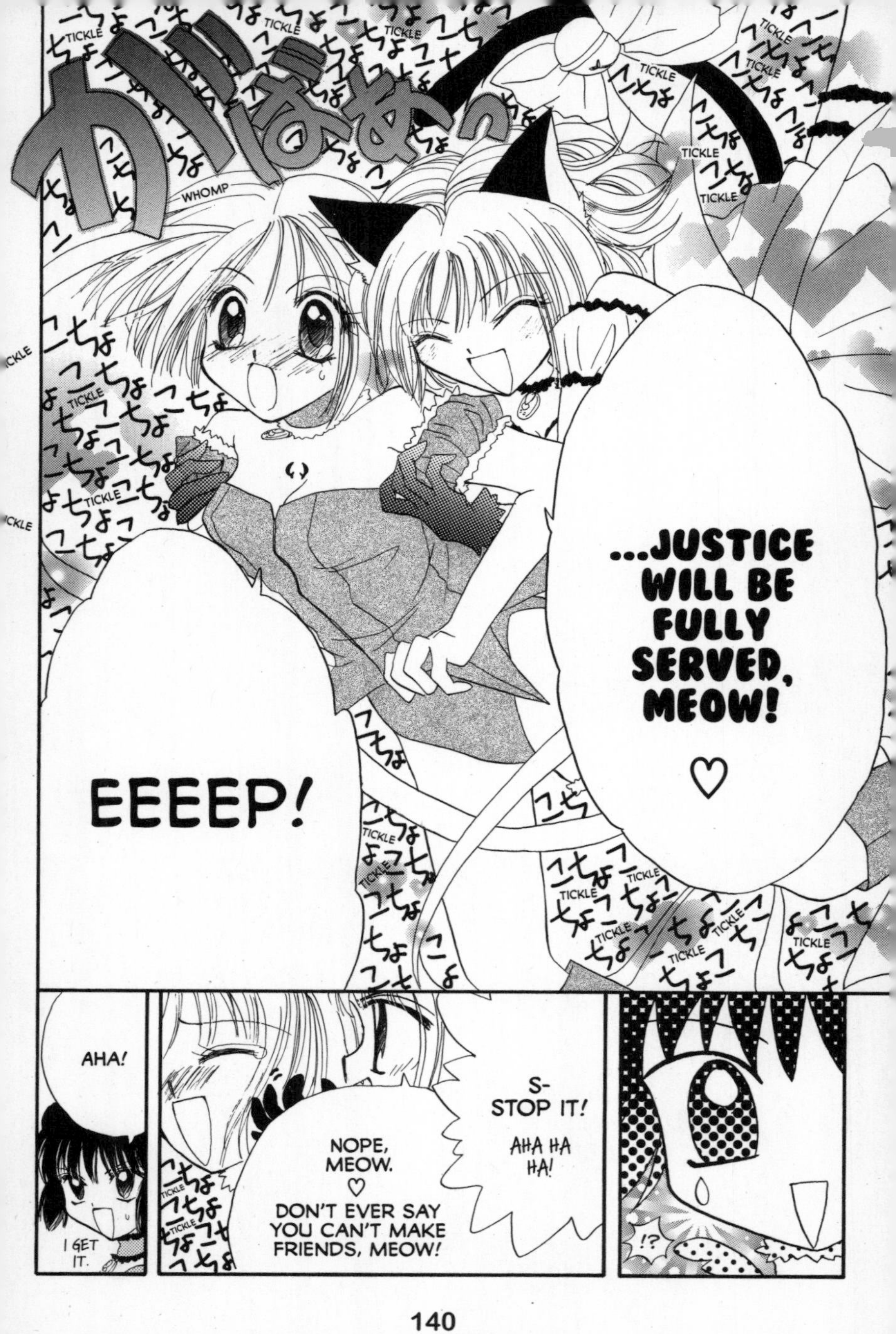
WHOMP
TICKLE
...JUSTICE WILL BE FULLY SERVED, MEOW! ♡
EEEEP!
!?
S- STOP IT!
AHA HA HA!
NOPE, MEOW. ♡ DON'T EVER SAY YOU CAN'T MAKE FRIENDS, MEOW!
AHA!
I GET IT.

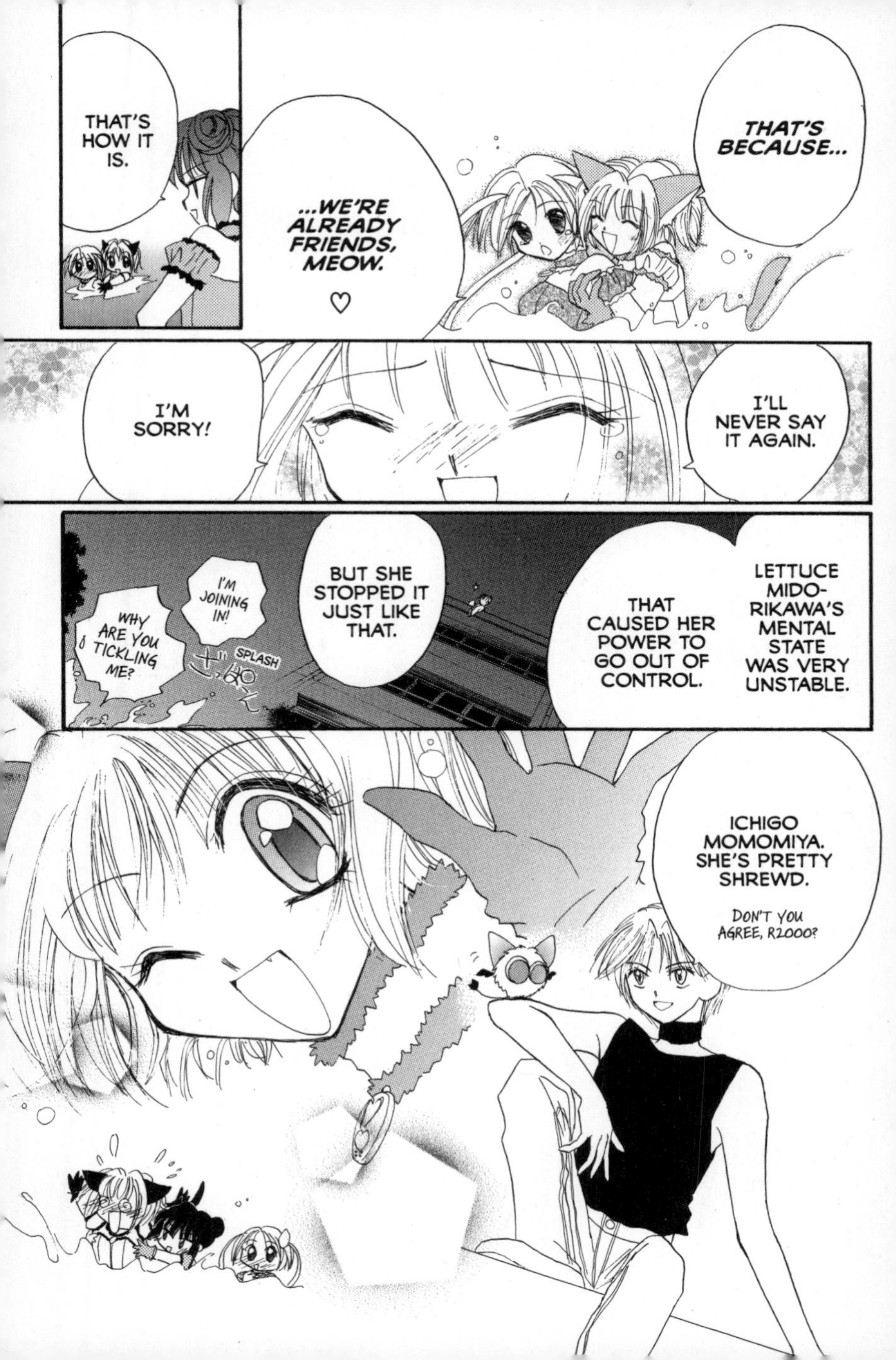
THAT'S BECAUSE...
...WE'RE ALREADY FRIENDS, MEOW. ♡
THAT'S HOW IT IS.
I'LL NEVER SAY IT AGAIN.
I'M SORRY!
LETTUCE MIDO-RIKAWA'S MENTAL STATE WAS VERY UNSTABLE.
THAT CAUSED HER POWER TO GO OUT OF CONTROL.
BUT SHE STOPPED IT JUST LIKE THAT.
I'M JOINING IN!
WHY ARE YOU TICKLING ME?
SPLASH
ICHIGO MOMOMIYA. SHE'S PRETTY SHREWD.
DON'T YOU AGREE, R2000?

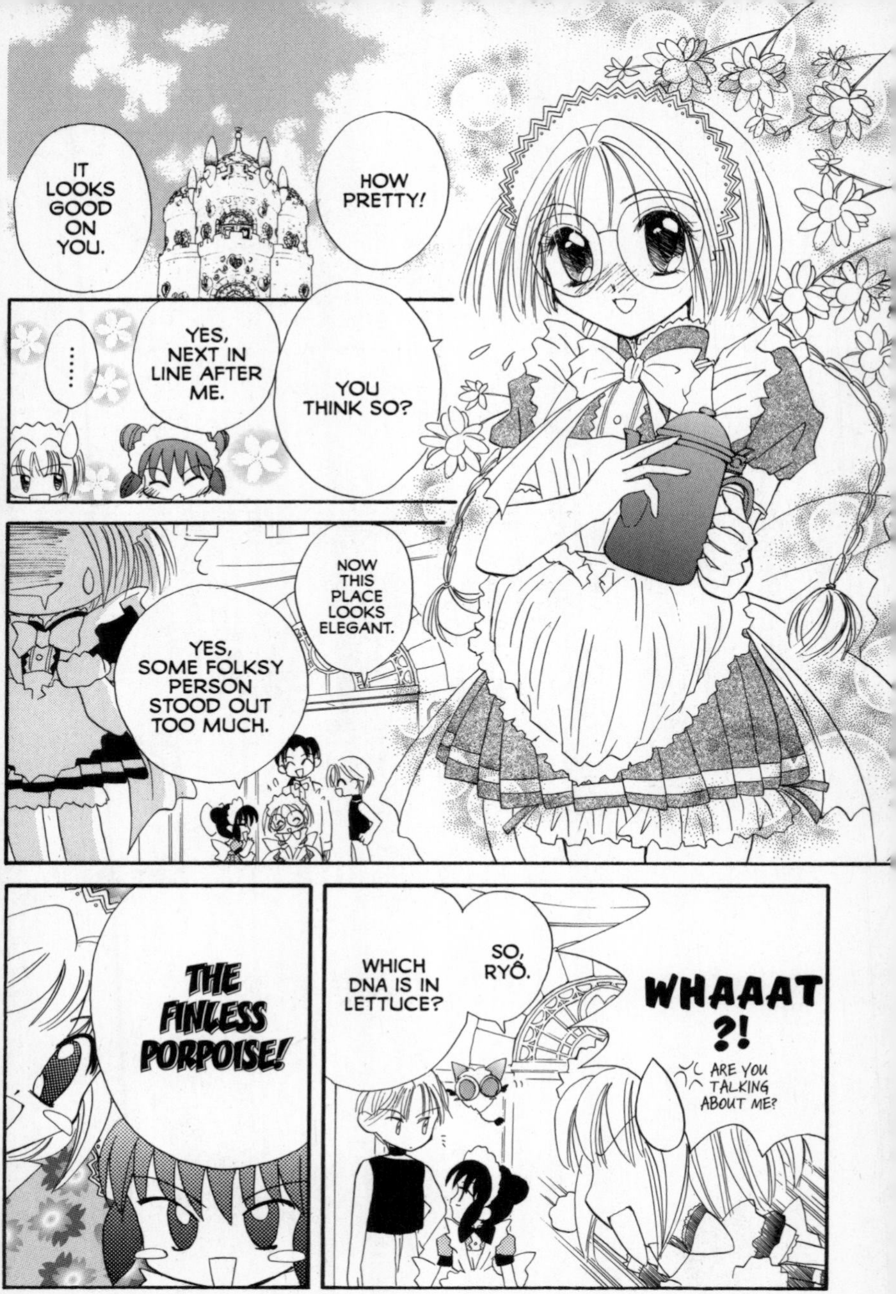
HOW PRETTY!
IT LOOKS GOOD ON YOU.
YOU THINK SO?
YES, NEXT IN LINE AFTER ME.
......
NOW THIS PLACE LOOKS ELEGANT.
YES, SOME FOLKSY PERSON STOOD OUT TOO MUCH.
SO, RYÔ.
WHICH DNA IS IN LETTUCE?
WHAAAT?!
ARE YOU TALKING ABOUT ME?
THE FINLESS PORPOISE!

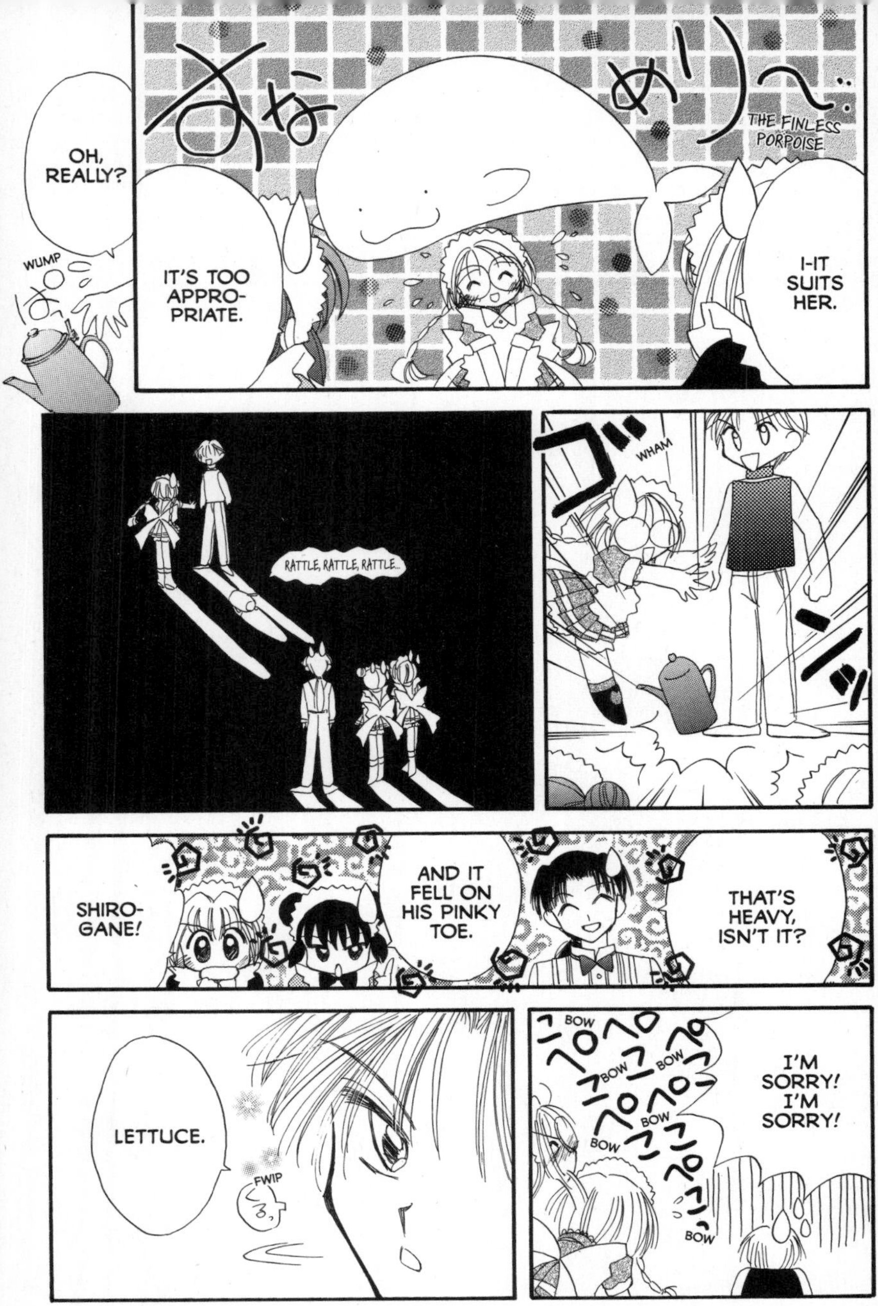
THE FINLESS PORPOISE
I-IT SUITS HER.
IT'S TOO APPROPRIATE.
OH, REALLY?
WUMP
WHAM
RATTLE, RATTLE, RATTLE...
THAT'S HEAVY, ISN'T IT?
AND IT FELL ON HIS PINKY TOE.
SHIRO-GANE!
I'M SORRY! I'M SORRY!
BOW
BOW
BOW
BOW
BOW
BOW
LETTUCE.
FWIP

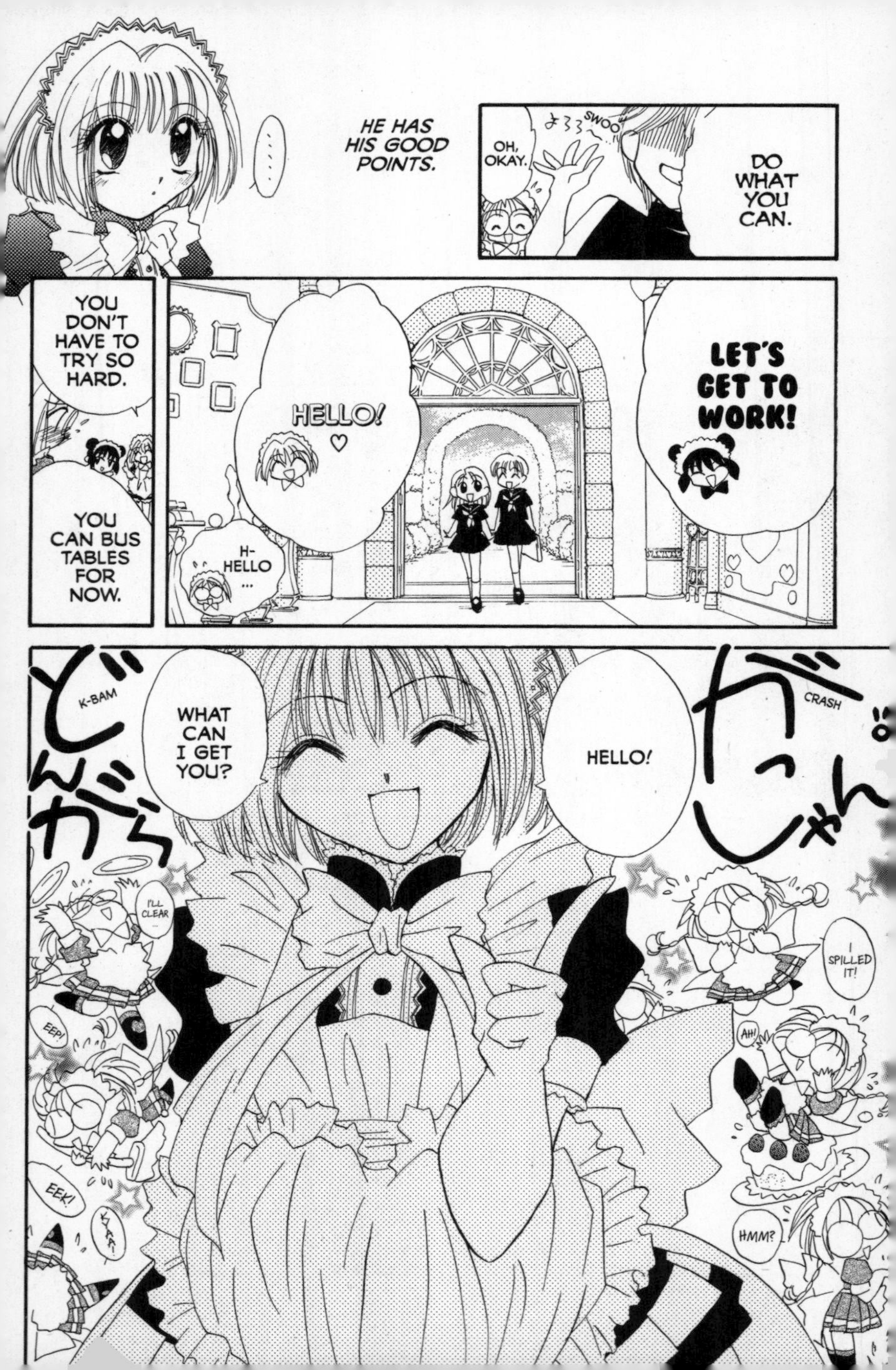

DO WHAT YOU CAN.
SWOO
よろろ~
OH, OKAY.
HE HAS HIS GOOD POINTS.
......
LET'S GET TO WORK!
HELLO! ♡
H-HELLO ...
YOU DON'T HAVE TO TRY SO HARD.
YOU CAN BUS TABLES FOR NOW.
がっしゃん
CRASH
HELLO!
WHAT CAN I GET YOU?
どんがら
K-BAM
I SPILLED IT!
AH!
HMM?
I'LL CLEAR ...
EEP!
EEK!
KYAA!

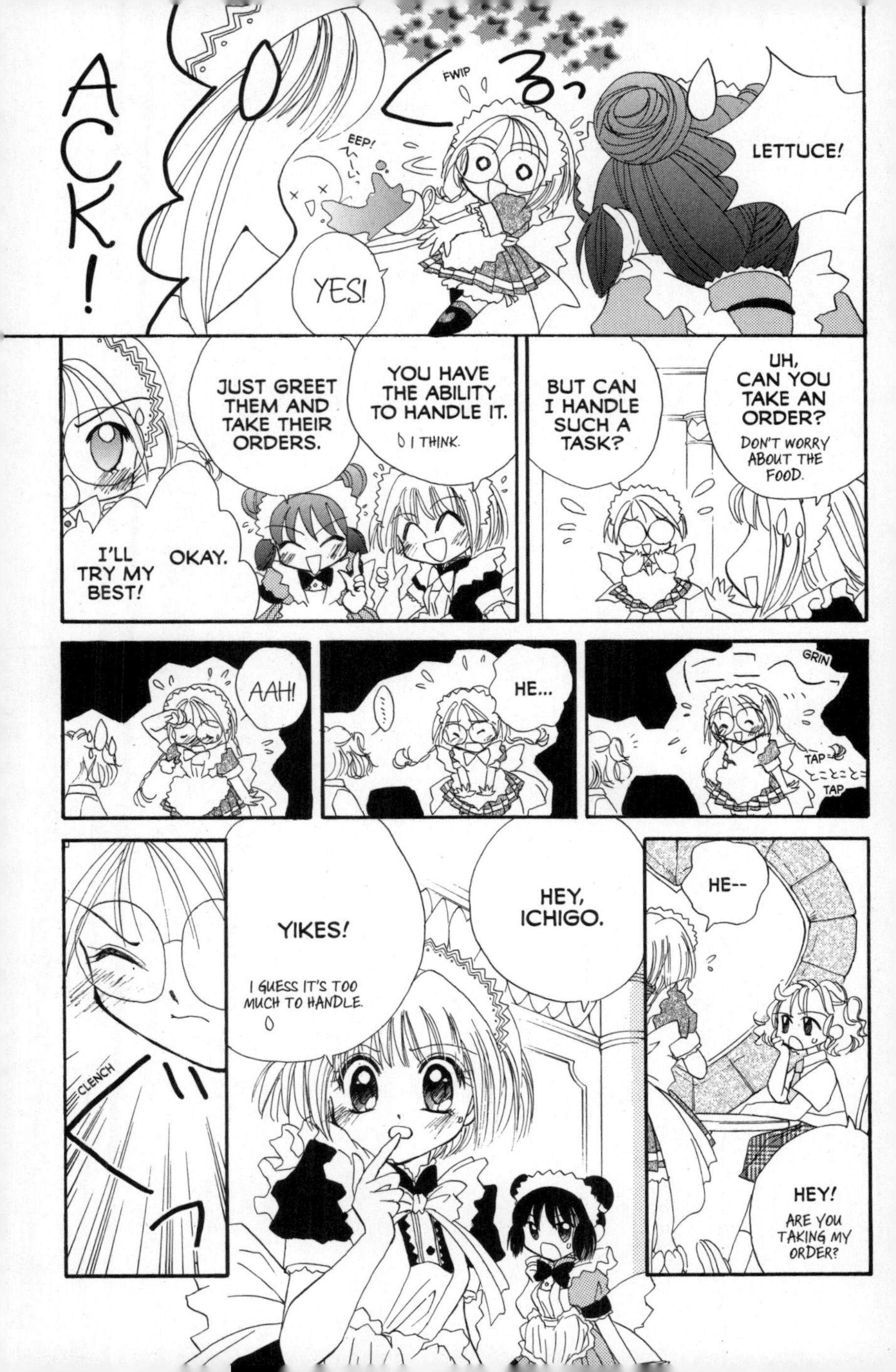
LETTUCE!
FWIP
EEP!
YES!
ACK!
UH, CAN YOU TAKE AN ORDER?
DON'T WORRY ABOUT THE FOOD.
BUT CAN I HANDLE SUCH A TASK?
YOU HAVE THE ABILITY TO HANDLE IT.
I THINK.
JUST GREET THEM AND TAKE THEIR ORDERS.
OKAY.
I'LL TRY MY BEST!
GRIN
TAP
TAP
HE...
...
AAH!
HE--
HEY!
ARE YOU TAKING MY ORDER?
HEY, ICHIGO.
YIKES!
I GUESS IT'S TOO MUCH TO HANDLE.
CLENCH

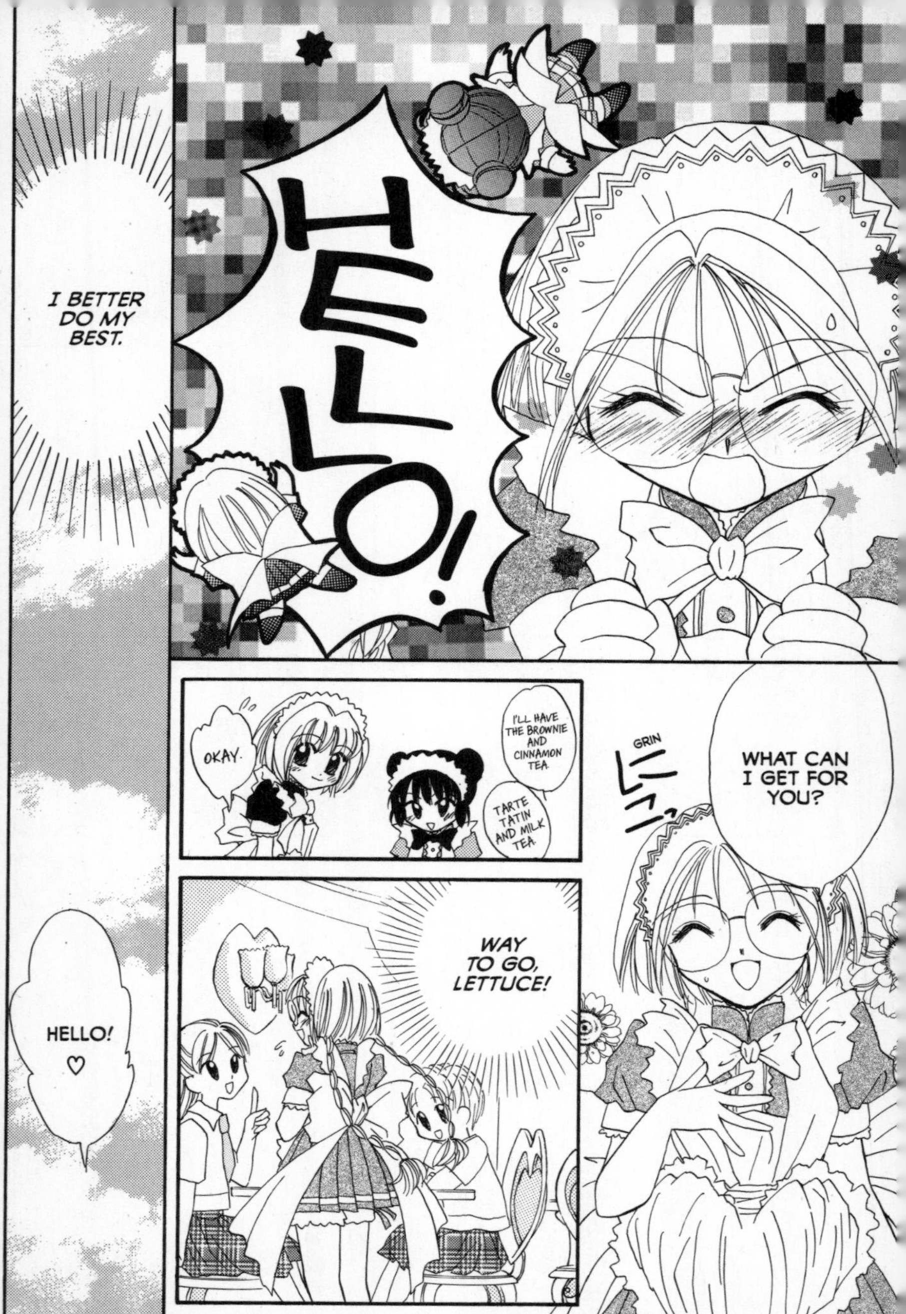
HELLO!
GRIN
WHAT CAN I GET FOR YOU?
I'LL HAVE THE BROWNIE AND CINNAMON TEA.
TARTE TATIN AND MILK TEA.
OKAY.
WAY TO GO, LETTUCE!
I BETTER DO MY BEST.
HELLO! ♡

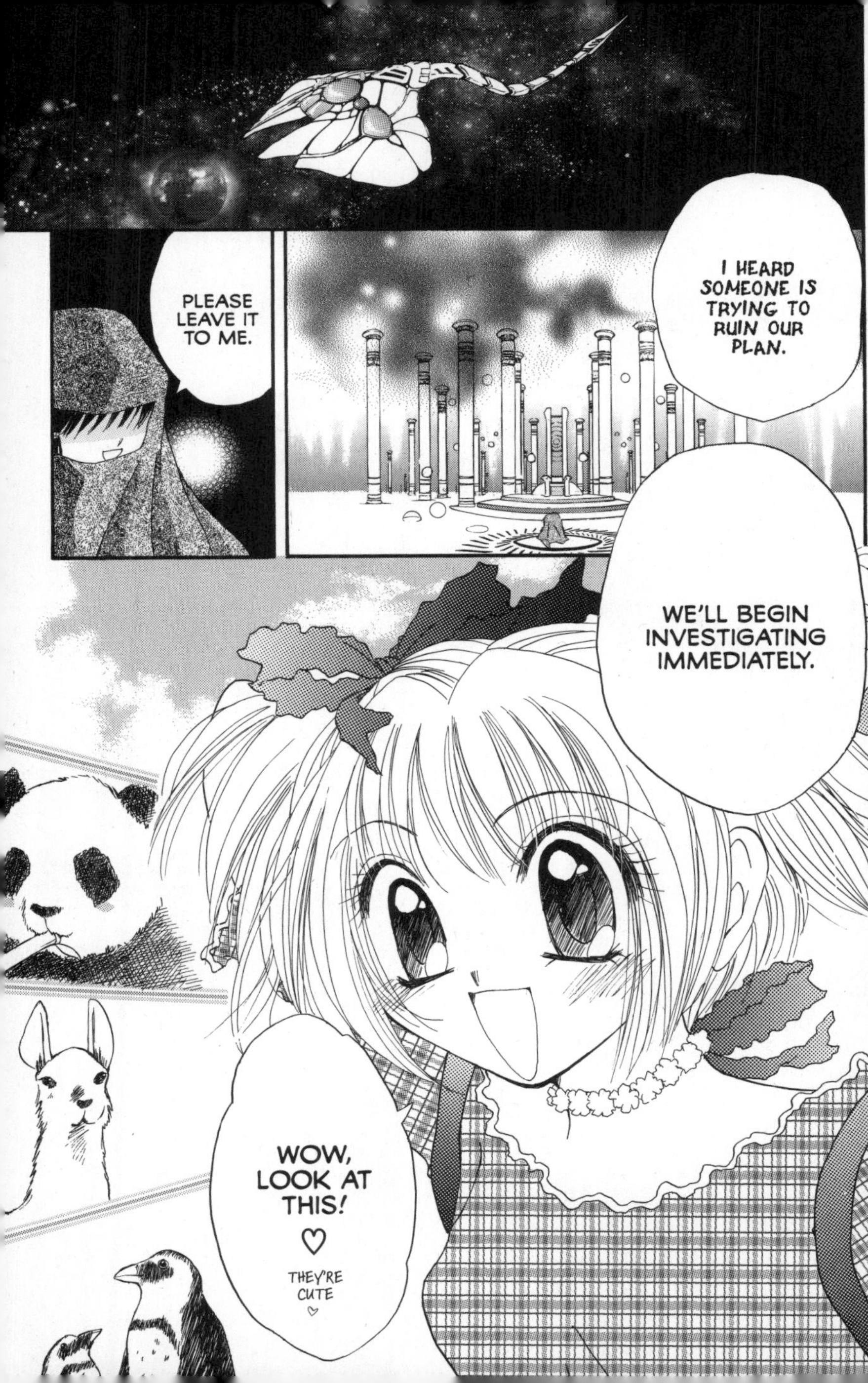
I HEARD SOMEONE IS TRYING TO RUIN OUR PLAN.
PLEASE LEAVE IT TO ME.
WE'LL BEGIN INVESTIGATING IMMEDIATELY.
WOW, LOOK AT THIS! ♡
THEY'RE CUTE ♡

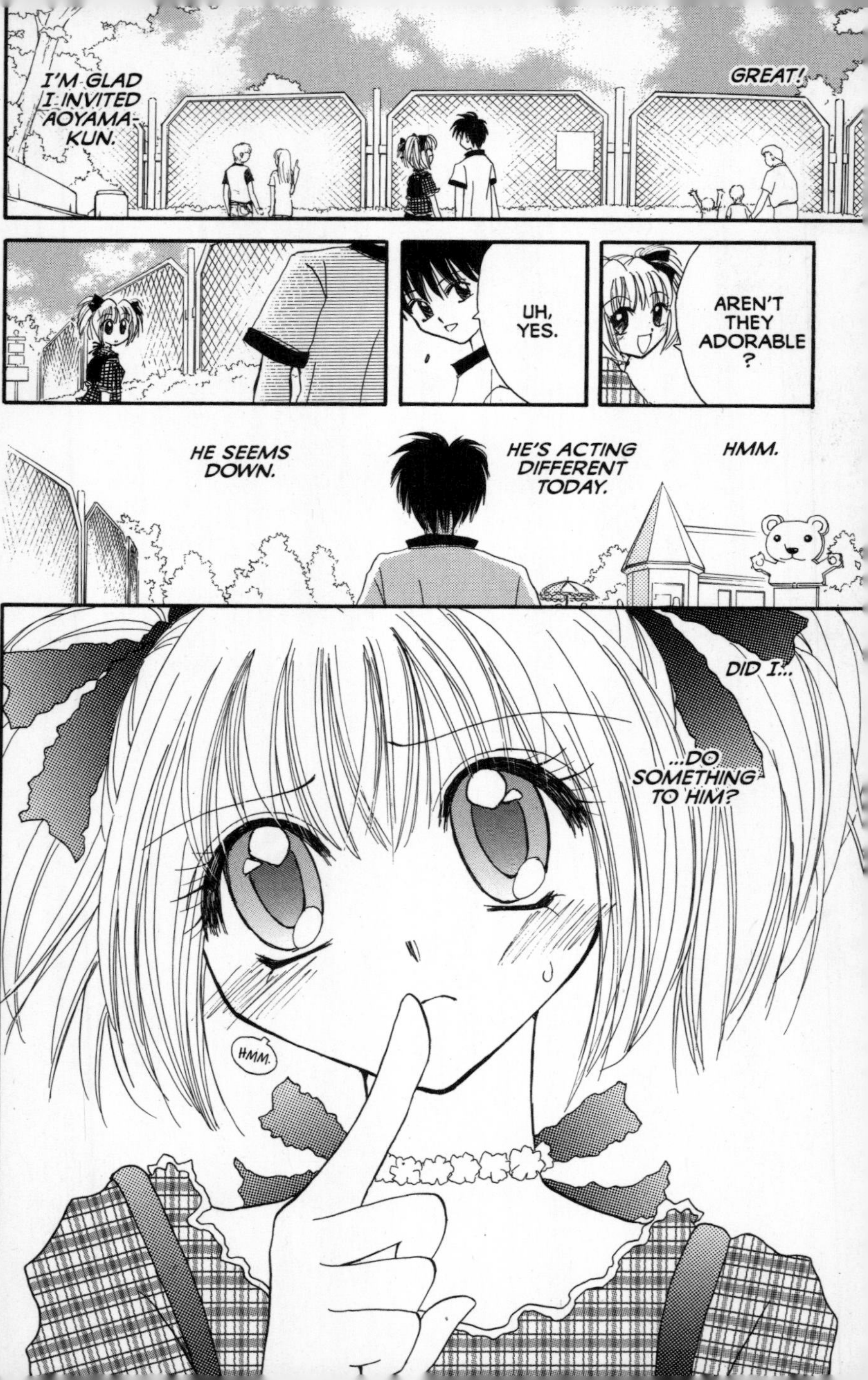
GREAT!
I'M GLAD I INVITED AOYAMA-KUN.
AREN'T THEY ADORABLE?
UH, YES.
HMM.
HE'S ACTING DIFFERENT TODAY.
HE SEEMS DOWN.
DID I...
...DO SOMETHING TO HIM?
HMM.

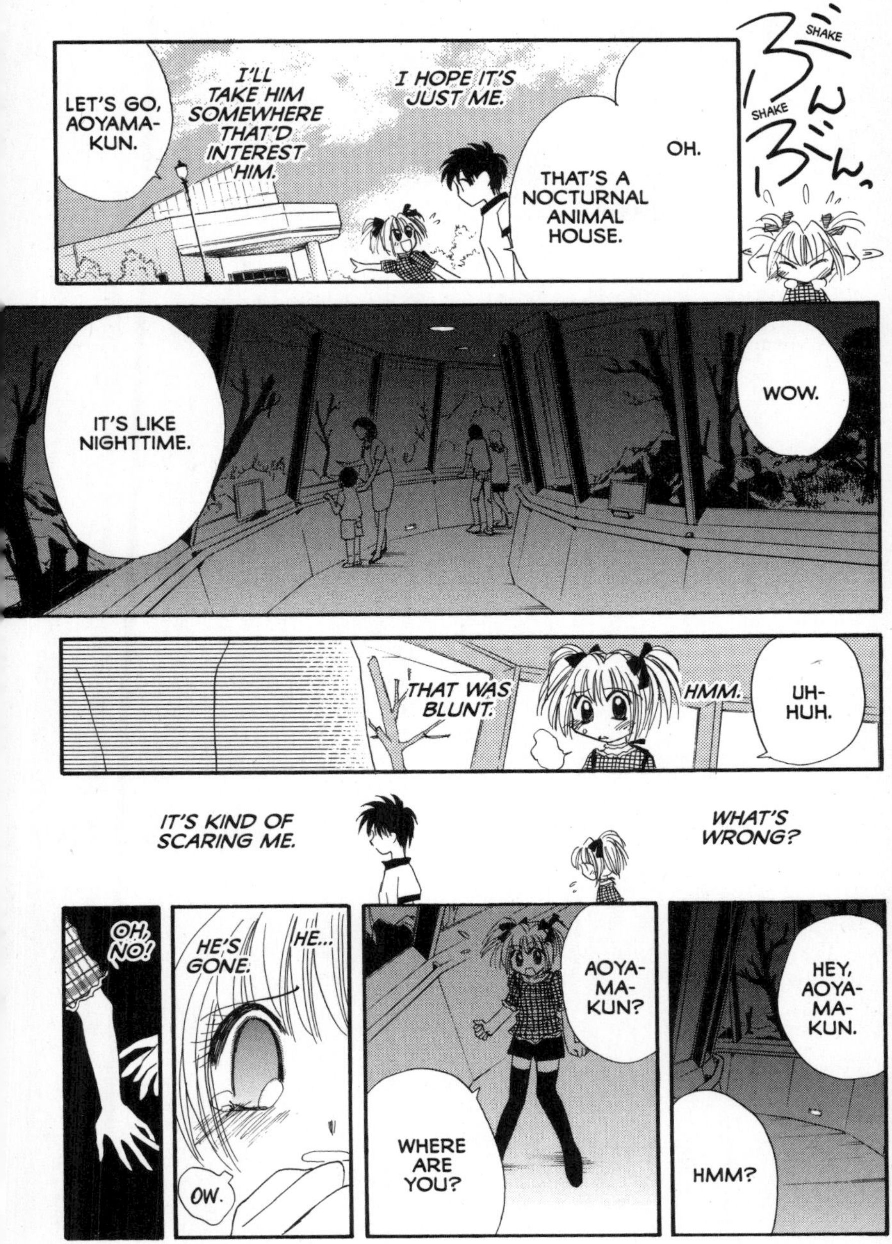
SHAKE
SHAKE
OH.
THAT'S A NOCTURNAL ANIMAL HOUSE.
I HOPE IT'S JUST ME.
I'LL TAKE HIM SOMEWHERE THAT'D INTEREST HIM.
LET'S GO, AOYAMA-KUN.
WOW.
IT'S LIKE NIGHTTIME.
UH-HUH.
HMM.
THAT WAS BLUNT.
WHAT'S WRONG?
IT'S KIND OF SCARING ME.
HEY, AOYAMA-KUN.
HMM?
AOYAMA-KUN?
WHERE ARE YOU?
HE...
HE'S GONE.
OW.
OH, NO!

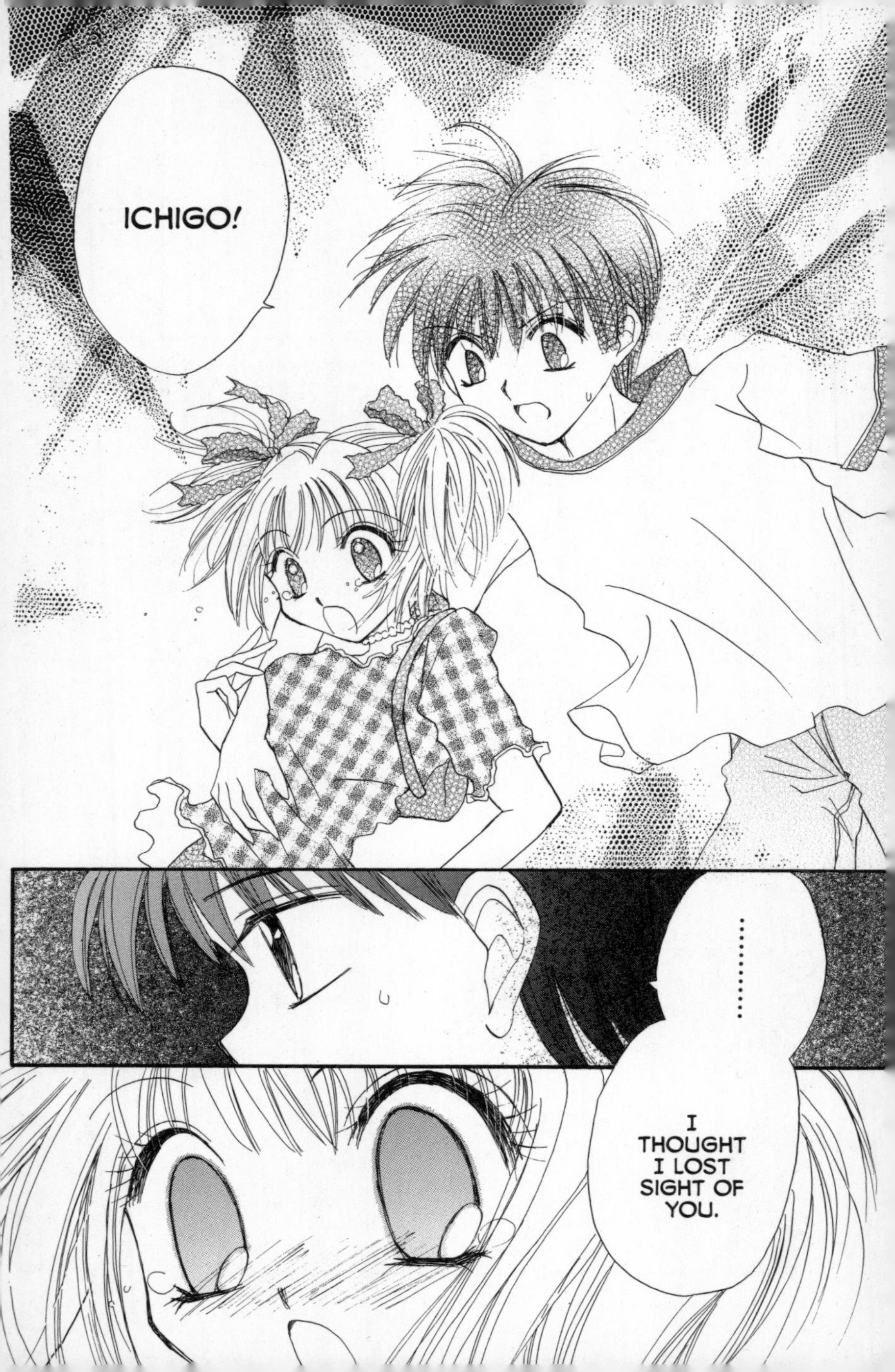
ICHIGO!
......
I THOUGHT I LOST SIGHT OF YOU.

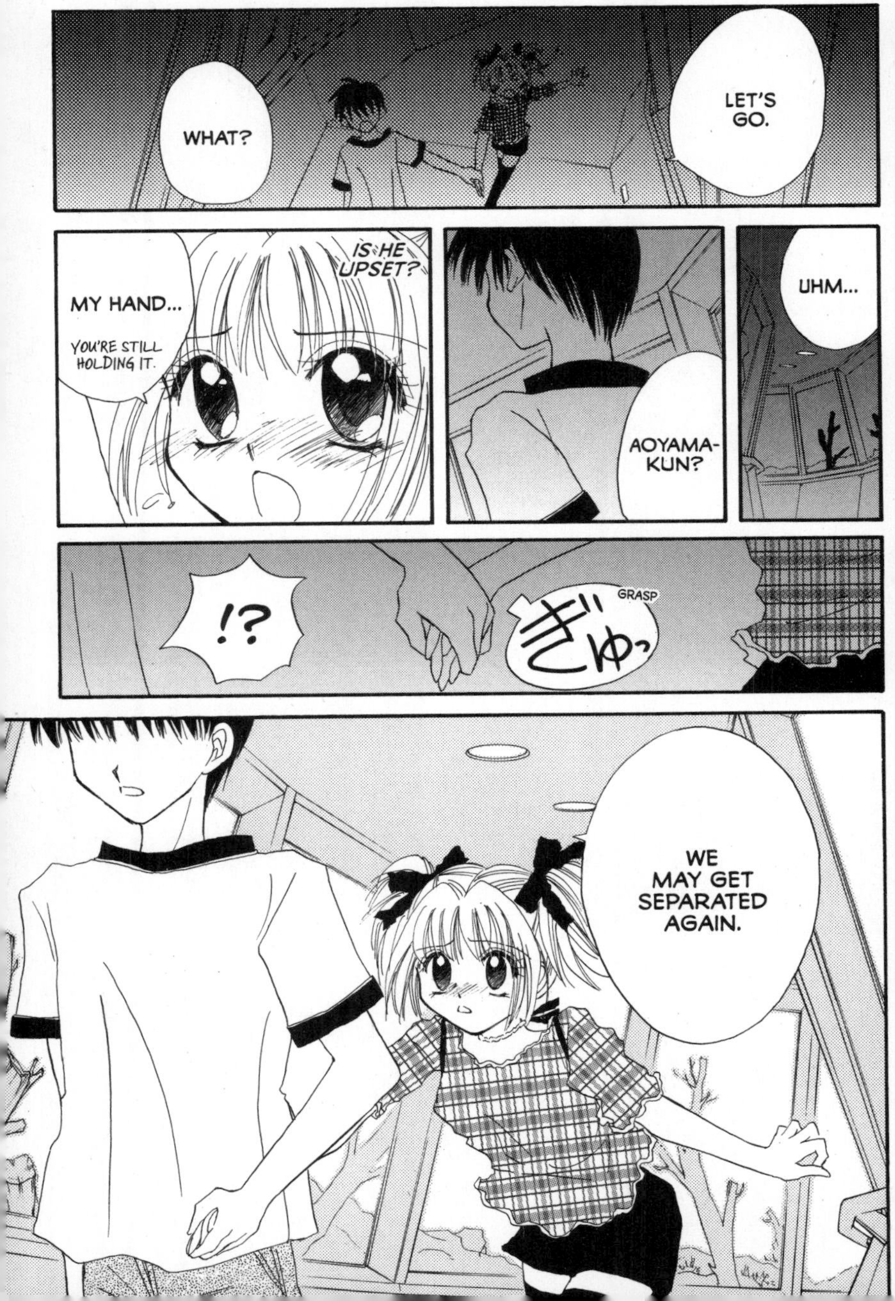
LET'S GO.
WHAT?
UHM...
AOYAMA-KUN?
IS HE UPSET?
MY HAND...
YOU'RE STILL HOLDING IT.
ぎゅっ
GRASP
!?
WE MAY GET SEPARATED AGAIN.

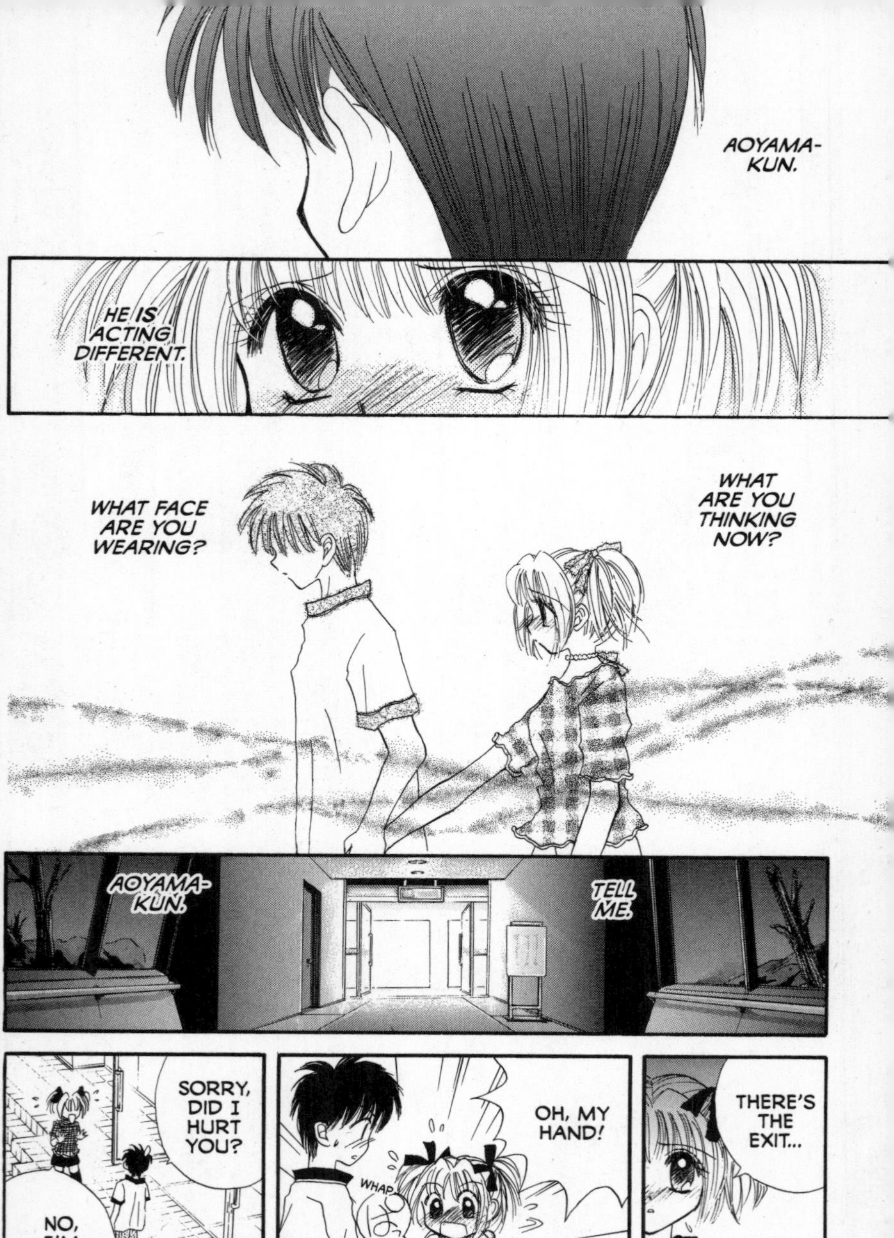
AOYAMA-KUN.
HE IS ACTING DIFFERENT.
WHAT ARE YOU THINKING NOW?
WHAT FACE ARE YOU WEARING?
TELL ME.
AOYAMA-KUN.
THERE'S THE EXIT...
OH, MY HAND!
WHAP
SORRY, DID I HURT YOU?
NO, I'M OKAY.

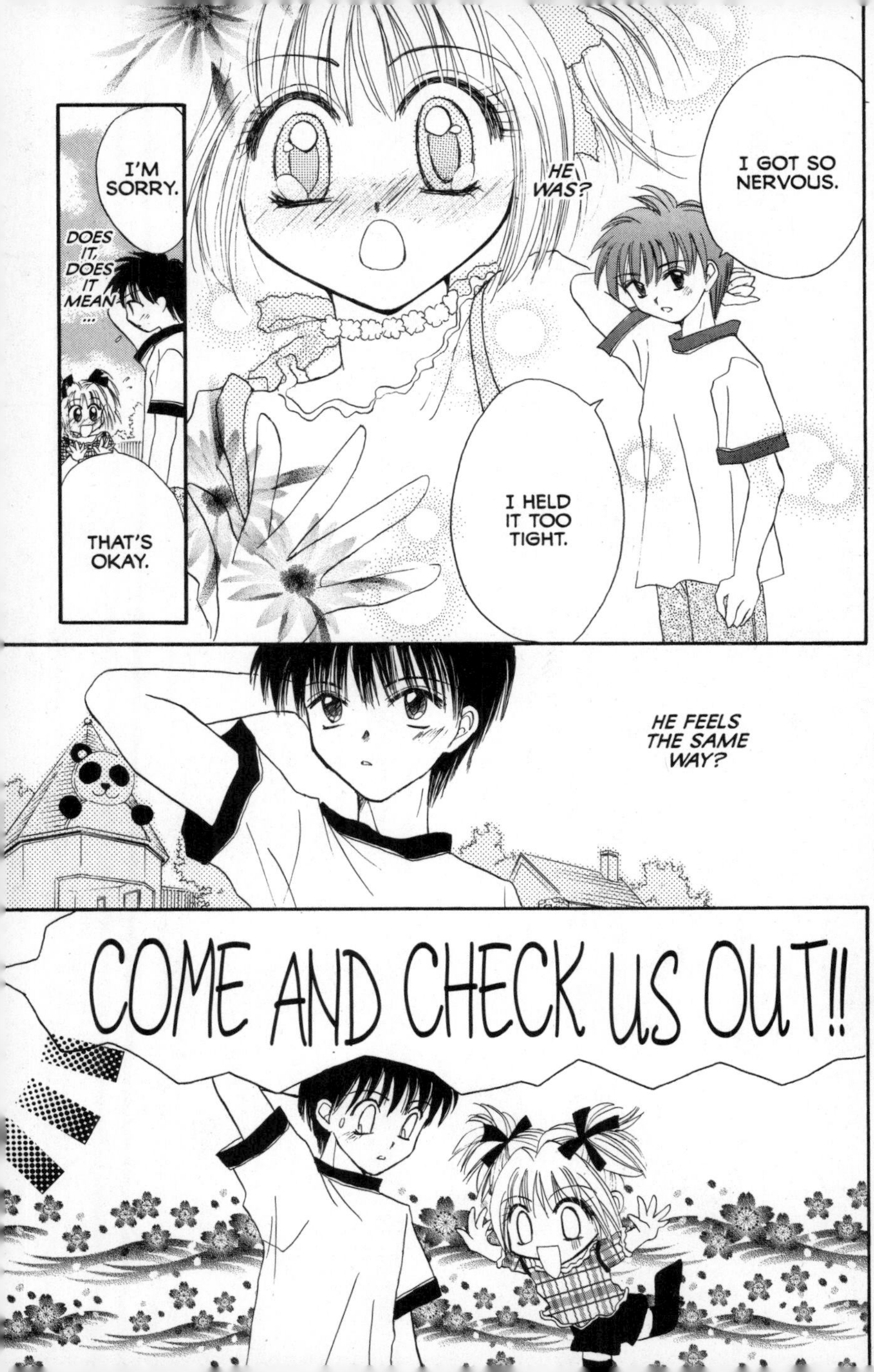

I GOT SO NERVOUS.
I HELD IT TOO TIGHT.
HE WAS?
I'M SORRY.
DOES IT, DOES IT MEAN ...
THAT'S OKAY.
HE FEELS THE SAME WAY?
COME AND CHECK US OUT!!

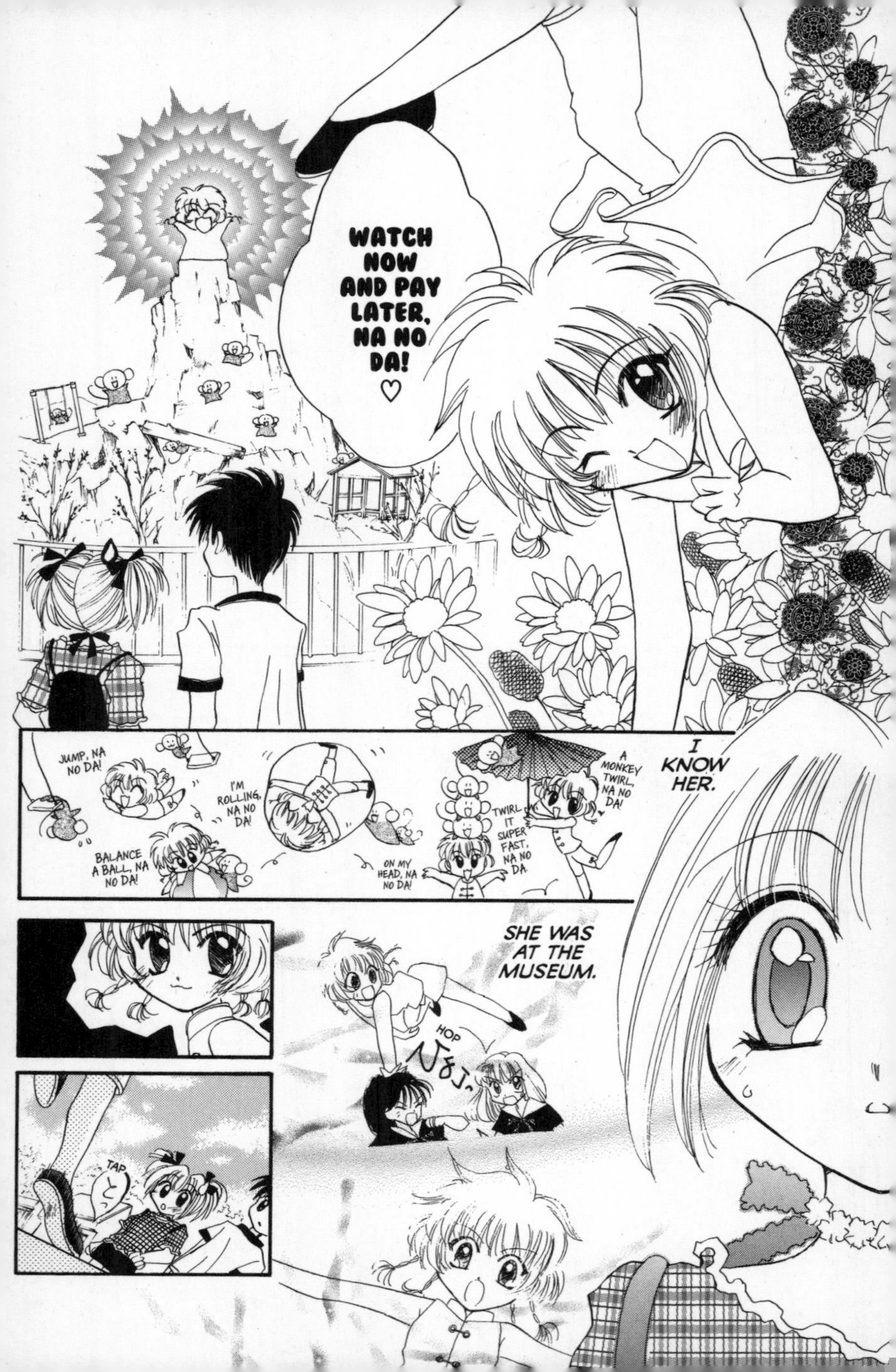
WATCH NOW AND PAY LATER, NA NO DA! ♡
I KNOW HER.
SHE WAS AT THE MUSEUM.
A MONKEY TWIRL, NA NO DA!
TWIRL IT SUPER FAST, NA NO DA.
ON MY HEAD, NA NO DA!
I'M ROLLING, NA NO DA!
BALANCE A BALL, NA NO DA!
JUMP, NA NO DA!
HOP
TAP

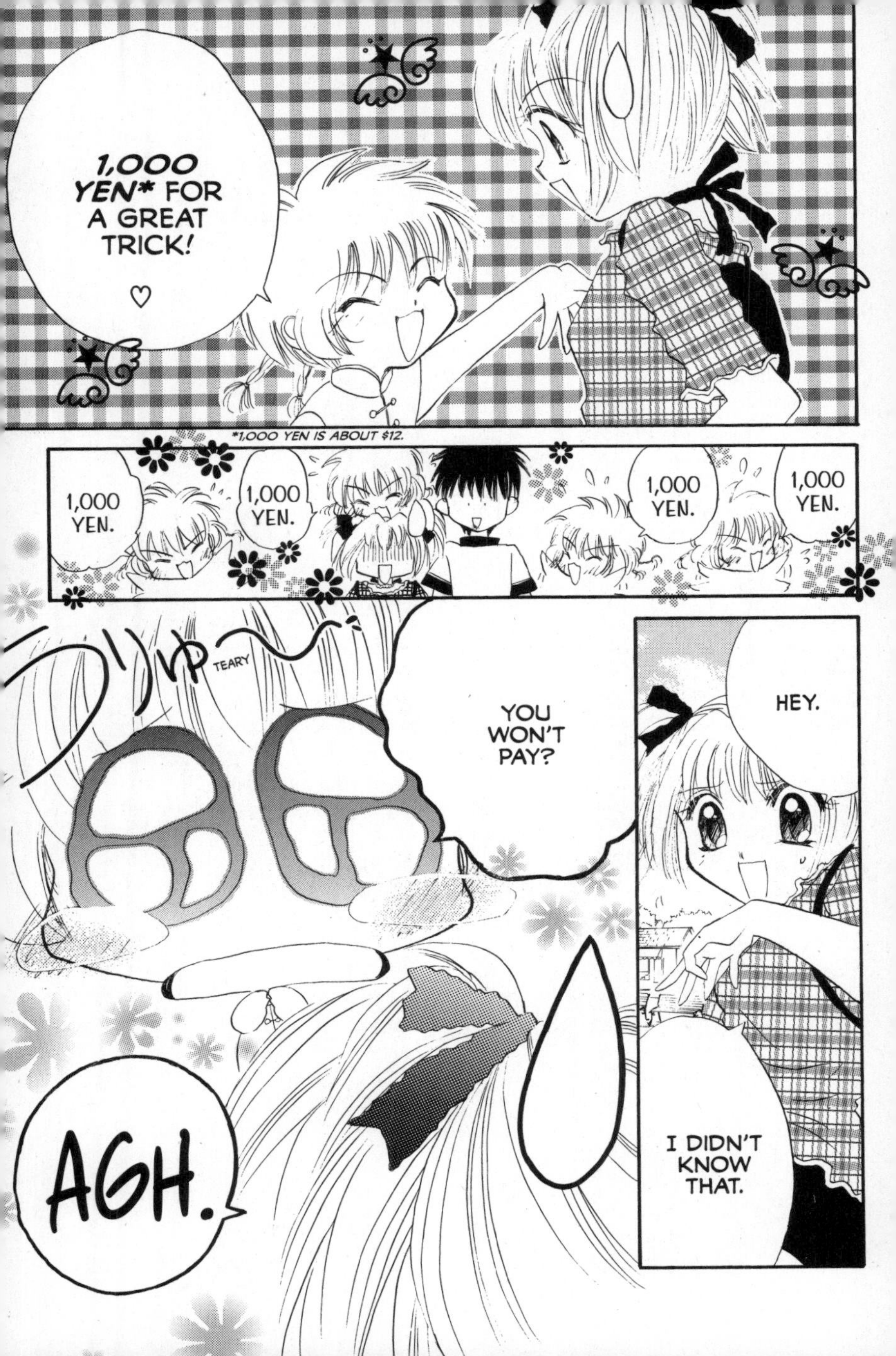
1,000 YEN* FOR A GREAT TRICK! ♡
1,000 YEN.
1,000 YEN.
1,000 YEN.
1,000 YEN.
HEY.
I DIDN'T KNOW THAT.
うりゅ～
TEARY
YOU WON'T PAY?
AGH.
*1,000 YEN IS ABOUT $12.

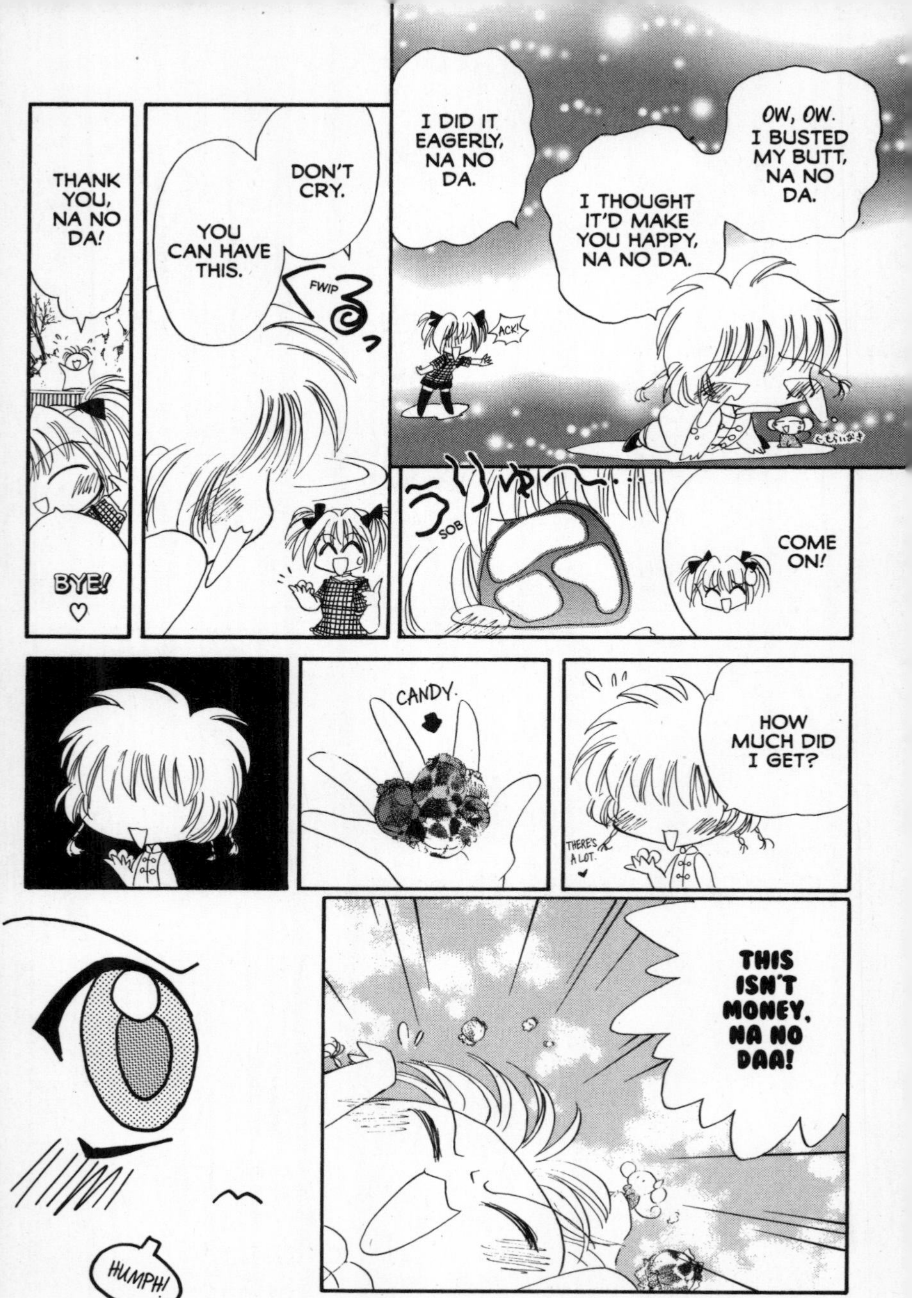
OW, OW. I BUSTED MY BUTT, NA NO DA.
I THOUGHT IT'D MAKE YOU HAPPY, NA NO DA.
I DID IT EAGERLY, NA NO DA.
ACK!
COME ON!
SOB
DON'T CRY.
YOU CAN HAVE THIS.
FWIP
THANK YOU, NA NO DA!
BYE! ♡
HOW MUCH DID I GET?
THERE'S A LOT. ♥
CANDY.
THIS ISN'T MONEY, NA NO DAA!
HUMPH!

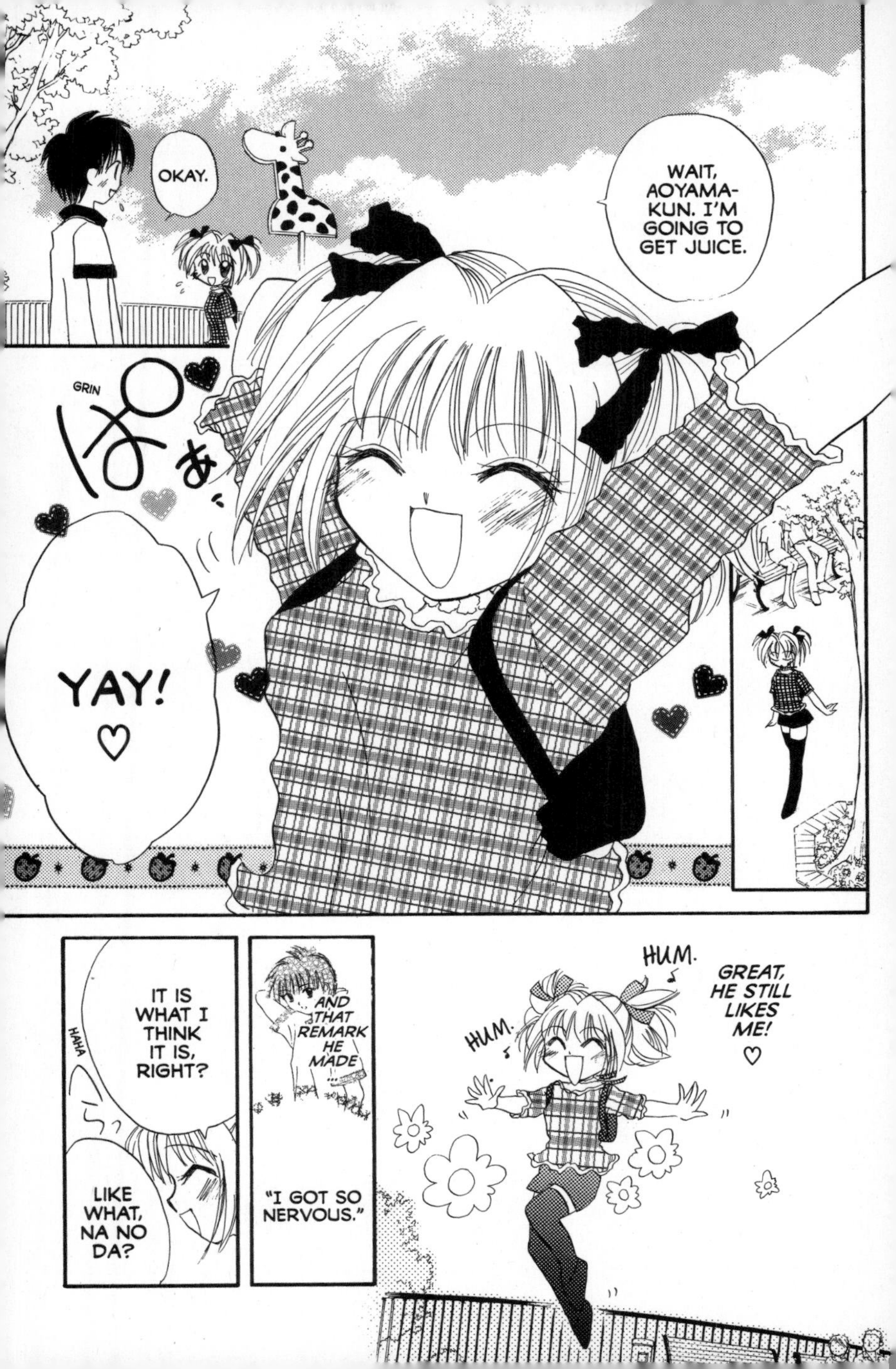
WAIT, AOYAMA-KUN. I'M GOING TO GET JUICE.
OKAY.
GRIN
YAY! ♡
HUM.
GREAT, HE STILL LIKES ME! ♡
HUM.
AND THAT REMARK HE MADE...
"I GOT SO NERVOUS."
IT IS WHAT I THINK IT IS, RIGHT?
HAHA
LIKE WHAT, NA NO DA?

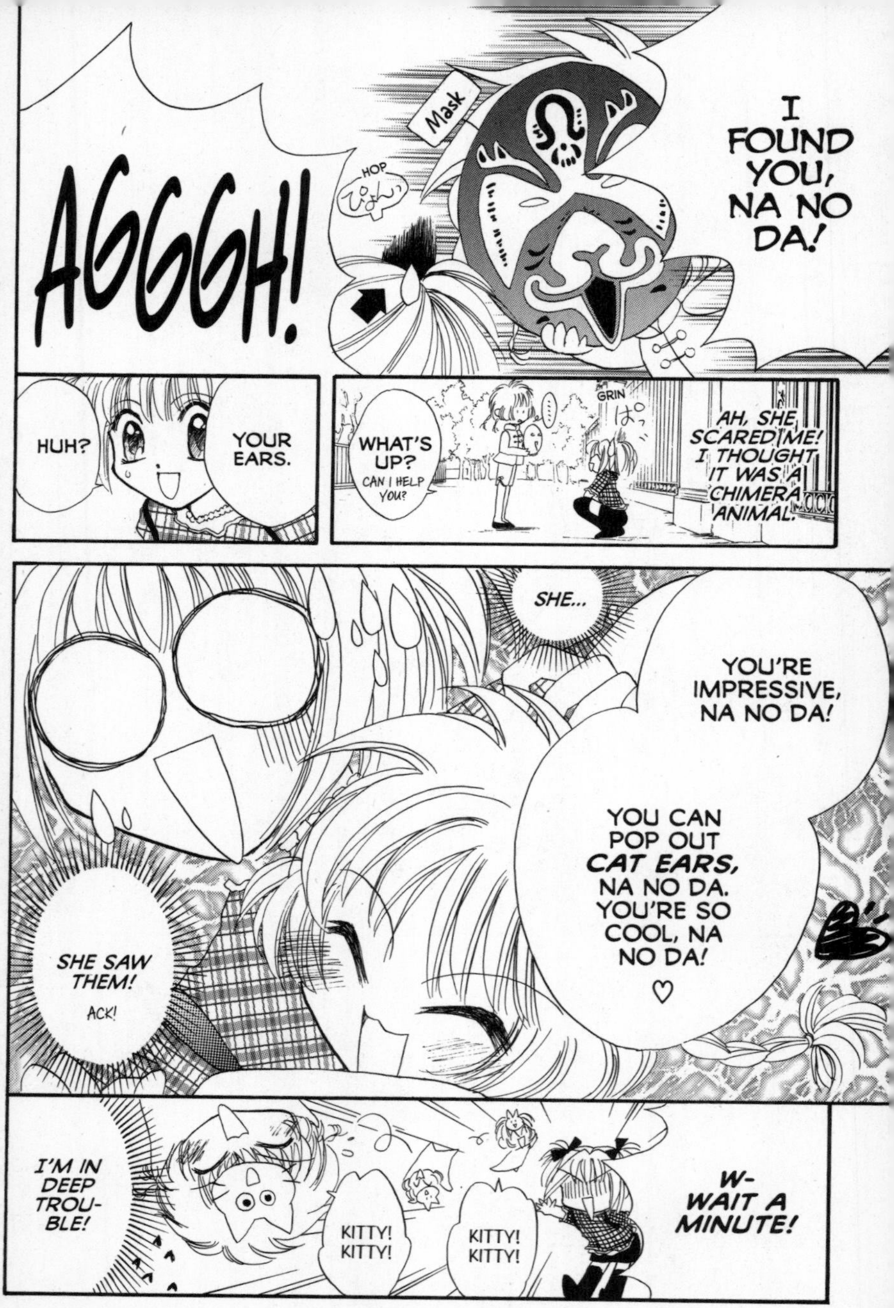
I FOUND YOU, NA NO DA!
Mask
HOP
ぴょんっ
AGGGH!
AH, SHE SCARED ME! I THOUGHT IT WAS A CHIMERA ANIMAL.
GRIN
ぱっ
...
WHAT'S UP?
CAN I HELP YOU?
YOUR EARS.
HUH?
SHE...
YOU'RE IMPRESSIVE, NA NO DA!
YOU CAN POP OUT CAT EARS, NA NO DA. YOU'RE SO COOL, NA NO DA! ♡
SHE SAW THEM!
ACK!
W-WAIT A MINUTE!
KITTY! KITTY!
KITTY! KITTY!
I'M IN DEEP TROUBLE!

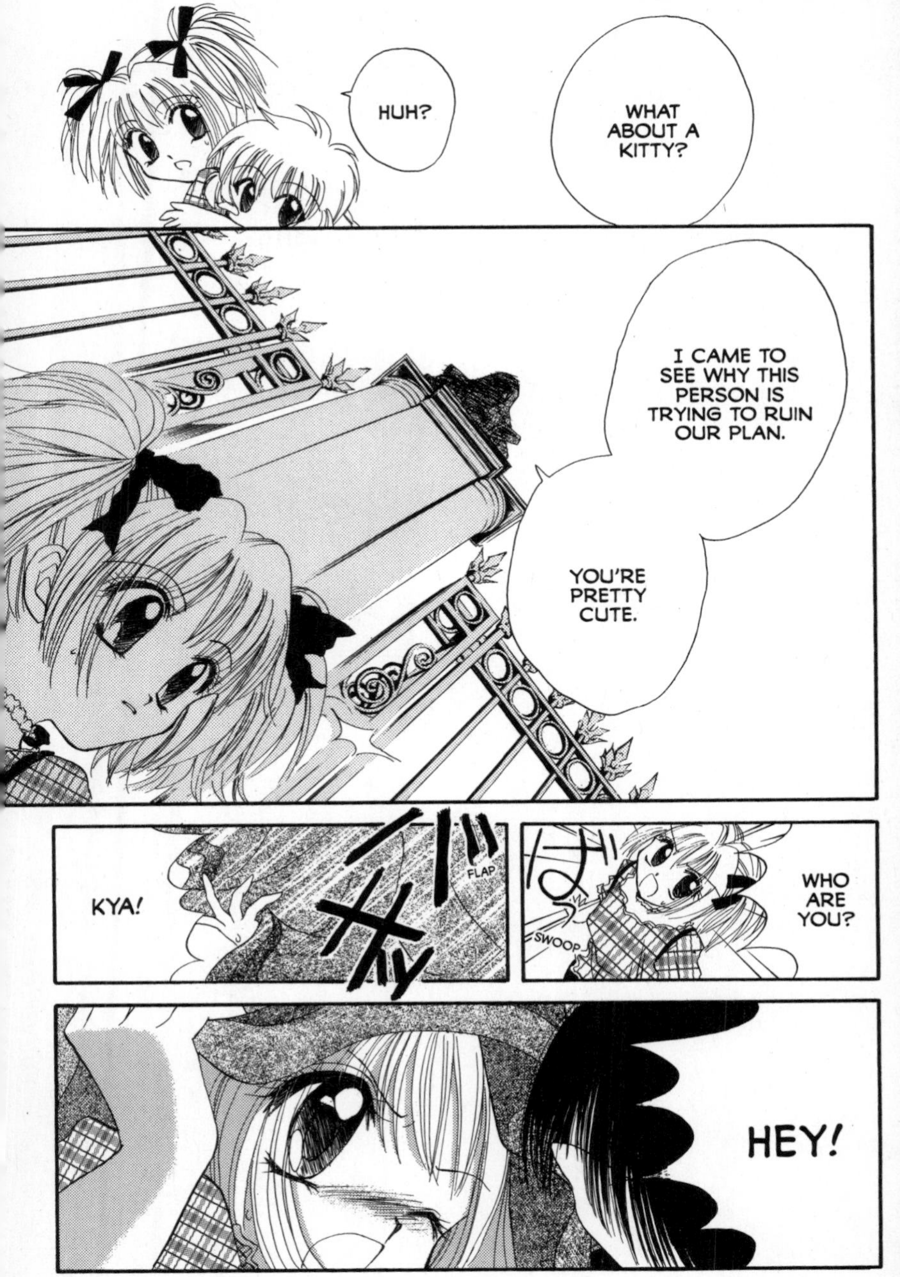
WHAT ABOUT A KITTY?
HUH?
I CAME TO SEE WHY THIS PERSON IS TRYING TO RUIN OUR PLAN.
YOU'RE PRETTY CUTE.
WHO ARE YOU?
SWOOP
FLAP
KYA!
HEY!

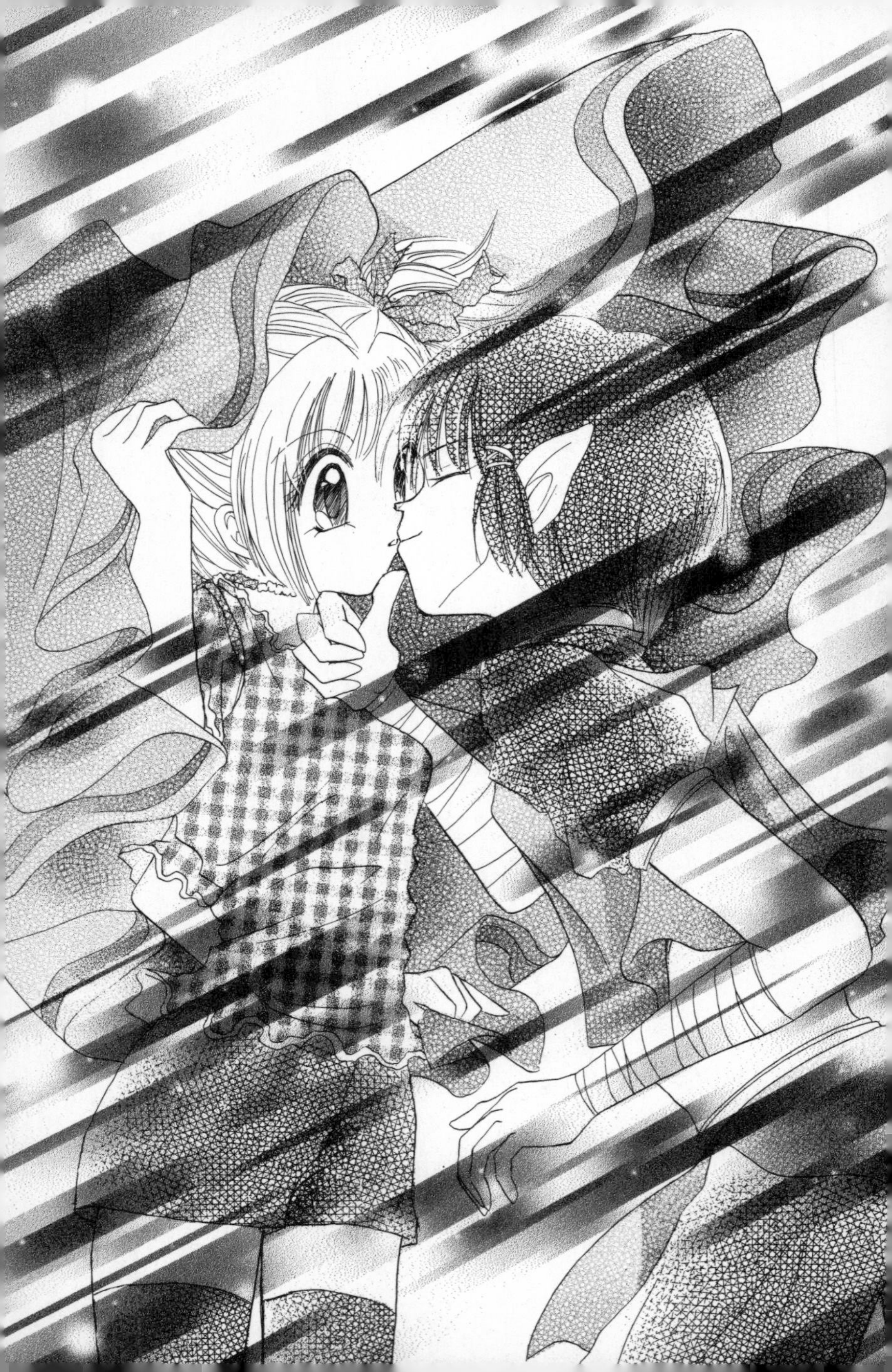

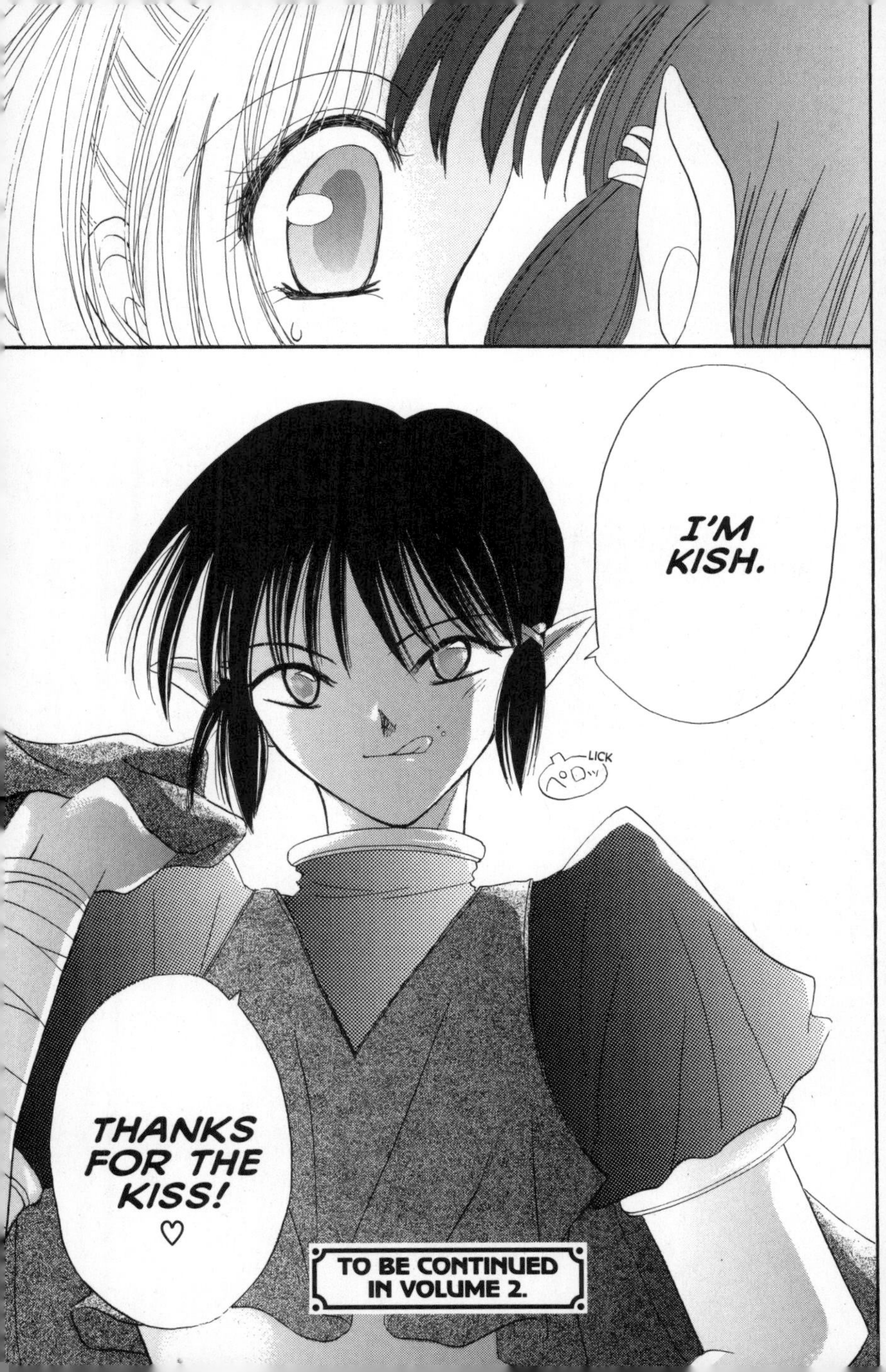
I'M KISH.
ペロッ
LICK
THANKS FOR THE KISS! ♡
TO BE CONTINUED IN VOLUME 2.

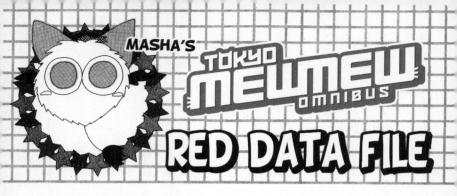

MASHA'S TOKYO MEW MEW OMNIBUS
RED DATA FILE

WHAT ARE "RED DATA" ANIMALS?

THEY'RE ANIMALS AT RISK OF EXTINCTION AND CURRENTLY THERE ARE 2,580 SPECIES WORLDWIDE. IT'S DUE TO OVERHUNTING AND ECOLOGICAL DESTRUCTION. LET'S COME TOGETHER AND SAVE THESE ENDANGERED ANIMALS!

FILE 3. FINLESS PORPOISE

SIZE: ABOUT 150 CM* IN HEAD AND BODY LENGTH AND ABOUT 40 KG* IN WEIGHT. HABITAT: INDO-PACIFIC OCEAN AND RIVERS FROM IRAN TO JAPAN.

RELATED TO DOLPHINS AND DESIGNATED AS A PROTECTED SPECIES IN 1930, FINLESS PORPOISES HAVE CUTE SMOOTH FACIAL FEATURES. UNLIKE DOLPHINS, THEY TRAVEL IN SMALL GROUPS OF ONE TO THREE ANIMALS. THEY'RE ENDANGERED BECAUSE THEY'RE SUBJECT TO OVERHUNTING FOR THEIR MEAT AND FAT OR DAMAGING FISHING NETS.

*50 CM IS ABOUT 19.7 IN. 25 CM IS ABOUT 9.8 IN.

THE DNA STRAINS OF THESE ENDANGERED SPECIES HAVE BEEN IMPLANTED IN ICHIGO-CHAN AND HER FRIENDS.

IRIOMOTE WILDCAT ------- ICHIGO
BLUE LORIKEET ----------- MINT
FINLESS PORPOISE -------- LETTUCE

THE OTHER TWO TEAMMATES WILL BE INTRODUCED IN *VOLUME 2.*

CHECK OUT THE WORK OF THE GIRLS WITH THESE DNA!

Bam with Ichigo☆

TOKYO MEW MEW MINI-STORY

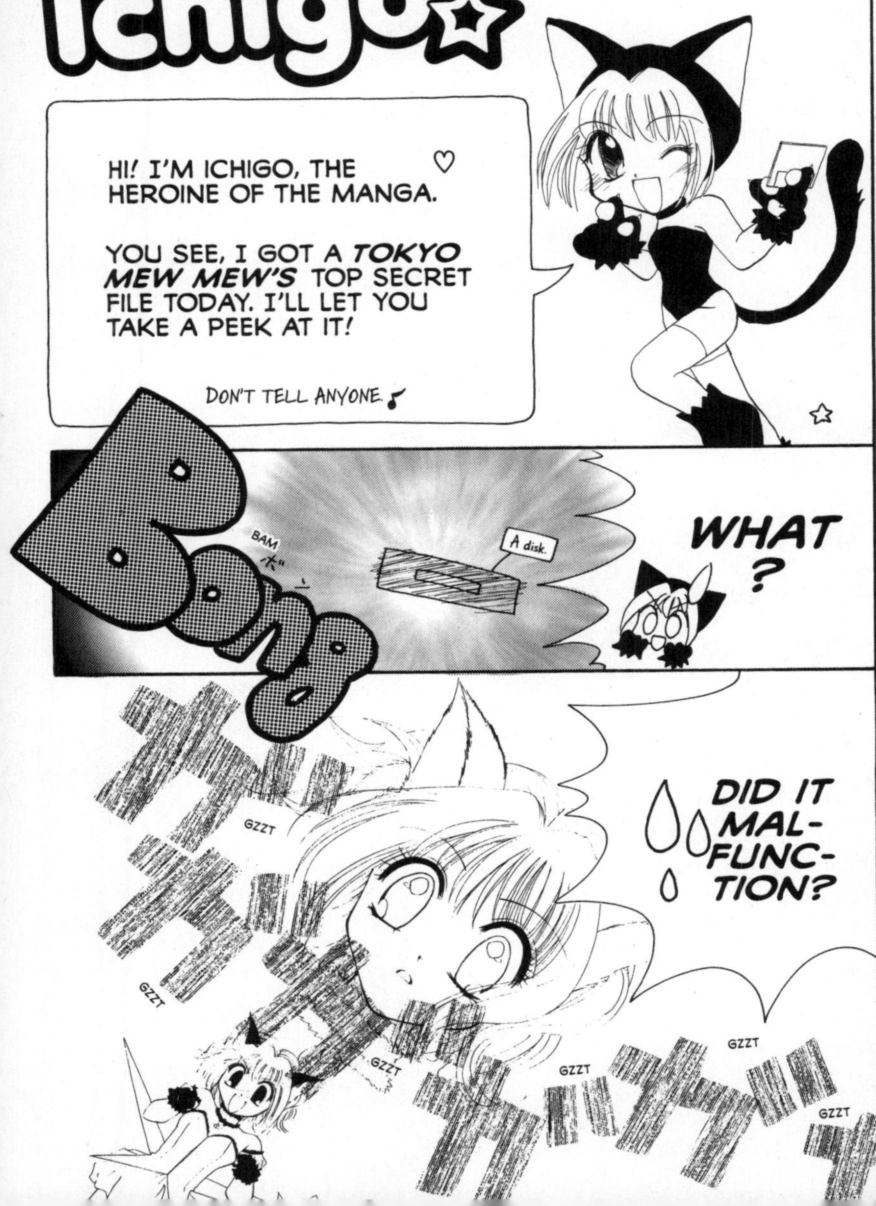

HI! I'M ICHIGO, THE HEROINE OF THE MANGA. ♡
YOU SEE, I GOT A *TOKYO MEW MEW'S* TOP SECRET FILE TODAY. I'LL LET YOU TAKE A PEEK AT IT!
DON'T TELL ANYONE. ♪
WHAT?
A disk.
BAM
Bang
DID IT MAL-FUNC-TION?
GZZT
GZZT
GZZT
GZZT
GZZT
GZZT

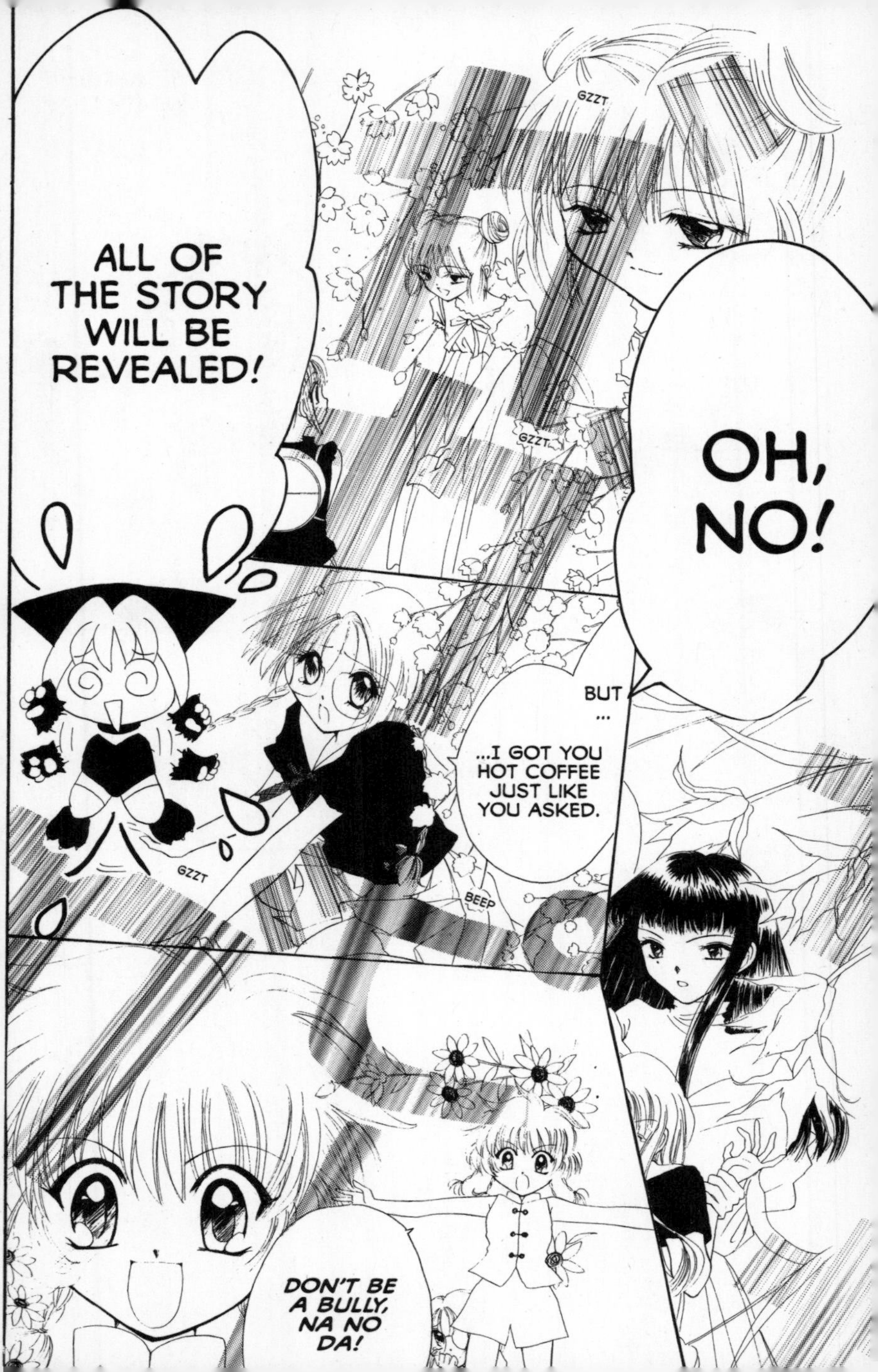
GZZT
OH, NO!
ALL OF THE STORY WILL BE REVEALED!
GZZT
BUT ...
...I GOT YOU HOT COFFEE JUST LIKE YOU ASKED.
BEEP
GZZT
DON'T BE A BULLY, NA NO DA!

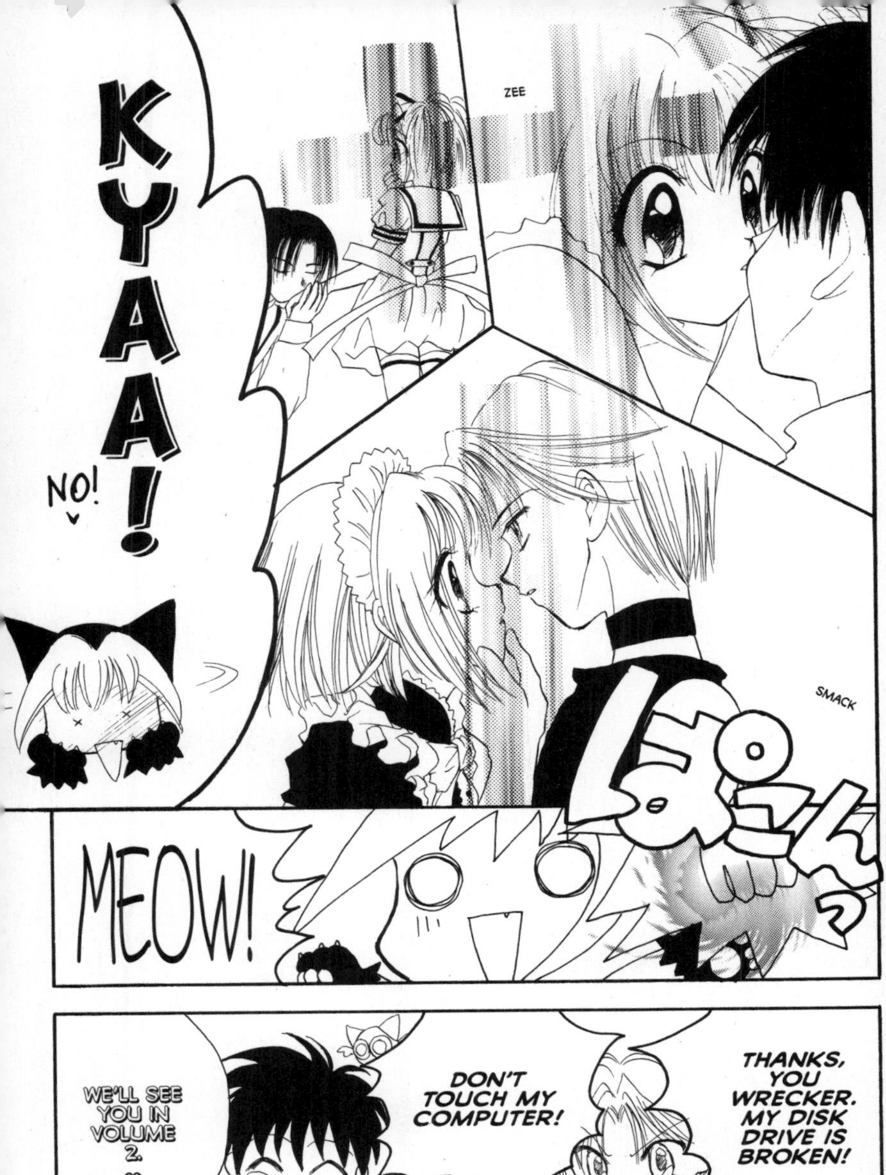
ZEE
SMACK
KYAA!
NO!
MEOW!
THANKS, YOU WRECKER. MY DISK DRIVE IS BROKEN!
FSST
FSST
DON'T TOUCH MY COMPUTER!
OKAY.
WE'LL SEE YOU IN VOLUME 2. ♡
Confiscated

THE END

CTION STAFF

TOKYO MEW MEW IS CREATED WITH A JOINT EFFORT BETWEEN VARIOUS PEOPLE. LET ME INTRODUCE YOU TO MEMBERS OF THIS POWERFUL TEAM!

GRAPHIC STAFF

MADOKA-ONESAMA,
BACKGROUND DESIGNER

SHE DESIGNS ELABORATE BACKGROUND FOR *TOKYO MEW MEW* AND HAS ALWAYS HELPED ME AS AN ASSISTANT. ♡

HER PEN WORK IS GREAT! ♡

RIMO-ONESAMA,
TECHNICAL ADVISER

A LADY WHO DEEPLY LOVES KISH. MOST OF THE TRICKS ARE INVENTED BY HER. NOWADAYS SHE WORKS AS MY MAIN ASSISTANT AS WELL. HER TONE TECHNIQUE IS SUPERB!

ASSISTANTS

HOSHINA-SAN

SHE'S MY MAIN ASSISTANT WHO'S GOOD AT TEMPLATES AND WHITE INK LAYER. AND HER HAMSTER DRAWING IS AMAZING!

ASUMIN

A RAINBOW MASKED WOMAN WHO ALWAYS BRINGS MINI-DISCS. SHE LOVES INOCCHI!

AND AYA SUZUKI-CHAN, MICHIYO KIKUTA-CHAN AND YAMASHITA-SAN.

THANKS FOR YOUR HELP!

WE'LL KEEP WORKING HARD, MEOW! ♡

MANGA CREATOR

IKUMI MIA,
COMIC ARTIST

AS WELL AS SUPERVISING MANGA CREATION, SHE DESIGNS CHARACTER AND ITEMS. RUMOR HAS IT THAT SHE'S THE MOST INCOMPETENT STA

TOKYO MEW MEW OMNIBUS PRODU

MEW MEW IS AMAZING. IT'S CREATED BY THE MIGHTY HANDS OF THESE PEOPLE!

ORIGINAL STORY STAFF

REIKO YOSHIDA, SCENARIO WRITER

I LOVE CRAB ROLLS!

A DEPENDABLE LADY WHOSE WORKS INCLUDE DIGITAL MONSTERS AND YUME NO CRAYON OKOKU. WE CAN'T CREATE MANGA WITHOUT HER DIALOGUES. SHE'S A MOTHER OF ONE. ♡

SEKIYACCHI, STRATEGIC DESIGNER

HE ORGANIZES THE OVERALL CONCEPT FOR THE MANGA. MY EDITOR SINCE I WAS A ROOKIE AND A SCARY INDIVIDUAL WHO FORCES ME TO WEAR CAT EARS AT EVENTS.

KAMAYAN, ADVANCED EDITOR

SHE SUGGESTS DETAILED IDEAS FOR MANGA SUCH AS CHARACTER BEHAVIOR, EPISODES AND DIALOGUES. A LADY WHO SECRETLY GAVE ME SHOES.

MECHANICAL STAFF

HIDEAKI OIKAWA, MECHANICAL DESIGNER

HE TAKES MY USELESS IMAGES AND RECREATES THEM INTO REALISTIC SPACESHIPS AND ELECTRONIC DEVICES IN *TOKYO MEW MEW.*

WHAT WOULD YOU DO IF YOU HAD CAT DNA IMPLANTED
INTO YOU, TRANSFORMED INTO A CAT AND WERE
ORDERED TO FIGHT?

A ...RESIGN YOURSELF TO FIGHTING THE ENEMIES.

B ...THINK OF THIS AS FATE AND AGGRESSIVELY
SAVE THE EARTH.

C ...WONDER WHAT TO DO IN THIS SITUATION.

D ...THINK OF HOW TO MAKE A LIVING,
NOT FIGHTING WITH YOUR ABILITY.

E ...GO ON YOUR WAY BECAUSE FIGHTING HAS
NOTHING TO DO WITH YOU.

IF YOU CHOSE A, YOU'RE EASILY INFLUENCED
AND SHOULD HAVE COURAGE TO SAY NO. IF YOU
CHOSE B, TRY NOT TO BECOME A MISUNDER-
STOOD PERSON. IF YOU CHOSE C, TAKE IT EASY
AND THINK POSITIVELY. IF YOU CHOSE D, HAVE
MORE PASSION FOR LIFE. IF YOU CHOSE E, DON'T
BECOME A LONER. EACH TYPE DESCRIBES ICHIGO,
MINT, LETTUCE, PUDDING AND ZACRO, IN THAT
ORDER. WHICH ONE ARE YOU? THEY'VE EACH
CHOSEN THE SAME FATE, BUT THEY CHOSE A
DIFFERENT PATH. I THINK THAT YOU'LL MANAGE
TO GET BY IF YOU MAKE THE MOST OF YOUR
PERSONALITY.

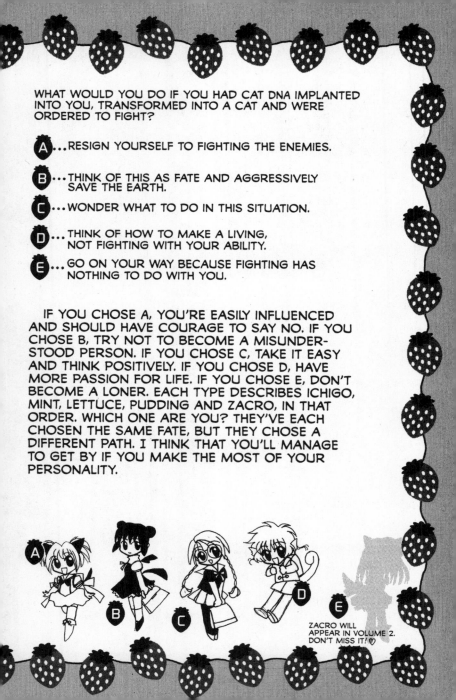

ZACRO WILL
APPEAR IN VOLUME 2.
DON'T MISS IT! ♡

MAKING OF

I FIRST MET IKUMI-SENSEI AT A CHINESE RESTAURANT IN A HOTEL IN TOKYO. SHE CAME DRESSED IN A PRETTY CHINA DRESS FOR THE OCCASION. SHE IS VERY PRETTY BUT IS SO NICE THAT SHE WOULD SHARE NIKUJAGA WITH HER NEIGHBORS. I HEARD THAT SHE WOULD NOT ONLY WEAR KITTY EARS BUT A KITTY TAIL AS WELL. I THOUGHT I COULD DO AN INTERESTING WORK WITH HER AND GLADLY TOOK CHARGE OF THE STORY.

THE PROCESS OF STORYMAKING BEGINS WITH A MEETING WITH A BRAINY EDITOR AND A GORGEOUS EDITOR IN WHICH WE CREATE SCENARIOS CONSISTING OF DIALOGUES AND STAGE DIRECTIONS. WE FINALIZE IT AFTER FURTHER DISCUSSION AND IKUMI-SENSEI CREATES A STORYBOARD BASED ON IT. THIS IS WHERE SHE ADDS HER IDEAS AND MAKES A GREAT MANGA.

WHO IS THIS CHARACTER? PART ONE

Is she a new member? Or Black Ichigo (laughs)? It's neither. The girl on the right is the memorable character I first presented to my editor for the series. At the time, I was suggested to do a horror manga. While I thought it sounded fun, I had always wanted to do a cat-type character even before my debut, prompting me to give it a shot. My editor liked her and quickly decided to do a story with her. As I was asked to create one character after another, I unintentionally ended up with a manga about a pretty girl squad (laughs).

I originally wanted to do a spunky heroine like her and had some skepticism about the final version of Ichigo. But, a heroine like this doesn't seem to be appropriate for Nakayoshi, either. °o To think that Mew Mew wouldn't exist if I hadn't created this character seems so weird.

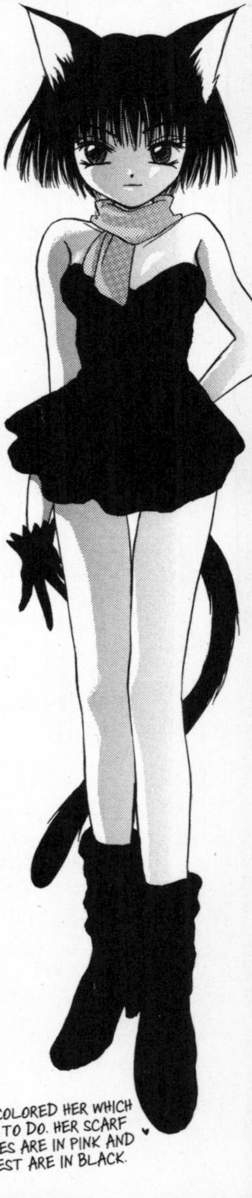

I EVEN COLORED HER WHICH I LOVE TO DO. HER SCARF AND EYES ARE IN PINK AND THE REST ARE IN BLACK. ♥

WHO IS THIS CHARACTER? PART TWO

This is another character I did per my editor's request. She's done in a similar color to Lettuce, grassy or light green. I had a personality like Izumi-chan from Super Doll Rika-Chan in my mind for her. She was my favorite character but she disappeared when I designed all five characters together. °o I want to do a mouse-type character someday!

These characters were created nearly two years ago. I was afraid the series wouldn't launch at first, but Tokyo Mew Mew turned into a humongous project after a scenario writer and a designer were added.

I've been offered to do magazine covers and cover pages and even colored pages for every chapter. I received lots of furoku and manga merchandise, too. They're treating me too well. They even made a television commercial. oo

MIA IKUMI'S SURPRISE COMMERCIAL FILMING REPORT

Story up to now: It's exciting to get Ichigo's uniform for the TV commercial, but I had to wear it and have my pictures taken.

I thought I'd talk about it getting into a manga newspaper.

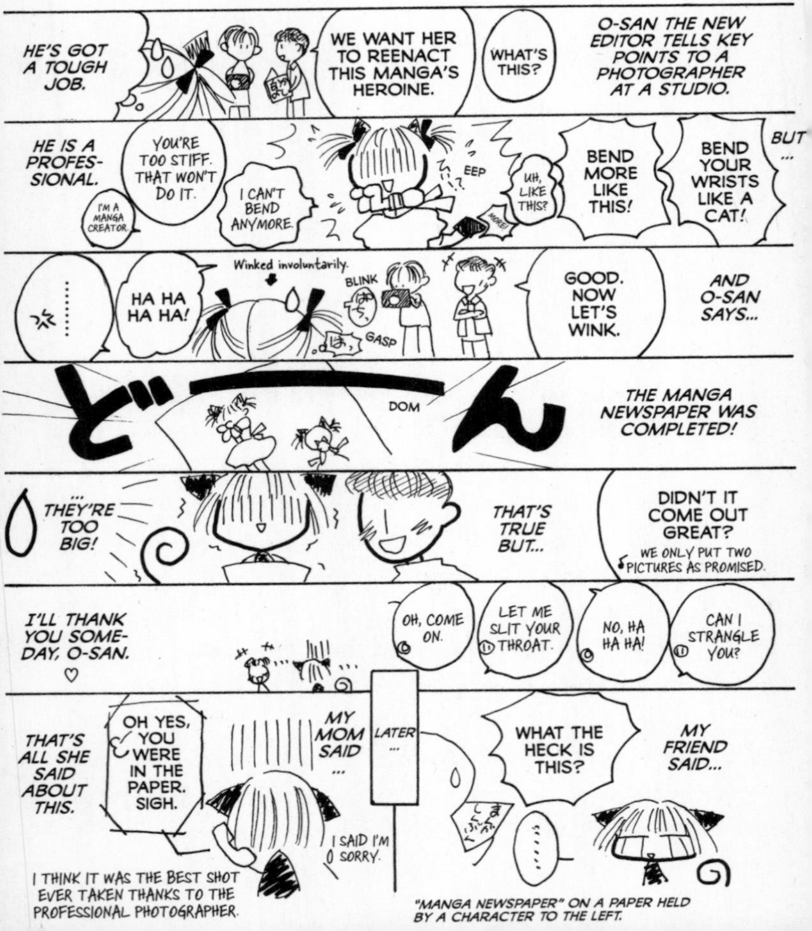

O-SAN THE NEW EDITOR TELLS KEY POINTS TO A PHOTOGRAPHER AT A STUDIO.
WHAT'S THIS?
WE WANT HER TO REENACT THIS MANGA'S HEROINE.
HE'S GOT A TOUGH JOB.
BUT ...
BEND YOUR WRISTS LIKE A CAT!
BEND MORE LIKE THIS!
MORE!
UH, LIKE THIS?
EEP
I CAN'T BEND ANYMORE.
YOU'RE TOO STIFF. THAT WON'T DO IT.
I'M A MANGA CREATOR.
HE IS A PROFESSIONAL.
AND O-SAN SAYS...
GOOD. NOW LET'S WINK.
BLINK
GASP
Winked involuntarily.
HA HA HA HA!
....
THE MANGA NEWSPAPER WAS COMPLETED!
DOM
DIDN'T IT COME OUT GREAT?
WE ONLY PUT TWO PICTURES AS PROMISED.
THAT'S TRUE BUT...
... THEY'RE TOO BIG!
CAN I STRANGLE YOU?
NO, HA HA HA!
LET ME SLIT YOUR THROAT.
OH, COME ON.
I'LL THANK YOU SOMEDAY, O-SAN. ♡
MY FRIEND SAID...
WHAT THE HECK IS THIS?
......
LATER ...
MY MOM SAID ...
OH YES, YOU WERE IN THE PAPER. SIGH.
I SAID I'M SORRY.
THAT'S ALL SHE SAID ABOUT THIS.
I THINK IT WAS THE BEST SHOT EVER TAKEN THANKS TO THE PROFESSIONAL PHOTOGRAPHER.
"MANGA NEWSPAPER" ON A PAPER HELD BY A CHARACTER TO THE LEFT.

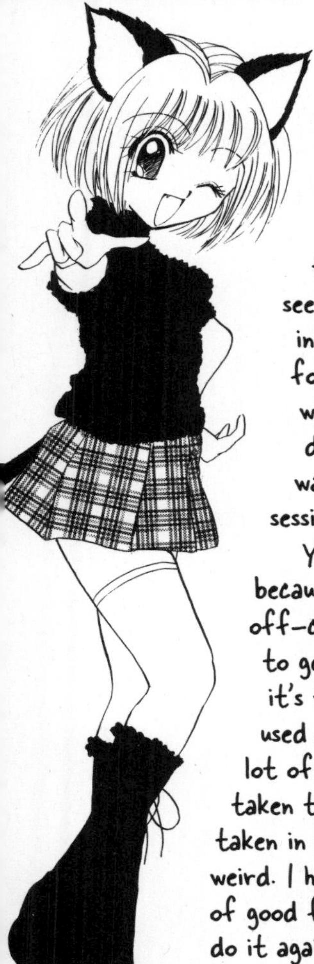
ACTING ICHIGO

It'd be worth attending events with my cat ears if everyone enjoys them in some way. Some who saw the paper may have thought they saw a rare thing and some may be glad they didn't see it. Anyone still willing to meet this inexperienced manga creator, please come for my autograph. I hope it's someone who wants to meet me. ♡ I'll be waiting dressed like the girl to the left. This was an outfit I wore to the autograph session in Nara.

You may not want to take my pictures because I don't look good in pictures or off-camera. Whenever I hear a fan failing to get a good shot of me, I don't believe it's the fault of the camera. it may be used as a charm. Anyway, I had an awful lot of pictures of me in my kitty outfit taken this year. While I rarely have my picture taken in private, it's all over Japan and it feels weird. I have fun meeting people and there's lots of good food at autograph sessions. ♡ I want to do it again. Thanks for coming, everyone. See you again!

Thank you to my friend, Ruka Hoshino-chan, for making the cat ears for me!

Finally, I want to give many thanks to everyone involved in this manga by creating, reading, supporting me, etc.

Thanks to the people I love. I'm here because of you. it's true. ♥

December 16, 2000   Mia Ikumi

Afterword ♥

I baked a chocolate cake the day I wrote this afterword and cookies on another day. I hadn't had time to make them for a few years since I began my career. it's been so long that I felt more thrilled than anything. Believing I would never bake again, I threw out all of my baking supplies when I got my own place, but I couldn't resist looking at them at stores. There was a time I got into trouble by giving away tons of homemade Christmas cakes. I'm about to get hooked on baking again.

   I've been too wrapped up in my work since my debut, but I finally got used to it that I could find time to do other things, which is a good thing. I love to do things for people like baking or creating manga to make them happy. I realize I'm fortunate to make a living out of it.

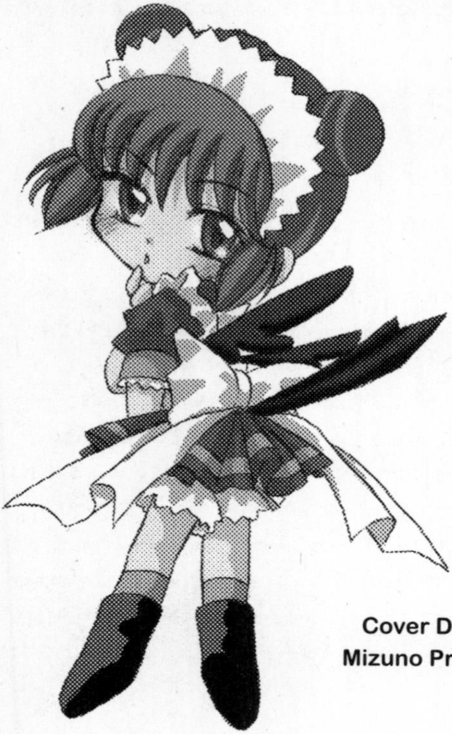

Cover Design by
Mizuno Productions

Born on March 27th, Aries, Blood type O, From Ôsaka Prefecture. She won the 24th Nakayoshi New Faces Manga Award with the manga Usagi no Furasu Hoshi in the year 1997, which made its debut in the January 1998 issue of Run-Run. Her featured works are Super Doll Rika-Chan and Ichigo no Mori no Nemurihime. She enjoys playing with her cat and wearing cute (weird?) clothes.

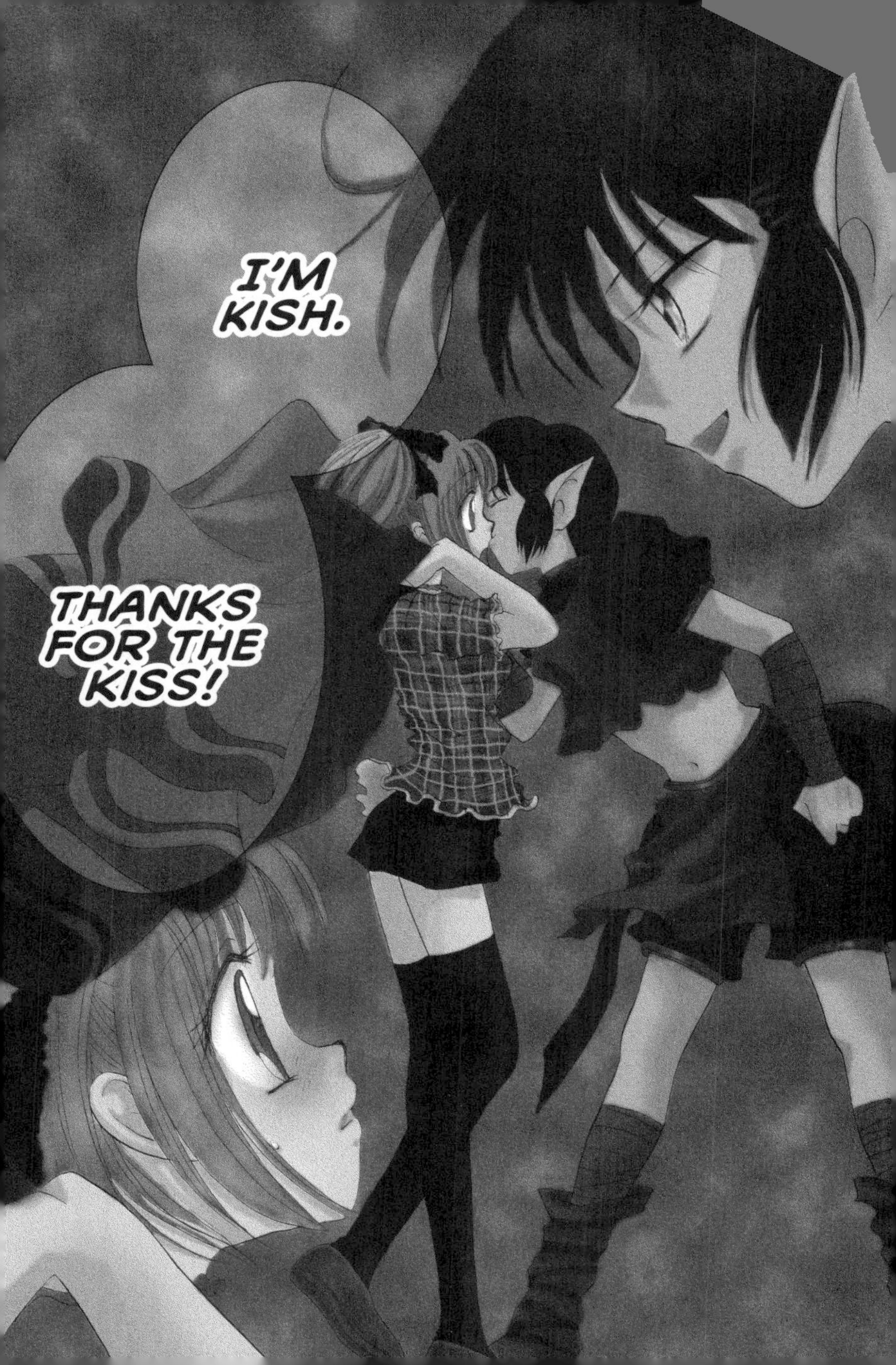
I'M KISH.
THANKS FOR THE KISS!

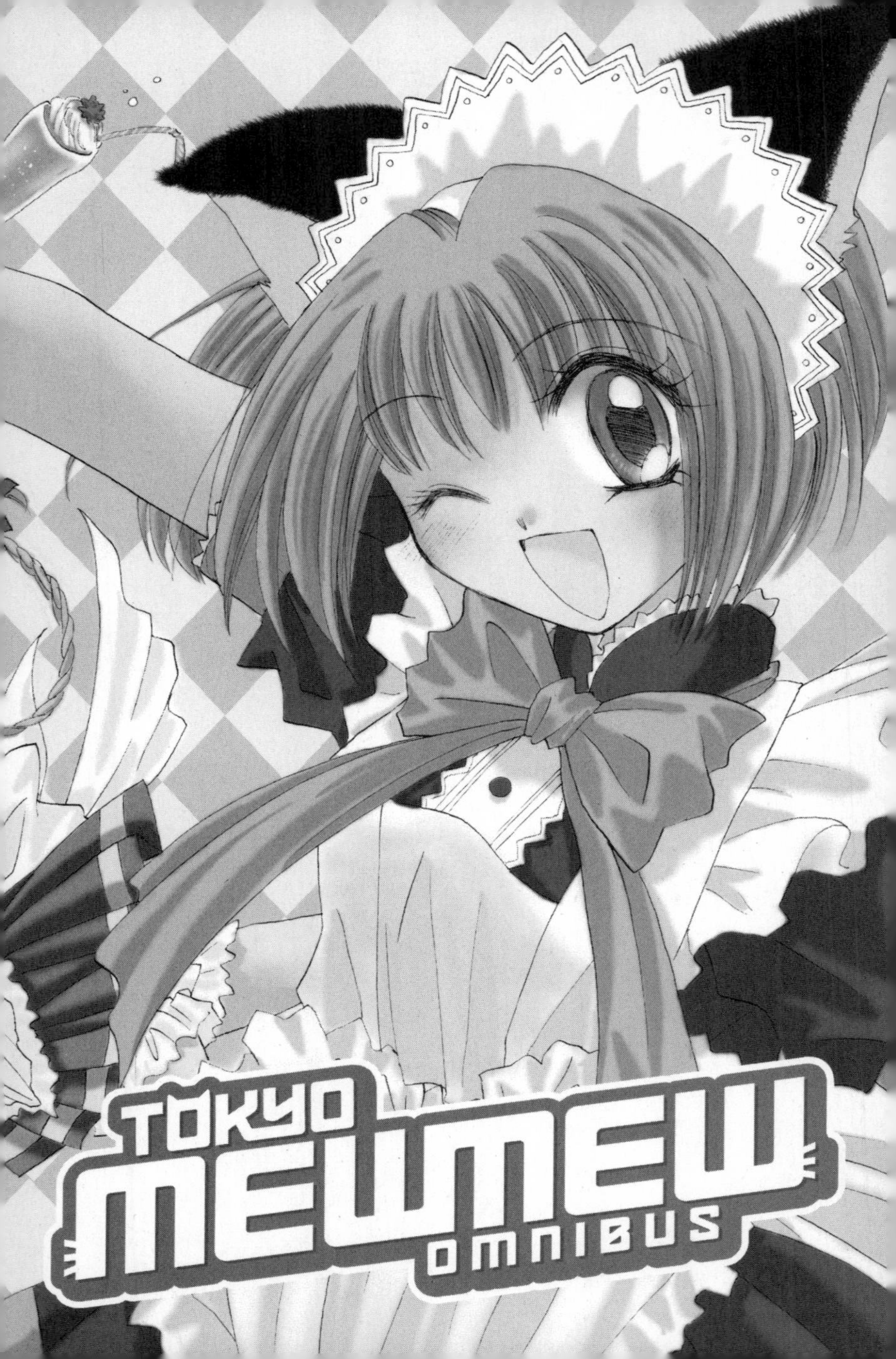
TOKYO
MEWMEW
OMNIBUS

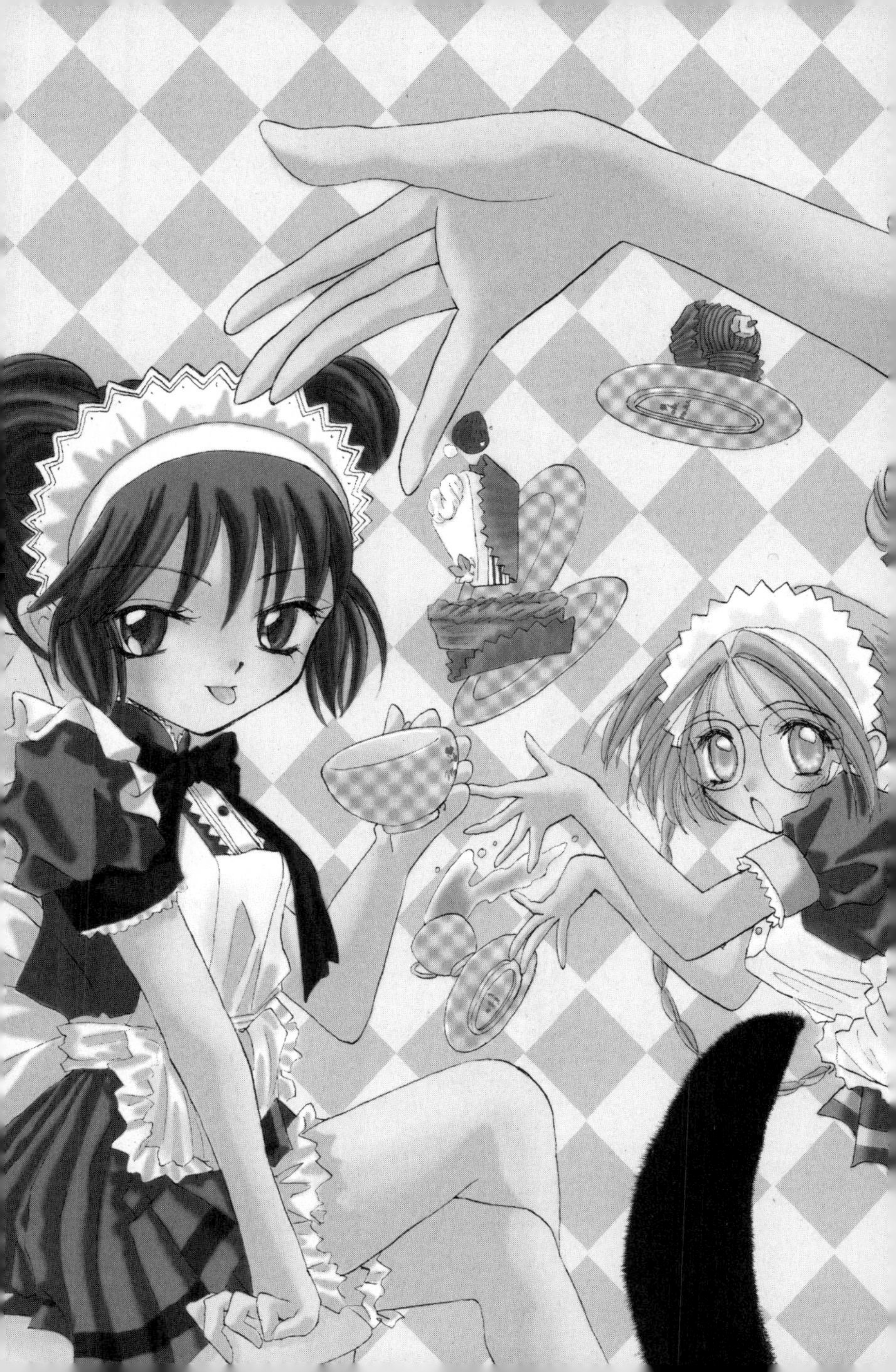

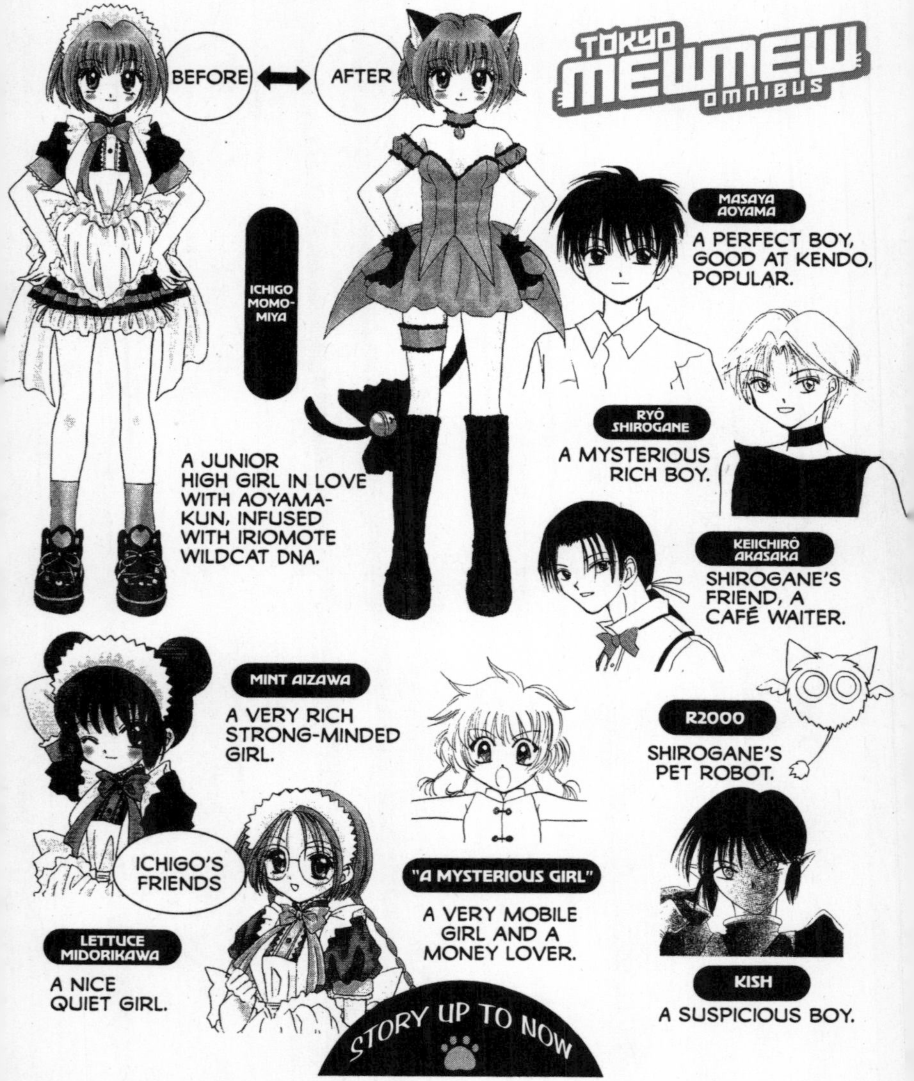
TOKYO MEWMEW OMNIBUS
BEFORE
AFTER
ICHIGO MOMOMIYA
A JUNIOR HIGH GIRL IN LOVE WITH AOYAMA-KUN, INFUSED WITH IRIOMOTE WILDCAT DNA.
MASAYA AOYAMA
A PERFECT BOY, GOOD AT KENDO, POPULAR.
RYÔ SHIROGANE
A MYSTERIOUS RICH BOY.
KEIICHIRÔ AKASAKA
SHIROGANE'S FRIEND, A CAFÉ WAITER.
MINT AIZAWA
A VERY RICH STRONG-MINDED GIRL.
R2000
SHIROGANE'S PET ROBOT.
ICHIGO'S FRIENDS
"A MYSTERIOUS GIRL"
A VERY MOBILE GIRL AND A MONEY LOVER.
LETTUCE MIDORIKAWA
A NICE QUIET GIRL.
KISH
A SUSPICIOUS BOY.

STORY UP TO NOW

☆ ICHIGO WAS AN ORDINARY JUNIOR HIGH GIRL, UNTIL ONE DAY, SHE BECAME MEW MEW THE PROTECTOR OF JUSTICE. SHE IS DOING HER BEST TO SAVE THE EARTH WHILE LOOKING FOR FOUR TEAMMATES.

☆ ONE DAY, ICHIGO GOES TO A ZOO WITH AOYAMA-KUN AND GETS CAUGHT WHILE IN MID-TRANSFORMATION BY A MYSTERIOUS FEMALE STREET PERFORMER. ON TOP OF THAT, SHE SUDDENLY GETS KISSED BY A SUSPICIOUS BOY!

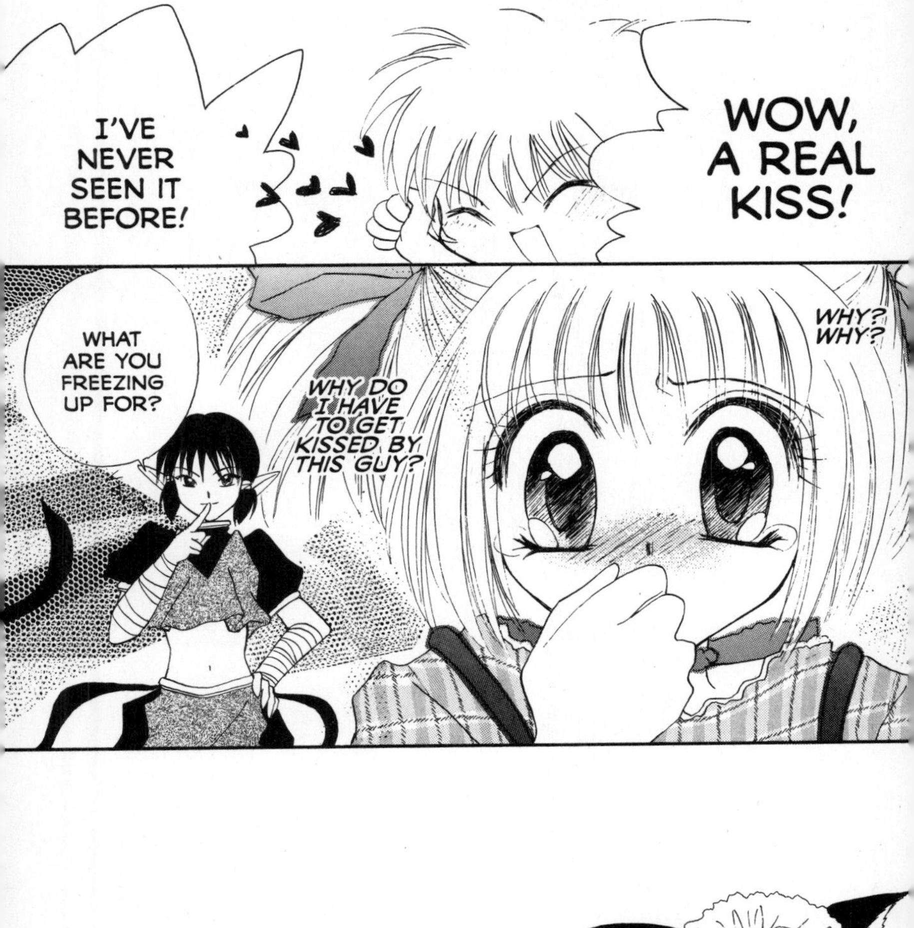
WOW, A REAL KISS!
I'VE NEVER SEEN IT BEFORE!
WHY? WHY?
WHY DO I HAVE TO GET KISSED BY THIS GUY?
WHAT ARE YOU FREEZING UP FOR?

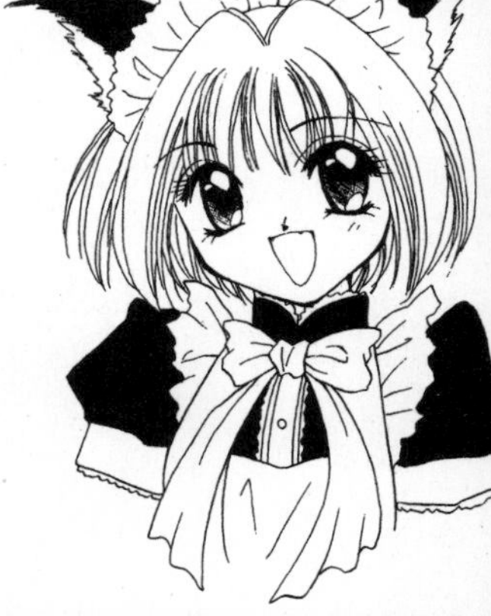

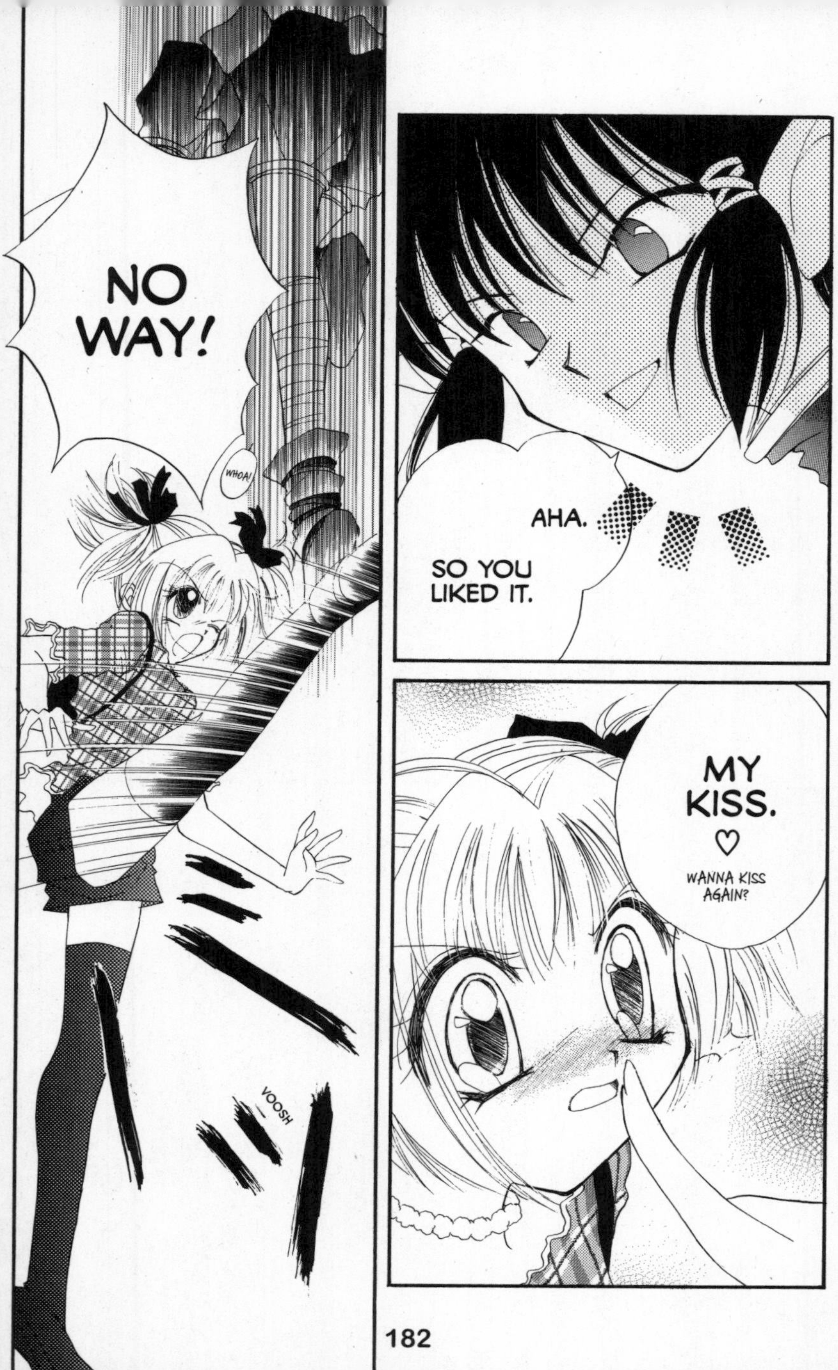
AHA.
SO YOU LIKED IT.
MY KISS. ♡
WANNA KISS AGAIN?
NO WAY!
WHOA!
VOOSH

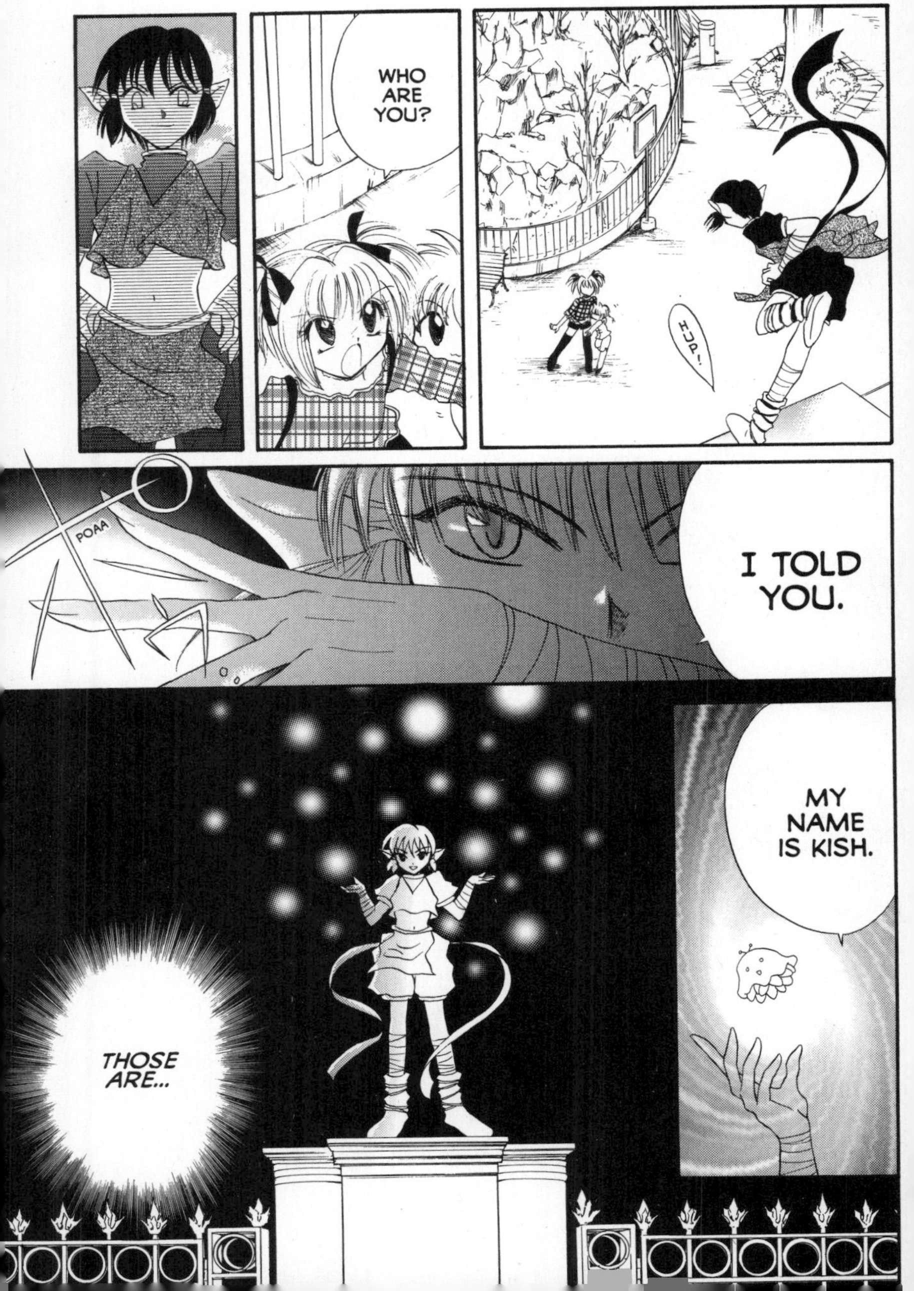
HUP!
WHO ARE YOU?
I TOLD YOU.
POAA
MY NAME IS KISH.
THOSE ARE...

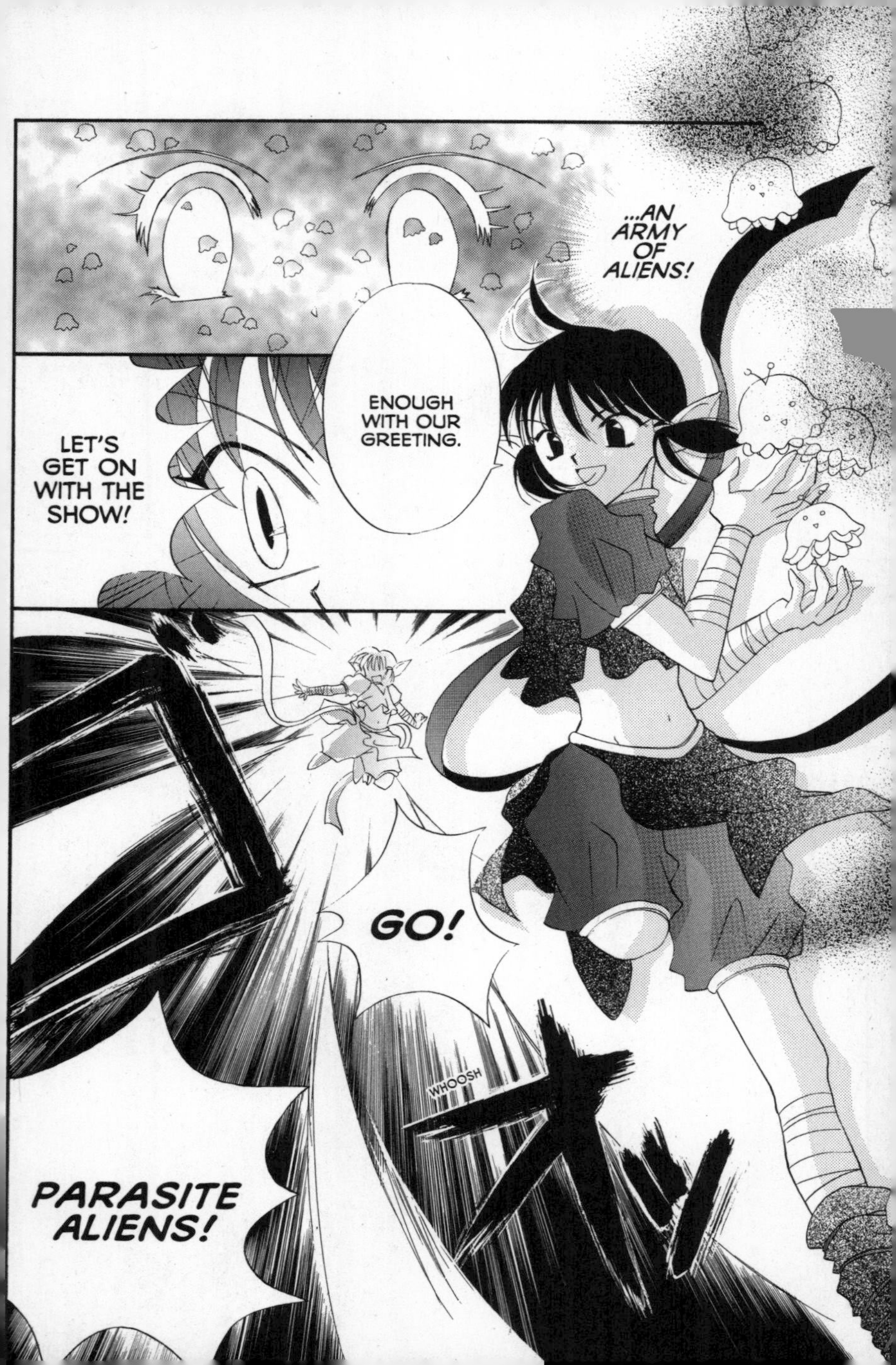
...AN ARMY OF ALIENS!
ENOUGH WITH OUR GREETING.
LET'S GET ON WITH THE SHOW!
GO!
WHOOSH
PARASITE ALIENS!

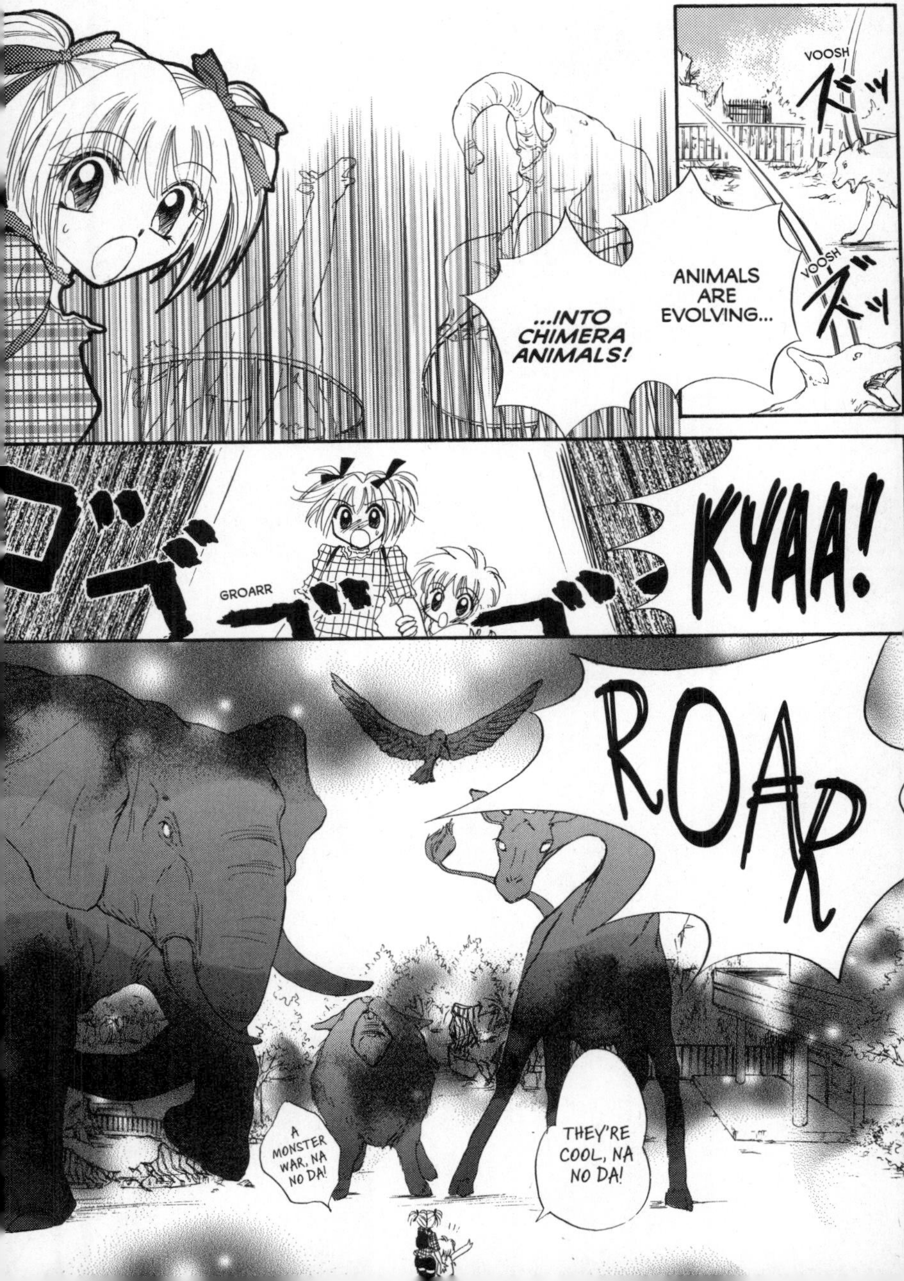
VOOSH
ズッ
VOOSH
ズッ
ANIMALS ARE EVOLVING...
...INTO CHIMERA ANIMALS!
KYAA!
GROARR
ROAR
THEY'RE COOL, NA NO DA!
A MONSTER WAR, NA NO DA!

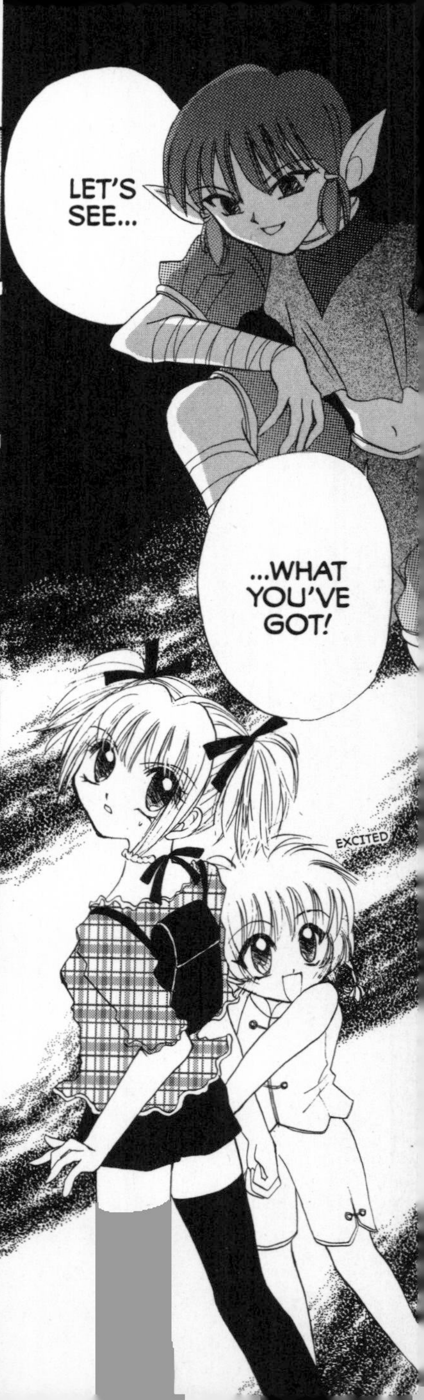
LET'S SEE...
...WHAT YOU'VE GOT!
EXCITED

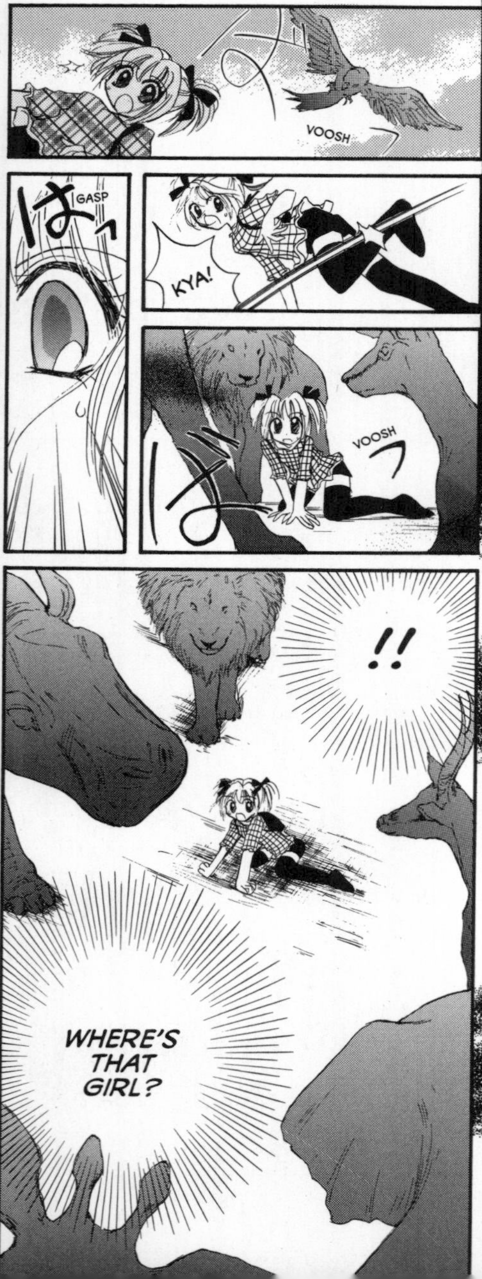
VOOSH
KYA!
VOOSH
GASP
!!
WHERE'S THAT GIRL?

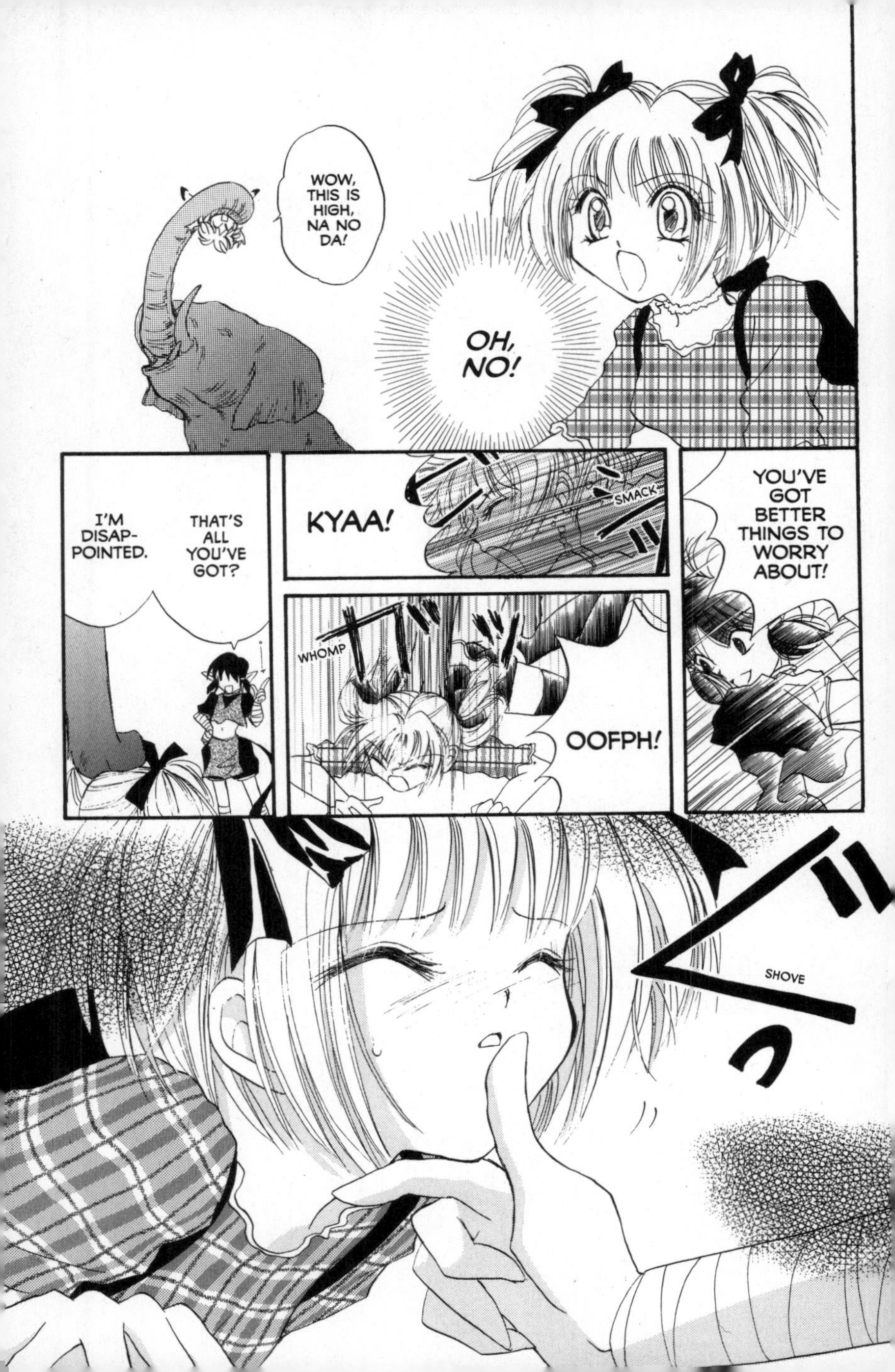
WOW, THIS IS HIGH, NA NO DA!
OH, NO!
YOU'VE GOT BETTER THINGS TO WORRY ABOUT!
SMACK
KYAA!
OOFPH!
WHOMP
THAT'S ALL YOU'VE GOT?
I'M DISAP-POINTED.
SHOVE

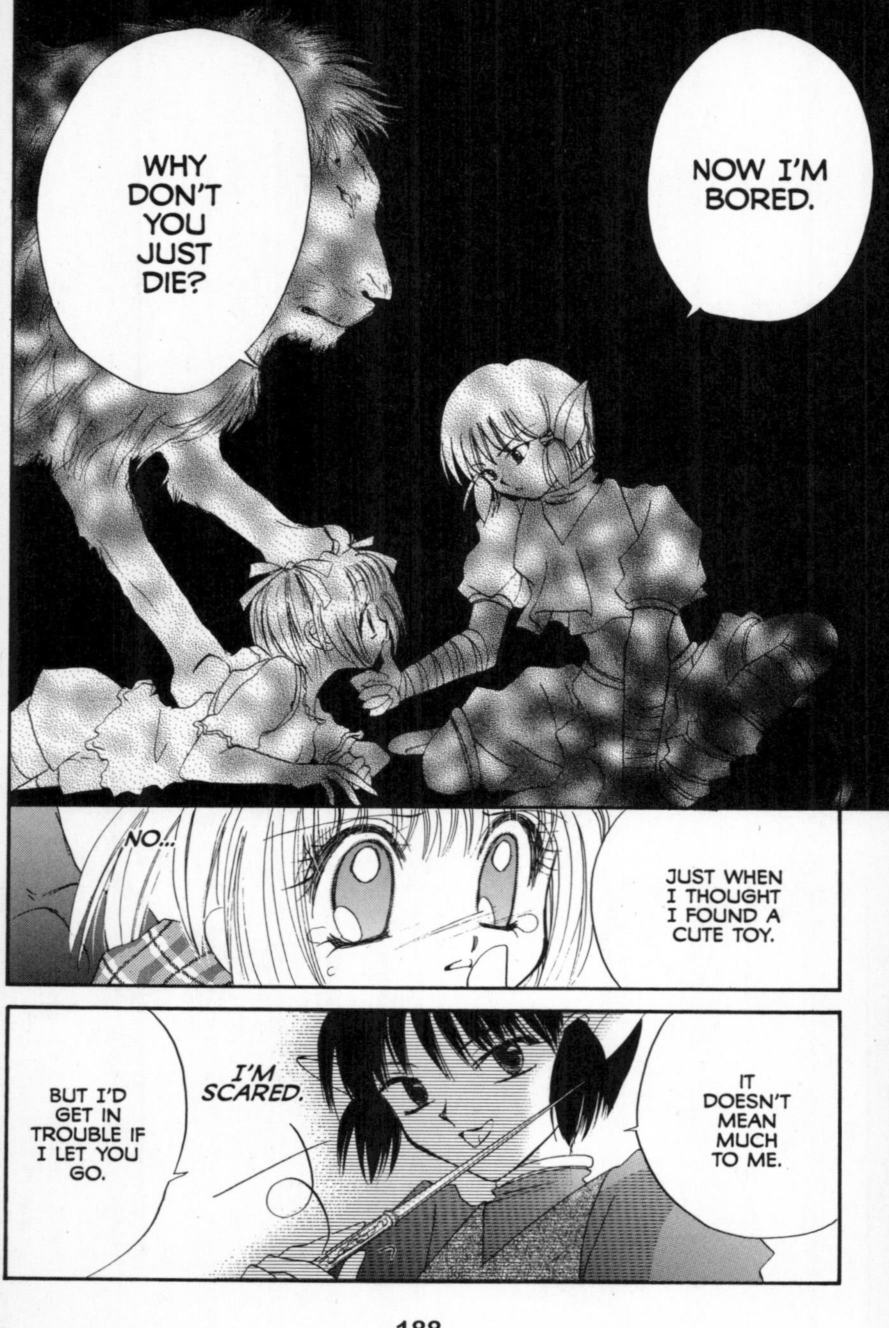
NOW I'M BORED.
WHY DON'T YOU JUST DIE?
JUST WHEN I THOUGHT I FOUND A CUTE TOY.
NO...
IT DOESN'T MEAN MUCH TO ME.
I'M SCARED.
BUT I'D GET IN TROUBLE IF I LET YOU GO.

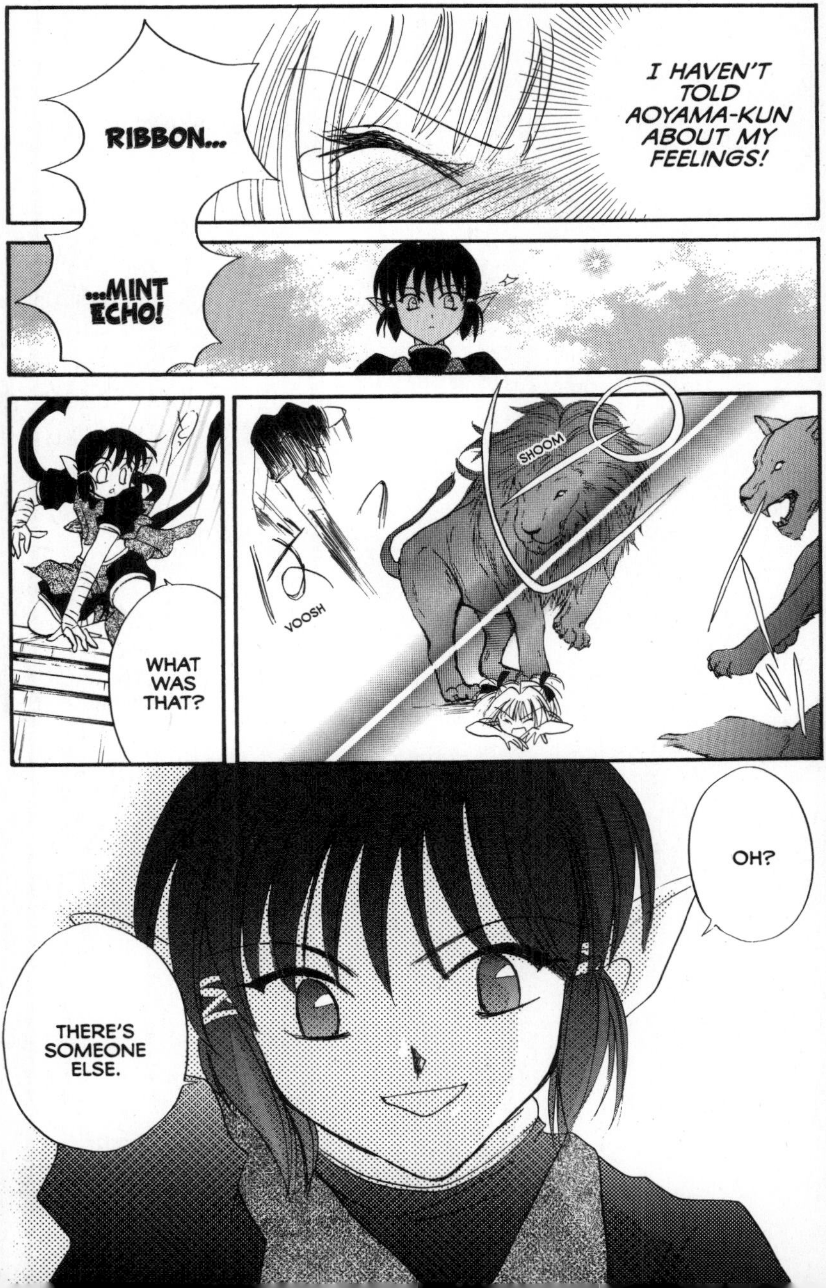
I HAVEN'T TOLD AOYAMA-KUN ABOUT MY FEELINGS!
RIBBON...
...MINT ECHO!
SHOOM
VOOSH
WHAT WAS THAT?
OH?
THERE'S SOMEONE ELSE.

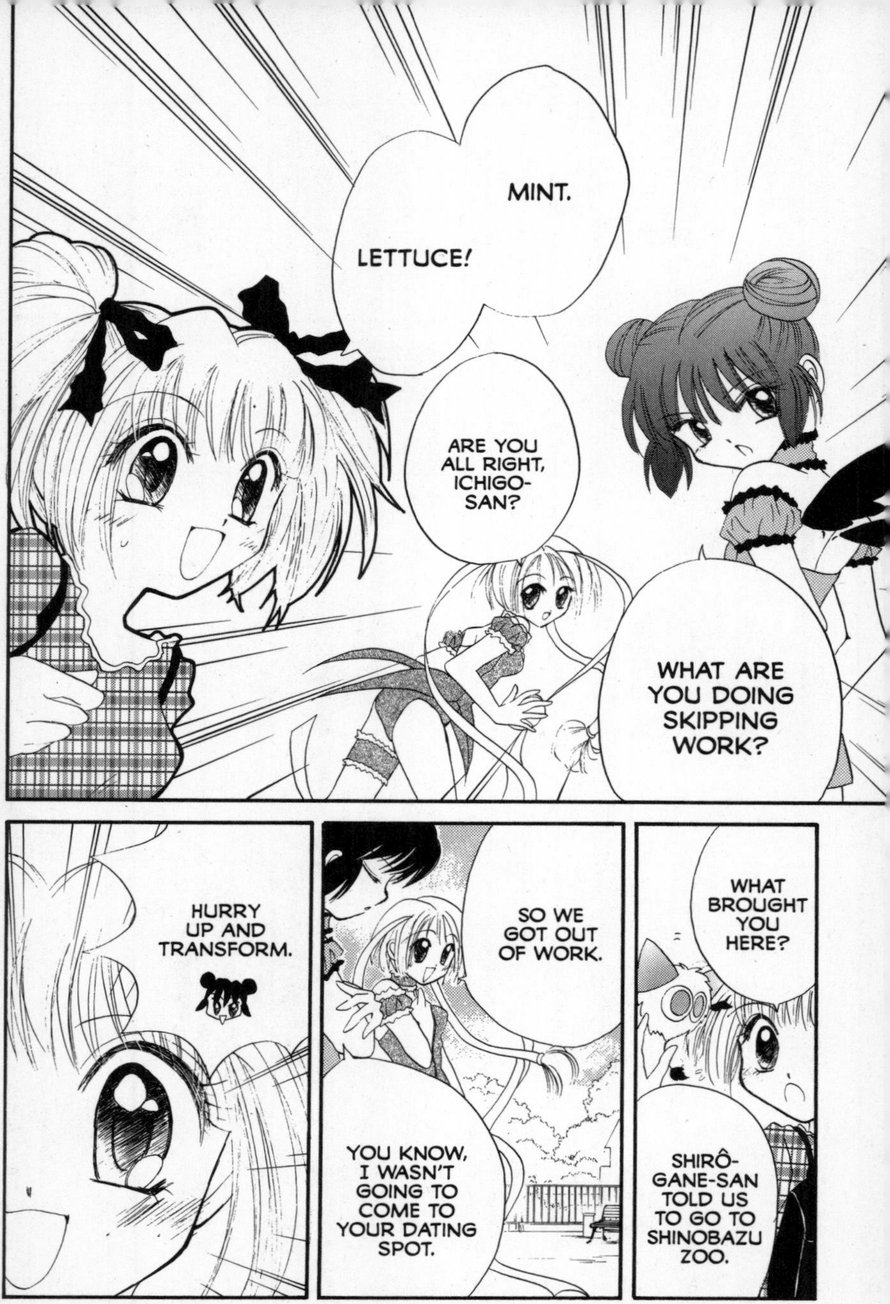
MINT.
LETTUCE!
ARE YOU ALL RIGHT, ICHIGO-SAN?
WHAT ARE YOU DOING SKIPPING WORK?
WHAT BROUGHT YOU HERE?
SHIRÔ-GANE-SAN TOLD US TO GO TO SHINOBAZU ZOO.
SO WE GOT OUT OF WORK.
YOU KNOW, I WASN'T GOING TO COME TO YOUR DATING SPOT.
HURRY UP AND TRANSFORM.

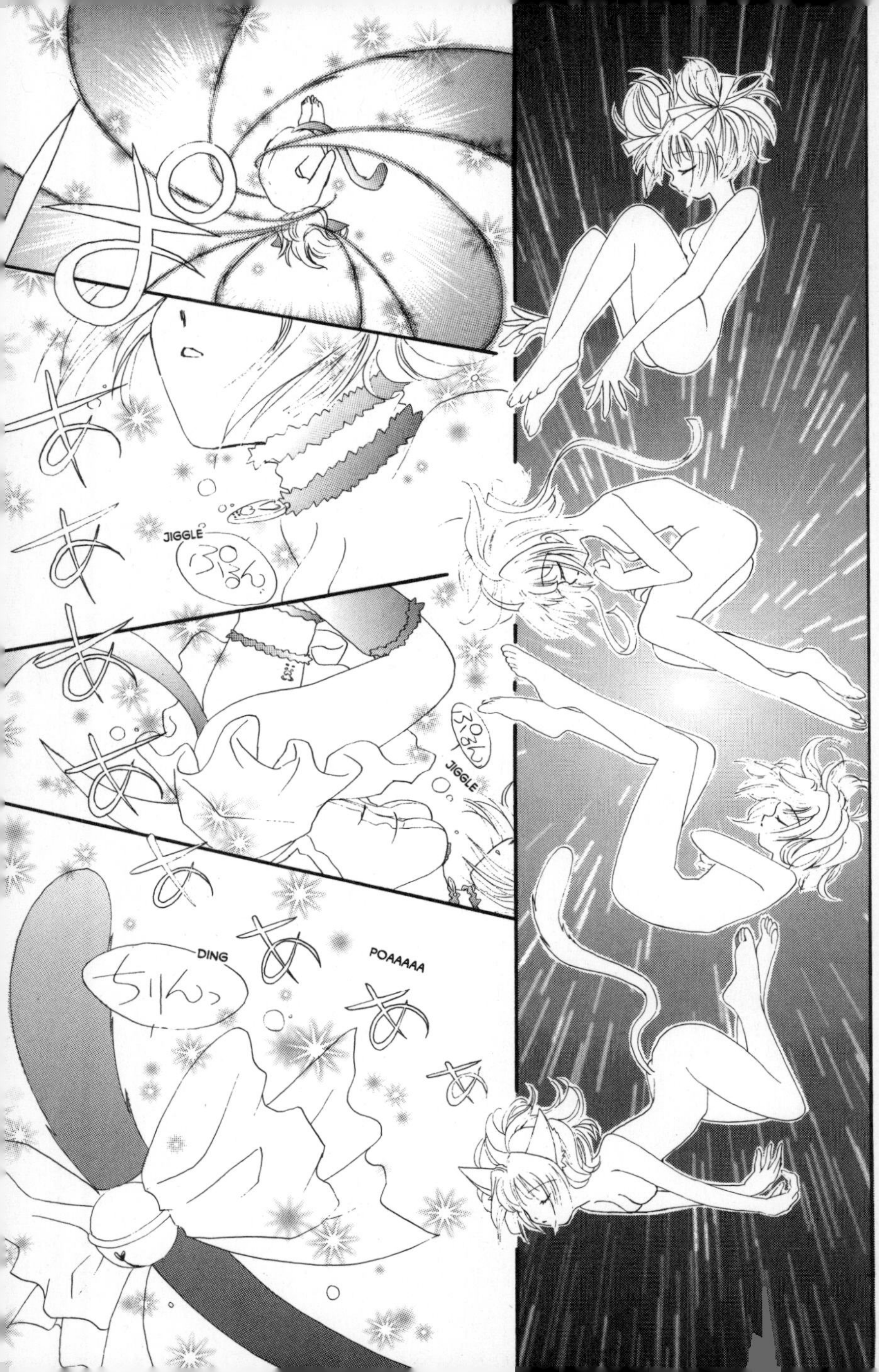

ぷああああああああ
ぷるん
JIGGLE
ぷるん
JIGGLE
ちりんっ
DING
POAAAAA

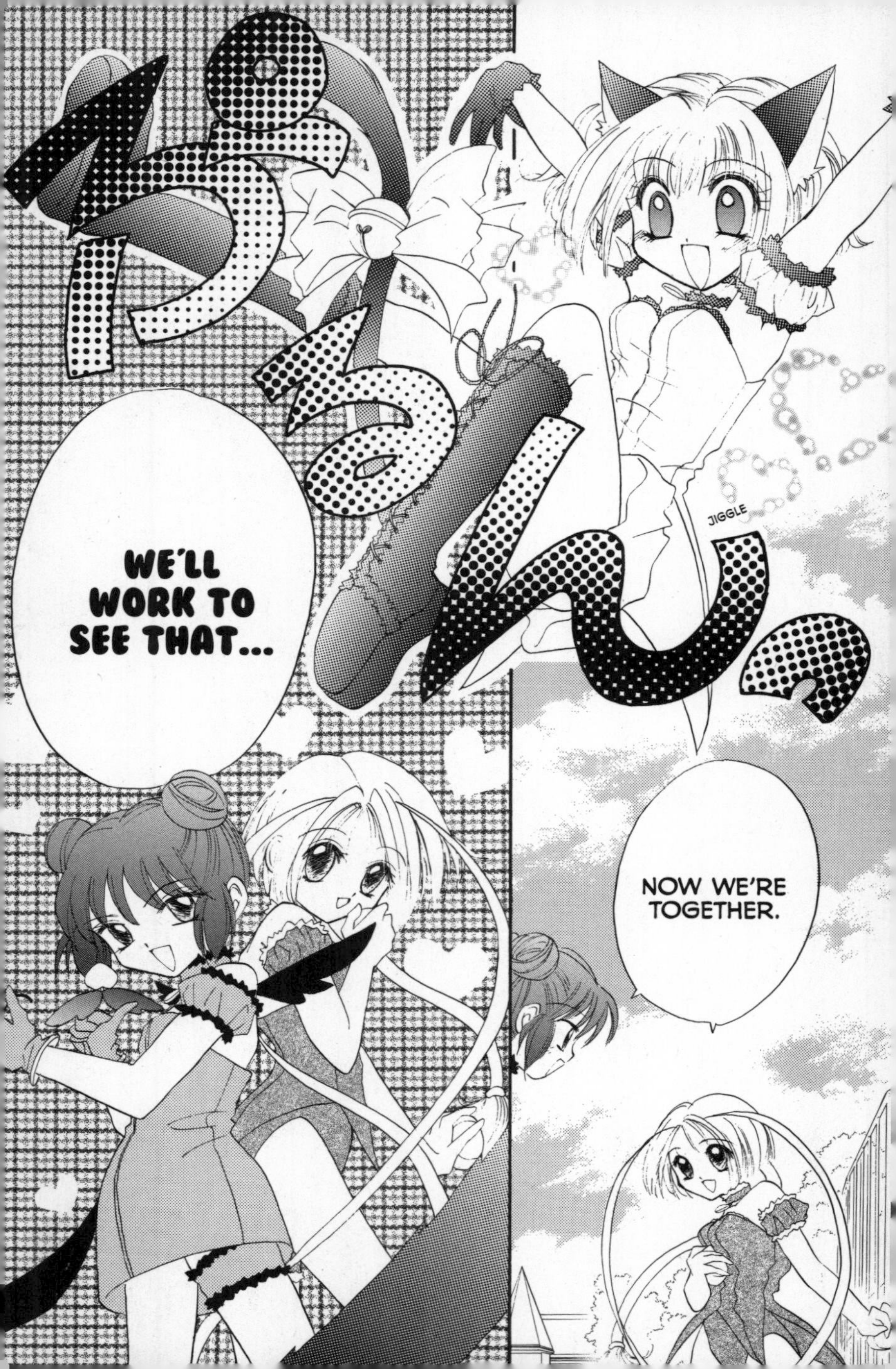
JIGGLE
NOW WE'RE TOGETHER.
WE'LL WORK TO SEE THAT...

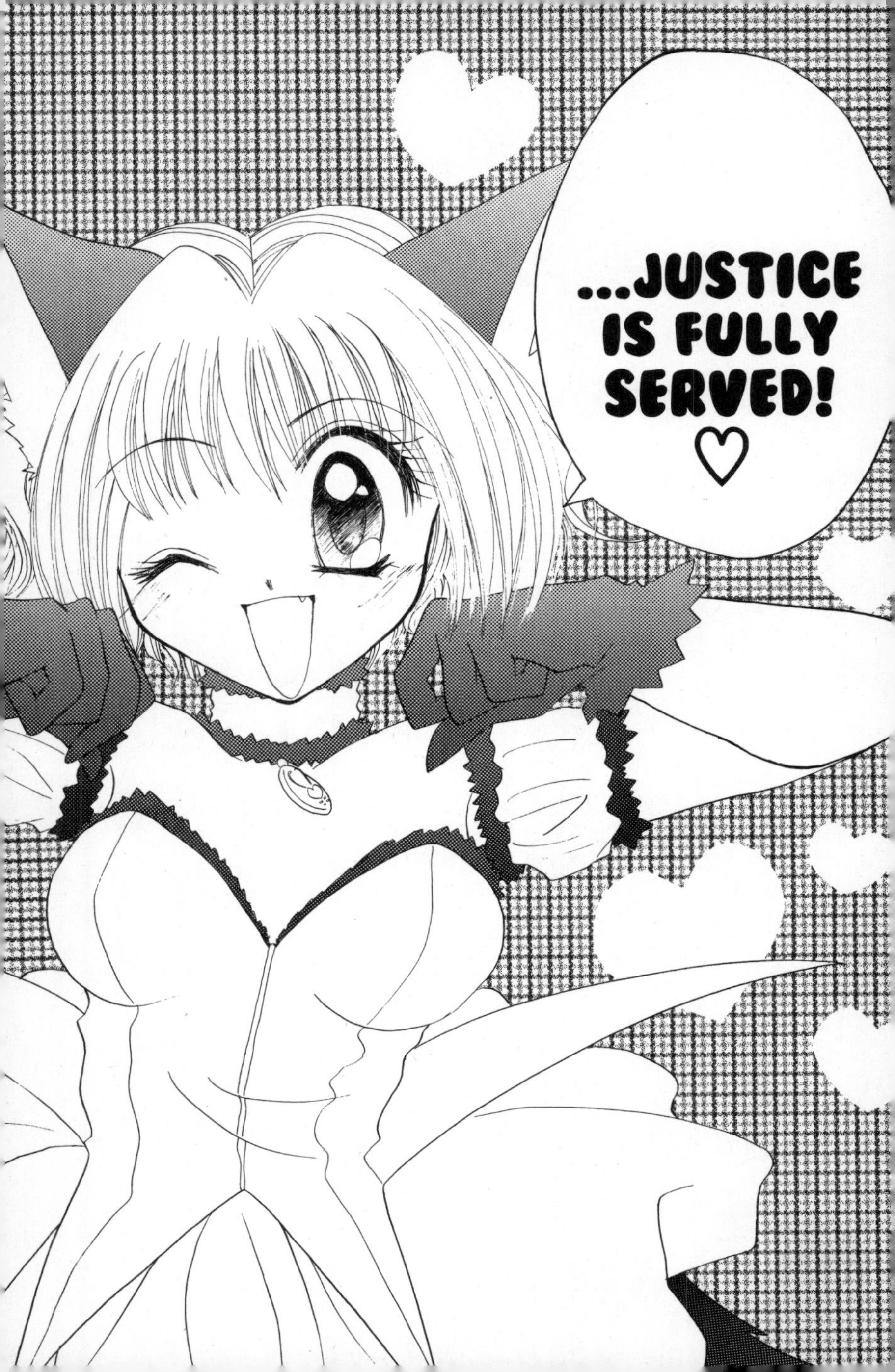
...JUSTICE IS FULLY SERVED! ♡

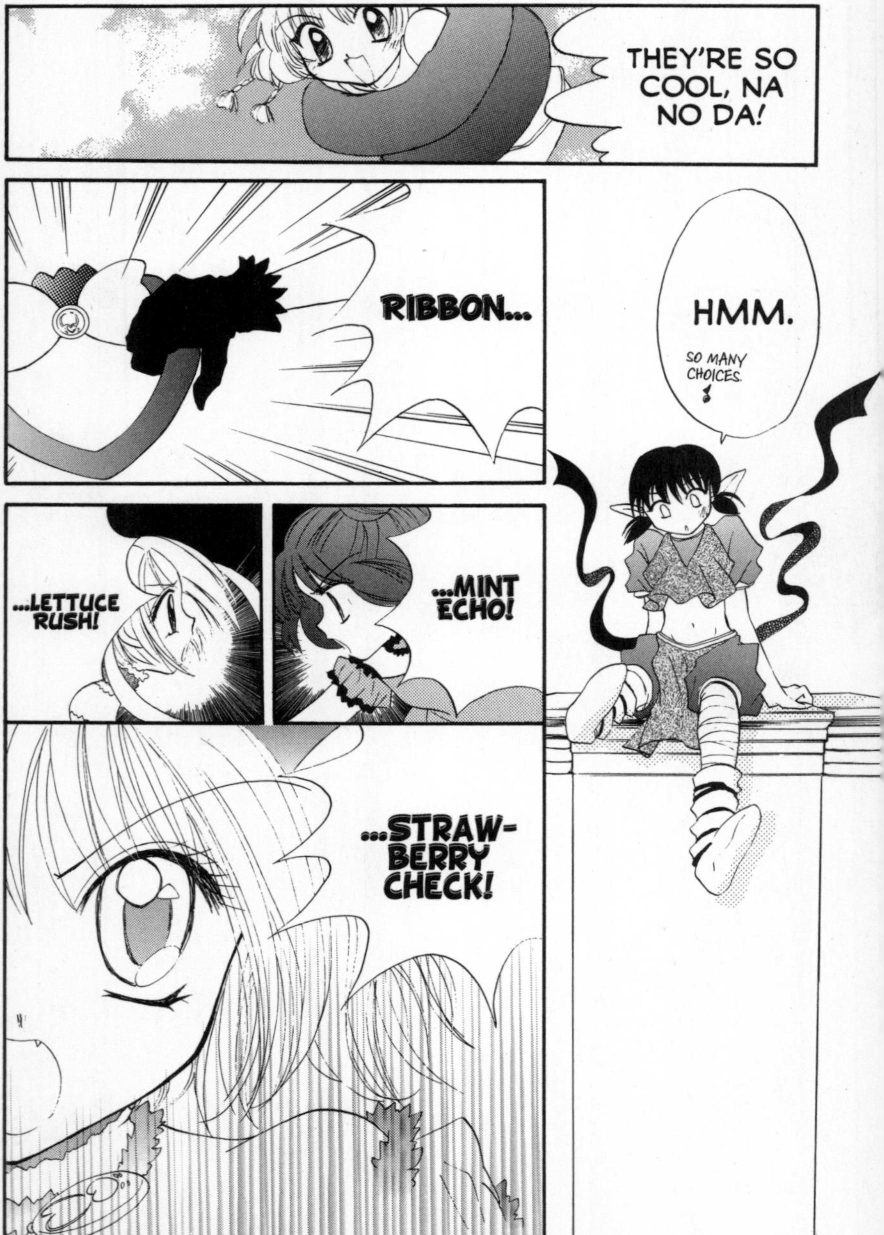
THEY'RE SO COOL, NA NO DA!
HMM.
SO MANY CHOICES.
RIBBON...
...MINT ECHO!
...LETTUCE RUSH!
...STRAWBERRY CHECK!

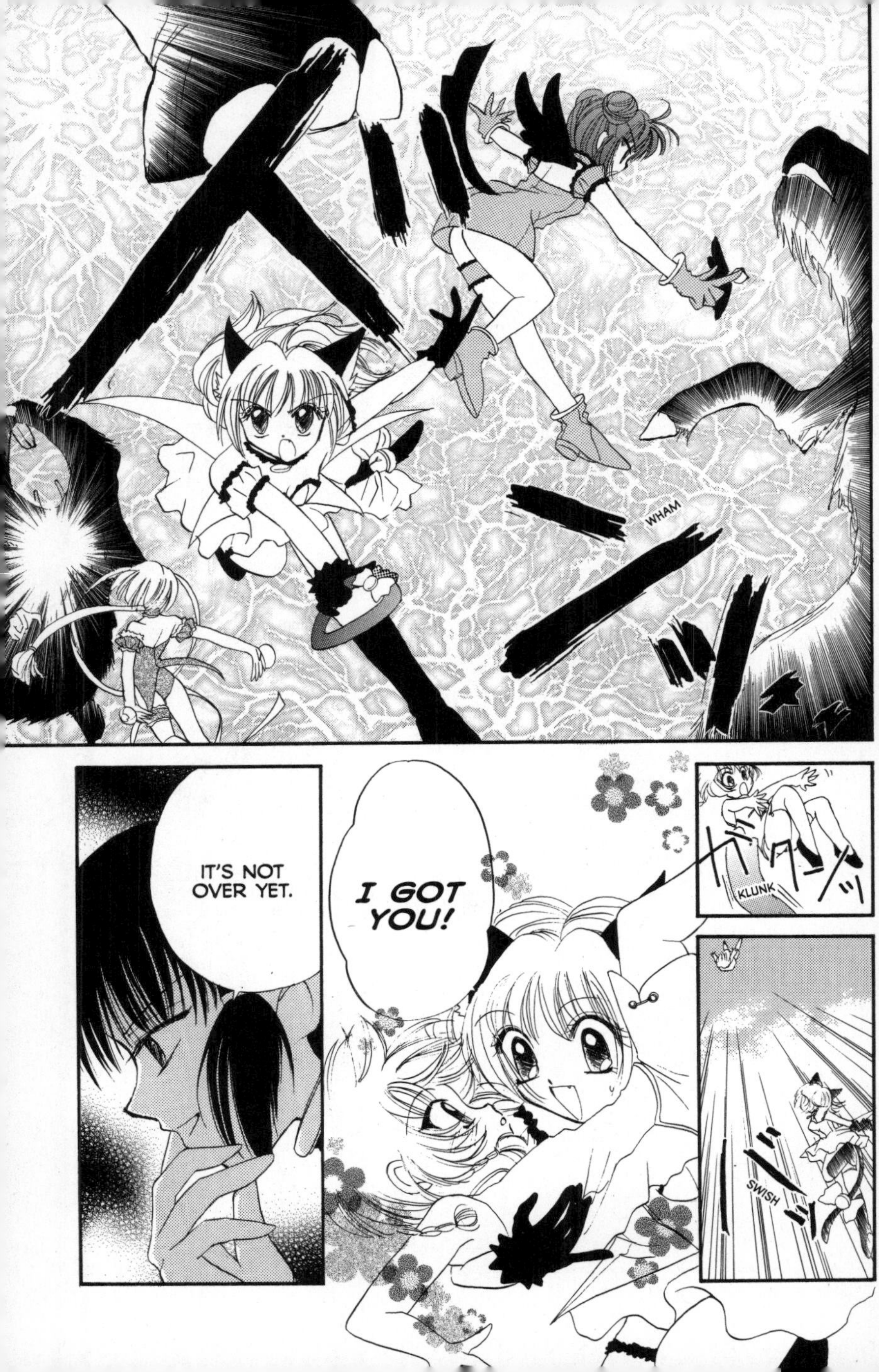
WHAM
KLUNK
SWISH
I GOT YOU!
IT'S NOT OVER YET.

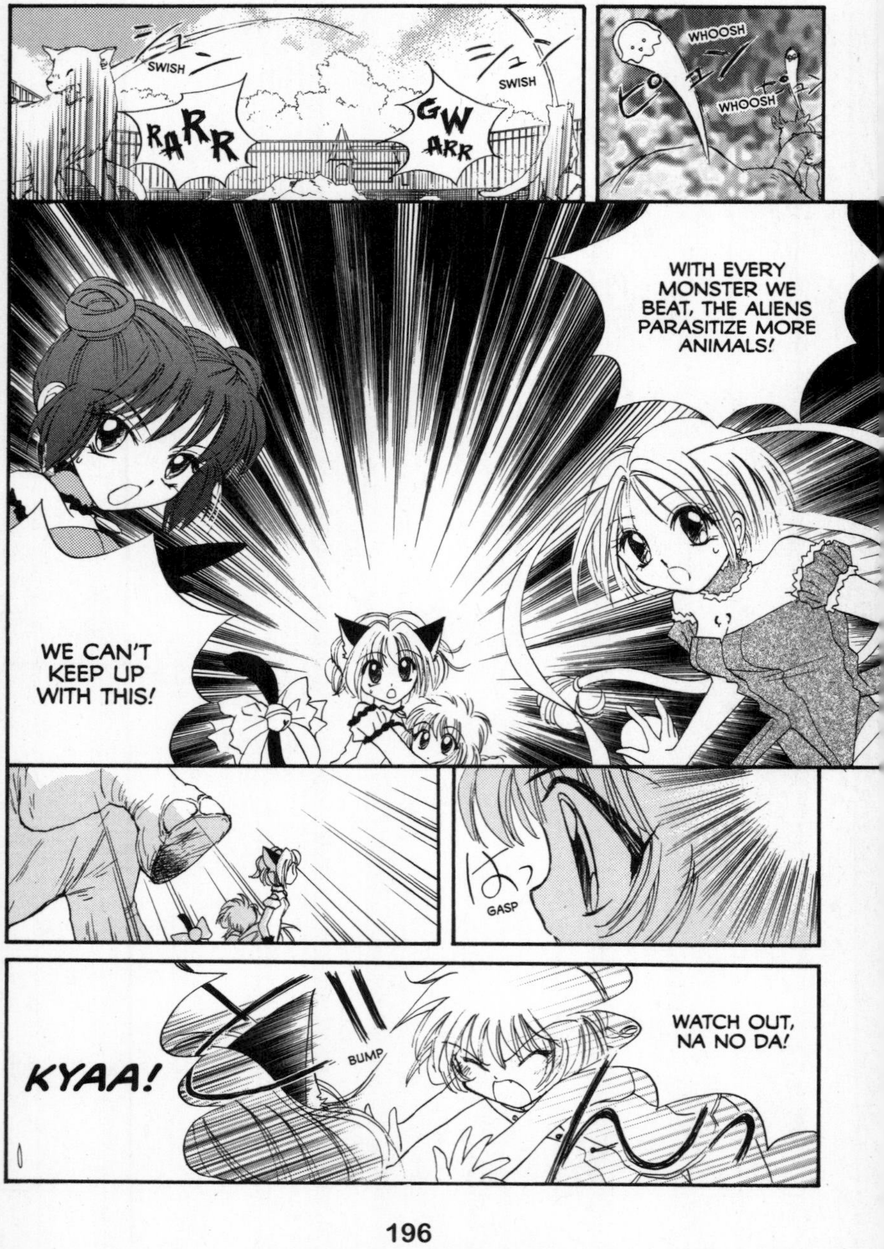
WHOOSH
WHOOSH
SWISH
GW ARR
SWISH
RARR
WITH EVERY MONSTER WE BEAT, THE ALIENS PARASITIZE MORE ANIMALS!
WE CAN'T KEEP UP WITH THIS!
はっ
GASP
WATCH OUT, NA NO DA!
BUMP
KYAA!

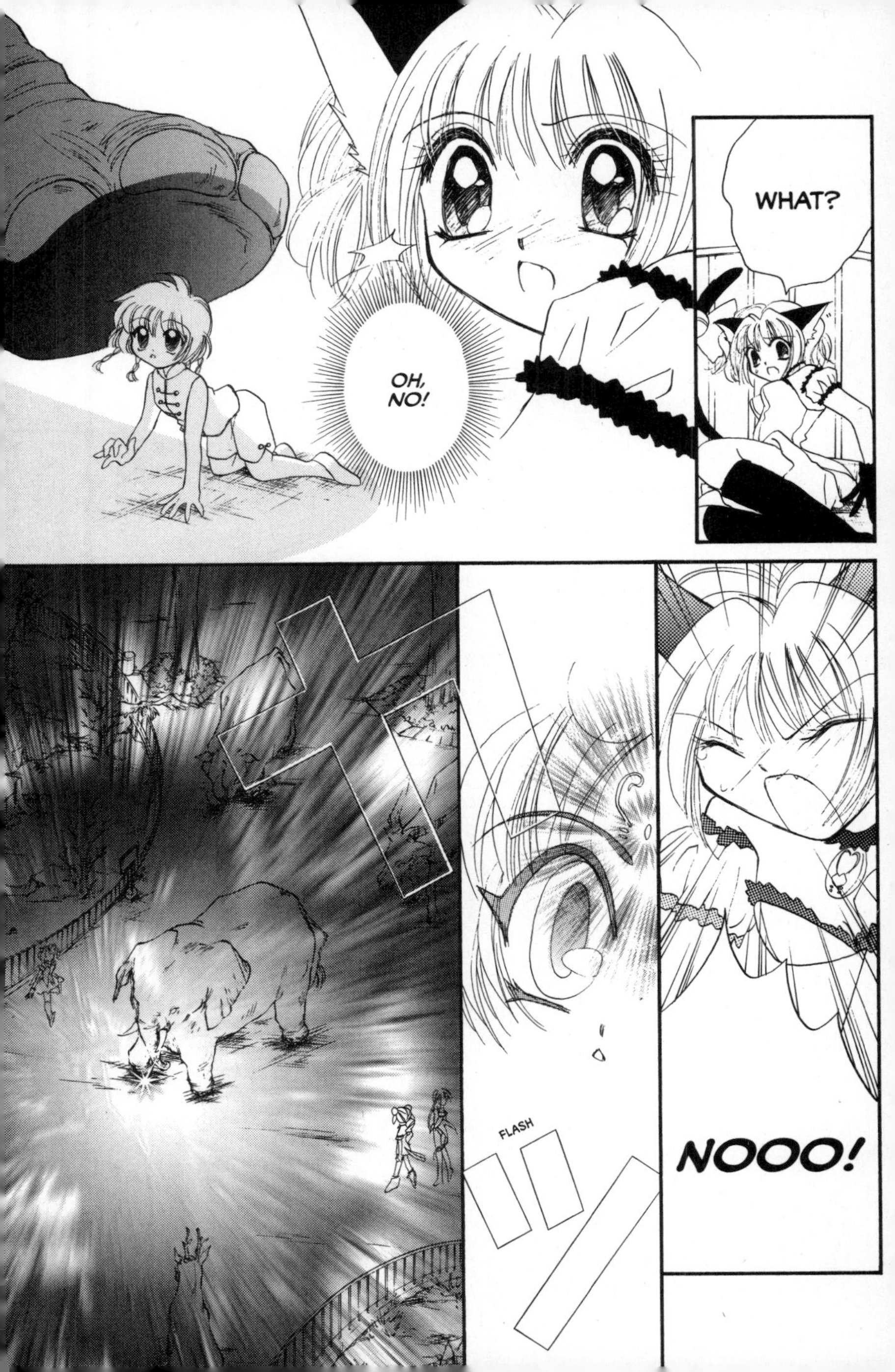
WHAT?
OH, NO!
NOOO!
FLASH

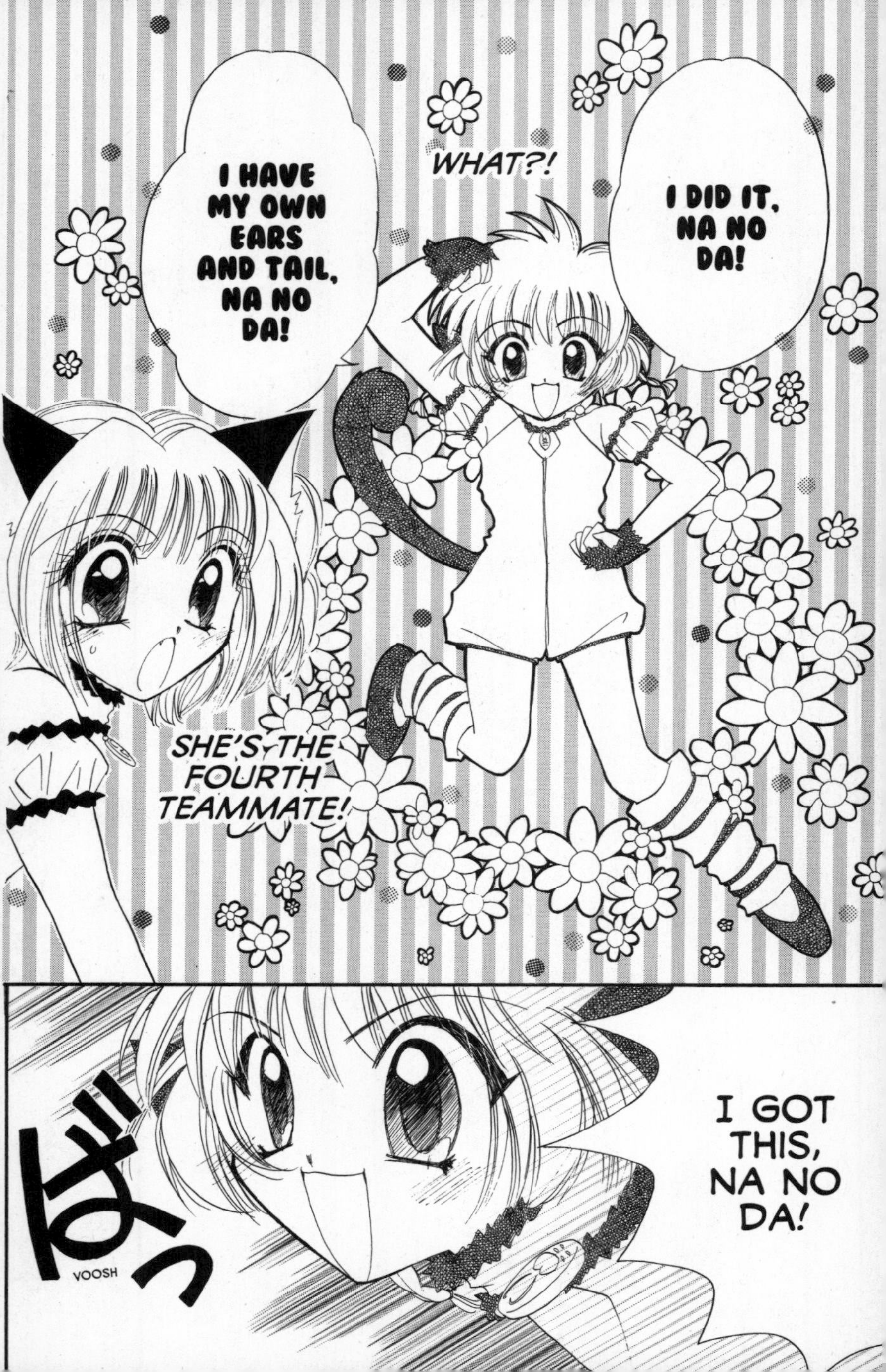
I DID IT, NA NO DA!
WHAT?!
I HAVE MY OWN EARS AND TAIL, NA NO DA!
SHE'S THE FOURTH TEAMMATE!
I GOT THIS, NA NO DA!
VOOSH

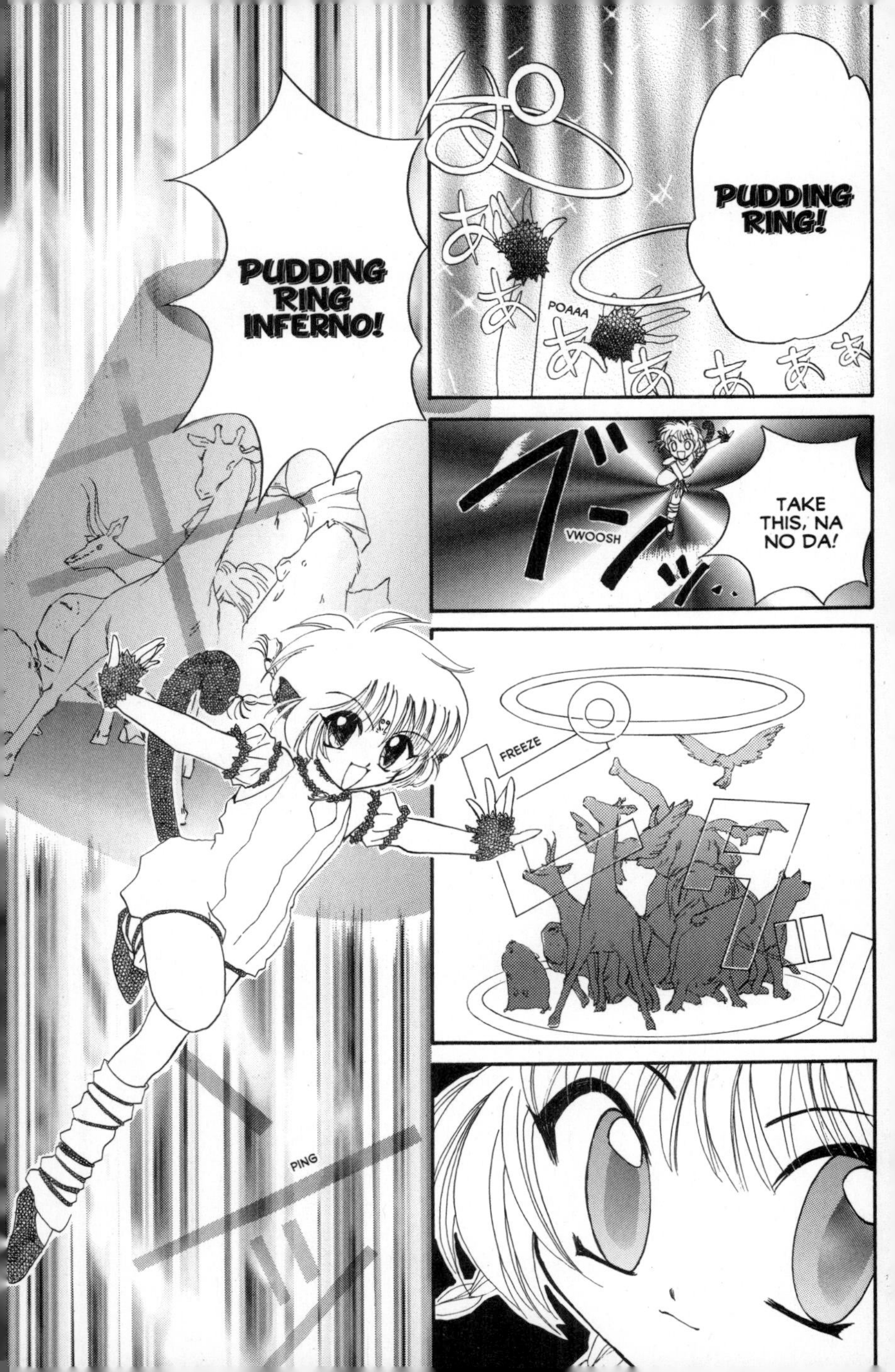
PUDDING RING!
POAAA
TAKE THIS, NA NO DA!
VWOOSH
FREEZE
PUDDING RING INFERNO!
PING

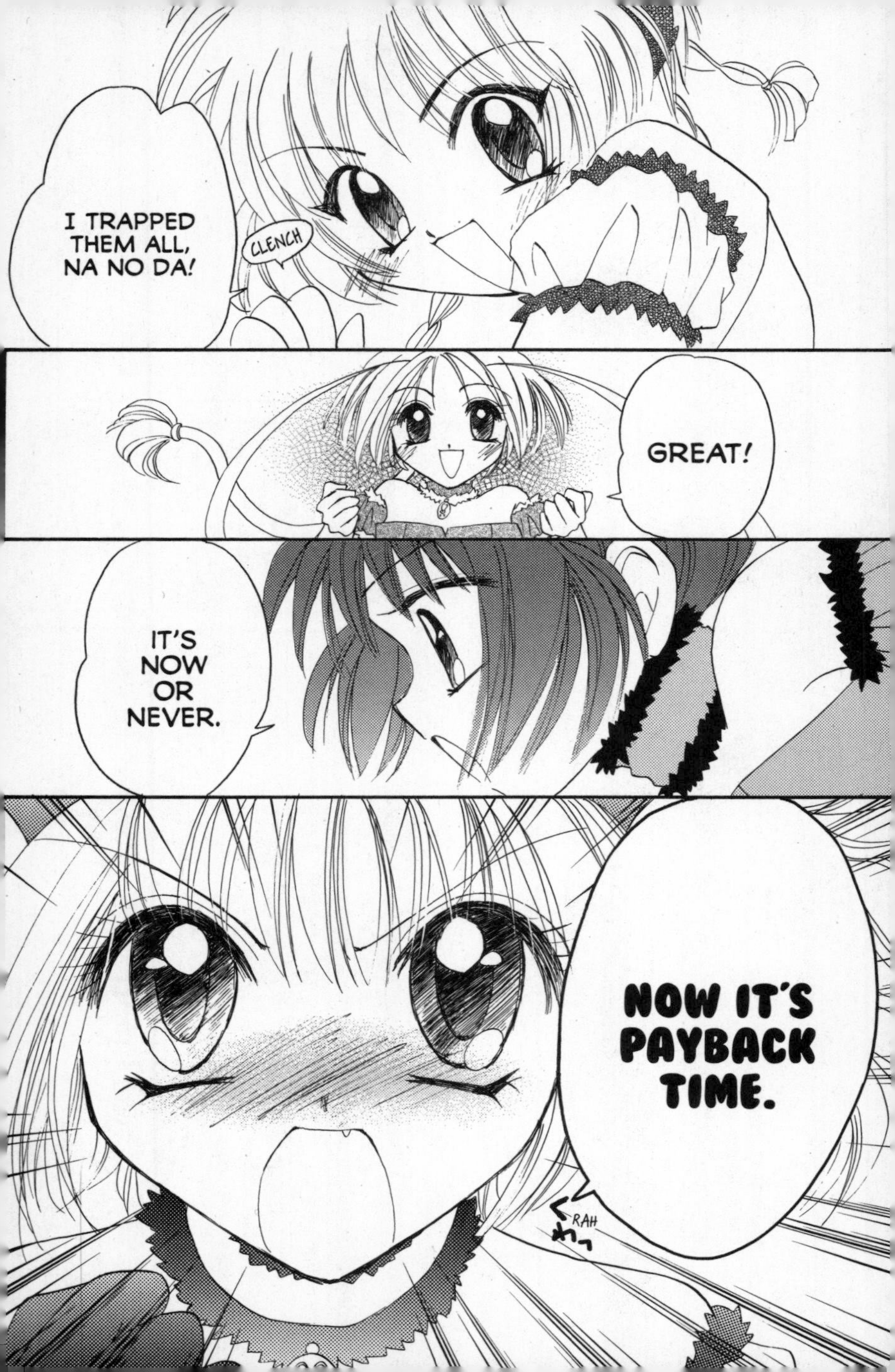
CLENCH
I TRAPPED THEM ALL, NA NO DA!
GREAT!
IT'S NOW OR NEVER.
NOW IT'S PAYBACK TIME.
RAH

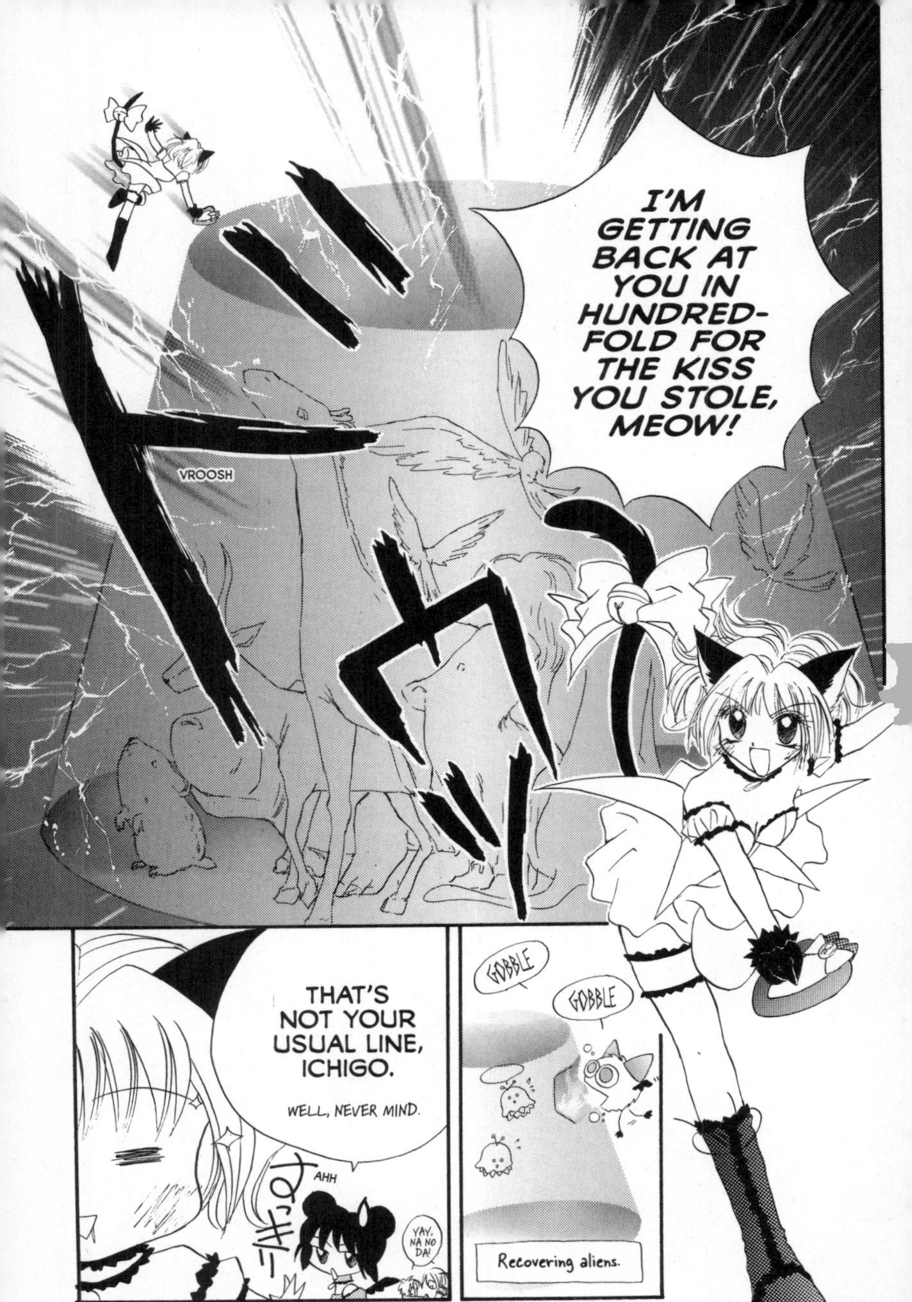
I'M GETTING BACK AT YOU IN HUNDRED-FOLD FOR THE KISS YOU STOLE, MEOW!
VROOSH
GOBBLE
GOBBLE
Recovering aliens.
THAT'S NOT YOUR USUAL LINE, ICHIGO.
WELL, NEVER MIND.
AHH
YAY, NA NO DA!

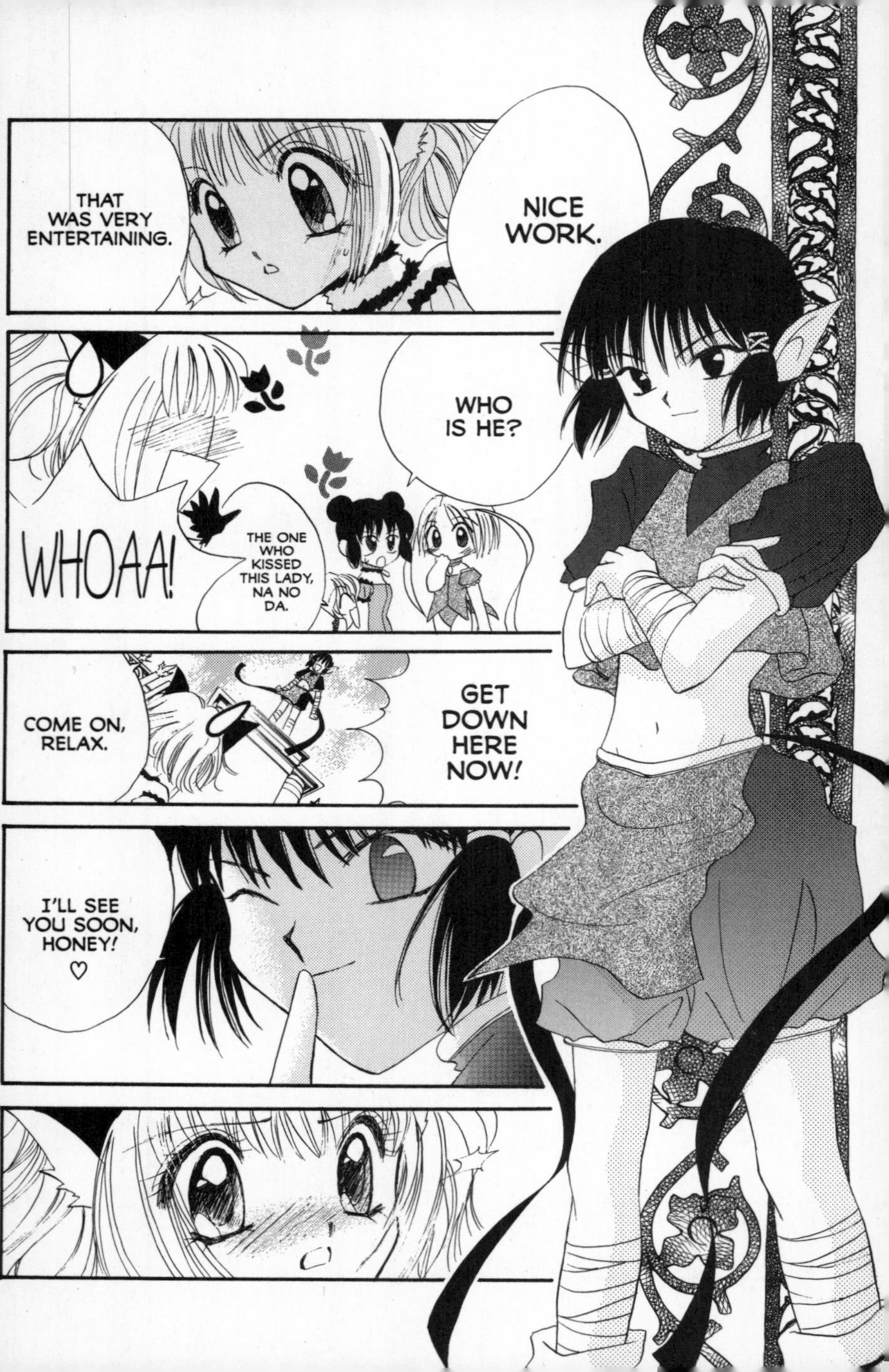
NICE WORK.
THAT WAS VERY ENTERTAINING.
WHO IS HE?
THE ONE WHO KISSED THIS LADY, NA NO DA.
WHOAA!
GET DOWN HERE NOW!
COME ON, RELAX.
I'LL SEE YOU SOON, HONEY! ♡

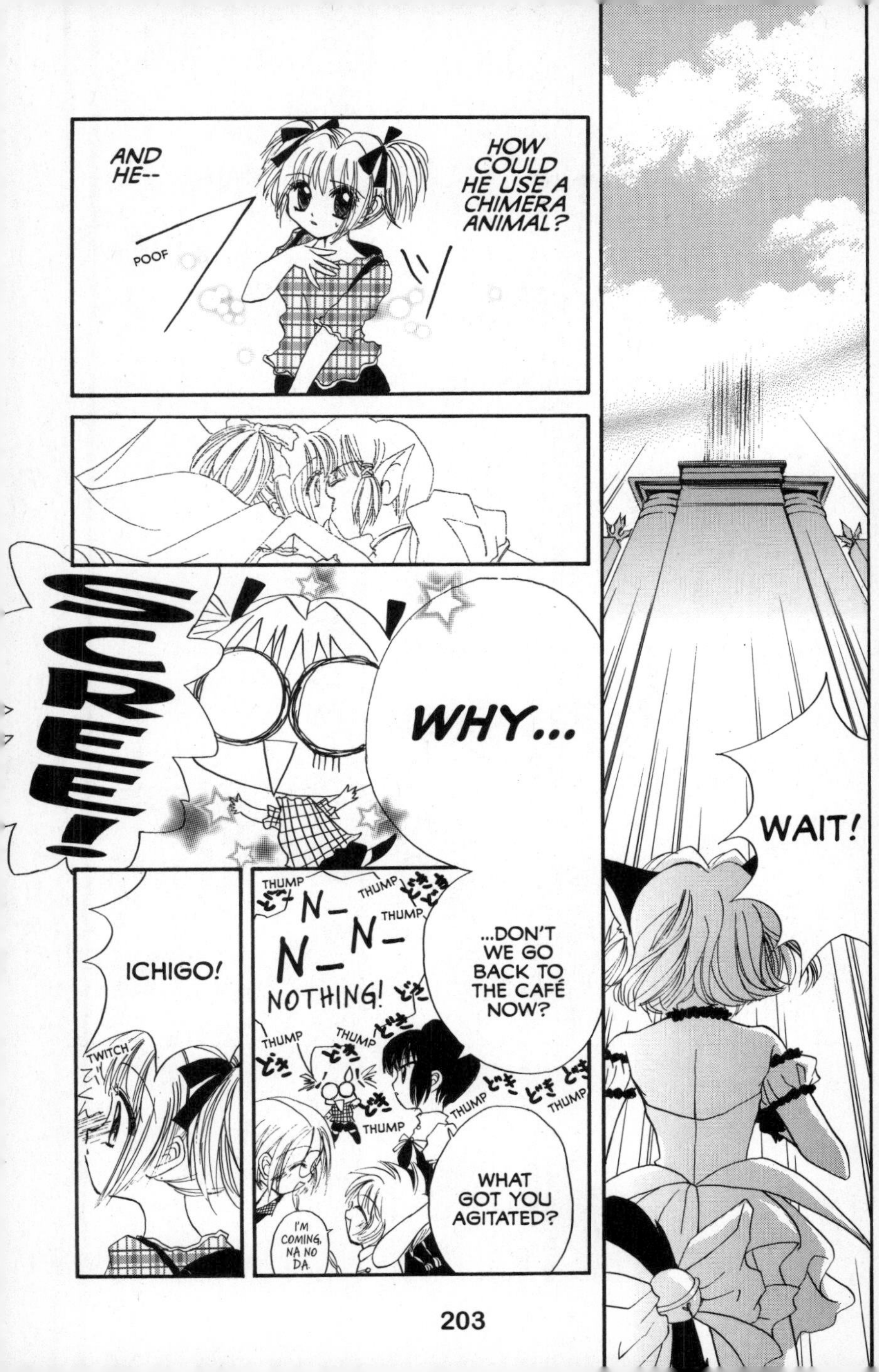
WAIT!
HOW COULD HE USE A CHIMERA ANIMAL?
AND HE--
POOF
WHY...
SCREEE!
...DON'T WE GO BACK TO THE CAFÉ NOW?
THUMP
THUMP
THUMP
N- N- N- NOTHING!
THUMP
THUMP
THUMP
THUMP
THUMP
WHAT GOT YOU AGITATED?
I'M COMING, NA NO DA.
ICHIGO!
TWITCH

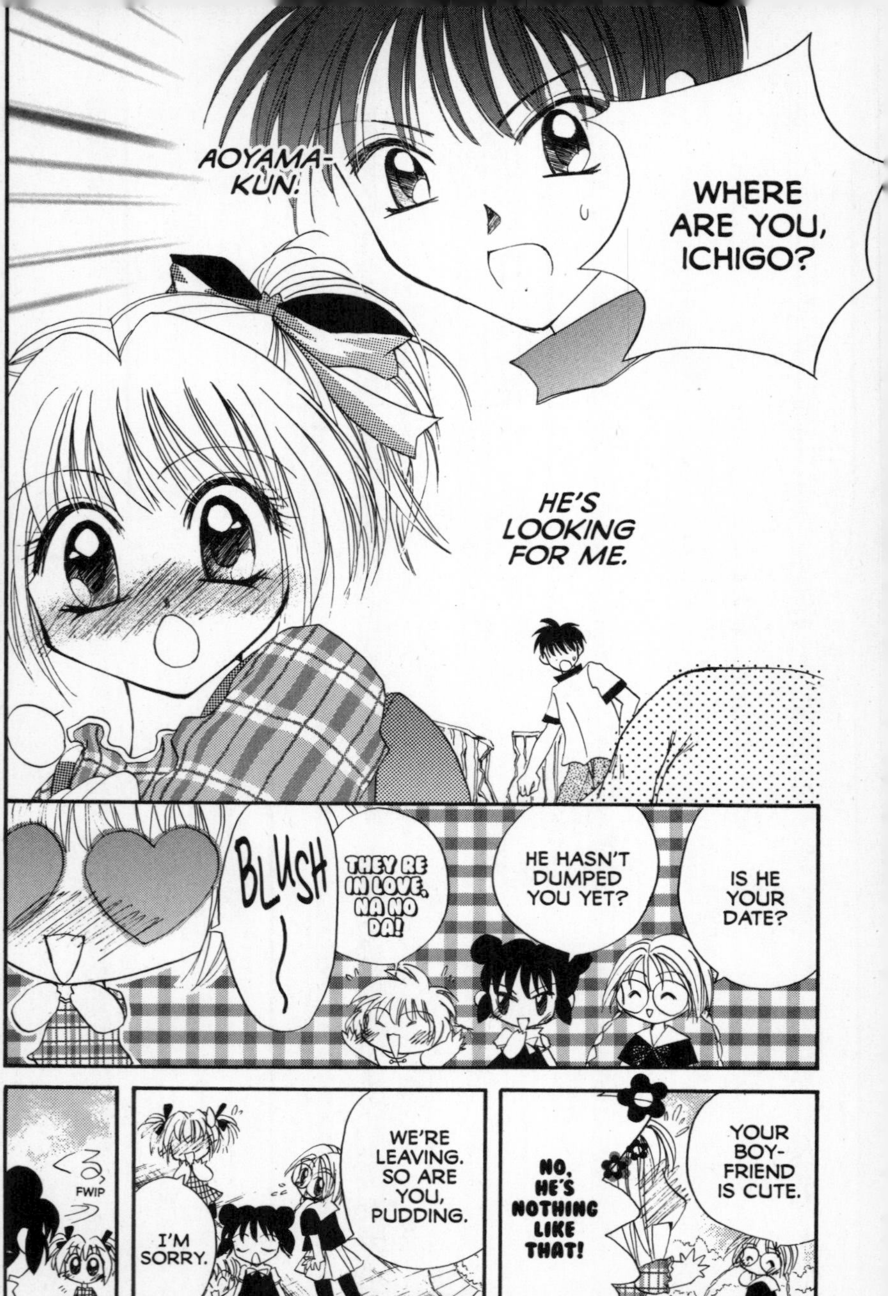
WHERE ARE YOU, ICHIGO?
AOYAMA-KUN.
HE'S LOOKING FOR ME.
IS HE YOUR DATE?
HE HASN'T DUMPED YOU YET?
THEY'RE IN LOVE, NA NO DA!
BLUSH
YOUR BOY-FRIEND IS CUTE.
NO, HE'S NOTHING LIKE THAT!
WE'RE LEAVING. SO ARE YOU, PUDDING.
I'M SORRY.
くるっ
FWIP

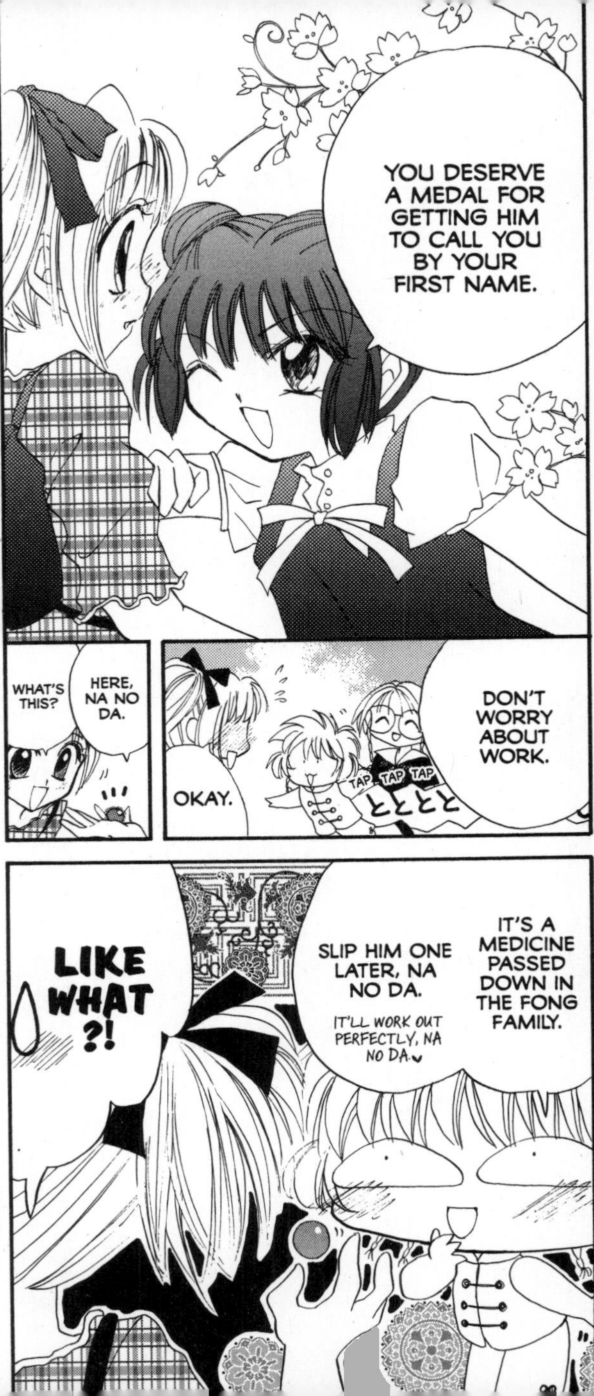

YOU DESERVE A MEDAL FOR GETTING HIM TO CALL YOU BY YOUR FIRST NAME.
DON'T WORRY ABOUT WORK.
TAP TAP TAP
とととと
OKAY.
HERE, NA NO DA.
WHAT'S THIS?
IT'S A MEDICINE PASSED DOWN IN THE FONG FAMILY.
SLIP HIM ONE LATER, NA NO DA.
IT'LL WORK OUT PERFECTLY, NA NO DA.
LIKE WHAT?!

Meeting with My Editors

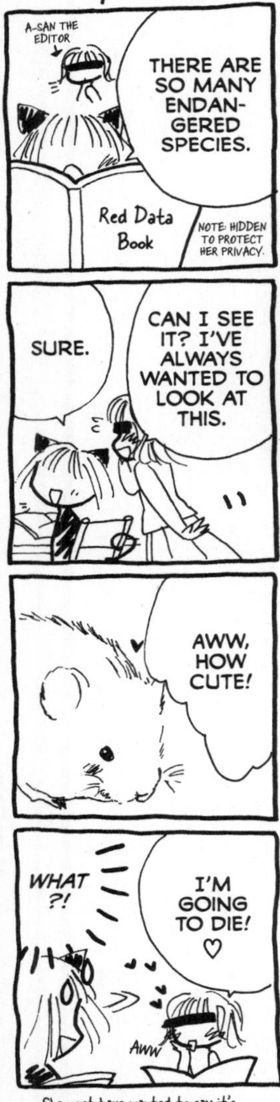

A-SAN THE EDITOR
THERE ARE SO MANY ENDANGERED SPECIES.
Red Data Book
NOTE: HIDDEN TO PROTECT HER PRIVACY.
CAN I SEE IT? I'VE ALWAYS WANTED TO LOOK AT THIS.
SURE.
AWW, HOW CUTE!
I'M GOING TO DIE! ♡
WHAT?!
AWW

She must have wanted to say it's so tiny and fragile that it's cute.

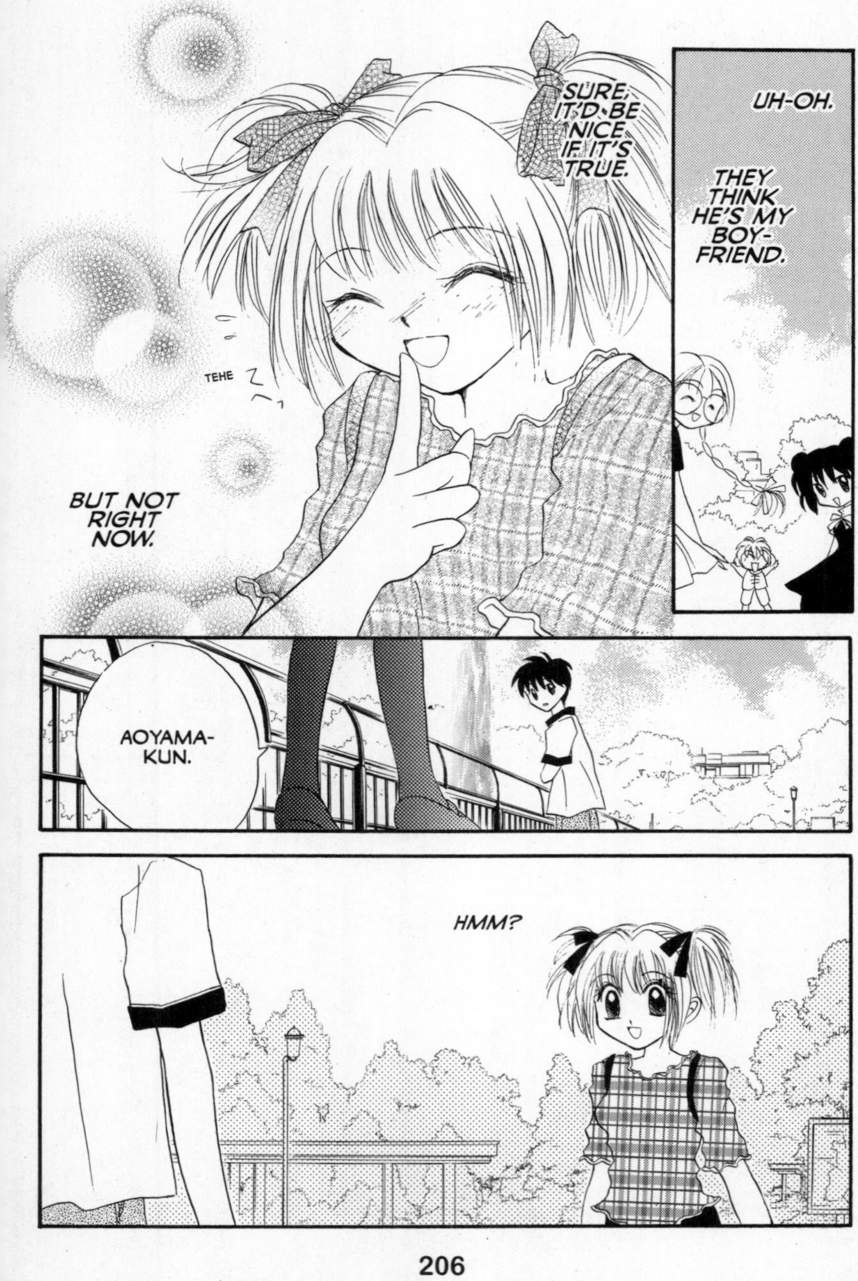
UH-OH.
THEY THINK HE'S MY BOY-FRIEND.
SURE, IT'D BE NICE IF IT'S TRUE.
TEHE
BUT NOT RIGHT NOW.
AOYAMA-KUN.
HMM?

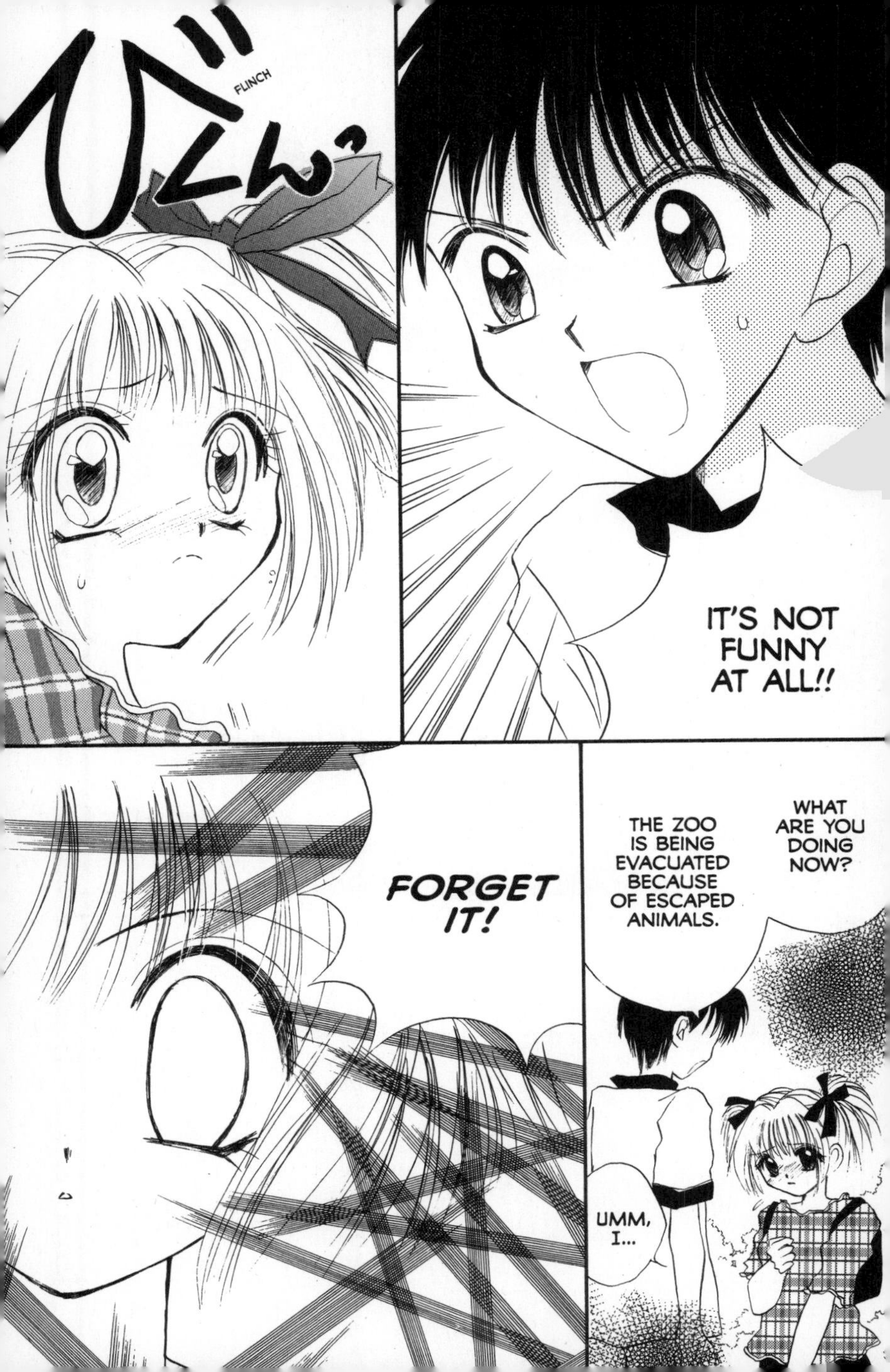
IT'S NOT FUNNY AT ALL!!
びくんっ
FLINCH
WHAT ARE YOU DOING NOW?
THE ZOO IS BEING EVACUATED BECAUSE OF ESCAPED ANIMALS.
UMM, I...
FORGET IT!

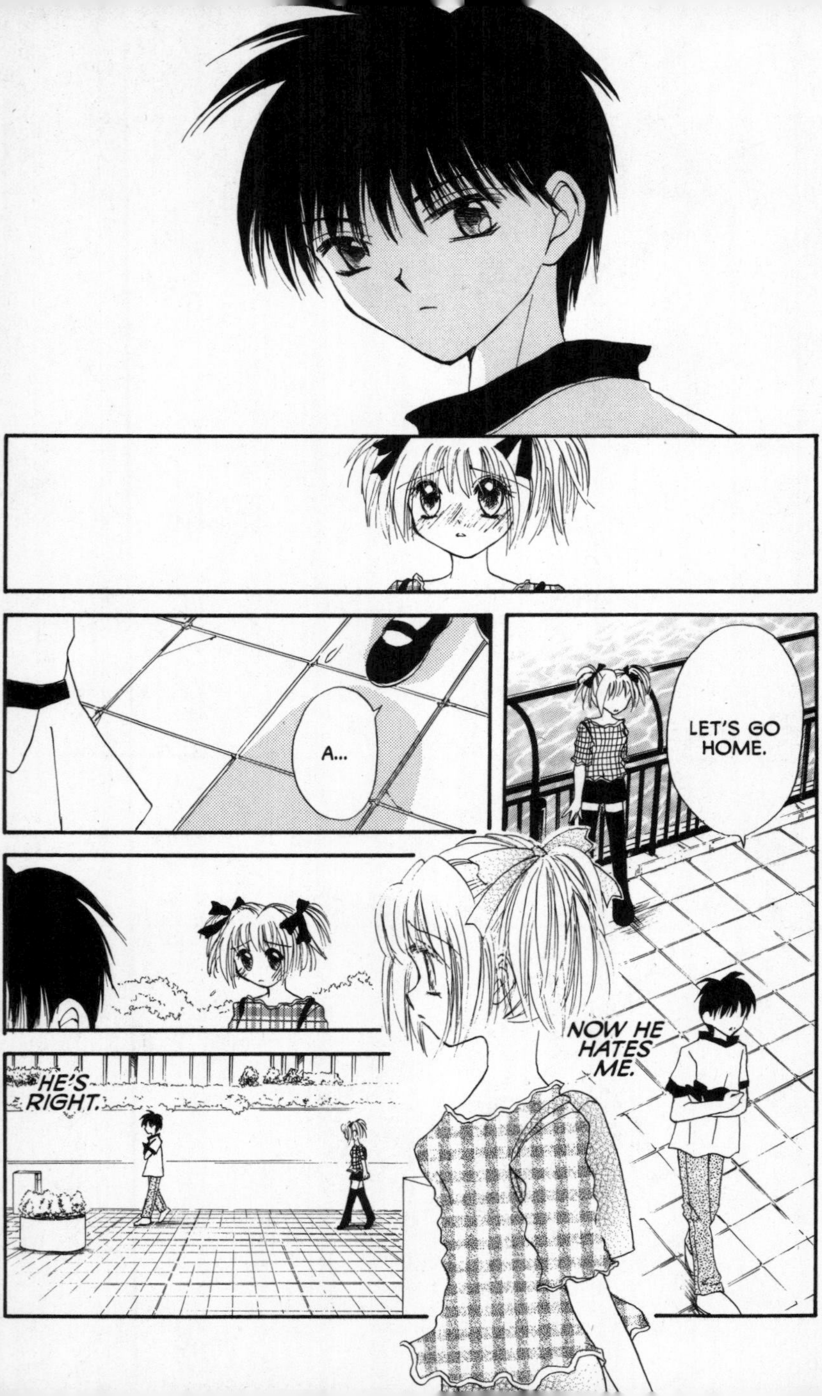
LET'S GO HOME.
NOW HE HATES ME.
A...
HE'S RIGHT.

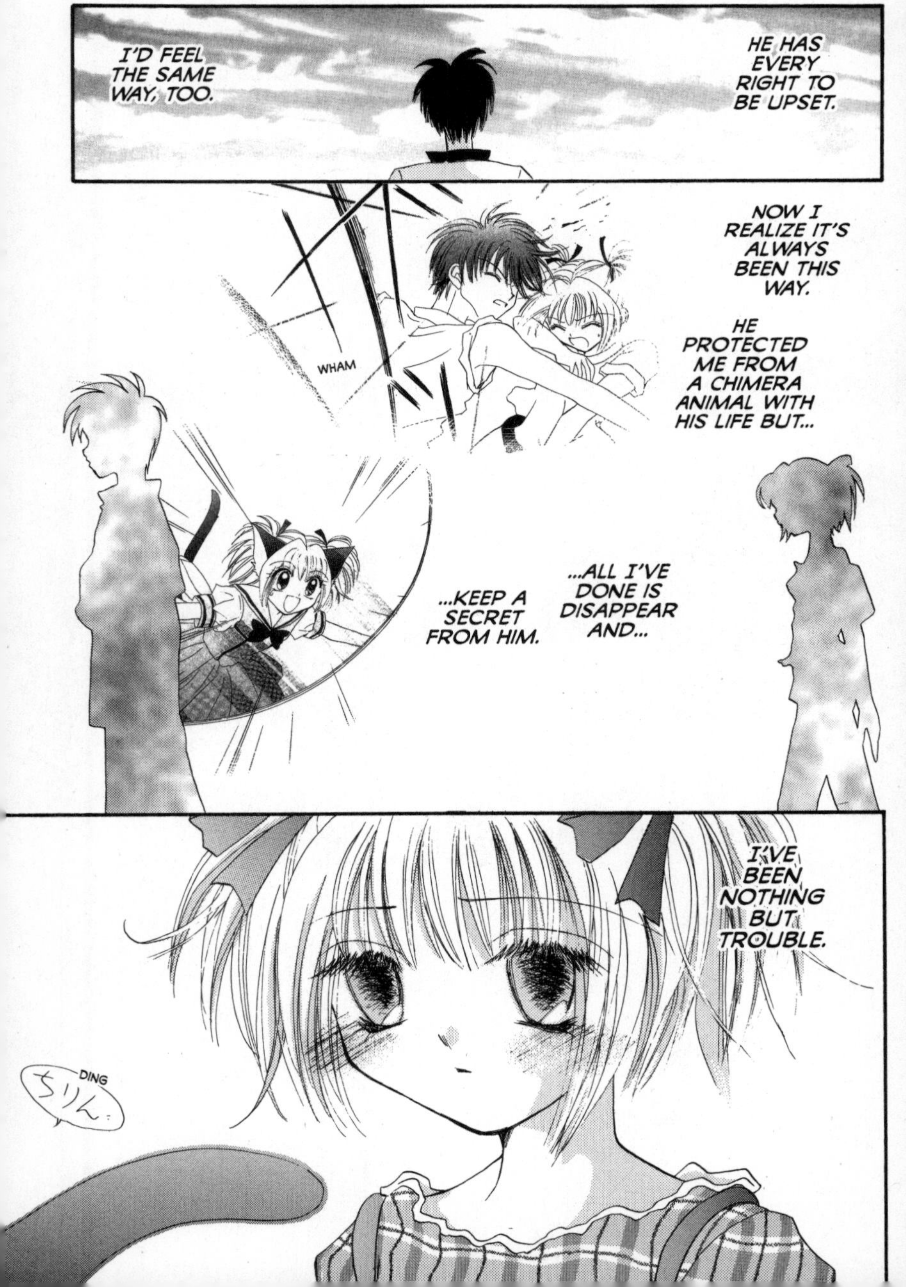
HE HAS EVERY RIGHT TO BE UPSET.
I'D FEEL THE SAME WAY, TOO.
NOW I REALIZE IT'S ALWAYS BEEN THIS WAY.
HE PROTECTED ME FROM A CHIMERA ANIMAL WITH HIS LIFE BUT...
WHAM
...ALL I'VE DONE IS DISAPPEAR AND...
...KEEP A SECRET FROM HIM.
I'VE BEEN NOTHING BUT TROUBLE.
DING
ちりん

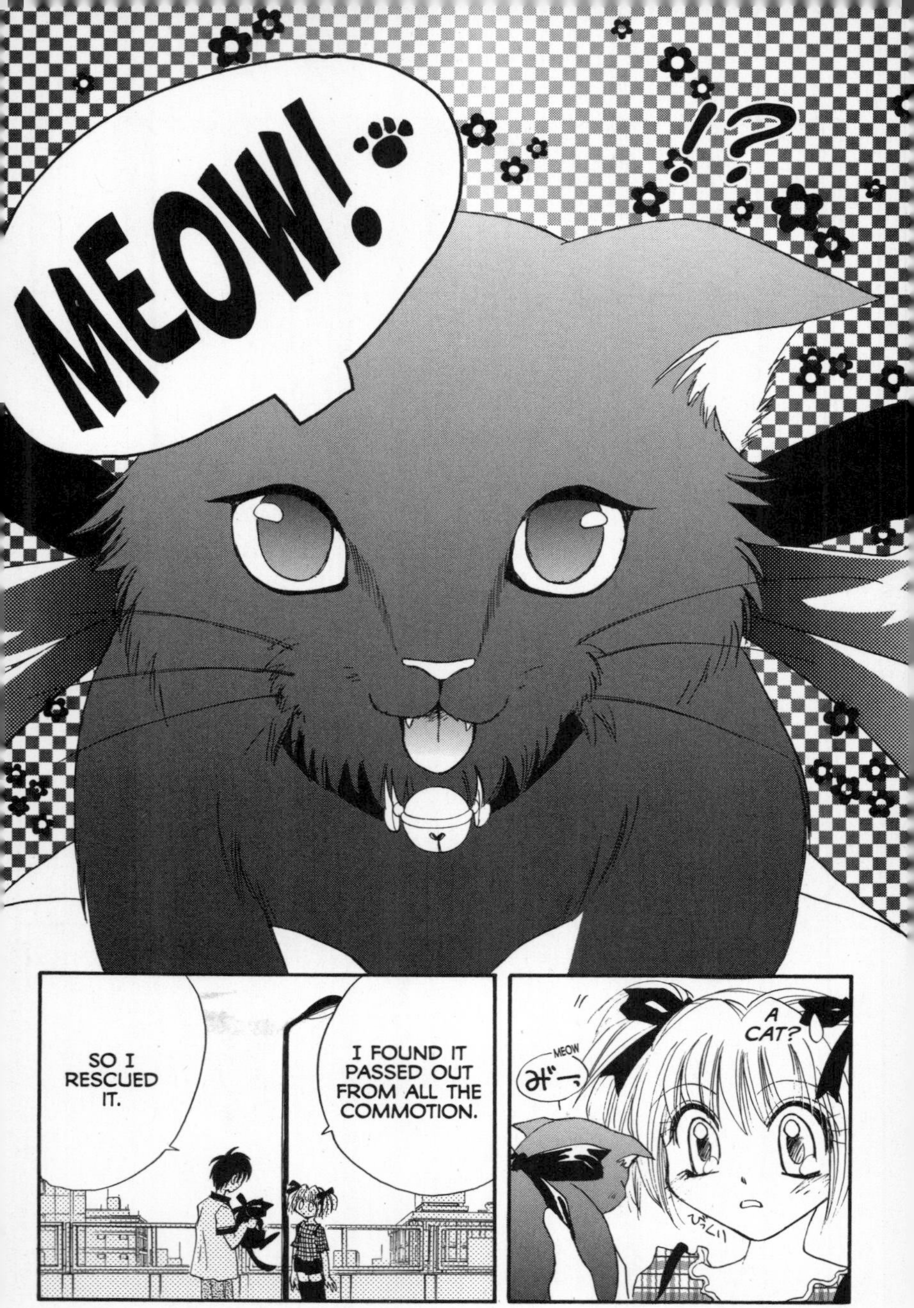
MEOW!
!?
A CAT?
MEOW
みー
I FOUND IT PASSED OUT FROM ALL THE COMMOTION.
SO I RESCUED IT.

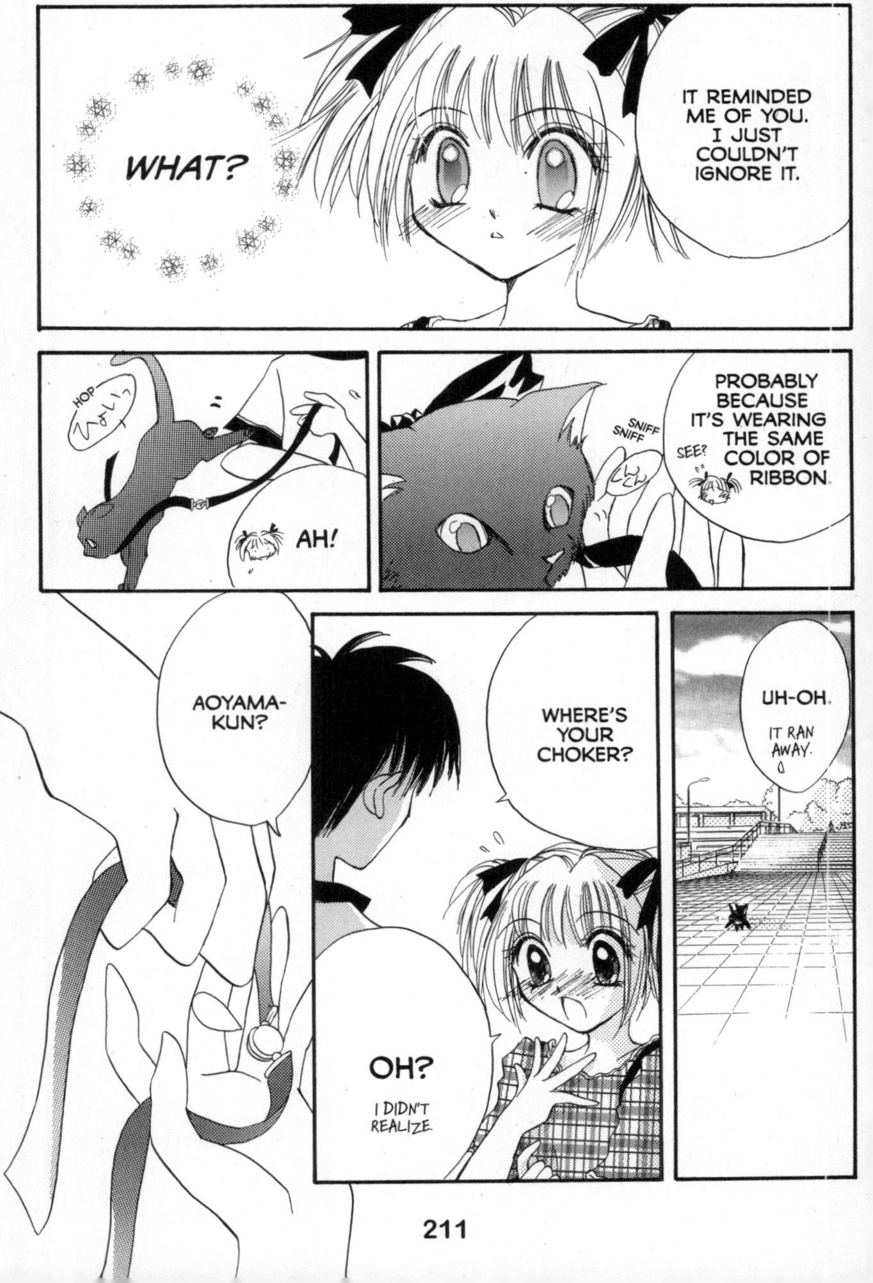
IT REMINDED ME OF YOU. I JUST COULDN'T IGNORE IT.
WHAT?
PROBABLY BECAUSE IT'S WEARING THE SAME COLOR OF RIBBON.
SEE?
SNIFF SNIFF
HOP
AH!
UH-OH.
IT RAN AWAY.
WHERE'S YOUR CHOKER?
OH?
I DIDN'T REALIZE.
AOYAMA-KUN?

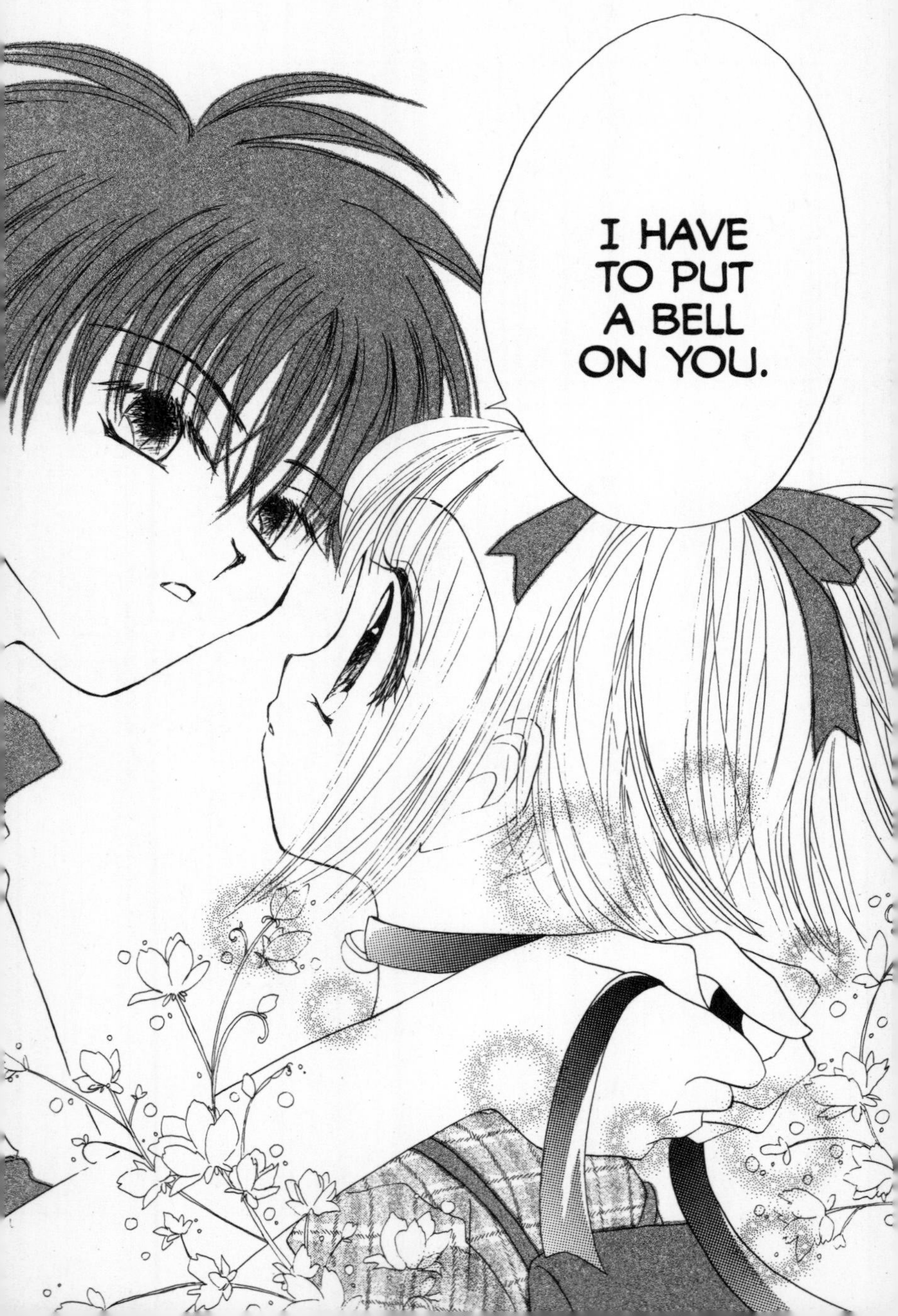
I HAVE TO PUT A BELL ON YOU.

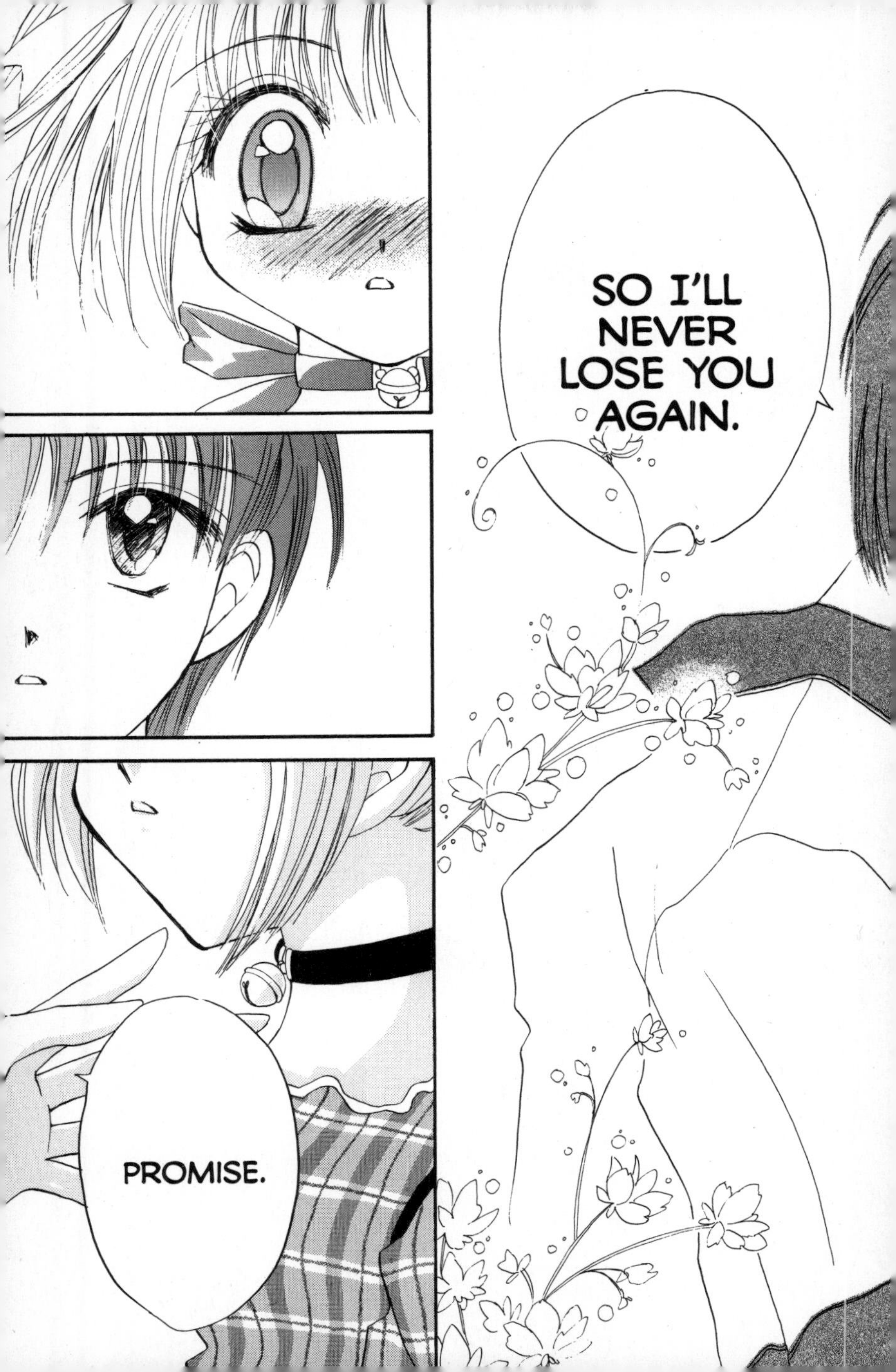
SO I'LL NEVER LOSE YOU AGAIN.
PROMISE.

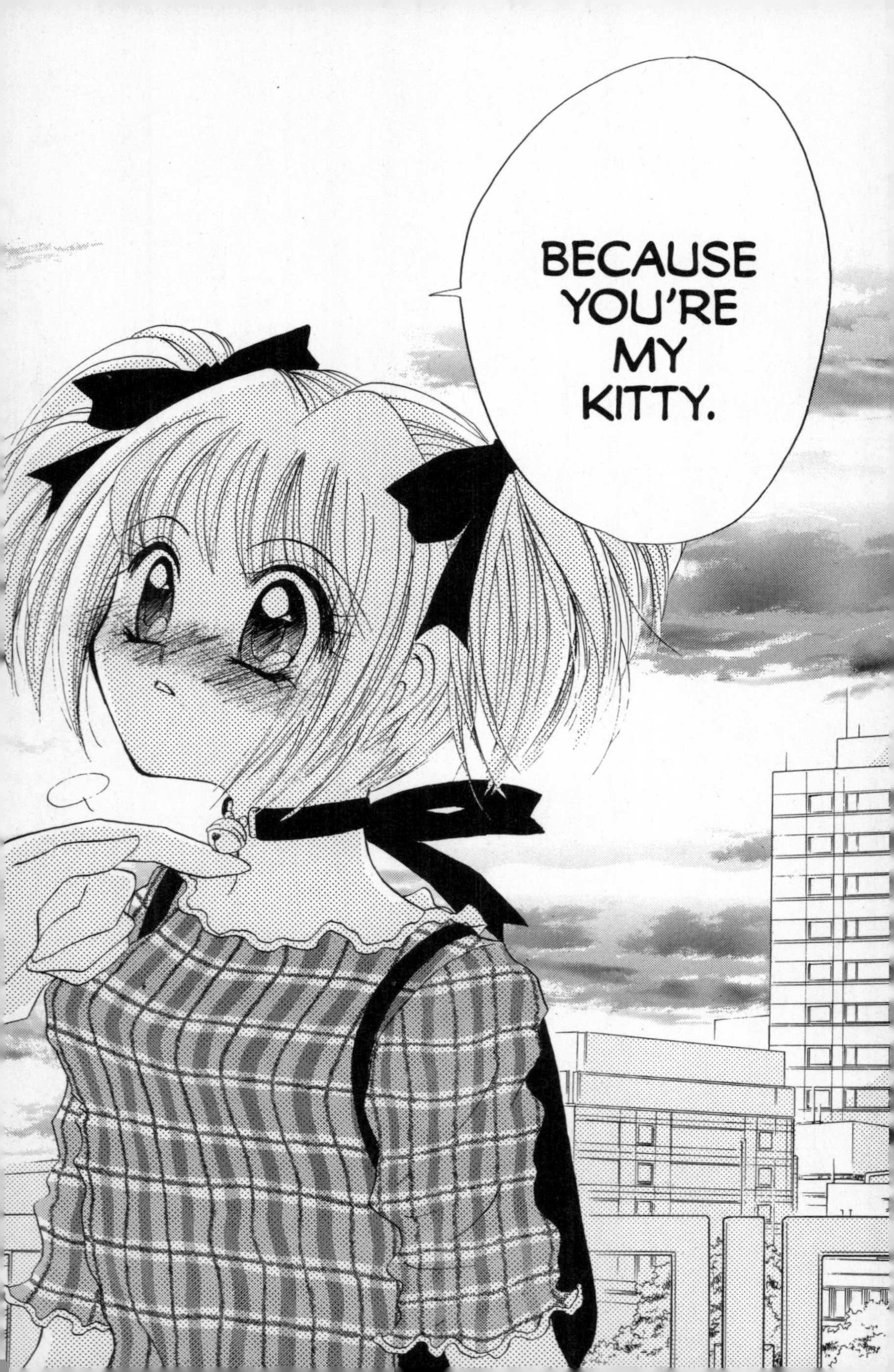
BECAUSE YOU'RE MY KITTY.

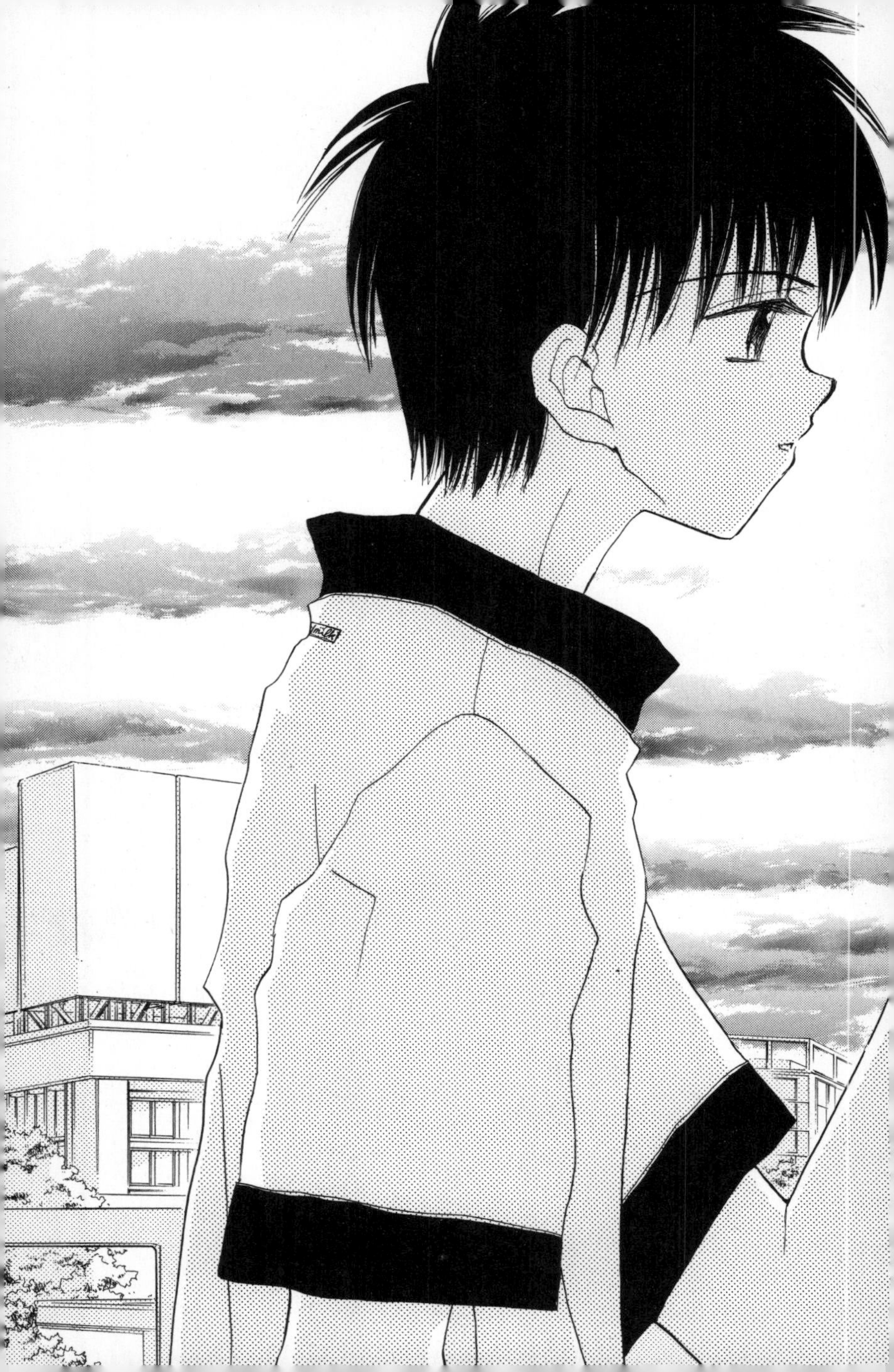

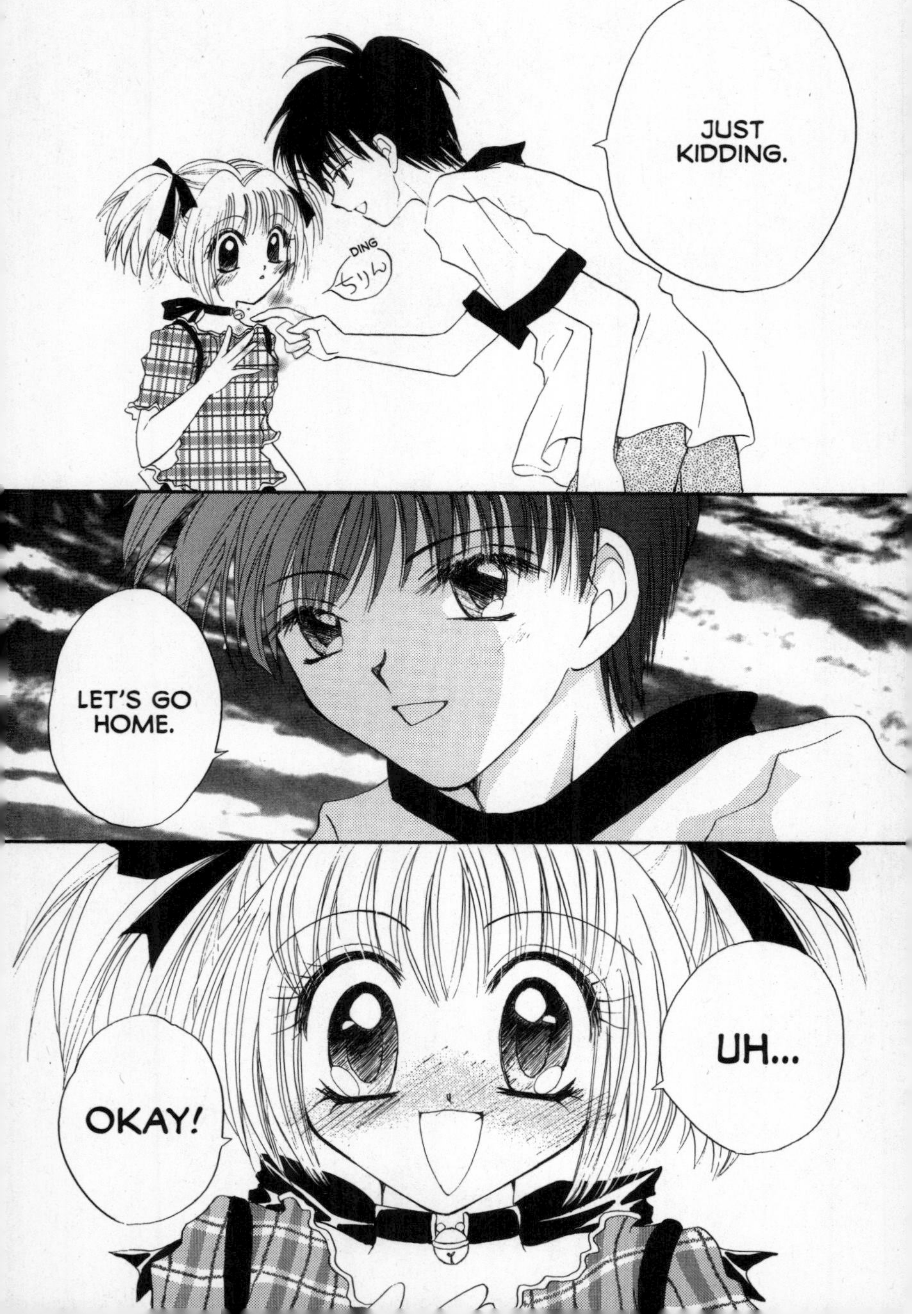
JUST KIDDING.
DING
ちりん
LET'S GO HOME.
UH...
OKAY!

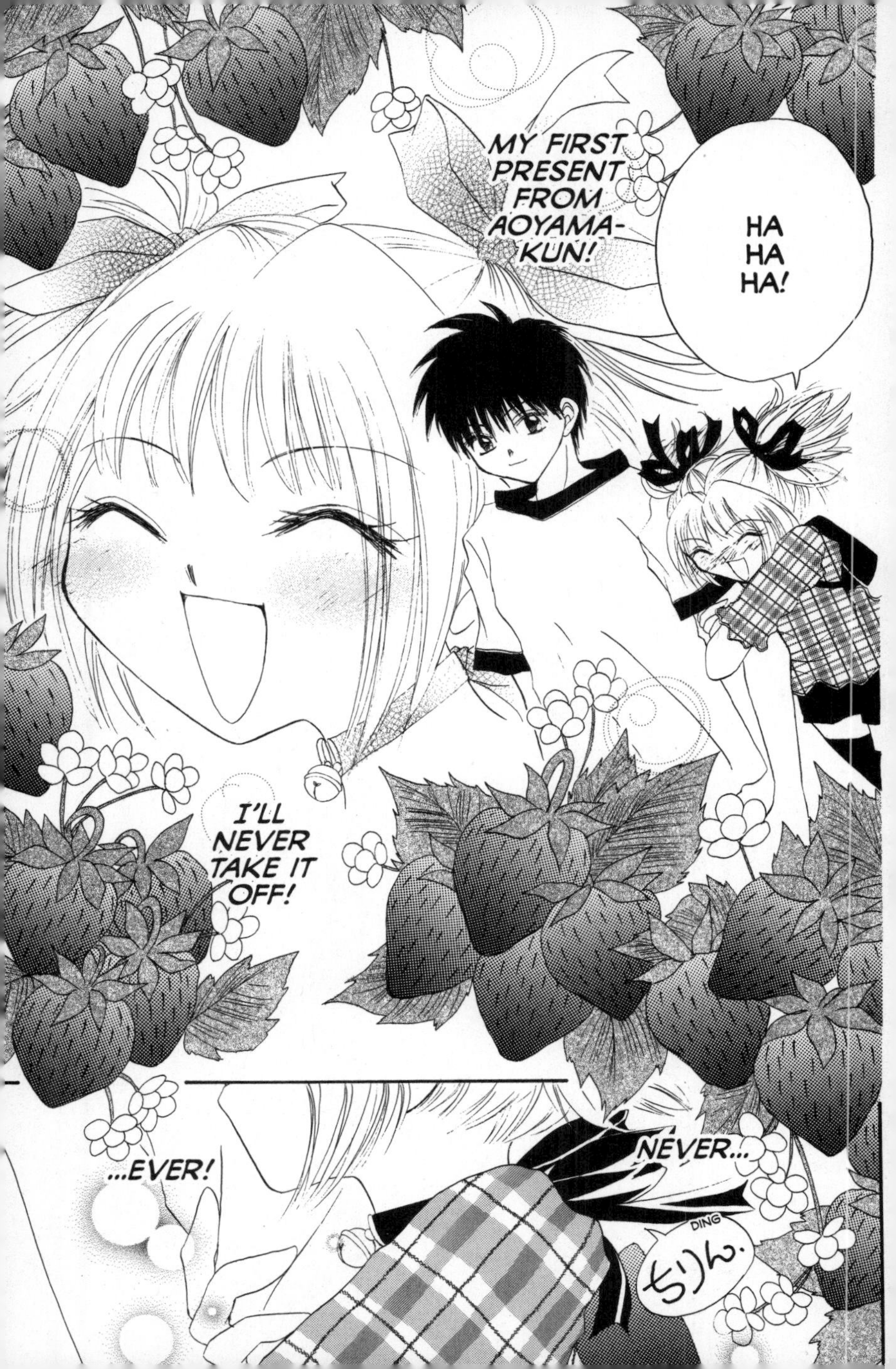
HA HA HA!
MY FIRST PRESENT FROM AOYAMA-KUN!
I'LL NEVER TAKE IT OFF!
NEVER...
DING
ちりん.
...EVER!

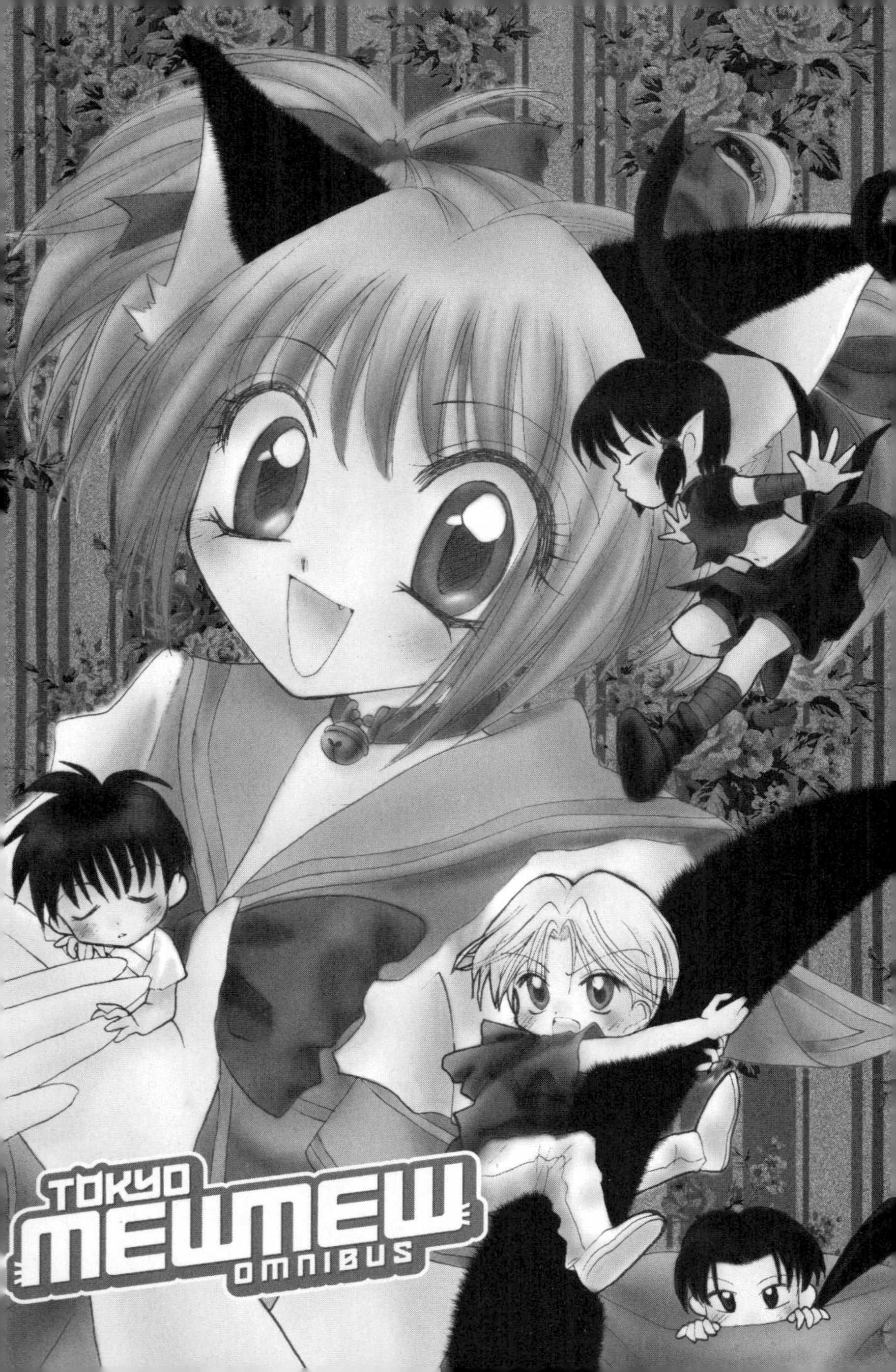
TOKYO
MEWMEW
OMNIBUS

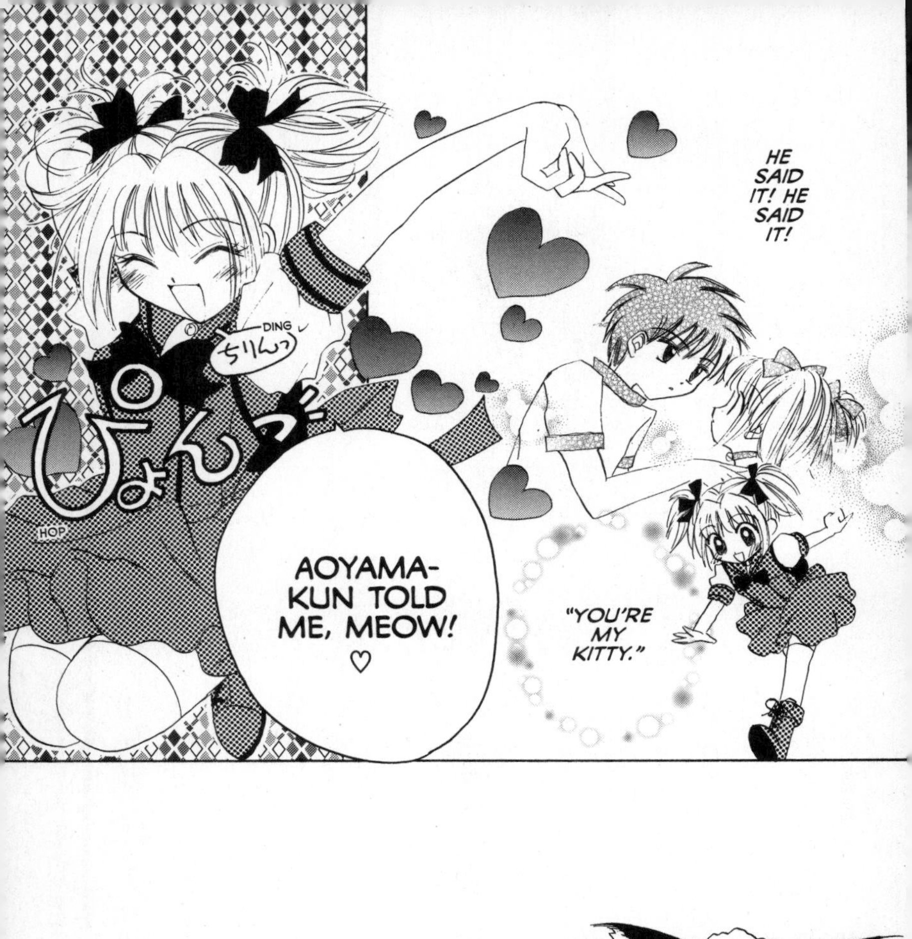
HE SAID IT! HE SAID IT!
DING
ちりんっ
"YOU'RE MY KITTY."
AOYAMA-KUN TOLD ME, MEOW! ♡
ぴょんっ
HOP

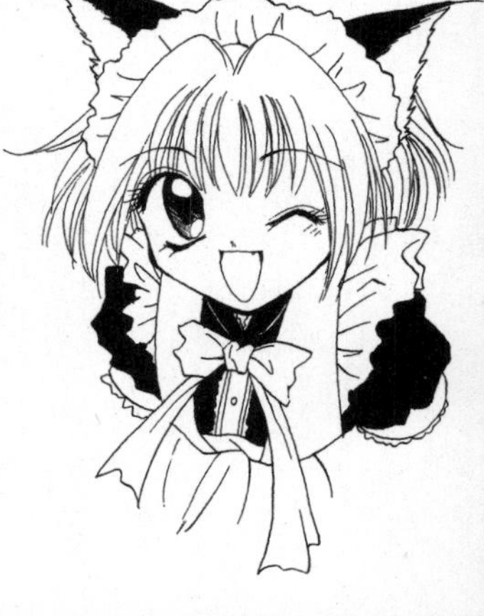

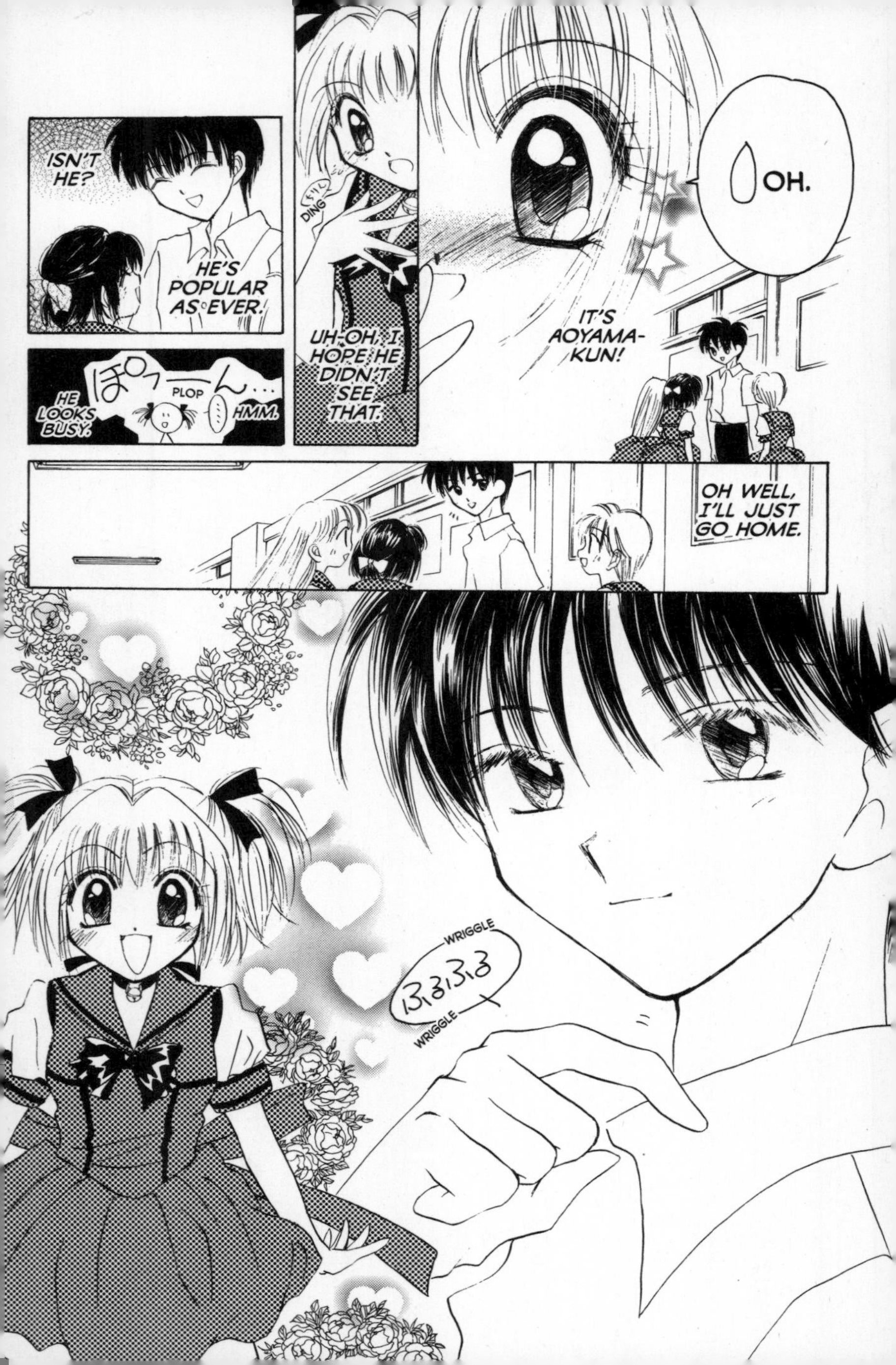
OH.
IT'S AOYAMA-KUN!
DING
UH-OH, I HOPE HE DIDN'T SEE THAT.
ISN'T HE?
HE'S POPULAR AS EVER.
ぽっーん…
PLOP
HMM.
HE LOOKS BUSY.
OH WELL, I'LL JUST GO HOME.
ふるふる
WRIGGLE
WRIGGLE

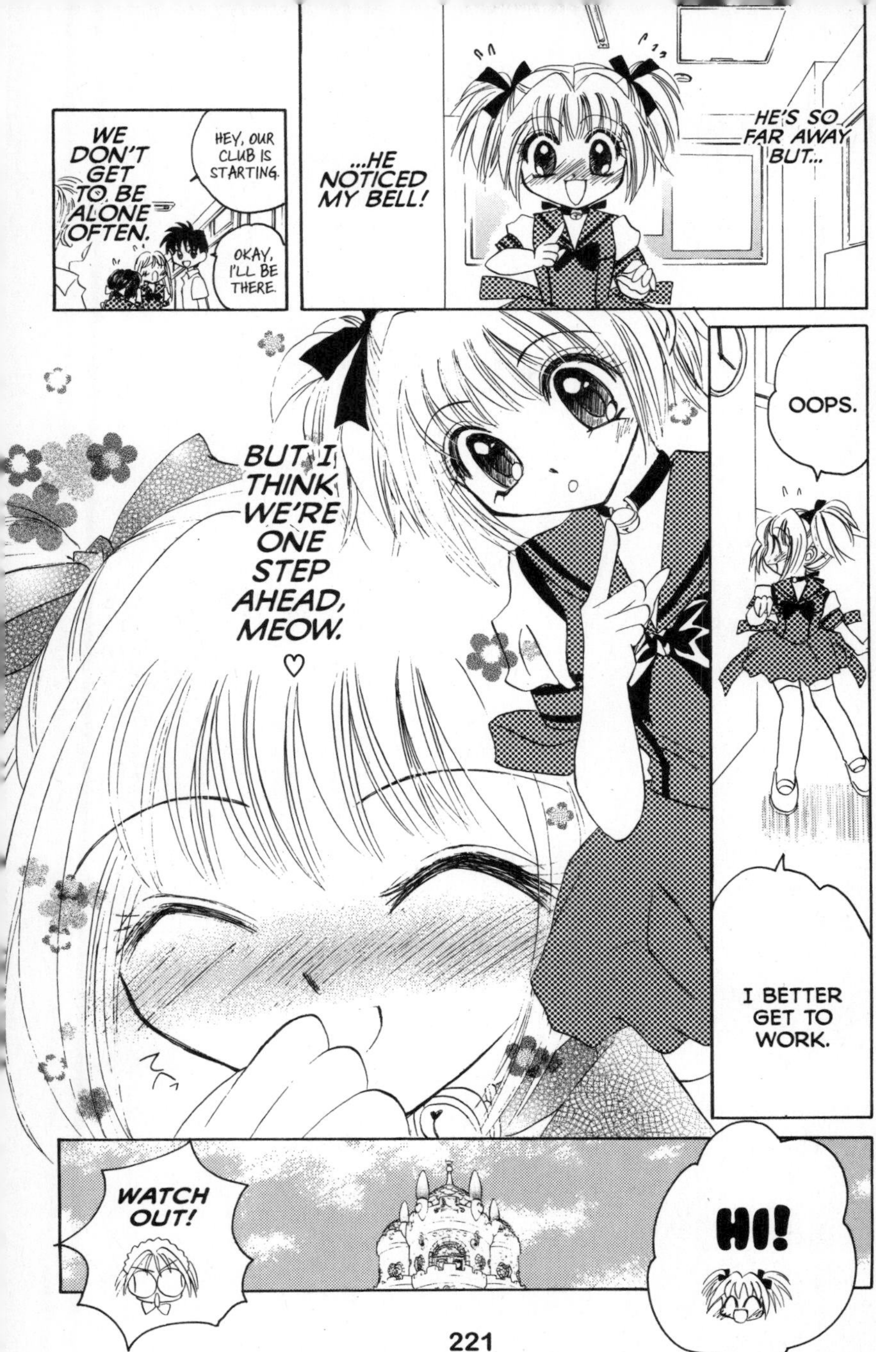

HE'S SO FAR AWAY BUT...
...HE NOTICED MY BELL!
HEY, OUR CLUB IS STARTING.
WE DON'T GET TO BE ALONE OFTEN.
OKAY, I'LL BE THERE.
OOPS.
I BETTER GET TO WORK.
BUT I THINK WE'RE ONE STEP AHEAD, MEOW. ♡
HI!
WATCH OUT!

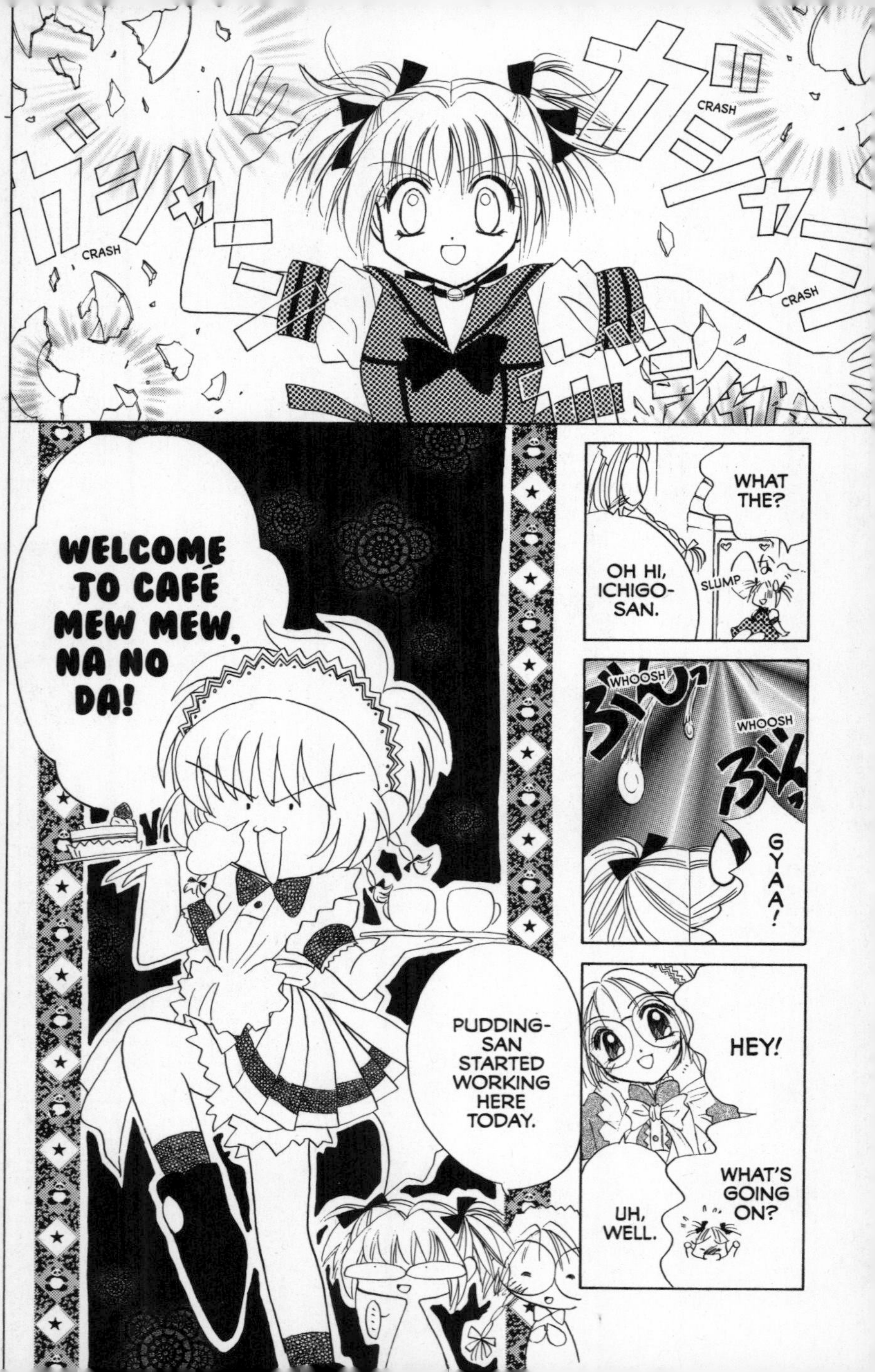
CRASH
CRASH
CRASH
WHAT THE?
OH HI, ICHIGO-SAN.
SLUMP
WHOOSH
WHOOSH
GYAA!
HEY!
WHAT'S GOING ON?
UH, WELL.
WELCOME TO CAFÉ MEW MEW, NA NO DA!
PUDDING-SAN STARTED WORKING HERE TODAY.

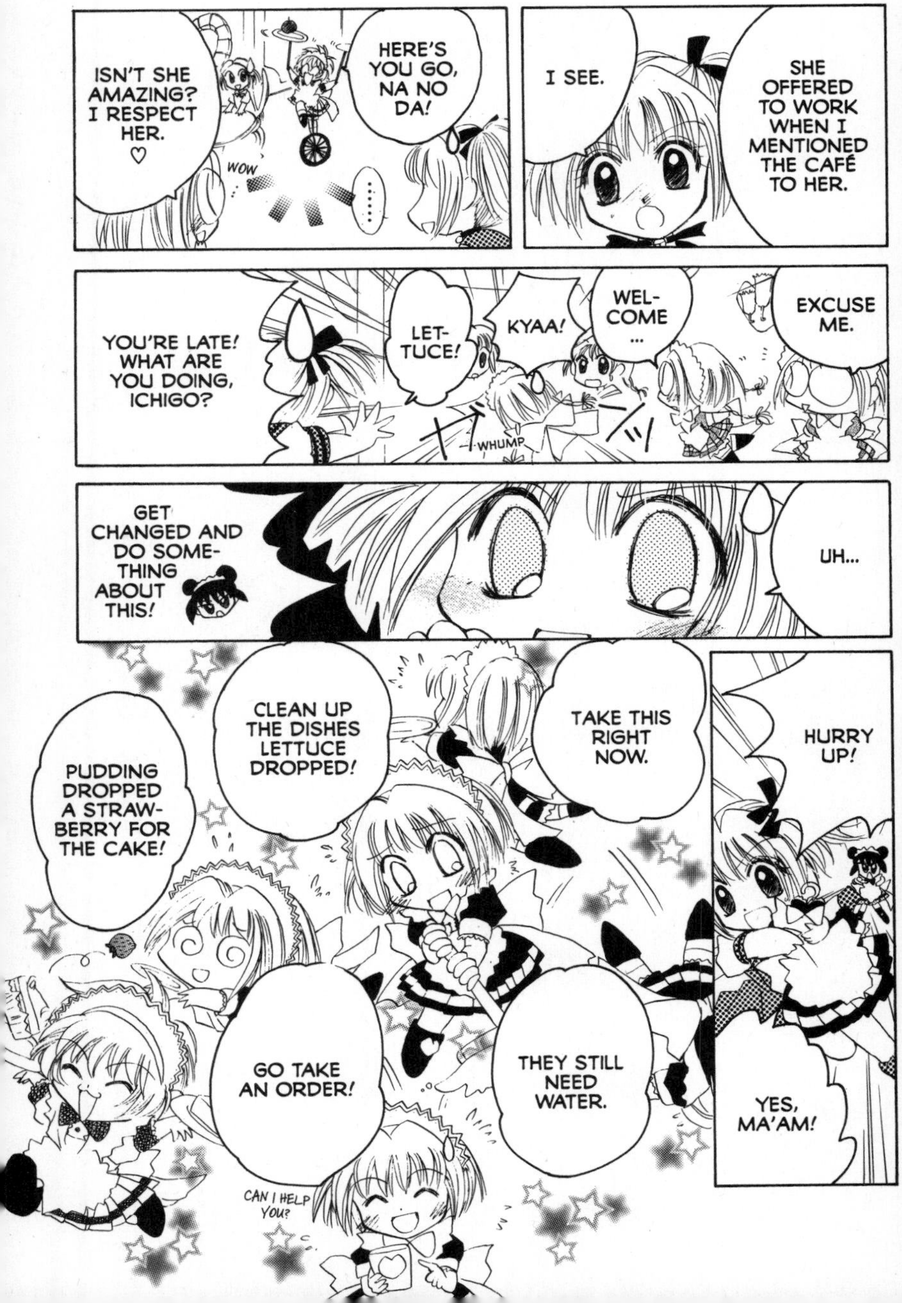
SHE OFFERED TO WORK WHEN I MENTIONED THE CAFÉ TO HER.
I SEE.
HERE'S YOU GO, NA NO DA!
ISN'T SHE AMAZING? I RESPECT HER. ♡
WOW
......
EXCUSE ME.
WEL-COME...
KYAA!
LET-TUCE!
YOU'RE LATE! WHAT ARE YOU DOING, ICHIGO?
WHUMP
UH...
GET CHANGED AND DO SOME-THING ABOUT THIS!
HURRY UP!
YES, MA'AM!
TAKE THIS RIGHT NOW.
CLEAN UP THE DISHES LETTUCE DROPPED!
PUDDING DROPPED A STRAW-BERRY FOR THE CAKE!
THEY STILL NEED WATER.
GO TAKE AN ORDER!
CAN I HELP YOU?

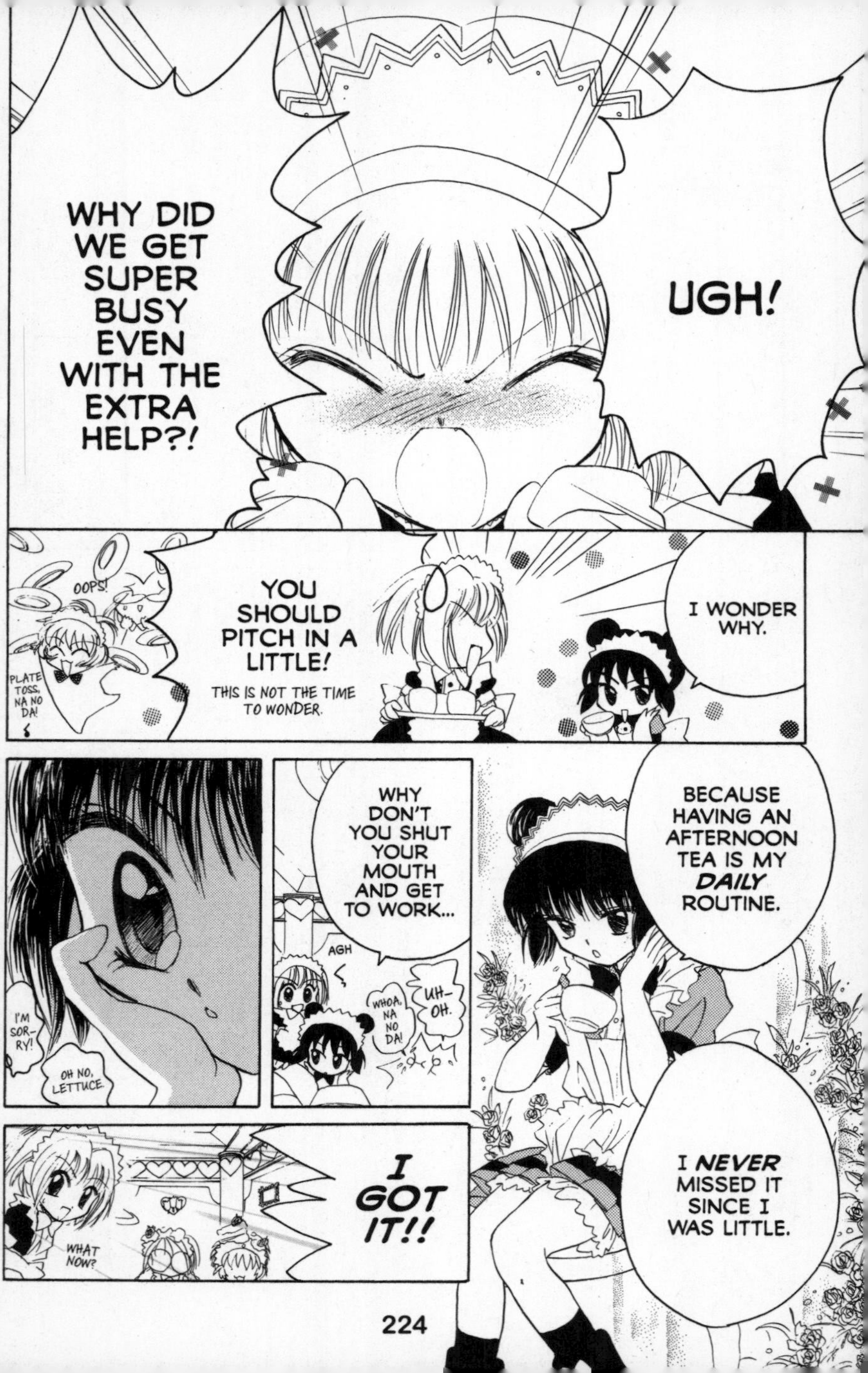
UGH!
WHY DID WE GET SUPER BUSY EVEN WITH THE EXTRA HELP?!
I WONDER WHY.
YOU SHOULD PITCH IN A LITTLE!
THIS IS NOT THE TIME TO WONDER.
OOPS!
PLATE TOSS, NA NO DA!
BECAUSE HAVING AN AFTERNOON TEA IS MY DAILY ROUTINE.
I NEVER MISSED IT SINCE I WAS LITTLE.
WHY DON'T YOU SHUT YOUR MOUTH AND GET TO WORK...
AGH
UH-OH.
WHOA, NA NO DA!
I'M SORRY!
OH NO, LETTUCE.
I GOT IT!!
WHAT NOW?

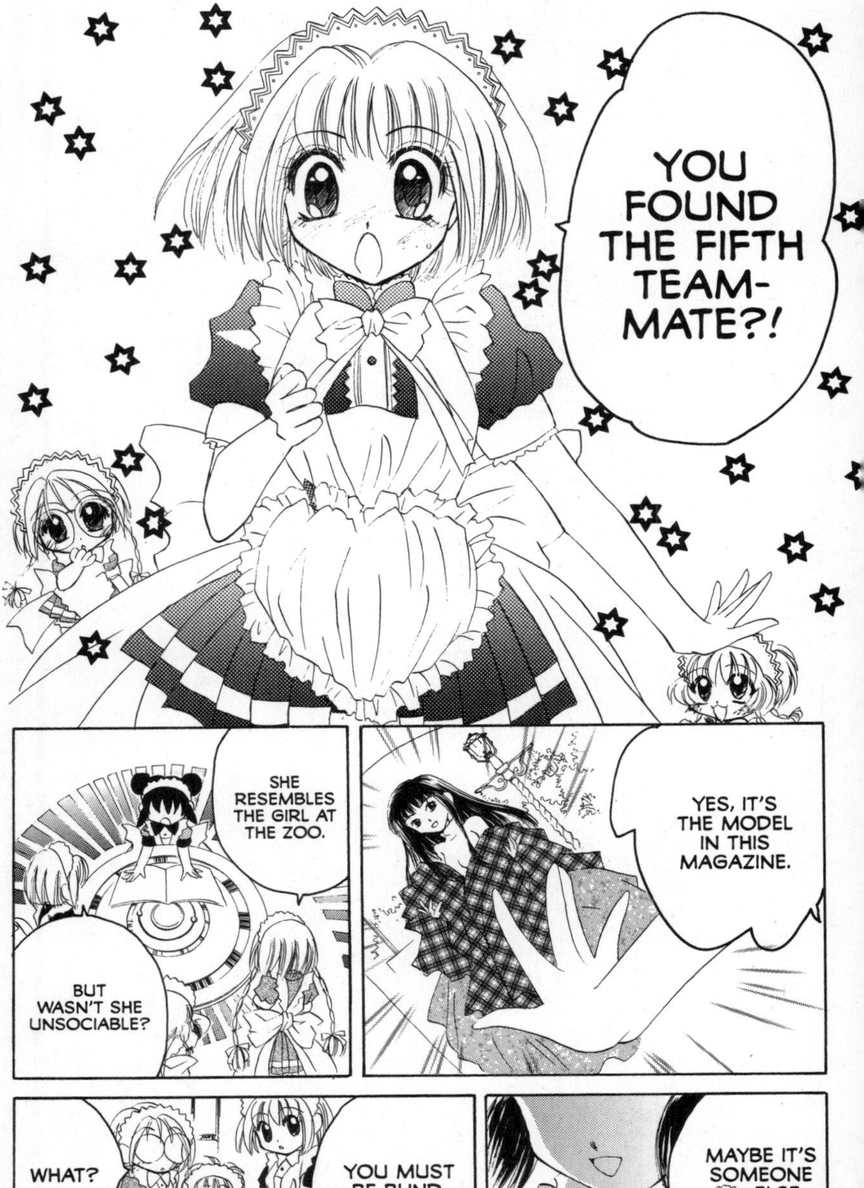
YOU FOUND THE FIFTH TEAM-MATE?!
YES, IT'S THE MODEL IN THIS MAGAZINE.
SHE RESEMBLES THE GIRL AT THE ZOO.
BUT WASN'T SHE UNSOCIABLE?
MAYBE IT'S SOMEONE ELSE.
HA
YOU MUST BE BLIND.
WHAT?

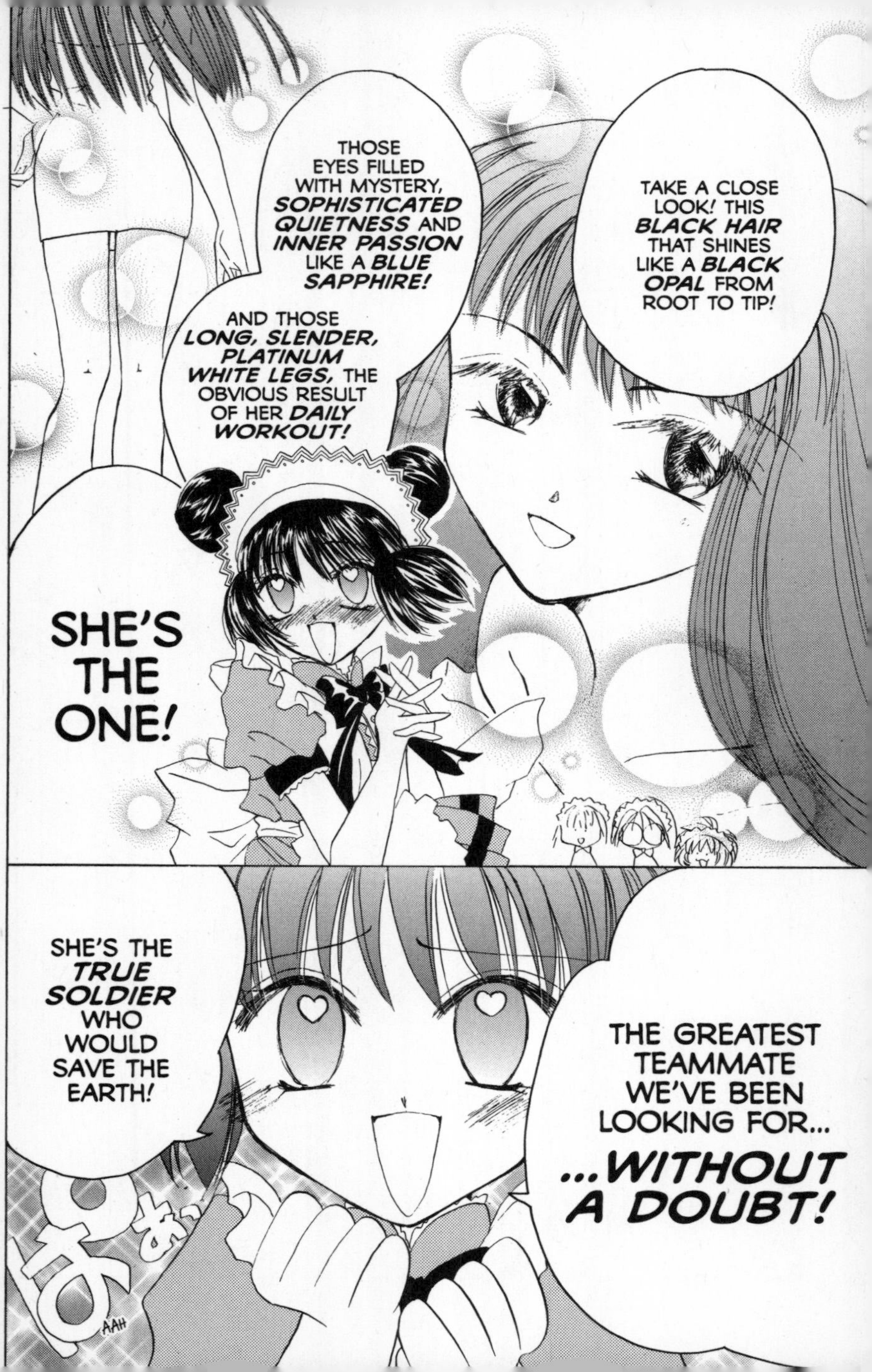
TAKE A CLOSE LOOK! THIS BLACK HAIR THAT SHINES LIKE A BLACK OPAL FROM ROOT TO TIP!
THOSE EYES FILLED WITH MYSTERY, SOPHISTICATED QUIETNESS AND INNER PASSION LIKE A BLUE SAPPHIRE!
AND THOSE LONG, SLENDER, PLATINUM WHITE LEGS, THE OBVIOUS RESULT OF HER DAILY WORKOUT!
SHE'S THE ONE!
THE GREATEST TEAMMATE WE'VE BEEN LOOKING FOR...
...WITHOUT A DOUBT!
SHE'S THE TRUE SOLDIER WHO WOULD SAVE THE EARTH!
AAH

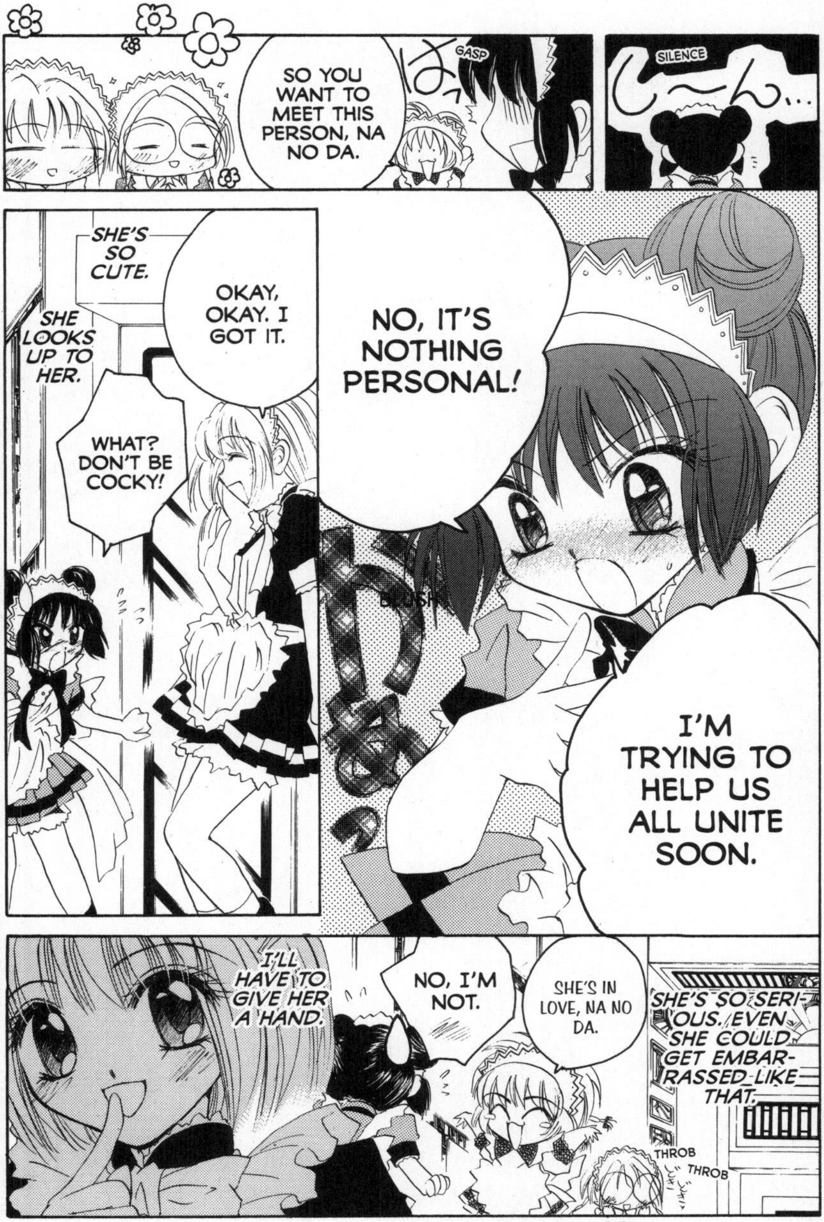
SILENCE
GASP
SO YOU WANT TO MEET THIS PERSON, NA NO DA.
NO, IT'S NOTHING PERSONAL!
BLUSH
I'M TRYING TO HELP US ALL UNITE SOON.
OKAY, OKAY. I GOT IT.
SHE'S SO CUTE.
SHE LOOKS UP TO HER.
WHAT? DON'T BE COCKY!
SHE'S SO SERIOUS. EVEN SHE COULD GET EMBARRASSED LIKE THAT.
THROB
THROB
SHE'S IN LOVE, NA NO DA.
NO, I'M NOT.
I'LL HAVE TO GIVE HER A HAND.

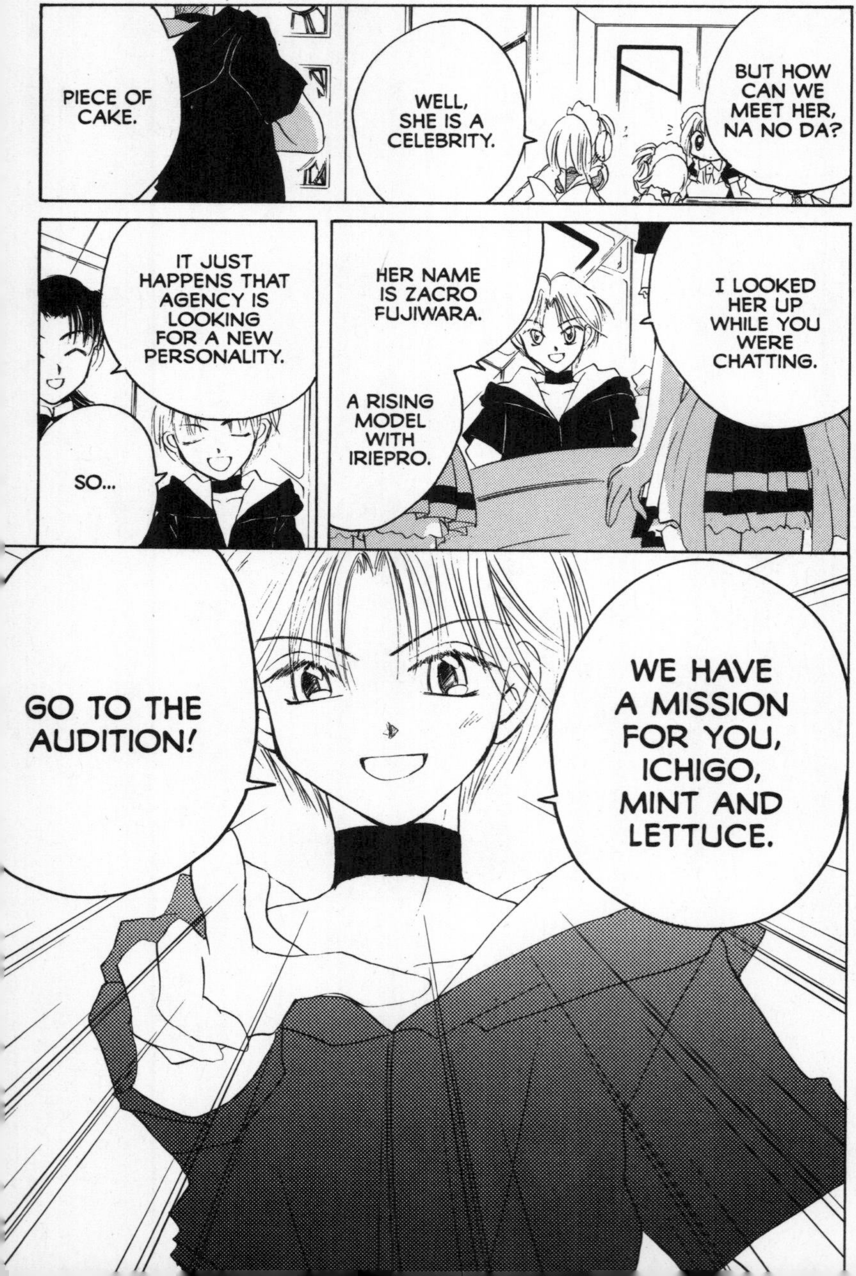
BUT HOW CAN WE MEET HER, NA NO DA?
WELL, SHE IS A CELEBRITY.
PIECE OF CAKE.
I LOOKED HER UP WHILE YOU WERE CHATTING.
HER NAME IS ZACRO FUJIWARA.
A RISING MODEL WITH IRIEPRO.
IT JUST HAPPENS THAT AGENCY IS LOOKING FOR A NEW PERSONALITY.
SO...
WE HAVE A MISSION FOR YOU, ICHIGO, MINT AND LETTUCE.
GO TO THE AUDITION!

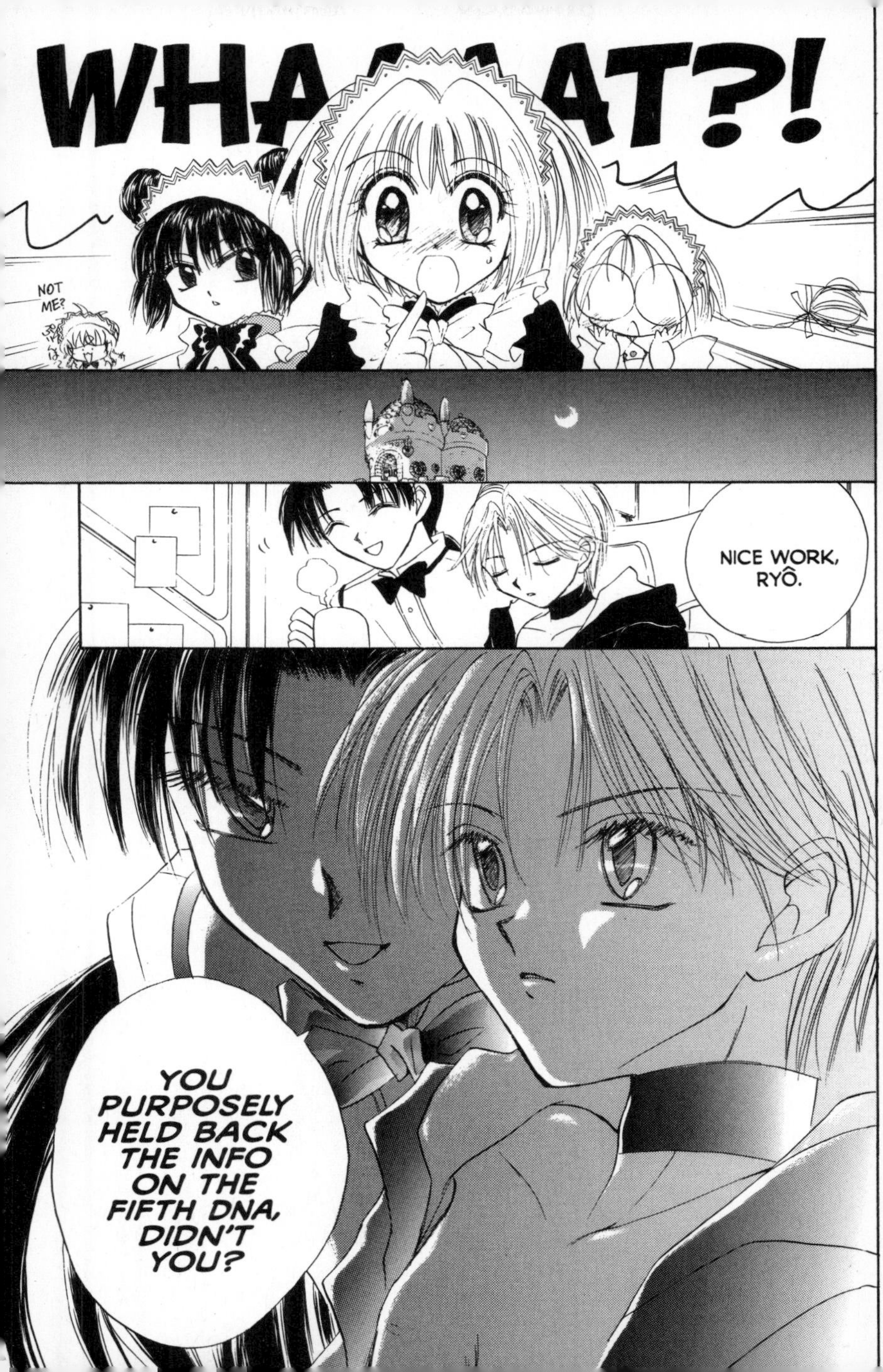
WHAAAAT?!
NOT ME?
NICE WORK, RYÔ.
YOU PURPOSELY HELD BACK THE INFO ON THE FIFTH DNA, DIDN'T YOU?

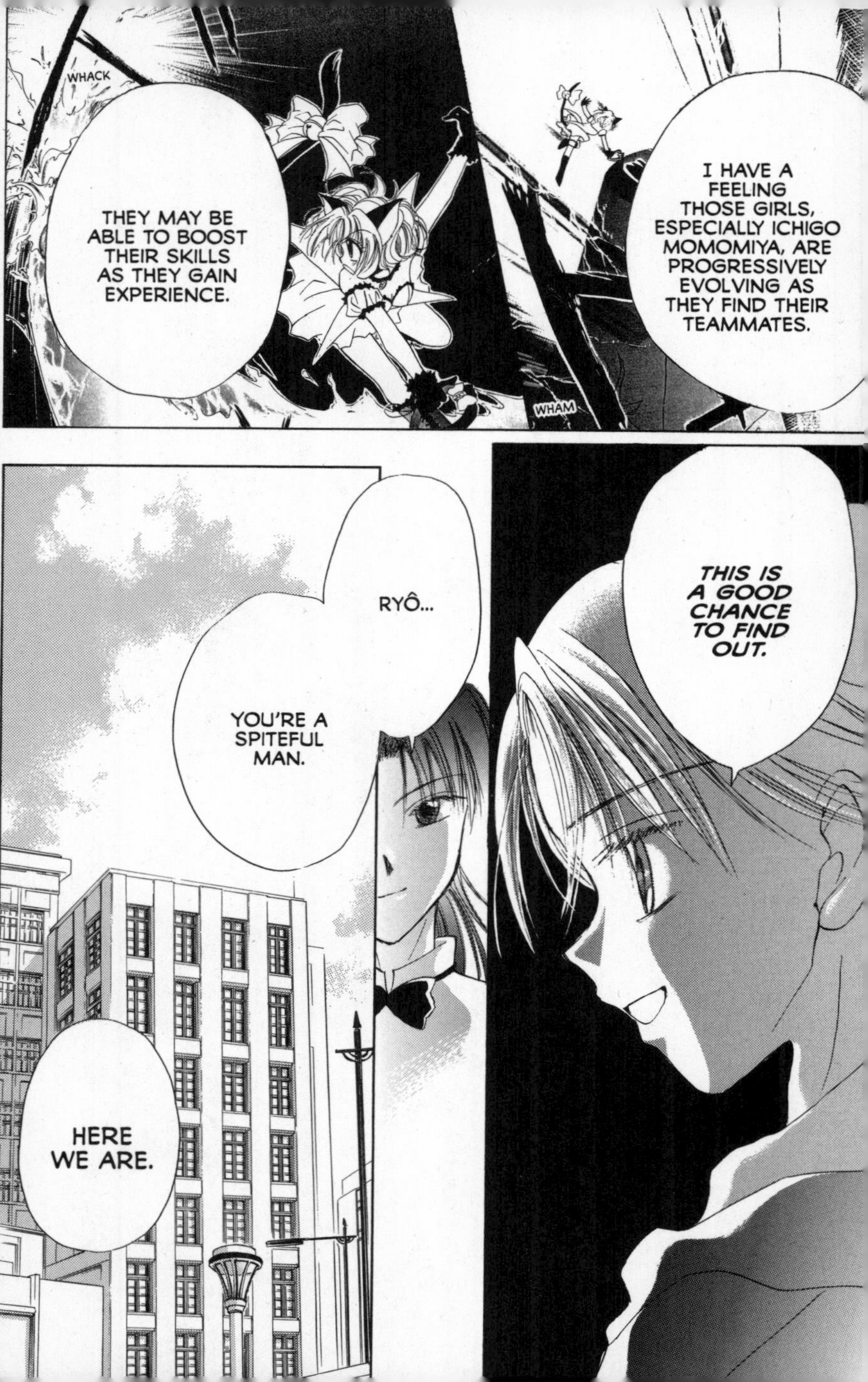
I HAVE A FEELING THOSE GIRLS, ESPECIALLY ICHIGO MOMOMIYA, ARE PROGRESSIVELY EVOLVING AS THEY FIND THEIR TEAMMATES.
WHAM
THEY MAY BE ABLE TO BOOST THEIR SKILLS AS THEY GAIN EXPERIENCE.
WHACK
THIS IS A GOOD CHANCE TO FIND OUT.
RYÔ...
YOU'RE A SPITEFUL MAN.
HERE WE ARE.

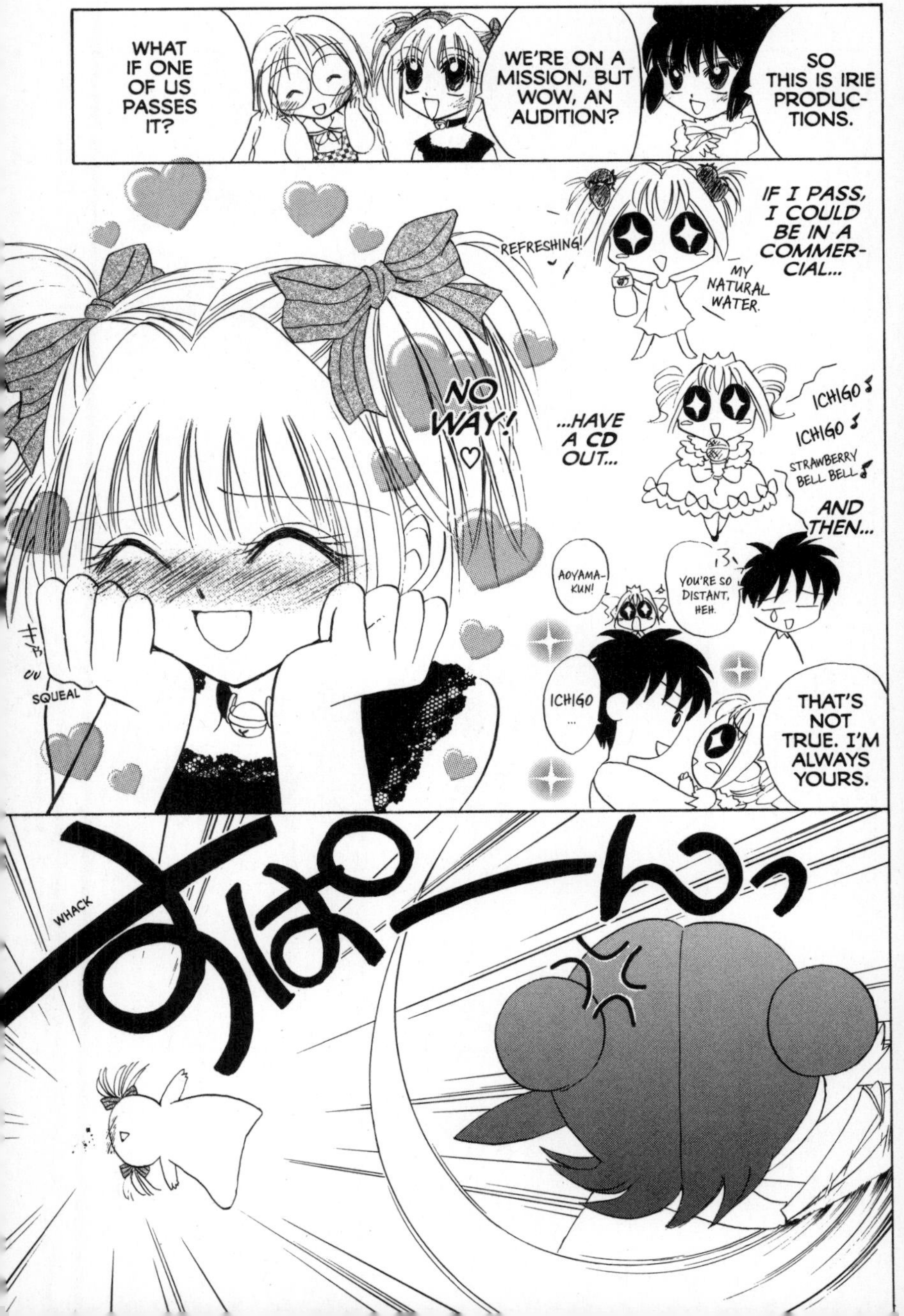
SO THIS IS IRIE PRODUCTIONS.
WE'RE ON A MISSION, BUT WOW, AN AUDITION?
WHAT IF ONE OF US PASSES IT?
IF I PASS, I COULD BE IN A COMMERCIAL...
MY NATURAL WATER.
REFRESHING!
ICHIGO ♪
ICHIGO ♪
STRAWBERRY BELL BELL ♪
...HAVE A CD OUT...
NO WAY! ♡
AND THEN...
YOU'RE SO DISTANT, HEH.
AOYAMA-KUN!
THAT'S NOT TRUE. I'M ALWAYS YOURS.
ICHIGO ...
SQUEAL
すぱーんっ
WHACK

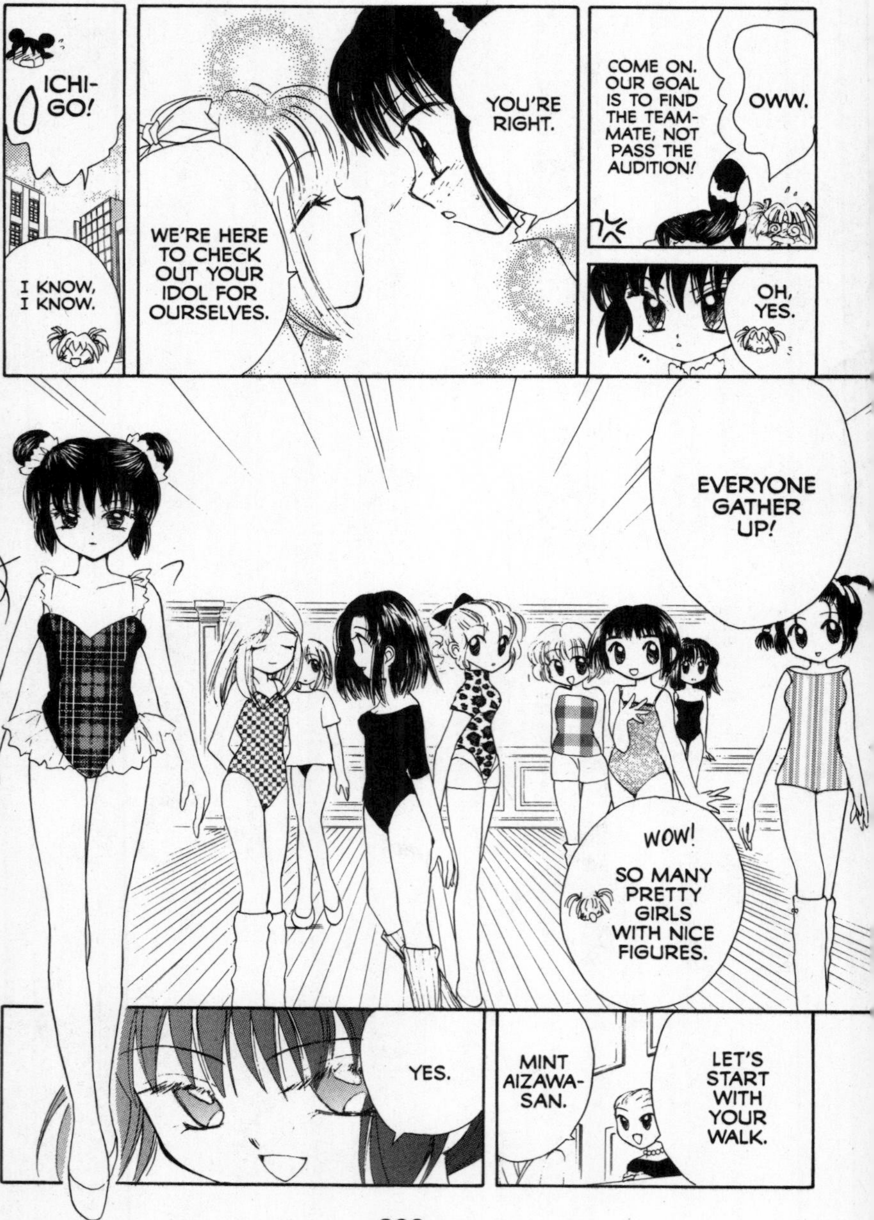
OWW.
COME ON. OUR GOAL IS TO FIND THE TEAM-MATE, NOT PASS THE AUDITION!
OH, YES.
YOU'RE RIGHT.
WE'RE HERE TO CHECK OUT YOUR IDOL FOR OURSELVES.
ICHI-GO!
I KNOW, I KNOW.
EVERYONE GATHER UP!
WOW!
SO MANY PRETTY GIRLS WITH NICE FIGURES.
LET'S START WITH YOUR WALK.
MINT AIZAWA-SAN.
YES.

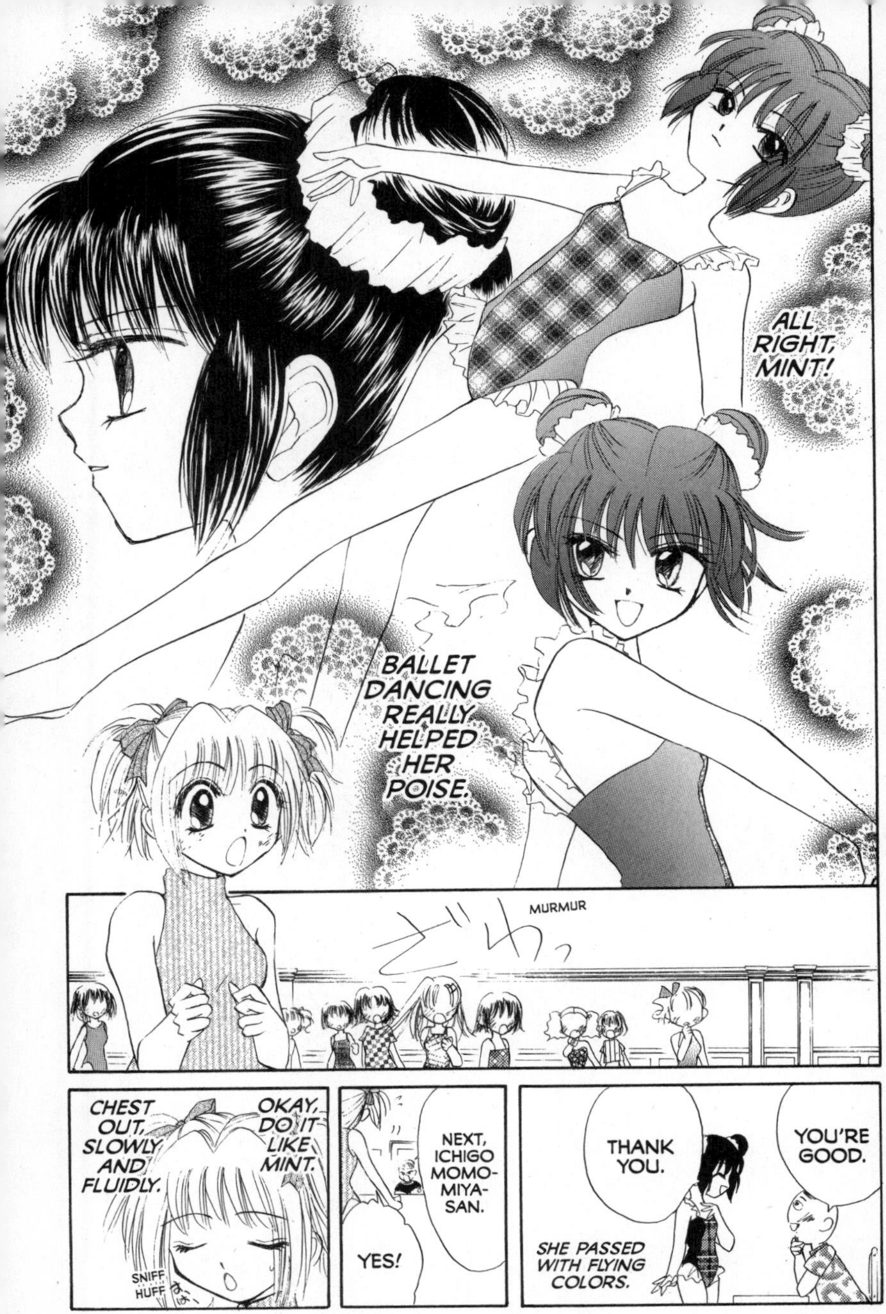
ALL RIGHT, MINT!
BALLET DANCING REALLY HELPED HER POISE.
MURMUR
ざわっ
YOU'RE GOOD.
THANK YOU.
SHE PASSED WITH FLYING COLORS.
NEXT, ICHIGO MOMOMIYA-SAN.
YES!
OKAY, DO IT LIKE MINT.
CHEST OUT, SLOWLY AND FLUIDLY.
SNIFF HUFF

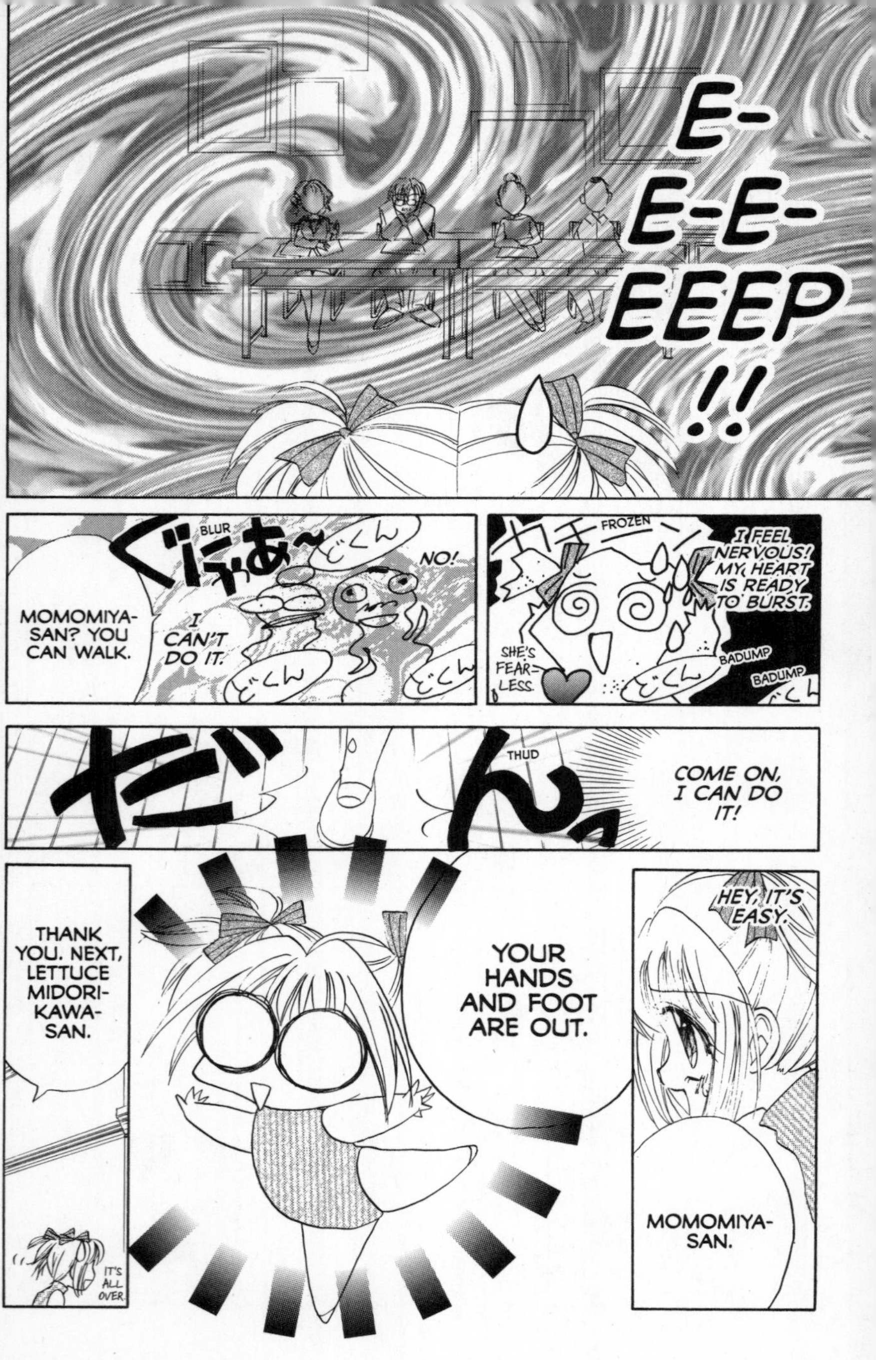
E-E-E-EEEP!!
FROZEN
I FEEL NERVOUS! MY HEART IS READY TO BURST.
SHE'S FEARLESS.
BADUMP
BADUMP
BLUR
NO!
I CAN'T DO IT.
MOMOMIYA-SAN? YOU CAN WALK.
COME ON, I CAN DO IT!
THUD
HEY, IT'S EASY.
MOMOMIYA-SAN.
YOUR HANDS AND FOOT ARE OUT.
THANK YOU. NEXT, LETTUCE MIDORIKAWA-SAN.
IT'S ALL OVER

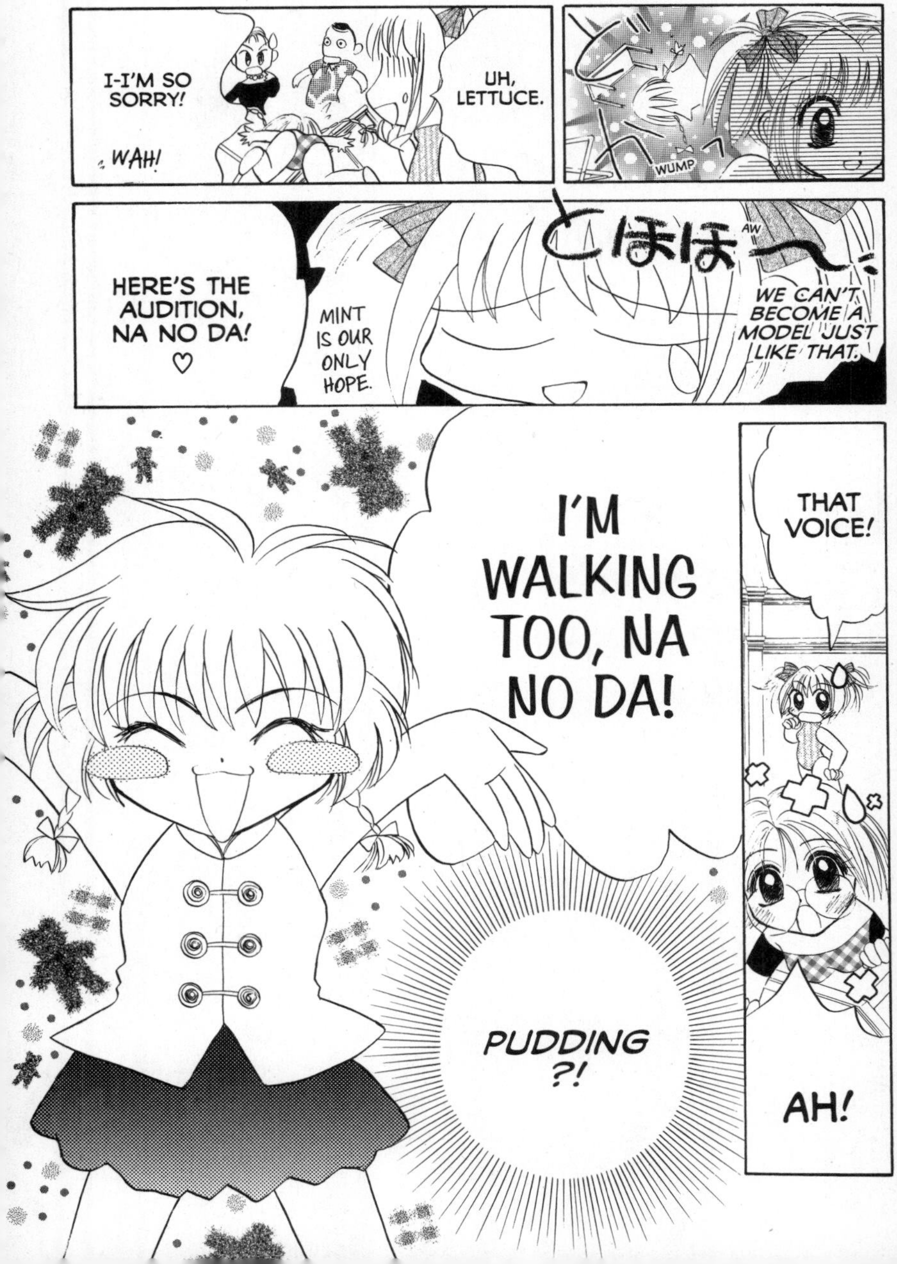

WUMP
UH, LETTUCE.
I-I'M SO SORRY!
WAH!
とほほ～
AW
WE CAN'T BECOME A MODEL JUST LIKE THAT.
MINT IS OUR ONLY HOPE.
HERE'S THE AUDITION, NA NO DA! ♡
THAT VOICE!
AH!
I'M WALKING TOO, NA NO DA!
PUDDING?!

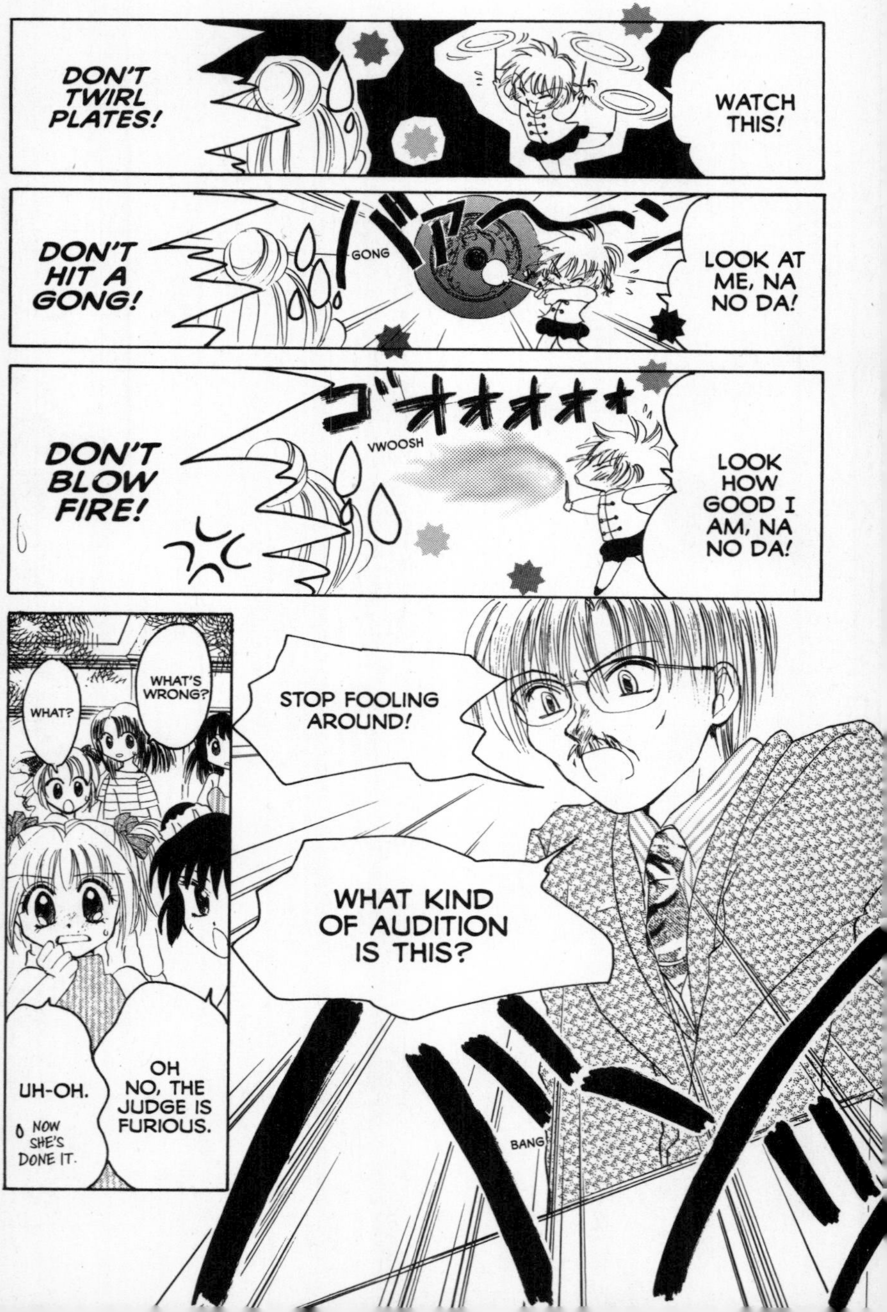

WATCH THIS!
DON'T TWIRL PLATES!
LOOK AT ME, NA NO DA!
GONG
DON'T HIT A GONG!
LOOK HOW GOOD I AM, NA NO DA!
VWOOSH
DON'T BLOW FIRE!
STOP FOOLING AROUND!
WHAT KIND OF AUDITION IS THIS?
BANG
WHAT'S WRONG?
WHAT?
OH NO, THE JUDGE IS FURIOUS.
UH-OH.
NOW SHE'S DONE IT.

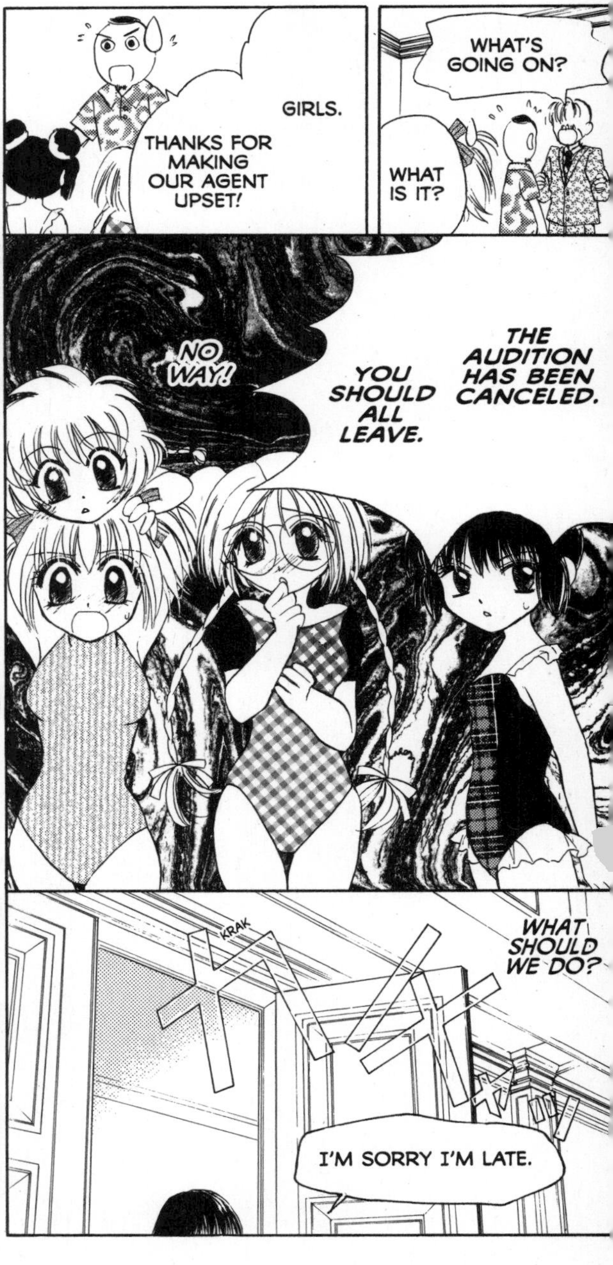
WHAT'S GOING ON?
WHAT IS IT?
GIRLS.
THANKS FOR MAKING OUR AGENT UPSET!
THE AUDITION HAS BEEN CANCELED.
YOU SHOULD ALL LEAVE.
NO WAY!
WHAT SHOULD WE DO?
KRAK
I'M SORRY I'M LATE.

Ikumin's Day

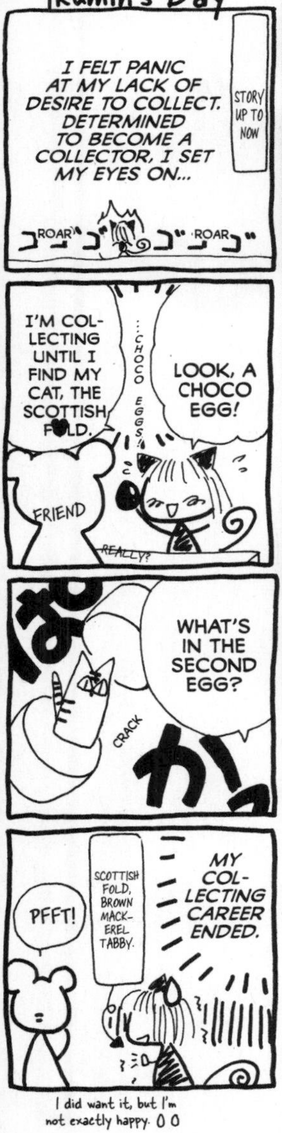
STORY UP TO NOW
I FELT PANIC AT MY LACK OF DESIRE TO COLLECT. DETERMINED TO BECOME A COLLECTOR, I SET MY EYES ON...
ROAR ROAR
LOOK, A CHOCO EGG!
...CHOCO EGGS!!
I'M COLLECTING UNTIL I FIND MY CAT, THE SCOTTISH FOLD.
FRIEND
REALLY?
WHAT'S IN THE SECOND EGG?
CRACK
MY COLLECTING CAREER ENDED.
SCOTTISH FOLD, BROWN MACKEREL TABBY.
PFFT!

I did want it, but I'm not exactly happy.

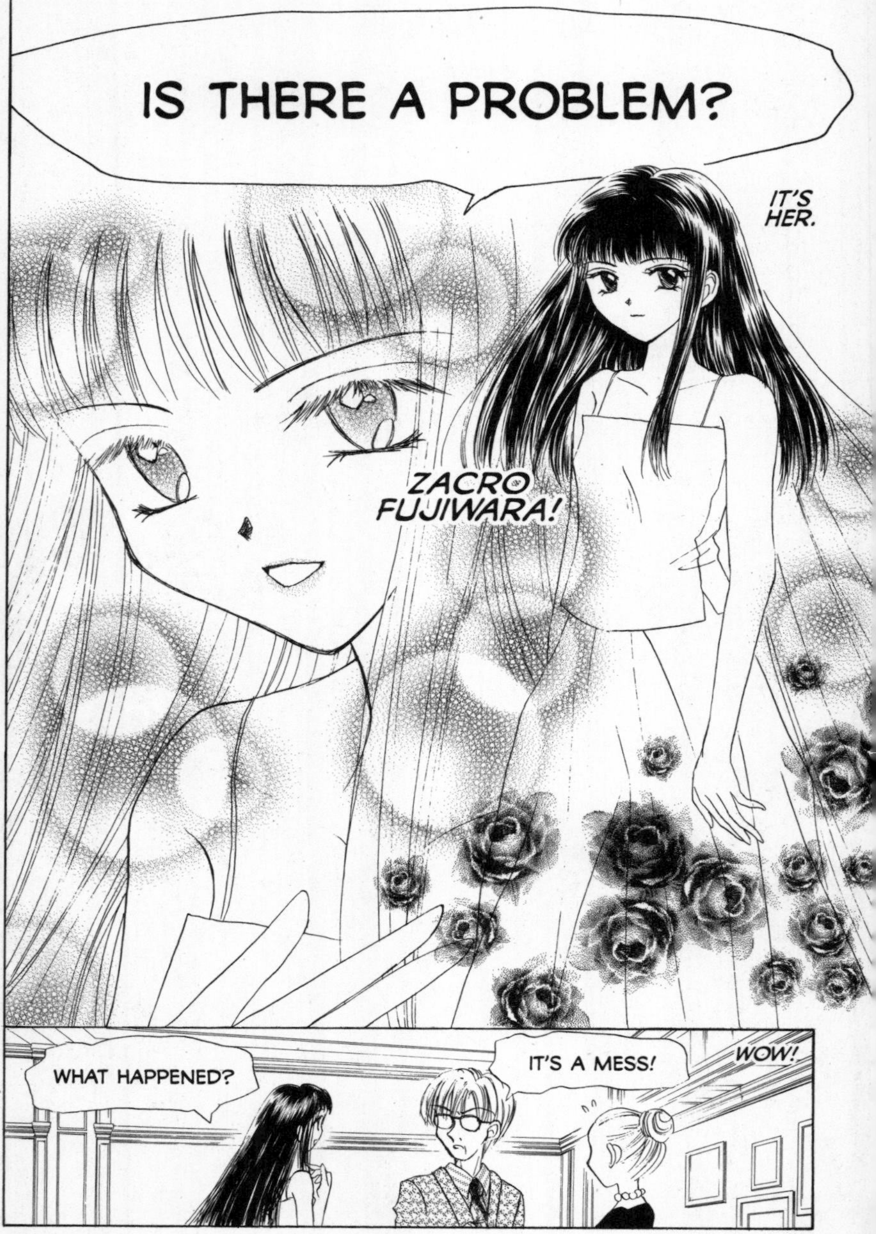
IS THERE A PROBLEM?
IT'S HER.
ZACRO FUJIWARA!
WOW!
IT'S A MESS!
WHAT HAPPENED?

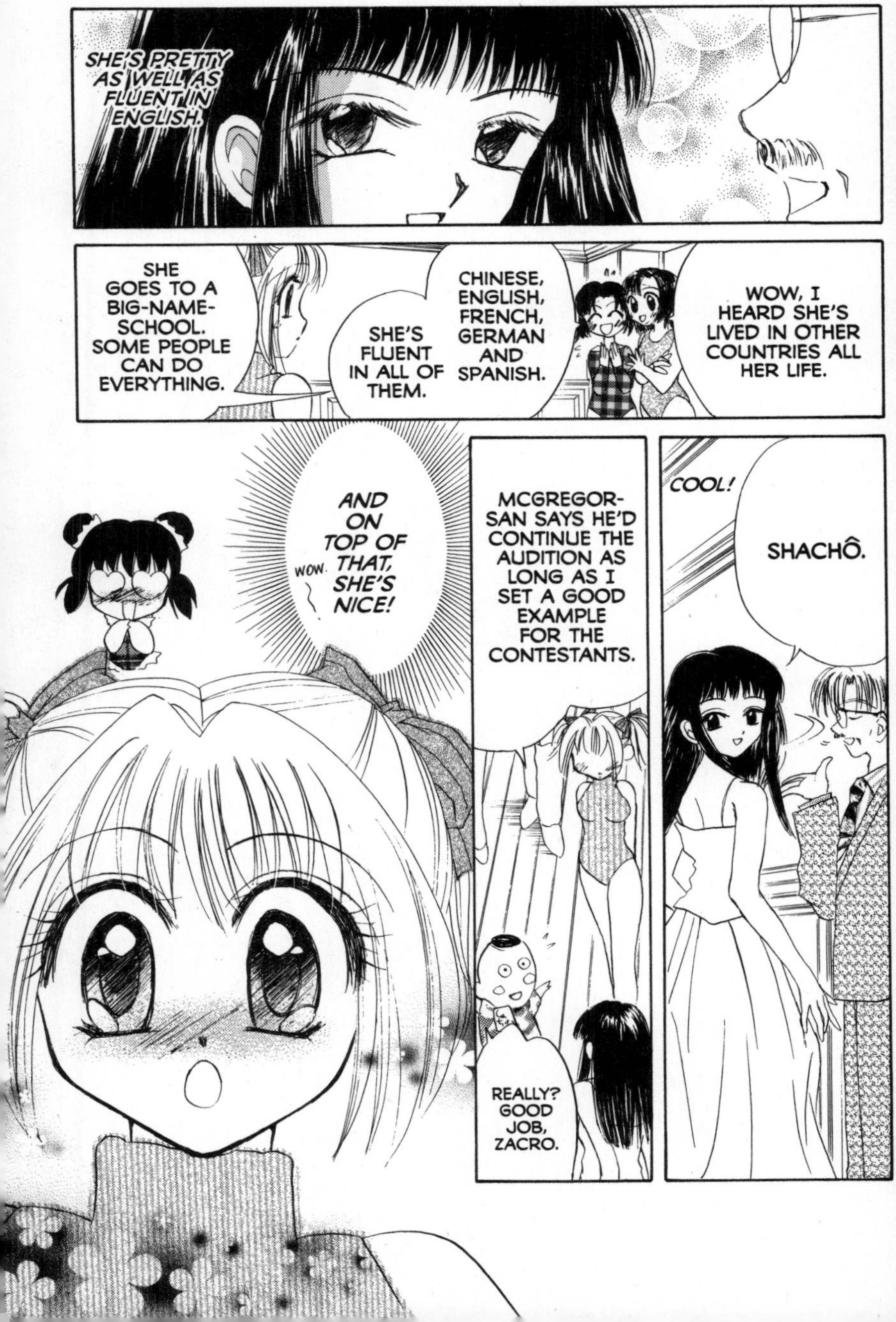
SHE'S PRETTY AS WELL AS FLUENT IN ENGLISH.
WOW, I HEARD SHE'S LIVED IN OTHER COUNTRIES ALL HER LIFE.
CHINESE, ENGLISH, FRENCH, GERMAN AND SPANISH.
SHE'S FLUENT IN ALL OF THEM.
SHE GOES TO A BIG-NAME-SCHOOL. SOME PEOPLE CAN DO EVERYTHING.
COOL!
SHACHÔ.
MCGREGOR-SAN SAYS HE'D CONTINUE THE AUDITION AS LONG AS I SET A GOOD EXAMPLE FOR THE CONTESTANTS.
REALLY? GOOD JOB, ZACRO.
AND ON TOP OF THAT, SHE'S NICE!
WOW.

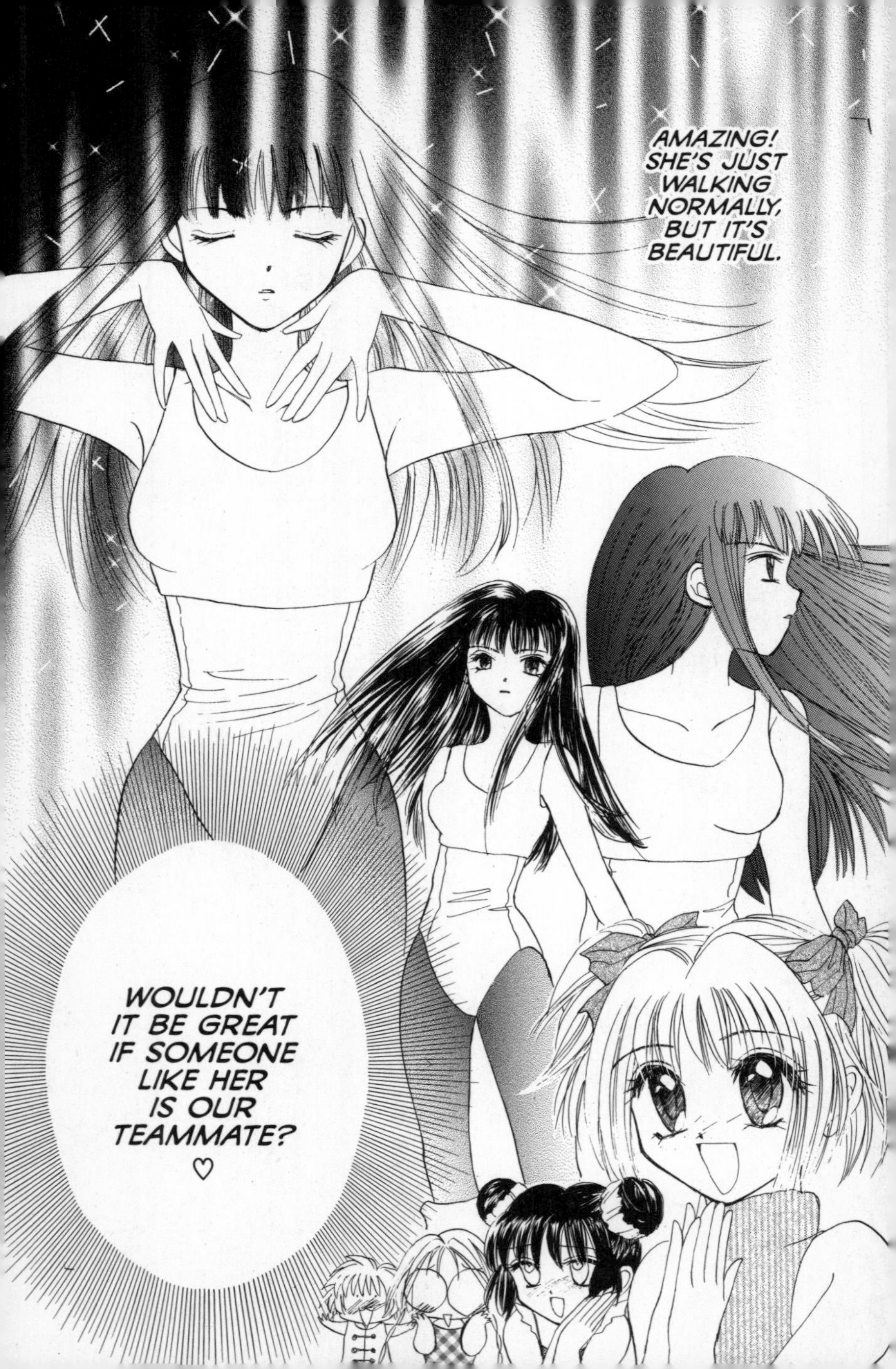
AMAZING! SHE'S JUST WALKING NORMALLY, BUT IT'S BEAUTIFUL.
WOULDN'T IT BE GREAT IF SOMEONE LIKE HER IS OUR TEAMMATE? ♡

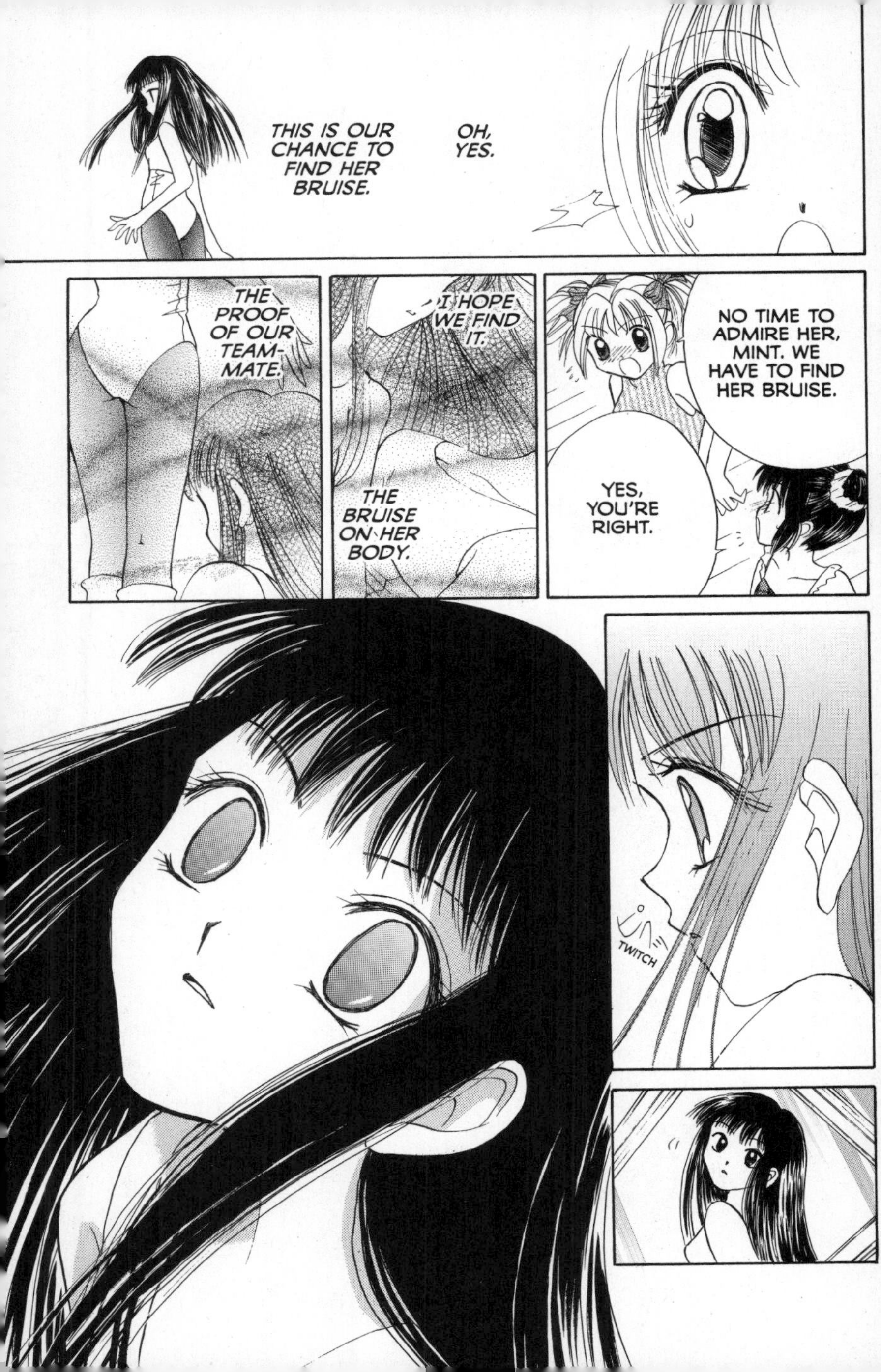
OH, YES.
THIS IS OUR CHANCE TO FIND HER BRUISE.
NO TIME TO ADMIRE HER, MINT. WE HAVE TO FIND HER BRUISE.
YES, YOU'RE RIGHT.
I HOPE WE FIND IT.
THE BRUISE ON HER BODY.
THE PROOF OF OUR TEAM-MATE.
TWITCH

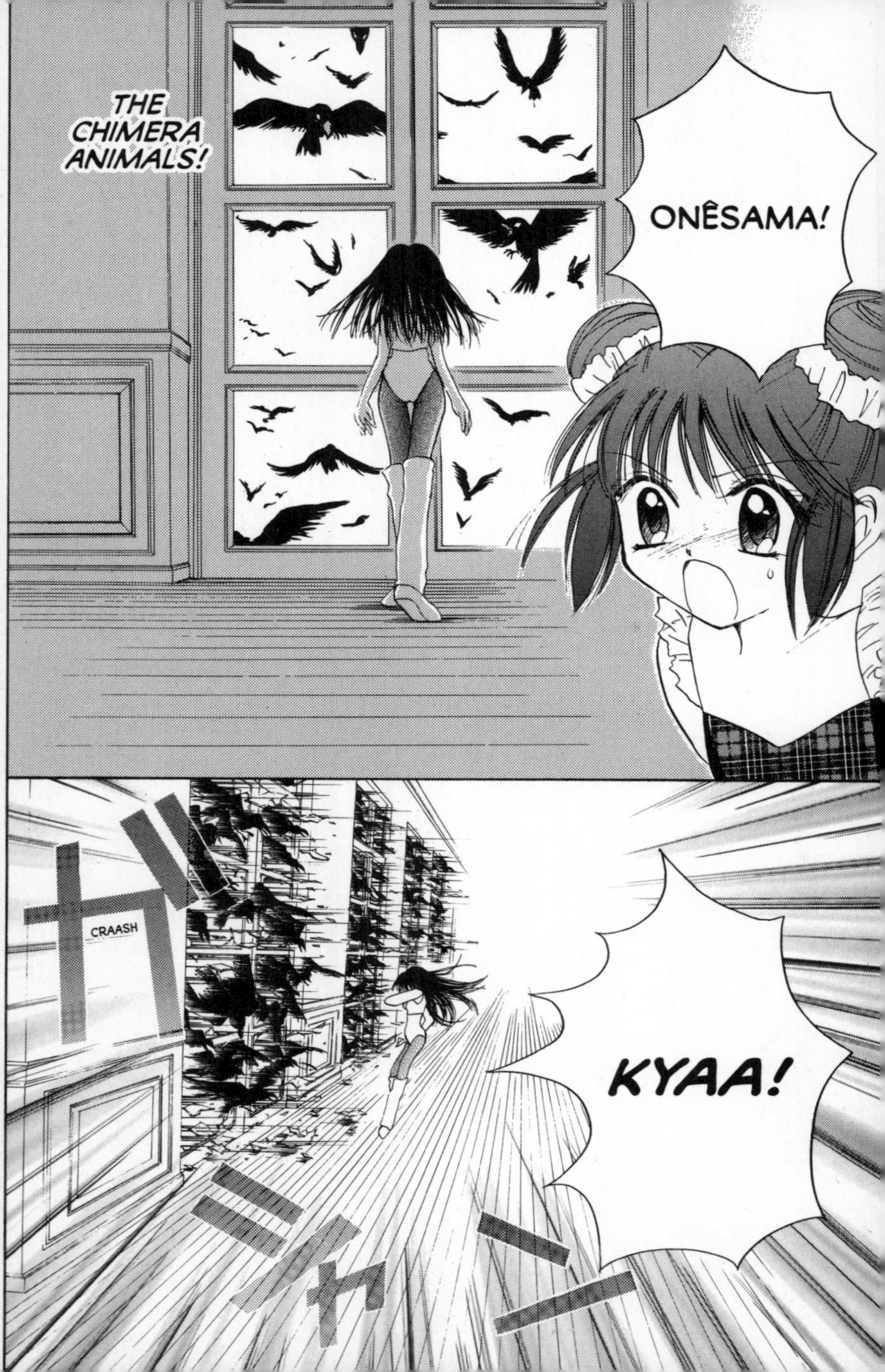
ONÊSAMA!
THE CHIMERA ANIMALS!
KYAA!
CRAASH

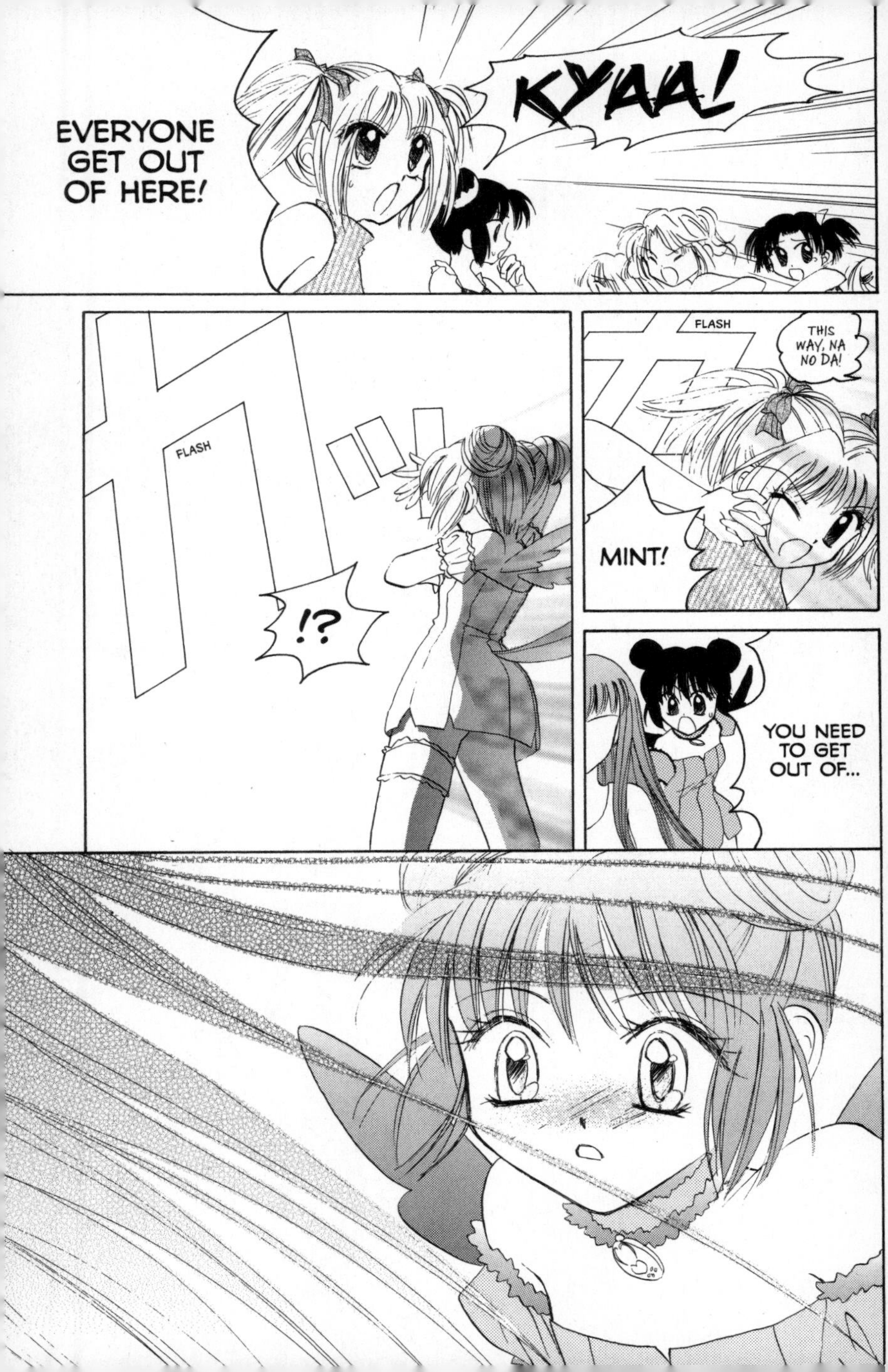
KYAA!
EVERYONE GET OUT OF HERE!
FLASH
THIS WAY, NA NO DA!
MINT!
YOU NEED TO GET OUT OF...
FLASH
!?

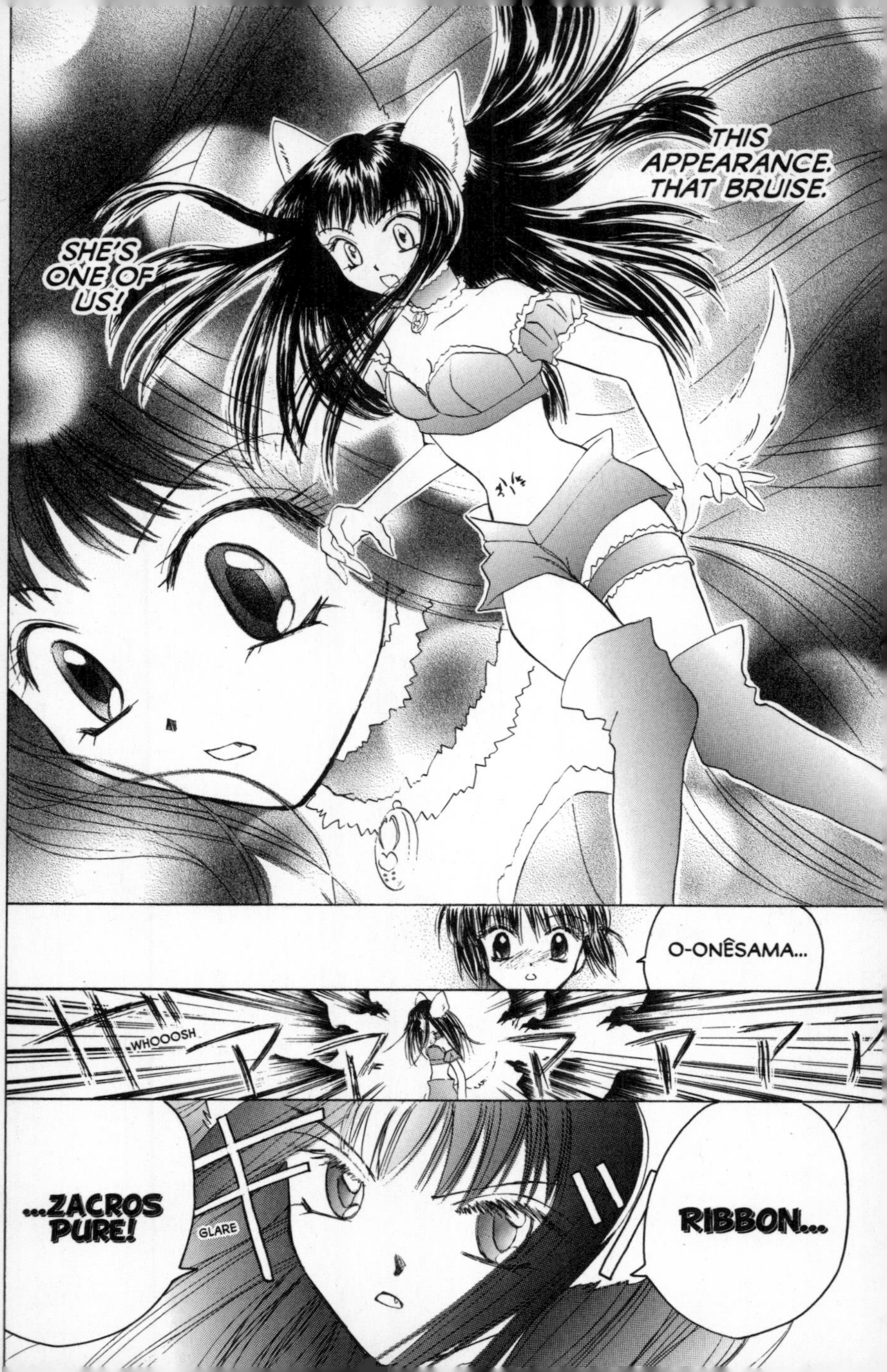
THIS APPEARANCE. THAT BRUISE.
SHE'S ONE OF US!
O-ONÊSAMA...
WHOOOSH
RIBBON...
GLARE
...ZACROS PURE!

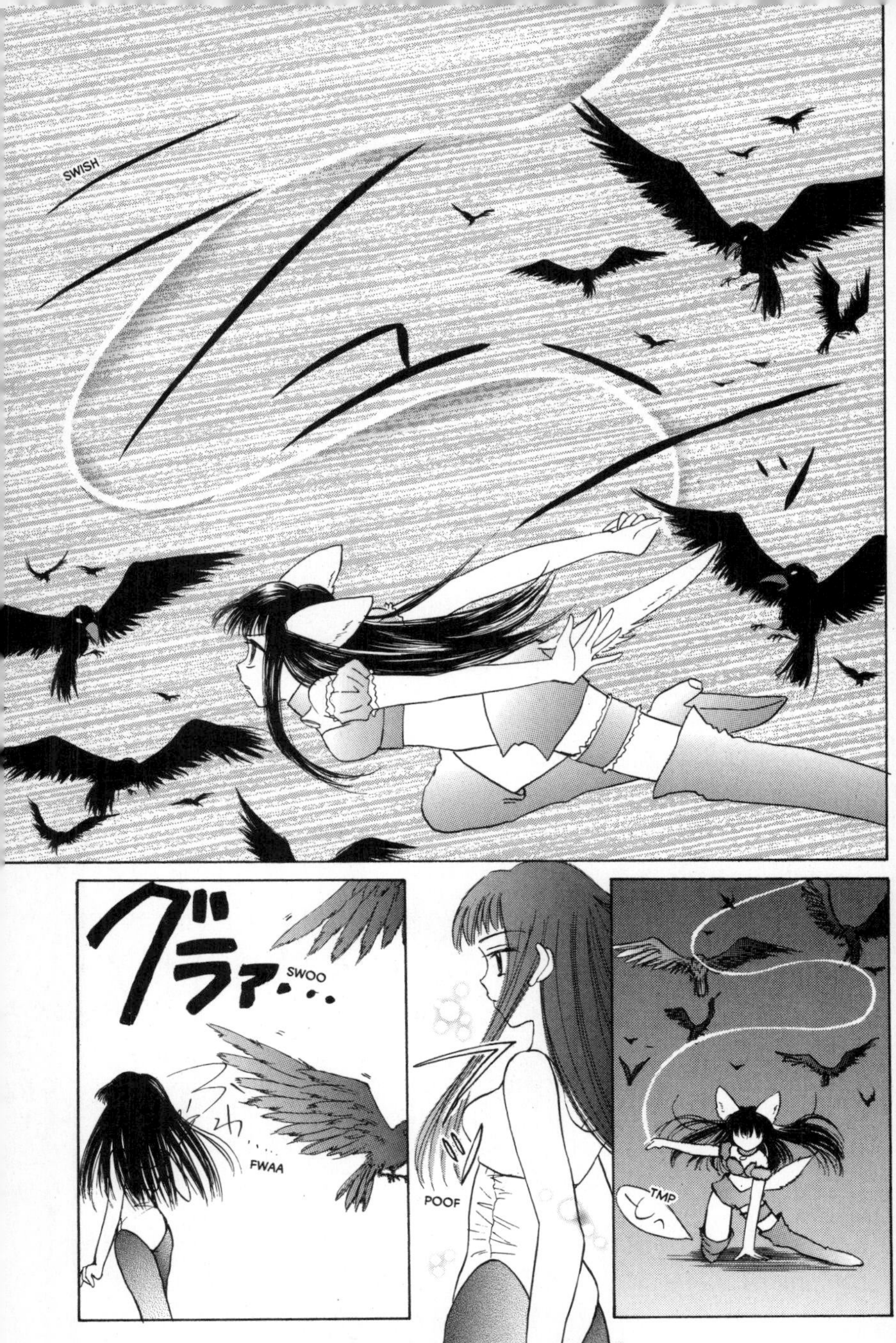
SWISH
TMP
POOF
グラァ…
SWOO
FWAA

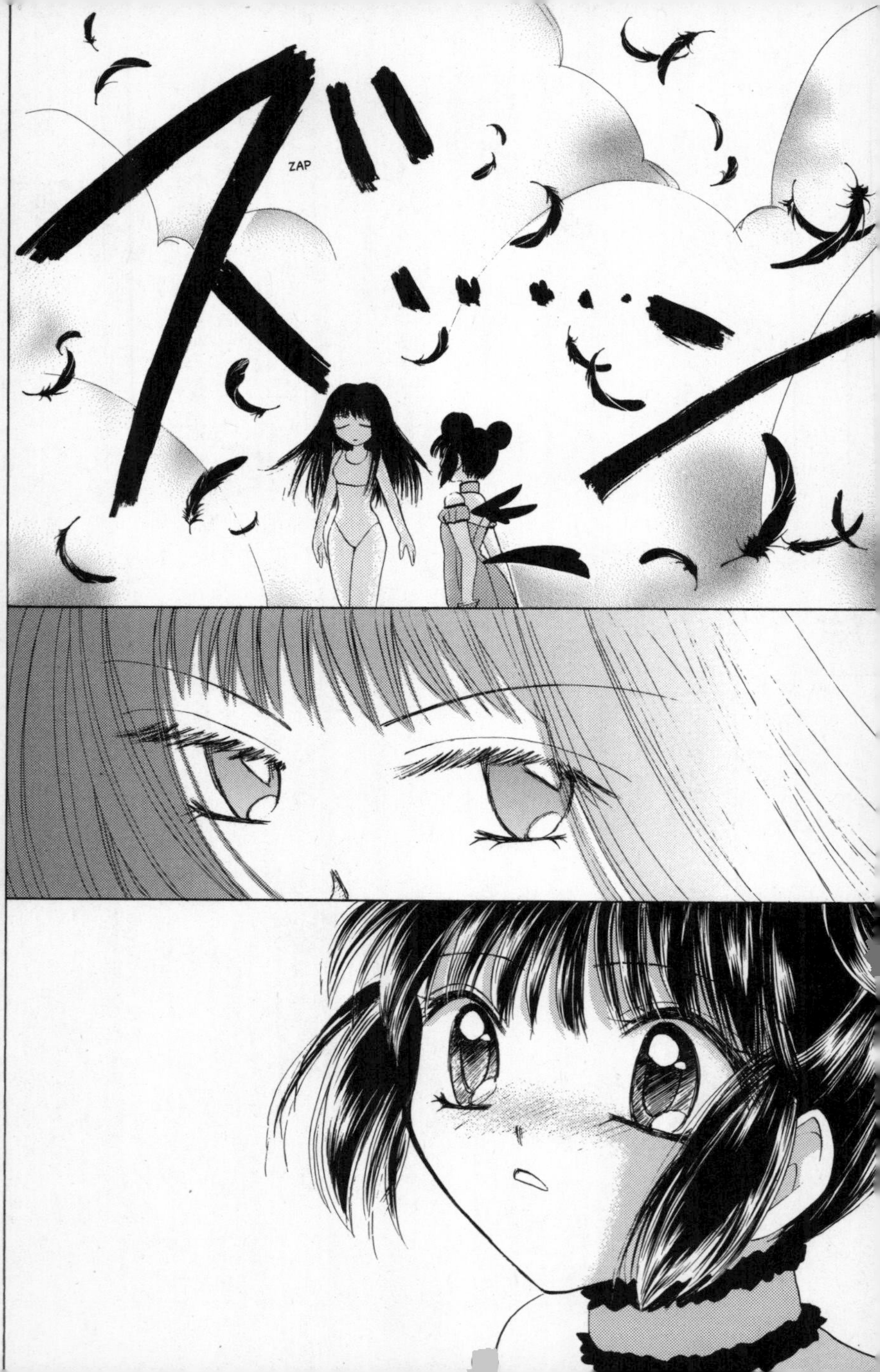
ZAP

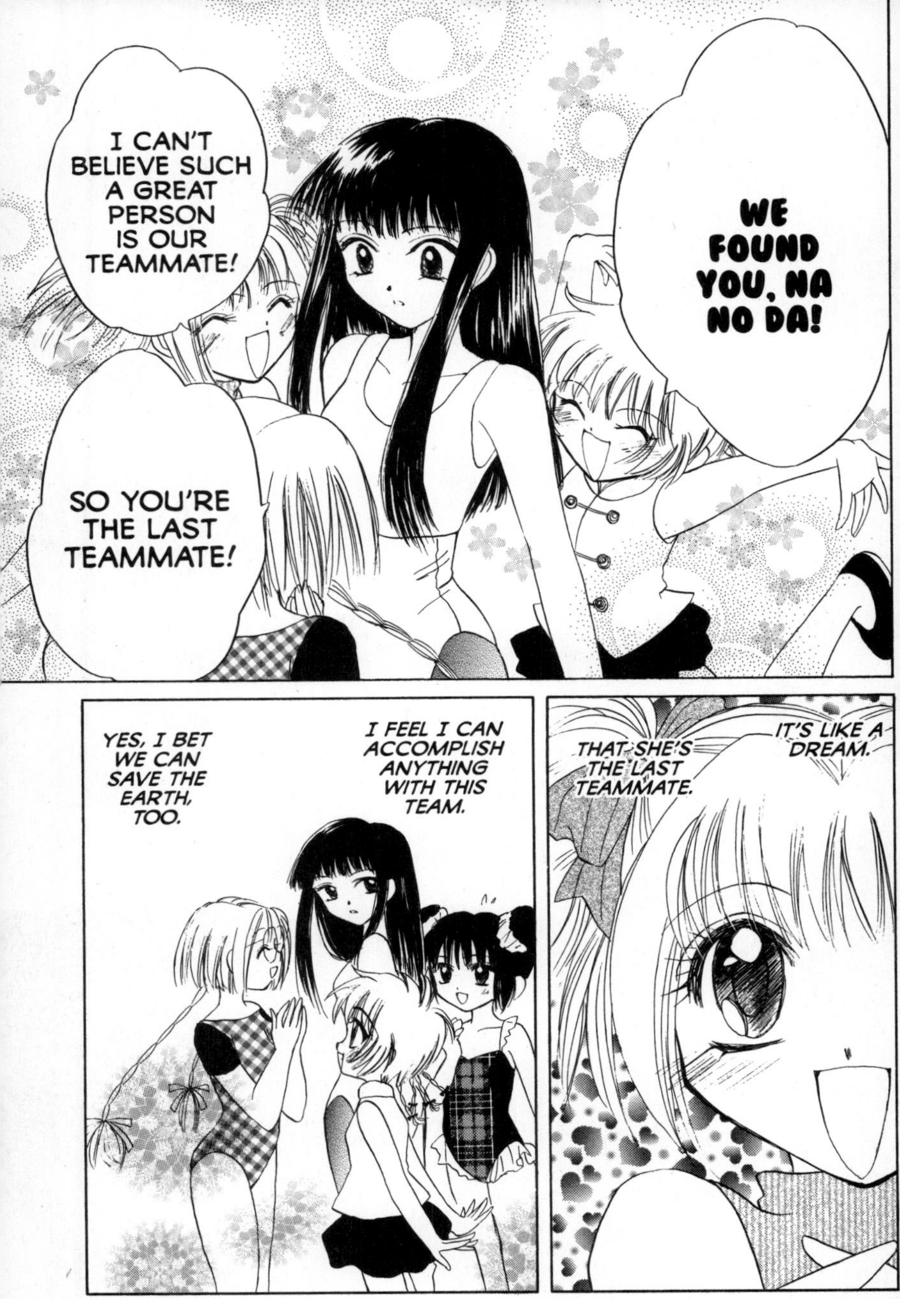
WE FOUND YOU, NA NO DA!
I CAN'T BELIEVE SUCH A GREAT PERSON IS OUR TEAMMATE!
SO YOU'RE THE LAST TEAMMATE!
IT'S LIKE A DREAM.
THAT SHE'S THE LAST TEAMMATE.
I FEEL I CAN ACCOMPLISH ANYTHING WITH THIS TEAM.
YES, I BET WE CAN SAVE THE EARTH, TOO.

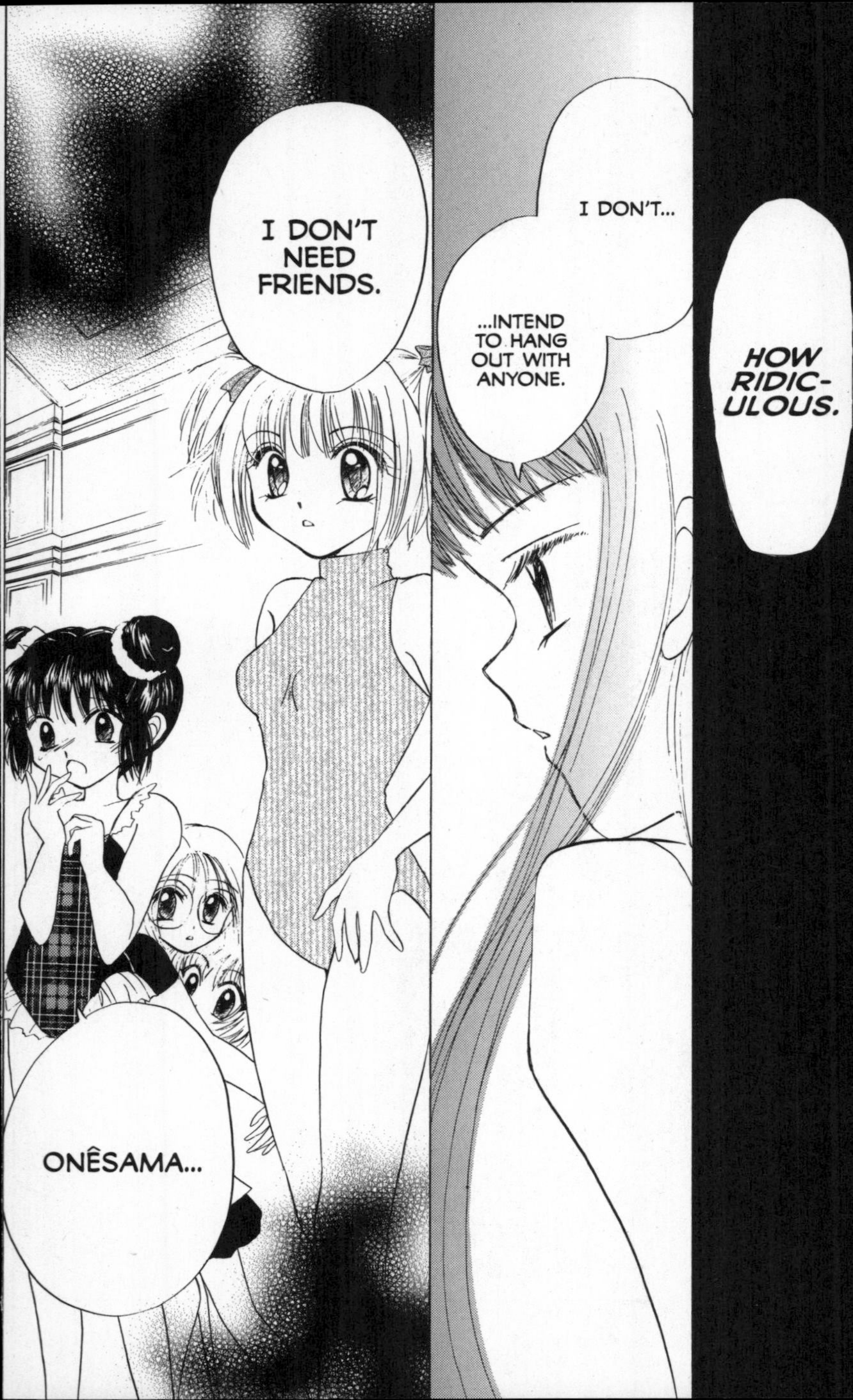
HOW RIDIC-ULOUS.
I DON'T...
...INTEND TO HANG OUT WITH ANYONE.
I DON'T NEED FRIENDS.
ONÊSAMA...

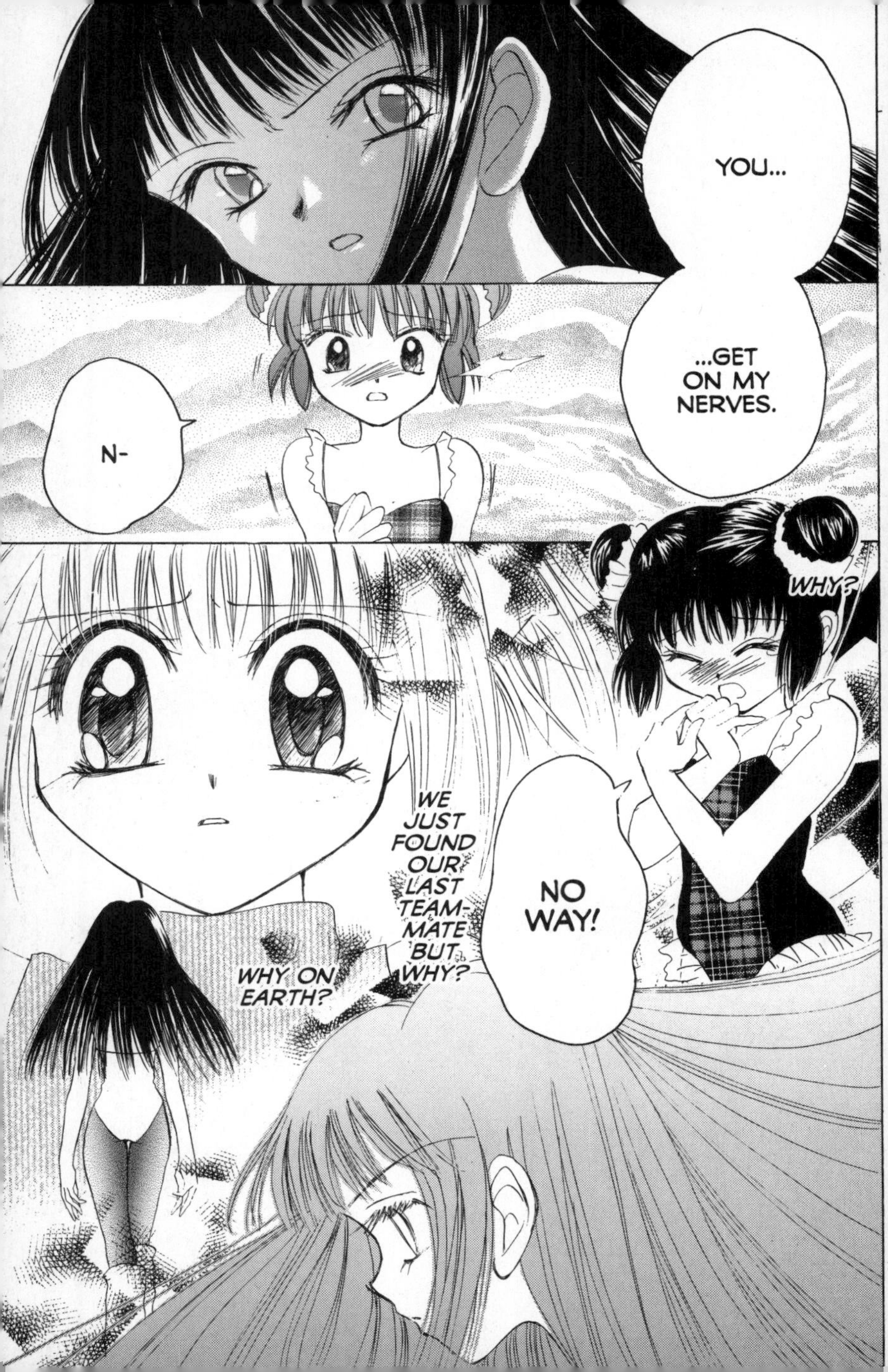
YOU...
...GET ON MY NERVES.
N-
WHY?
NO WAY!
WE JUST FOUND OUR LAST TEAM-MATE BUT WHY?
WHY ON EARTH?

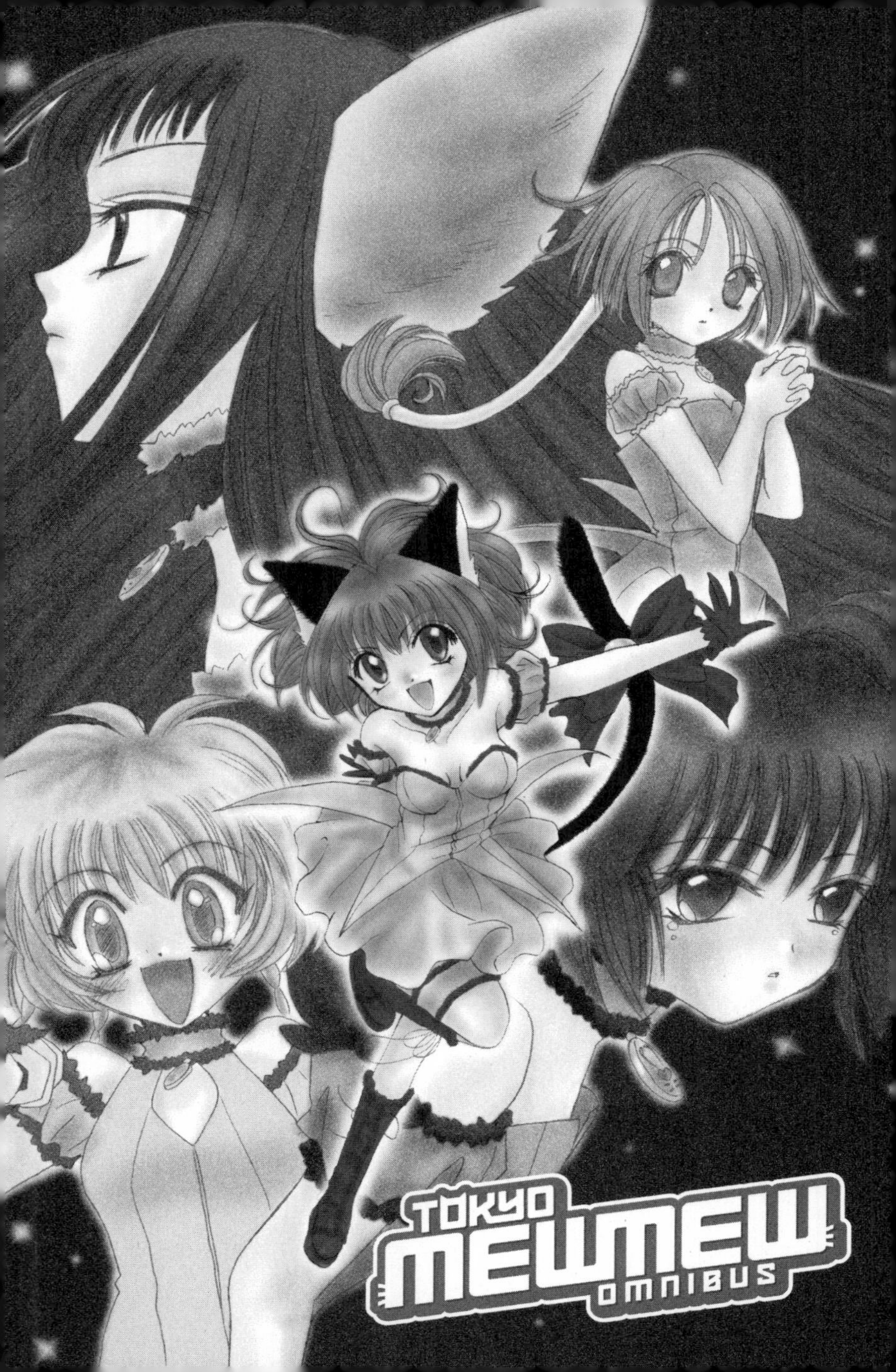
TOKYO MEWMEW OMNIBUS

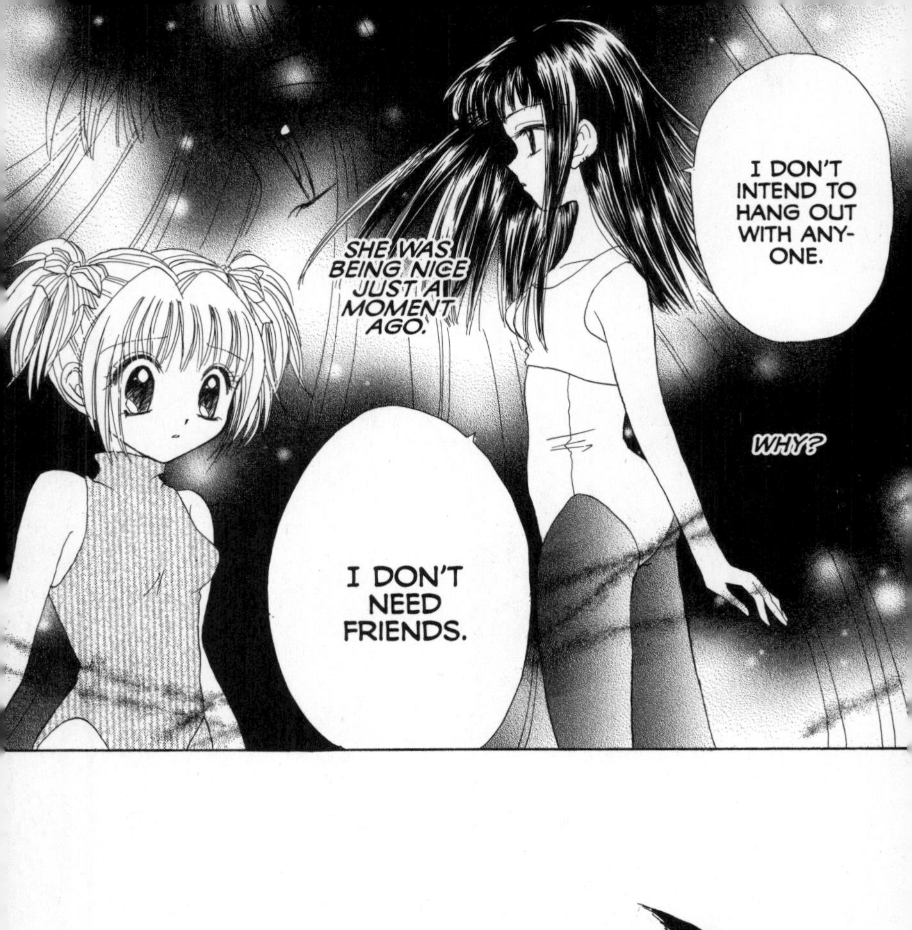
I DON'T INTEND TO HANG OUT WITH ANY-ONE.
SHE WAS BEING NICE JUST A MOMENT AGO.
WHY?
I DON'T NEED FRIENDS.

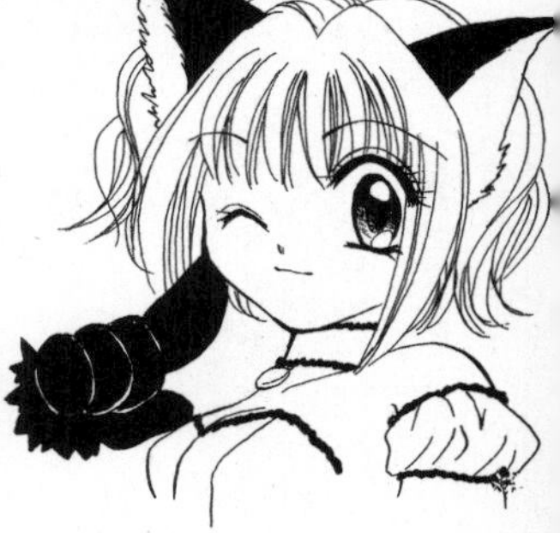

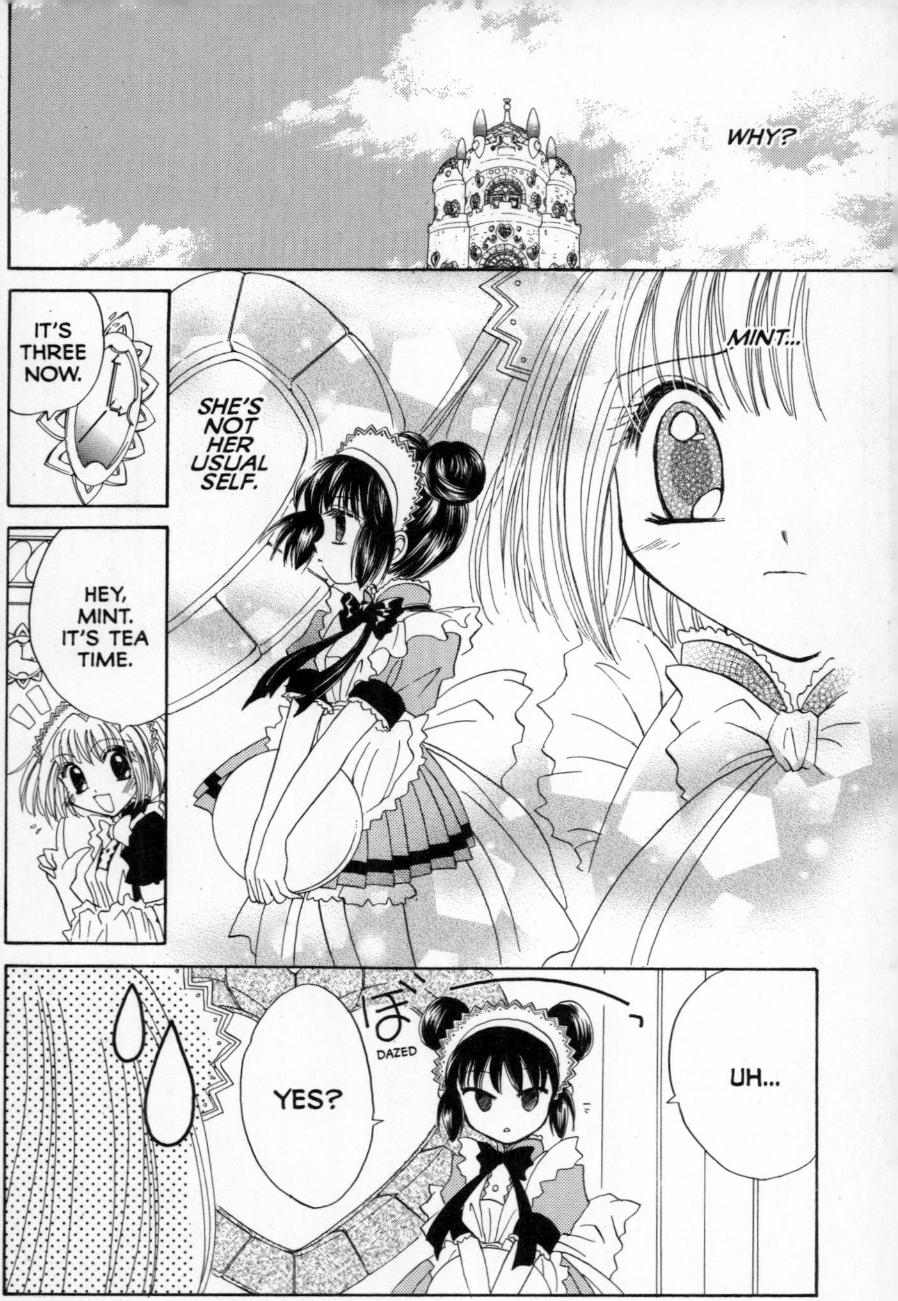
WHY?
MINT...
SHE'S NOT HER USUAL SELF.
IT'S THREE NOW.
HEY, MINT. IT'S TEA TIME.
UH...
ぼ
DAZED
YES?

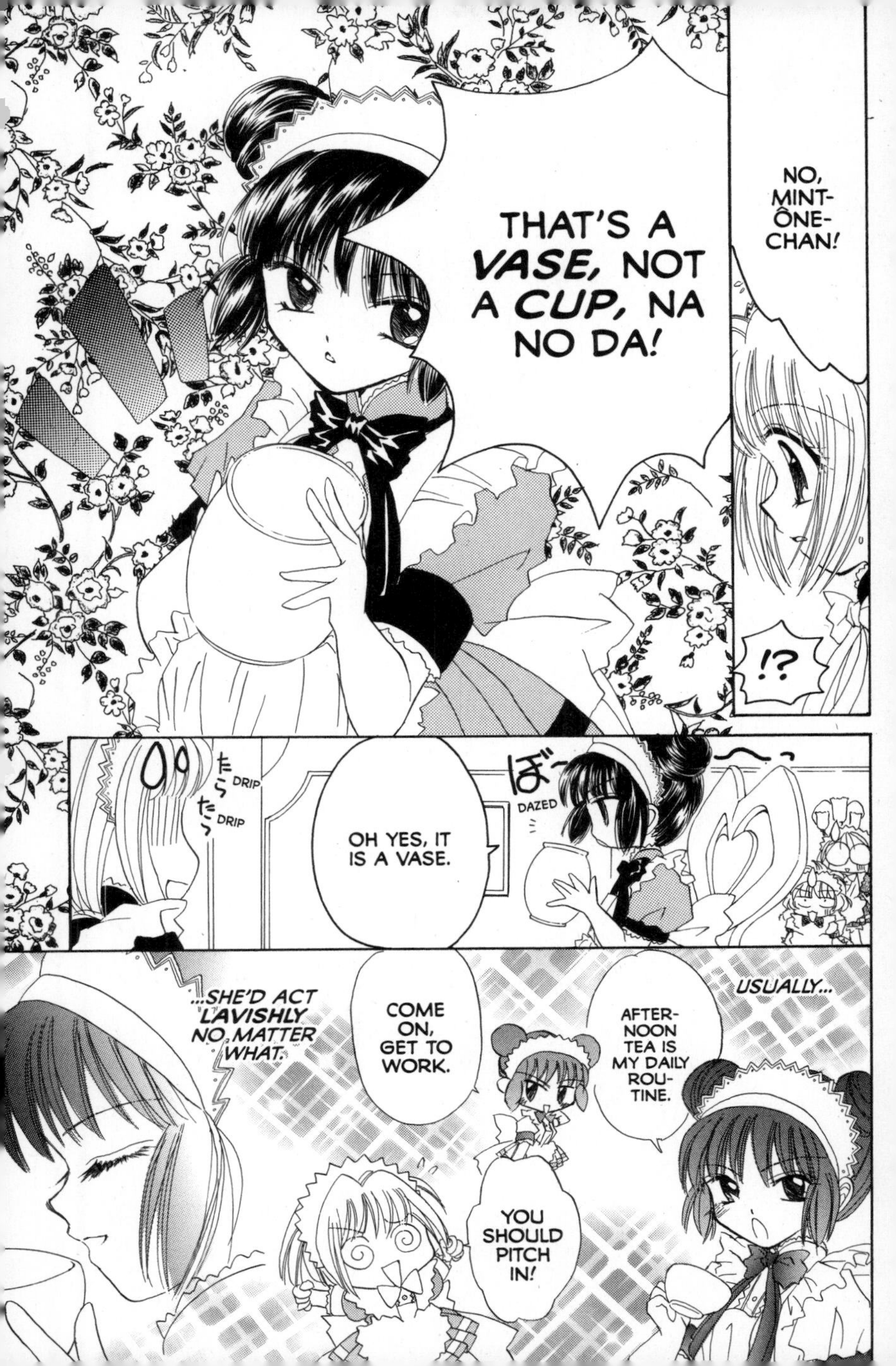
NO, MINT-ÔNE-CHAN!
!?
THAT'S A *VASE,* NOT A *CUP,* NA NO DA!
ぼ~ DAZED
OH YES, IT IS A VASE.
たら DRIP
たら DRIP
USUALLY...
AFTER-NOON TEA IS MY DAILY ROU-TINE.
COME ON, GET TO WORK.
...SHE'D ACT LAVISHLY NO MATTER WHAT.
YOU SHOULD PITCH IN!

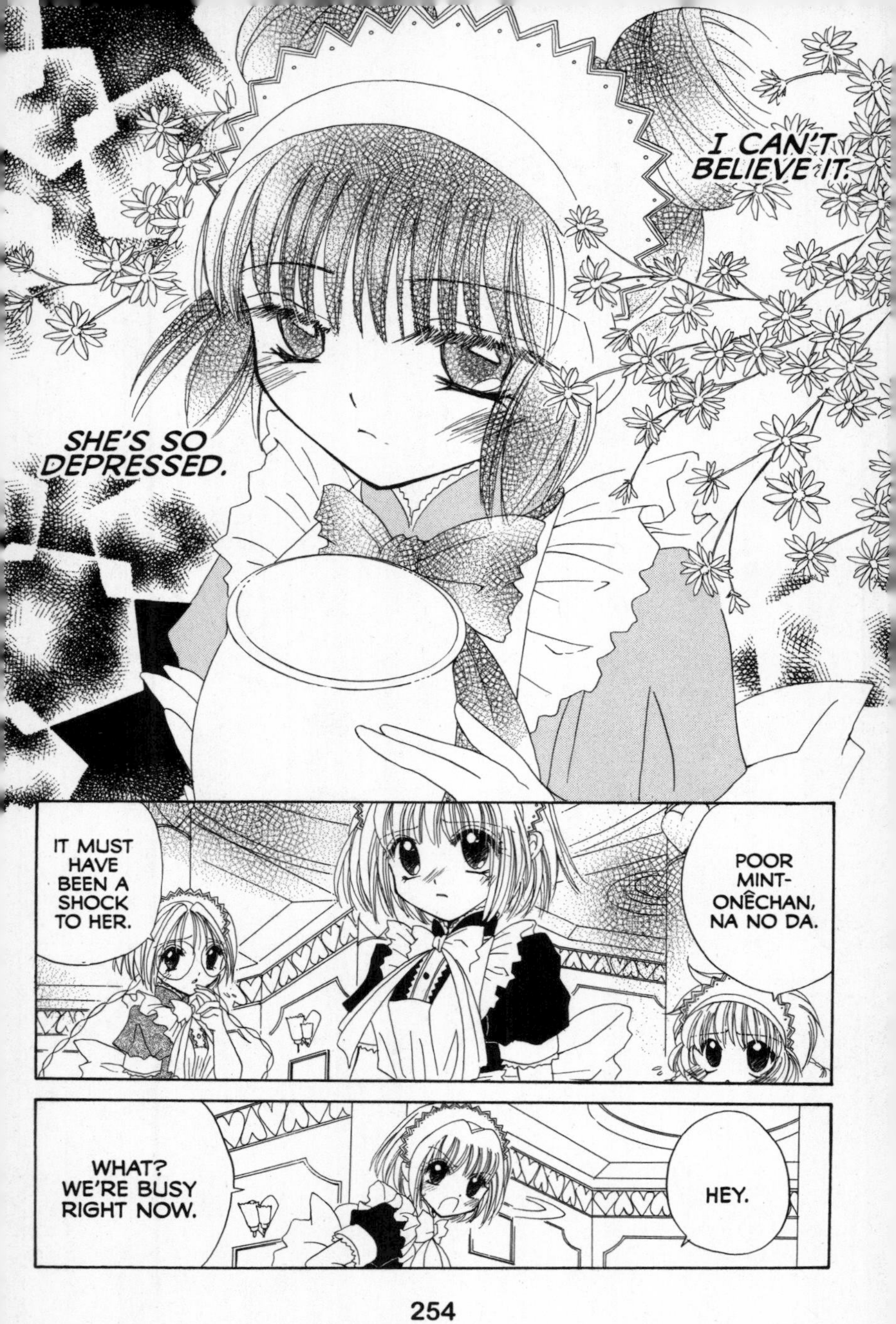
I CAN'T BELIEVE IT.
SHE'S SO DEPRESSED.
POOR MINT-ONÊCHAN, NA NO DA.
IT MUST HAVE BEEN A SHOCK TO HER.
HEY.
WHAT? WE'RE BUSY RIGHT NOW.

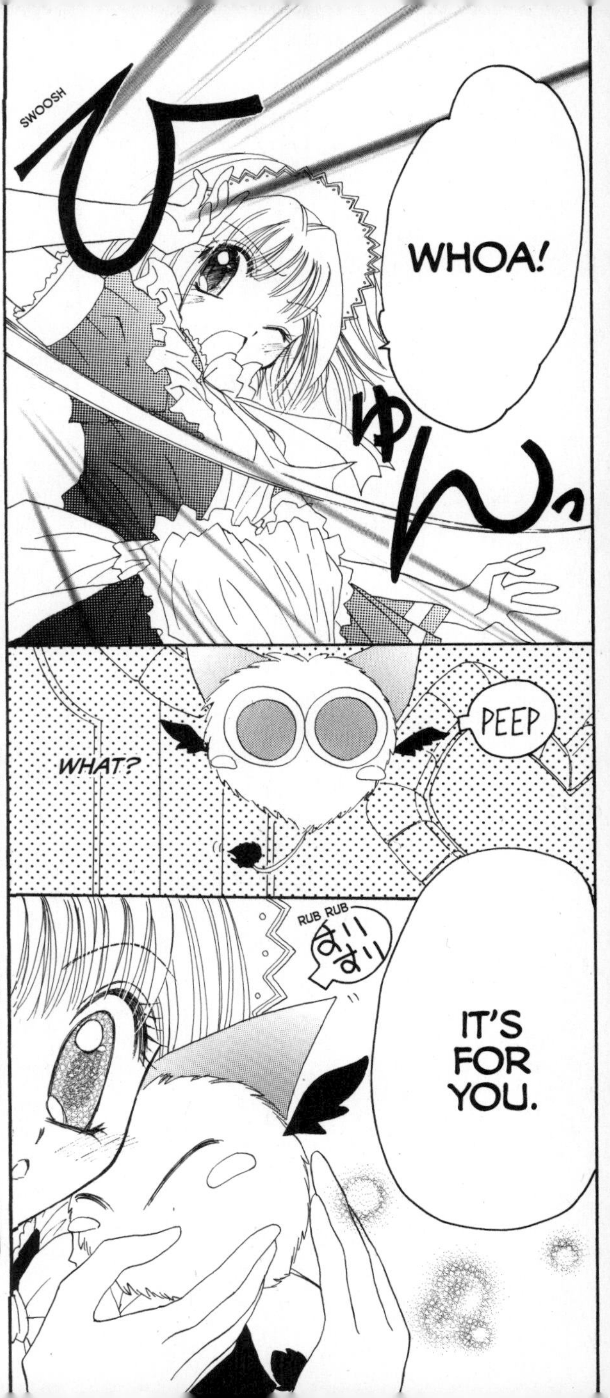
WHOA!
SWOOSH
PEEP.
WHAT?
IT'S FOR YOU.
RUB RUB

Meeting with My Editors

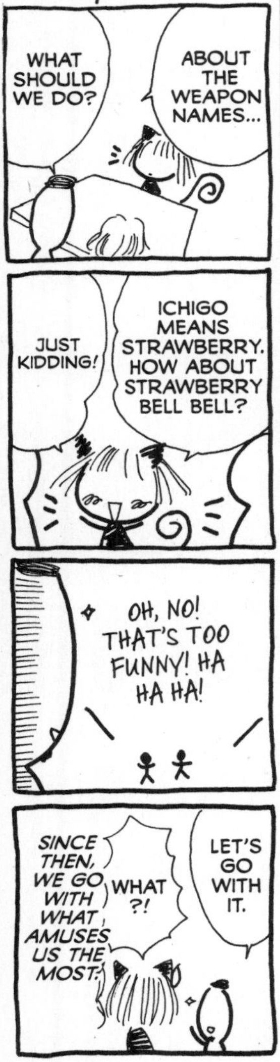
ABOUT THE WEAPON NAMES...
WHAT SHOULD WE DO?
ICHIGO MEANS STRAWBERRY. HOW ABOUT STRAWBERRY BELL BELL?
JUST KIDDING!
OH, NO! THAT'S TOO FUNNY! HA HA HA!
LET'S GO WITH IT.
WHAT?!
SINCE THEN, WE GO WITH WHAT AMUSES US THE MOST.

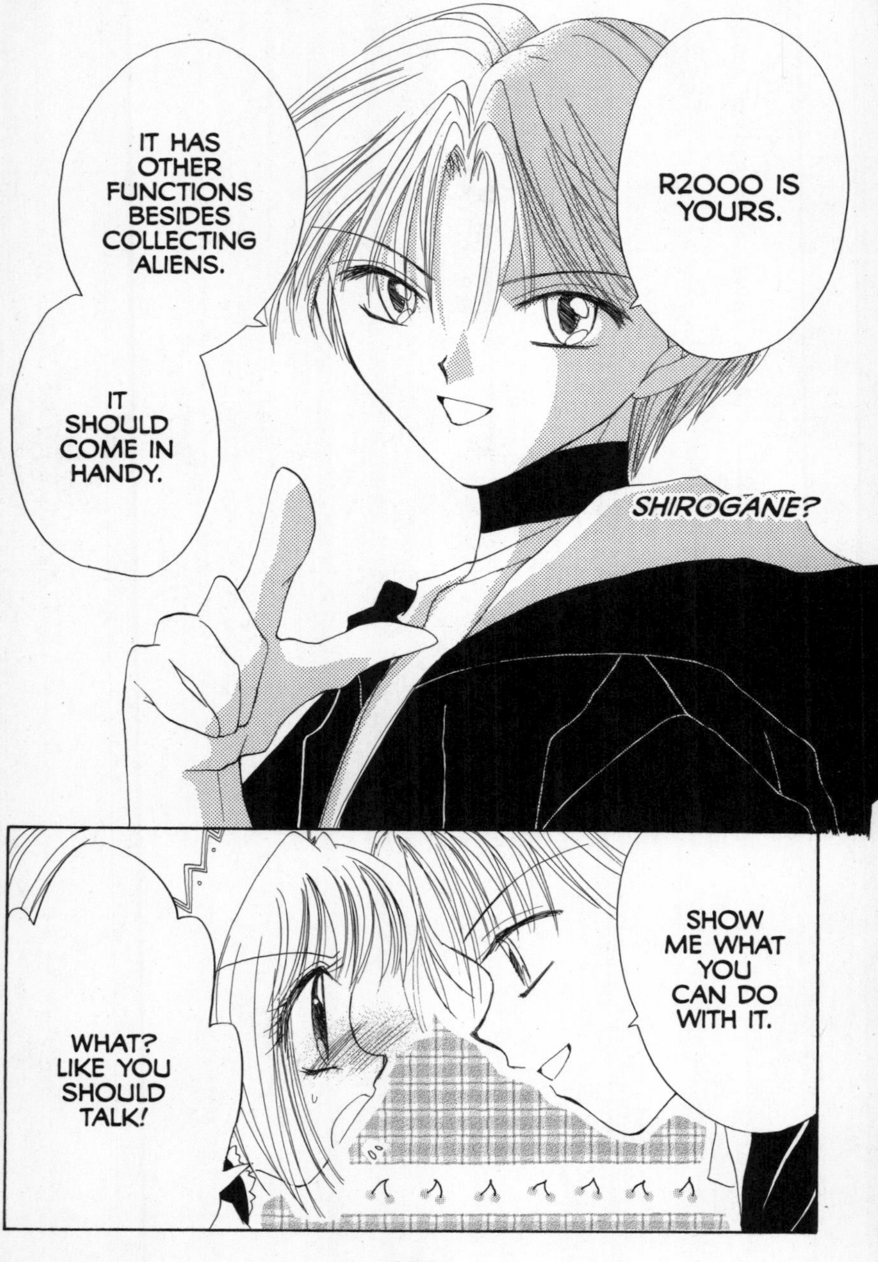
R2000 IS YOURS.
IT HAS OTHER FUNCTIONS BESIDES COLLECTING ALIENS.
IT SHOULD COME IN HANDY.
SHIROGANE?
SHOW ME WHAT YOU CAN DO WITH IT.
WHAT? LIKE YOU SHOULD TALK!

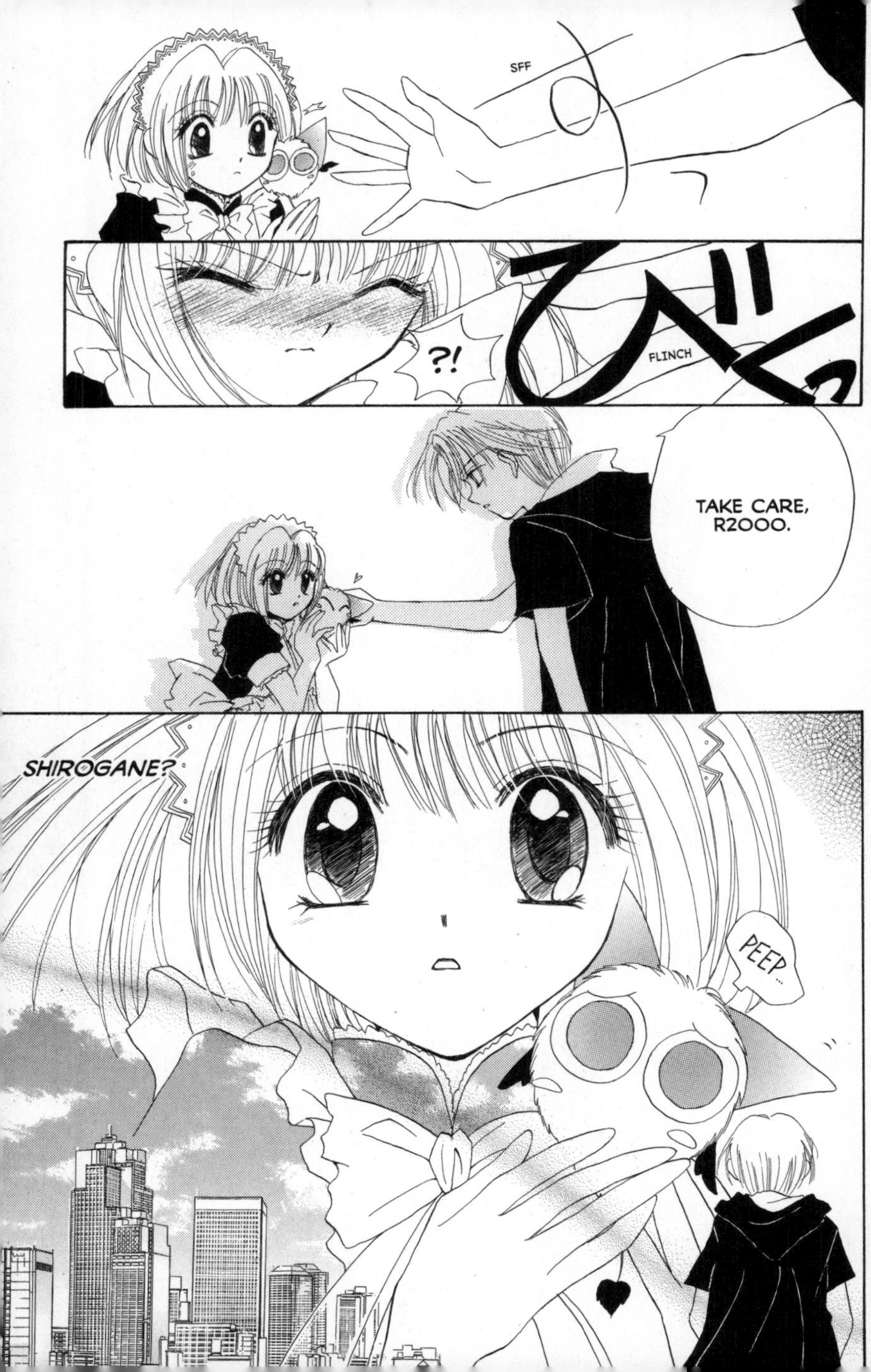
SFF
FLINCH
?!
TAKE CARE, R2000.
SHIROGANE?
PEEP...

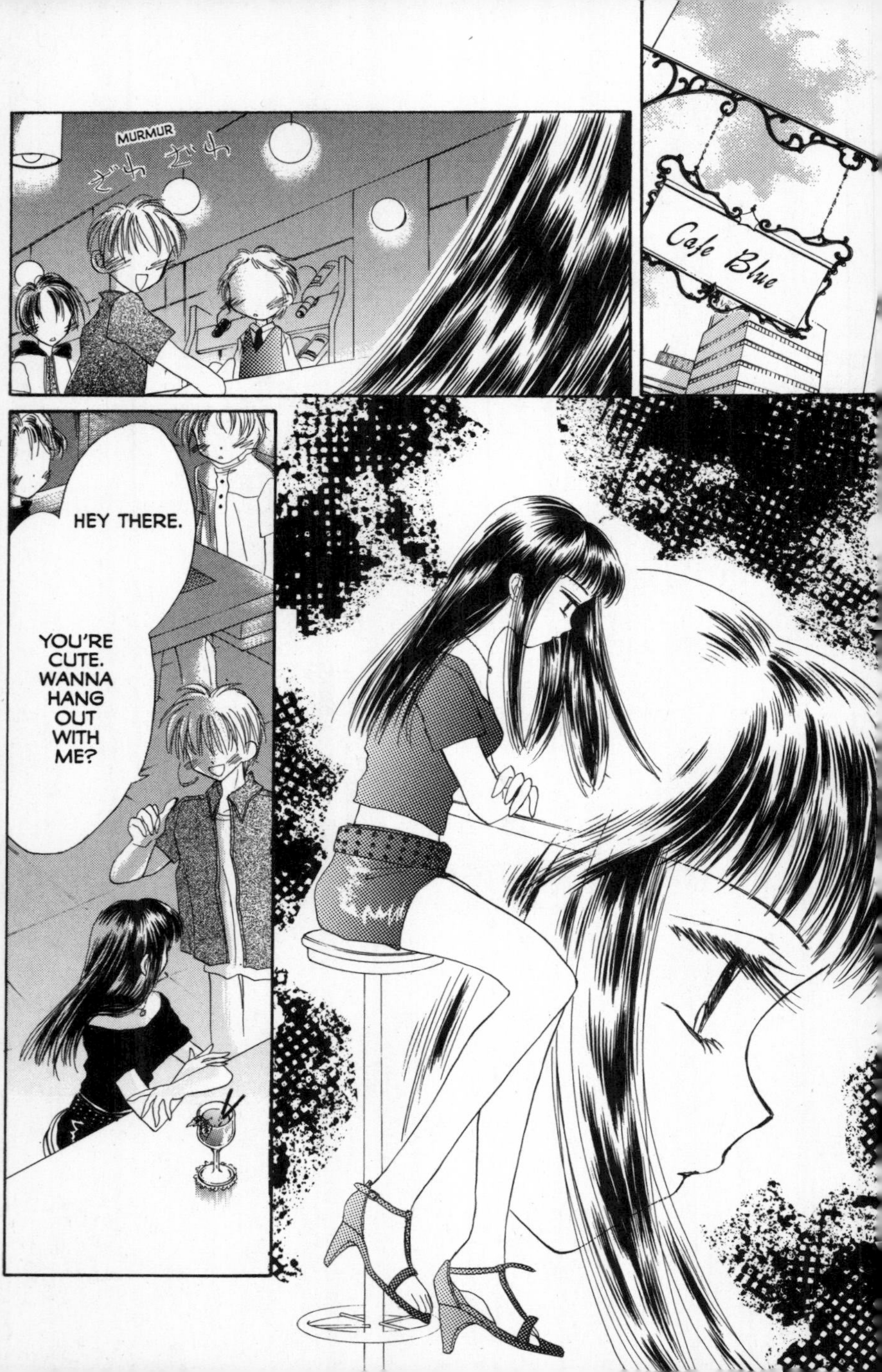
Cafe Blue
MURMUR
ざわざわ
HEY THERE.
YOU'RE CUTE. WANNA HANG OUT WITH ME?

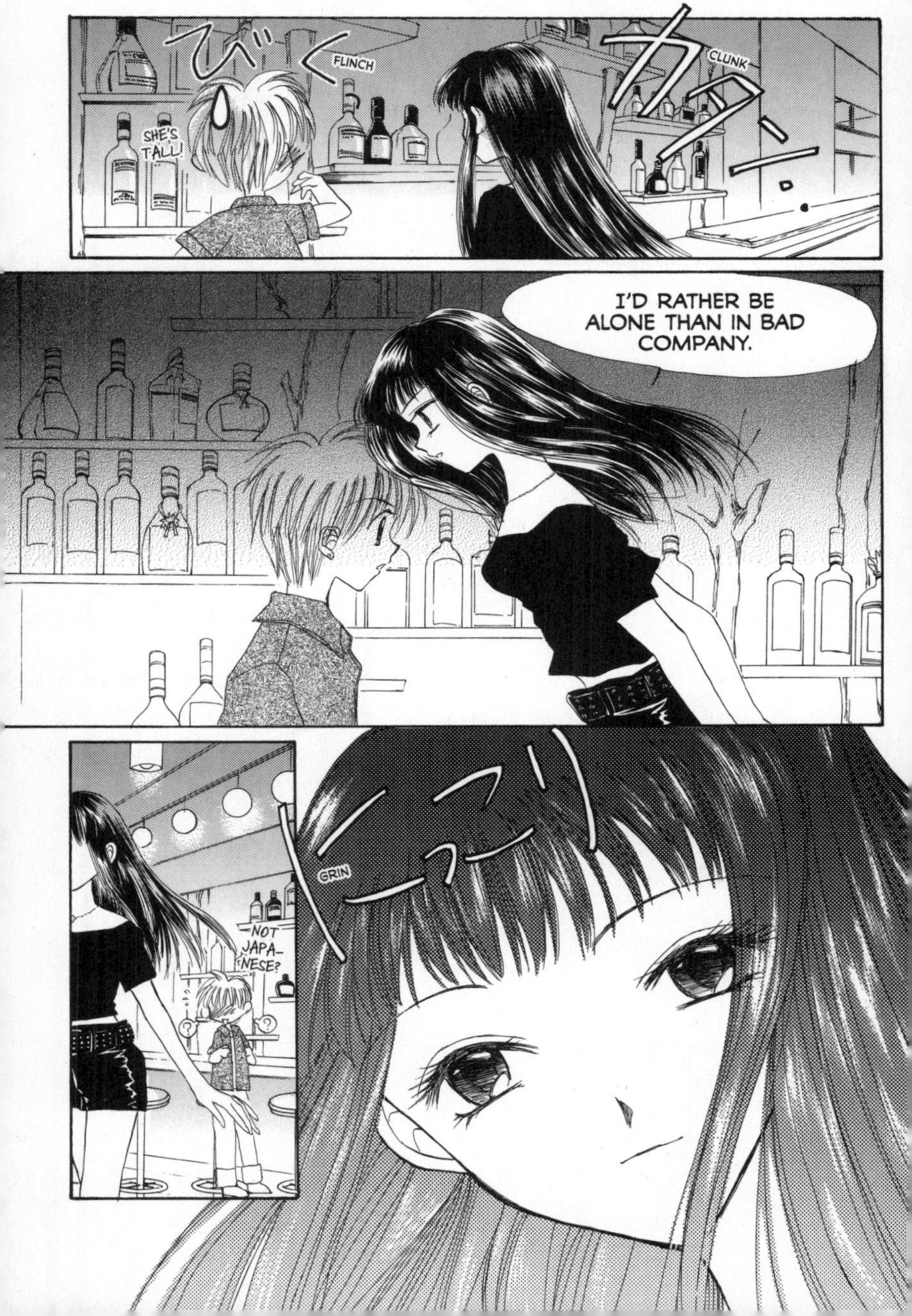
CLUNK
FLINCH
SHE'S TALL!
I'D RATHER BE ALONE THAN IN BAD COMPANY.
GRIN
NOT JAPA-NESE?

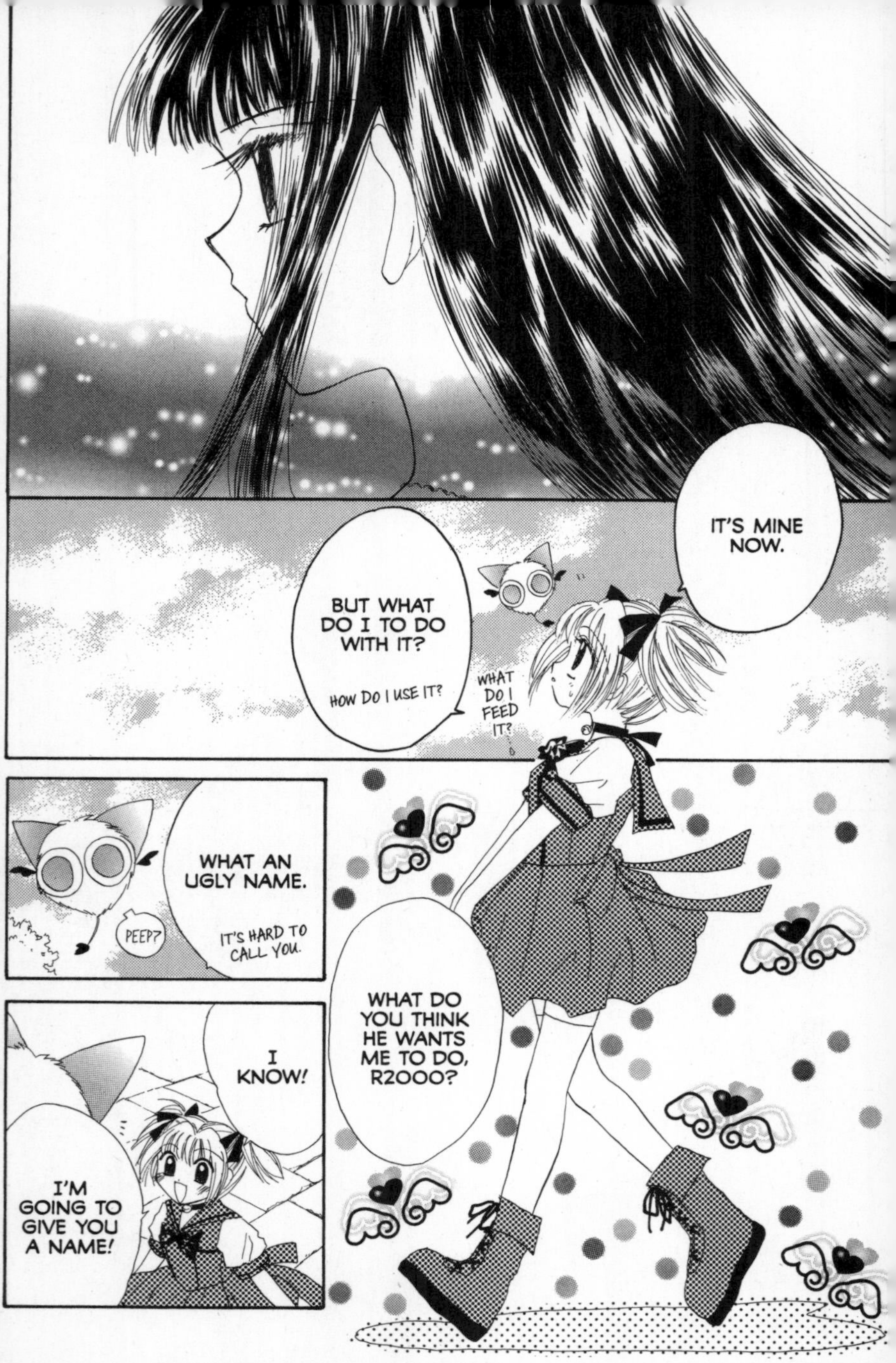
IT'S MINE NOW.
BUT WHAT DO I TO DO WITH IT?
HOW DO I USE IT?
WHAT DO I FEED IT?
WHAT DO YOU THINK HE WANTS ME TO DO, R2000?
WHAT AN UGLY NAME.
IT'S HARD TO CALL YOU.
PEEP?
I KNOW!
I'M GOING TO GIVE YOU A NAME!

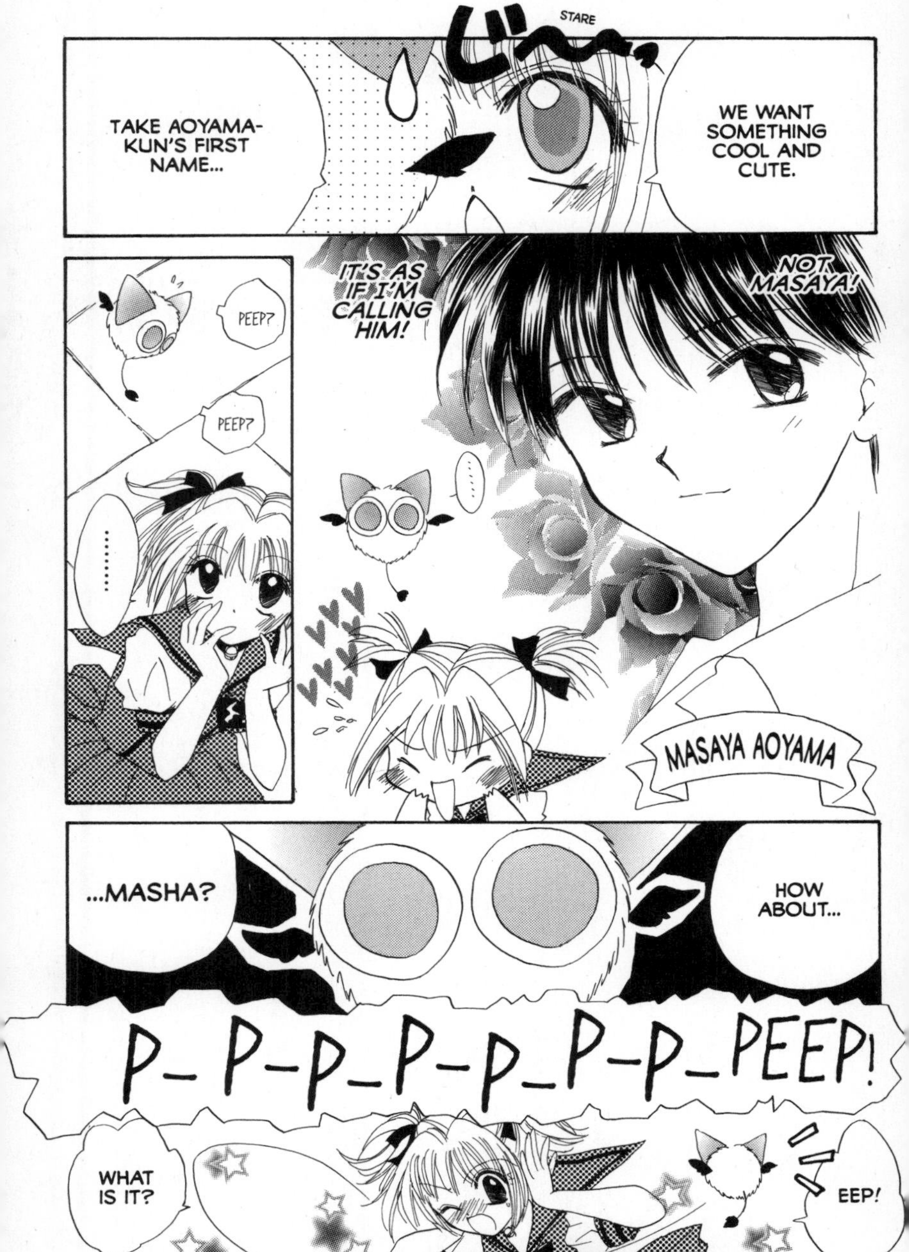

STARE
WE WANT SOMETHING COOL AND CUTE.
TAKE AOYAMA-KUN'S FIRST NAME...
NOT MASAYA!
IT'S AS IF I'M CALLING HIM!
......
MASAYA AOYAMA
PEEP?
PEEP?
......
HOW ABOUT...
...MASHA?
P- P-P-P-P-P-P-P-PEEP!
EEP!
WHAT IS IT?

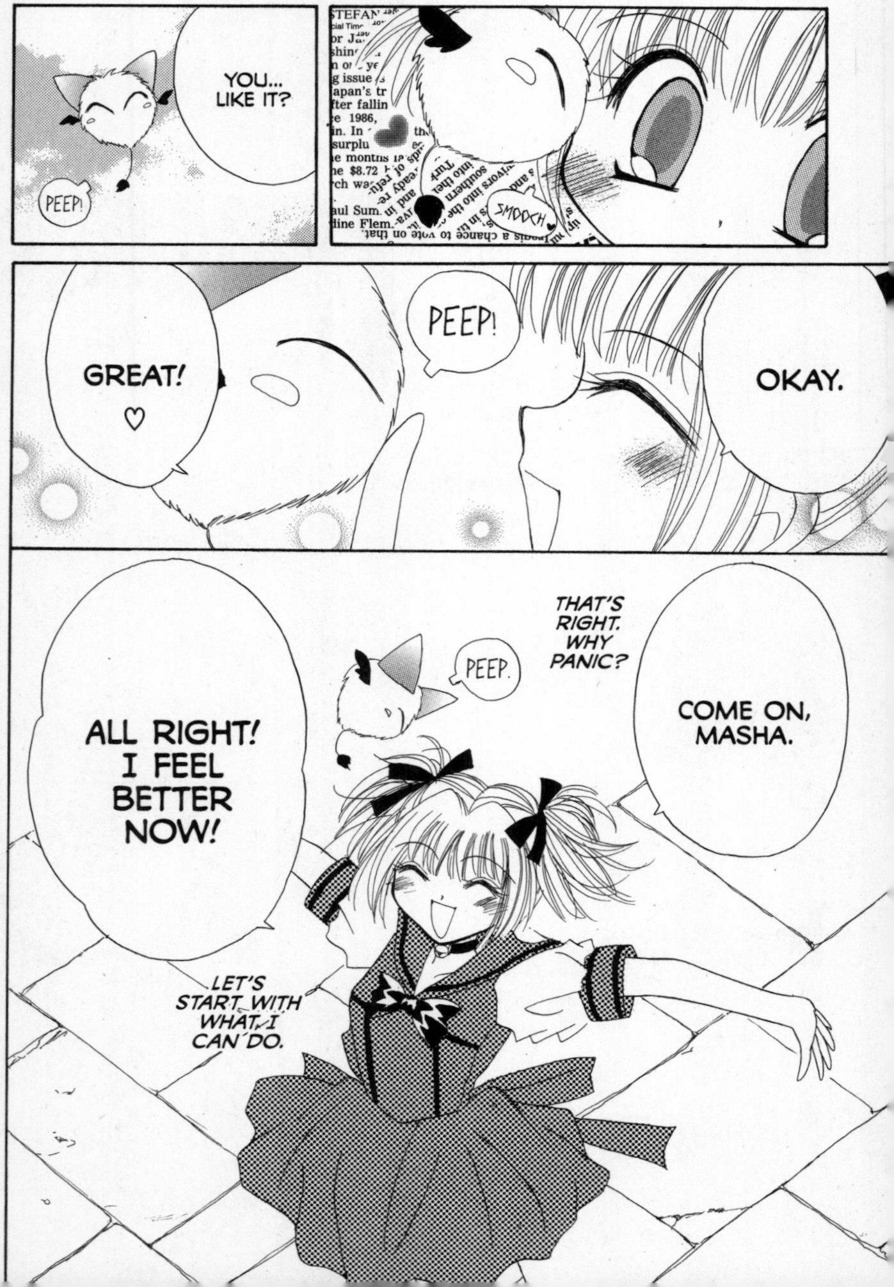
SMOOCH
YOU... LIKE IT?
PEEP!
OKAY.
PEEP!
GREAT! ♡
THAT'S RIGHT. WHY PANIC?
COME ON, MASHA.
PEEP.
ALL RIGHT! I FEEL BETTER NOW!
LET'S START WITH WHAT I CAN DO.

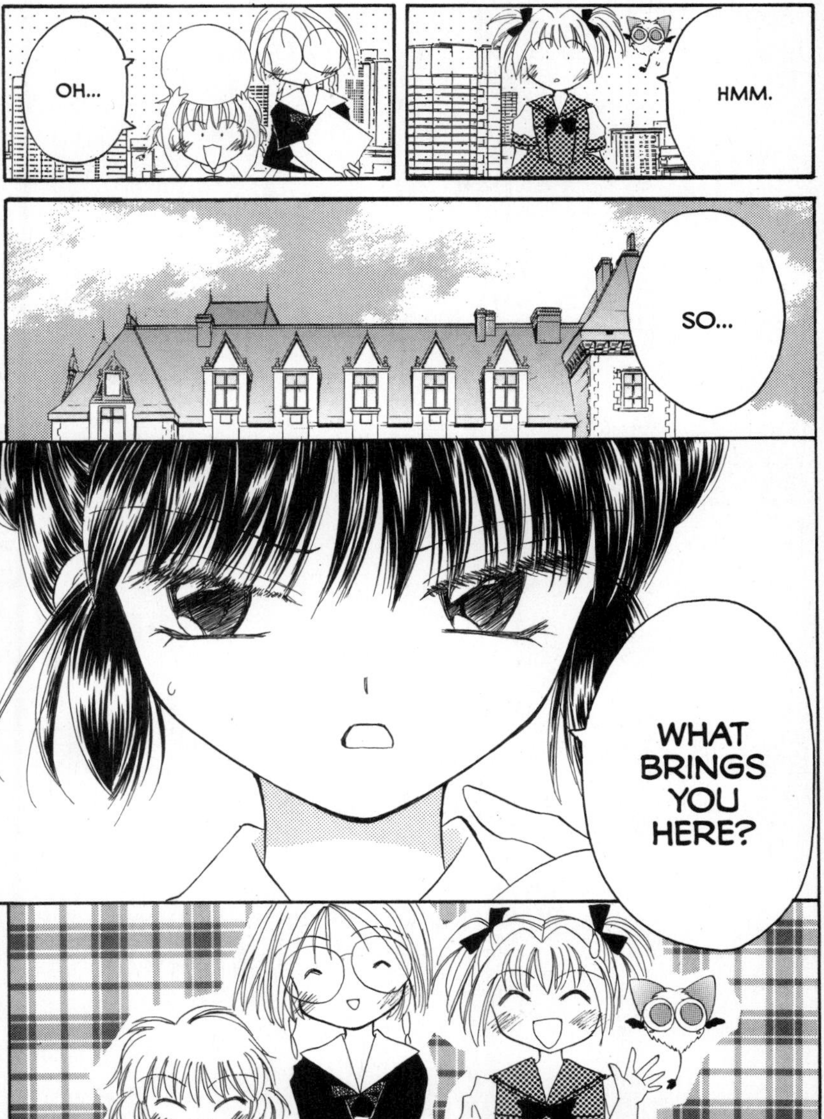
HMM.
OH...
SO...
WHAT BRINGS YOU HERE?

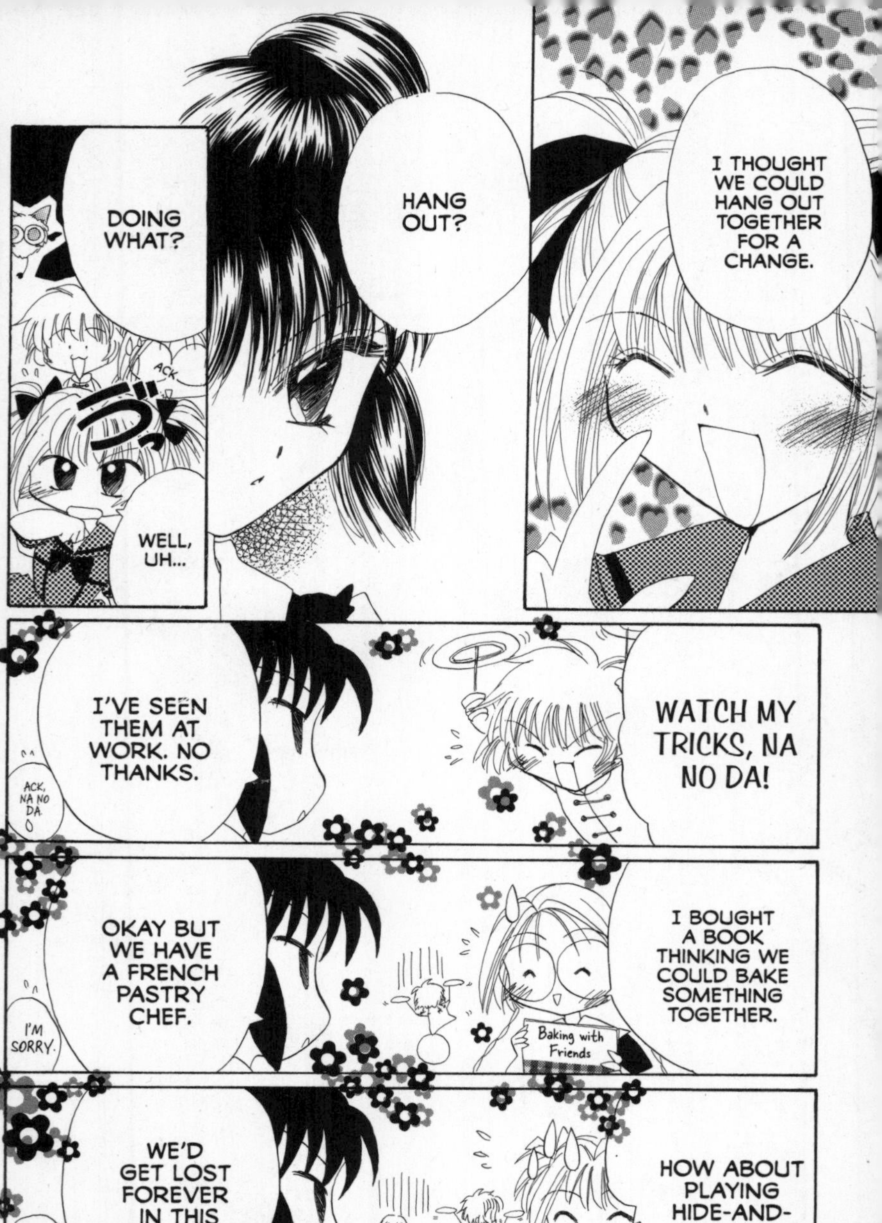
I THOUGHT WE COULD HANG OUT TOGETHER FOR A CHANGE.
HANG OUT?
DOING WHAT?
ACK
うっ
WELL, UH...
WATCH MY TRICKS, NA NO DA!
I'VE SEEN THEM AT WORK. NO THANKS.
ACK, NA NO DA.
I BOUGHT A BOOK THINKING WE COULD BAKE SOMETHING TOGETHER.
Baking with Friends
OKAY BUT WE HAVE A FRENCH PASTRY CHEF.
I'M SORRY.
HOW ABOUT PLAYING HIDE-AND-SEEK?
WE'D GET LOST FOREVER IN THIS MANSION.
RIGHT.

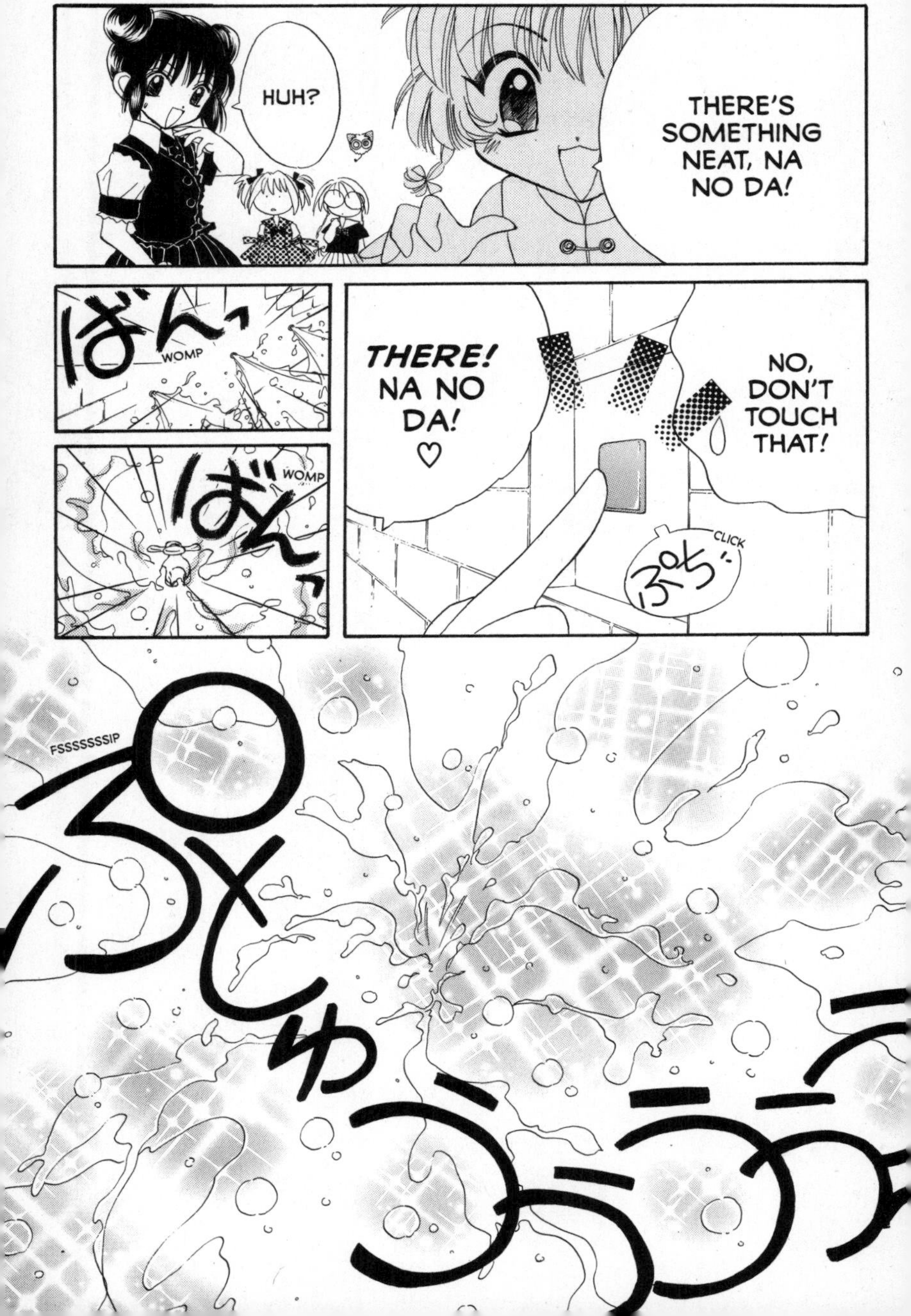
THERE'S SOMETHING NEAT, NA NO DA!
HUH?
NO, DON'T TOUCH THAT!
THERE! NA NO DA! ♡
ぷち
CLICK
ばん
WOMP
ばん
WOMP
FSSSSSSSIP

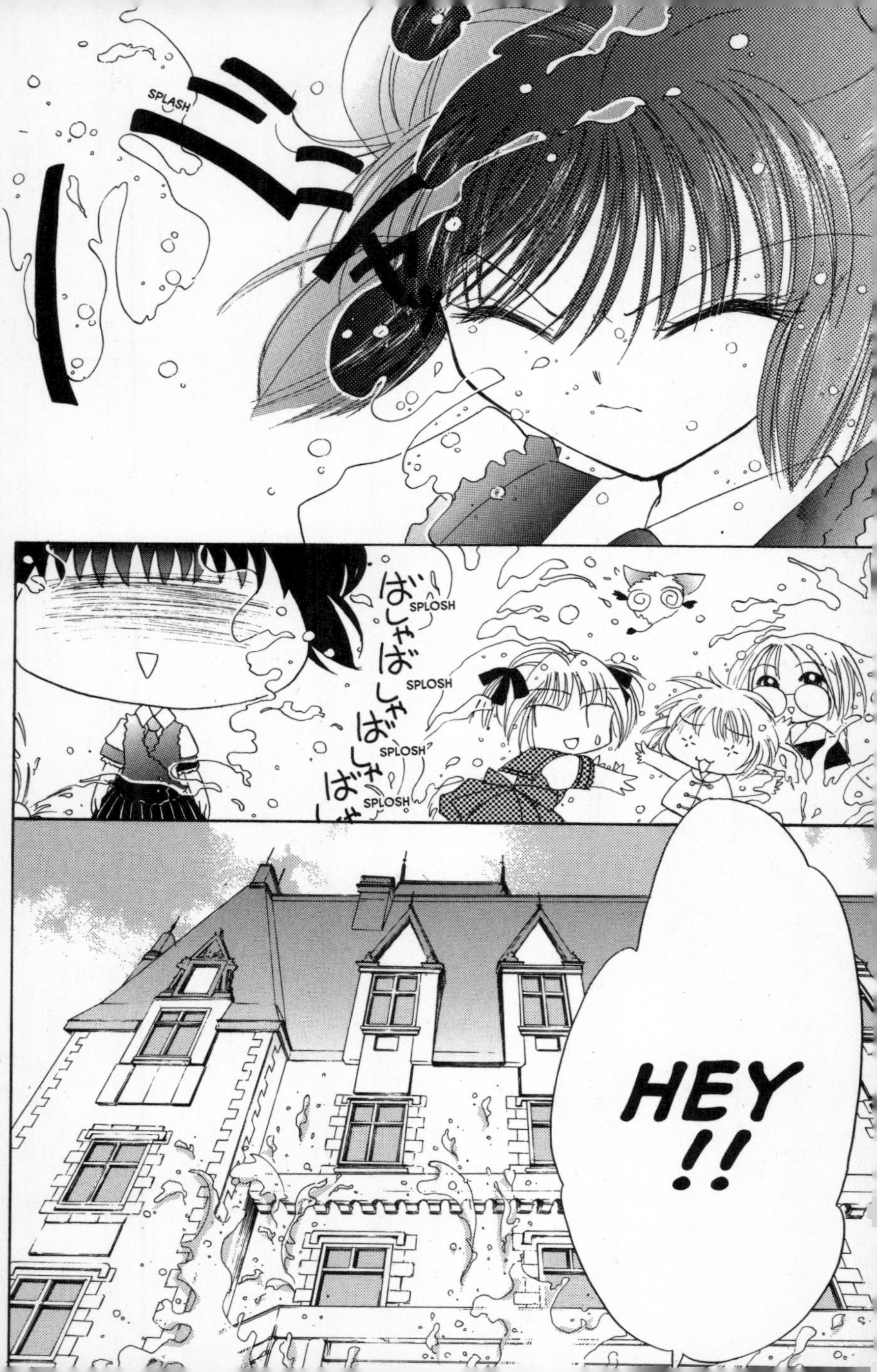
SPLASH
SPLOSH
SPLOSH
SPLOSH
SPLOSH
HEY !!

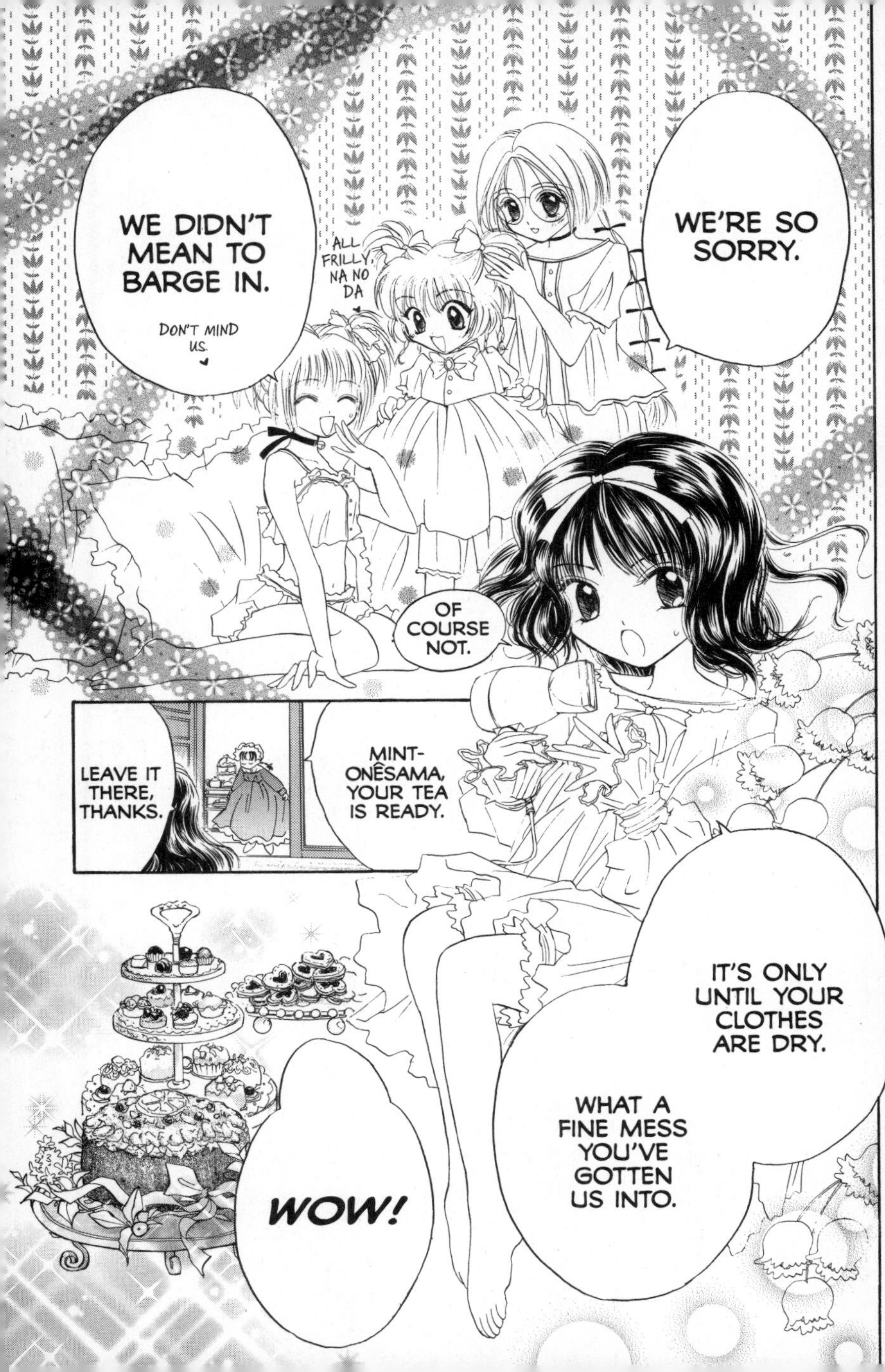
WE'RE SO SORRY.
ALL FRILLY, NA NO DA
WE DIDN'T MEAN TO BARGE IN.
DON'T MIND US.
OF COURSE NOT.
MINT-ONÊSAMA, YOUR TEA IS READY.
LEAVE IT THERE, THANKS.
IT'S ONLY UNTIL YOUR CLOTHES ARE DRY.
WHAT A FINE MESS YOU'VE GOTTEN US INTO.
WOW!

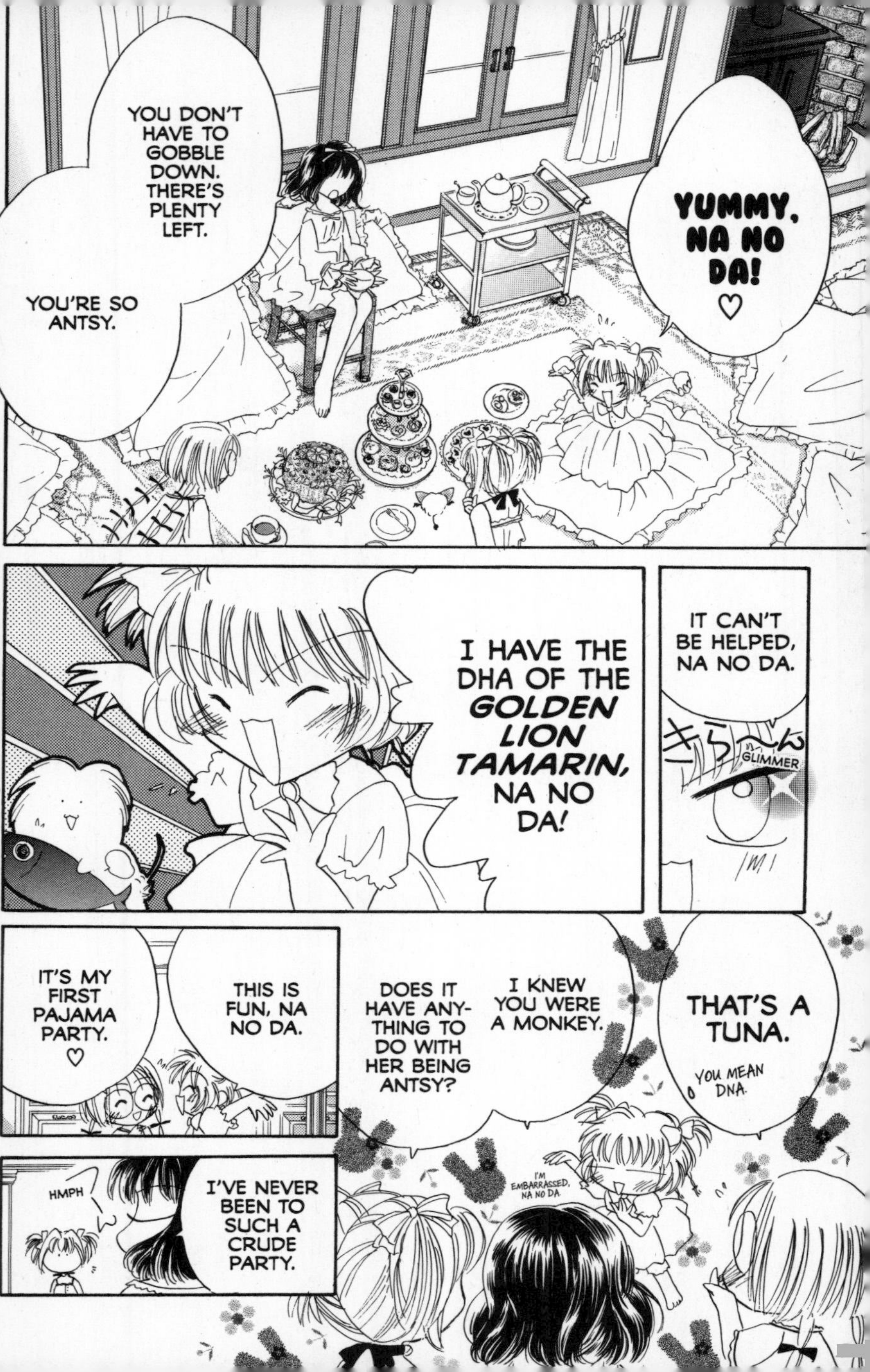
YUMMY, NA NO DA! ♡
YOU DON'T HAVE TO GOBBLE DOWN. THERE'S PLENTY LEFT.
YOU'RE SO ANTSY.
IT CAN'T BE HELPED, NA NO DA.
きらーん GLIMMER
I HAVE THE DHA OF THE *GOLDEN LION TAMARIN,* NA NO DA!
THAT'S A TUNA.
YOU MEAN DNA.
I KNEW YOU WERE A MONKEY.
DOES IT HAVE ANY-THING TO DO WITH HER BEING ANTSY?
I'M EMBARRASSED, NA NO DA
THIS IS FUN, NA NO DA.
IT'S MY FIRST PAJAMA PARTY. ♡
I'VE NEVER BEEN TO SUCH A CRUDE PARTY.
HMPH

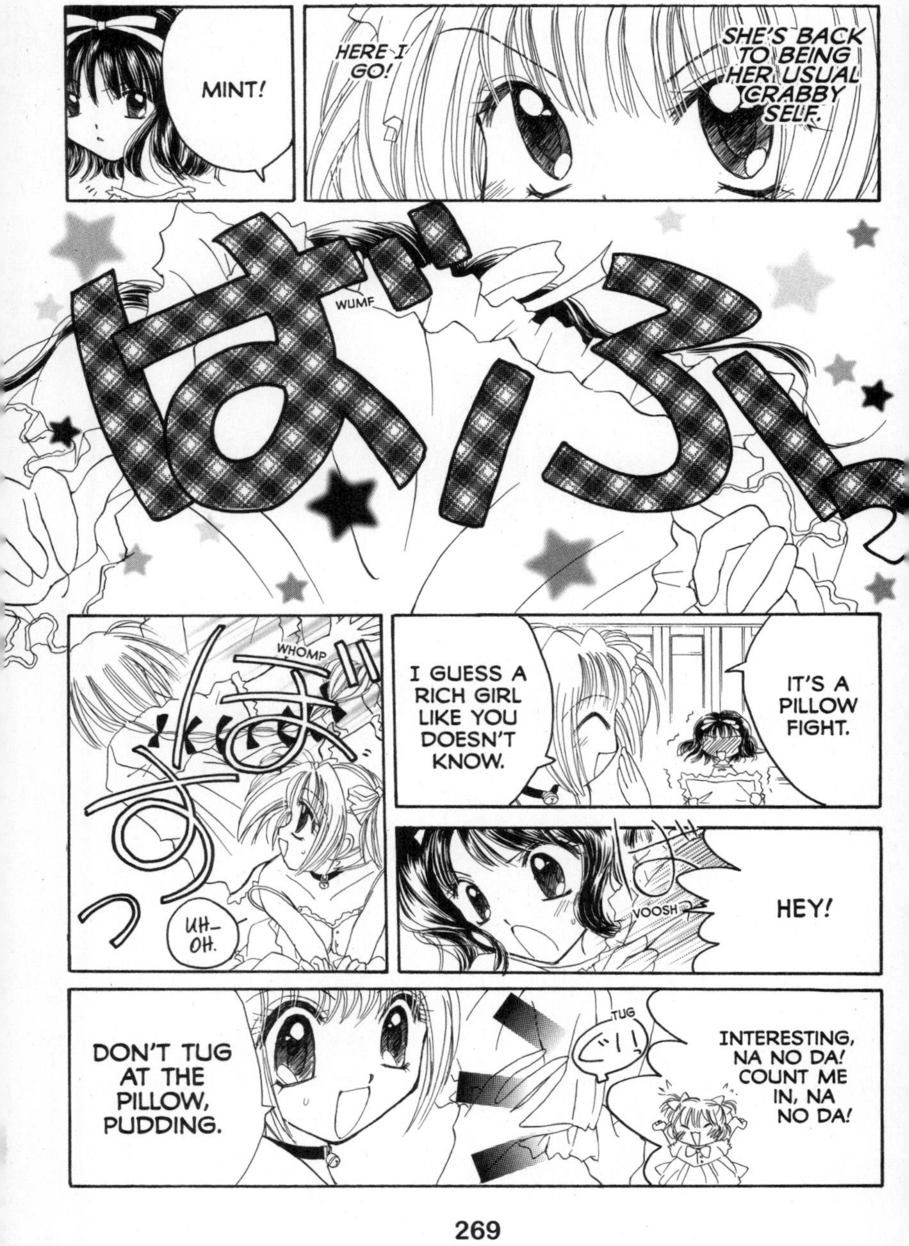
SHE'S BACK TO BEING HER USUAL CRABBY SELF.
HERE I GO!
MINT!
WUMF
IT'S A PILLOW FIGHT.
I GUESS A RICH GIRL LIKE YOU DOESN'T KNOW.
HEY!
VOOSH
WHOMP
UH-OH.
INTERESTING, NA NO DA! COUNT ME IN, NA NO DA!
TUG
DON'T TUG AT THE PILLOW, PUDDING.

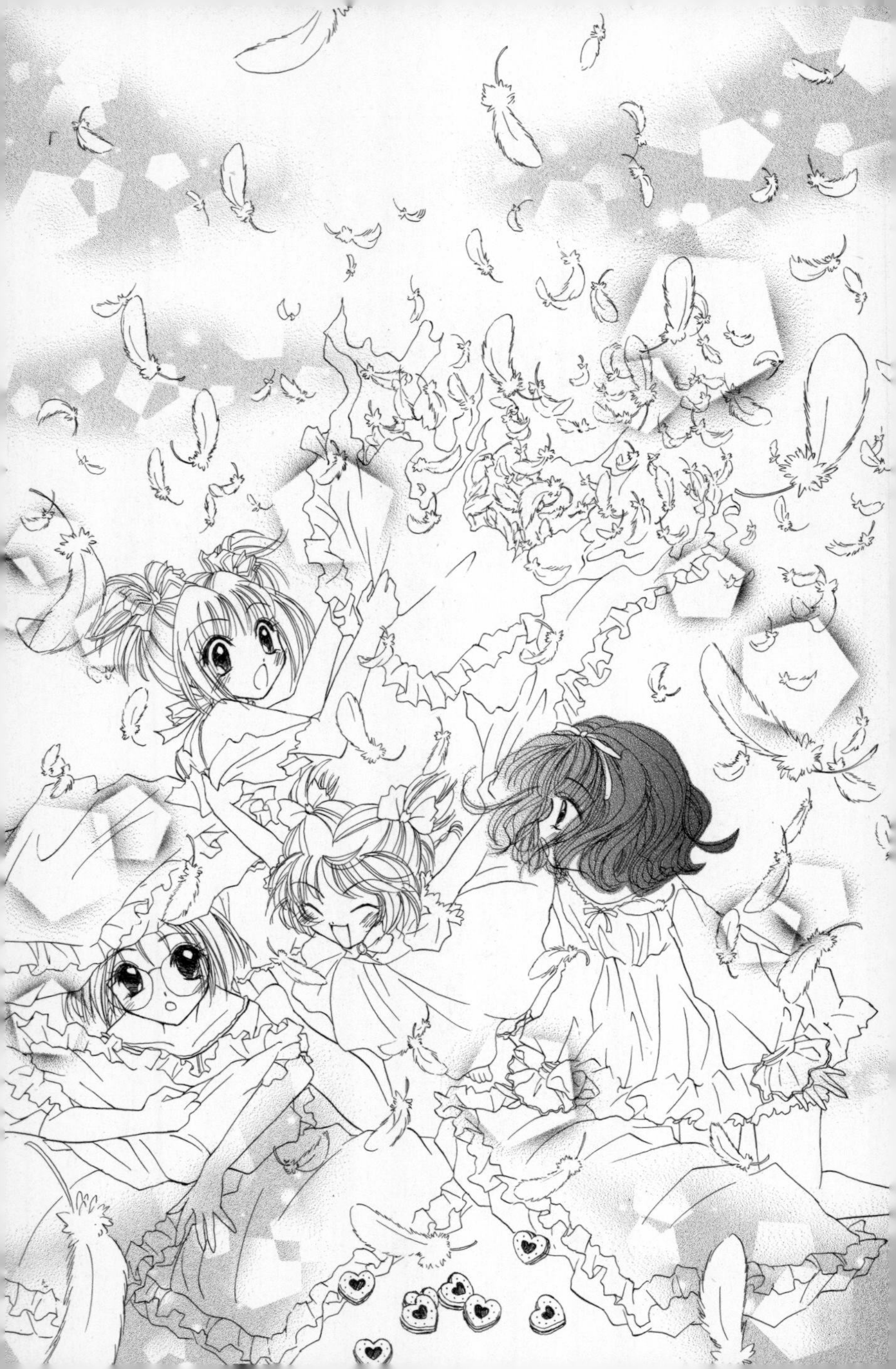

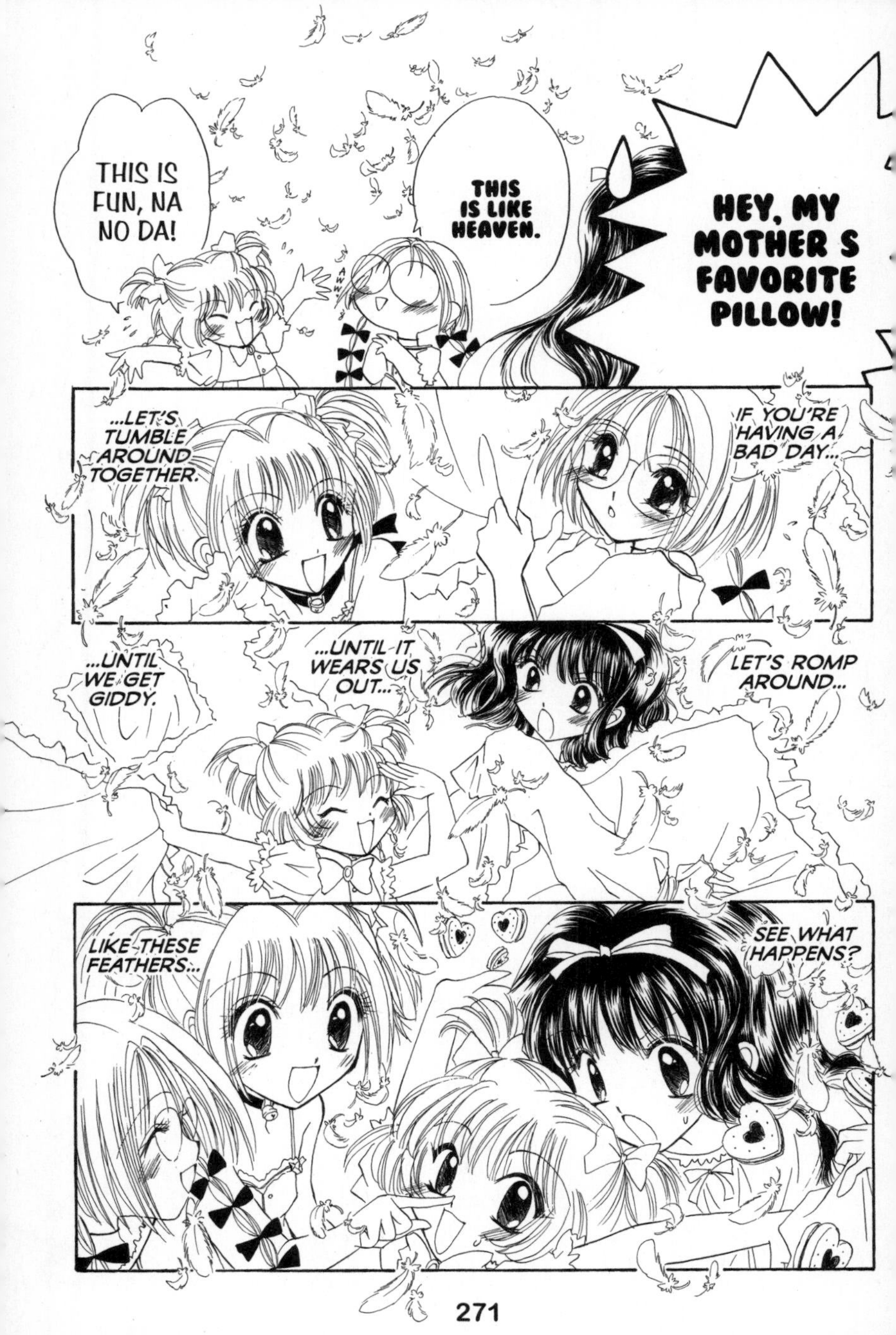
HEY, MY MOTHER S FAVORITE PILLOW!
THIS IS LIKE HEAVEN.
THIS IS FUN, NA NO DA!
IF YOU'RE HAVING A BAD DAY...
...LET'S TUMBLE AROUND TOGETHER.
LET'S ROMP AROUND...
...UNTIL IT WEARS US OUT...
...UNTIL WE GET GIDDY.
SEE WHAT HAPPENS?
LIKE THESE FEATHERS...

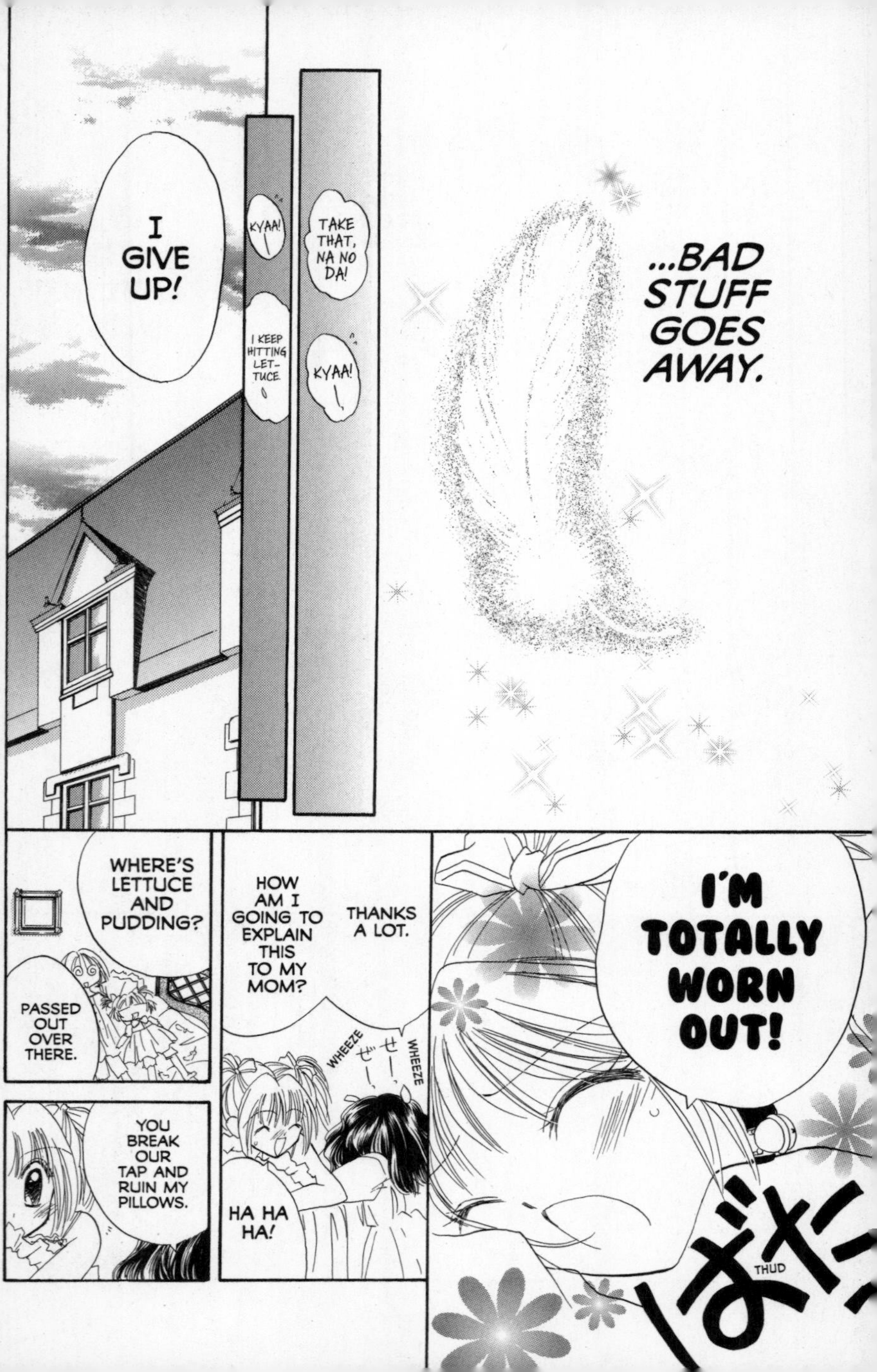
...BAD STUFF GOES AWAY.
TAKE THAT, NA NO DA!
KYAA!
KYAA!
I KEEP HITTING LET-TUCE.
I GIVE UP!
I'M TOTALLY WORN OUT!
THUD
THANKS A LOT.
HOW AM I GOING TO EXPLAIN THIS TO MY MOM?
WHEEZE
WHEEZE
HA HA HA!
WHERE'S LETTUCE AND PUDDING?
PASSED OUT OVER THERE.
YOU BREAK OUR TAP AND RUIN MY PILLOWS.

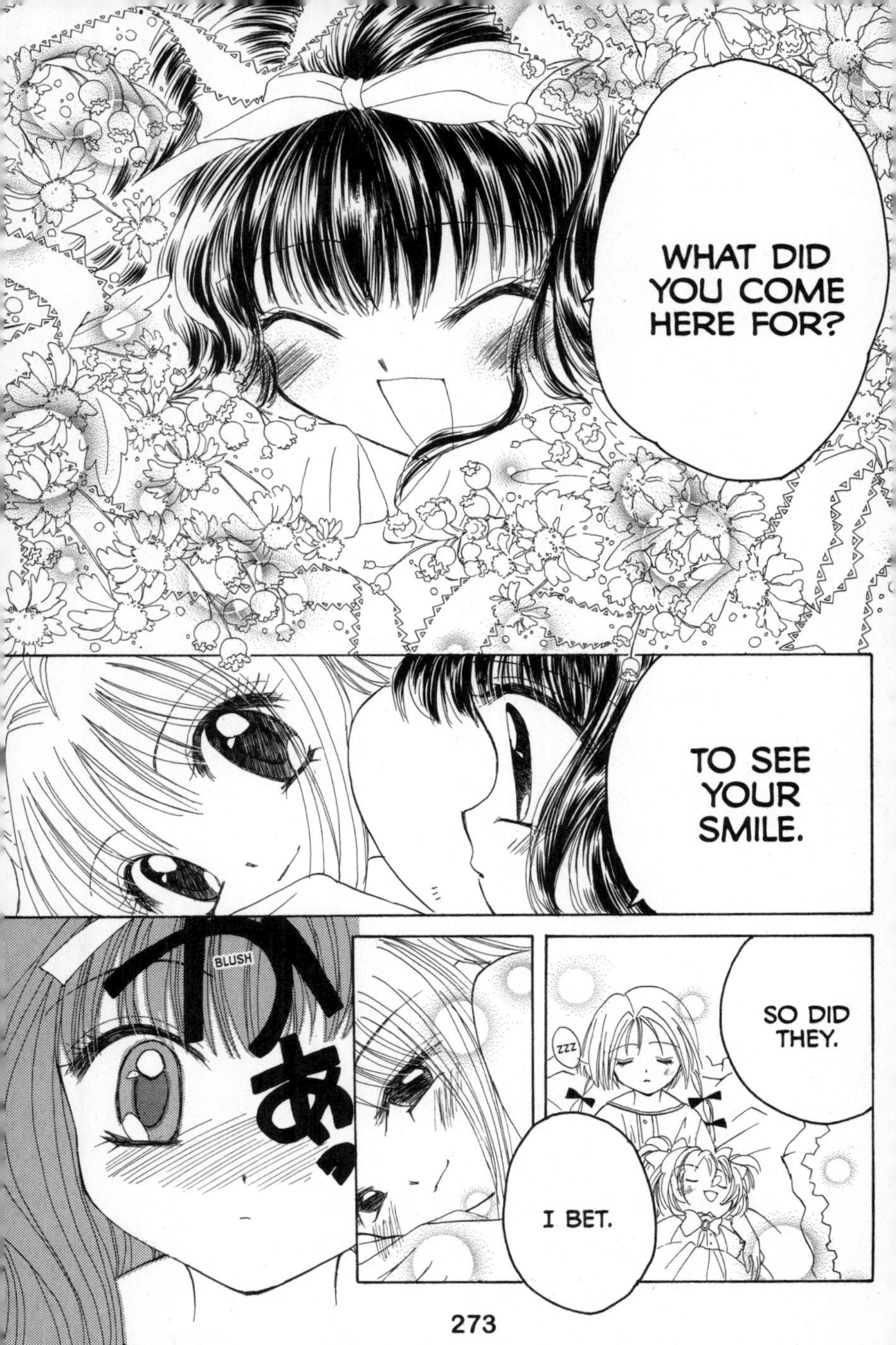
WHAT DID YOU COME HERE FOR?
TO SEE YOUR SMILE.
ZZZ
SO DID THEY.
I BET.
BLUSH

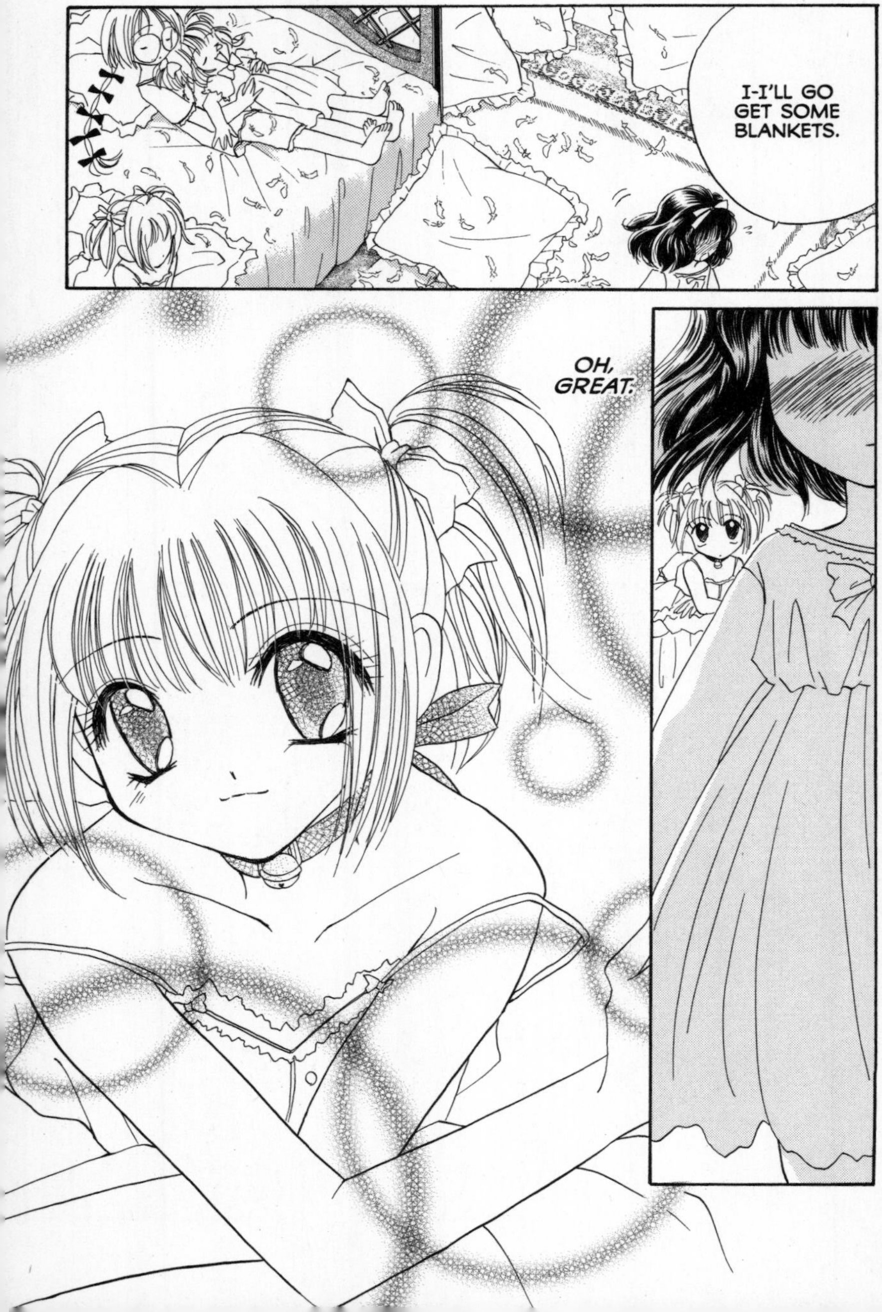
I-I'LL GO GET SOME BLANKETS.
OH, GREAT.

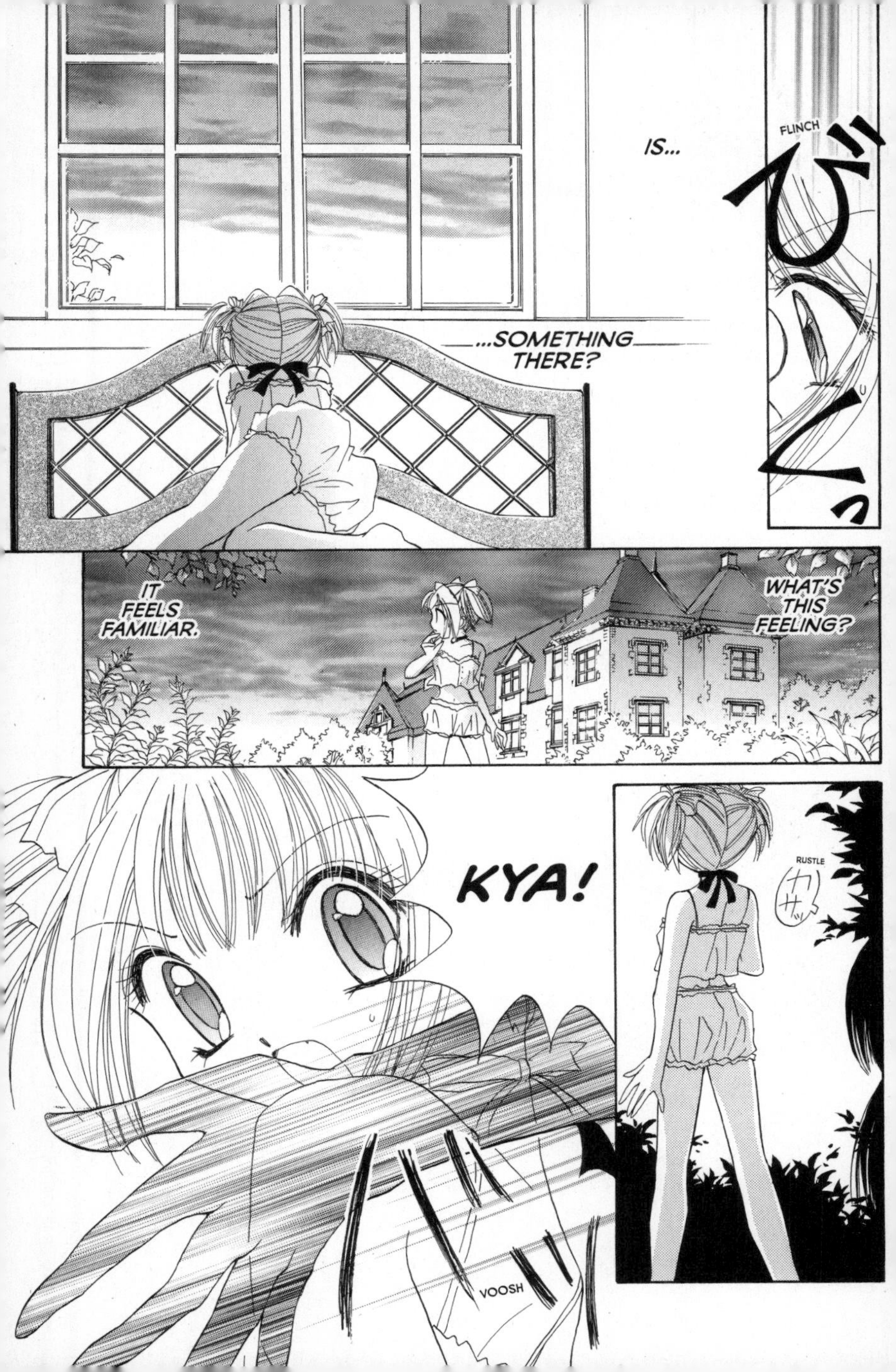
FLINCH
びくっ
IS...
...SOMETHING THERE?
WHAT'S THIS FEELING?
IT FEELS FAMILIAR.
RUSTLE
カサッ
KYA!
VOOSH

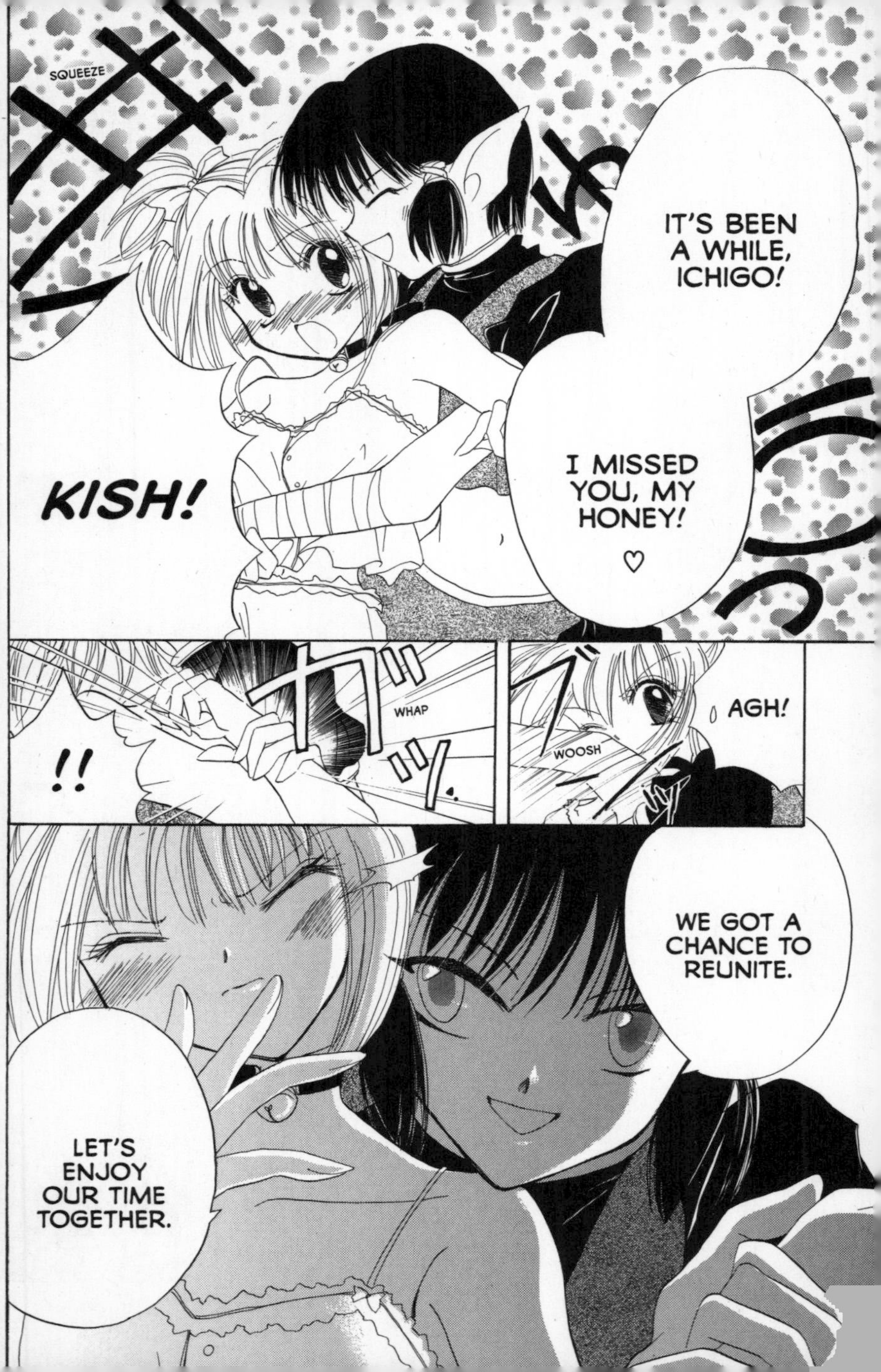
IT'S BEEN A WHILE, ICHIGO!
I MISSED YOU, MY HONEY! ♡
SQUEEZE
KISH!
AGH!
WOOSH
WHAP
!!
WE GOT A CHANCE TO REUNITE.
LET'S ENJOY OUR TIME TOGETHER.

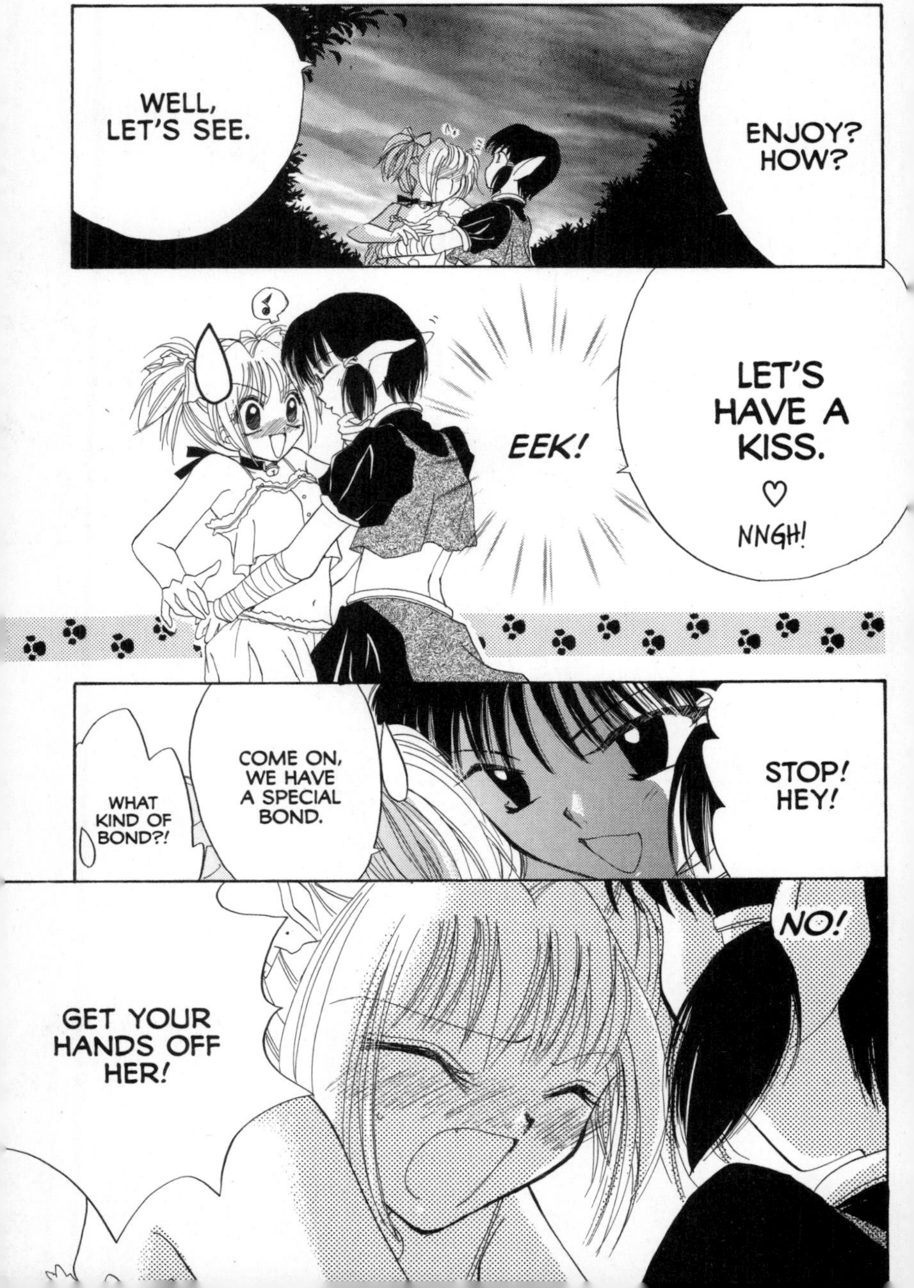
ENJOY? HOW?
WELL, LET'S SEE.
LET'S HAVE A KISS. ♡
NNGH!
EEK!
STOP! HEY!
COME ON, WE HAVE A SPECIAL BOND.
WHAT KIND OF BOND?!
NO!
GET YOUR HANDS OFF HER!

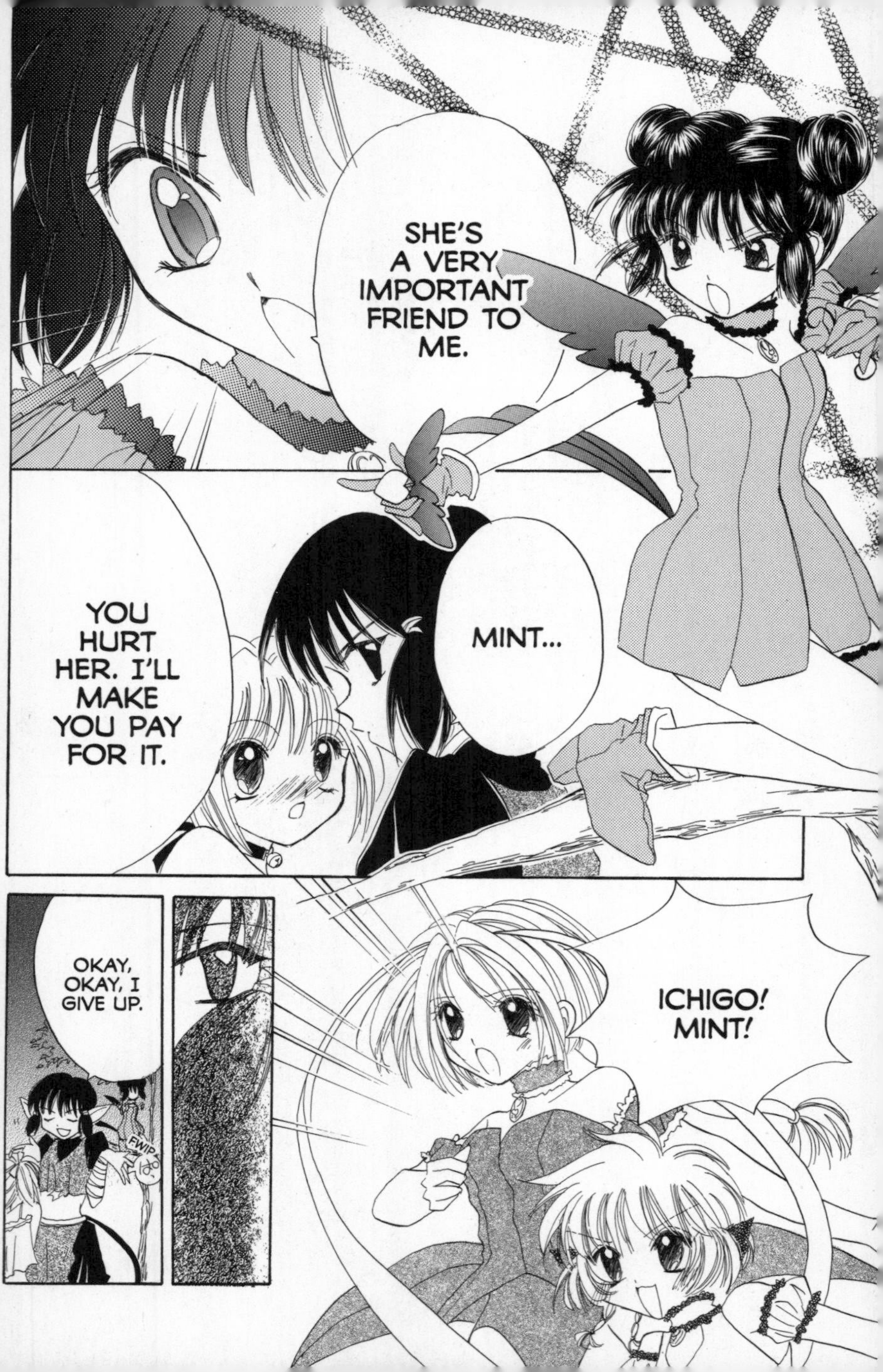
SHE'S A VERY IMPORTANT FRIEND TO ME.
YOU HURT HER. I'LL MAKE YOU PAY FOR IT.
MINT...
ICHIGO! MINT!
OKAY, OKAY, I GIVE UP.
FWIP
ぱっ

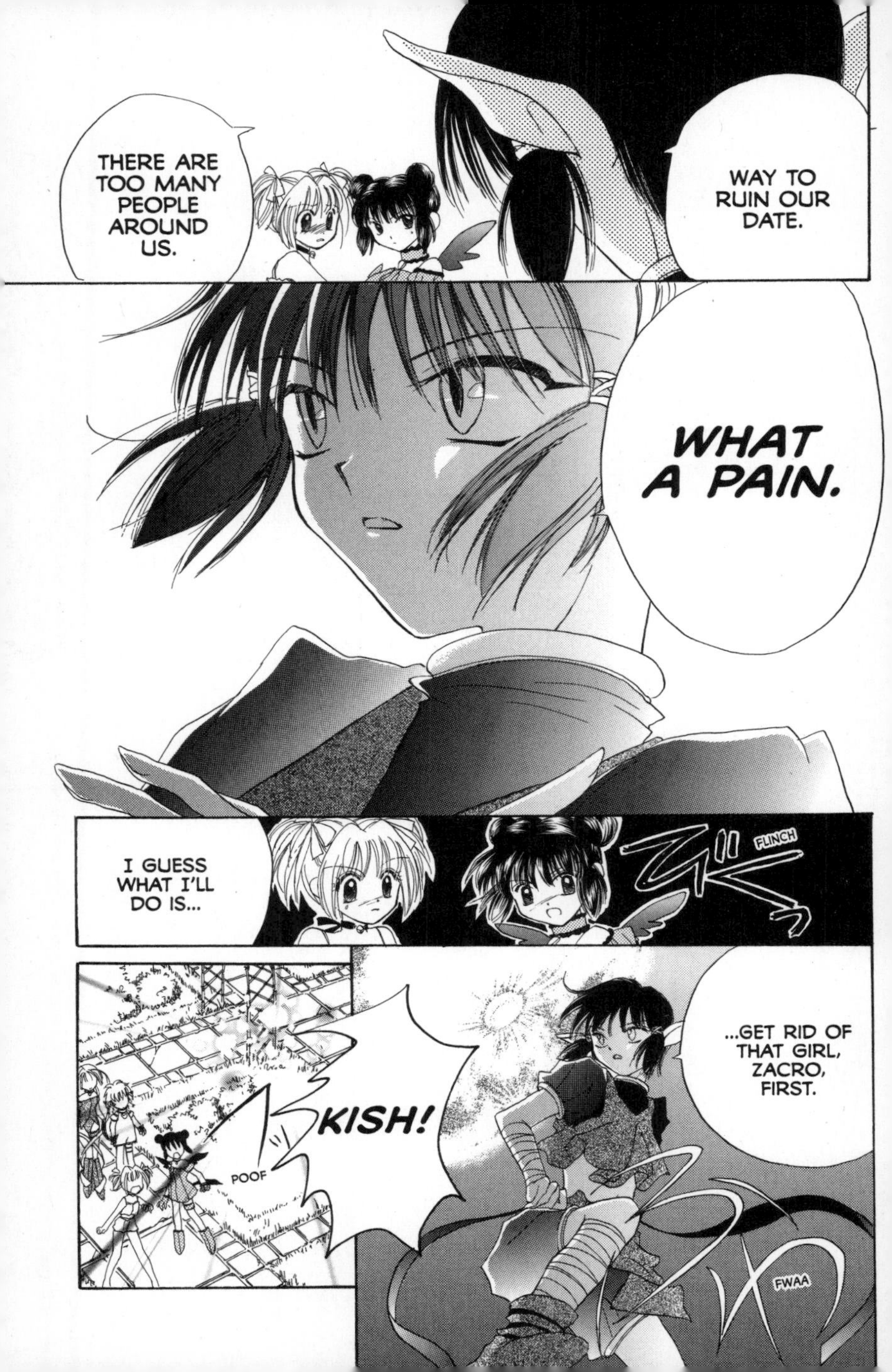
WAY TO RUIN OUR DATE.
THERE ARE TOO MANY PEOPLE AROUND US.
WHAT A PAIN.
FLINCH
I GUESS WHAT I'LL DO IS...
...GET RID OF THAT GIRL, ZACRO, FIRST.
FWAA
KISH!
POOF

SHIRO-GANE!

CAN YOU HEAR ME, ICHIGO?

RELAX, MINT.

O-ONÊSAMA...

YOU CAN STILL MAKE IT.

HURRY!

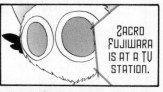

ZACRO FUJIWARA IS AT A TV STATION.

YOU KNOW OUR ANSWER.

OH NO, ONÊSAMA IS IN DANGER.

ICHIGO...

GRASP

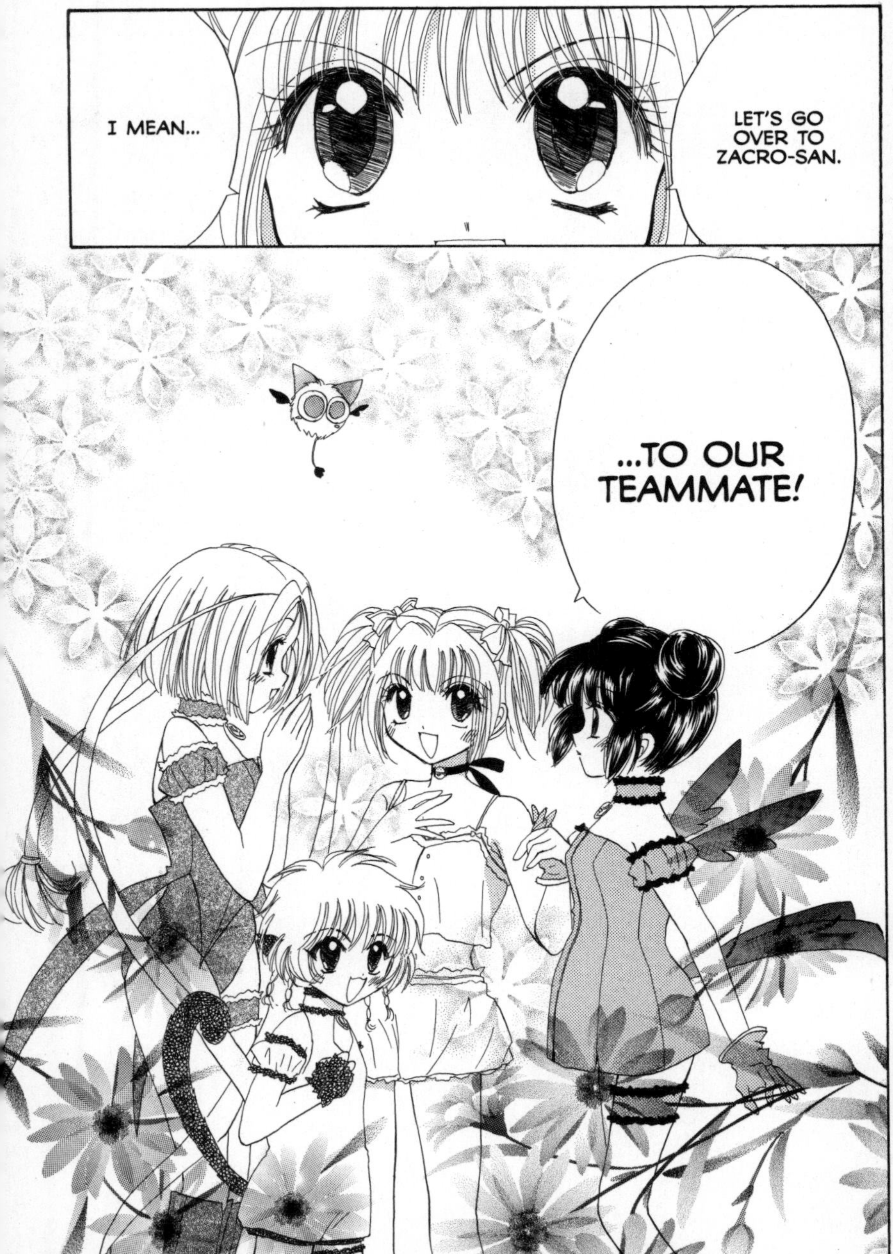
LET'S GO OVER TO ZACRO-SAN.
I MEAN...
...TO OUR TEAMMATE!

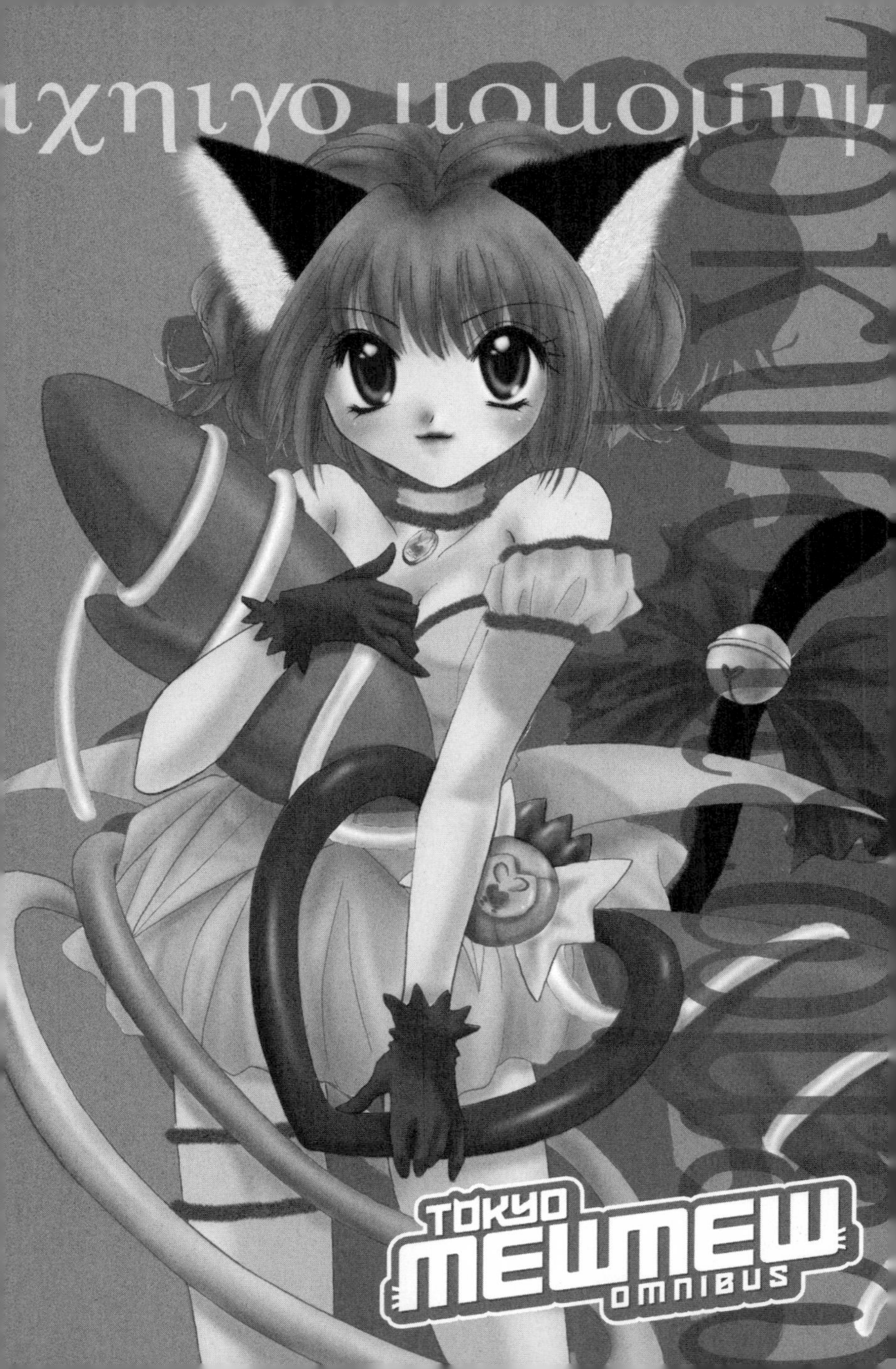
TOKYO MEWMEW OMNIBUS

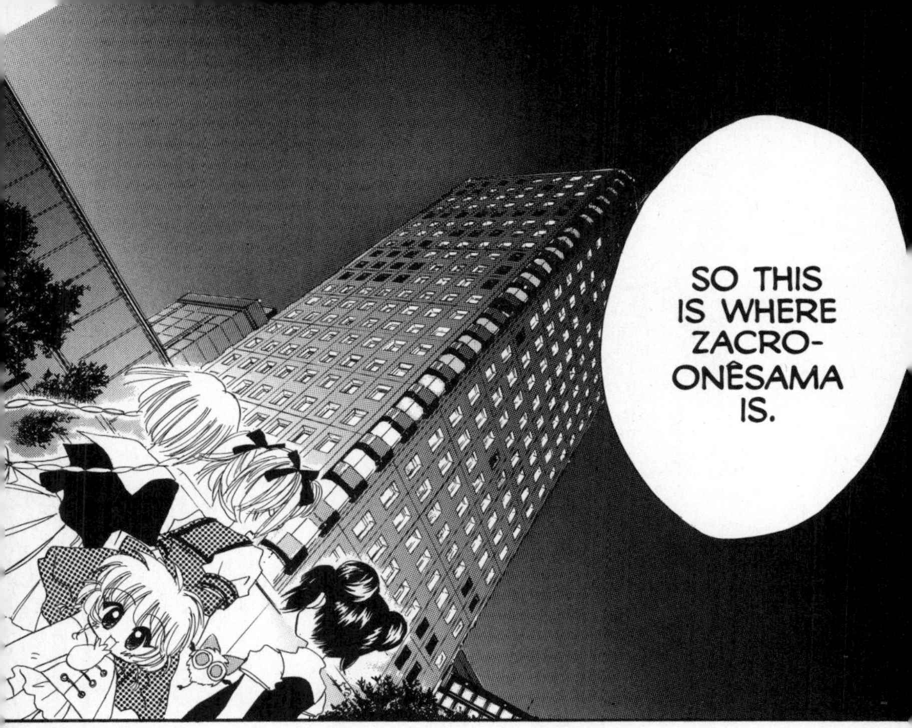
SO THIS IS WHERE ZACRO-ONÊSAMA IS.

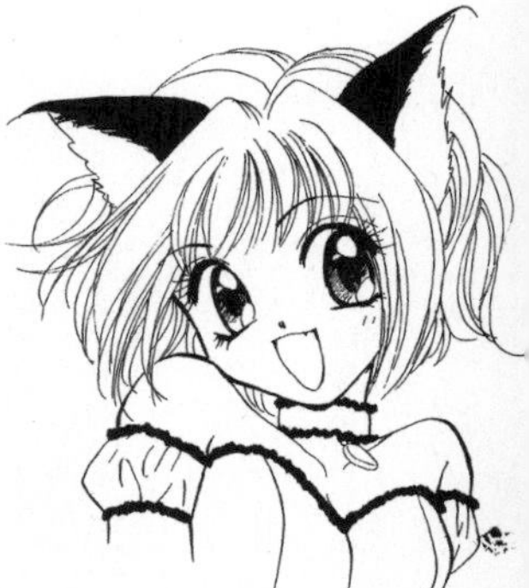

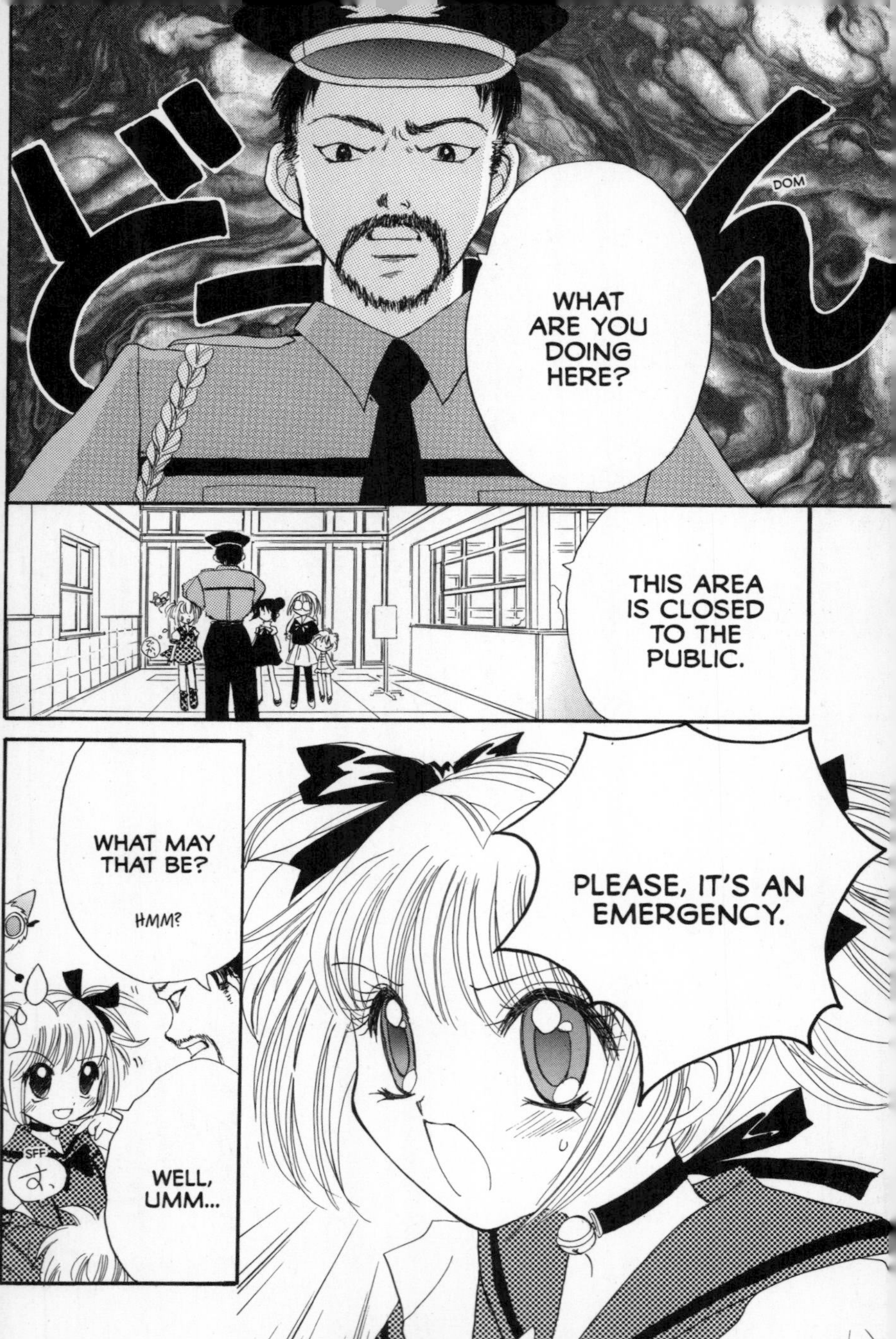

どーん
DOM
WHAT ARE YOU DOING HERE?
THIS AREA IS CLOSED TO THE PUBLIC.
PLEASE, IT'S AN EMERGENCY.
WHAT MAY THAT BE?
HMM?
WELL, UMM...
SFF
す、

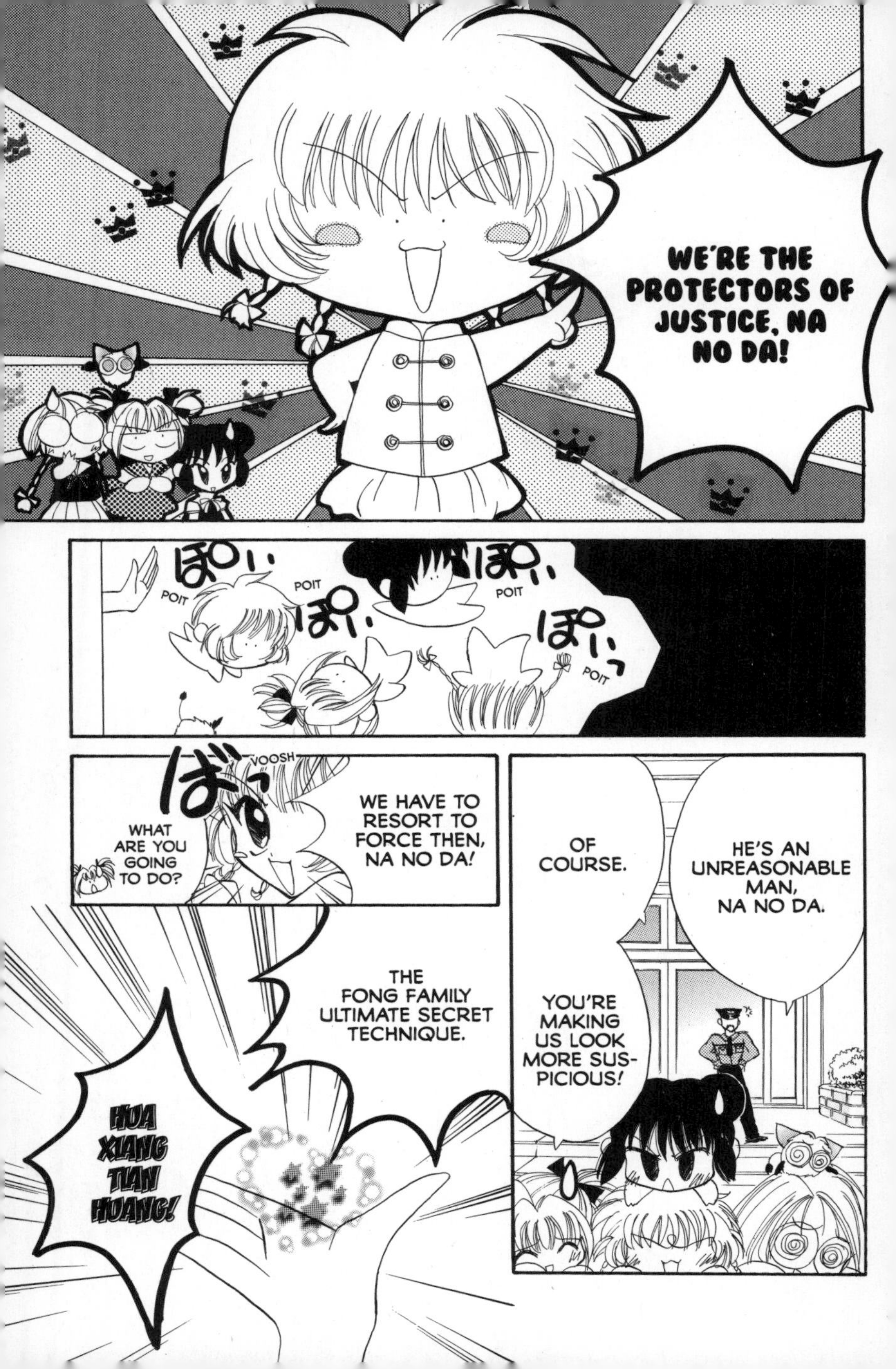
WE'RE THE PROTECTORS OF JUSTICE, NA NO DA!
ぽいっ
POIT
ぽい
POIT
ぽい
POIT
ぽい
POIT
HE'S AN UNREASONABLE MAN, NA NO DA.
OF COURSE.
YOU'RE MAKING US LOOK MORE SUS-PICIOUS!
ばっ
VOOSH
WE HAVE TO RESORT TO FORCE THEN, NA NO DA!
WHAT ARE YOU GOING TO DO?
THE FONG FAMILY ULTIMATE SECRET TECHNIQUE.
HUA XIANG TIAN HUANG!

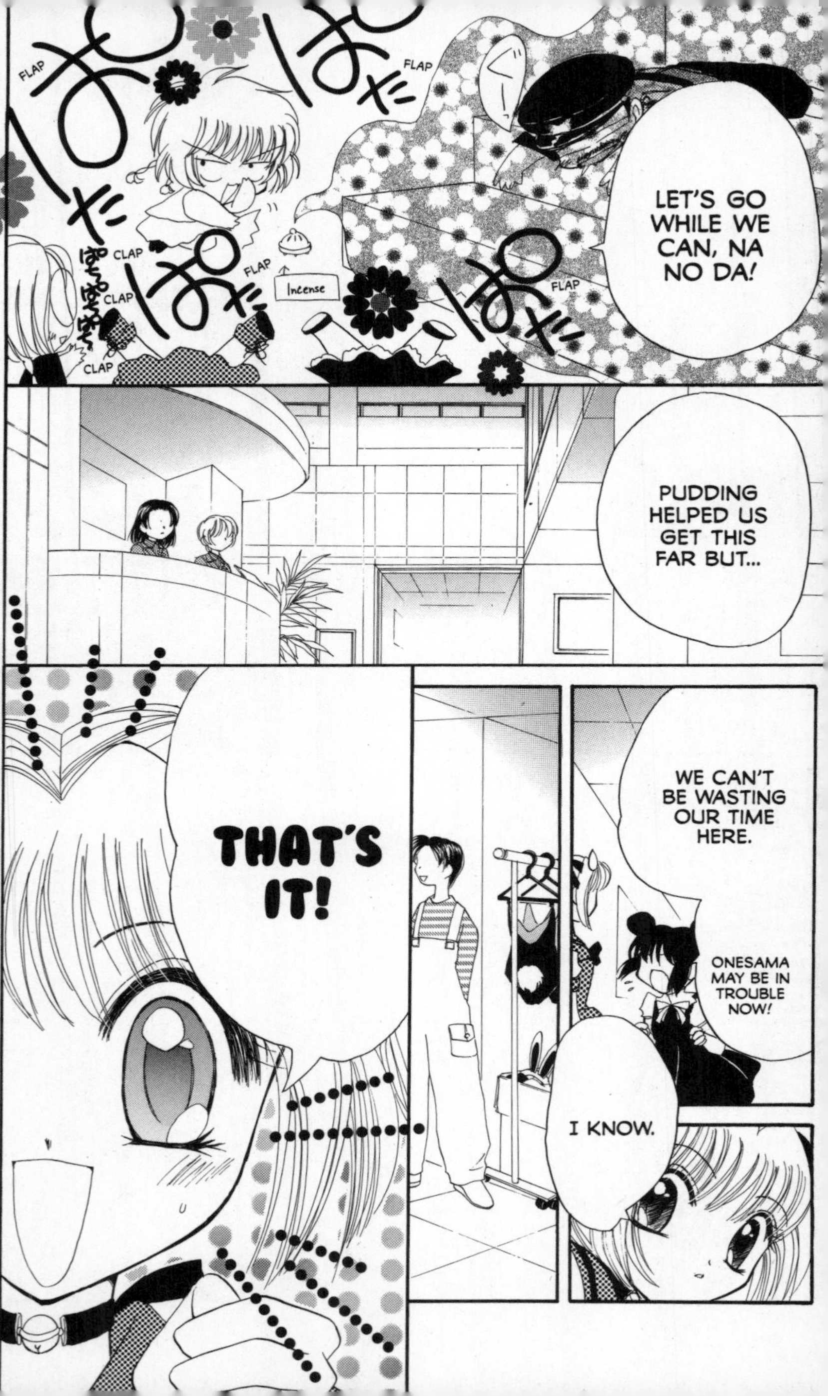
LET'S GO WHILE WE CAN, NA NO DA!
FLAP
FLAP
FLAP
FLAP
Incense
CLAP
CLAP
CLAP
PUDDING HELPED US GET THIS FAR BUT...
WE CAN'T BE WASTING OUR TIME HERE.
ONESAMA MAY BE IN TROUBLE NOW!
I KNOW.
THAT'S IT!

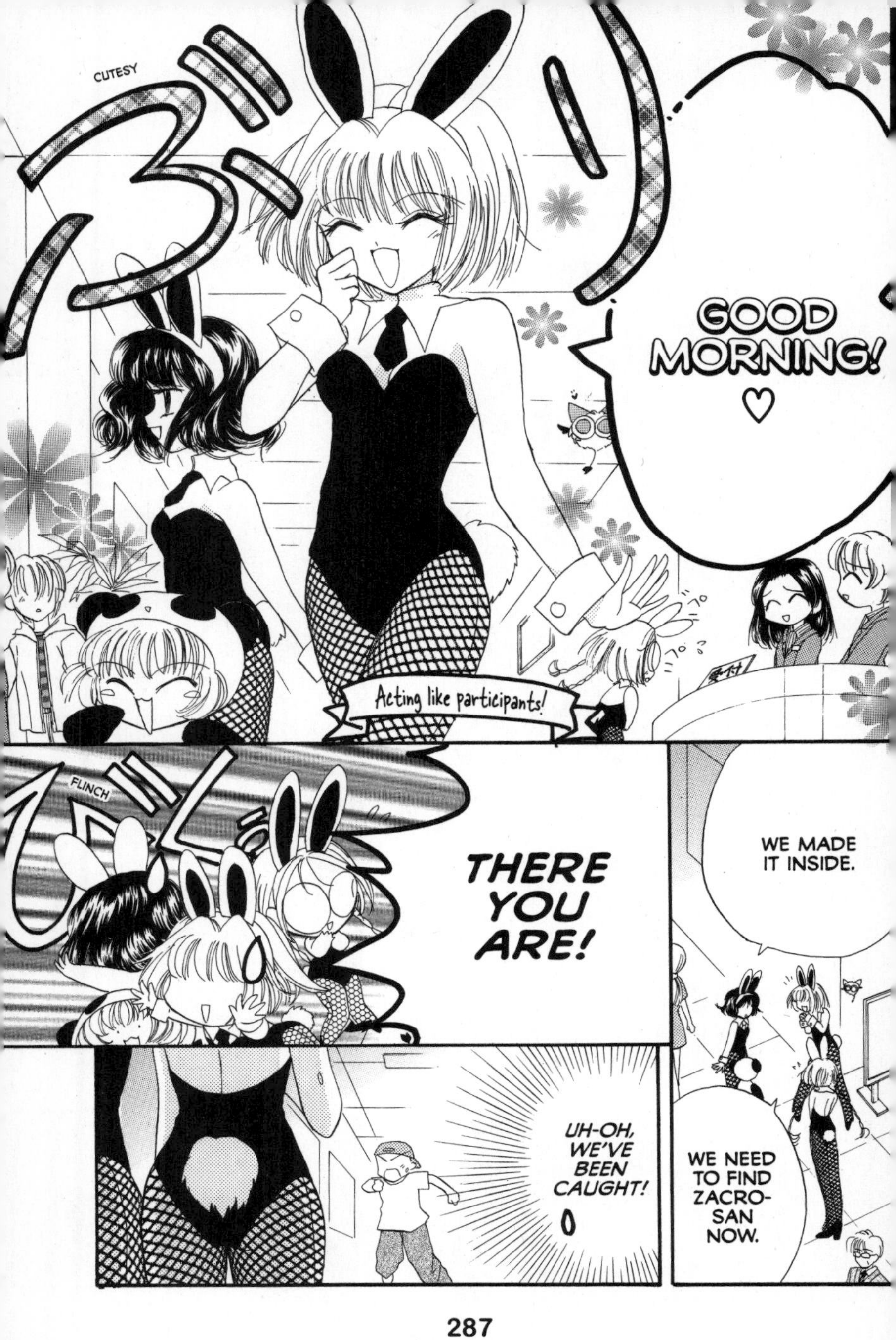
GOOD MORNING! ♡
CUTESY
Acting like participants!
WE MADE IT INSIDE.
WE NEED TO FIND ZACRO-SAN NOW.
THERE YOU ARE!
FLINCH
UH-OH, WE'VE BEEN CAUGHT!

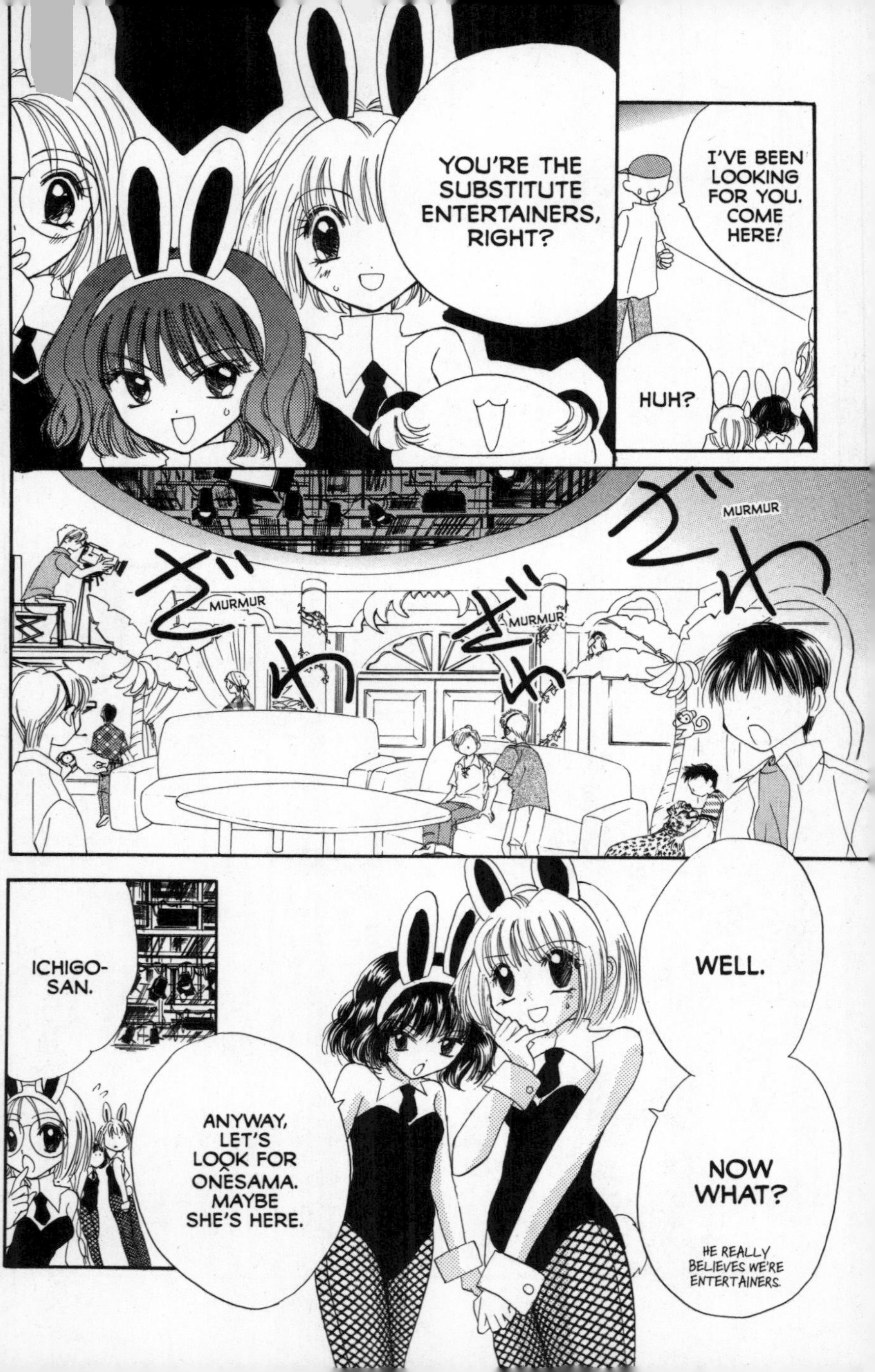
I'VE BEEN LOOKING FOR YOU. COME HERE!
HUH?
YOU'RE THE SUBSTITUTE ENTERTAINERS, RIGHT?
MURMUR
MURMUR
MURMUR
WELL.
NOW WHAT?
HE REALLY BELIEVES WE'RE ENTERTAINERS.
ANYWAY, LET'S LOOK FOR ONÊSAMA. MAYBE SHE'S HERE.
ICHIGO-SAN.

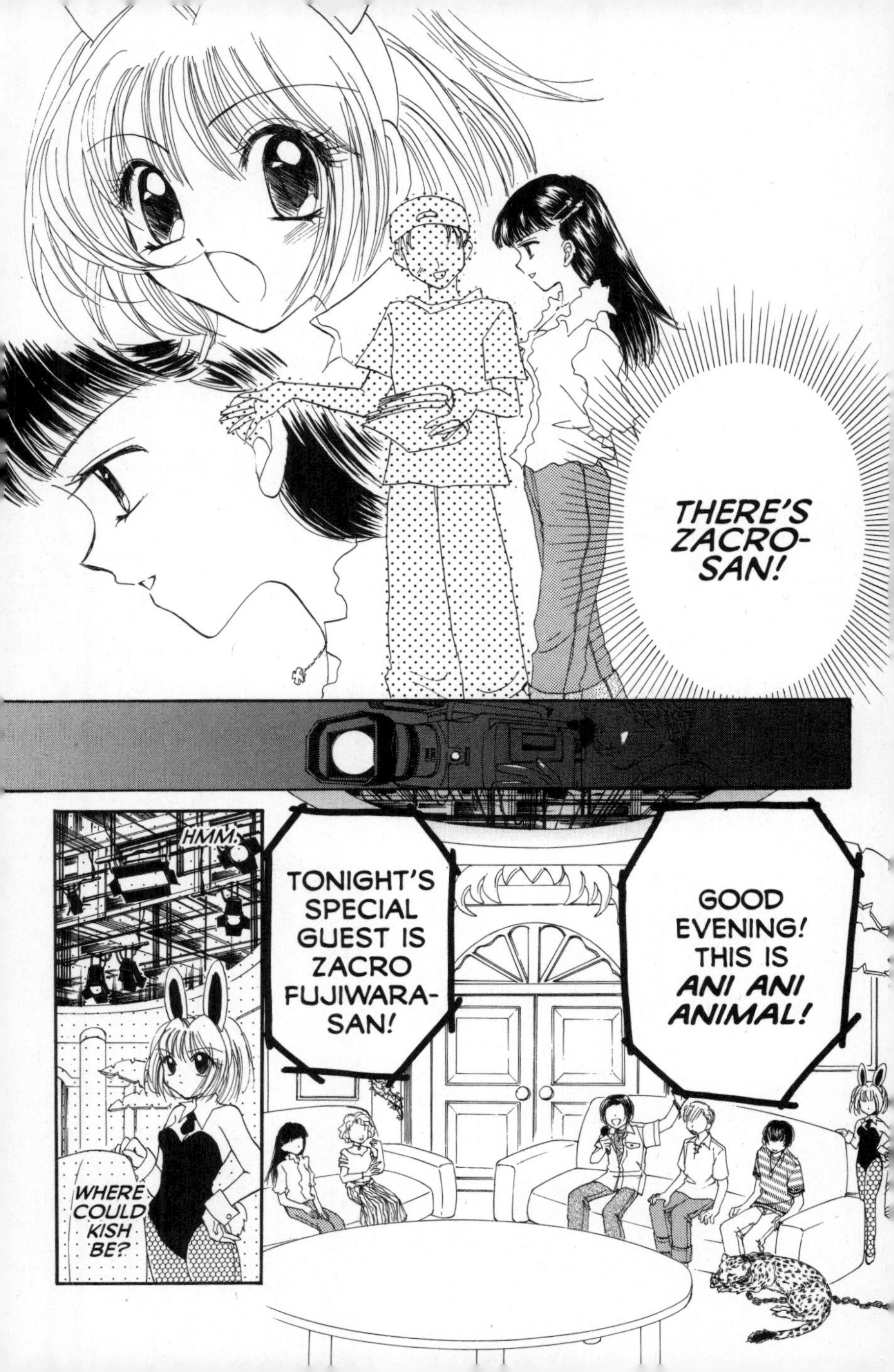
THERE'S ZACRO-SAN!
GOOD EVENING! THIS IS *ANI ANI ANIMAL!*
TONIGHT'S SPECIAL GUEST IS ZACRO FUJIWARA-SAN!
HMM.
WHERE COULD KISH BE?

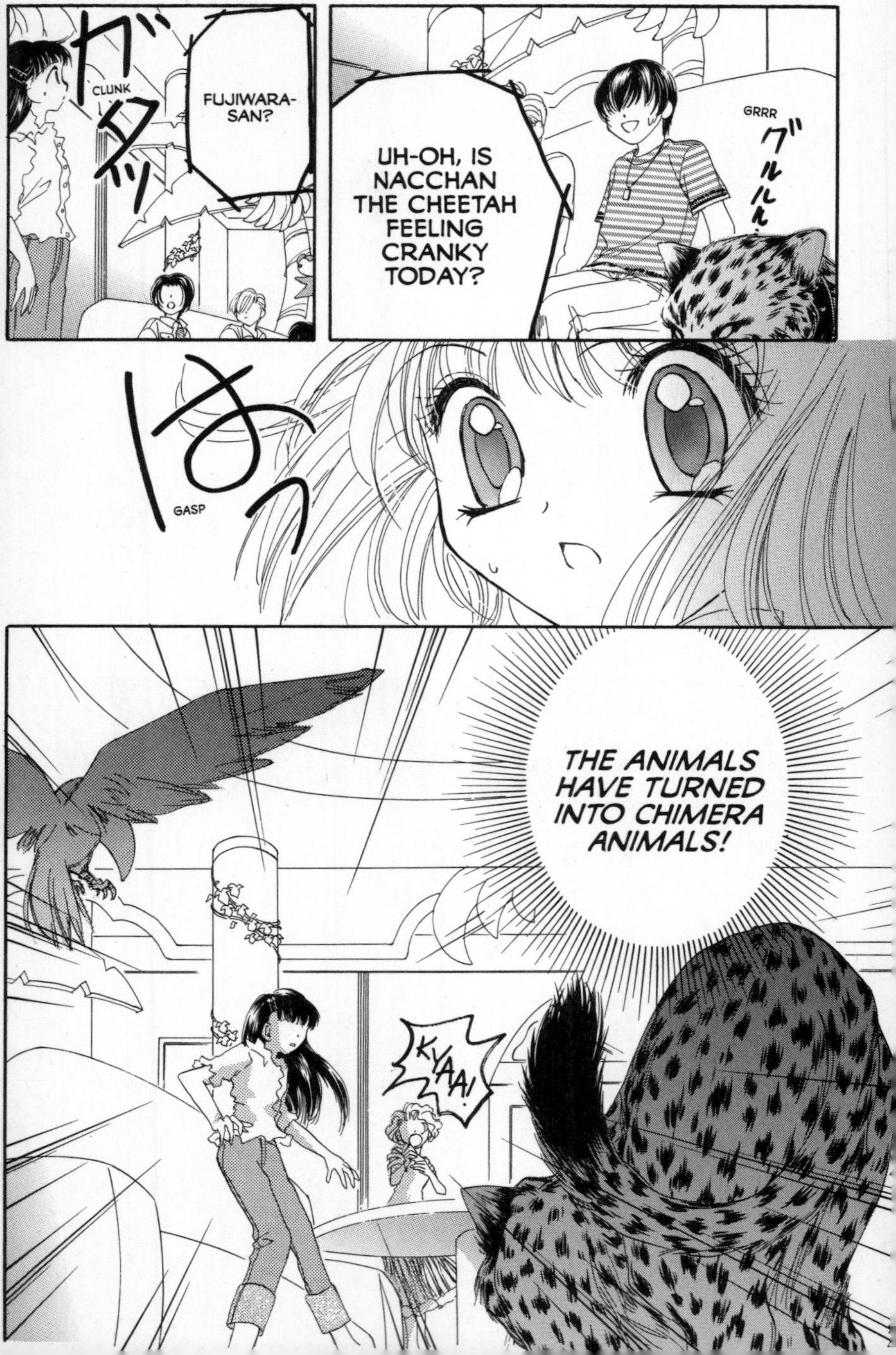

GRRR
グルルル
UH-OH, IS NACCHAN THE CHEETAH FEELING CRANKY TODAY?
FUJIWARA-SAN?
ガタッ
CLUNK
はっ
GASP
THE ANIMALS HAVE TURNED INTO CHIMERA ANIMALS!
KYAAA!

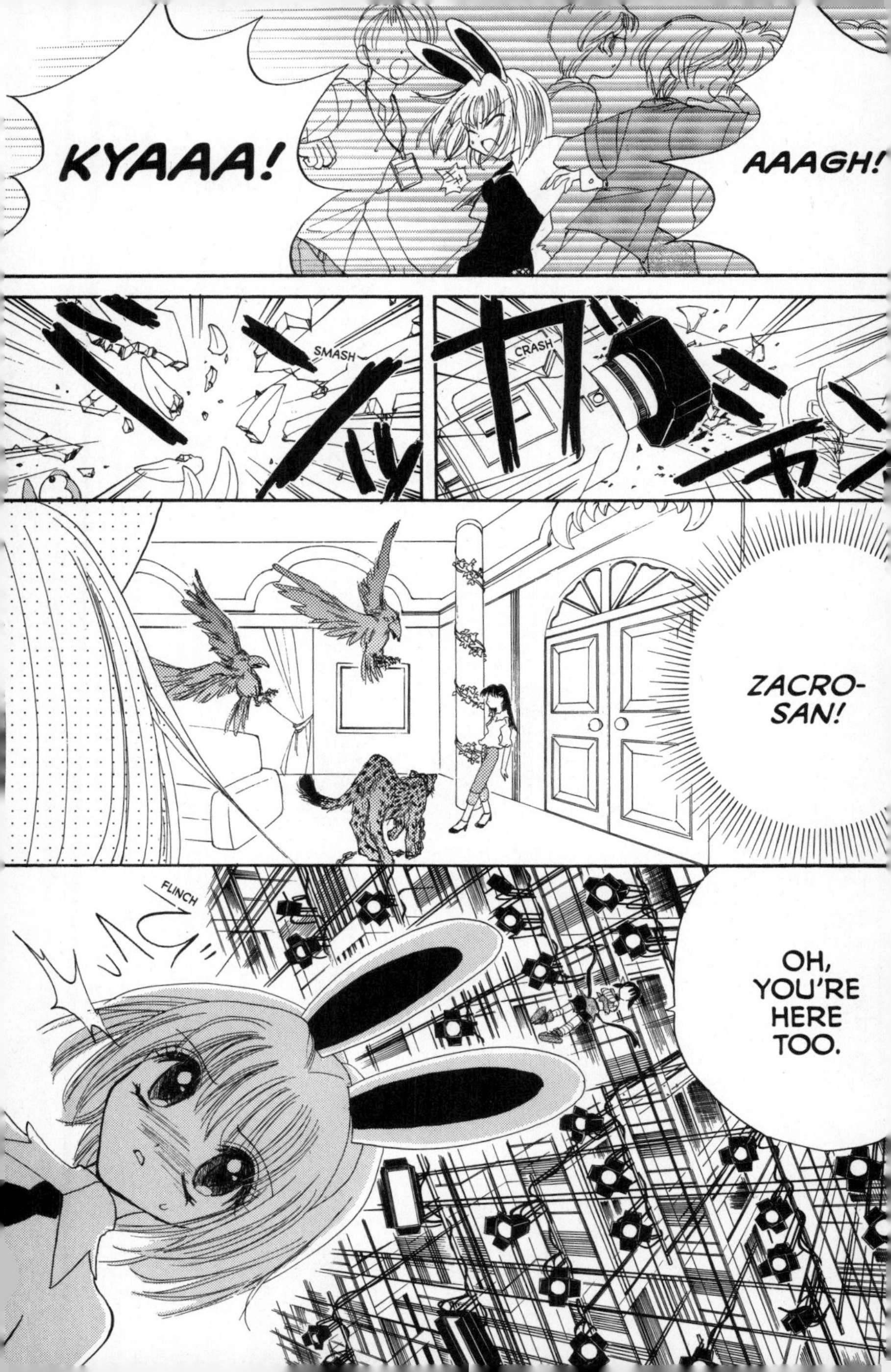
AAAGH!
KYAAA!
CRASH
SMASH
ZACRO-SAN!
OH, YOU'RE HERE TOO.
FLINCH

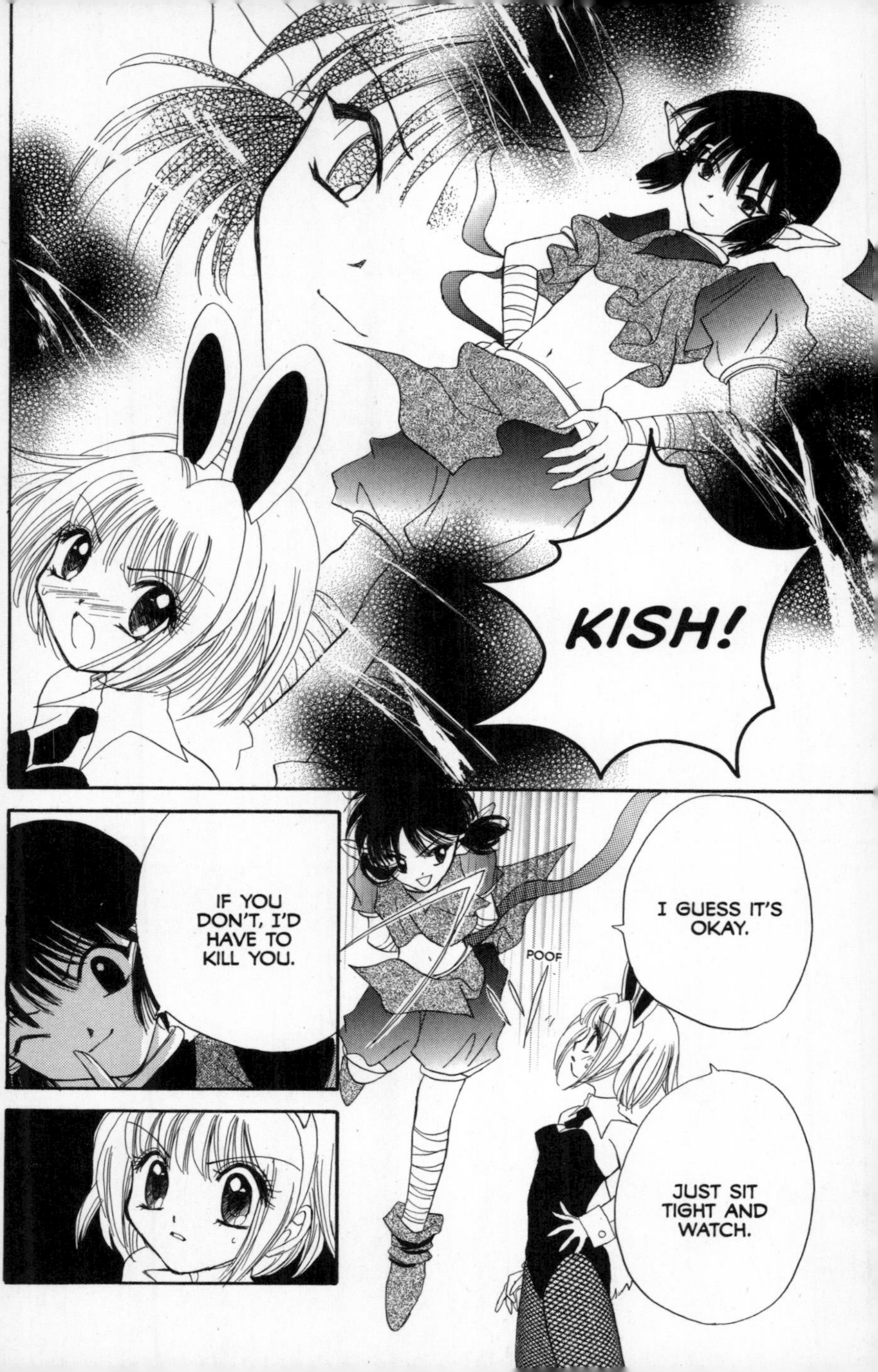
KISH!
I GUESS IT'S OKAY.
POOF
JUST SIT TIGHT AND WATCH.
IF YOU DON'T, I'D HAVE TO KILL YOU.

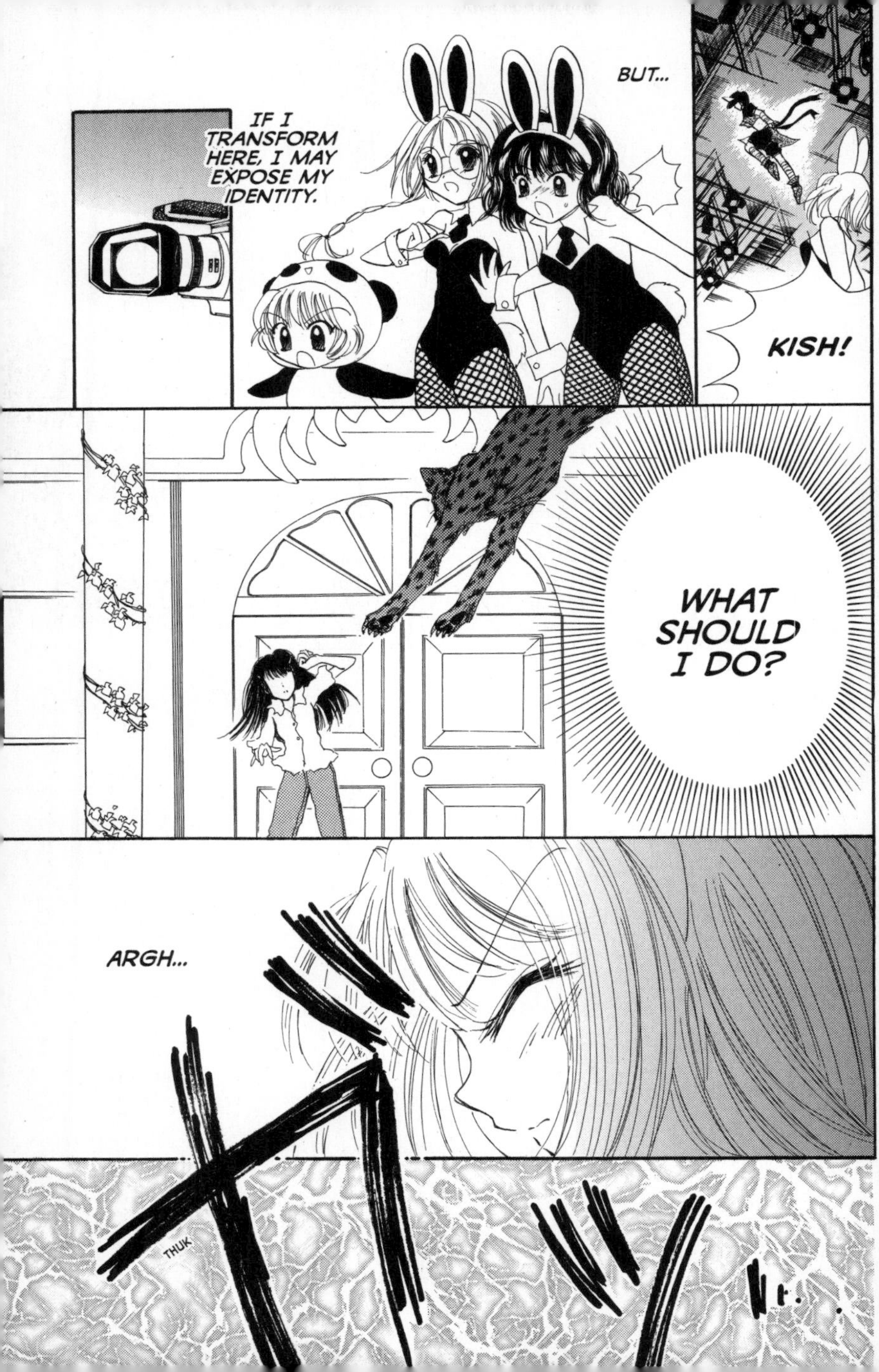
KISH!
BUT...
IF I TRANSFORM HERE, I MAY EXPOSE MY IDENTITY.
WHAT SHOULD I DO?
ARGH...
THUK

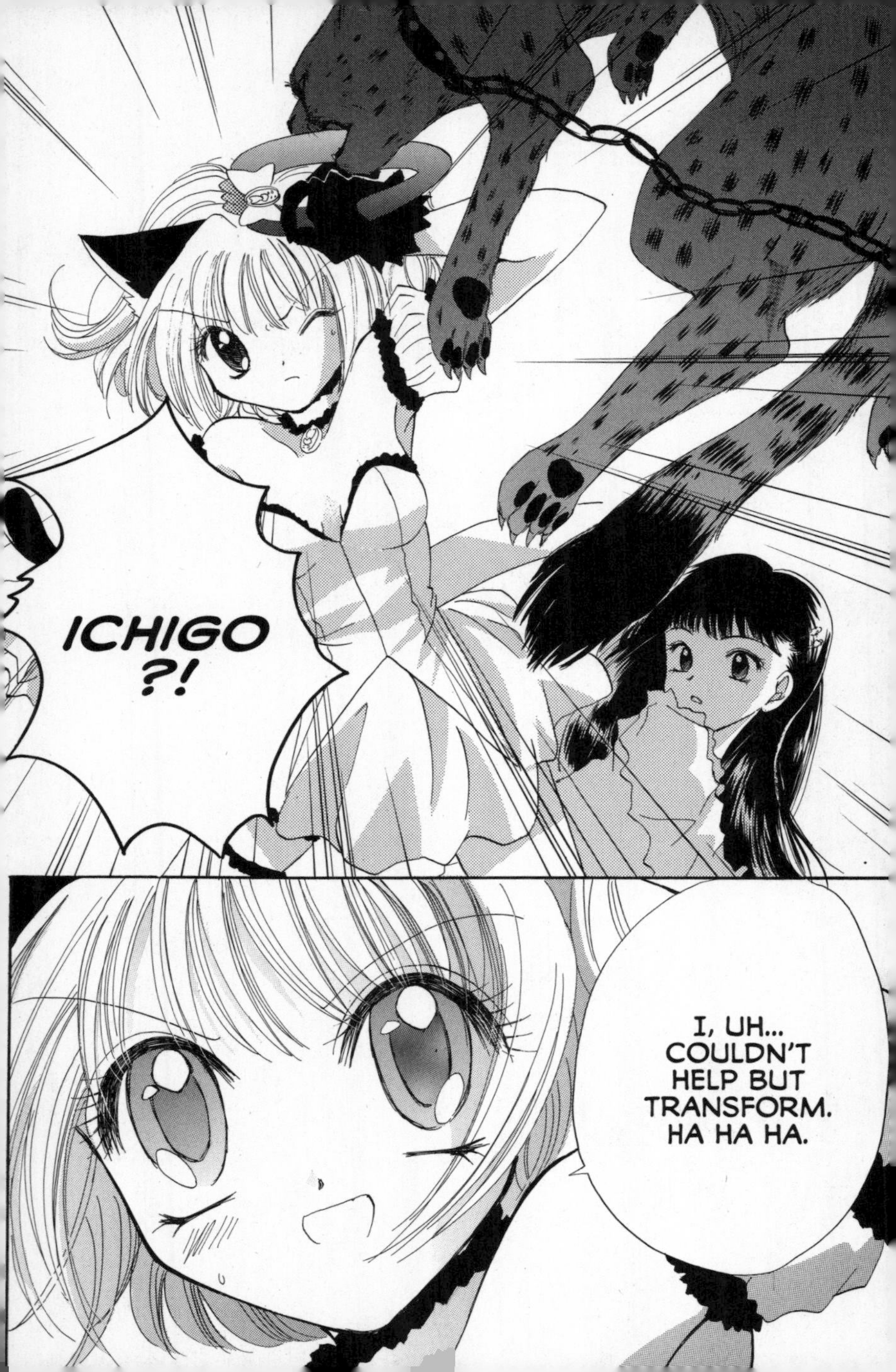
ICHIGO ?!
I, UH... COULDN'T HELP BUT TRANSFORM. HA HA HA.

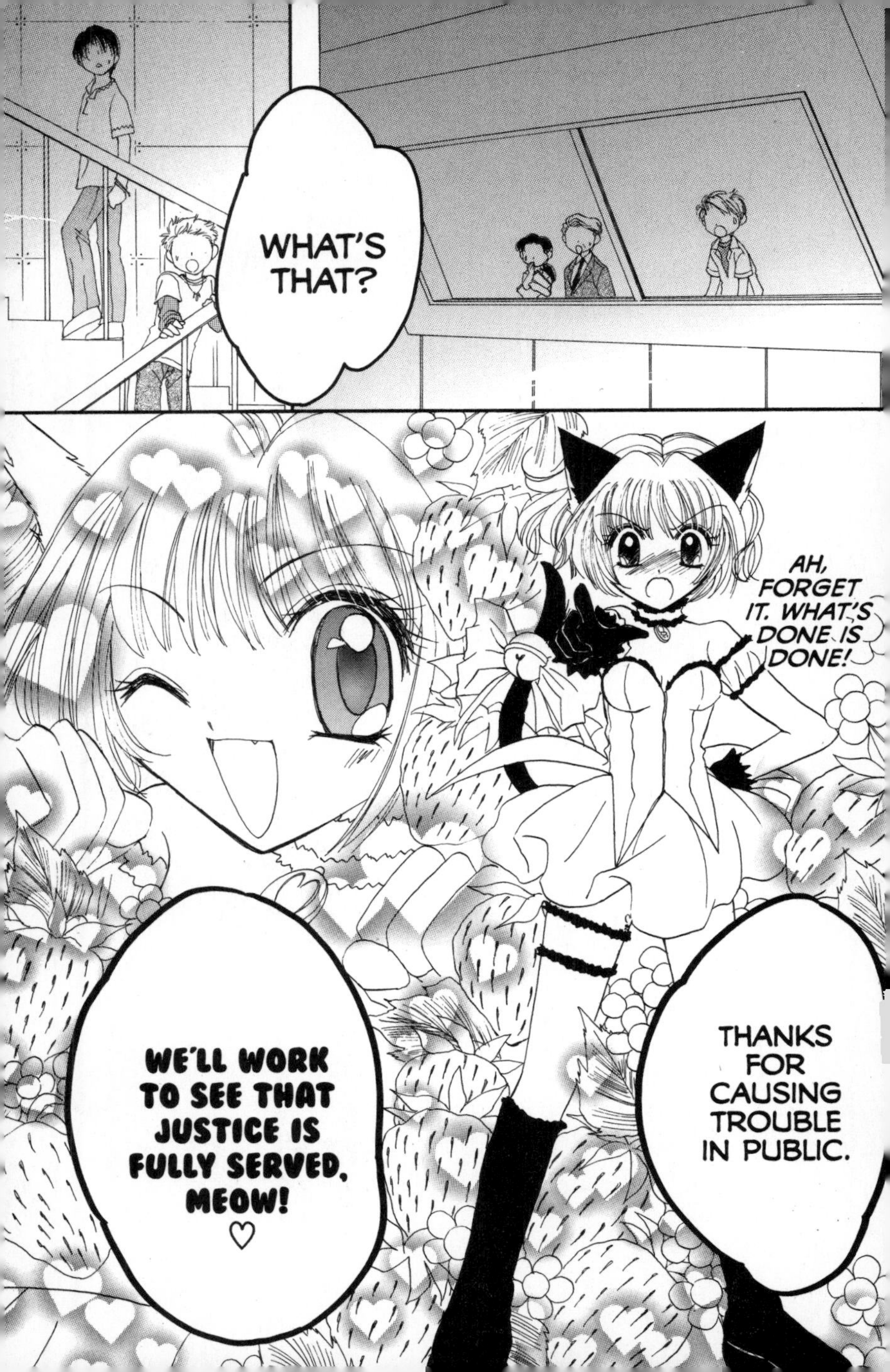
WHAT'S THAT?
AH, FORGET IT. WHAT'S DONE IS DONE!
THANKS FOR CAUSING TROUBLE IN PUBLIC.
WE'LL WORK TO SEE THAT JUSTICE IS FULLY SERVED, MEOW! ♡

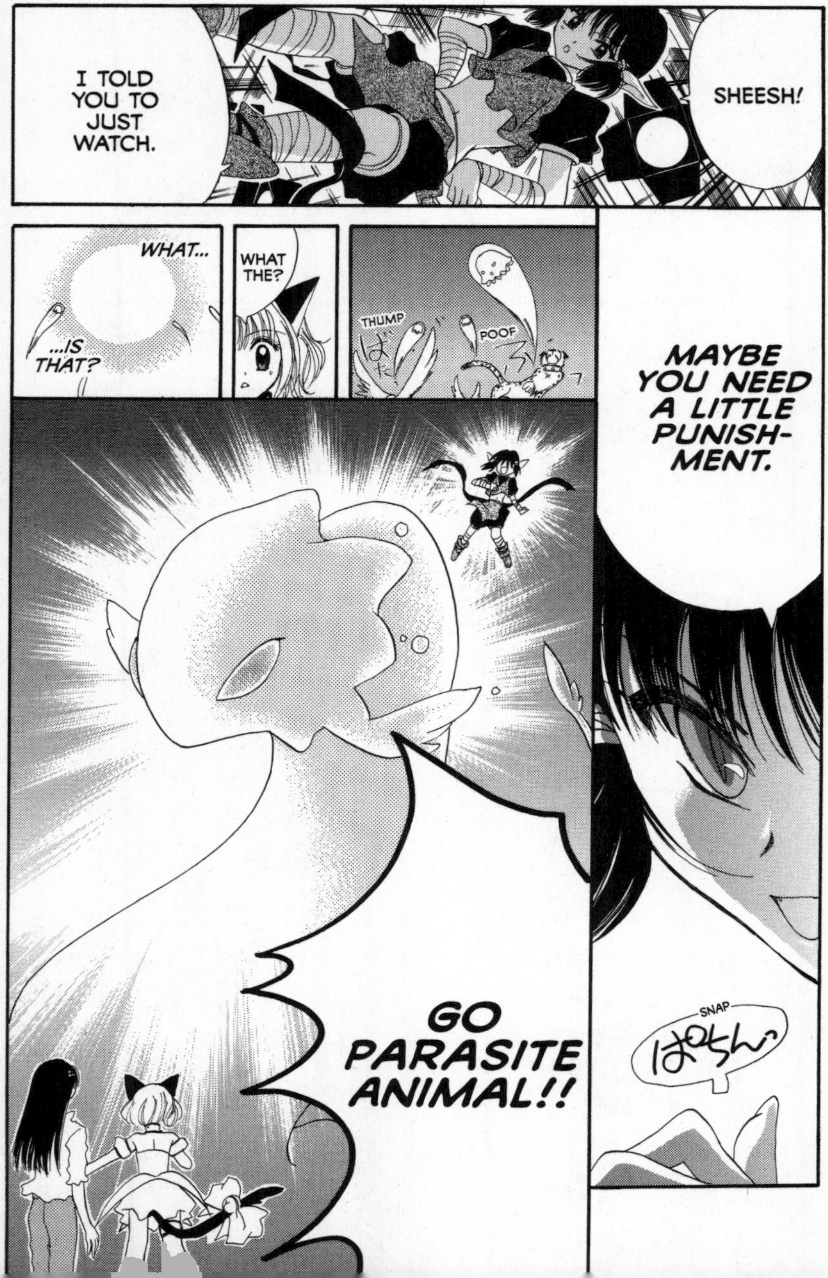
SHEESH!
I TOLD YOU TO JUST WATCH.
MAYBE YOU NEED A LITTLE PUNISHMENT.
SNAP
ぱちん
THUMP
POOF
WHAT THE?
WHAT...
...IS THAT?
GO PARASITE ANIMAL!!

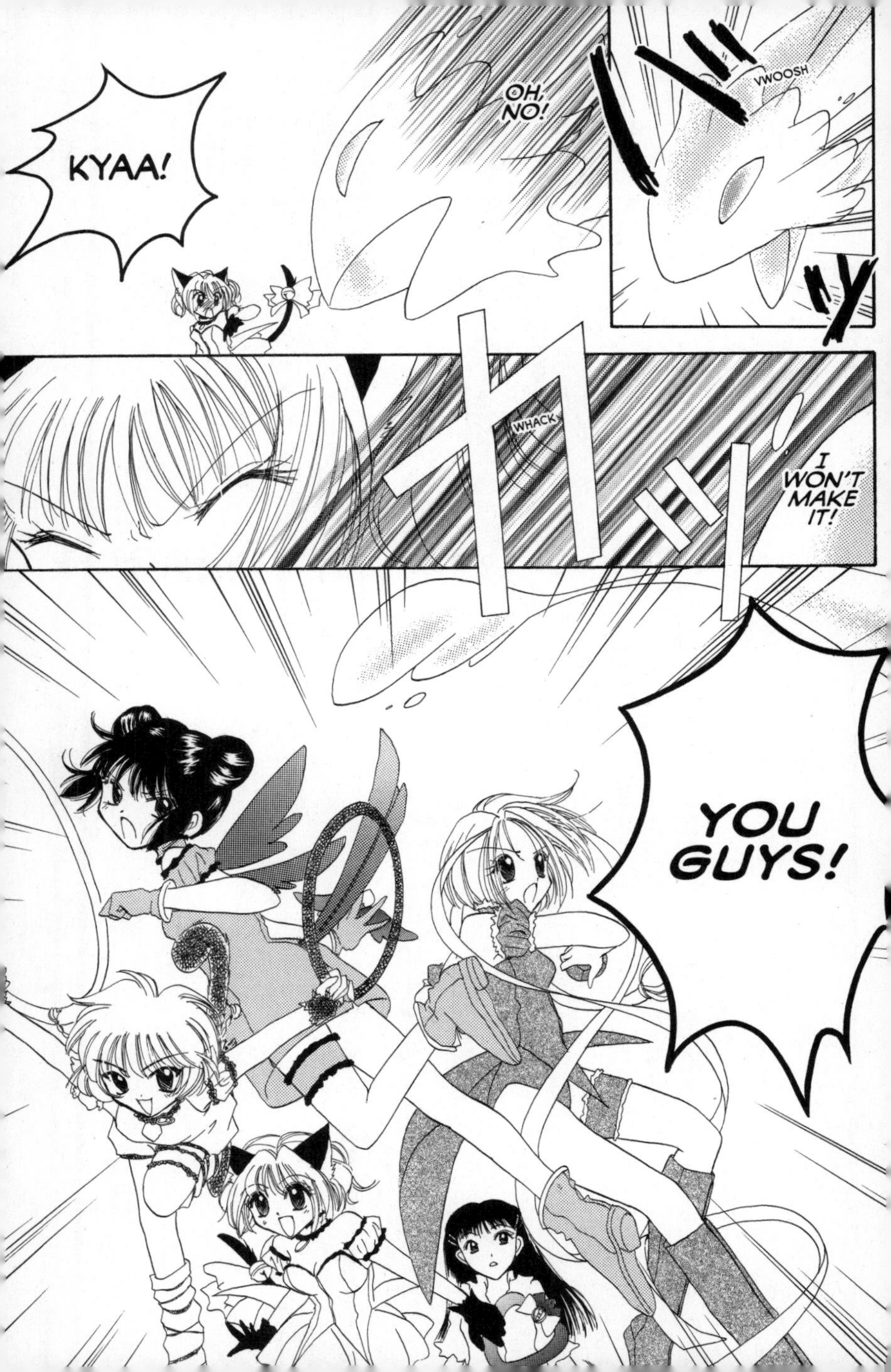
VWOOSH
OH, NO!
KYAA!
I WON'T MAKE IT!
WHACK
YOU GUYS!

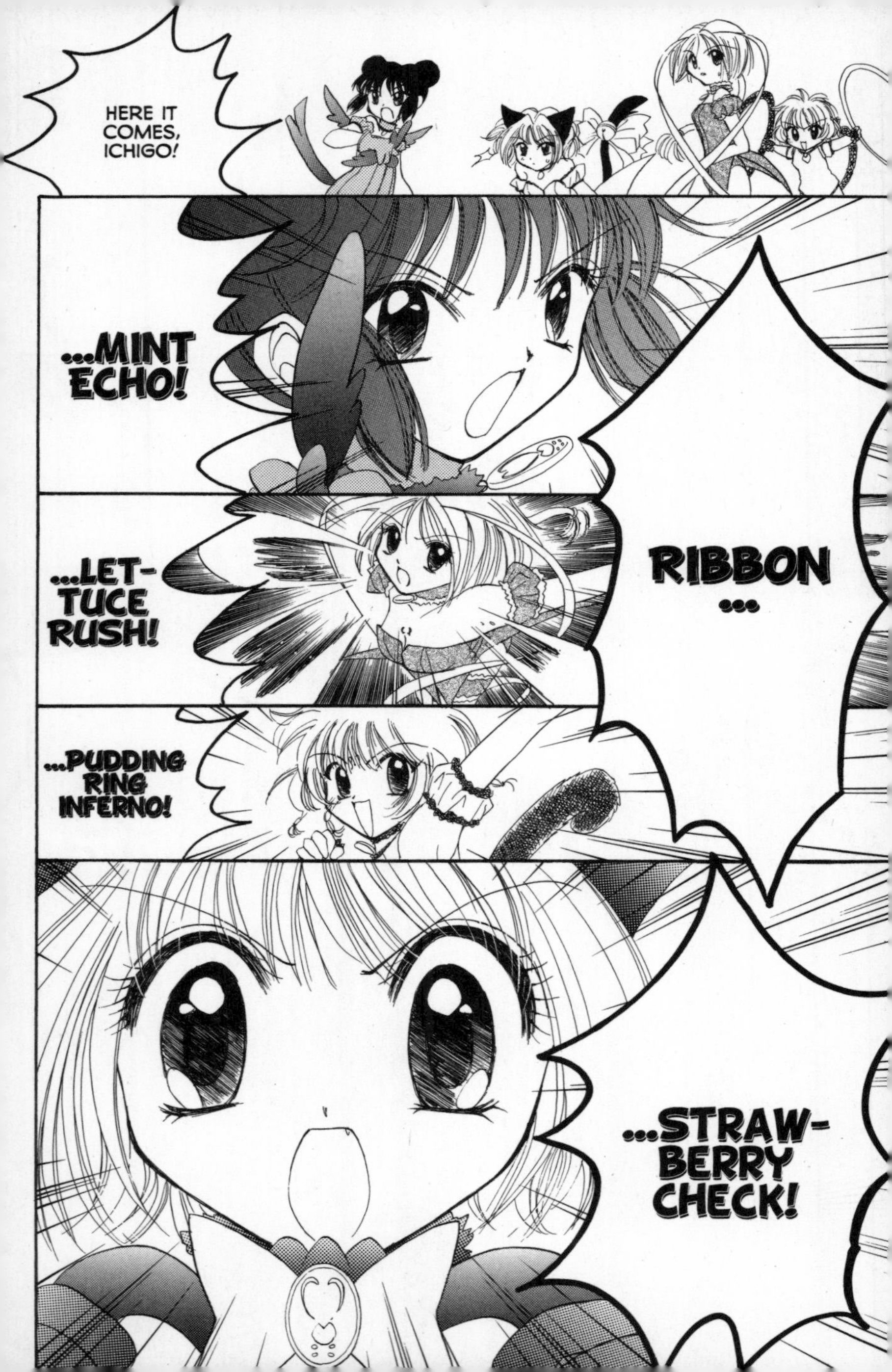
HERE IT COMES, ICHIGO!
RIBBON ...
...MINT ECHO!
...LET-TUCE RUSH!
...PUDDING RING INFERNO!
...STRAW-BERRY CHECK!

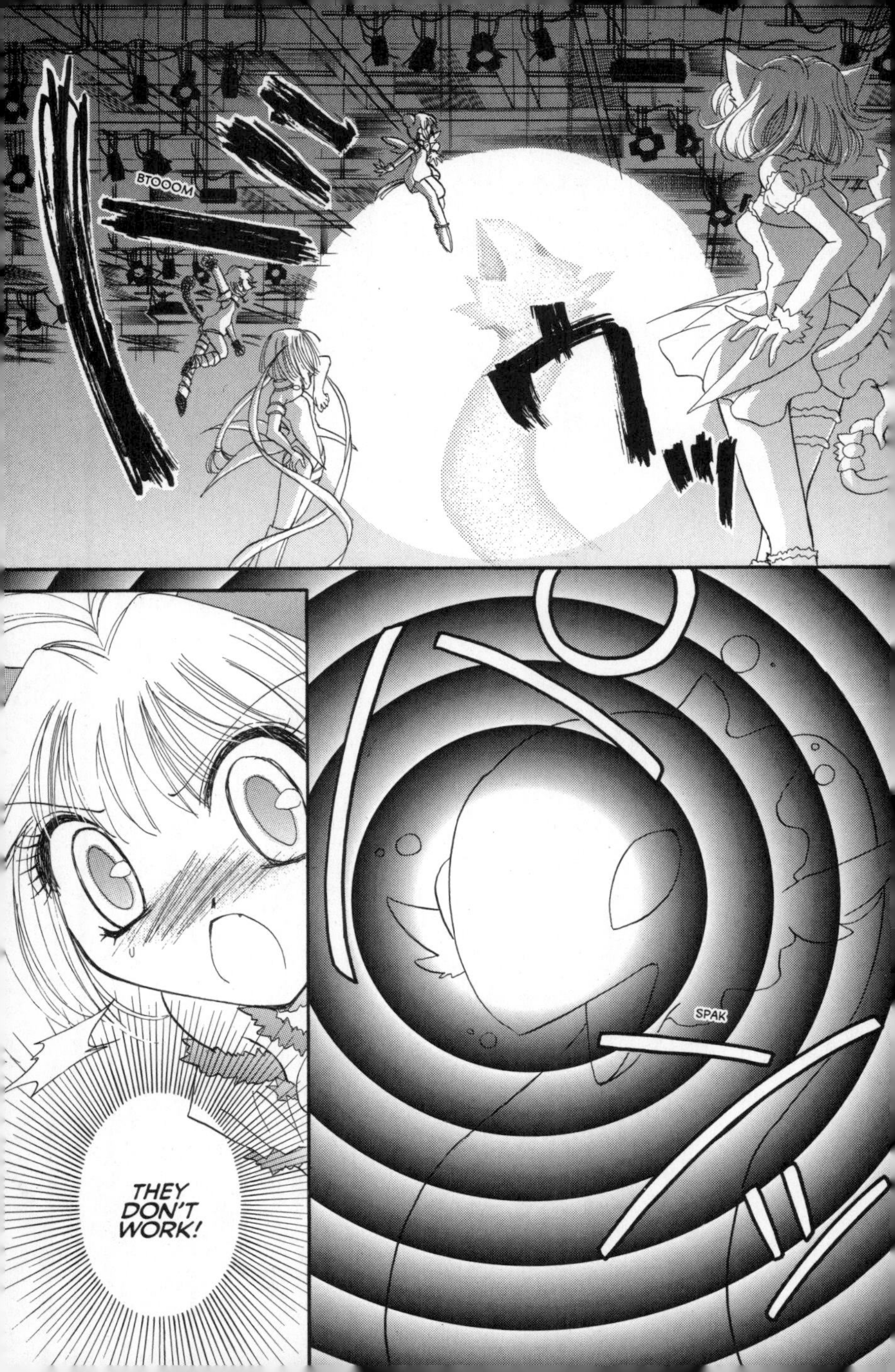
BTOOOM
SPAK
THEY DON'T WORK!

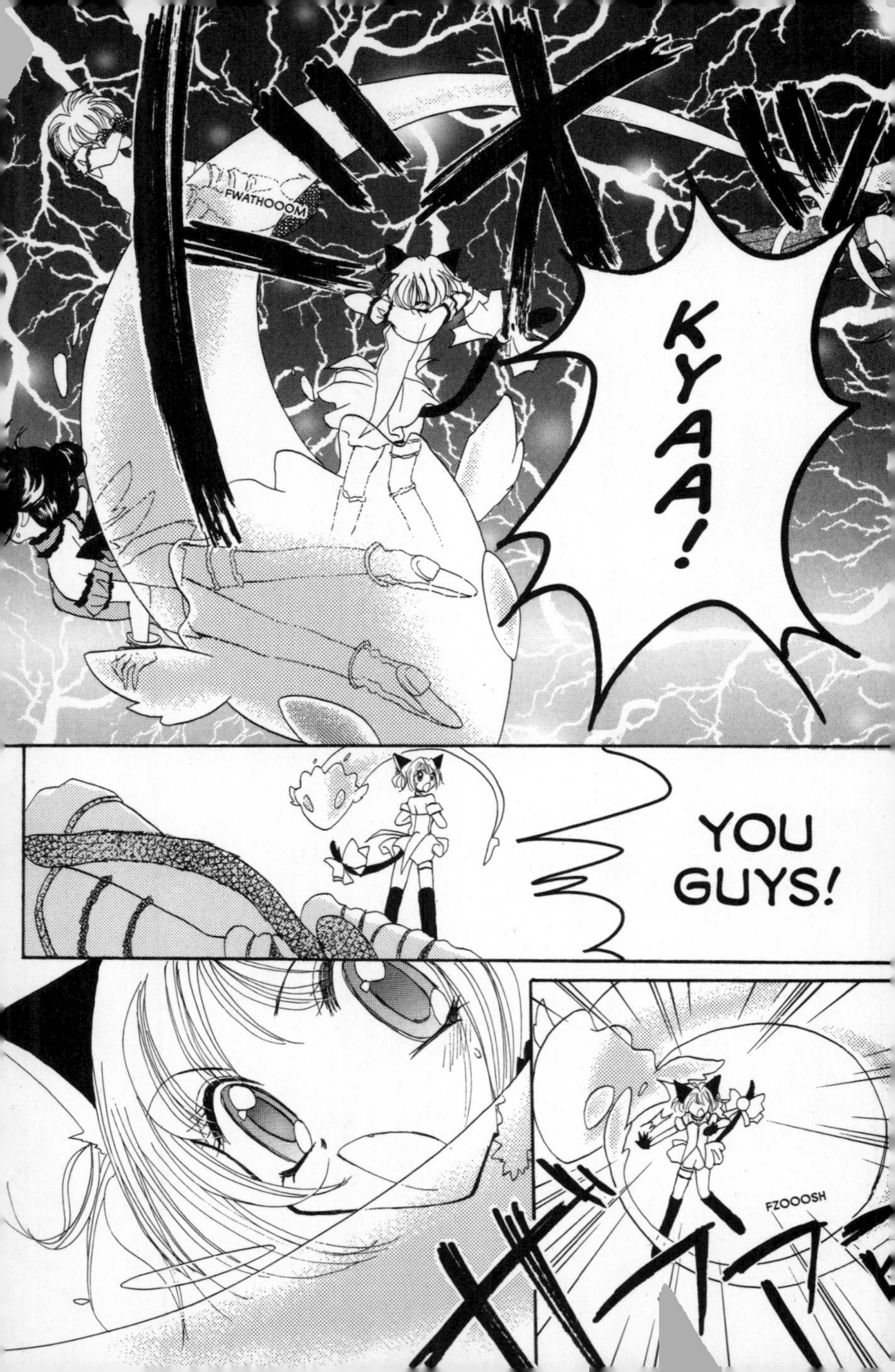
FWATHOOOM
KYAA!
YOU GUYS!
FZOOOSH

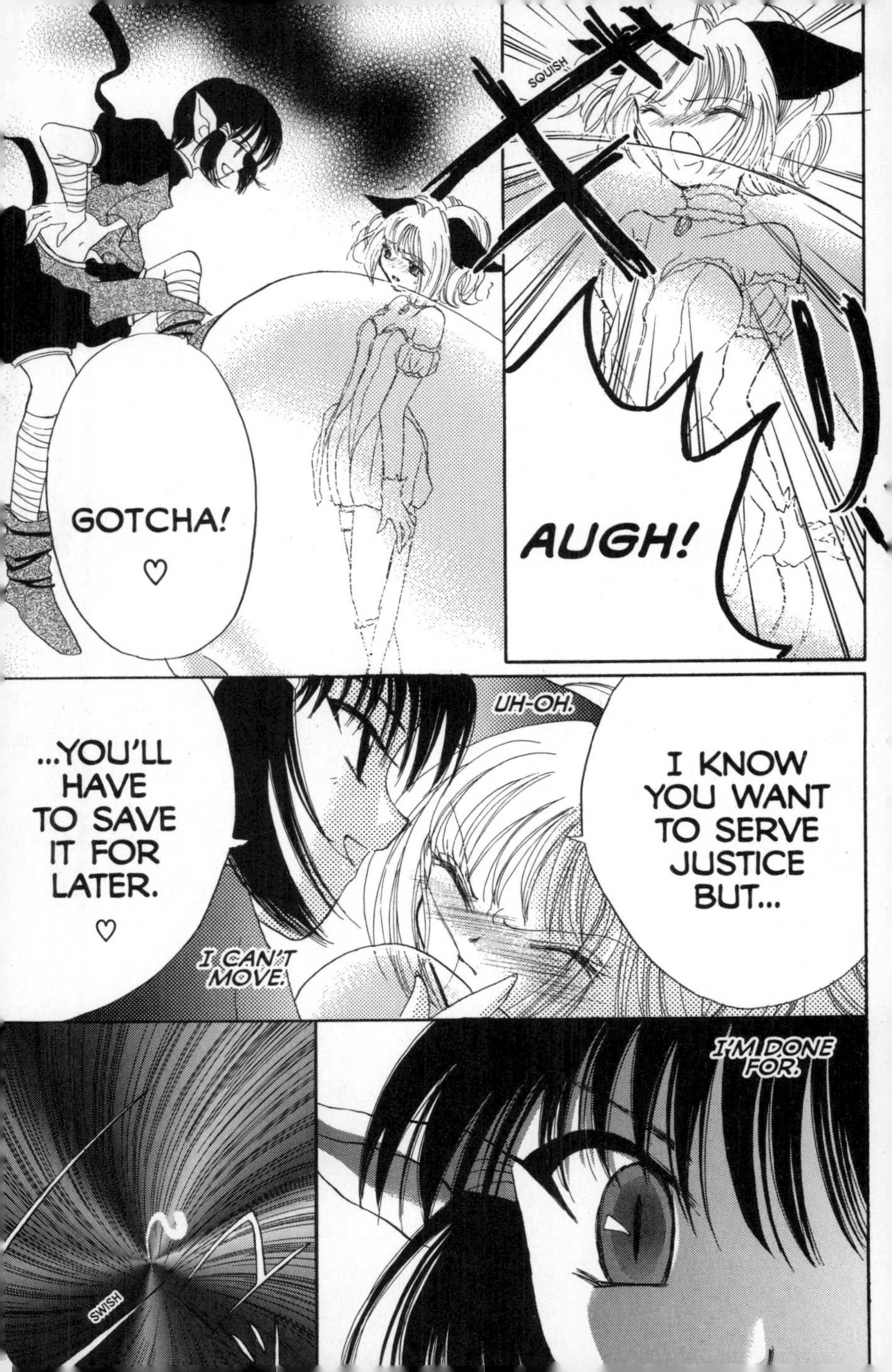
SQUISH
AUGH!
GOTCHA! ♡
I KNOW YOU WANT TO SERVE JUSTICE BUT...
UH-OH.
...YOU'LL HAVE TO SAVE IT FOR LATER. ♡
I CAN'T MOVE.
I'M DONE FOR.
SWISH

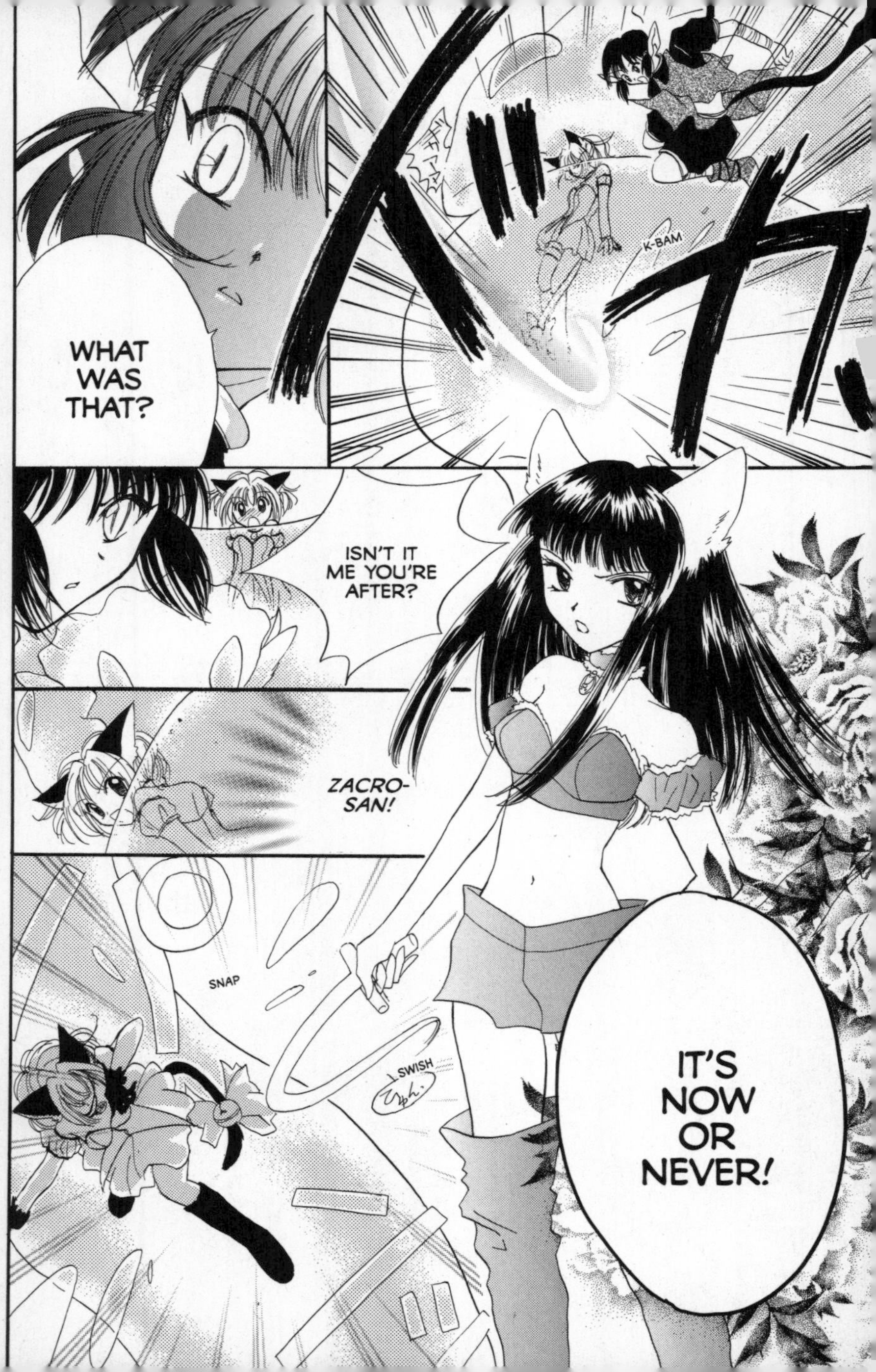
K-BAM
WHAT WAS THAT?
ISN'T IT ME YOU'RE AFTER?
ZACRO-SAN!
IT'S NOW OR NEVER!
SNAP
SWISH

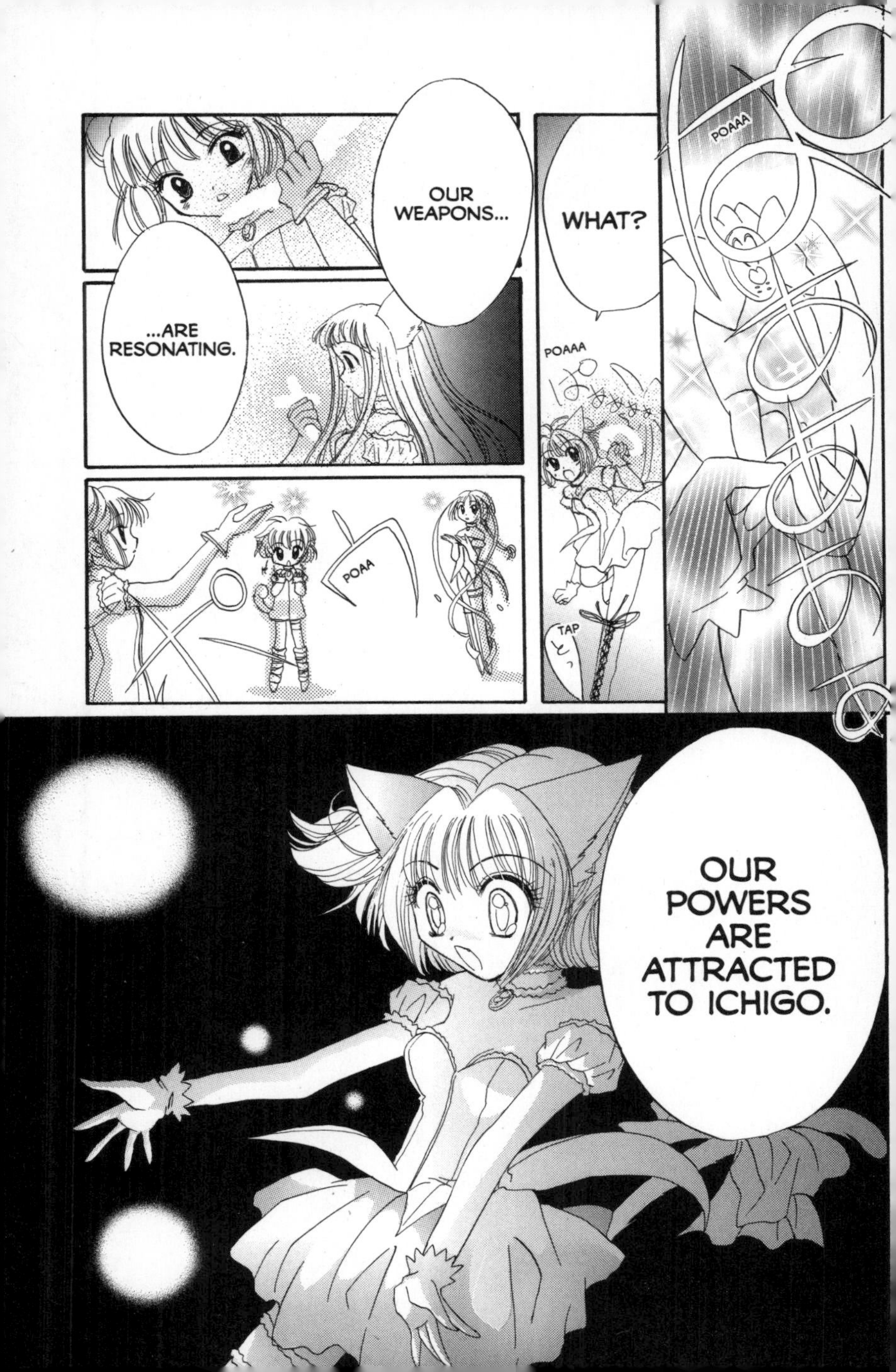
POAAA
WHAT?
POAAA
TAP
とっ
OUR WEAPONS...
...ARE RESONATING.
POAA
OUR POWERS ARE ATTRACTED TO ICHIGO.

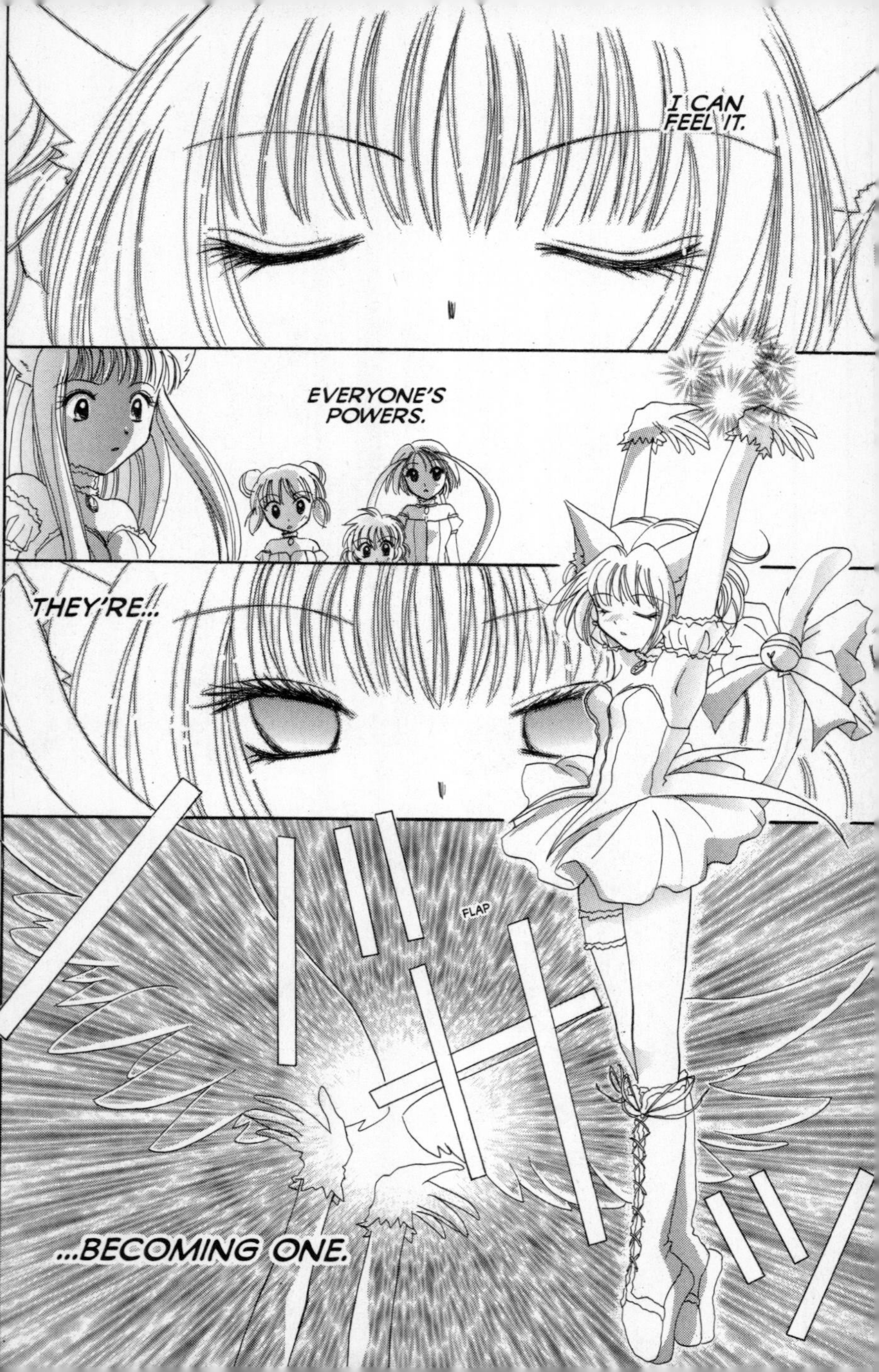
I CAN FEEL IT.
EVERYONE'S POWERS.
THEY'RE...
FLAP
...BECOMING ONE.

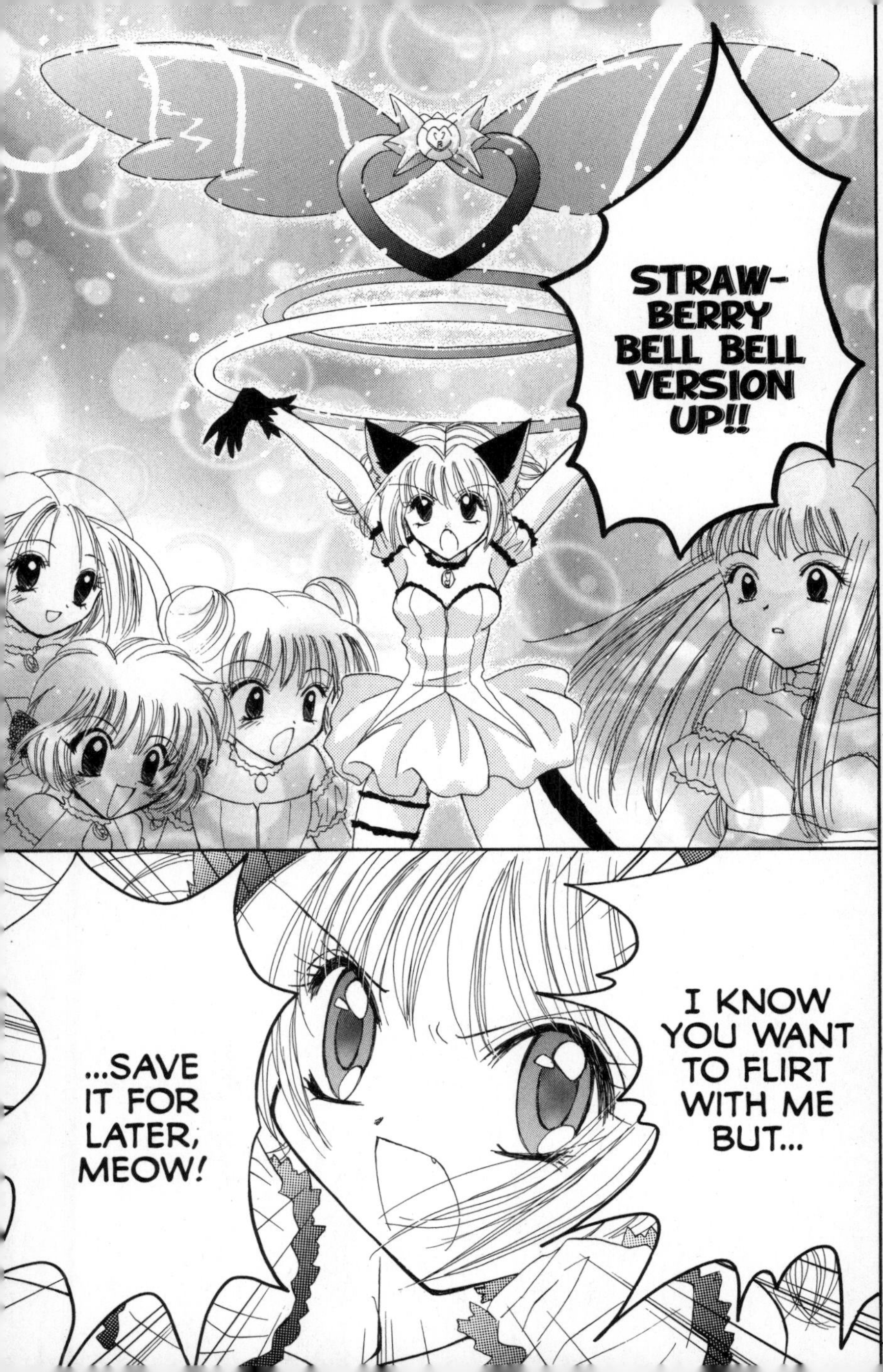
STRAW-BERRY BELL BELL VERSION UP!!
I KNOW YOU WANT TO FLIRT WITH ME BUT...
...SAVE IT FOR LATER, MEOW!

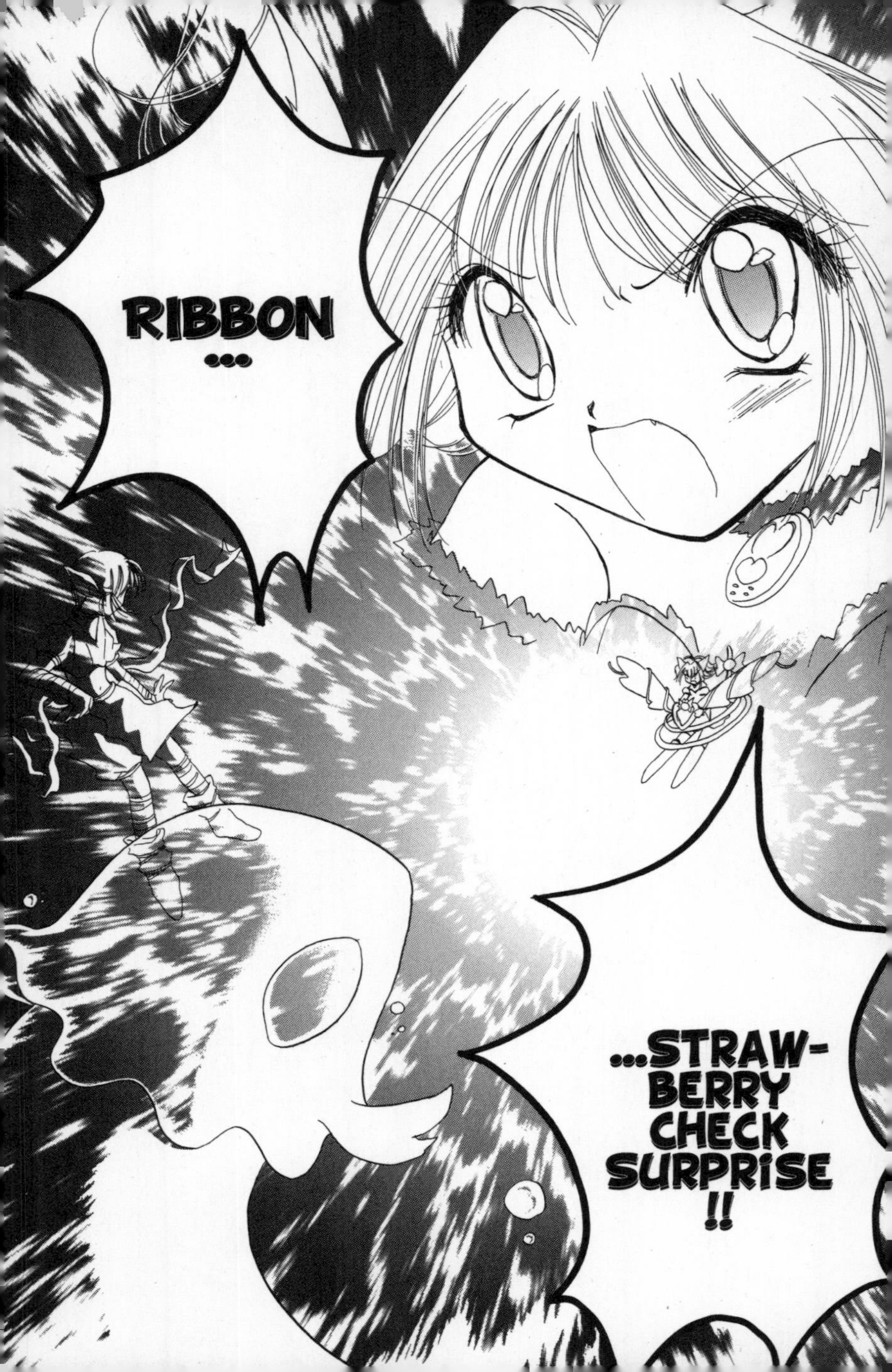
RIBBON ...
...STRAW-BERRY CHECK SURPRISE !!

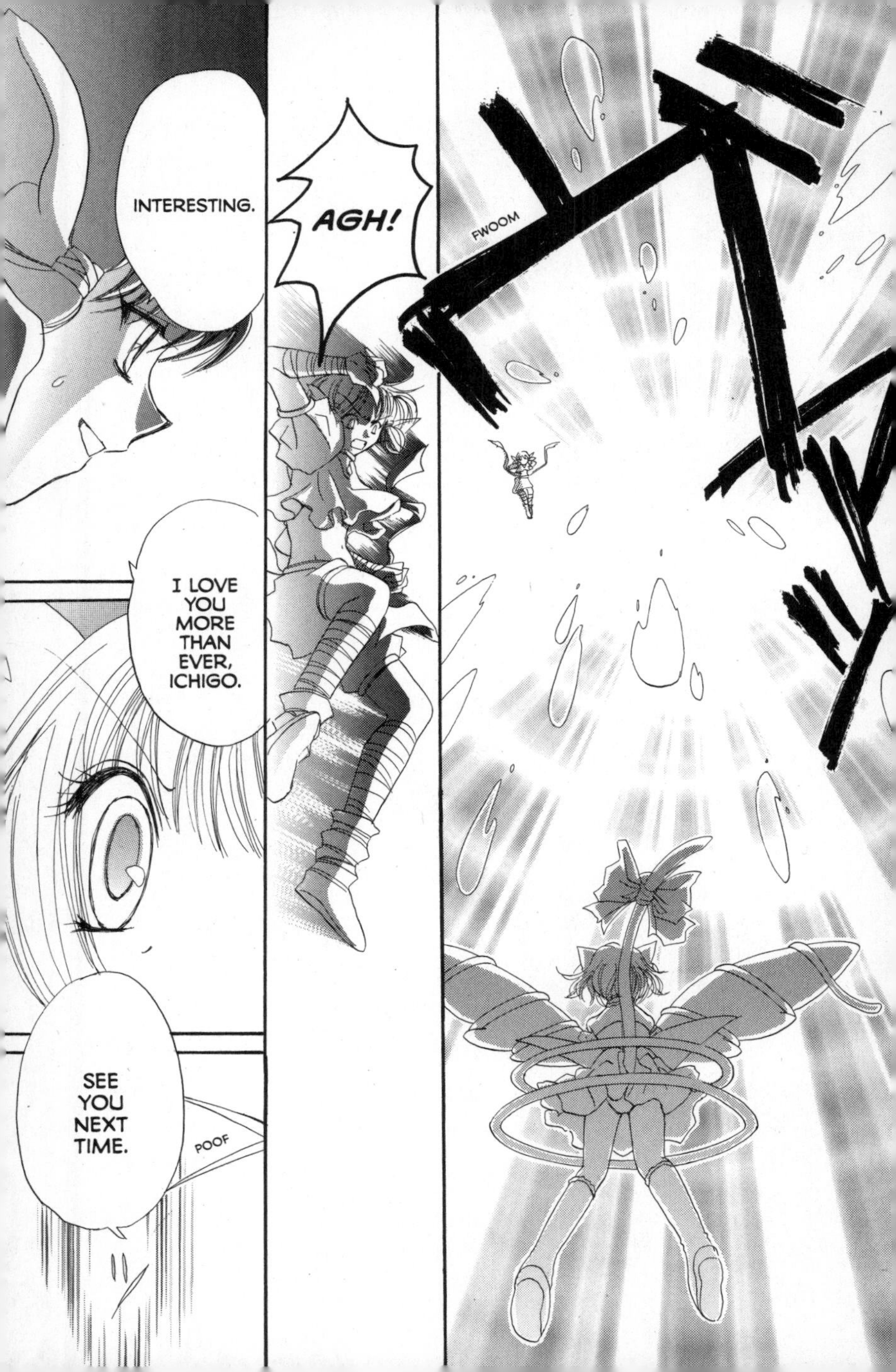
FWOOM
AGH!
INTERESTING.
I LOVE YOU MORE THAN EVER, ICHIGO.
SEE YOU NEXT TIME.
POOF

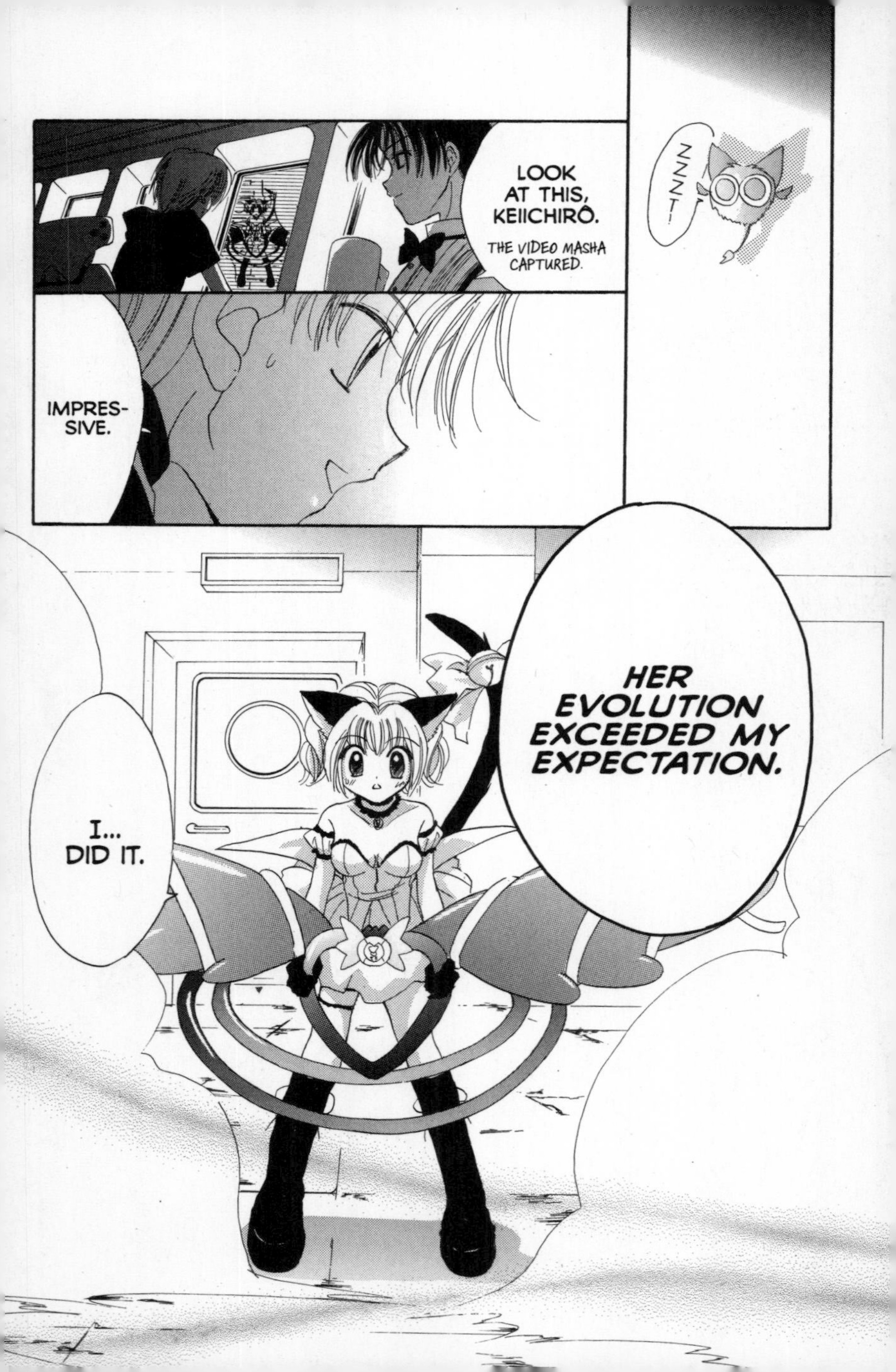
ZZZT!
LOOK AT THIS, KEIICHIRÔ.
THE VIDEO MASHA CAPTURED.
IMPRES-SIVE.
HER EVOLUTION EXCEEDED MY EXPECTATION.
I... DID IT.

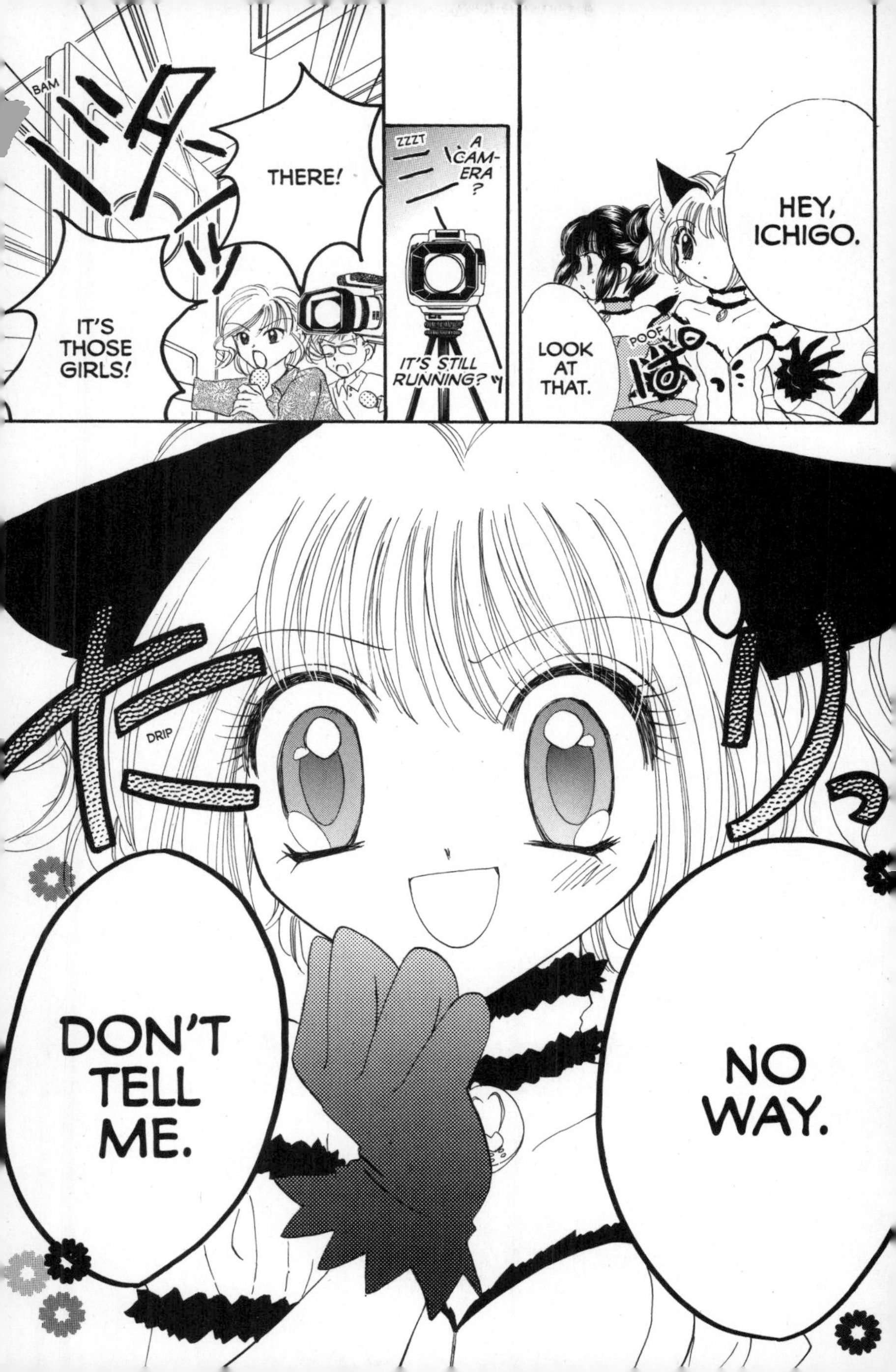
HEY, ICHIGO.
LOOK AT THAT.
POOF
ZZZT
A CAM-ERA?
IT'S STILL RUNNING?
BAM
THERE!
IT'S THOSE GIRLS!
DRIP
NO WAY.
DON'T TELL ME.

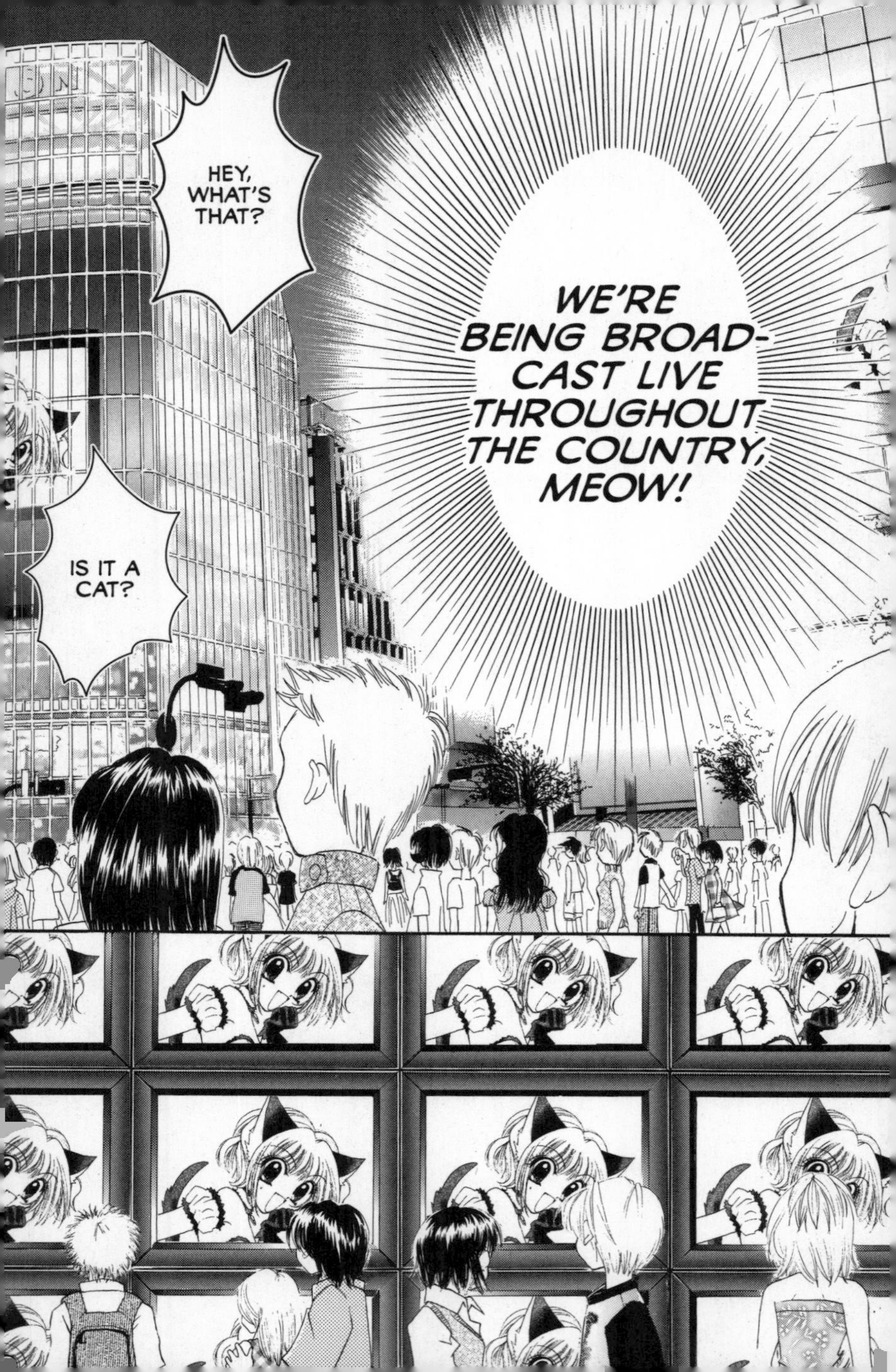
WE'RE BEING BROAD-CAST LIVE THROUGHOUT THE COUNTRY, MEOW!
HEY, WHAT'S THAT?
IS IT A CAT?

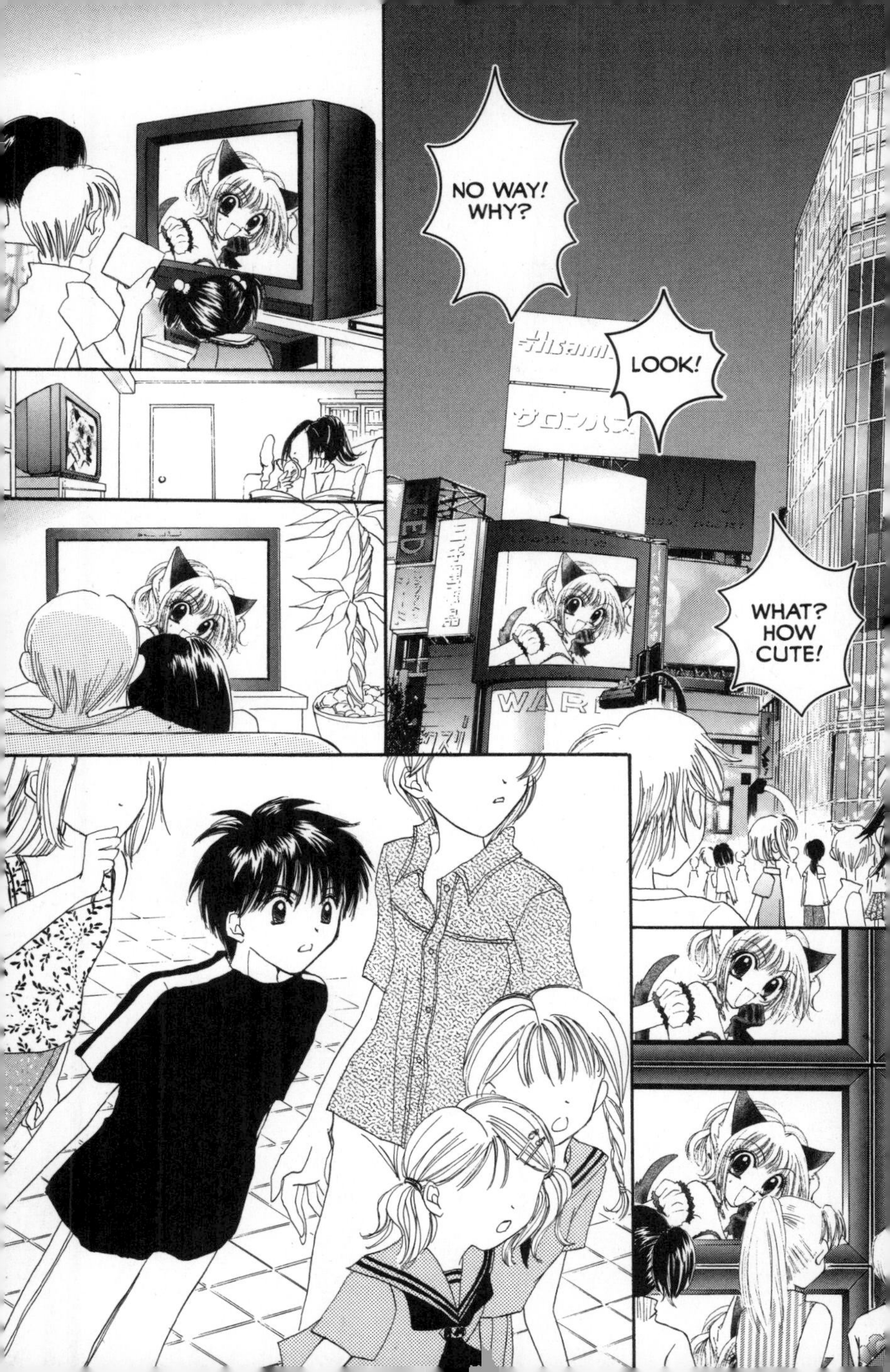
NO WAY! WHY?
LOOK!
WHAT? HOW CUTE!

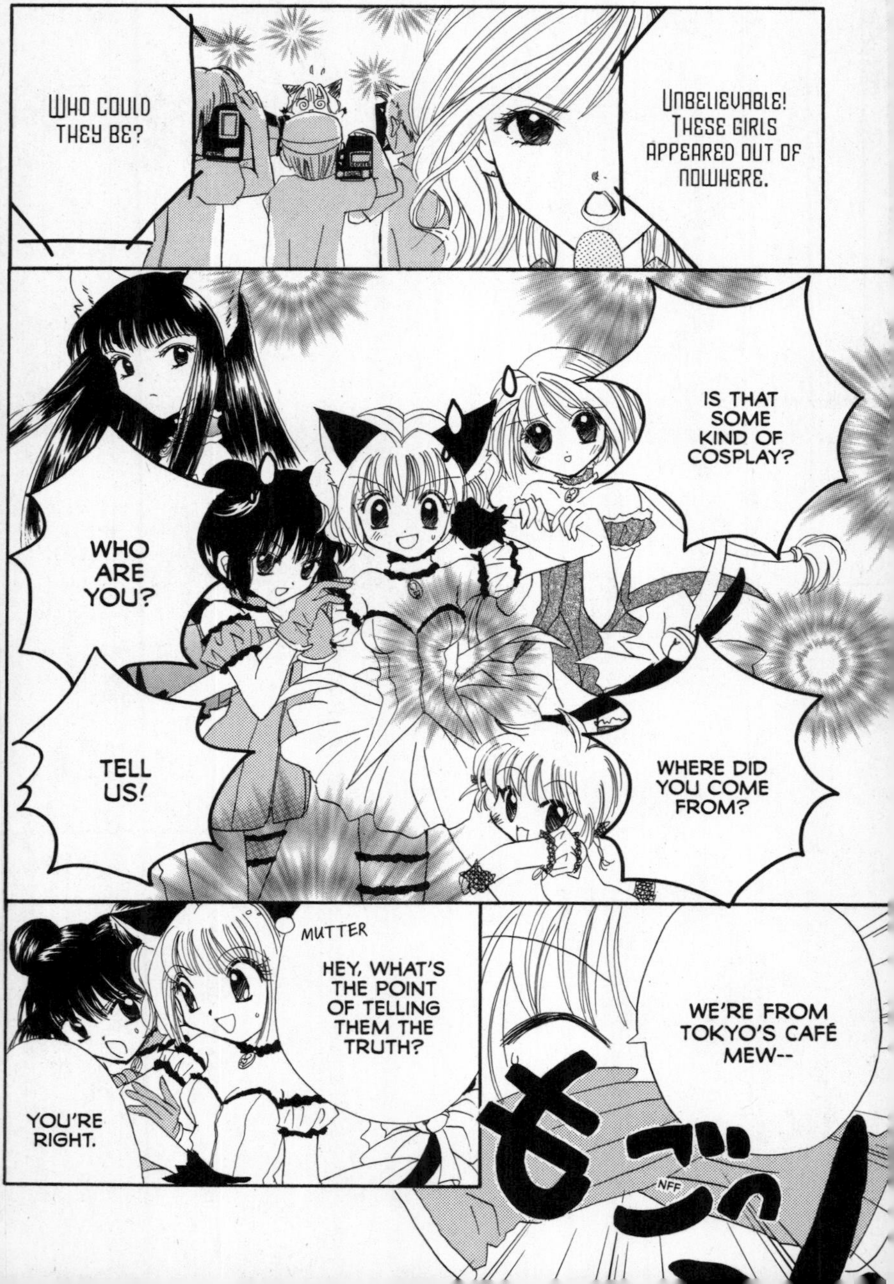

Unbelievable! These girls appeared out of nowhere.
Who could they be?
Is that some kind of cosplay?
Who are you?
Where did you come from?
Tell us!
We're from Tokyo's Café Mew--
NFF
MUTTER
Hey, what's the point of telling them the truth?
You're right.

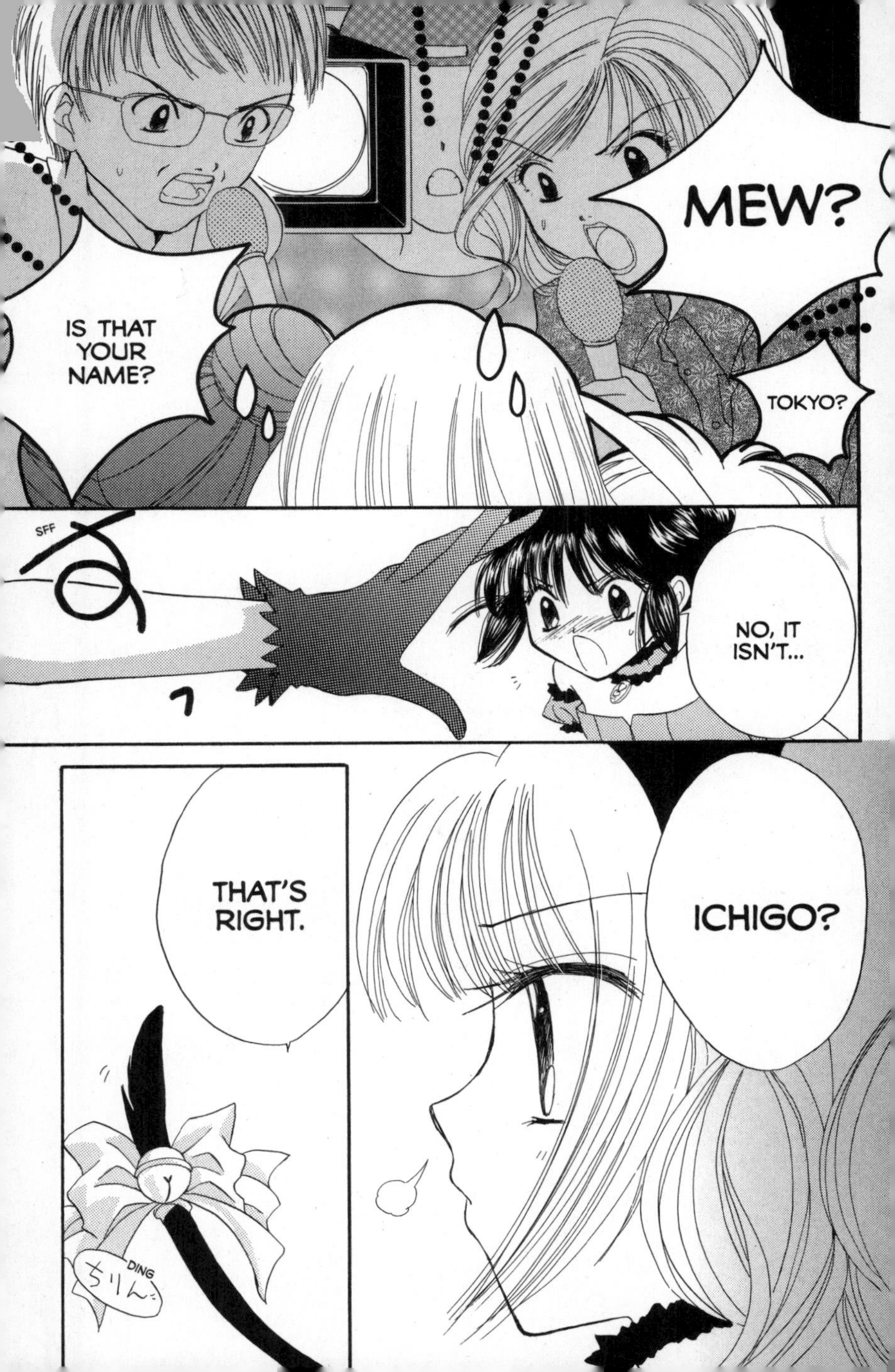
MEW?
TOKYO?
IS THAT YOUR NAME?
NO, IT ISN'T...
SFF
ICHIGO?
THAT'S RIGHT.
DING
ちりん

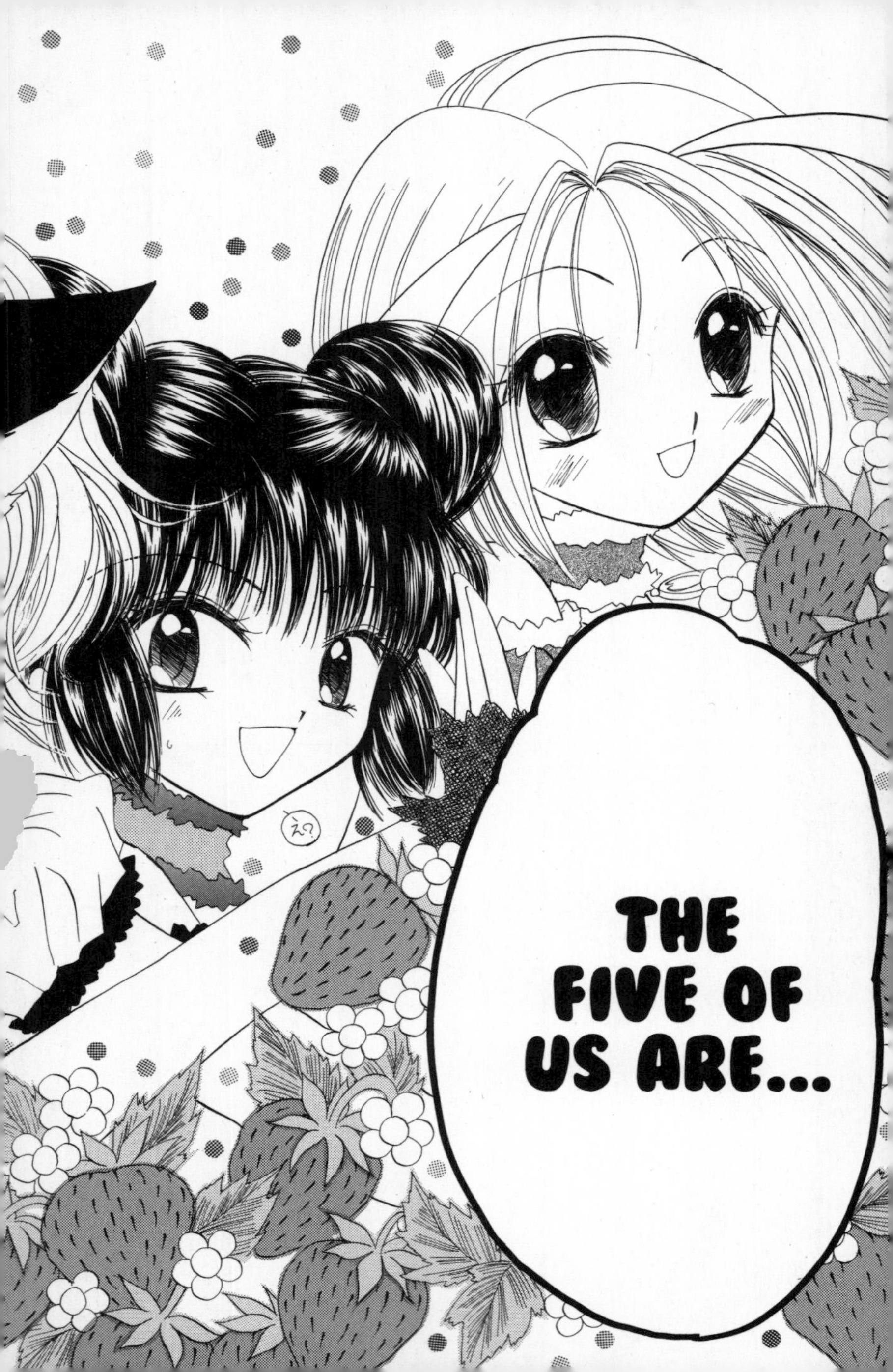
THE FIVE OF US ARE...
え?

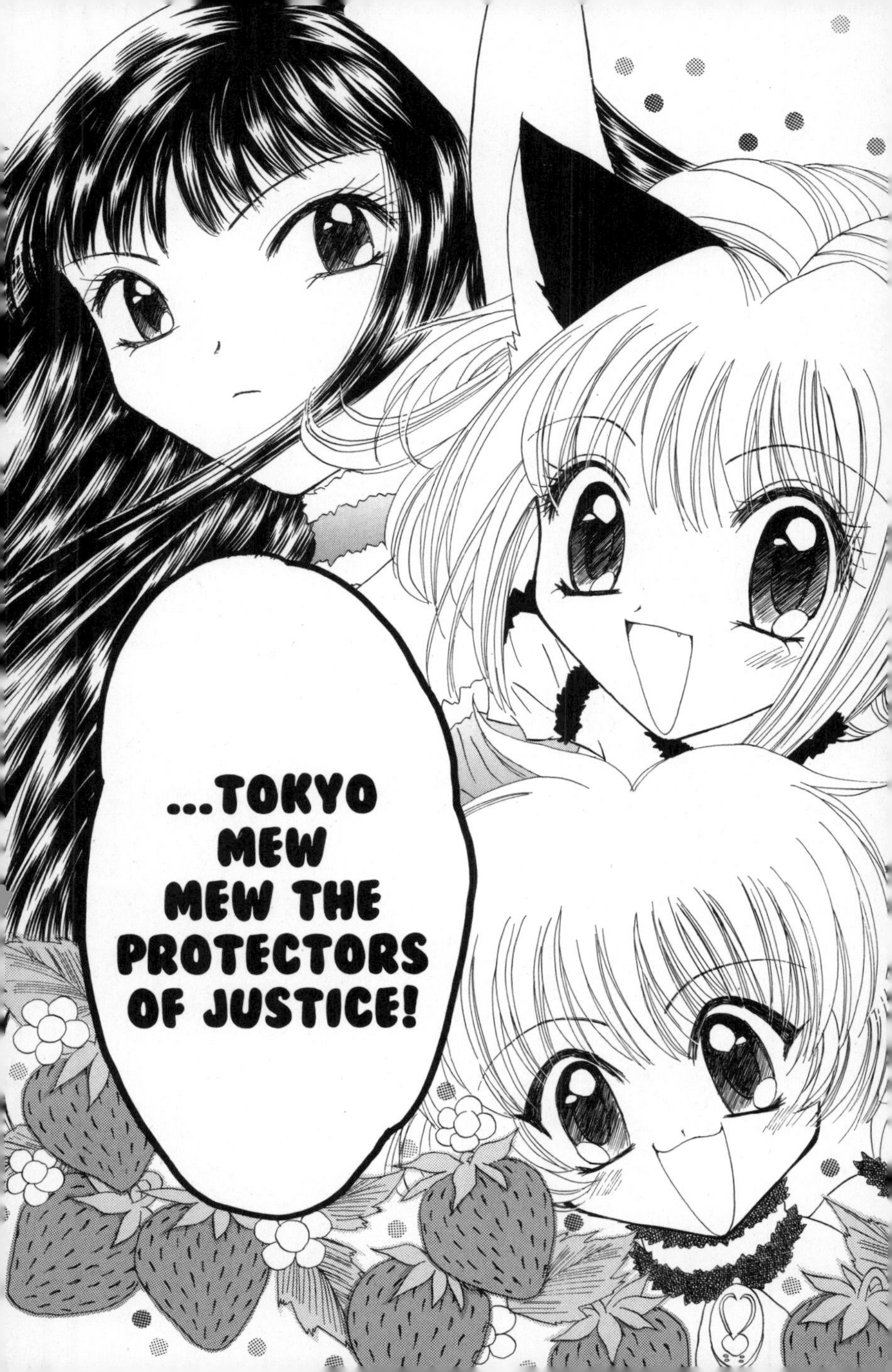
...TOKYO MEW MEW THE PROTECTORS OF JUSTICE!

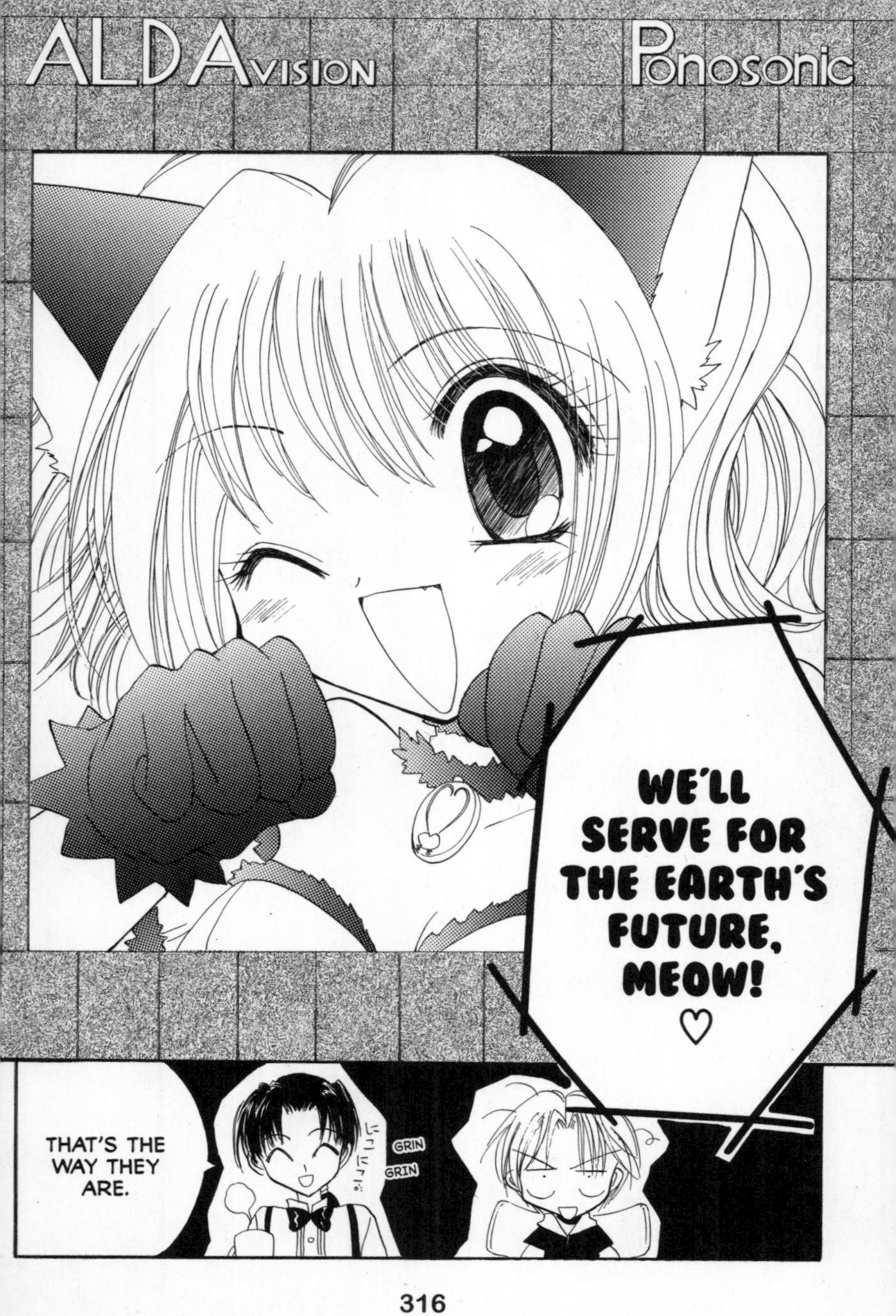
ALDA vision
Ponosonic
WE'LL SERVE FOR THE EARTH'S FUTURE, MEOW! ♡
THAT'S THE WAY THEY ARE.
GRIN
GRIN

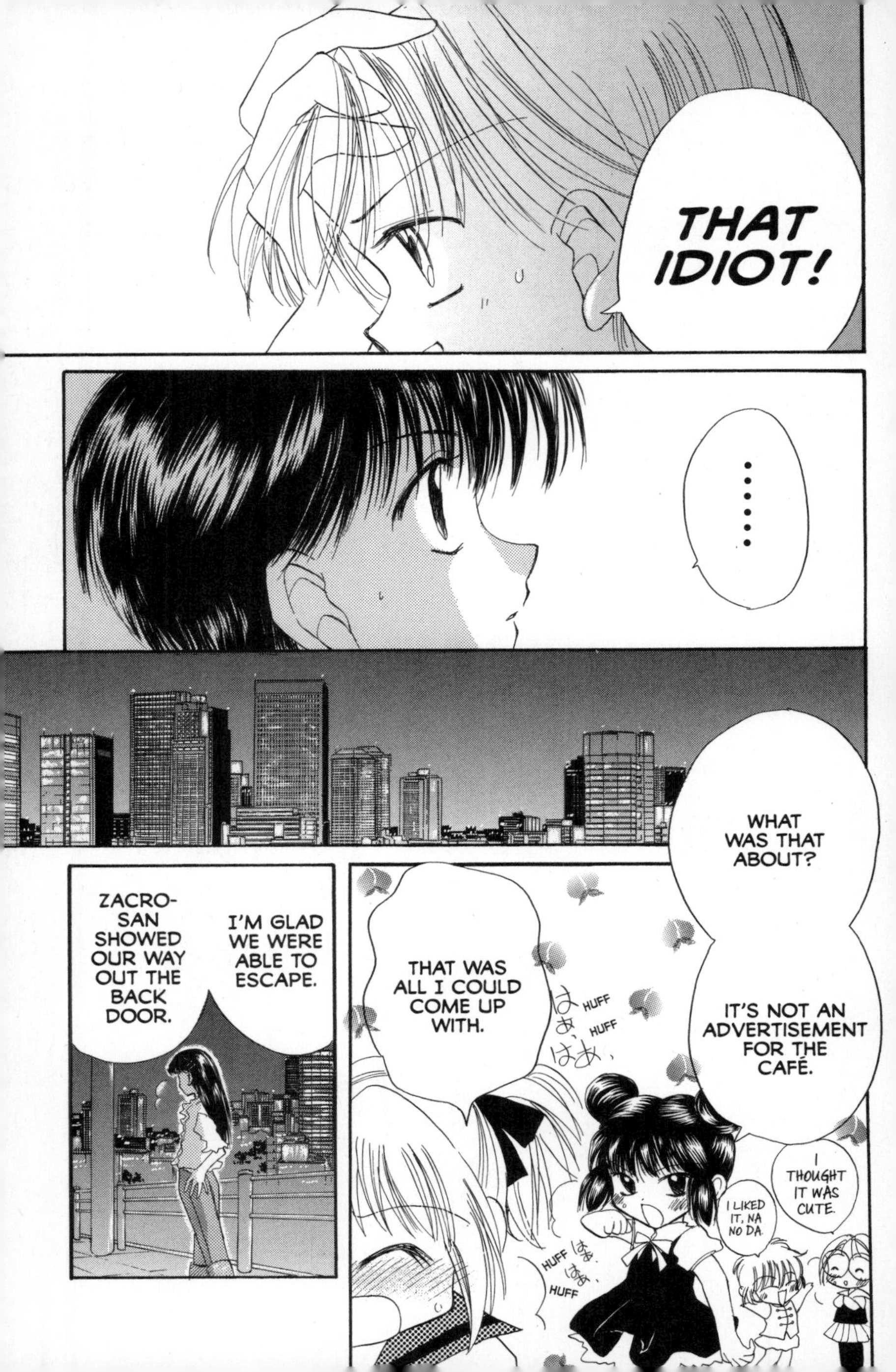
THAT IDIOT!
......
WHAT WAS THAT ABOUT?
IT'S NOT AN ADVERTISEMENT FOR THE CAFÉ.
THAT WAS ALL I COULD COME UP WITH.
はあ、はあ、
HUFF HUFF
I THOUGHT IT WAS CUTE.
I LIKED IT, NA NO DA.
はぁ、はぁ、
HUFF HUFF
I'M GLAD WE WERE ABLE TO ESCAPE.
ZACRO-SAN SHOWED OUR WAY OUT THE BACK DOOR.

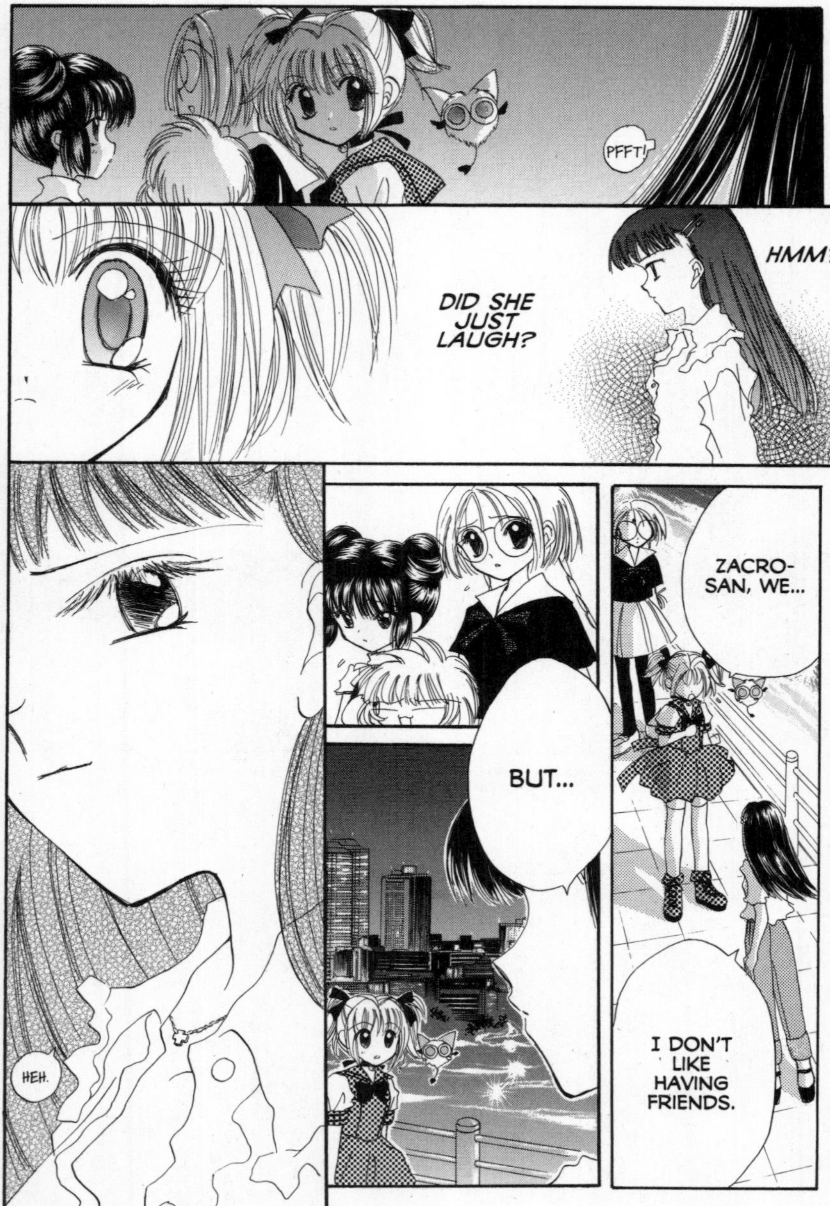
PFFT!
HMM?
DID SHE JUST LAUGH?
ZACRO-SAN, WE...
I DON'T LIKE HAVING FRIENDS.
BUT...
HEH.

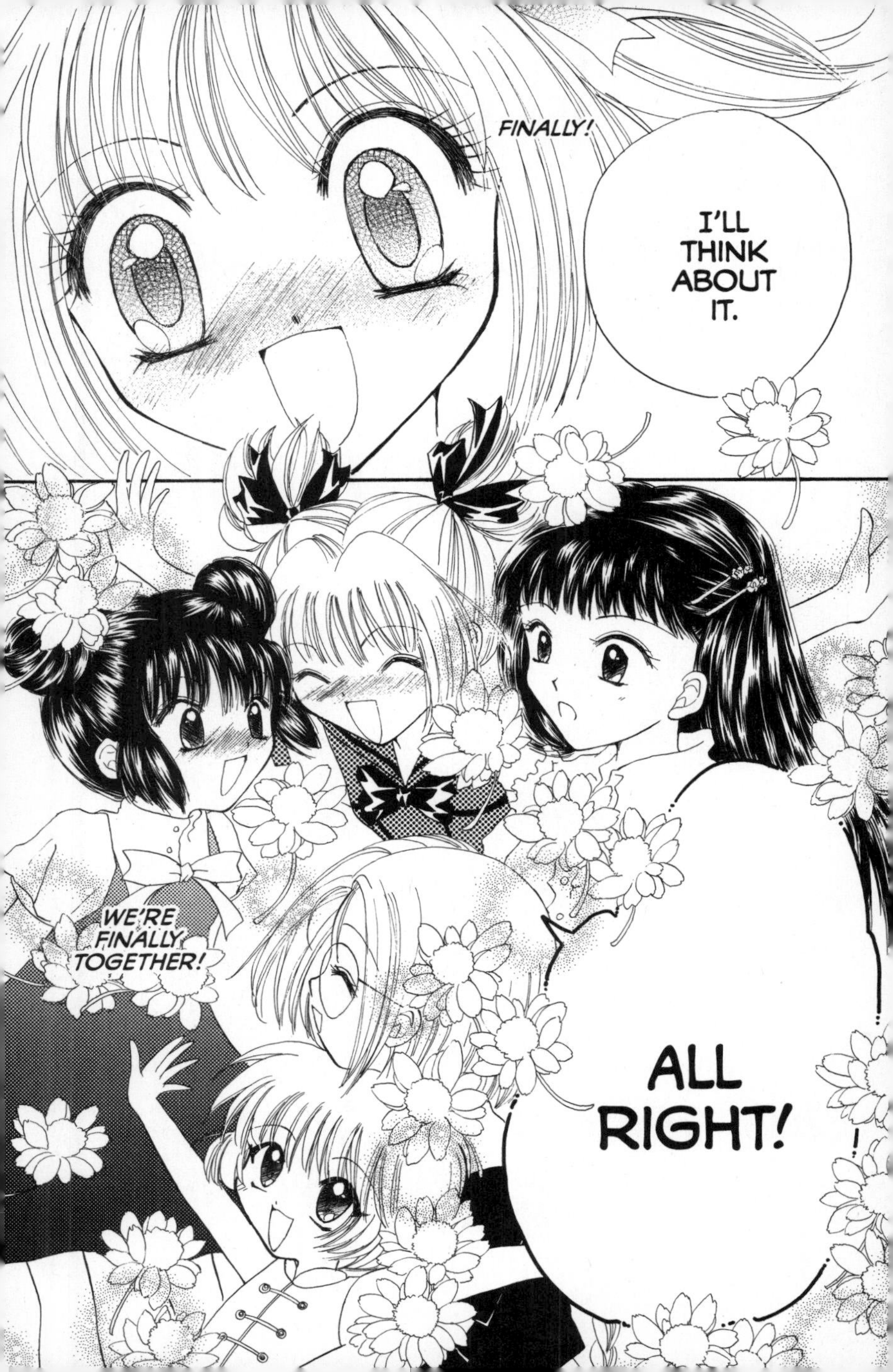
I'LL THINK ABOUT IT.
FINALLY!
ALL RIGHT!
WE'RE FINALLY TOGETHER!

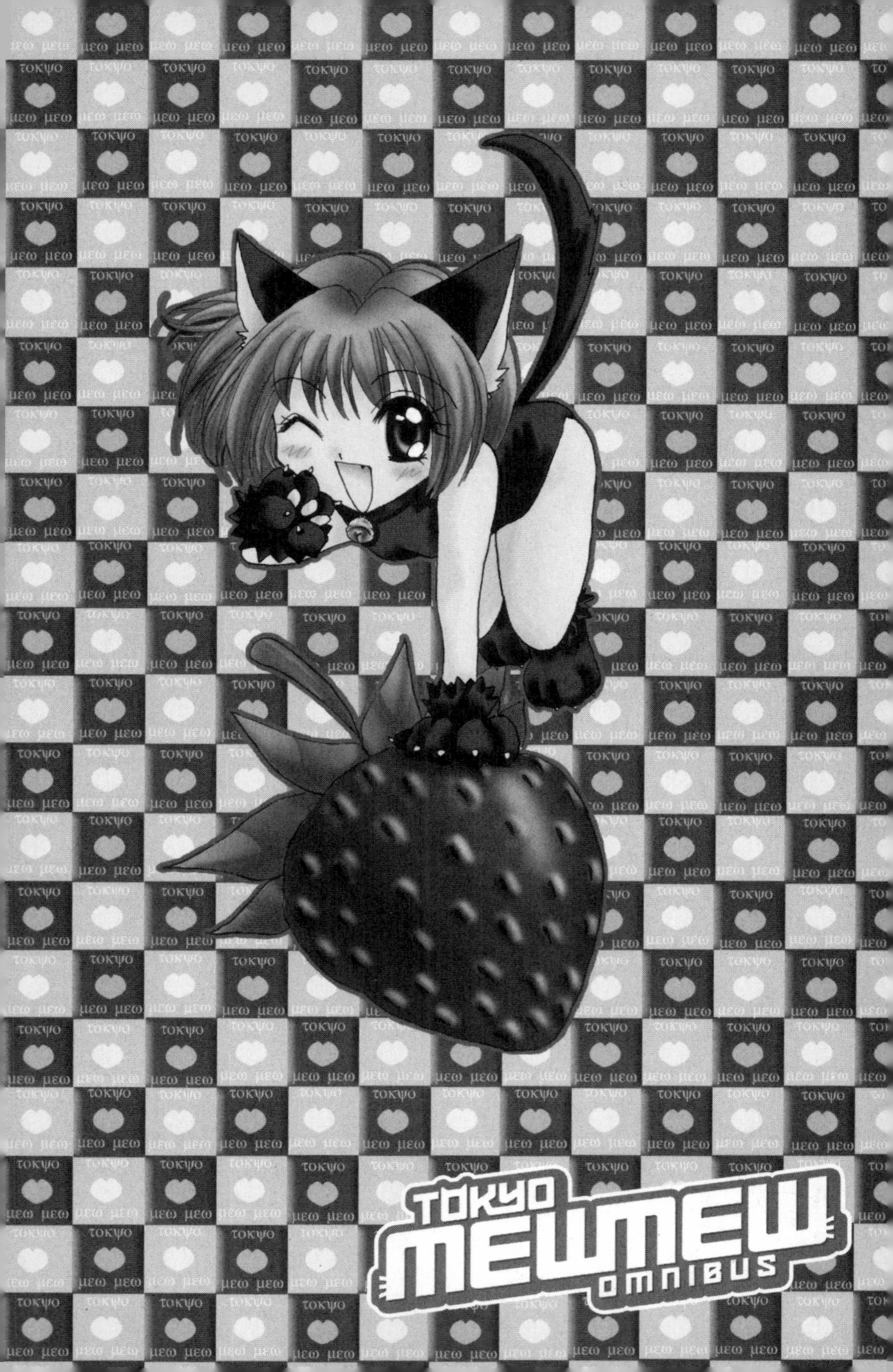
TOKYO MEWMEW OMNIBUS

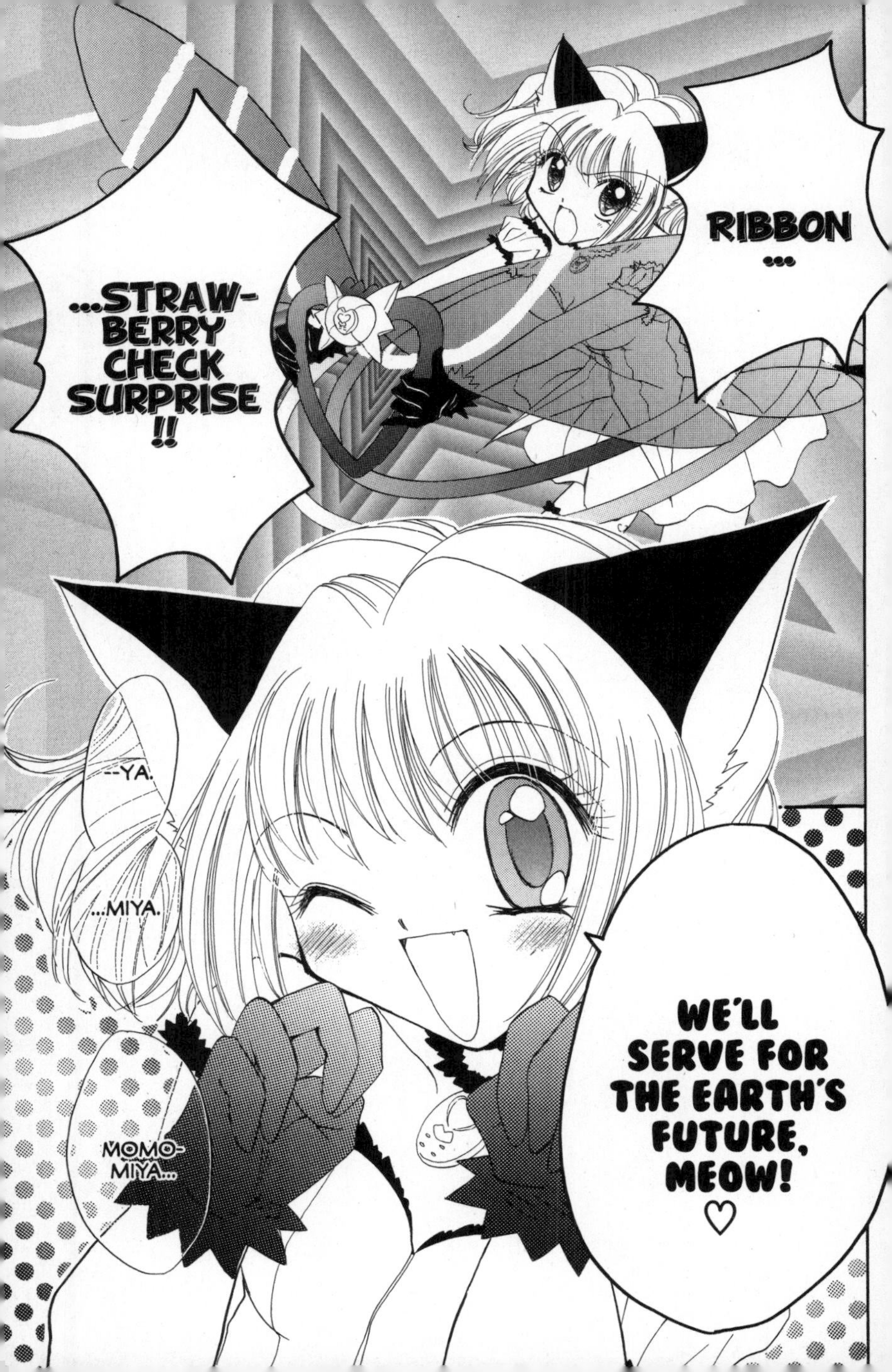
RIBBON ...
...STRAW-BERRY CHECK SURPRISE !!
WE'LL SERVE FOR THE EARTH'S FUTURE, MEOW! ♡
--YA.
...MIYA.
MOMO-MIYA...

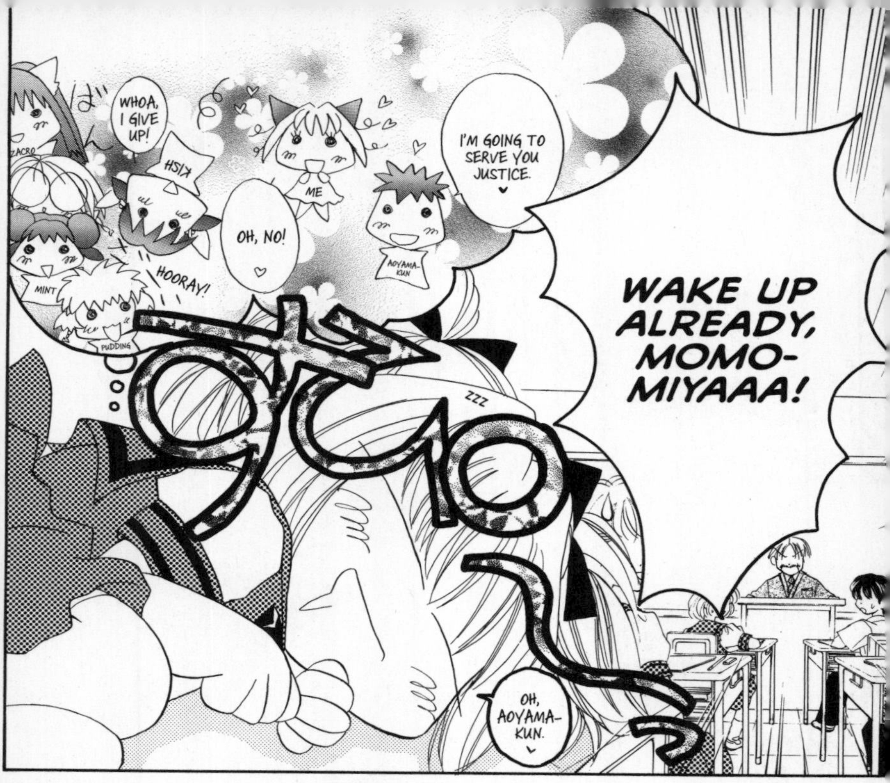

WAKE UP ALREADY, MOMO-MIYAAA!
I'M GOING TO SERVE YOU JUSTICE.
AOYAMA-KUN
ME
OH, NO!
KISH
WHOA, I GIVE UP!
ZACRO
HOORAY!
MINT
PUDDING
ZZZ
OH, AOYAMA-KUN.

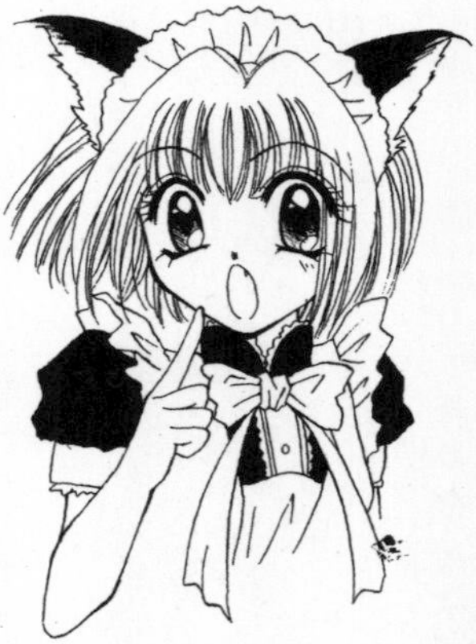

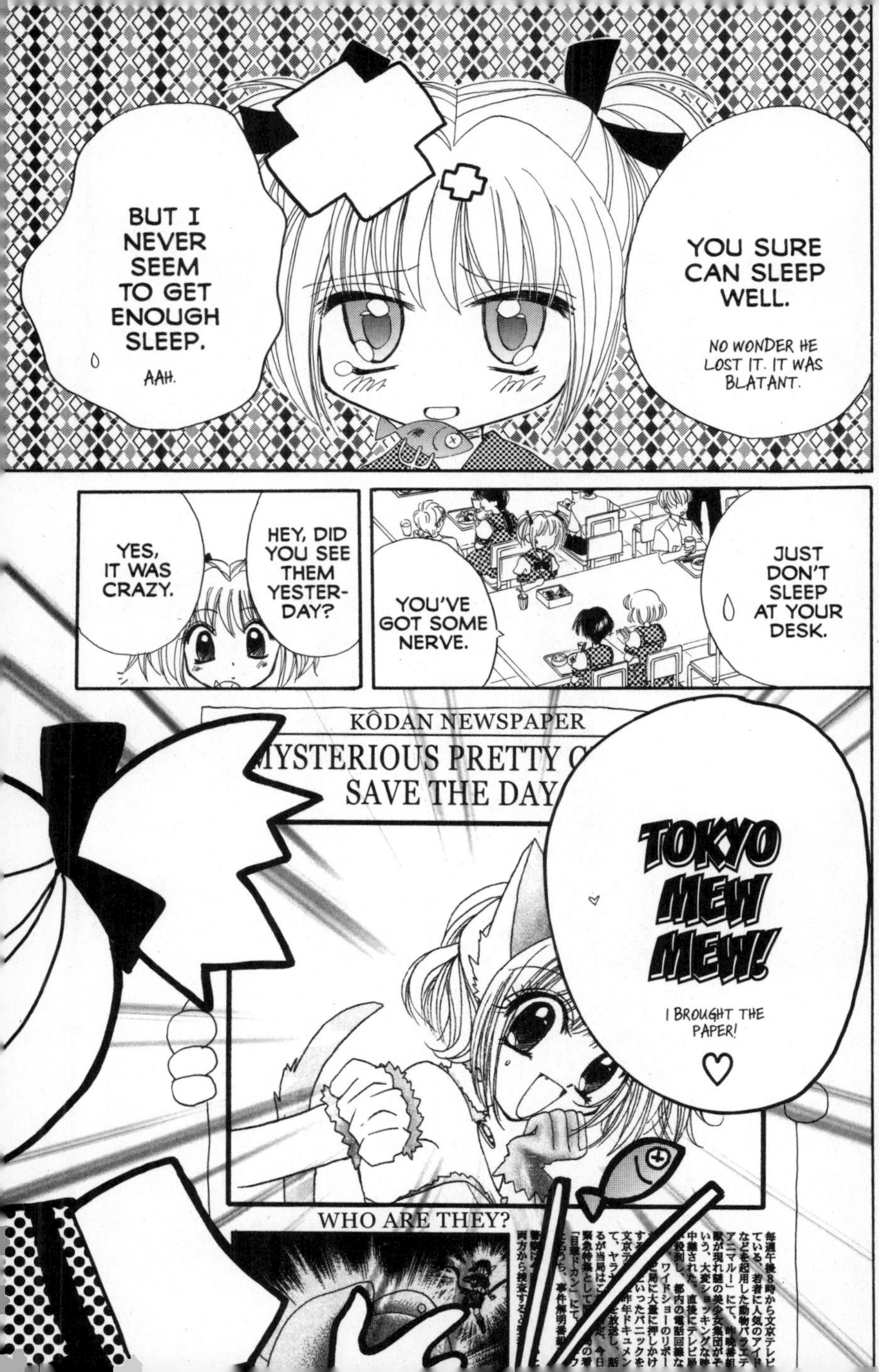

YOU SURE CAN SLEEP WELL.
NO WONDER HE LOST IT. IT WAS BLATANT.
BUT I NEVER SEEM TO GET ENOUGH SLEEP.
AAH.
JUST DON'T SLEEP AT YOUR DESK.
YOU'VE GOT SOME NERVE.
HEY, DID YOU SEE THEM YESTER-DAY?
YES, IT WAS CRAZY.
TOKYO MEW MEW!
I BROUGHT THE PAPER! ♡
KÔDAN NEWSPAPER
MYSTERIOUS PRETTY
SAVE THE DAY
WHO ARE THEY?

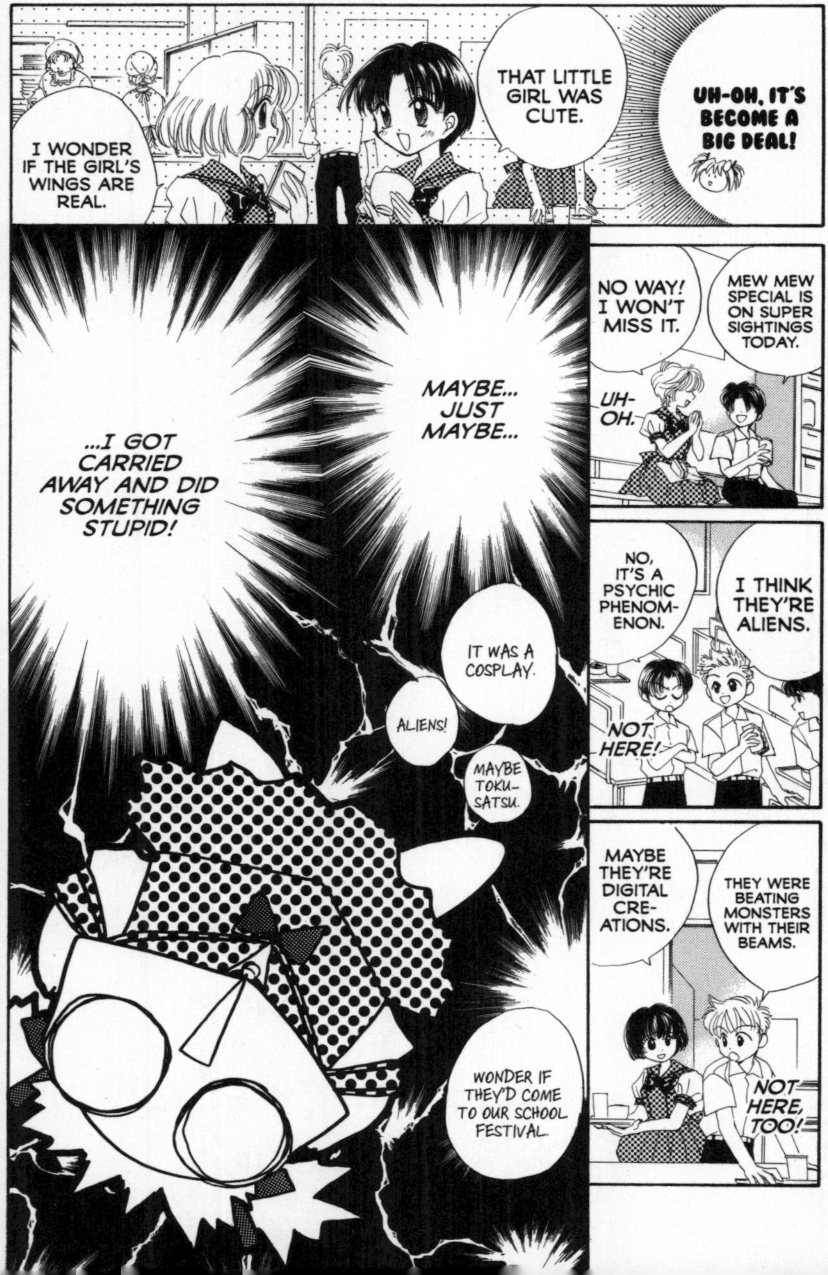
UH-OH, IT'S BECOME A BIG DEAL!
THAT LITTLE GIRL WAS CUTE.
I WONDER IF THE GIRL'S WINGS ARE REAL.
MEW MEW SPECIAL IS ON SUPER SIGHTINGS TODAY.
NO WAY! I WON'T MISS IT.
UH-OH.
I THINK THEY'RE ALIENS.
NO, IT'S A PSYCHIC PHENOMENON.
NOT HERE!
THEY WERE BEATING MONSTERS WITH THEIR BEAMS.
MAYBE THEY'RE DIGITAL CREATIONS.
NOT HERE, TOO!
MAYBE... JUST MAYBE...
...I GOT CARRIED AWAY AND DID SOMETHING STUPID!
IT WAS A COSPLAY.
ALIENS!
MAYBE TOKUSATSU.
WONDER IF THEY'D COME TO OUR SCHOOL FESTIVAL.

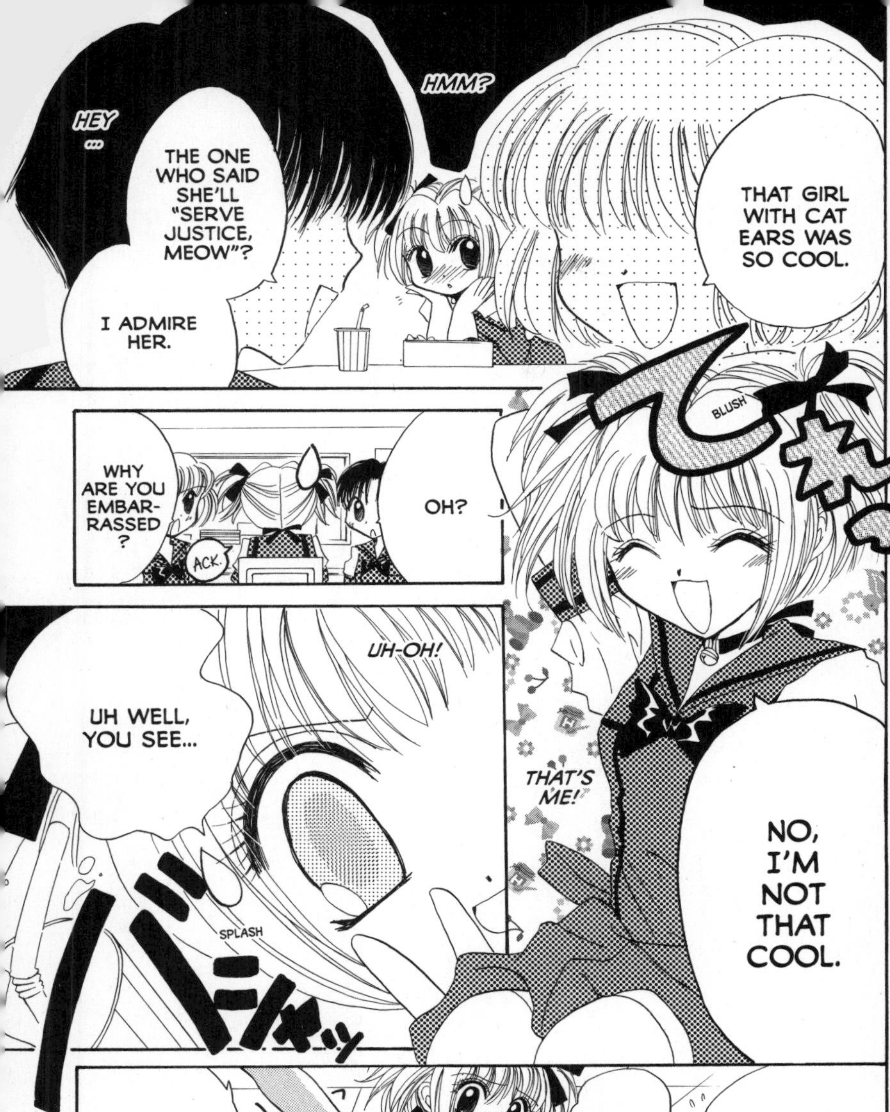
THAT GIRL WITH CAT EARS WAS SO COOL.
HMM?
HEY...
THE ONE WHO SAID SHE'LL "SERVE JUSTICE, MEOW"?
I ADMIRE HER.
BLUSH
THAT'S ME!
NO, I'M NOT THAT COOL.
OH?
WHY ARE YOU EMBARRASSED?
ACK.
UH-OH!
UH WELL, YOU SEE...
SPLASH
WHAT ARE YOU DOING, ICHIGO?
I'M SORRY--
SFF
REALLY, WHAT ARE YOU DOING?

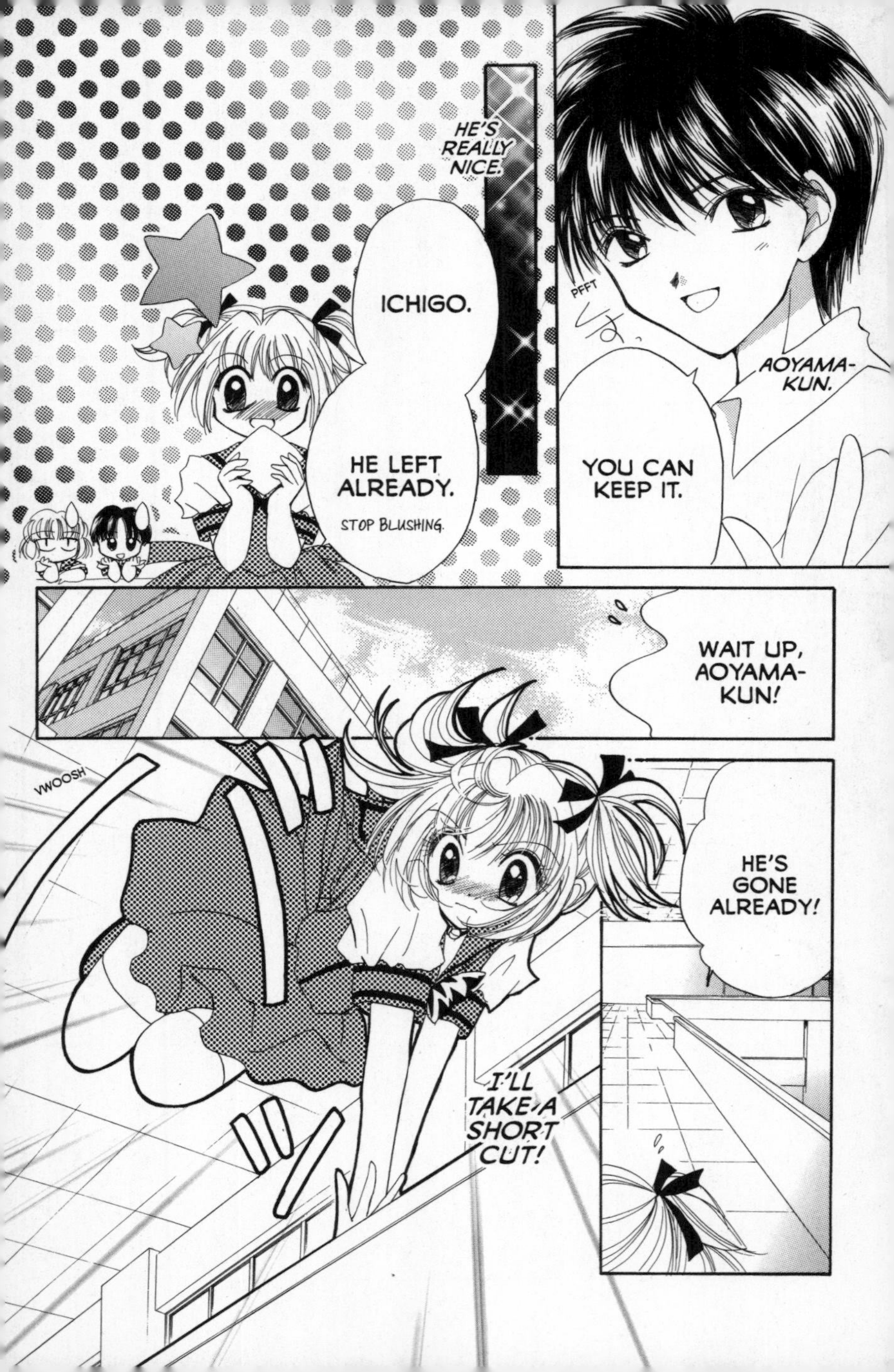
PFFT
AOYAMA-KUN.
YOU CAN KEEP IT.
HE'S REALLY NICE.
ICHIGO.
HE LEFT ALREADY.
STOP BLUSHING.
WAIT UP, AOYAMA-KUN!
HE'S GONE ALREADY!
I'LL TAKE A SHORT CUT!
VWOOSH

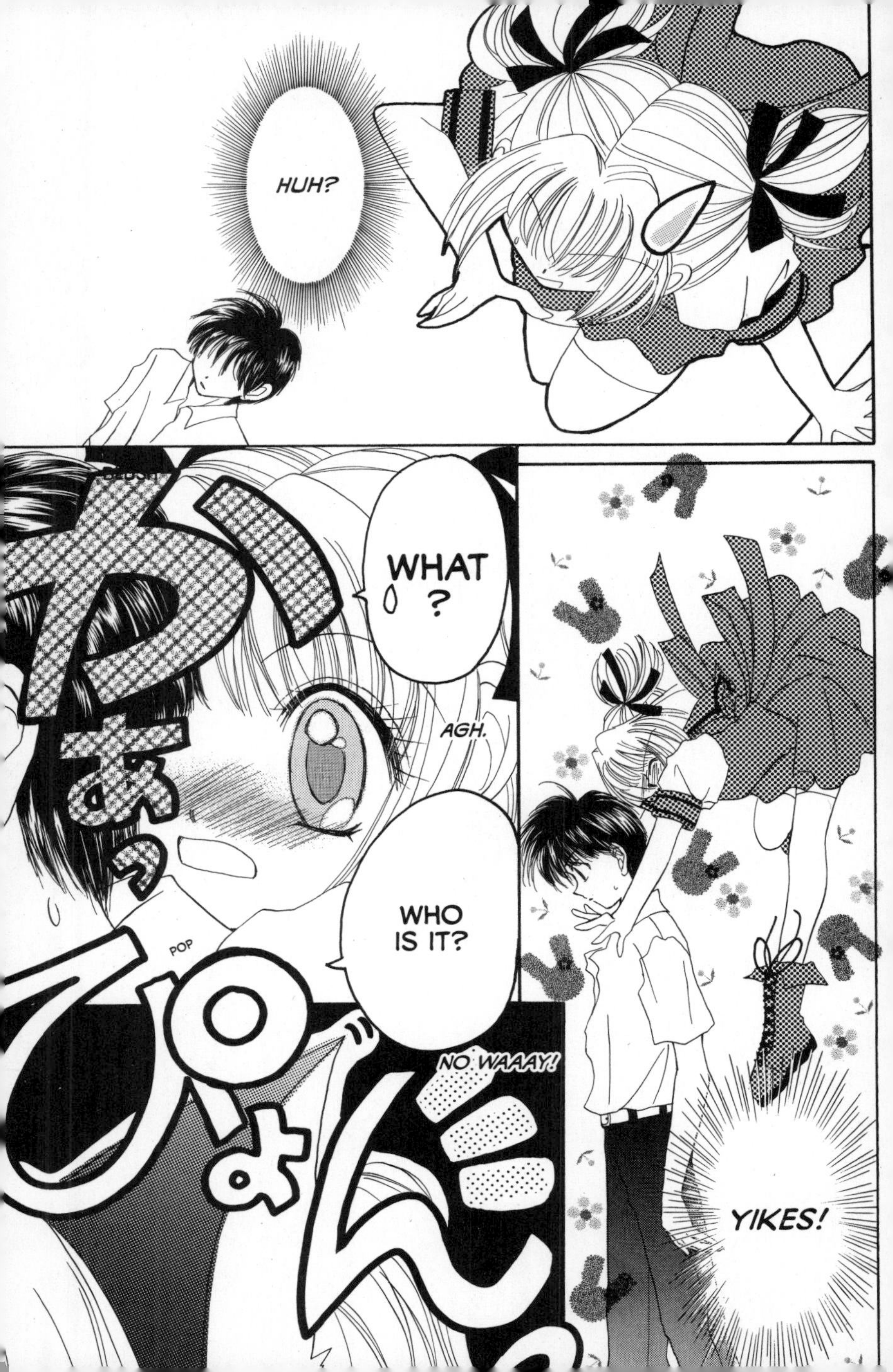
HUH?
YIKES!
WHAT ?
AGH.
WHO IS IT?
POP
NO WAAAY!

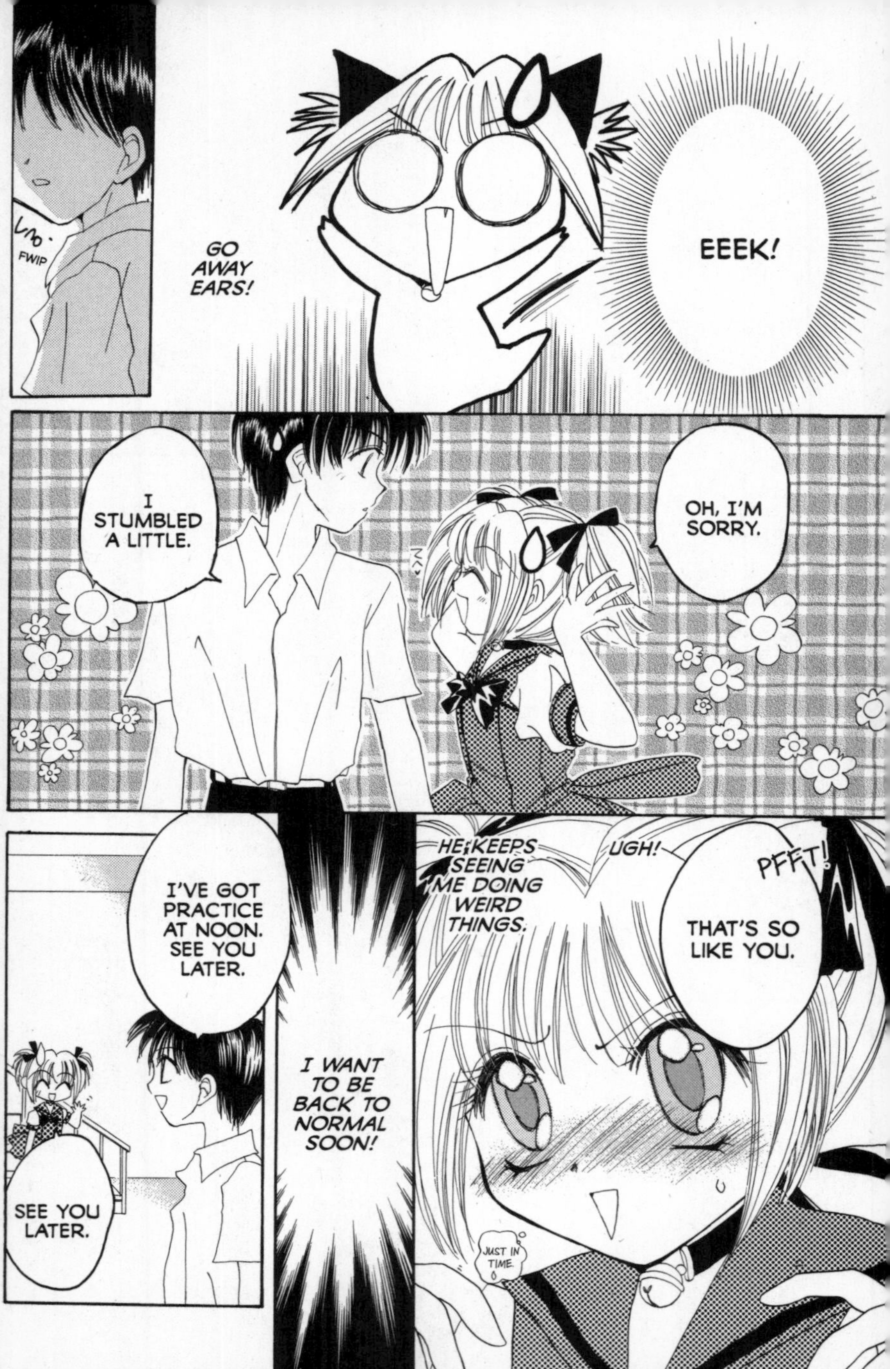
EEEK!
GO AWAY EARS!
FWIP
OH, I'M SORRY.
I STUMBLED A LITTLE.
PFFT!
THAT'S SO LIKE YOU.
UGH!
HE KEEPS SEEING ME DOING WEIRD THINGS.
JUST IN TIME.
I WANT TO BE BACK TO NORMAL SOON!
I'VE GOT PRACTICE AT NOON. SEE YOU LATER.
SEE YOU LATER.

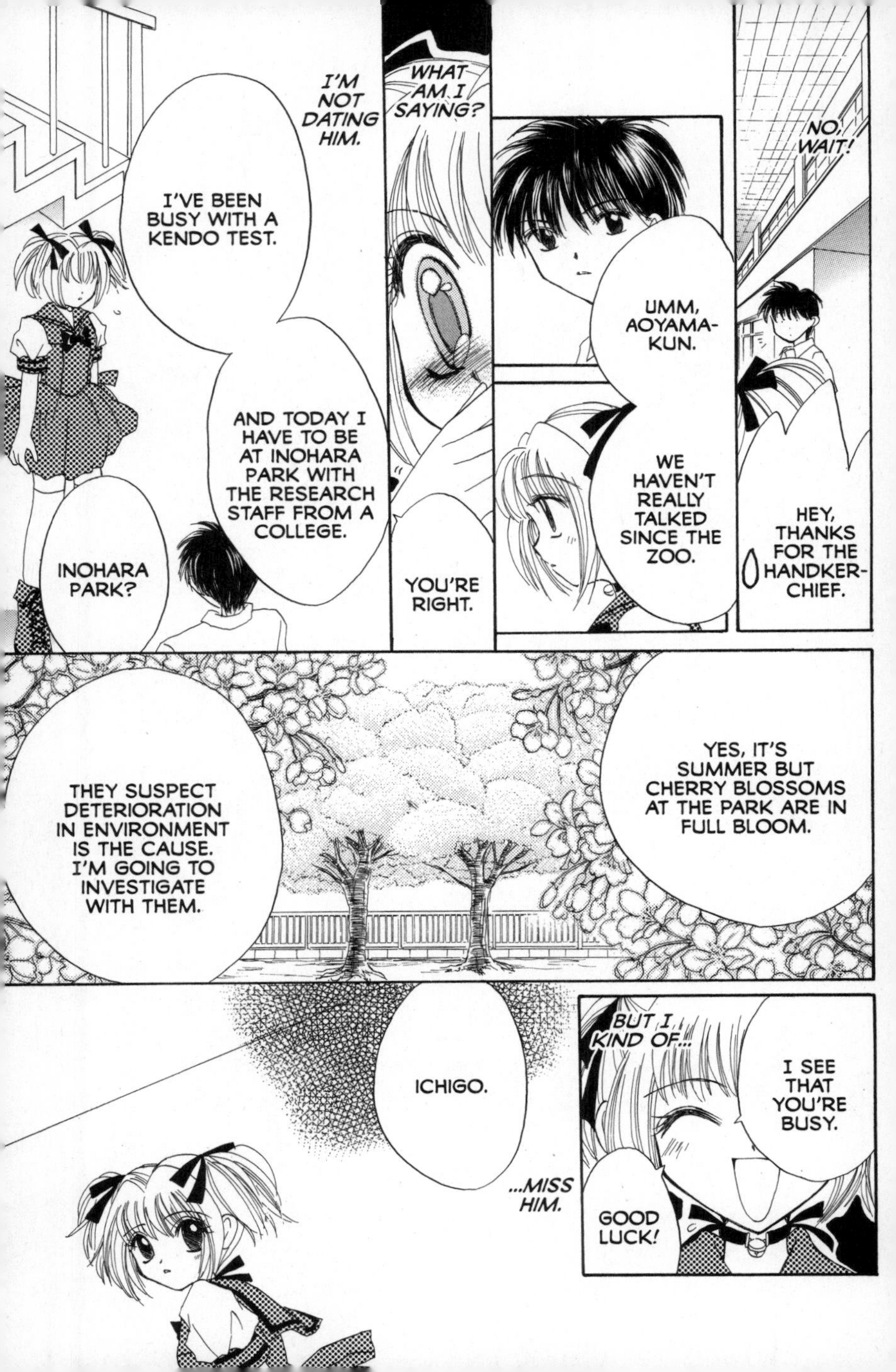
NO, WAIT!
HEY, THANKS FOR THE HANDKERCHIEF.
UMM, AOYAMA-KUN.
WE HAVEN'T REALLY TALKED SINCE THE ZOO.
WHAT AM I SAYING?
I'M NOT DATING HIM.
YOU'RE RIGHT.
I'VE BEEN BUSY WITH A KENDO TEST.
AND TODAY I HAVE TO BE AT INOHARA PARK WITH THE RESEARCH STAFF FROM A COLLEGE.
INOHARA PARK?
YES, IT'S SUMMER BUT CHERRY BLOSSOMS AT THE PARK ARE IN FULL BLOOM.
THEY SUSPECT DETERIORATION IN ENVIRONMENT IS THE CAUSE. I'M GOING TO INVESTIGATE WITH THEM.
I SEE THAT YOU'RE BUSY.
BUT I KIND OF...
GOOD LUCK!
...MISS HIM.
ICHIGO.

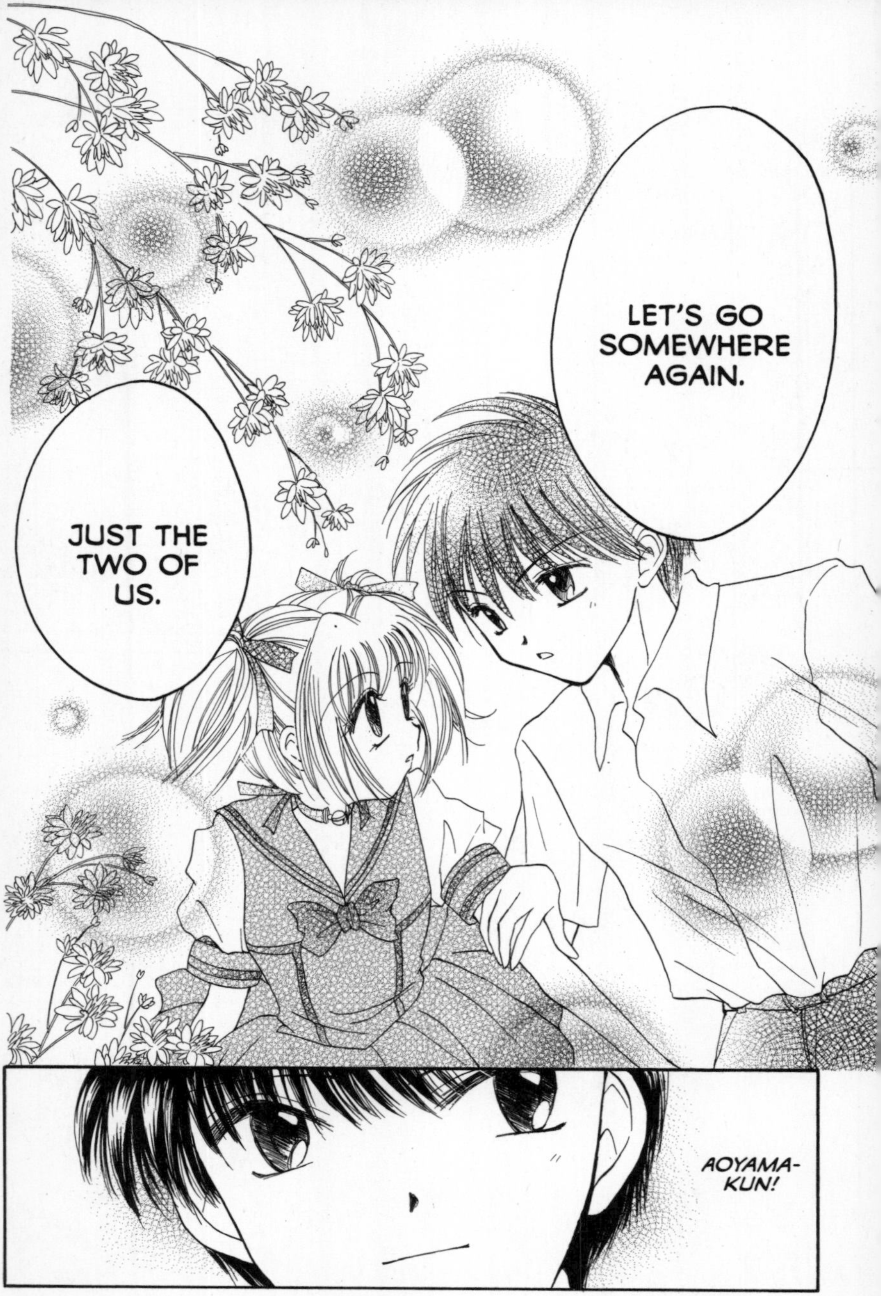
LET'S GO SOMEWHERE AGAIN.
JUST THE TWO OF US.
AOYAMA-KUN!

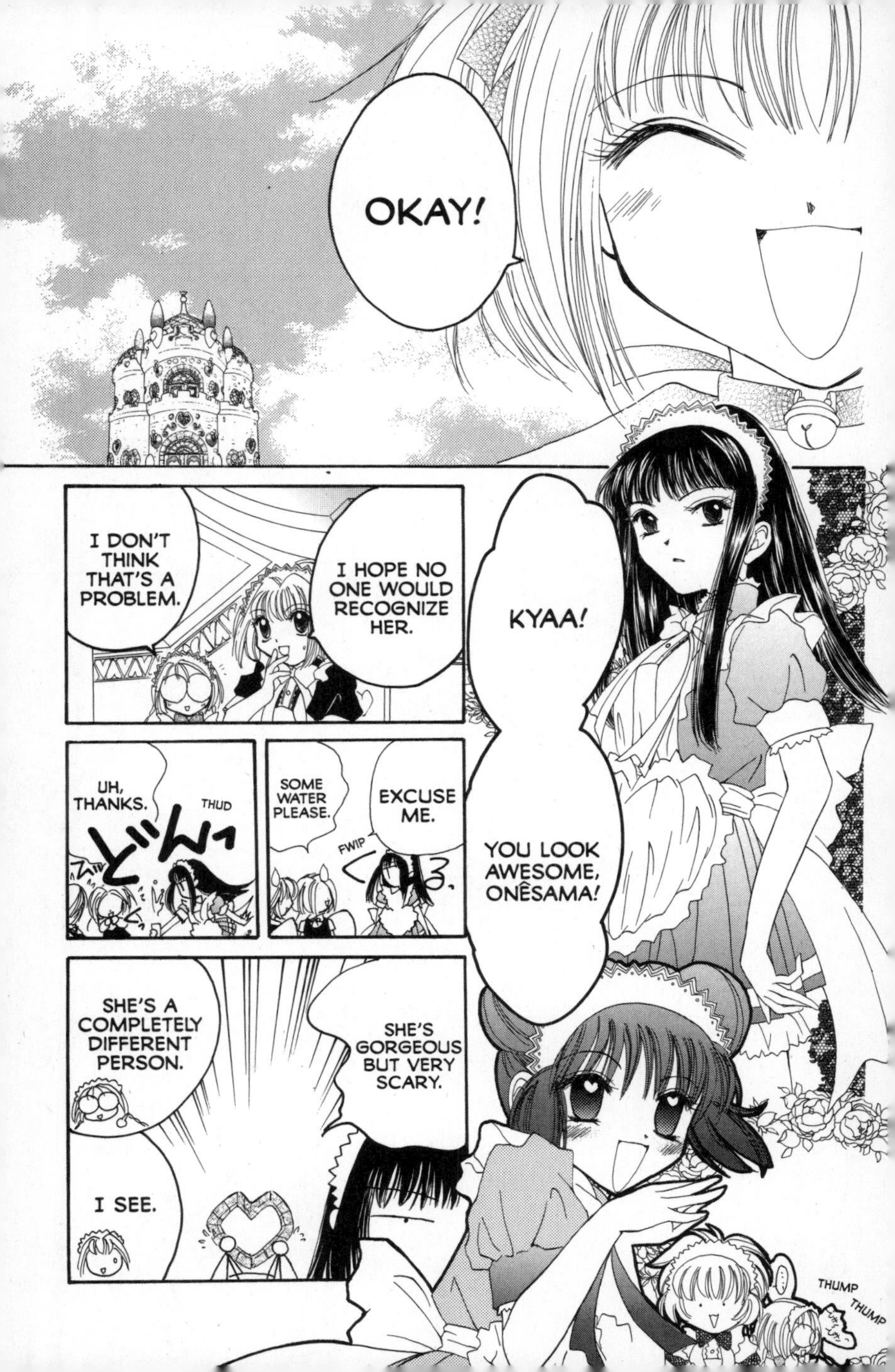
OKAY!
KYAA!
YOU LOOK AWESOME, ONÊSAMA!
I HOPE NO ONE WOULD RECOGNIZE HER.
I DON'T THINK THAT'S A PROBLEM.
EXCUSE ME.
SOME WATER PLEASE.
FWIP
UH, THANKS.
THUD
SHE'S GORGEOUS BUT VERY SCARY.
SHE'S A COMPLETELY DIFFERENT PERSON.
I SEE.
THUMP THUMP

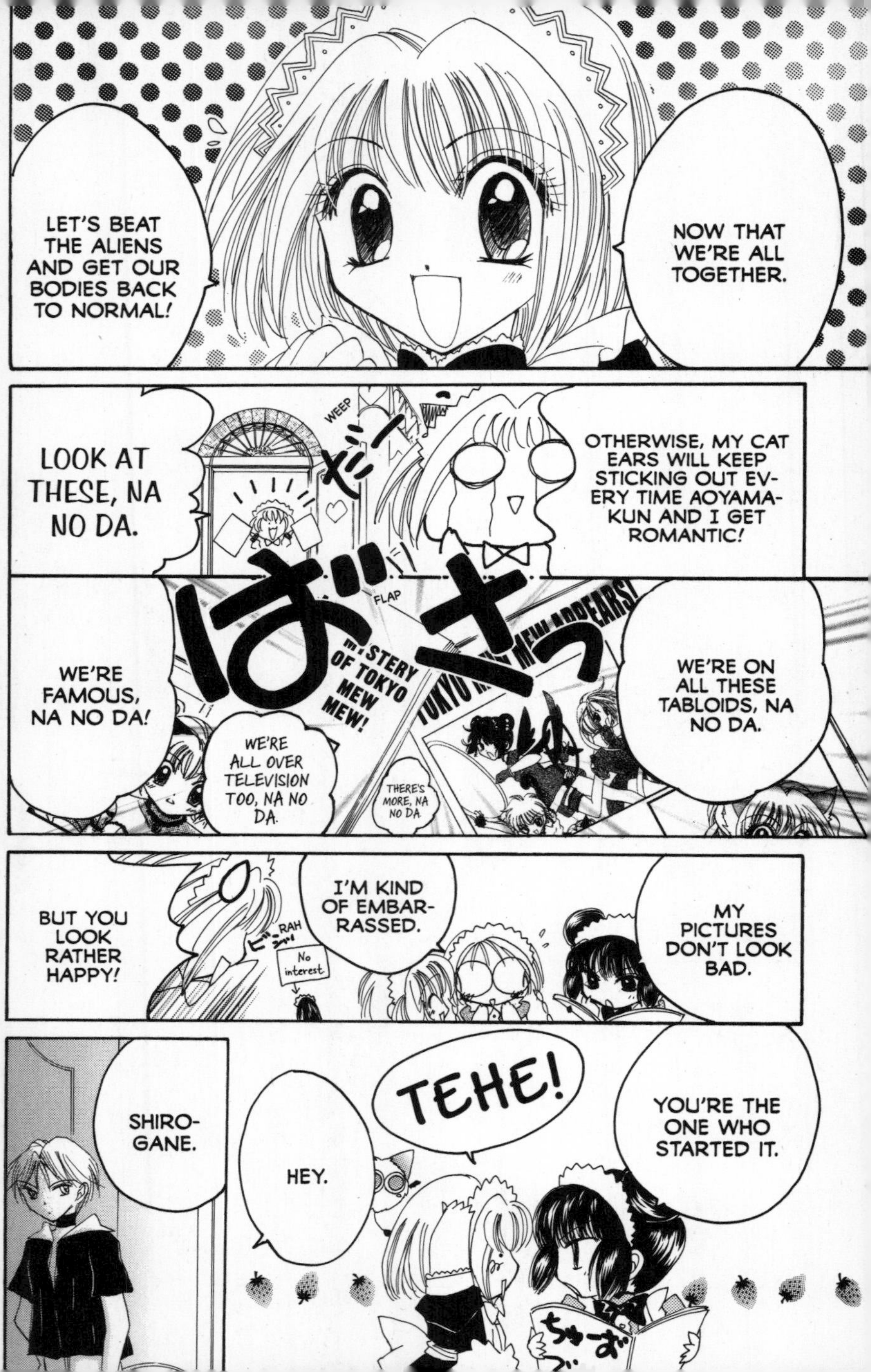
NOW THAT WE'RE ALL TOGETHER.
LET'S BEAT THE ALIENS AND GET OUR BODIES BACK TO NORMAL!
OTHERWISE, MY CAT EARS WILL KEEP STICKING OUT EV-ERY TIME AOYAMA-KUN AND I GET ROMANTIC!
WEEP
LOOK AT THESE, NA NO DA.
WE'RE ON ALL THESE TABLOIDS, NA NO DA.
ばさっ
FLAP
MEW APPEARS!
MYSTERY OF TOKYO MEW MEW!
THERE'S MORE, NA NO DA.
WE'RE ALL OVER TELEVISION TOO, NA NO DA.
WE'RE FAMOUS, NA NO DA!
MY PICTURES DON'T LOOK BAD.
I'M KIND OF EMBAR-RASSED.
No interest.
RAH
BUT YOU LOOK RATHER HAPPY!
YOU'RE THE ONE WHO STARTED IT.
TEHE!
HEY.
SHIRO-GANE.

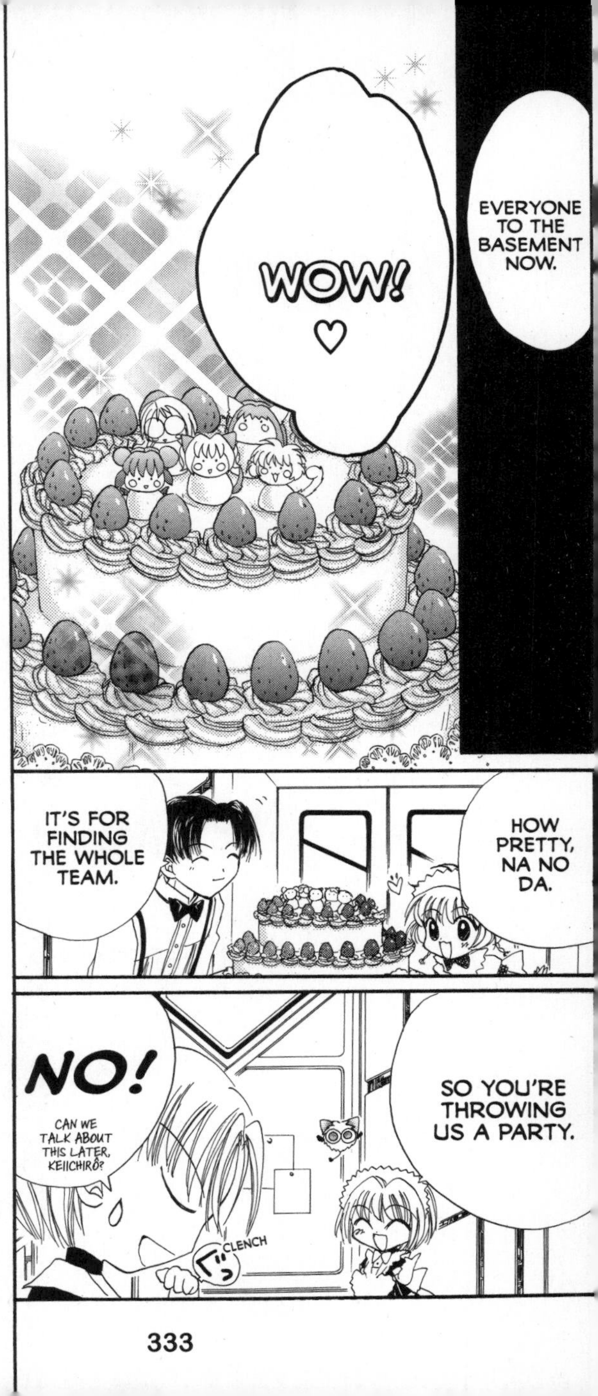
EVERYONE TO THE BASEMENT NOW.
WOW! ♡
HOW PRETTY, NA NO DA.
IT'S FOR FINDING THE WHOLE TEAM.
SO YOU'RE THROWING US A PARTY.
NO!
CAN WE TALK ABOUT THIS LATER, KEIICHIRŌ?
CLENCH

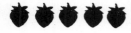

SPECIAL THANKS!!

REIKO YOSHIDA

RIMO MIDORIKAWA
MADOKA OMORI

HIDEAKI OIKAWA

HIJIRI MATSUMOTO
AYA SUZUKI

IZUMI UEDA

ASUMI HARA

M. SEKIYA
T. KAMAGATA

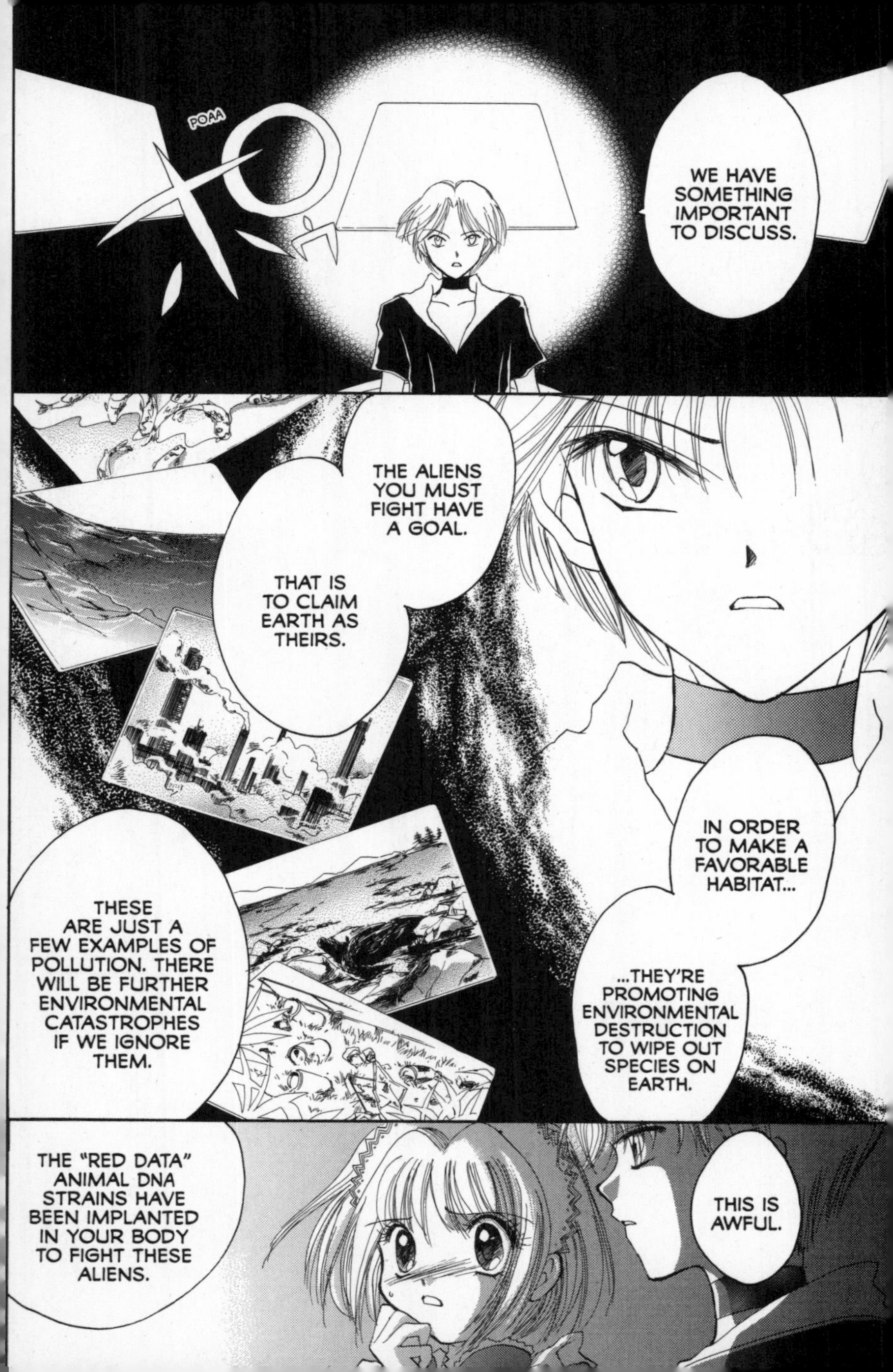
WE HAVE SOMETHING IMPORTANT TO DISCUSS.
POAA
THE ALIENS YOU MUST FIGHT HAVE A GOAL.
THAT IS TO CLAIM EARTH AS THEIRS.
IN ORDER TO MAKE A FAVORABLE HABITAT...
...THEY'RE PROMOTING ENVIRONMENTAL DESTRUCTION TO WIPE OUT SPECIES ON EARTH.
THESE ARE JUST A FEW EXAMPLES OF POLLUTION. THERE WILL BE FURTHER ENVIRONMENTAL CATASTROPHES IF WE IGNORE THEM.
THIS IS AWFUL.
THE "RED DATA" ANIMAL DNA STRAINS HAVE BEEN IMPLANTED IN YOUR BODY TO FIGHT THESE ALIENS.

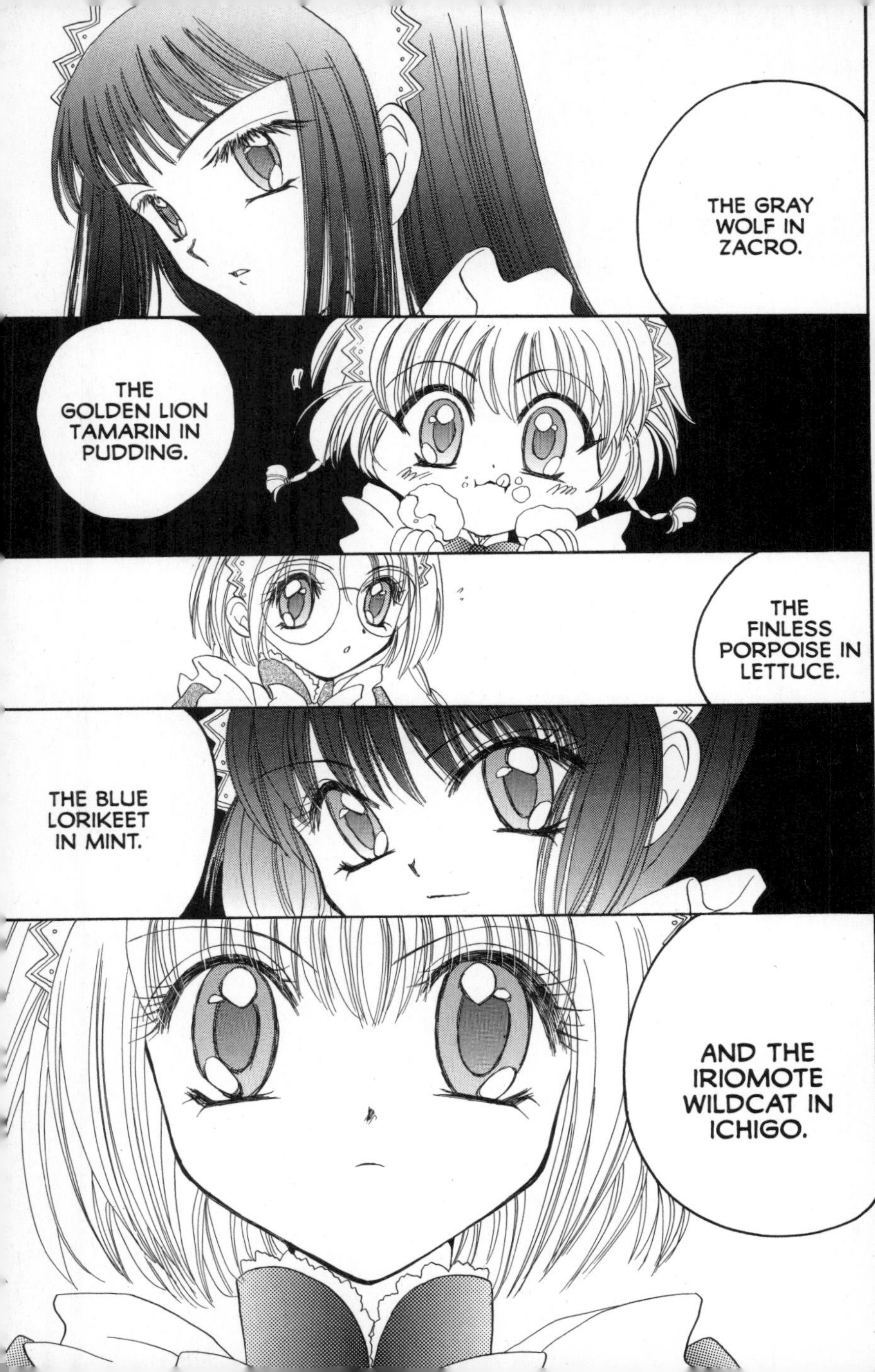
THE GRAY WOLF IN ZACRO.
THE GOLDEN LION TAMARIN IN PUDDING.
THE FINLESS PORPOISE IN LETTUCE.
THE BLUE LORIKEET IN MINT.
AND THE IRIOMOTE WILDCAT IN ICHIGO.

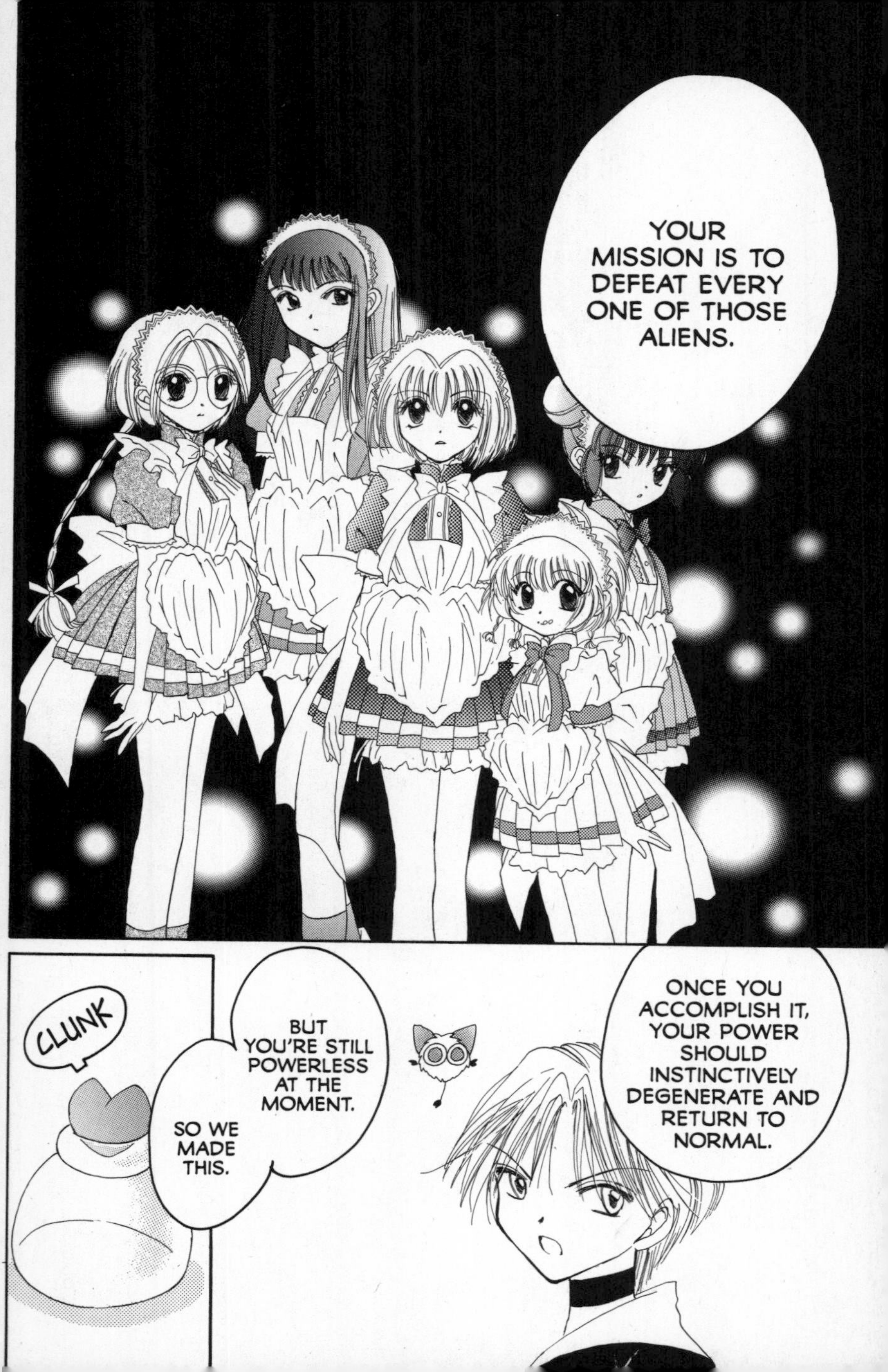
YOUR MISSION IS TO DEFEAT EVERY ONE OF THOSE ALIENS.
ONCE YOU ACCOMPLISH IT, YOUR POWER SHOULD INSTINCTIVELY DEGENERATE AND RETURN TO NORMAL.
BUT YOU'RE STILL POWERLESS AT THE MOMENT.
SO WE MADE THIS.
CLUNK

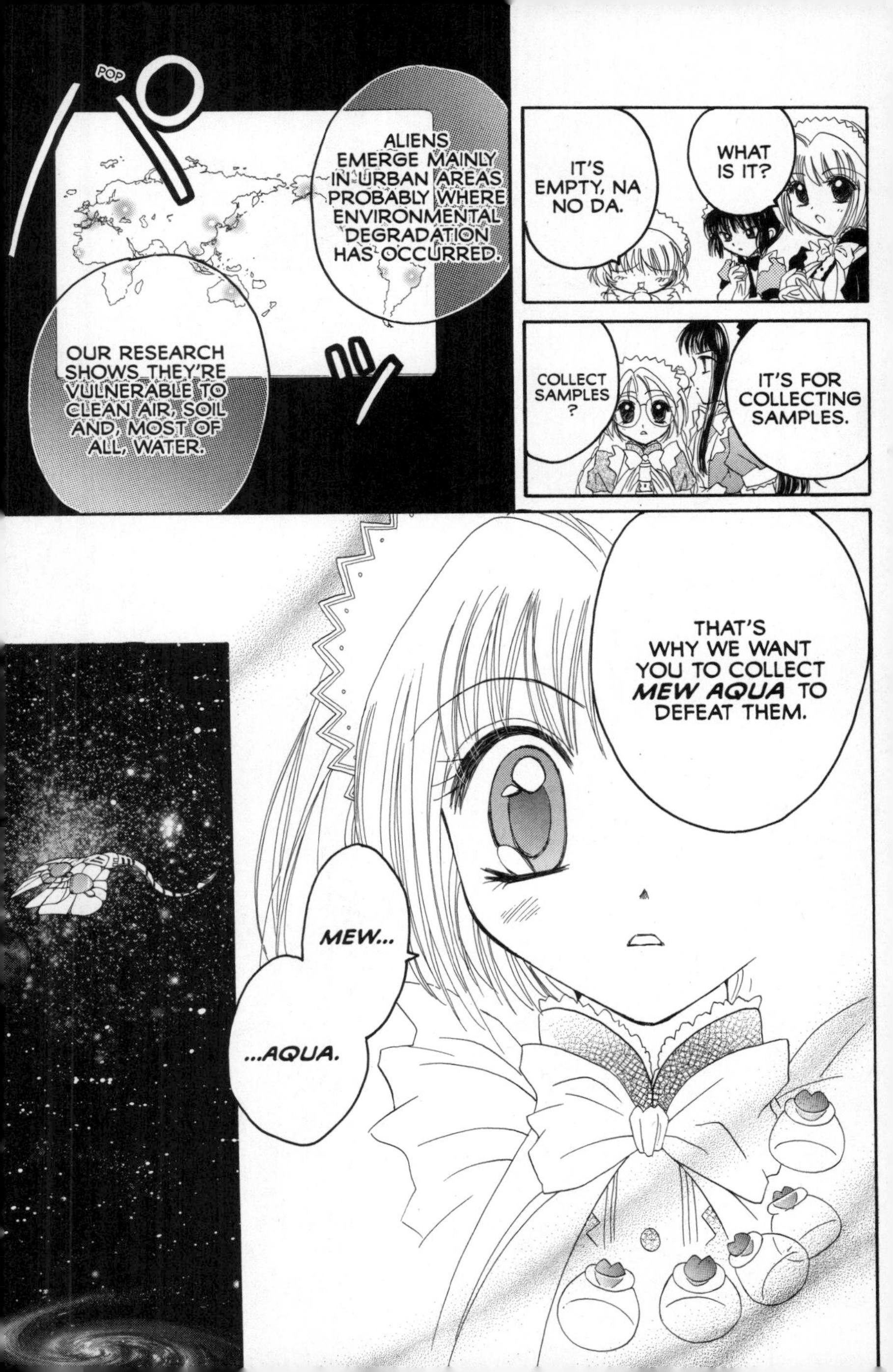
WHAT IS IT?
IT'S EMPTY, NA NO DA.
IT'S FOR COLLECTING SAMPLES.
COLLECT SAMPLES?
POP
ALIENS EMERGE MAINLY IN URBAN AREAS PROBABLY WHERE ENVIRONMENTAL DEGRADATION HAS OCCURRED.
OUR RESEARCH SHOWS THEY'RE VULNERABLE TO CLEAN AIR, SOIL AND, MOST OF ALL, WATER.
THAT'S WHY WE WANT YOU TO COLLECT *MEW AQUA* TO DEFEAT THEM.
MEW...
...AQUA.

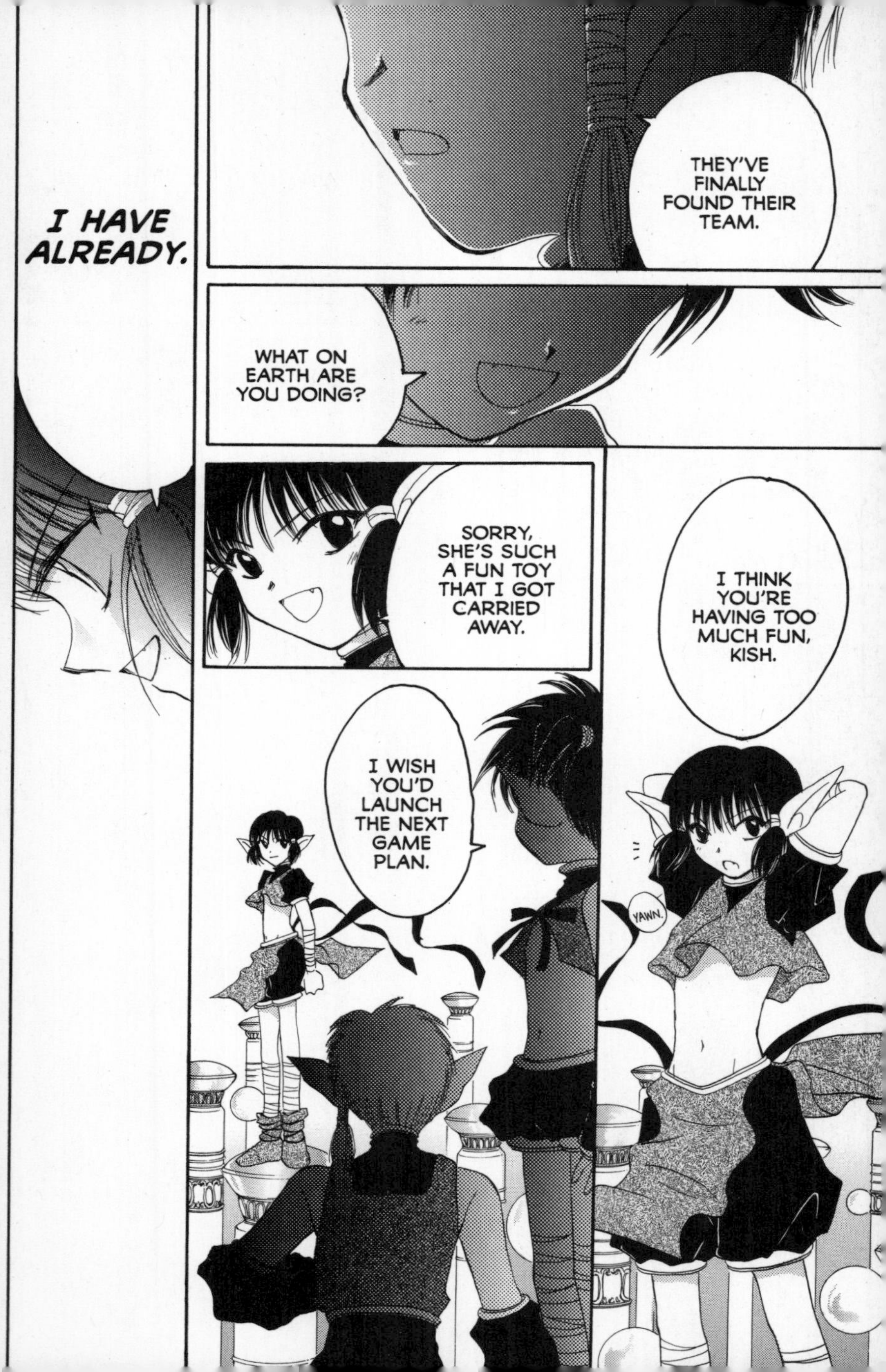
THEY'VE FINALLY FOUND THEIR TEAM.
WHAT ON EARTH ARE YOU DOING?
I THINK YOU'RE HAVING TOO MUCH FUN, KISH.
YAWN.
SORRY, SHE'S SUCH A FUN TOY THAT I GOT CARRIED AWAY.
I WISH YOU'D LAUNCH THE NEXT GAME PLAN.
I HAVE ALREADY.

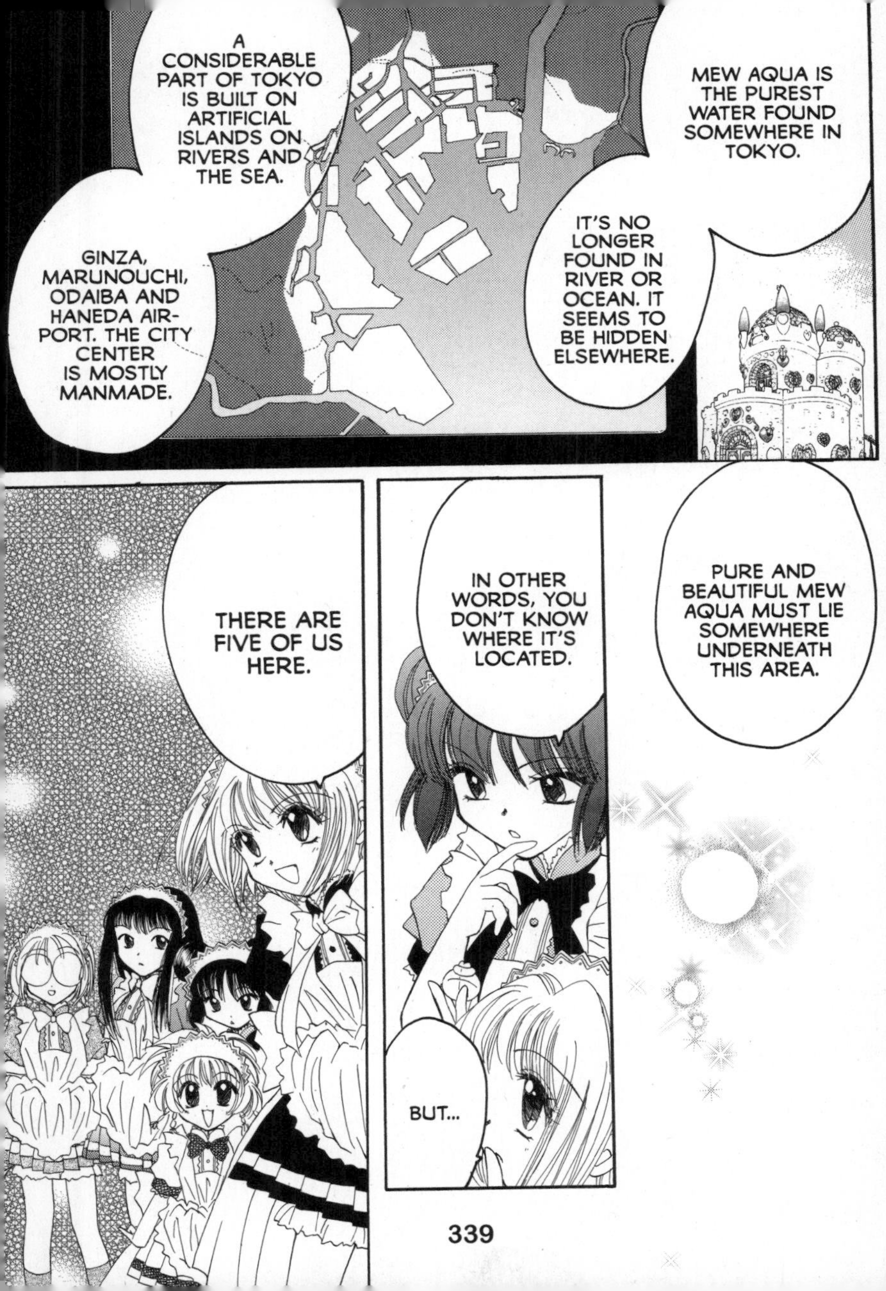
MEW AQUA IS THE PUREST WATER FOUND SOMEWHERE IN TOKYO.
IT'S NO LONGER FOUND IN RIVER OR OCEAN. IT SEEMS TO BE HIDDEN ELSEWHERE.
A CONSIDERABLE PART OF TOKYO IS BUILT ON ARTIFICIAL ISLANDS ON RIVERS AND THE SEA.
GINZA, MARUNOUCHI, ODAIBA AND HANEDA AIR-PORT. THE CITY CENTER IS MOSTLY MANMADE.
PURE AND BEAUTIFUL MEW AQUA MUST LIE SOMEWHERE UNDERNEATH THIS AREA.
IN OTHER WORDS, YOU DON'T KNOW WHERE IT'S LOCATED.
BUT...
THERE ARE FIVE OF US HERE.

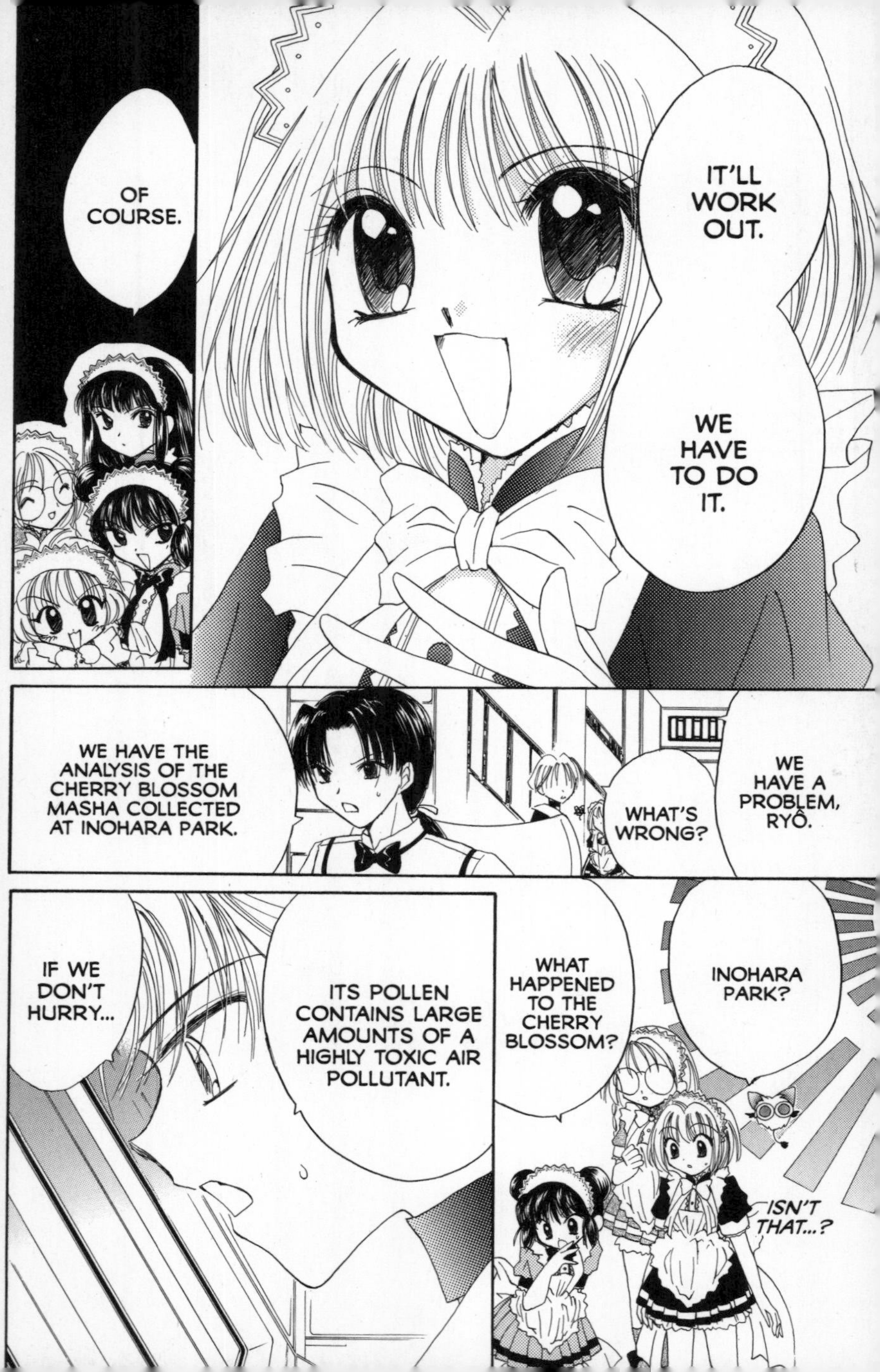
IT'LL WORK OUT.
WE HAVE TO DO IT.
OF COURSE.
WE HAVE A PROBLEM, RYÔ.
WHAT'S WRONG?
WE HAVE THE ANALYSIS OF THE CHERRY BLOSSOM MASHA COLLECTED AT INOHARA PARK.
INOHARA PARK?
WHAT HAPPENED TO THE CHERRY BLOSSOM?
ISN'T THAT...?
ITS POLLEN CONTAINS LARGE AMOUNTS OF A HIGHLY TOXIC AIR POLLUTANT.
IF WE DON'T HURRY...

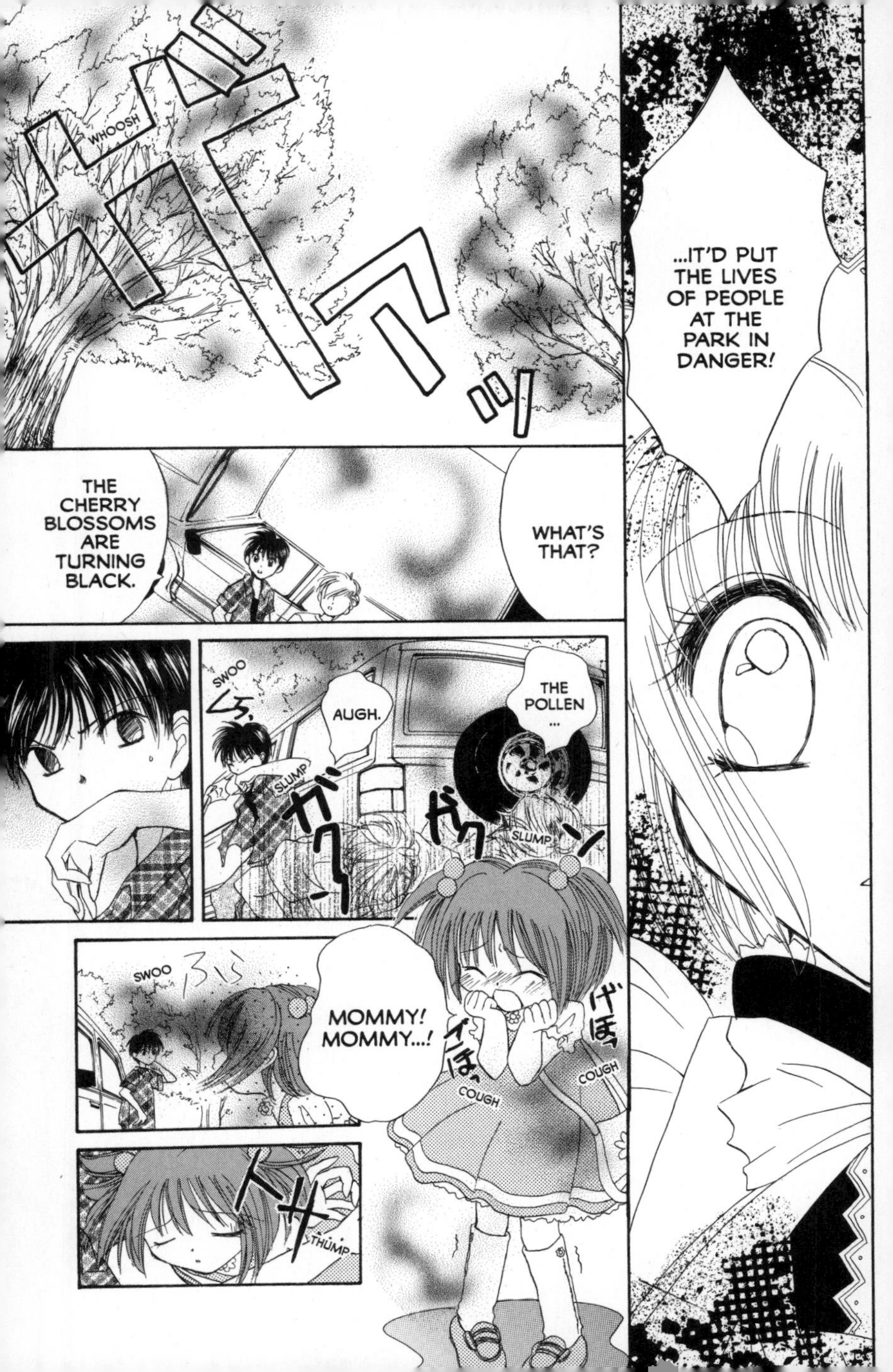
...IT'D PUT THE LIVES OF PEOPLE AT THE PARK IN DANGER!
WHOOSH
WHAT'S THAT?
THE CHERRY BLOSSOMS ARE TURNING BLACK.
THE POLLEN ...
SLUMP
AUGH.
SWOO
SLUMP
COUGH
COUGH
MOMMY! MOMMY...!
SWOO
THUMP

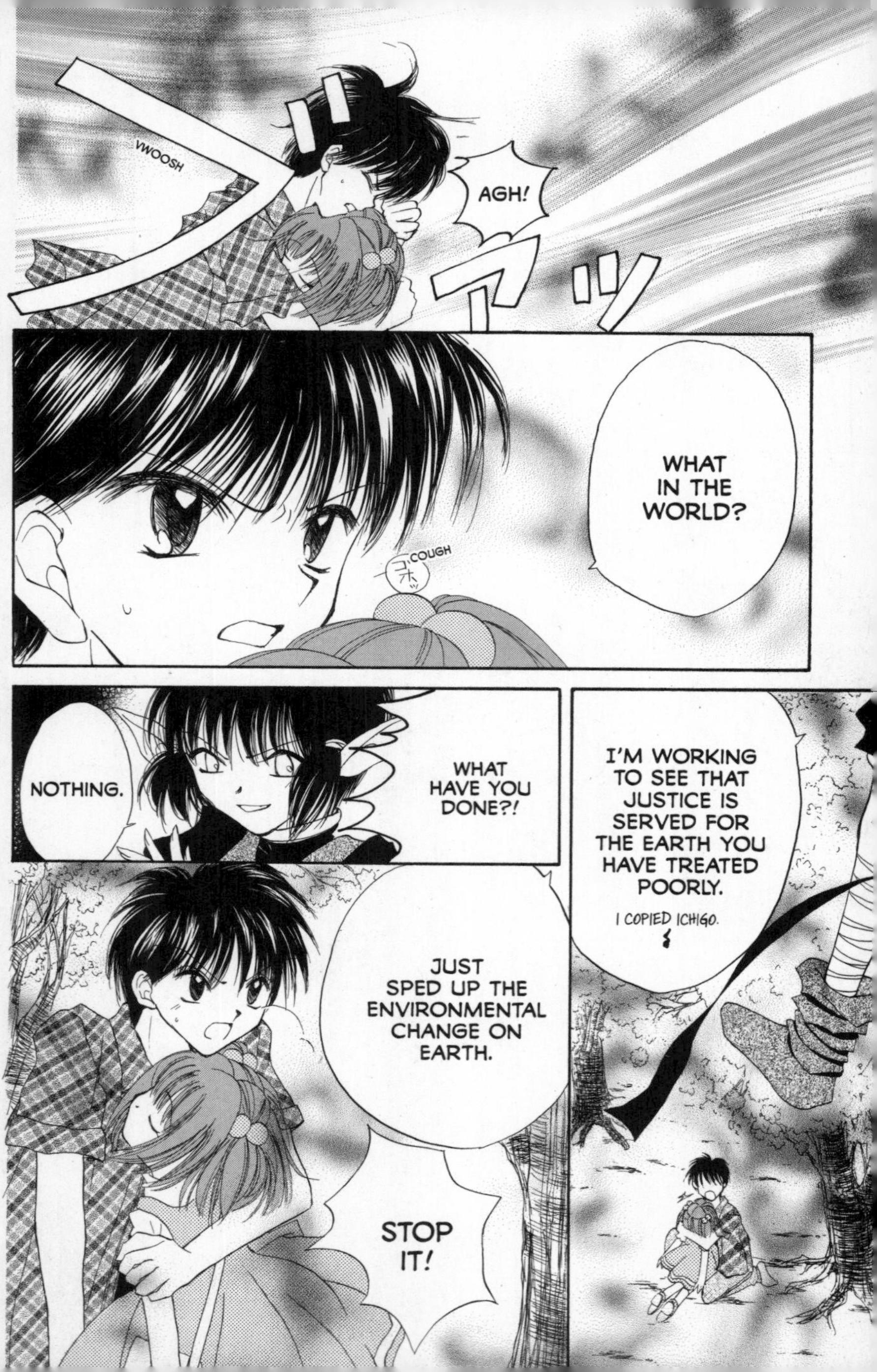
AGH!
アッ
VWOOSH
WHAT IN THE WORLD?
COUGH
ゴホッ
I'M WORKING TO SEE THAT JUSTICE IS SERVED FOR THE EARTH YOU HAVE TREATED POORLY.
I COPIED ICHIGO.
WHAT HAVE YOU DONE?!
NOTHING.
JUST SPED UP THE ENVIRONMENTAL CHANGE ON EARTH.
STOP IT!

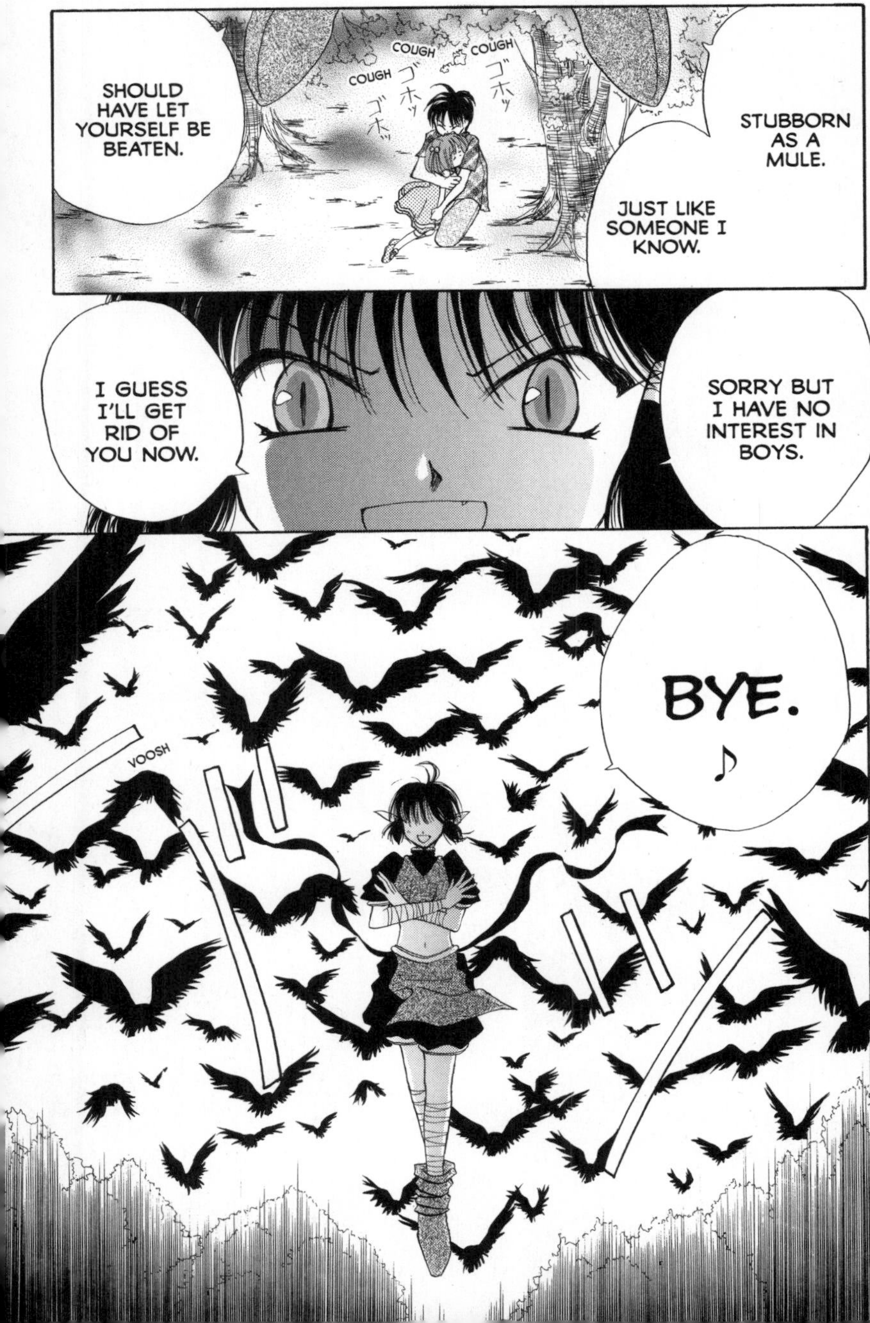
STUBBORN AS A MULE.
JUST LIKE SOMEONE I KNOW.
COUGH ゴホッ
COUGH ゴホッ
COUGH ゴホッ
SHOULD HAVE LET YOURSELF BE BEATEN.
SORRY BUT I HAVE NO INTEREST IN BOYS.
I GUESS I'LL GET RID OF YOU NOW.
BYE. ♪
VOOSH

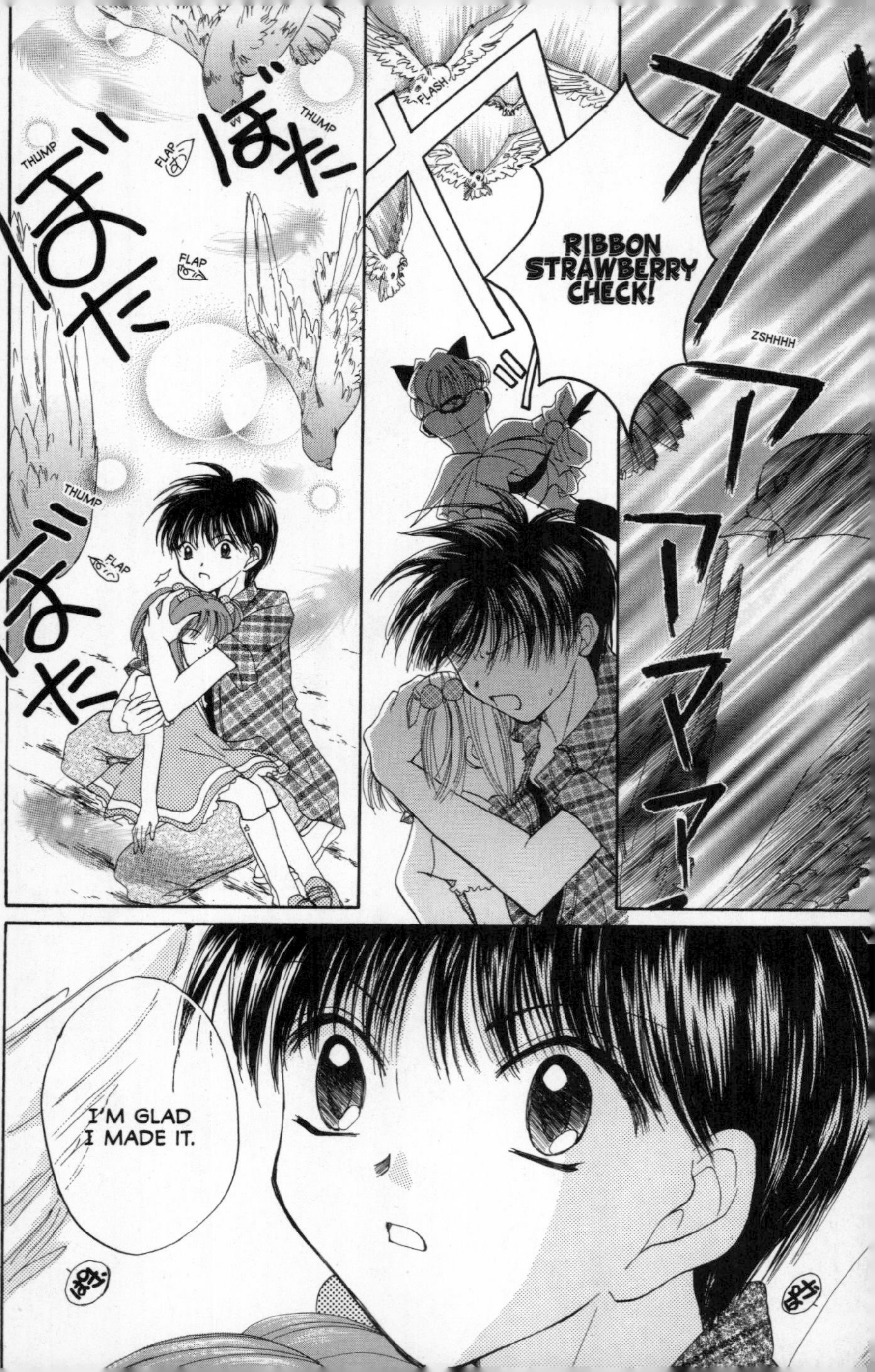
RIBBON STRAWBERRY CHECK!
ZSHHHH
FLASH
THUMP
FLAP
THUMP
FLAP
THUMP
FLAP
I'M GLAD I MADE IT.

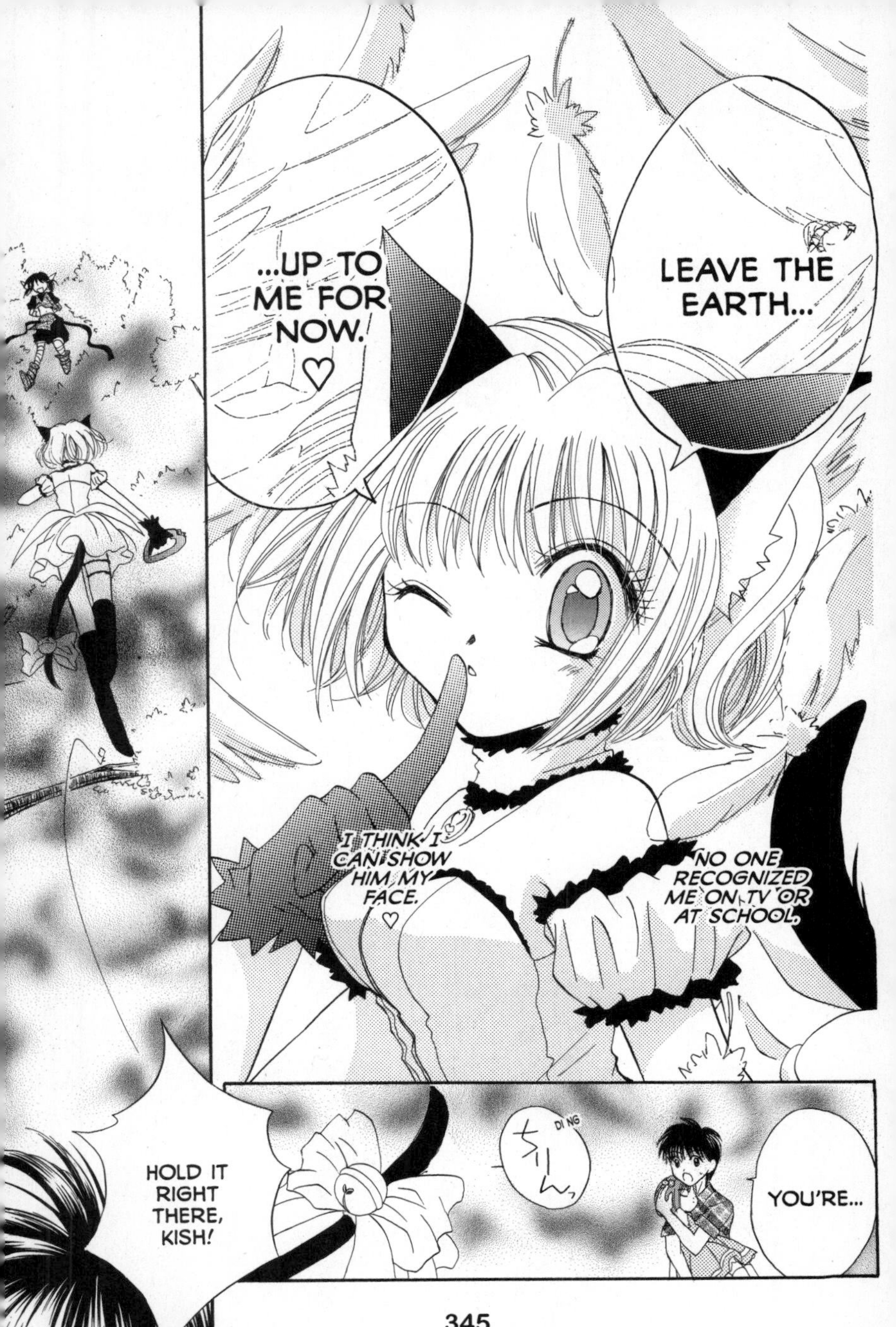
LEAVE THE EARTH...
...UP TO ME FOR NOW. ♡
NO ONE RECOGNIZED ME ON TV OR AT SCHOOL,
I THINK I CAN SHOW HIM MY FACE. ♡
YOU'RE...
ちりんっ
DING
HOLD IT RIGHT THERE, KISH!

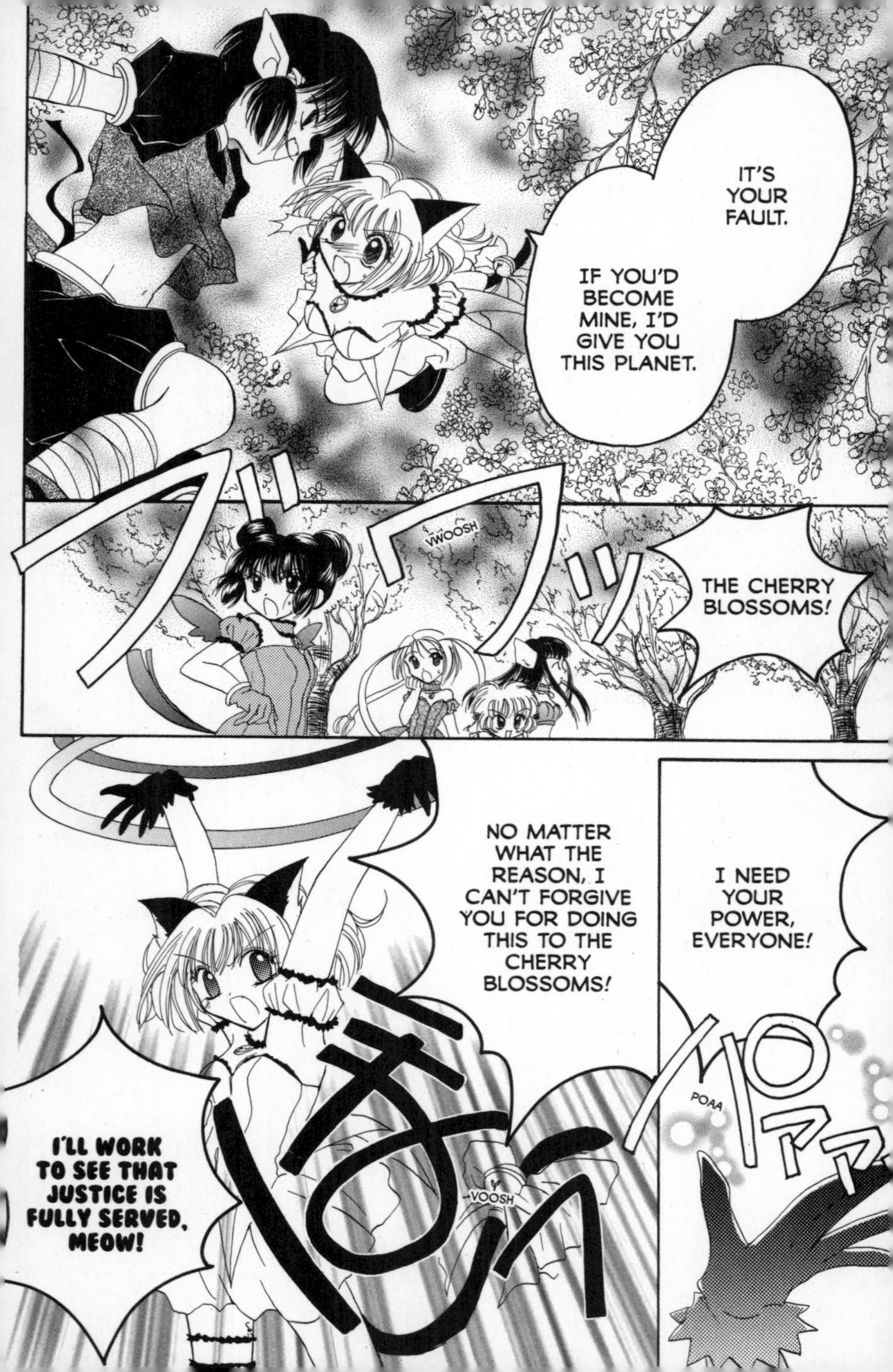
IT'S YOUR FAULT.
IF YOU'D BECOME MINE, I'D GIVE YOU THIS PLANET.
THE CHERRY BLOSSOMS!
VWOOSH
I NEED YOUR POWER, EVERYONE!
POAA
NO MATTER WHAT THE REASON, I CAN'T FORGIVE YOU FOR DOING THIS TO THE CHERRY BLOSSOMS!
I'LL WORK TO SEE THAT JUSTICE IS FULLY SERVED, MEOW!
VOOSH

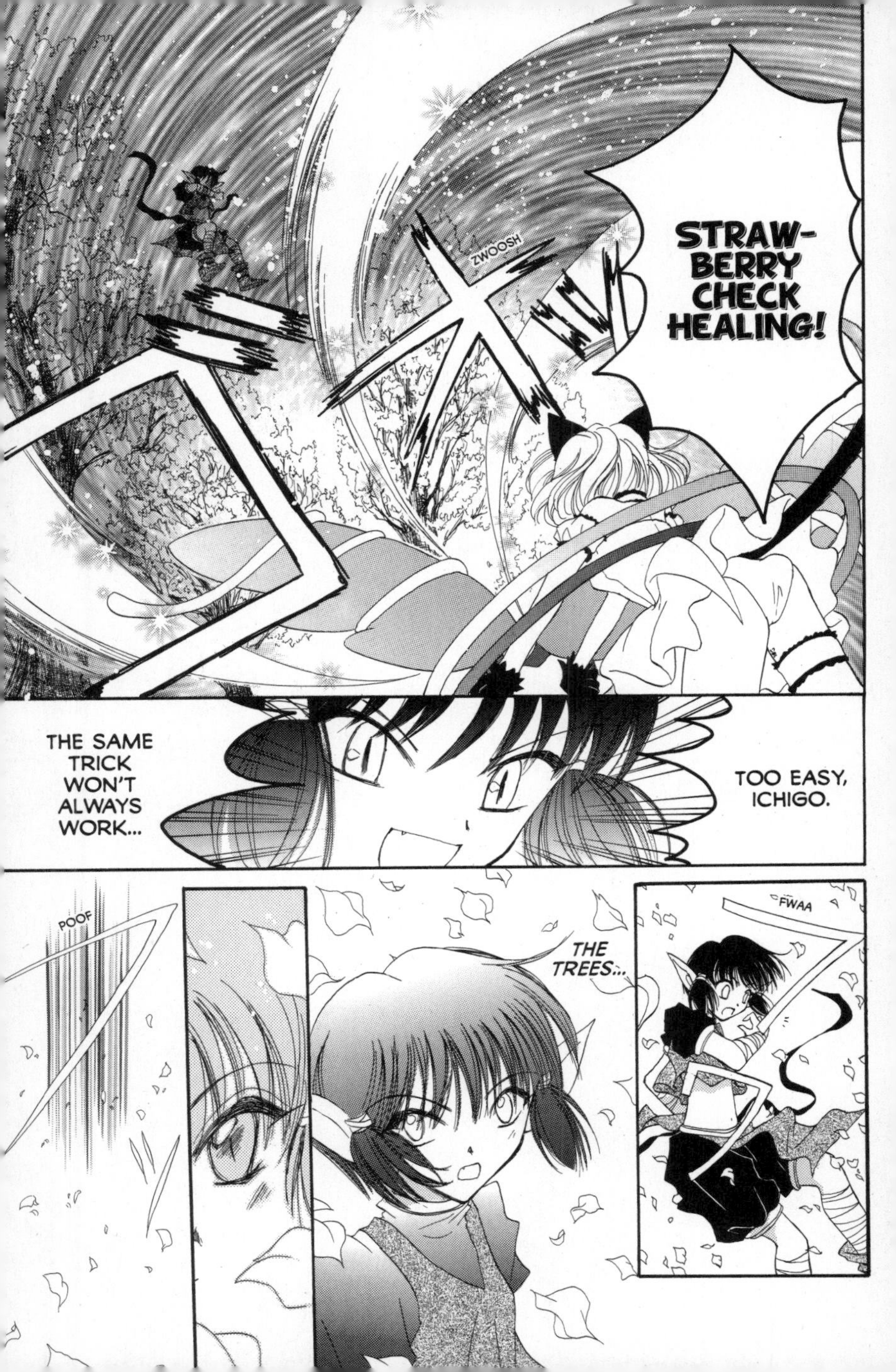
STRAW-BERRY CHECK HEALING!
ZWOOSH
TOO EASY, ICHIGO.
THE SAME TRICK WON'T ALWAYS WORK...
FWAA
THE TREES...
POOF

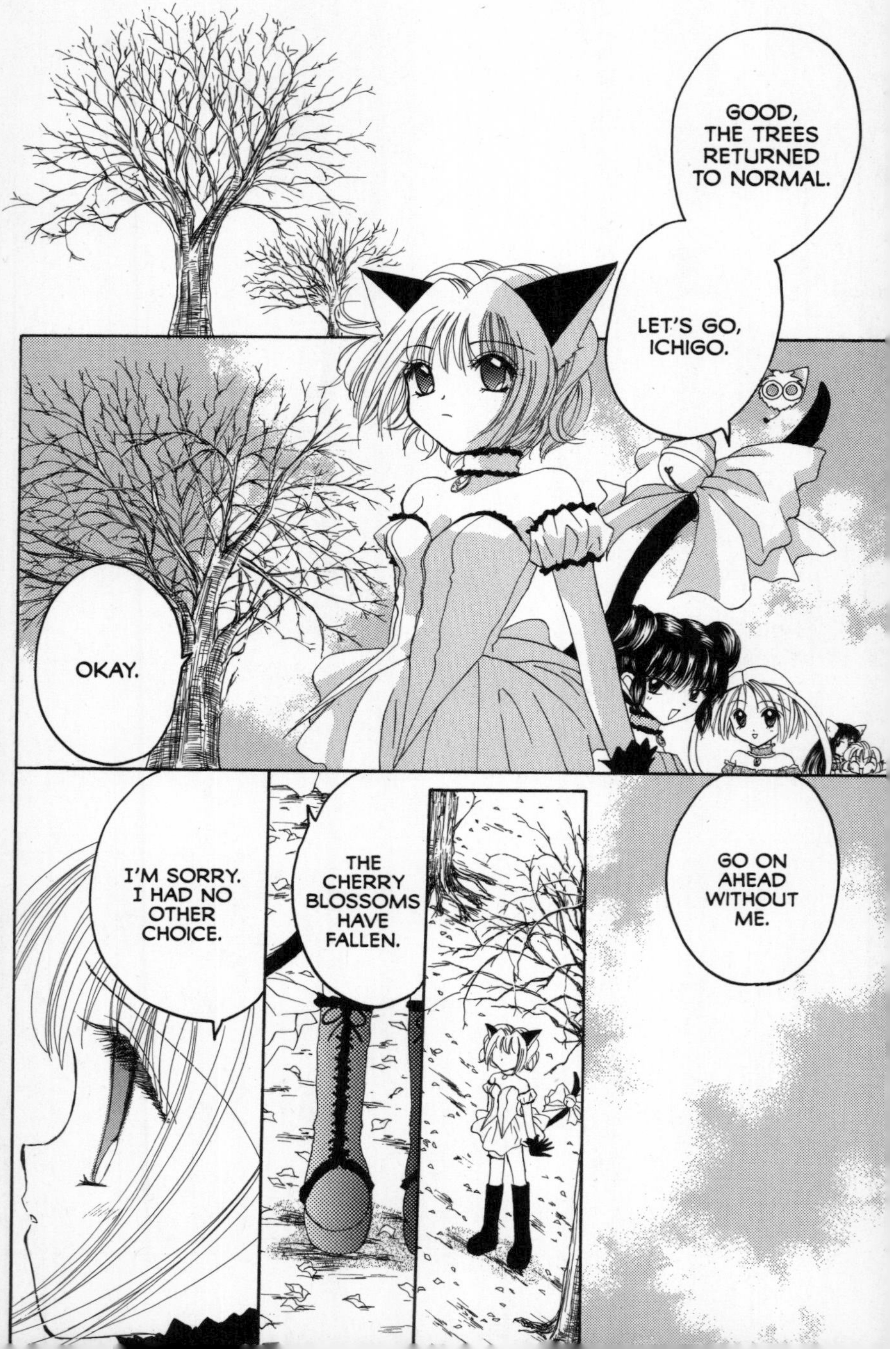
GOOD, THE TREES RETURNED TO NORMAL.
LET'S GO, ICHIGO.
OKAY.
GO ON AHEAD WITHOUT ME.
THE CHERRY BLOSSOMS HAVE FALLEN.
I'M SORRY. I HAD NO OTHER CHOICE.

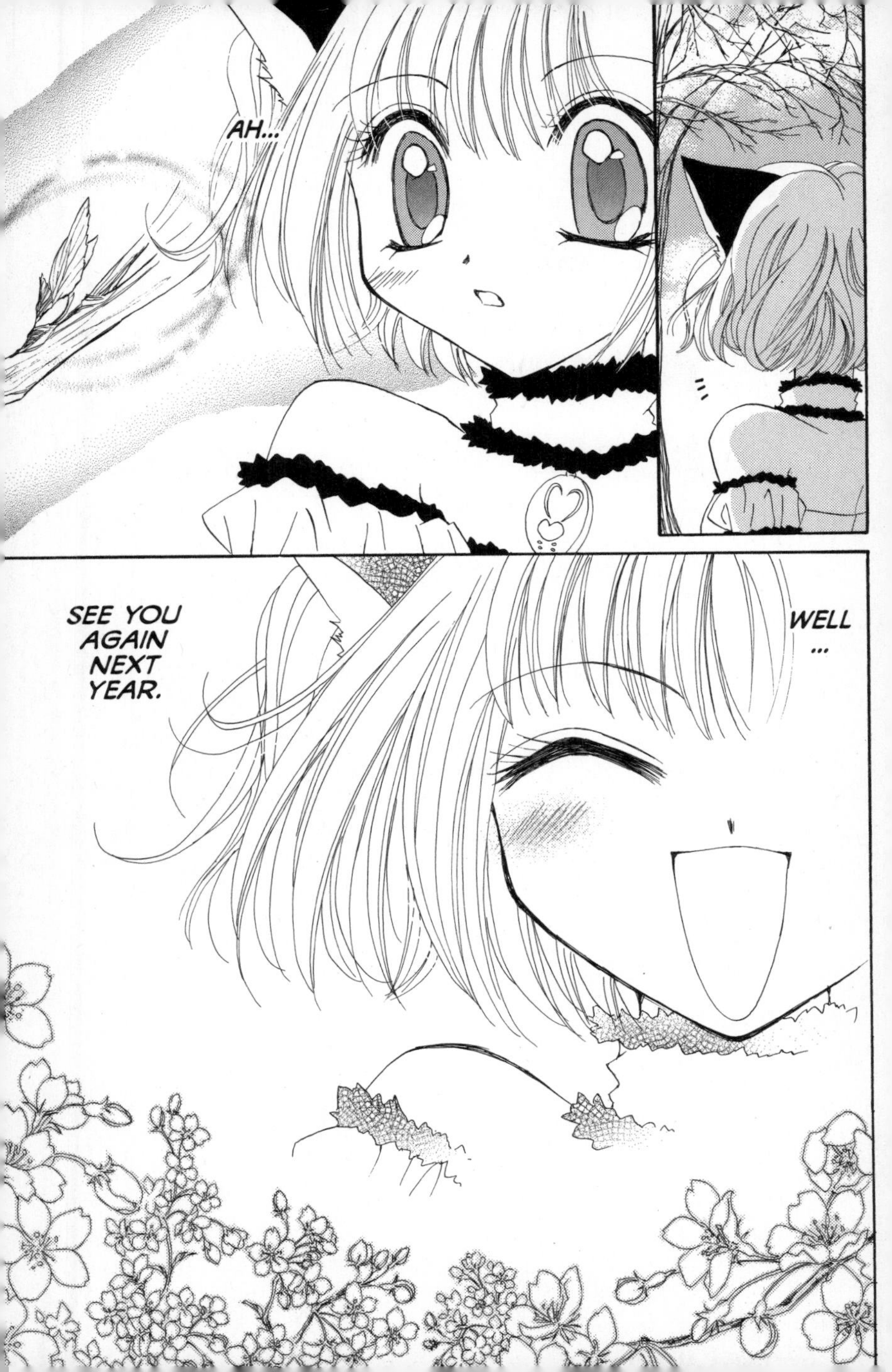
AH...
WELL
...
SEE YOU AGAIN NEXT YEAR.

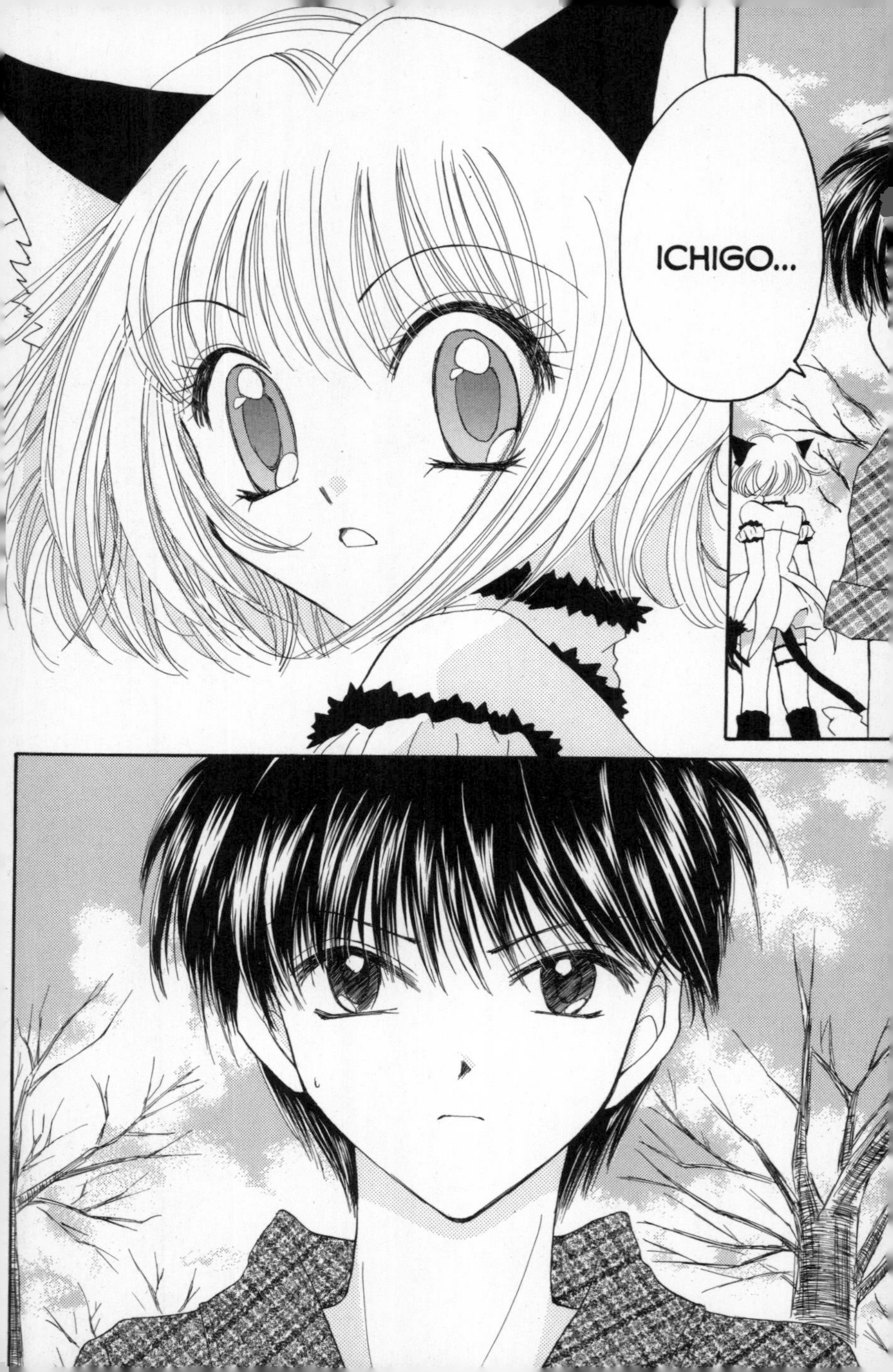
ICHIGO...

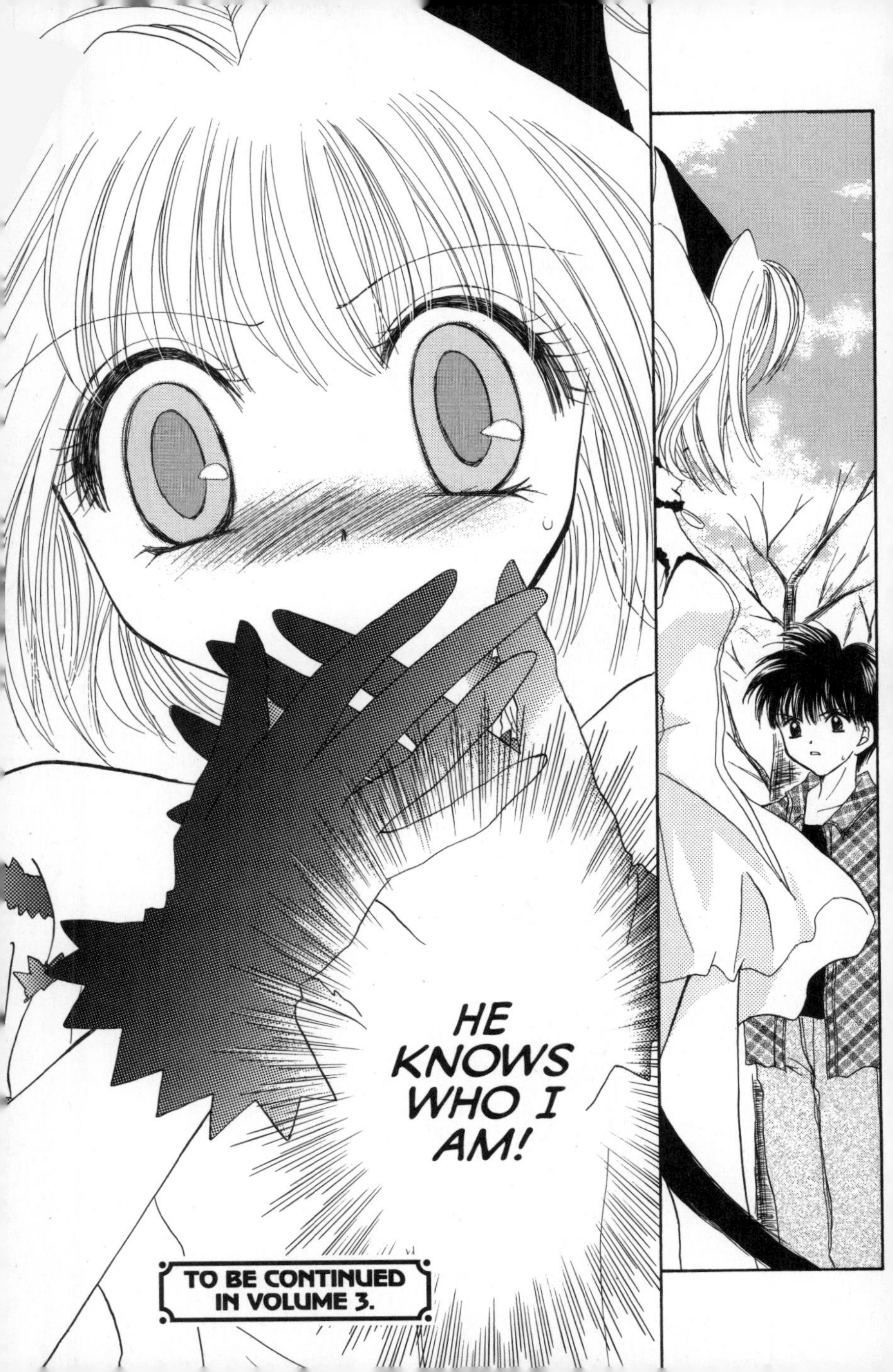
HE KNOWS WHO I AM!
TO BE CONTINUED IN VOLUME 3.

MASHA'S TOKYO MEW MEW OMNIBUS RED DATA FILE

WHAT ARE "RED DATA" ANIMALS?

THEY'RE ANIMALS AT RISK OF EXTINCTION AND CURRENTLY THERE ARE 2,580 SPECIES WORLDWIDE. IT'S DUE TO OVERHUNTING AND ECOLOGICAL DESTRUCTION. LET'S COME TOGETHER AND SAVE THESE ENDANGERED ANIMALS!

FILE 3: GOLDEN LION TAMARIN

SIZE: 20-33 CM* IN HEAD AND BODY LENGTH, 20-30 CM* IN TAIL LENGTH AND 600-800 G* IN WEIGHT.
HABITAT: STATE OF RIO DE JANEIRO, BRAZIL ONLY.

IT'S A TYPE OF MARMOSET, A SMALL MONKEY, WHICH HAS A LION-LIKE GOLDEN MANE. RECOGNIZED AS A SYMBOL OF RAINFOREST CONSERVATION, ONLY 400 OF THIS SPECIES REMAIN IN THE WILD AND THERE HAS BEEN MUCH EFFORT TO CREATE FORESTS AND RAISE THEM BY HUMAN HANDS IN BRAZIL.

*20-33 CM IS ABOUT 8-13 IN. 20-30 CM IS ABOUT 8-12 IN. 600-800 G IS ABOUT 21-28 OZ.

FILE 5: GRAY WOLF

SIZE: 82-160 CM* IN HEAD AND BODY LENGTH AND 20-80 KG* IN WEIGHT FOR MALES AND 18-55 KG* FOR FEMALES.
HABITAT: NORTH AMERICA AND EURASIA.

THE GRAY WOLF IS THE LARGEST MEMBER OF THE CANINE FAMILY. CONSIDERED A GREAT HUNTER, IT CAN PREY ON LARGER ANIMALS INCLUDING DEER. THE HUNTING OF GRAY WOLVES FOR THEIR PRIZED FURS OR DANGER TO PEOPLE REDUCED THEIR POPULATION TO ABOUT 100,000. THEY'RE LARGER IN THE FURTHER NORTH.

*82-160 CM IS ABOUT 32-63 IN. 20-80 KG IS ABOUT 44-176 LB. 18-55 KG IS ABOUT 40-121 LB.

THE FOLLOWING PEOPLE HAVE THESE DNA STRAINS:

GOLDEN LION TAMARIN ------- PUDDING
GRAY WOLF ------------ ZACRO

TOKYO MEW MEW OMNIBUS

ABOUT VOLUME 2

吉田玲子

ANIMAL FORTUNE-TELLING WAS POPULAR IN JAPAN A WHILE GO. WHICH ANIMAL DO YOU THINK MATCHES YOU? A FICKLE BUT ADORABLE CAT, AN ELEGANT AND GORGEOUS PARAKEET, A SPACEY PORPOISE THAT LIKES TO DO THINGS ITS OWN WAY, AN ACTIVE AND LIVELY MONKEY OR A KEEN STRONG WOLF?

CATS MAY BE ADORED BY MANY PEOPLE, BUT PRINCESS-LIKE PARAKEETS MAY BE POPULAR AS WELL. PORPOISES MAKE YOU WANT TO PROTECT THEM. MONKEYS SEEM TO BE FUN TO HANG OUT AS FRIENDS AND WOLVES LOOK INTIMIDATING BUT COOL AND ADMIRABLE.

I FEEL AN AFFINITY TO PORPOISES FOR BEING LAIDBACK. AT ONE POINT I WAS HOOKED ON SNORKELING AND SWAM LIMPLY IN THE SEA. I DIDN'T REALIZE THERE WERE MANY SEA CREATURES UNTIL I SAW A LOT OF FISH ON THE SHORES OF TOKYO. I WANT TO TRANSFORM INTO A PORPOISE LIKE LETTUCE AND SWIM IN THE SEA!

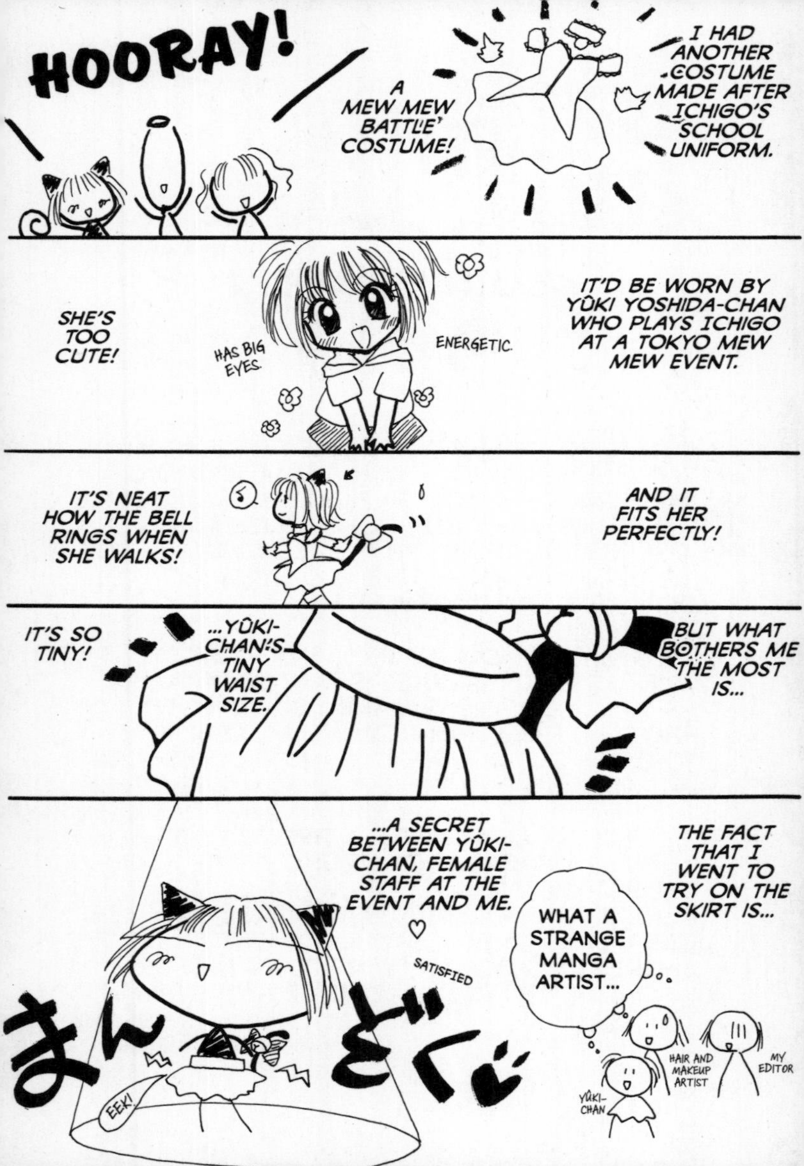
I HAD ANOTHER COSTUME MADE AFTER ICHIGO'S SCHOOL UNIFORM.
A MEW MEW BATTLE COSTUME!
HOORAY!
IT'D BE WORN BY YÛKI YOSHIDA-CHAN WHO PLAYS ICHIGO AT A TOKYO MEW MEW EVENT.
ENERGETIC.
HAS BIG EYES.
SHE'S TOO CUTE!
AND IT FITS HER PERFECTLY!
IT'S NEAT HOW THE BELL RINGS WHEN SHE WALKS!
BUT WHAT BOTHERS ME THE MOST IS...
...YÛKI-CHAN'S TINY WAIST SIZE.
IT'S SO TINY!
THE FACT THAT I WENT TO TRY ON THE SKIRT IS...
MY EDITOR
HAIR AND MAKEUP ARTIST
...A SECRET BETWEEN YÛKI-CHAN, FEMALE STAFF AT THE EVENT AND ME. ♡
WHAT A STRANGE MANGA ARTIST...
YÛKI-CHAN
SATISFIED
まんぞく
EEK!

HOWDY!
IT'S ME, IKUMI!

ACTING
LETTUCE

ACTING
MINT

I like Chinese style outfits.

Spontaneously bought it as a reference at a discount shop.

Hello and nice to meet you. I'm Mia Ikumi. I bring you Tokyo Mew Mew Volume 2. Can you believe it? Time flies too fast!

A few months since the release of Volume 1, I had an unimaginable experience being an audition judge and going on a lunch cruise on Tokyo Bay (laughs). The most amazing event was Tokyo Mew Mew Festival held at Animate in Ikebukuro during Golden Week. There was an exhibition of my original drawings and new manga related merchandise made. I was particularly thrilled that I got to draw a special poster featuring all 12 characters for it.

I couldn't believe we had a two-day autograph session, either. The outfits in the picture to the left are what I wore to this event. I know I'm nuts, but a professional hair and makeup artist volunteered to give me a makeover, which was out of this world! I looked nothing like myself. I had the typical "I can't believe it's me" moment often seen in shôjo manga (laughs). I was glad I dressed up just to have this once in a lifetime experience. On the second day, the hair and makeup artist brought makeup just for me! She was so nice and I'm very grateful to her.

You know, there's a limit to what even the best hair and makeup artist can do. I thought I looked my best, but other people may feel differently. A few older male staff at the festival seemed to have liked it though (giggle nervously).

I drew pictures on the next two pages based on Yûki Yoshida-chan's photos published in Nakayoshi. I think they look a little like an 11 year old and their outfits are realistic. Can you tell? But I realized they don't resemble Yûki-chan after meeting her. They look more like Ichigo in the manga for real.

My first impression of Yûki-chan was that she has big eyes. They're remarkably bigger than anyone's I've seen. I also thought she is pretty and energetic and reminds me of Ichigo. The more I look at her, the more she strangely looks like Ichigo. It feels like I'm drawing Yûki-chan in manga, too. I don't know if it's because she resembles Ichigo or I fell for her beauty (laughs). There will be more opportunities for everyone to meet her, so check her out for yourself. She'll be at Tokyo Character Show where four other Mew Mew members will appear. Don't miss it!

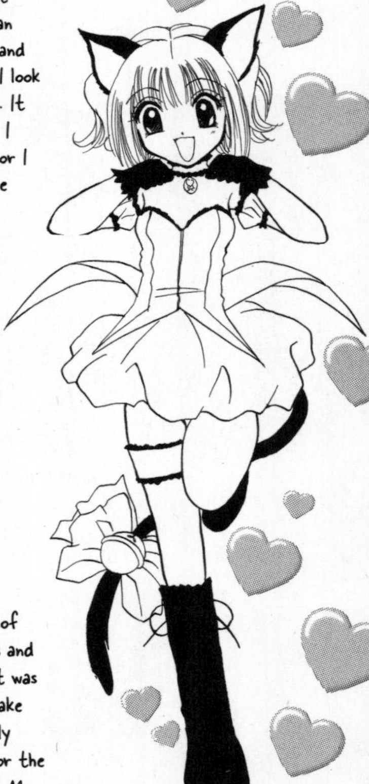

I actually met the last four members at an audition. They all have such a nice figure and good looks that I can't wait to see all five dressed in their costumes. I saw in my editor's schedule that I'll be attending an event called Tokyo Character Show. I doubt I'd get on stage. I'll probably watch the show from a special seat.

A few days ago, I drew up rough sketches of costumes for the remaining Mew Mew members and it wasn't easy to do for four characters. If it was this hard to draw them, it can't be easy to make them, either. Since they were able to faithfully reproduce Ichigo's costume, I have high hopes for the remaining costumes.☆I'm going to support Mew Mew with everyone this summer!

My editor asked me to write about my secret, but I can't think of any. I was asked to include something in common with Ichigo as well. I guess we have the same height, wear cat ears, work like a maid wherever we go and like caramel popcorn. (What in the world?)

I get pushed around by my editor at work and treated like a maid by my friend. I fix meals and clean around her house when I visit her. Just kidding! I do these things at my own will.

At work, I'd do a sketch or create names and ask my editor to turn them into merchandise or let me do a side story. This is how I create more work for myself. Yet I complain that I need a break. I'm a hopeless case.

At my friend's house, I'd ignore my friend who doesn't do anything, clean around and fix meals if there's food on my own. I don't know if that's the reason, but her mother gives me bags, clothes and jewelry. I'm so lucky! I like bringing grocery to fix something for a friend and invite myself to help out a fellow manga artist as well.

It seems I'm just doing whatever pleases me, but my place looks neglected lately on the contrary. When I'm home, I sit at my desk or in front of my computer for a long time while feeling obligated to do work. I seriously want to dust my house sometime soon. Lately, I feel I've become more domesticated since I moved into my own place. I think that's my secret.

Speaking of domesticating, my friend, Asumi Hara-sensei, told me I'm like a mom. I hope it was a compliment.

Afterword

Yesterday, my friend told me Disneyland needs cast members and even offers a three-day work week with weekends included. Why am I talking about this? I love Disneyland and seriously thought of working there. I don't mind wearing a costume or acting as a female character, but I was dying to work as a friendly ice cream vendor at a fantasy land cart. The smile on a female vendor's face was priceless! She was really like a Disneyland member. At the moment, I want to be a caramel popcorn vendor in front of the Cinderella Castle and then eat caramel popcorn and watch the parade to my heart's content. Yay! ☆ (It'll never happen!)

I gave it a serious consideration, but I'll forget it before my editor kills me. It was a short-lived dream (laughs).

I almost forgot. Fantallusion, a nighttime parade at Tokyo Disneyland, ended the other day. I went to see it numerous times until the very end so I won't have any regrets. The next parade is Electrical Dream Parade Lights. I'm going to check it out as soon as I finish the next chapter! ☆

It's off topic, but I like a pair of female comediennes from another country called Isabelle and Bene. Though I've only seen their short skits in the evening on Fuji TV, they're surprisingly fluent in Japanese and I love their very stereotypical jokes. There's no other program I look more forward to. I turn on my TV for this program only. ◊

MY ASSISTANT'S ONE WORD WAS THE DECIDING FACTOR FOR CHOOSING LAMBS. WHAT TO DO NEXT?

I was lucky enough to become a manga artist and be one among the few to get to meet her characters. I don't know if I'm blessed or fortunate, but I don't think I should be too dependent on it. I don't believe happiness can be found easily. It's something we gain with desire and a lot of effort.

Lastly, I want to give lots of thanks to everyone helping me create this manga, everyone involved in this project and everyone reading this manga!

Because we want to bring happiness to our loved ones, because we want to bring happiness to ourselves

Let's work hard together.

May 23, 2001   Mia Ikumi

VOLUME 1 NOTES

Kyaa and *Gyaa*
Kyaa is a girlish scream. Although it can be used when a character is frightened or surprised, it's usually heard as a scream of delight. *Gyaa* nearly always indicates real fright, embarrassment or pain, and hardly ever has a good meaning.

I'll be here, page 14
In Japan, it is customary to say *Itterasshai* ("Go on" or "Have a nice day"), when you see someone off. We don't have such custom and to help read the scene smoothly, we chose to use the phrase, "I'll be here," instead.

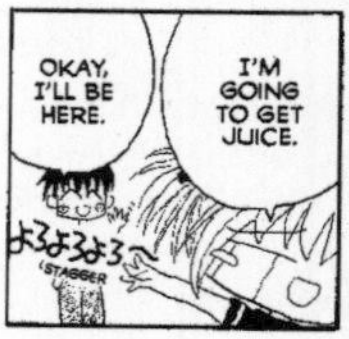
I'M GOING TO GET JUICE.
OKAY, I'LL BE HERE.
STAGGER

Na no da, page 18
Pudding has a habit of ending all her lines of dialogue with the word Na no da, which literally means "it is that." While it is has no particular meaning in the way Pudding uses it, she applies it to her statement to put more emphasis.

Onigokko, page 18
Pudding actually says, "This way, oni-san." She is playing a Japanese version of "tag" game called onigokko. Oni is the equivalent of "it".

Onêsama, page 21
While onêsama means an "older sister," it also refers to a highly respected older female such as in the scene where Mint admires Zacro.

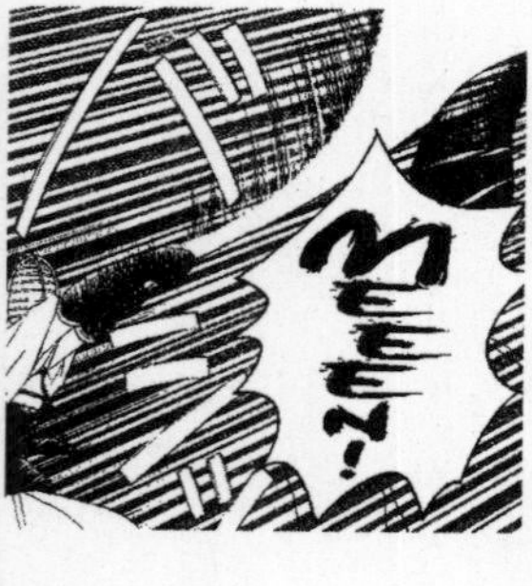
MEEEN!

Kendo and Men, page 28
Kendo is a Japanese martial art of sword-fighting. It is practiced wearing a Japanese clothing and protective armor and using a bamboo sword called *shinai*. Men is a protective helmet as well as a vertical strike to the head.

Let's Eat, page 32
People in Japan have the custom of beginning their meals with a phrase *itadakimasu*, which means "Let's eat!"

COD, page 34
COD stands for chemical oxygen demand and it is a test that determines the amount of water pollutants found in water.

Parts per Million, page 34
"Parts per million" or "ppm" is a term used to describe a concentration of substance in water or soil. 1 ppm is equivalent to 1 milligram per liter.

Soft serve at Kihachi, page 34
Kihachi is a chain ice cream shop that specializes in soft serve in Japan.

Ichigo and Strawberry, page 42
Ichigo's name means "strawberry" in Japanese.

UMA, page 60
UMA stands for unidentified mysterious animal.

Tsuchinoko, page 61
The Tsuchinoko is a mythical snake-like creature from Japan. Though its sightings have been reported all over Japan, no one has caught it alive or dead to this day.

Momo, Ao and Midori, page 69
Momo, literally meaning "peach" in Japanese, comes from Japanese pink called *momoiro*. Ao and midori mean "blue" and "green" respectively. Instead, the manga artist creates last names that represent the color for each character such as Momomiya for *momoiro* or "pink," Aizawa for *aiiro* or "blue" and Midorikawa for *midori* or "green."

See You Later, page 113
Otsukaresama, which literally means, "You must be tired," is used to acknowledge someone completing a task in Japan. Since such custom doesn't exist in English-speaking countries, we used the phrase, "See you later," instead.

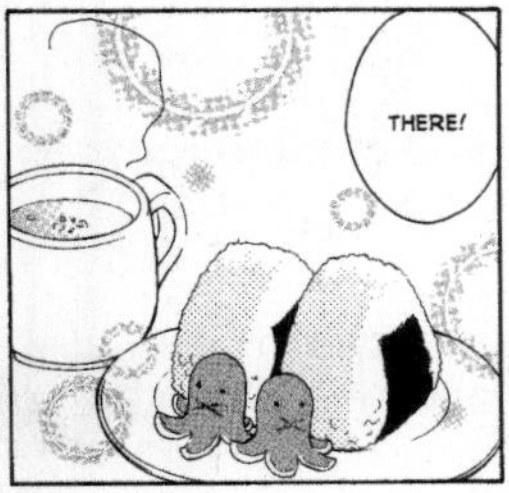
THERE!

Nigiri-Meshi, page 117
Also known as *onigiri* or *omusubi* in Japan, nigiri-meshi is cooked rice (*meshi*) that is often stuffed with a salty or sour filling, molded into a triangular or oval shape and wrapped with nori ("dried seaweed").

Yôkai, page 138
Yôkai are Japanese folklore creatures that have spiritual or supernatural power. The most well-known yôkai are evil oni ("ogre") and shape-shifting animals such as kitsune ("fox") and tanuki ("raccoon dog").

Tarte Tatin, page 146
Tarte Tatin is a fruit tart served upside down.

Inocchi, page 167
Inocchi is a nickname for Yoshihiko Inohara, a member of a popular Japanese idol group, V6.

Nikujaga, page 168
Short for *niku* and *jagaimo*, nikujaga literally means, "meat and potato" in Japanese and is a dish of meat and potatoes simmered in a soy sauce-based sauce.

Nakayoshi, page 170
Nakayoshi is a monthly shôjo manga magazine published by Kodansha in Japan.

Furoku, page 171
Furoku, which literally means "supplement," is a bonus item that is included in some magazines in Japan. Furoku for manga magazines range anything from a mechanical pencil to plastic bag designed by a manga artist.

VOLUME 2 NOTES

Kyaa and *Gyaa*
Kyaa is a girlish scream. Although it can be used when a character is frightened or surprised, it's usually heard as a scream of delight. Gyaa nearly always indicates real fright, embarrassment or pain, and hardly ever has a good meaning.

Ichigo and Strawberry
Ichigo's name means "strawberry" in Japanese.

Last Names
Each character's last name represents a color: Momomiya for *momoiro* or "pink," Aizawa for *aiiro* or "blue," Midorikawa for *midori* or "green," Fujiwara for *fujiiro* or "purple" and Fong means "yellow" in Chinese.

Na no da
Pudding has a habit of ending all her lines of dialogue with the word Na no da, which literally means "it is that." While it is has no particular meaning in the way Pudding uses it, she applies it to her statement to put more emphasis.

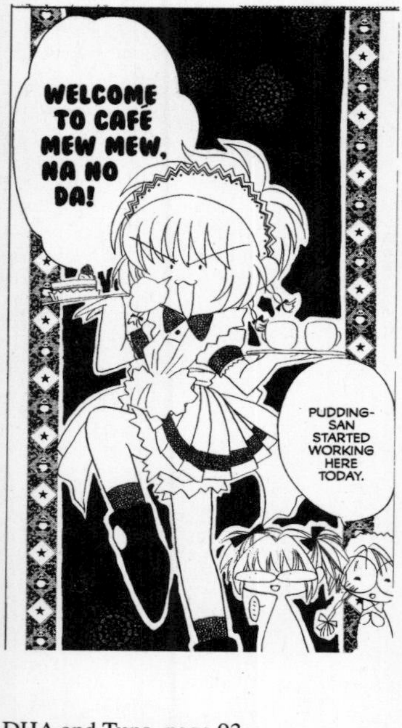
WELCOME TO CAFÉ MEW MEW, NA NO DA!
PUDDING-SAN STARTED WORKING HERE TODAY.

Welcome to Café Mew Mew, page 46
Irasshaimase, which literally means, "Come on in," is a standard greeting used at most place of business in Japan. To make the scene read more smoothly, we used the phrase, "Welcome to Café Mew Mew," instead.

Choco Egg, page 61
Choco Egg is a chocolate egg with a toy. This candy-toy product in Japan comes in different series ranging from animals to cars.

Sachô, page 63
Literally meaning "head of a company," sachô is a title used for company presidents.

Onêsama and onêchan, page 66
Onêsama and onêchan literally mean "older sister" as well as an older female of great respect. While onêsama refers to someone of great respect, onêchan expresses someone endearing to a speaker.

Ojôsama, page 91
Ojôsama, which literally means "a young lady," is a title used for a girl from a well off family.

DHA and Tuna, page 93
DHA, which stands for docosahexaenoic acid, is an omega-3 fatty acid. Tuna is known to have a rich amount of DHA.

Hua Xiang Tian Huang, page 109
Pudding uses a Chinese command and it means, "Magnificent Fragrance, Sky Sway."

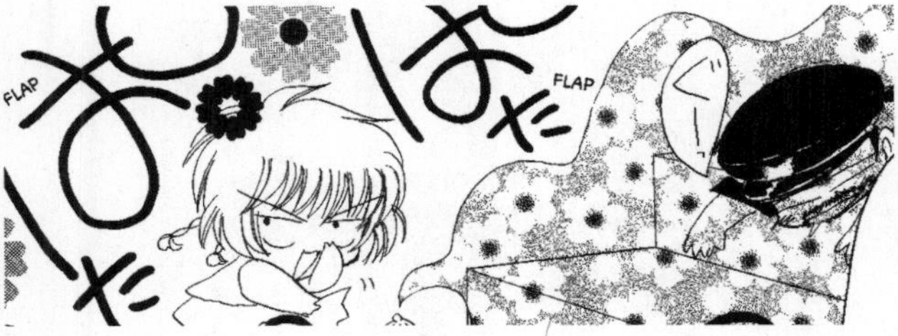
FLAP
FLAP

Cosplay, page 136
Short for "costume" and "play," cosplay is a type of performance where someone dresses up in a costume to represent a fictitious character.

Tokusatsu, page 143
Tokusatsu is a shortened term for *tokushu satsuei*, which literally means "special photography." It refers to live-action films or television drama that relies heavily on special effects.

Animal fortune-telling, page 177
Dôbutsu uranai or "animal fortune-telling" is a Japanese divination based on animal horoscope. It uses the person's birth date to determine the person's animal character--there are 12--and personality differentiated by colors.

Golden Week, page 179
Golden Week is a Japanese term that applies to several national holidays within seven days at the end of April to beginning of May in Japan. Since many businesses close during this period, many businesses close and people take vacation.

TOMARE!

止まれ
[STOP!]

You're going the wrong way!

Manga is a completely different type of reading experience.

To start at the *beginning,* go to the *end!*

That's right! Authentic manga is read the traditional Japanese way—from right to left, exactly the *opposite* of how American books are read. It's easy to follow: Just go to the other end of the book and read each page—and each panel—from right side to left side, starting at the top right. Now you're experiencing manga as it was meant to be!